RESTA
NEW ENGLAND

A Guide to Good Eating
By Nancy Webster & Richard Woodworth

Wood Pond Press
365 Ridgewood Road
West Hartford, Conn. 06107

Prices, hours and menu offerings at restaurants change seasonally and with business conditions. Readers should call or write ahead to avoid disappointment. The details reported in this book were correct at presstime and are subject, of course, to change. They are offered as a relative guide to what to expect.

The authors have personally researched the places recommended in this edition. There is no charge for inclusion.

The authors welcome readers' reactions and suggestions.

What the book's symbols mean:
* exceptional food.
♥ exceptional atmosphere.
$ exceptional value.

First Printing, February 1990.

Cover Design by Bob Smith the Artsmith

Cover Photo by Ronald Dahle of Biddeford, Me.: Window table setting at Seascapes, Kennebunkport, Me.

Contents

VERMONT

NEW HAMPSHIRE

MAINE

To Our Readers

We are forever being asked, "where should we eat when we're in (fill in the blank)?" We've faced the same question time after time. The big national guidebooks generally stick with the tried-and-true, the places that tourists seek out. The Yellow Pages and the Chamber of Commerce listings are usually just that. What you need is an informed consensus by knowledgeable residents familiar with the ins and outs of the local restaurant scene where you are or where you're going.

This book fills that need. In twenty years of touring and writing about New England, we've visited almost every city and hamlet, accruing dining information and informants along the way. In the past year, we've revisited restaurants and scouted out new ones. Although we could not possibly eat in every one, we've eaten in many and we've relied on the local consensus — that of restaurateurs, chefs, diners, innkeepers, gourmet shop owners, and others who know what's going on — so that our recommendations are as trustworthy and timely as possible. (If we have missed your favorite, please advise for our next edition).

The book is arranged geographically, generally from south to north and east to west. In each town, restaurants are reported roughly in order of personal preference.

Three symbols are used to point out places of exceptional merit:

✱ for food.

♥ for atmosphere.

$ for value.

Rather than waffle in generalities, we are specific. Prices listed indicate the range for dinner entrees. Prix-fixe means the price for a set meal. Table d'hote indicates the price of a complete meal. Dinner hours often vary: when they are listed as 5 to 9 or 10, it usually means weekdays to 9, weekends to 10. The style of cuisine reflects either what the restaurant says it is or what its menu indicates. We report specific menu items to indicate what the chef is up to; we recognize that many items change.

The choices are a selective process. And we had to be more selective in places like Boston and Connecticut's Fairfield County, where good restaurants are a dime a dozen, than in remote areas like Block Island or Caribou. Part of this book's value lies in its territorial reach; in your travels, you will never be far from a recommended restaurant. The restaurant we list for Podunk may not measure up to some that we left out in Cambridge or Greenwich, however. The same goes for our symbols for stars and value between states; they tend to be relative to each other within the state or region, although each is noteworthy in its own right.

The primary measure, of course, is the food. While many establishments reported here fall into the category of fine *dining,* we call this a guide to good *eating* because we cover far more than the citadels to haute cuisine. Lobster pounds, lunch spots, ethnic eateries, and even a few takeout-delis are included. We also stress that these aren't intended to be restaurant critiques as much as descriptions, for we are reporters here rather than reviewers.

The New England restaurant scene is changing as it moves into the 1990s. New restaurants proliferate, but too many others close. Our journalistic background and desktop publishing system give us a timeliness that few guidebook authors enjoy. Although this book is as up-to-date as its 1990 publication date, menus, hours, prices, chefs, owners, and restaurants change. It's a fact of their business and ours. To avoid disappointment, call ahead to confirm details.

We hope you'll enjoy our guide to good eating across New England. We welcome your reactions and recommendations.

Nancy Webster and Richard Woodworth
February 1990

About the Authors

Nancy Webster began her dining experiences in her native Montreal and as a waitress in summer resorts across Canada during her McGill University years. She worked in London and hitchhiked through Europe on $3 a day before her marriage to an American newspaper editor, whom she met while skiing at Mont Tremblant. She started writing her "Roaming the Restaurants" column for the West Hartford (Conn.) News in 1972. That led to half of the book, *Daytripping & Dining in Southern New England,* written in collaboration with Betsy Wittemann in 1978. She since has co-authored three editions of *Weekending in New England;* three more editions in the *Daytripping & Dining* series; two editions of *Getaways for Gourmets in the Northeast,* two editions of *Inn Spots & Special Places in New England,* and *Water Escapes in the Northeast.* She and her husband have two grown sons and live in West Hartford.

Richard Woodworth was raised on wholesome American food in suburban Syracuse, N.Y., where his early wanderlust took him on birthday travel outings with friends for the day to Utica or Rochester. After graduation from Middlebury College, he was a reporter for upstate New York newspapers in Syracuse, Jamestown, Geneva and Rochester before moving to Connecticut to become editor of the West Hartford News and executive editor of Imprint Newspapers. He now is editor and publisher of Wood Pond Press and co-author with his wife of *Getaways for Gourmets in the Northeast* and *Inn Spots & Special Places in New England.* With wife Nancy Webster and their sons, he has traveled to the four corners of this country, Canada and portions of Europe, writing their findings for Imprint Newspapers and others. Between adventures and publishing ventures, he tries to find time to weed the garden in summer and ski in the winter.

Fairfield County

Greenwich

✱ Bertrand, 253 Greenwich Ave., Greenwich. (203) 661-4459.
French. $22.75 to $28.50.

Widely acclaimed since it opened in 1987 as one of Connecticut's best restaurants, if not *the* best, this is the creation of Christian Bertrand, executive chef for twelve years at Lutece in New York, and his wife Michelle, who oversees the front of the house. The building, which formerly housed a restaurant called Greenstreet, was originally that of the 70-year-old Putnam Bank and Trust Co., and the honey-colored brick, Romanesque arched and vaulted ceiling soaring two stories is truly amazing. From the main floor, wide oak staircases lined with gleaming brass rails lead to dining balconies on two sides. On our January visit, Michelle had replaced her Christmas decorations with lavish displays of primroses, cyclamen and branches of apple blossoms forced into bloom. This is not a pretentious place, but everything is impeccable, as it should be when you are paying top dollar. If you were celebrating a great occasion, you might like to start with diced lobster with spring vegetables ($19.50) or fresh foie gras poached in consomme with sherry ($26). From the eleven entrees, roasted red snapper with a fresh coriander sauce on homemade pasta, and dover sole meuniere with diced artichoke and white mushrooms (the most expensive entree) sound fabulous. But a roasted gigot of rabbit and confit of duck with sorrel sauce might tempt, too. For dessert there are five versions of souffles, baked alaska with a black cherry coulis, golden apple shortcake with raisins, orange confite and calvados sauce, and an assortment of homemade sorbets with fresh fruit. Most of the desserts are available at lunch, when entrees like steamed salmon steak and salmon sausage with sauerkraut, noisettes of lamb with nicoise olives and tomatoes, and beef mignonette forestiere are in the $16 to $19 range. At night, a tasting menu (minimum of two people) offers eight courses for $70 each. Those without bulging wallets might try the $35 prix-fixe dinner on Thursday nights, when dishes of different regions of France are prepared more in a country style. The wines match the food, with bottles starting at $18 and rising rapidly.

Lunch, Monday-Friday noon to 2:30; dinner, Monday-Saturday 6 to 10, Sunday 5 to 8. Reservations imperative (a week ahead) for weekends.

✱ Restaurant Jean-Louis, 61 Lewis St., Greenwich. (203) 622-8450.
New and Classic French. $25 to $29, or Prix-Fixe, $48.

For a small, 38-seater, this esteemed restaurant harbors an awesome wine list that would be hard to maintain in a place many times its size. The wine cellar fills half the basement and cops Wine Spectator's "best of award of excellence," one of only two in Connecticut. "We like our wines," understates personable, young chef-owner Jean-Louis Gerin, who helped celebrated Paris chef Guy Savoy open his Greenwich sensation and changed its name to his own upon purchasing it in 1986. He and wife Linda also like their foods, and present meals of great tastes and originality in a pleasant room where tables are set with white cloths over lace, Villeroy & Boch china, sterling silver, and red roses. The majority of patrons select the menu degustation ($48 per person, two-person minimum), four courses that change daily and aren't decided until 5 o'clock. What about tonight? we asked. Jean-Louis thought a moment, and responded: sweetwater prawns, filet of pompano, sweetbreads with saffron, and wood pigeon. Otherwise, you can expect expensive, exotic treats on the a la carte menu. The four appetizers start at $16 for endive salad folded in a cream fraiche and American caviars dressing or a fresh duck foie gras terrine with salad. The four soups ($9 or $10) include diced vegetables and mussels in a saffron broth, and mushroom, bacon and flageolet bean soup. For main courses, we hear great things about the medallions of lotte (monkfish) in a red wine, bacon and tomato sauce; the sliced breast of duck and foie gras sauteed with orange vinaigrette sauce, and the medallions of venison in a grand veneur sauce. Typical of the restaurant's personal touches, the dessert menu notes that "each of us has a special dessert that we love and prepare every day for you. Try one or try them all!" ($7 or $19, respectively). You might try praline cheesecake by Linda, creme brulee by Victor, chocolate lover's surprise by Keith, fresh fruits mosaic by Birte, or thin warm apple tart, pear and lemon gratin, and dessert du jour by Jean-Louis. Afterward, Jean-Louis likely will come to your table to discuss the meal and bid you good night. Then he's off to nearby South Salem, N.Y., to say good evening to guests at Rene Chardain Restaurant. The Gerins took over management of the restaurant run by Linda's father after he retired in 1989.

Dinner, Monday-Friday 6 to 9:30, Saturday, seatings at 6:30 and 9; lunch, Friday only, noon to 2.

∗ La Grange at The Homestead Inn, 420 Field Point Road, Greenwich.
(203) 869-7500.
Contemporary French. $24 to $29.50.

The refined, lovely dining room at this urbane country inn in the Belle Haven section beside Long Island Sound occupies what once was an 18th-century barn that gives the restaurant its name. So it retains the original beams, barnwood and brick hearth for an unexpectedly historic feeling, while appearing airy and more contemporary, thanks to a wraparound veranda in which the windows open to let in summer's breezes and close to capture winter's sunshine. Floral china, rattan or antique chairs, fresh flowers, and formal service are the rule. Longtime chef Jacques Thiebeult, formerly executive chef at New York's Le Cirque and Le Cygne, changes the menu two or three times a year and says he likes "to play with the food" on daily specials. But his customers demand that he always offer certain dishes: medallions of lobster and vegetables in a cream sauce, roast duck with a black currant sauce and wild rice, sweetbreads sauteed with wild mushrooms and madeira, and rack of lamb garnished with fresh vegetables. For dinner, you might choose a couple of signature appetizers, the cassolette of snails with pernod and herbs or the country pate of coarsely ground veal and pork, or crabmeat Belle Haven, crab cakes with tartar sauce, or billi-bi soup. The pastry chef is known for her triple chocolate cake, fruit tarts with kiwi and raspberries, creme brulee, linzer tortes, and homemade ice creams and sorbets.

Lunch, Monday-Friday noon to 2:30; dinner, nightly 6 to 9:30, weekends to 10:15.

La Strada, 48 West Putnam Ave., Greenwich. (203) 629-8484.
Northern Italian. $17.75 to $24.75.

Only a discreet sign marks the entrance to this new bastion of Italian cuisine, the sole branch of a downtown Chicago institution. Inside, all is rich and elegant, matching the lunchtime clientele parading in the day we visited. Serene and sophisticated with lavish woods, the main dining room is separated from two more intimate dining areas by glass-paneled, red wood dividers. Marble floors, marbelized artworks, crystal chandeliers, comfortable booths, high-back chairs, peach-bordered china, and a tapestry and a grand piano in the bar set the stage. Dining is by candlelight, even at noon, when the menu is slightly reduced from the dinner version in scope and price. The oversize menu holds few surprises, but everything is prepared to perfection. Pastas are available as appetizers or entrees, although this is the kind of splurgey place where you'd be more likely to order salmon steak with green peppercorns, scampi, one of the eight veal dishes, or the broiled sirloin steak. Among desserts are chocolate mousse, zabaglione, and strawberries with vintage vinegar. The extensive wine list, categorized by the regions of Italy, offers quite a few for under $15 as well as one for $650. All the solicitous staff are Italian, too.

Lunch, Monday-Friday 11:30 to 2:30; dinner, Monday-Saturday 5 to 10 or 11.

Tapestries, 554 Old Post Road No. 3, Greenwich. (203) 629-9204.
Contemporary American/International. $19.95 to $26.95.

There are tapestries here, though not as many as you might expect from the name. The name really reflects the menu, which is designed as a tapestry, a blend of different cuisines. The setting is quite unexpected: a dark gray stone house that looks like a residence, its main floor containing a large reception foyer with deep mulberry walls and a grand piano, a small dining room, and a lavish cocktail lounge. A stairway leads beneath a crystal chandelier, its chain enshrouded in an ecru fabric, to the open upstairs dining room, where white linens and china are set off by deep violet orchids, a slide of leaves is projected on one wall, and sunlight casts striking pastel stripes through windows curtained in plastic behind sheer. The short menu is deceptively simple, offering such dinner entrees as Idaho brook trout meuniere with polenta, New Orleans spicy shrimp, breast of duck with apple and caraway, loin of veal with lobster-scallop champagne cream, sweetbreads with sherry vinegar and pancetta, beef and kidney pie, and breast of chicken with sesame and Japanese eggplant. Appetizers include blackened scallops with Cajun beurre blanc, sweetbreads and wild mushrooms in puff pastry, and fresh mozzarella with grilled eggplant and roasted peppers. Desserts reflect an Italian influence: mascarpone ricotta cheesecake, berries and zabaglione, tirami su, and budino al praline. The expansive wine list starts at $22 and rises rapidly. Regular lunch is a smaller version of the dinner menu, and a casual luncheon menu offers the type of fare (and prices) one expects everywhere but in Greenwich.

Lunch, Monday-Friday noon to 2; dinner, Monday-Saturday 6 to 9 or 10.

Cafe du Bec Fin, 199 Sound Beach Ave., Old Greenwich. (203) 637-4447.
French. $24 to $27.

In an area where haute French reigns, this delightful cafe appeals as user-friendly. The long, narrow room has colorful wall murals depicting French citizens of various centuries, a rear bookcase displaying tomes on food and wine, cane and wood chairs, and white linens and service plates, with pink napkins resting in the wine glasses. Polish chef-owner Joseph Cizynski is known for mixing wines with food, as in tenderloin of beef with zinfandel and roasted shallots, calves liver with roasted shallots and merlot, roast baby guinea hen with grapes and white port, and scallops with hard cider and almonds. Breast of duck is a specialty; it might be done with fresh black figs, cranberries and oranges, or with wild blackberries and huckleberries. Begin your feast with lobster pate, smoked vegetable raviolis, or butternut squash soup with steamed lobster dumplings. Finish with persimmon pudding with creme anglaise and clementines, white chocolate mousse napoleon with fresh berries, or something called "three tastes of pears:" pear ice cream in a caramel bird's nest, a pear tart with brown butter, and poached Chinese pear in zinfandel. The wine list starts at $12 and goes to $1,000, but Joseph takes pride in finding little-known wines from unusual regions that are great values.

Lunch, Tuesday-Friday noon to 2; dinner, Monday-Saturday 6 to 9 or 10.

Conte, 44 Old Field Point Road, Greenwich. (203) 622-4387.
Italian. $12.95 to $18.95.

Here is a typical Italian family operation — parents, four offspring and their spouses. But don't expect checkered tablecloths, hanging chianti bottles and spaghetti with meatballs. In 1989, the Conti family fashioned two handsome dining areas with a mix of brick and stucco, in colors reflecting their vision of the Italian countryside, terra cotta and green, blue and white. The indigo color of the hand-painted family crest on the menu is repeated on the service plates and china atop the white-over-blue tables. A few artworks and copper molds adorn the walls. The Contis lured as chef Fabrizio Bottero from Rome, by way of Paoli in New York City. He puts out highly regarded fare, from grilled calves liver with sauteed red onions and rosemary to shrimp in spicy tomato sauce, from veal scaloppine with eggplant and fontina cheese to roasted suckling pig with fresh applesauce. The homemade pastas are excellent, particularly the fettuccine with crabmeat, leeks, tomato and cream. Tempting starters are three cheeses in a pastry shell, mussels fra diavolo, and a fine crostino romano (toasted bread with prosciutto, mozzarella, anchovies and mushrooms). Vegetables star in their own appetizer listing in the form of grilled radicchio, sauteed spinach with pine nuts and raisins, and sauteed escarole with garlic, olives and pine nuts. The dessert shelf yields such delectables as raspberry tart, budino al chocolate, mascarpone and ricotta cheesecakes, and tirami su.

Lunch, Monday-Friday 11:30 to 2:30; dinner nightly, 5:30 to 10.

Boxing Cat Grill, 1392 East Putnam Ave., Old Greenwich. (203) 698-1995.
New American. $13.95 to $16.95.

Some new restaurants meet instant success; others don't. This new-in-1988 venture did, and has been packing them in ever since (we faced a half-hour wait for lunch on a midwinter Friday and thought better of it when we saw the hubbub all around). The wait would have been worth it, perhaps, for the Jersey Shore cheese steak, the chicken pot pie or the sole molokai (sauteed in a pineapple-ginger butter with macadamia nuts and snow peas). But instead we came back for a less crowded look at the dramatic interior, which focuses on six tables on a raised dining platform centered with a palmetto tree under a large skylight and looks out a wall of windows onto a rock garden beneath a wall of boulders. Modern acrylic paintings, green and white tablecloths striped on the diagonal, and cacti in clay pots on each table enhance the decor. The with-it menu with California-Southwest accents is a mixed bag, from appetizers through pizzas and salads to entrees and grills. You could start with almond fried calamari or yellowfin tuna maki roll (wrapped in nori with radish sprouts, smelt roe and vinegar rice), Caribbean black bean soup or Louisiana crab bisque, a four-seasons or margherita pizza, or a Ty Cobb or pacifico spinach salad (the last harboring bay scallops, sliced beets, walnuts, smoked cheeses and more). On to the main courses, perhaps shepherd's pie with a strange-sounding but good-tasting sweet potato crust, pan-fried red snapper with sauce of crabmeat and leeks, grilled saddle of lamb with tortilla lasagna, or grilled medallion of salmon with a watercress sauce. Or simply settle for the cadillac burger (jalapeno cheese, guacamole and salsa), with a side order of zucchini strings or coleslaw. Finish with an angel food cake sandwich with vanilla ice cream and lemon cream, chocolate ganache cake or a fresh fruit cobbler.

Lunch, Monday-Friday 11:30 to 3:30; dinner, Monday-Saturday 6 to 10:30 or 11, Sunday 5:30 to 9:30; weekend brunch, noon to 3.

Tucson, 130 East Putnam Ave., Greenwich. (203) 661-2483.
Southwest. $11.95 to $17.

"Bar food," the purists scoff. "A singles place." Not so, though some of both were evident when we were there. The appealing two-level interior with big exposed black pipes, pictures of the Southwest, and glass-topped peach tables is the arena for some interesting fare, particularly at night when full-fledged entrees supplement the "starters" and "light stuff" that make up the lunch menu. Possibilities include grilled salmon filet on a bed of tomatillo sauce topped with a fresh basil and black olive relish, seafood ravioli with grilled salmon, wild mushrooms and scallions and served with a roasted tomato and vodka sauce, broiled lamb chops with a jalapeno-mint sauce, and grilled chicken breasts heady with cumin, garlic, oregano and coriander. Start with fried calamari with salsa fresca or angel-hair pasta with shrimp and roasted pine nuts on a bed of sweet red pepper puree. If you're not up to a full meal, try a pizzette, beef enchilada, or one of the interesting salads. Tucson mud pie, oreo mousse cake and apple-cinnamon chimichanga are among desserts.

Lunch, Monday-Saturday 11:30 to 3; dinner nightly, 6 to 11; Sunday brunch, noon to 3:30.

Morgan, 265 Glenville Road, Greenwich. (203) 531-5100.
New American. $14.95 to $20.95.
This neighborhood bistro in the Glenville-Byram section doesn't get much press or even a bold-face listing in the phone book. But it's a favorite of local restaurateurs of our acquaintance, and obviously popular with regulars who packed the two small dining rooms on either side of the bar-lounge the day we were there. The decor is a mix of parquet floors, paneled walls, black ceiling, pale yellow bentwood armchairs, and white linens. We enjoyed a lunch of sauteed mahi-mahi with a ginger-lime sauce, accompanied by pasta and spaghetti squash with a side salad, and the huge seasonal salad of grilled chicken strips, bacon, brie and hearts of palm, delicious with its Mexican-style dressing. The desserts were ordinary enough to skip, but we'd go back for such dinner entrees as grilled Norwegian salmon with lemon-pepper mayonnaise, chicken valencia, sauteed shrimp with red curry paste and coconut milk, and grilled veal chop with piccata-pine nut butter.

Lunch, Monday-Friday 11:30 to 3:30; dinner nightly, 6 to 11:30; weekend brunch, noon to 3:30.

La Maison Indochine, 107 Greenwich Ave., Greenwich. (203) 869-2689.
Gourmet Vietnamese. $15.50 to $20.50.
This upstairs restaurant, hidden in an alley and up a flight of stairs from the Dress Barn, is more exotic than most Vietnamese restaurants we've seen. An overhead skylight sheds light on fabulous colorful fabric hangings from Vietnam, mother-of-pearl inlaid wood screens, oriental paintings, close-together tables dressed with heavy white linens, gleaming glassware and silverware, and lots of greenery. The menu is exotic as well, from the wonderful soups, Vietnamese country pate, spring rolls and dumplings to deep-fried shrimp beignets and a feuilletee of shrimp wrapped around sugar cane over angel-hair pasta. The grilled chicken with curry, sweet and sour pork, and grilled beef sate come highly recommended. Eating here is an experience, especially if the Vietnamese owner is on hand to guide you.

Lunch, Tuesday-Saturday 11 to 2:30; dinner, Tuesday-Sunday 6 to 10:30.

Stamford

Columbus Park Trattoria, 205 Main St., Stamford. (203) 967-9191.
Italian. $9.50 to $18.50.
Across from a statue of Christopher Columbus in a postage-stamp park, this high-ceilinged downtown storefront is part of a family-run operation that started with Maria's Trattoria in Norwalk and Apulia in South Norwalk. This is considered the best of the three, and was mobbed when others in Stamford were half-empty the day we lunched there. It's a small, convivial room where customers and waiters seem to know each other and we newcomers felt a bit overlooked. Decor is spare: bare walls with a few small cacti in recessed side niches, plants hanging from track-light rails,

and a tall bar whose bottles lend color. Pastas are featured, but for $9.95 at lunch we felt they should have come with a salad as well as the thin, crusty Italian bread that was good enough to request seconds. We liked the penne with radicchio and smoked mozzarella better than the orecchiette with broccoli, sun-dried tomatoes and garlic. At night, you can get the same pastas plus an expanded list of entrees, including red snapper genovese, veal chop with vinegar peppers, quail with wild mushrooms, rabbit with mushrooms and garlic, and lamb chops with rosemary and garlic. Desserts are few and standard: Italian cheesecake, ice cream tartuffo, strawberries and whipped cream, and tirami su.

Lunch, Monday-Friday 11:30 to 2:30; dinner, Monday-Saturday 5 to 10 or 11.

The Magnificent J's, Sheraton Stamford Hotel, One First Stamford Place, Stamford. (203) 967-2222.
New American. $14.95 to $23.95.
Like so many others in Stamford, hotel restaurants come and go — mostly go — but this one seems to have found the right formula. That formula is a setting of restful opulence, professional service, and an interesting menu that's affordably priced. The J boats of America's Cup racing fame set the theme, from the photo murals on the high ceilings that slope inward like those of a sailboat cabin to the logo on the service plates. All is subdued in beige and white with plush armchairs, extravagant chandeliers, and pictures of yachts on the walls. The dinner menu tempts: grilled swordfish with fire-roasted onions, chilies, cilantro and black beans; spicy skillet shrimp with sweet potato hush puppies, creme fraiche and hickory-smoked salmon; red snapper steamed in a corn husk with smoked tomato and corn relish; pork chops with cranberry and black walnut relish, and veal chop with roasted shallots, wild mushrooms and leek compote. Blackened lamb, Maryland crab cakes, mesquite-grilled shrimp with foie gras and cranberries, oyster roast soup, and a salad of smoked salmon with black pasta appeal as starters. The Connecticut clambake brings lobster, clams, mussels, shrimps, sea scallops, and chorizo sausage for $23.95. Desserts range from hot blueberry cobbler to poached saffron pear with hazelnut paste in a phyllo nest.

Dinner, Monday-Saturday 5:30 to 10 or 10:30.

Bourbon Street, 20 Summer St., Stamford. (203) 356-1467.
Cajun/Continental. $14.95 to $18.95.
This is a mix of all those New Orleans restaurants with tile floors, dark wood, a big raw bar, dining areas separated by brass rails, lots of mirrors and coat hooks, a solarium in back, and a very busy bar. Tables are covered with glass, which we don't appreciate, but some of the glass covers are handsomely etched with piano notes. We visited during Mardi Gras, were served by someone costumed as "The Fonz" and enjoyed music by a wandering banjo player. Except for rock-hard rolls, we had a fine lunch of a house specialty, coconut and beer batter shrimp, served with good hot mustardy fruit sauce; a delicious file gumbo chock full of oysters, clams, mussels and scallops, and a smallish Creole-style stew from the trunnion kettles. At dinner, there's plenty of choice: broiled Cajun scallops, blackened fish, trout en papillote, crab au gratin, cornish hen poivrade, roast duckling bigarade, veal paneed with fettuccine, chicken oscar and more. Desserts include such treats as homemade pecan pie, fresh fruit with palmiers and blackened ice cream, whatever that is.

Lunch, Monday-Saturday 11:30 to 3:30; dinner, 5 to 10 or 11, Sunday 5 to 9.

La Bretagne, 2010 West Main St., Stamford. (203) 324-9539.
French. $19 to $26.
Ensconced in a former Chinese restaurant near the Old Greenwich line (and with

something of an old continental feel) is a French restaurant that has endured, which alone sets it apart in a city where others have come and gone. The three dining rooms with well-spaced tables are formal, fairly brightly lit, and enhanced by paintings done by owner Jean Daniel's wife. The menu is classic French, and the kitchen is known for its seafood dishes, especialy mussels served three ways as appetizers. Dover sole (amandine or meuniere, deboned tableside), bay scallops, poached salmon with choron sauce, sweetbreads, roast duckling, and rack of lamb are among recommended choices. Homemade desserts include sour cream cheesecake, carrot cake, creme caramel, and chocolate mousse.

Lunch, Monday-Saturday noon to 2:30; dinner, Monday-Saturday 6 to 9:30 or 10:30.

Sichuan Pavilion, 60 Strawberry Hill Ave., Stamford. (203) 967-9000.
Szechuan. $9.95 to $14.95.

Le Pavillon, the luxury European-style hotel, is now the Royal Pavilion apartments and Aux Beaux Jardins, a stunning Hong Kong-style Far Eastern restaurant, is no more. Its place has been taken by Sichuan Pavilion, a branch of a Manhattan establishment. Though stylish, it doesn't seem to have quite the remarkable ambience of its exotic predecessor, the pinpoint-lighted flower arrangements and many of the Eastern plates and porcelains missing. Authentic Szechuan food is featured, prepared by Chinese government-rated (and furnished) chefs. The menu is lengthy and sufficiently obscure as to require some explanation. Most dishes marked hot and spicy are only mildly so, but the chicken chunks with garlic, lamb Szechuan style and double cooked pork slices come highly recommended. Otherwise, put yourself in the hands of the hosts and trust.

Lunch, Monday-Friday 12:30 to 4; Saturday and Sunday 1 to 4; dinner nightly, 4 to 10 or 11.

Rusty Scupper, 104 Harbor Plaza Drive, Stamford. (203) 964-1235.
Seafood. $12.95 to $18.95.

From almost every table in this angled, multi-level two-story restaurant one may gaze onto Stamford's boat-filled harbor. In summer, the tiered, outdoor deck is the place to be, and at all times the upstairs lounge is the place where locals seem to be. Decor is contemporary and unobtrusive, light and airy. The typical Rusty Scupper menu offers all things for all people. Dinner is preceded by French bread and a large mixed salad. A special of poached salmon and the shrimp tempura were fine, and when we couldn't decide between the mixed vegetables or red-skinned potatoes, our waiter offered both. The specials are usually best: perhaps peppered shark steak, catfish with oriental ginger sauce, grilled yellowfin tuna with a warm tequila-tomato vinaigrette, and fresh mahi-mahi with a robust tomato-cilantro sauce. Prime rib, filet mignon and chicken dishes are available for landlubbers. Desserts tend to the toll house cookie pie and hot fudge brownie a la mode ilk.

Lunch, Monday-Friday 11:30 to 2; dinner, Monday-Saturday 5:30 to 10 or 11; Sunday, brunch 11 to 2, dinner from 4:30.

Darien

Black Goose Grille, 972 Post Road, Darien. (203) 655-7107.
Regional American. $10.95 to $17.95.

Geese on the menu, on the brass door handles, on the lace curtains and atop a shelf in the high-ceilinged dining room are the motif here. With its attractive artwork and tempting offerings, the menu posted outside is guaranteed to draw one in. But inside, the old Hinkel's where we once enjoyed Sunday brunch seems to have gone somewhat downscale. A small, spare dining room with bare wood tables and bentwood chairs competes with a larger, rather more inviting bar. Here is a restaurant in search of a theme. Witness the dinner appetizers: saute of wild mushrooms, two kinds of wontons with spicy currant sauce, nachos with salsa and sour cream, chicken fingers with honey-mustard sauce, Maryland crab cake with pesto mayonnaise, orecchiette pasta with plum tomatoes, wild mushrooms, shallots, basil and ricotta cheese, and two-color fettuccine with prosciutto, sun-dried tomatoes, shiitake mushrooms, romano, cream and cracked pepper. Both of the last also turn up under pastas. Entrees range from chicken pot pie to roast Idaho rainbow trout stuffed with shrimp and scallions, from filet of sole to cassoulet. The grill yields hamburgers, swordfish, sirloin steak with cabernet sauce, and boneless breast of turkey with pear and roquefort cream sauce. These guys must know what they're doing, for they also own the popular Black Bass in Rye, N.Y. And they sure know how to dress up a menu.

Open Monday-Saturday 11:30 to 11, Sunday 11:30 to 10.

Backstreet, 22 Center St., Darien. (203) 655-9944.
American. $10.95 to $17.95.
If ever a restaurant were correctly named, it's this, hidden behind stores on a back street in downtown Darien. Small and intimate, it is half bar and half solarium, with crammed-together tables sporting colorful patchwork cloths under glass and, in season, doubling in size when it spills outside and adds a sidewalk cafe. Salads and appetizers take up half the menu at dinner. The rest is devoted to a dozen or so entrees ranging from fish and chips or shrimp stir-fry to chicken romana and calves liver pommery. Confit of duck, tournedos of beef choron, grilled swordfish, and roast New Zealand rack of lamb with a green peppercorn and brandy sauce are pricier possibilities. White and dark chocolate mousse, carrot cake and cheesecake with white chocolate cassis are favored desserts.

Open daily, 11:30 to 9 or 10.

Newport Grill, 154 Boston Post Road, Darien. (203) 656-0386.
Seafood/Steaks. $8.95 to $18.95.
The decorator had a field day in this cavernous place, converted by the owner of the Tanglewoods group from a Chi-Chi's and, earlier, a Red Coach Grill. On two levels with dark green and dark brown accents against beige walls and ceiling, all is tasteful: a mix of booths and large tables, four neon signs, maritime prints, hanging lamps, track lights, and votive candles. A pianist plays in the luxurious lounge. The menu has been upscaled lately, offering such things as Newport martini scallops sauteed with olive oil and extra dry vermouth, grilled mako shark, seafood pie in a bechamel sauce, cornish game hen with Rhode Island red raspberry sauce, tournedos rossini, "gourmet sandwiches," and pastas, along with basic steak, seafood and prime ribs.

Open Monday-Saturday, 11:30 to 9 or 10, Sunday noon to 9.

Rowayton

Five Mile River Grille, 148 Rowayton Ave., Rowayton. (203) 855-0025.
New American. $10.95 to $19.95.
We expected this establishment to have a view of Rowayton's busy waterfront, but no such luck. It's across the street, and the only water visible here is in an aquarium in the corner of the dining room, where a wall of brick and glass separates it from the bar. But the two-level room is pleasant enough with dark green leather banquettes, fanned white napkins on dark wood tables, tiny oil lamps, fresh flowers, and track lights illuminating pictures of fish and seascapes. All the better to view the food. You might start with gumbo ya ya, Maryland crab cakes with red pepper puree,

Louisiana crayfish and Monterey jack quesadilla with vera cruz sauce, mussels cataplana, tequila chicken grilled with cilantro pesto, or chicken wontons with a diablo sauce. Continue with salmon sauteed in a whole-grain mustard-cognac sauce, sea scallops with blue corn cakes, sole stuffed with shrimp in a tomato coulis, California cioppino, filet mignon with a seasonal relish, or medallions of beef with a pink peppercorn and raspberry demi-glace. Finish with a fresh fruit tart, apple-walnut and cinnamon strudel, or amaretto and chocolate-chip cheesecake.

Lunch, Monday-Friday noon to 3; dinner nightly, 6 to 10 or 11.

New Canaan

✱ L'Abbee Ltd., 62 Main St., New Canaan. (203) 972-6181. Contemporary International. $14.95 to $22.95.

The newest, smallest restaurant in New Canaan was such a smash success that it moved next door in February 1990 to larger quarters to meet demand, extending its hours and adding a bar. Local caterer Paul L'Abbee, of French-Canadian descent, obviously was onto a good thing in 1989 when he opened a small retail store with a few cafe tables and chairs for people who wanted to sip a cup of his tasty hazelnut coffee and nibble on a pastry as they awaited their order for takeout. He moved the takeout area lock, stock and counter to the front of a building that once had been a church, where customers still can order lunch from the deli cases outlined in white della robia and sit at cafe tables covered with strawberry-print cloths or come in for afternoon high tea. Beyond a waiting area with two loveseats is an intimate dining room with little round tables seating a total of 40 and a small bar. In back is a kitchen that fills half the building and is headquarters for the catering operation. Paul was display director at Bergdorf Goodman for years, a talent that shows in the hunter green and white decor, the all-white bar, the pedestal with a showy floral arrangement, the dark green carpeting and the pale green tinted Spanish glassware, the brass candelabra with hurricane lamps, and the brass service plates. Here is the arena for some mighty interesting fare, perhaps salmon poached in court bouillon with sour cream-dill sauce, pork chop with fruit stuffing and apricot sauce, individual beef wellington, boneless duck with tawny port sauce and cracklings on the side, sliced filet mignon with bearnaise, and rack of lamb with rosemary sauce. Starters might be wild mushroom raviolis, penne with asparagus in tomato cream, and Southwestern chicken salad in an edible tortilla basket. Desserts are a L'Abbee forte, perhaps caramelized bread pudding with hard sauce, pear and almond crisp with whipped cream, creme brulee, and sour cream fudge cake with raspberry and chocolate leaves. The small, select wine list is tilted toward Californias.

Open daily except Monday, 8:30 a.m. to 9:30 p.m.

✱ Roger Sherman Inn, 195 Oenoke Ridge, New Canaan. (203) 966-4541. French. $19.75 to $24.75.

This venerable inn, built in 1740, was given a badly needed facelift and a culinary shot in the arm in 1988 by new owner Henry Prieger, formerly of the Inn at Ridgefield. There are six dining rooms of different themes (one a wine cellar for private parties) and a flagstone terrace for outdoor meals. Crisp linens, Dudson china and upholstered chairs in a tapestry look add to the elegant decor. For dinner, the oversize menu that is a Prieger trademark starts with such appetizers as two terrines in port wine aspic, smoked Nordic salmon a la russe, cassolette of snails in garlic cream, grilled clams provencale, and ravioli of lobster with mariniere sauce. Among entrees, you might find navarin of lobster and sweetbreads, casserole of scampis, medallions of veal with chanterelles and ginger, eventail of duck with pear and cassis sauce, and sirloin steak with three mustards. The luscious desserts are homemade, including a trio of sorbets (raspberry, lemon and lime), souffles, creme brulee, and crepes suzette. The extensive wine list is priced from $16 to $500. The lunch menu embraces pastas, salads and entrees ranging from omelets to Maryland crab cakes.

Lunch, Monday-Saturday noon to 2; dinner, 6 to 9 or 10:30; Sunday, brunch noon to 2, dinner 3 to 8.

Gates, 10 Forest St., New Canaan. (203) 966-8666.
American/International. $12.95 to $17.95.

Authentic Austrian gates at the entrance lead to more gates inside at one of New Canaan's more interesting restaurants. Towering ficus trees in the two-story greenhouse section, interior arches, red tile and parquet floors, a veritable art gallery on the walls, and newspapers on racks in the bar enliven a bright, eclectic and noisy place. Cuban black bean soup, burgers and salads like Mediterranean, Greek and vaucluse (with string beans, zucchini, new potatoes, and sun-dried tomatoes) are served all day. So are changing entrees from a lengthy list of specials. Lunch might be chicken oriental, golden snapper aioli or a swordfish sandwich. Dinner includes lemon or curried chicken, filet of sole with soy and ginger served with snow peas, calves liver sesame, a mixed grill of shrimp, chicken and veal sausage, and grilled lamb chops. The beer list numbers countless varieties from the Philippines to Czechoslovakia, and the wines are among the area's more reasonably priced.

Lunch daily, 11:30 to 3:30; dinner from 6.

Nantucket Cafe, 15 Elm St., New Canaan. (203) 972-0831.
American/Continental. $13.95 to $17.95.

Owners Pieter and Elizabeth Van Munching like to vacation on Nantucket, which explains the name and theme of this little place with two dozen seats and so small that smoking is banned. Gray shingled walls evoke a Nantucket beach cottage, and a mirror the length of one wall adds dimension. Framed Nantucket photos and prints, a couple of booths for two with bright floral cushions opposite the bar, white molded chairs, glass over white tablecloths, and a brass bar that has to be polished every day complete the summery Nantucket look. A few menu items bear Nantucket names, some inexplicably as in Brant Point baked brie and Nantucket chicken wings, and some understandably as in Madaket clam chowder and Siasconset scallop salad, which along with shrimp pesto salad is available at both lunch and dinner. Dinner entrees include sole vera cruz, grilled tuna or swordfish, seafood primavera, chicken chasseur, and veal normande. Key lime pie, creme caramel and oreo decadence are likely desserts. All but two of the seldom-seen vintages on the short wine list are available by the glass and are nicely priced in the teens.

Lunch, Monday-Saturday 11:30 to 2:30; dinner, Monday-Saturday 5:30 to 9 or 10; Sunday brunch, 9 to 1. No smoking.

The Little Kitchen of New Canaan, 64 Main St., New Canaan.
(203) 972-6881.
Chinese/Indonesian. $5.95 to $25.

Part of the late, fashionable Mr. Lee restaurant gave way in 1989 to this small establishment with two colorful dining rooms with rattan chairs, wild print tablecloths under glass, Chinese celadon tableware, and posters and big fans on the melon-colored walls. Indonesian, Malaysian and Vietnamese specialties reflecting the cooks' varied backgrounds turn up on the menu. Unusual dishes include crispy eggplant pancakes with ground beef as an appetizer and South China Sea entrees like prawns Bali style, sliced lamb with scallions and red peppers in a spicy basil sauce, mixed seafood with basil in a garlic sauce, Renbang beef stew with coconut, tumeric and lemon grass, and a choice of beef, chicken or shrimp sauteed with mixed vegetables and shallots in a spicy tamarind sauce. Ginger duck, prawns with mustard sauce, orange-flavored beef or chicken, and Peking duck are other possibilities. Desserts are black bean rice pudding, lychees and kumquats.

Lunch, Monday-Saturday 11:30 to 3; dinner nightly, 3 to 10 or 11, Sunday noon to 10.

Ridgefield

★♥ Stonehenge, Route 7, Ridgefield. (203) 438-6511.
New French. $19 to $26; Weekends, Prix-Fixe, $44.

Stonehenge has been known for distinguished cuisine since the days of its famed Swiss chef, Albert Stockli. Owners David Davis and Douglas Seville have enhanced the tradition, surviving a disastrous fire but reopening in grand new quarters in 1989. The rebuilt restaurant is patterned after its original early 19th-century, white Colonial-style edifice. But it is smaller than the original and designed with a new side entrance and a layout that gives virtually every table a view of the lake and bucolic surroundings that make the inn so special. Handsome swagged draperies and corner cabinets filled with rare china and silver enhance the beautiful main dining room done in a peachy coral, green and white scheme. English sporting prints and wall sconces made from hunting horns adorn the walls of the cozy tavern outfitted in hunter green. The a la carte menu gives way on weekends to prix-fixe meals of four courses for $44. Dinner begins with complimentary canapes, a miniature asparagus spear wrapped in prosciutto and a tiny new potato stuffed with caviar and sour cream at our latest visit. We like to start with Stonehenge's hearty barley soup and its classic shrimp in beer batter with pungent fruit sauce. Among other appetizers, a crepe of wild mushrooms with a mornay sauce and gruyere cheese was out of this world, as was a sizzling sausage, smoked in the Stonehenge kitchen, served with a mustard-wine sauce and garnished with grapes. Entrees could be broiled brook trout deboned at tableside, rack of Kentucky lamb with fresh rosemary, medallions of pork with sweet ginger and vermouth, crisply roasted duckling with a raspberry sauce, sauteed filet of Norwegian salmon with a leek and champagne sauce, and noisettes of veal loin with foie gras and morels. In season, you can get pate-stuffed roast quail with truffles and saddle of venison. Luscious desserts include a remarkable sweet pastry basket with fresh fruits cascading over the sides into creme anglaise, creamy cheesecake with white chocolate sauce, and orange creme caramel.

Dinner nightly, 6 to 9:30; Sunday, brunch 11:30 to 3, dinner 4 to 8:30

La Cave, Big Shop Lane, Ridgefield. (203) 431-3060.
French. $16.25 to $18.50.

Serenely pretty and intimate in the lower level of a 19th-century blacksmith shop at the end of a row of stores, this restaurant evolved from the old Le Coq Hardi in 1989 with the same ownership and new management. Billed as a French bistro, it takes its name from its rough fieldstone walls. But a glamorous cave is this: a sophisticated country look in burgundy and green, with lace curtains and vases of alstroemeria. The lunch menu is written daily on a white board: omelets, turkey melt, garden burger (no bun) on a bed of lettuce, and a couple of entrees like liver and onions or grilled salmon with sorrel. At night, the mood turns convivial and/or romantic for dining on such entrees as grilled salmon, roast duck with orange sauce, calves liver with raspberry vinegar, choucroute, grilled lamb chops, and pepper steak with sauteed shallots. Warm goat cheese salad and garlic sausage served on a green salad are a couple of starters. Among desserts are chocolate truffle cake and praline torte. A light bar menu is served in the new greenhouse bar in front.

Lunch, Monday-Friday noon to 2; dinner nightly, 6 to 10; Sunday, brunch noon to 3, dinner 3 to 9.

The Inn at Ridgefield, 20 West Lane (Route 35), Ridgefield. (203) 438-8282.
French. $18.75 to $25.75; Prix-Fixe, $39.

A profusion of flowers brightens the canopied entrance to this formal restaurant founded in 1947. The entrance is lined with the sides of wine crates from across the world. Three dining rooms plus a small bar are attractively furnished in turn-of-the-century style with rich fabric wallpaper, chandeliers and comfortable upholstered chairs at large, well-spaced tables. The striking pewter service plates are emblazoned with a picture of the inn. Except for the change of faces, regulars barely noted a difference when new chef Johannes Brugger and partner Ray Kuhnt bought the inn from longtime owner Henry Prieger. The ambitious, oversize dinner menu is prix-fixe at $39 for one side that favors the new French cuisine and a la carte for the traditional continental side. It's supplemented by a variety of specials listed on a white board — everything from a pate of pistachios and truffles with spiced cassis sauce to medallions of venison Baden-Baden on a recent visit. Chef Brugger has maintained some of the inn's traditional dishes, among them such appetizers as smoked eel with dill sauce and Peruvian shrimp cocktail. Entrees include filet of sole caprice, breast of chicken catalane, Spanish red-tail shrimp, wiener schnitzel, flambeed roast duckling, chateaubriand, and rack of lamb. On the prix-fixe side, you might start with a pate of salmon, sole and lobster with a fresh basil sauce, feast on filet mignon with pistachio and truffle sauce or sliced duck with green peppercorns and sweet and sour sauce, and finish with one of the acclaimed desserts, perhaps a chocolate mousse cake or an almond tart with raspberry and marzipan.

Lunch, Monday-Saturday noon to 2; dinner nightly, 6 to 9:30 or 10:30; Sunday, brunch noon to 3, dinner 3 to 8.

The Elms, 500 Main St., Ridgefield. (203) 438-2541.
American/Continental. $17 to $26.

This is Ridgefield's oldest operating inn (1799), and traditionalists still favor it for lunch on the enclosed front porch or dinner in one of the older dining rooms. Robert Scala has continued the reputation for solid American and continental cuisine built by his father, John, a former master chef at the St. Regis in New York. Robert says his aim is "to remain traditional in a world of change." We note, however, that a few trendies like arugula salad have crept in. The large a la carte menu lists appetizers from salade russe to clams casino. Among entrees are filet of sole amandine, scampi romani, curry of sliced capon, veal marsala, English lamb chop with kidney and bacon, sweetbreads, steak au poivre, and chateaubriand for two. Desserts include a selection from the cart as well as cherries jubilee and peaches flambeed in brandy. Robert Scala is proud of his wine cellar of more than 8,000 bottles — some are attractively displayed on a table in the main foyer. A pianist plays on weekends in the Music Room.

Lunch, noon to 2:30; dinner, 6 to 9:30 or 10; Sunday, brunch noon to 2:30, dinner 5 to 8:30. Closed Wednesday.

Scrimshaw's of Ridgefield, 5 Bailey Ave., Ridgefield. (203) 438-1774.
Seafood. $10.95 to $15.95.

The former storeroom of a hardware store has been transformed into a bright, intimate seafood restaurant containing two long, narrow dining rooms with raw wood trim, heavy wooden tables and small lanterns on the walls. Dusty pink linens and fanned napkins add elegance at night. Chef Dave Hammond oversees a vast menu, supplemented by daily specials — perhaps sauteed sea bass with tomato concasse and herbs, lemon sole with spinach and scallop stuffing and dill hollandaise sauce, grilled swordfish with salsa picante, broiled Norwegian salmon with lobster sauce, and baked brook trout with salmon mousse in puff pastry. Regular entrees include everything from baked bay scallops and shrimp parmigiana a la grecque to paella and bouillabaisse. Good starters are marinated squid, conch and octopus or a seafood sampler platter (shrimp, clams, smoked trout, cheese and marinated eggplant salad served over lettuce). Half a dozen pastas harbor seafood treats. The seafood is fresh from New York's Fulton Fish Market, the cooking simple with light sauces made from homemade stocks, and the abundant portions include vegetable, potato and house salad. Desserts include passion fruit cake, almond-praline delice, ganache cake, and white chocolate mousse cake. The wine list carries some excellent vineyards and values.

Lunch, Monday-Friday 11:30 to 2:30; dinner nightly, 5:30 to 9:30 or 10:30.

Southwest Cafe, 109 Danbury Road, Copps Hill Common, Ridgefield. (203) 431-3398.
Mexican/Southwest. $7.95 to $8.95.

Just in time to capitalize on the trend toward Southwest cooking, New Mexican restaurateur Cheryl Guerrie came to town and opened the Southwest Charcuterie with Barbara Nevins. A couple of name changes later, the cafe emerged with highly rated Southwest and Mexican foods. Tortilla soup, enchiladas, tacos, tostadas and gringo salads (including shrimp and vegetables, tuna and cucumber) are offered at lunch. The dinner menu brings much of the same, plus (inexplicably) huevos rancheros. That's also on the Sunday brunch menu, with blue corn pancakes, green chile stew, nachos grande and more. Try the blue coyote, kind of a margarita made with wine and colored with curacao, and save room for a Mexican flan or kahlua-pecan pie. Patrons sit at a counter or at an assortment of tables each topped with a cactus.

Lunch daily, 11 to 5 (Sunday to 4); dinner nightly, 5 to 9:30 or 10.

West Redding

★ **L'Hotellerie des Bois,** 4 Long Ridge Road, West Redding. (203) 938-8585.
French. $18 to $25.

It's almost like a fairy tale, finding a mini-chateau, not exactly in the woods, but certainly not where you would expect to see a gorgeous restaurant straight out of the French countryside. Frenchman Gerard Sebban, whose family owns several restaurants in France, spared no expense on the building nor the furnishings. An auberge-style, tiled front hall filled with fencing swords, tapestries and hunting guns gives way to an airy lounge with a marble bar and six dining tables on one side, a beamed dining room with a terra-cotta tiled floor and handsome sideboards and corner cabinets on the other. Everything from the door knobs and curtains to the chairs and bar stools was imported from France. Except for the handsome china and glassware, the tables are set entirely with silver: flatware, salt and pepper shakers, vases, ramekins of butter, wine holders — and plates of food are covered with silver domes that are removed with a flourish. Flourishes prevail in the kitchen as well. Our dinner started with an endive leaf filled with salmon mousse garnished with black caviar and dill, "compliments of the chef." We shared an appetizer of a masterful lobster pate, presented with a full fish service for two. Sweetbreads sauteed with Westphalian ham and capers and two grilled quails with mushroom sauce came with exquisite vegetables: a puree of squash, cauliflower with a crumb topping, a timbale of spinach, and tiny sauteed potato balls or wild rice. Under new chef Andrew Klein from the Hotel Pierre in New York, entrees could include bouillabaisse and noisettes of veal with asparagus and tomato chive sauce. Among desserts on the cylindrical silver cart, we succumbed to a nougat glace and a chocolate-praline meringue cake topped with fresh raspberries. The bill, presented on a silver tray, came with bitter chocolate truffles and caramel nut squares on shortbread.

Lunch, Tuesday-Friday noon to 3; dinner, Tuesday-Sunday 6 to 9 or 10; Sunday brunch, noon to 3.

Norwalk

✳ Pasta Nostra, 116 Washington St., Norwalk. (203) 854-9700.
Contemporary Italian. $14 to $20.

Pass by the three pasta machines in the window (the energetic young man making the raviolis might well be chef-owner Joe Bruno himself) and the cases filled with goodies to take out. Settle into the long and narrow back room with its tiled floor, high ceilings and track lighting. The room is unadorned, tables are bare, chairs are uncomfortable bentwood, and it's noisy. But no one seems to mind, for the food is the star here. This may well be the best Italian food in Connecticut, from the Italian bread with just the right amount of crispy crust to the chocolate sponge cake with raspberries and whipped cream. Both lunch and dinner menus change daily. Pastas might include pork loin with hot and sweet pickled peppers with linguini, puttanesca, shrimp sauce with spicy red linguini, and the one we tried, fettuccine with pesto, riccota and pignoli, which was superb. From the intriguing antipasti list, we chose one of soft bel paese cheese, sliced tomato and prosciutto, the best we've ever had. The other marvelous appetizer that made half a lunch was a ball of robiola cheese dusted with herbs in the middle of toasted croutons covered with a black olive spread. At dinner, the menu expands a bit. Try the crostini with a puree of black olives and goat cheese, swordfish spiedini with braised scallions or cheese-stuffed steak with potato gnocchi. Chef Joe, quite a character, ranges from outrageous to inspired. A self-trained cook who grew up in New York, he likes to add items like clams oreganata alla Mom and Aunt Nancy's ravioli of spinach, cheese and meat to a menu that is often at the cutting edge.

Lunch, Tuesday-Friday 11:45 to 2:45; dinner, Thursday-Saturday 6 to 9:30.

✳ $ La Provence, 86 Washington St., South Norwalk. (203) 855-8958.
French. $13 to $15.

This new-in-1989 storefront restaurant looks as if it's straight out of the south of France. It's charming with brick and beam walls, ladderback chairs at tables draped in white over rose cloths, old French posters and Quimper plates on the walls, stuffed dolls on the shelves, and baskets of dried flowers everywhere. The setting is mere backdrop for the food, which prompted the New York Times to award an "excellent" rating and ensure that its tables would be booked days to weeks in advance. The kitchen is the domain of Patrick Benrezkellah, co-owner with maitre d'hotel Patrick Ravanello, both formerly with Guy Savoy in Greenwich. Their prix-fixe meals are extraordinary bargains — $17 for a three-course dinner that could be $25 if ordered separately, and $12.50 for a three-course lunch. A typical prix-fixe dinner might offer a choice of four starters: soup du jour, four-leaf salad, imported prosciutto, and salad of fresh green lentils with bacon. The main course could be beef daube baked in red wine provencale style with potato gnocchi, homemade chicken sausage boudin blanc with leek and spinach sauce, or bouillabaisse vallon des auffes. Crepes suzette, creme brulee, or chocolate mousse could end a meal to remember. Other a la carte entrees might be Algerian couscous with lamb and vegetables, duck confit with potatoes anna and wild mushrooms, savoy cabbage stuffed with homemade sausage, roquefort and pecan nuts, and shrimp and sea scallops in garlic and olive oil on green lentils. Heady stuff, this, daring to embrace North African touches and served in robust portions. The short French wine list starts at $15, but most are over

14

$20, making wine the most expensive part of the average dinner tab at this charmer of a place.

Lunch, Tuesday-Friday noon to 2:30; dinner, Tuesday-Saturday 6:30 to 9:30 or 10.

✴ Meson Galicia, 250 Westport Ave. (Route 1), Norwalk. (203) 846-0223. Spanish. $14.50 to $22.

This prize of five years' standing in a shopping center is unexpectedly lavish, its two-level dining room dressed with blond wood, white over peach linens, booths in striped velvet, curved banquettes, well-spaced tables with windsor chairs, and a ficus tree rising into an atrium skylight. The food is the match for the setting, consistently earning raves for the finest Spanish fare in Connecticut. Ignacio Blanco oversees a kitchen known for seafood specialties from the oceanside Galician region, especially a light sea bass Galician style, the fish and shellfish Catalan style, and grilled salmon with red bell peppers and aioli. Other entrees entice: the classic paella valencia, veal sweetbreads with shrimp, loin of lamb Navarra style, and filets of duck breast with chestnuts. The nightly specials might include hake in a green sauce with clams, stuffed squid in its own ink, and beef tenderloin with goat cheese and juniper berries. Start with Galician or black bean soup, endive and radicchio salad with tetilla cheese, octopus in olive oil and Spanish paprika, grilled Spanish sausages with mushrooms, or baked goat cheese with fennel, basil and tomatoes. Among fabulous desserts are flan, chocolate mango mousse and a raspberry-straw-berry-kiwi tart. The Spanish wine list includes about 100 entries.

Lunch, Monday-Friday 11:30 to 2:30; dinner nightly, 5 to 9:30 or 10:30.

Apulia, 70 North Main St., South Norwalk. (203) 852-1168. Italian. $9.95 to $21.95.

An offshoot of Maria's Trattoria across town, this is more than twice its size and offers an oversize menu with high aspirations. You'll find about fifteen pastas, including tubettini with seafood and tomato sauce, and ravioli filled with spinach and filet of sole in red shrimp sauce. The most expensive entrees are mixed grills of assorted fish (swordfish, sole, shrimp, salmon and clams) and meat (beef, lamb and veal). Other possibilities are grilled red snapper, filet of sole in orange-lemon sauce with capers and anchovies, grilled shrimp with broccoli, veal saltimbocca, lamb stew, and cornish hen roasted with garlic and rosemary. The changing desserts might include mascarpone cake, Italian cheesecake and tirami su. All this is served in two side-by-side dining rooms at well-spaced tables with white cloths and dark green napkins, bentwood chairs, hanging plants, and a few prints and plates on the walls.

Lunch, Monday-Friday 11:30 to 3; dinner, Monday-Saturday 5 to 10 or 11.

Sweptaway, 2 South Main St., South Norwalk. (203) 852-1716. American. $8.95 to $14.95.

The folks from Breakaway in Fairfield run this vast place about quadruple its size, with two dining rooms separated from a huge, noisy lounge that has a square bar in the center. The dining rooms are mod in black and white, with black tables and chairs with gray tweed seats, gray sponged wainscoting, and paned mirrors on the walls. The casual, all-day menu has something for everyone, and is particularly strong on salads and sandwiches. At night the kitchen shines with such entrees as grilled tuna topped with chopped vegetables in a light vinaigrette, poached Nor-wegian salmon with dijon butter sauce, shrimp and scallop stir-fry over orange-ginger linguini, grilled flank steak on garlic toast, and charbroiled lamb chops. Desserts run to chocolate mousse, coconut cream pie and brownies.

Open daily, 11:30 to 11 or 11:30.

Fairfield County

Portofino Clam House, 18 South Main St., South Norwalk. (203) 838-8605.
Seafood/Italian. $9.95 to $16.95.
Clams, of course, are the star at this sister of a Greenwich restaurant. They're available six ways as appetizers, on a fried platter, or as steamers in a clambake for two. But there's much more: fried seafood, the specialty tortellini Portofino, warm salmon salad over a bed of spinach, shrimp fra diavolo, veal parmigiana, barbecued ribs, seafood brochette, and angus sirloin steak. Finish with New York creamy cheesecake, peach melba or triple layer chocolate cake. The decor in several dining rooms is casual: red bentwood chairs at tables of inlaid green and red, small hurricane lamps on blocks of wood, and old posters on brick walls.
Lunch, Monday-Friday 11:45 to 3; dinner, Monday-Thursday 6 to 10, Friday-Sunday 5 or 5:30 to 10 or 11.

Westport

★ **Francine's,** 7 Sconset Square, Westport. (203) 454-9531.
Contemporary. $17 to $21.
This intimate space in a suave shopping center has housed many a restaurant, but none better than Francine's, which opened to good reviews in 1989. Moving here from their restaurant — Jessica's House — in the Hamptons, Francine Garb and her husband Isaac, the chef and the artist, cater to serious foodies with original cooking and chutzpah. The striped, uncovered tables are striking, each washed in acrylic to become its own abstract painting and "to really show the food," according to Isaac, who did each one along with some of the paintings on the walls. The hand-printed menu changes, but you might start with a cilantro and parsnip soup, an onion tart, pasta with sun-dried tomatoes, or a goat cheese salad with sauteed mushrooms, tomatoes and basil. Move on to shrimp with caramelized garlic served with linguini, spicy crusty seared salmon over arugula, succulent sea scallops sauced with lemon and tomato, roast loin of pork stuffed with prunes and apricots in a lemon-cognac sauce, or loin lamb chops seared in sweet and hot spices with mint jelly. Snow pea pods and couscous are possible accompaniments. For dessert, how about mango mousse, chocolate ganache with fresh fruit, or chocolate-orange cake? A good wine list starts in the low teens. Although Isaac has cooked most cuisines, he says all his dishes are now his own creations. Francine adds that their aim is to serve the best food in Connecticut.
Dinner, Wednesday-Sunday 6 to 10.

★ **Da Pietro,** 36 Riverside Ave., Westport. (203) 454-1213.
Northern Italian. $15.25 to $24.95.
Standing out among Westport's sea of restaurants is this little gem with 22 coveted seats in a stylish dining room, handsome as can be with oak wainscoting, patterned banquettes, ladderback chairs, Villeroy & Boch china, brass hurricane lamps, and tapestries on the walls. Since opening in 1989, chef-owner Pietro Scotti and his staff have kept those seats filled nightly (and booked way ahead), such is the renown of the fare. Stellar starters include bruschetta (toasted bread drizzled with diced tomatoes, olive oil and basil), coquilles St. Jacques, and any of the salads, particularly the radicchio, baby bibb, arugula, and gorgonzola dressed with olive oil and balsamic vinegar. All the pastas are highly rated, as are such entrees as sweetbreads, veal medallions with chanterelles and cognac, roasted duck with lingonberries and calvados, and saddle of lamb with garlic and leeks. Cappuccino and chocolate velvet cakes, profiteroles, ricotta cheesecake, and fruit tarts are among desserts. A three-course prix-fixe dinner with several choices is available for

$36.95. Italian opera music plays in the background as you sip an Italian wine and partake of the good life.

Dinner, Monday-Saturday 5:30 to 10.

Le Chambord, 1572 Post Road East, Westport. (203) 255-2654.
French. $14.50 to $21.50.

Other restaurants come and go, but this local institution remains a fixture on the haute dining scene. Chef Robert Pouget and maitre-d Oscar Basler run a beautiful place in the classic manner, with a traditional menu that rarely changes. Several dining areas on different levels are glamorous in beige and pink, with lattice work and mirrors at once dividing and making the space look bigger. Three-course table d'hote dinners are featured, the price ($20.95 to $29.95) depending on choice of entree, from frog's legs provencale to dover sole and filet of wild boar poivrade. Duckling a l'orange, coq au vin, veal kidneys, calves brains, veal chop, venison, and chateaubriand bouquetiere are among the possibilities on the seemingly endless menu. Desserts are a particularly strong suit. Souffle grand marnier, cherries jubilee, coupe aux marrons — all the classics are there at, surprisingly for Fairfield County, not unreasonable prices. No wonder the traditionalists love Le Chambord.

Lunch, Tuesday-Friday noon to 2; dinner, Tuesday-Saturday 5:30 to 9 or 10. Jackets required.

Chez Pierre, 142 Main St., Westport. (203) 227-5295.
French. $15.50 to $19.50.

Where the other veteran French institution in town is elegant French, this charming oldtimer has a casual cafe atmosphere. Proprietor Pierre Nelli founded the place in 1958 in an early American farmhouse; now it's surrounded by chic shops. The second-story walkup opens into a cozy lounge with cafe tables for dining. Beyond is a beamed dining room with red and white checkered tablecloths, bentwood chairs, wine racks on the walls and copper pots everywhere, all dark and intimate and like a French bistro. A rear terrace provides al fresco dining in summer. Pierre says the menu has hardly changed in 30 years. There's no need for it to change, when regulars pack the place for such specialties as coquilles St. Jacques with tarragon glace, dover sole amandine, grilled veal chop with prosciutto and fresh pasta, sweetbreads with spinach and black currants, filet au roquefort, and rack of lamb for two. Start with classic French onion soup or a crepe of chicken and mushrooms. Finish with profiteroles, chocolate mousse or creme caramel. The wine list is an interesting mix, most priced in the upper teens.

Lunch, Monday-Saturday noon to 2; dinner, Monday-Saturday from 6. No Saturday lunch in summer.

Dameon, 32 Railroad Place, Westport. (203) 226-6580.
French. $10.95 to $25.95.

As if Westport needed another French restaurant! This relative newcomer (fifteen years) has survived very nicely, thank you, behind its jaunty canopies facing the Westport train station. In a bistro atmosphere beneath a high tin ceiling, chef-owner George Llorens and partner Lisa Reese serve a slightly updated French menu. That is, the printed menu is updated: lemon sole dijonnaise, swordfish with wine and capers, sweetbreads in a green peppercorn sauce, medallions of pork with apples in applejack sauce, and pasta au pesto and lobster raviolettes as entrees. The blackboard menu is traditional and staggering: duck two ways, red snapper four ways, possibly 40 or 50 variations on the theme, and even the waiter isn't sure of all the variations. Suffice to say that the Norwegian salmon may come with julienne of leeks and mustard seed sauce or en croute. Among delectable desserts are raspberry nut cake, strawberry crepes, cheesecake with two sauces, and frozen lime pie.

Lunch, Monday-Friday noon to 3; dinner, Monday-Saturday 6 to 10.

Stone's Throw, 323 North Main St., Westport. (203) 226-1799.
Contemporary American. $12.95 to $18.95.

Located a long stone's throw from downtown and the Post Road where most Westport restaurants hang out, this newcomer occupies a white building that looks like a house and acts like a contemporary country cafe with wainscoted walls, balloon-curtained windows, hanging ribbed-glass lamps, windsor chairs, and floral red and black tablecloths topped (the only jarring note) by glass. It's a pretty setting for chef-partner Laurie Vander Woude's fresh fare. Likely dinner entrees are sauteed catfish garnished with leeks and tomatoes, grilled turkey paillard with juniper berries and port wine sauce, roasted duckling with ginger and soy sauce, sauteed calves liver with bacon, onions and mustard seeds, and grilled lamb chops with roasted shallots, endive and mint. Grilled tuna on a bed of fresh fennel with capers and leeks was a special the night we were there. For starters, try the interesting sweet potato and apple soup, grilled oysters with cognac and leek butter, cold peppered sirloin with basil and caper sauce, or angel-hair pasta with rock shrimp and sun-dried tomatoes. The signature dessert is creme brulee, followed by chocolate chip pie and apple oatmeal cake. Good old meatloaf with mashed potatoes and gravy vies with more modern items for attention on the lunch menu.

Lunch, Monday-Friday 11:30 to 3; dinner nightly, 6 to 10 or 11, Sunday to 9; weekend brunch, 11:30 to 3.

Saratoga, 1563 Post Road, Westport. (203) 254-7777.
American. $11.95 to $17.95.

Yet another restaurant opening in food-crazed Westport, this one emerged in November 1989 along Post Road's restaurant row. The folks from Backstreet in Darien branched out here, favoring a country cafe look in an airy dining room and lounge, with stenciled columns, etched glass, teal carpeting, and glass over patterned tablecloths. A patio was in the works for summer dining. The menu includes Cajun blackened fish, stir-fried shrimp and vegetables, filet of sole with almonds and grapes, chicken with melted brie and a puree of raspberries, sauteed calves liver with shallots, scallions and balsamic vinegar, and grilled lamb chops with a spinach, tomato and madeira wine sauce. You also can make a meal out of soups and appetizers, say Cuban black bean soup and country pate with a red currant sauce, and a cobb or warm chicken and watercress salad. The same goes for lunch, when more salads, sandwiches, burgers and omelets appear. White and dark chocolate mousse, pumpkin spice cake and varying cheesecakes are among desserts.

Open daily from 11:30 to 10 or 11; weekend brunch, 11:30 to 4.

Fairfield

Centro, 1435 Post Road, Fairfield. (203) 255-1210.
New Italian. $6.50 to $14.95.

The folks from Gates in New Canaan and the Pompano Grill in Westport opened this trendy Italian eatery in 1989 in the center of Fairfield. Enter through a takeout area where the deli case displays delectable salads and hearty Italian breads into an airy, long and narrow room with large windows along the side and pale peach walls accented with trompe l'oeil columns. There is whimsy here: pictures of one of the owner's young children framed atop the columns and drawings of olives, a broken wine glass, pennies and a pizza slice here and there on the tiled floor, a painting of a shark's mouth in the men's room urinal and another of fishes in the ladies' sink. Mod black chairs flank tables with white paper over white cloths, each sporting crayons for doodling, a dish of marinated olives, and a carafe of water with a whole lemon (slice it if you wish) on top. A generous glass of the house Italian chardonnay and a basket of crusty, loose-textured peasant bread started our lunches — a chicken pancetta salad with an assertive garlic and olive oil dressing, and a tasty farfalle al forno pasta with three cheeses, sausages and peas. We were so full we could only look longingly at the sweet potato pecan pie and the tirami su being devoured for dessert at the next table. The dinner menu lists ten European pizzas (the seafood version is especially choice), big enough to serve as appetizers for four, and eight pastas, plus a handful of specials like tuna catania and veal taranto. The with-it wine list is priced primarily in the teens.

Lunch, Monday-Saturday 11:30 to 3; dinner nightly, 5:30 to 10 or 11; Sunday brunch.

Gregory's, 1599 Post Road, Fairfield. (203) 259-7417.
New American. $14.95 to $21.95.

An extremely knowledgeable staff and fresh, new American cuisine are the hallmarks of this elegant, mod eatery operated by Starr Zuckerman in partnership with daughter Reina, the pastry chef, and named for her son Greg. Theirs is a sophisticated yet casual room, long and narrow with oriental rugs, four huge columns, linened tables, blond wood chairs with rush seats, flowers in Perrier bottles, and sconces interspersed between framed prints of fruits and vegetables on the cream-colored and mirrored walls. There's a convivial bar in the rear. Lentil soup plus a hot duck salad over arugula and roasted veal hash are appealing items from the winter lunch menu. Veal is highly rated at dinner — perhaps sauteed with shrimp in a lime and tomato cream with fresh basil, or with sun-dried tomatoes, garlic and sweet peppers. Other possibilities might be grilled pork spiced with garlic and cilantro and served with red onions, black beans and Mayan sauce; roasted duckling with apples in an apple brandy and peppercorn cream sauce; sauteed shrimp served with garlic and herbs, and grilled chicken marinated in Indian spices and yogurt, served with a fresh fruit chutney. Start perhaps with grilled homemade sausage or medallions of beef sauteed with onion, garlic, cilantro and lime. Assertive fare, this, and eminently respected by the clientele. Wonderful desserts include hazelnut mocha torte and cranberry streusel cake with white chocolate sauce. The inspired wine list covers all price ranges.

Lunch, Monday-Saturday 11:30 to 3; dinner nightly, 5:30 to 10 or 11.

Breakaway, 2316 Post Road, Fairfield. (203) 255-0026.
American. $10.95 to $14.95.

Everyone hereabouts loves Breakaway, first of a chain that now includes Sweptaway in Norwalk and Thataway in Greenwich. They love it for casual food, low prices and a convivial — make that crowded — eating and drinking scene. The building is unexpectedly small, looking from the outside like an art deco Southwest grill from yesteryear. Inside, all is vaguely deco and very close: blue and black seats and banquettes, high tables in the bar, and the noise echoing off a pressed-tin ceiling. The all-day menu features slurpers, snackers, crispers, beefers, stackers, double deckers and standbys (for those sandwiches that don't fit other categories), plus spectaculars (barbecues and strip steak with house salad) and sensations, the day's blackboard specials, perhaps grilled salmon steak with hollandaise or chicken breast in mustard cream sauce. Mississippi mud pie, tollhouse pie, peachy berry pie and oreo fudge pie were among the eight pies chalked up on the blackboard when we were there. The only other dessert offered: a brownie.

Open Monday-Saturday, 11:30 to 10 or 11; Sunday, 4 to 10.

Bridgeport

Wellingtons Market Restaurant, 2521 Main St., Bridgeport. (203) 335-9431.
Continental. $9.50 to $16.95.

Chef Paul Murphy took over this storefront space with two side-by-side dining rooms in 1989 after the well-regarded Tavern on the Main closed. He dressed up the interior, added all kinds of artworks and baskets for sale (hence the market name), and drew a receptive following with a sophisticated menu of manageable size. The high tin ceilings are painted gray; the chair seats match the runners on the tables covered with mulberry cloths and pastel napkins. A painted wooden tulip and a candle in a fancy glass holder are on each table. Likely appetizers are escargots wellington, clams casino, scungilli salad, mussels and plum tomatoes, and smoked fish. A loaf of Italian bread sprinkled with sesame seeds and a house salad accompany the entrees, perhaps grilled chicken soy, sauteed bay scallops with julienne of zucchini and carrots, Cajun shrimp, roast duckling with mandarin orange sauce, veal medallions with sliced eggplant, ham and mozzarella, and pena pasta with ham, mushrooms, peas and romano cheese. Favored desserts are cappuccino mousse cake and white pistachio ice cream in a pastry shell on strawberry sauce with fresh mint. Wines from five countries are offered at fair prices.

Lunch, Monday-Friday 11:30 to 2:30; dinner, Monday-Saturday 5:30 to 10.

Ocean Sea Grill, 1328 Main St., Bridgeport. (203) 336-2132.
Seafood. $10.50 to $18.50.

"Our customers expect quality, but they don't want a lot of frills," said the longtime waiter at this downtown institution of 55 years. What they get are fresh seafood, generous portions and reasonable prices in a solid, art deco building of the old school in a rather rundown neighborhood. The two large dining rooms have been slightly upscaled since we dined here a decade ago. The main one has two levels, brick walls interspersed with beige fabric, bentwood arm chairs, peach lalique-style lamps, and peach and green linens whose colors somehow seem out of place. The lengthy menu pairs broiled and fried seafood with such fancier items as shrimp newburg, frog's legs, lobster au gratin, and lobster and shrimp provencale over linguini. You can start with tomato juice or fruit cocktail, fried mozzarella or smoked salmon. Special vegetables and salads are a la carte, although some also come with the entree. We liked the impeccably fresh oysters from the restaurant's fish market and lobster thermidor served en coquille. Among modest desserts are chocolate mousse, rice pudding and carrot cake.

Lunch, Monday-Saturday 11:30 to 5; dinner, 5 to 10 or 10:30. Closed Sunday.

Stratford

The Shell Station, West Main Street at the Railroad Station, Stratford.
(203) 377-1648.
Seafood/Continental. $9.25 to $18.

Trains rumble by, only a few feet from the windows of this old waiting room-turned-restaurant. It's a crowded melange of tables with white linens under glass, mulberry napkins, carved-back chairs, and wooden grooved walls bearing a bit of art. Shellfish is the specialty, as the name suggests. It comes many ways, from baked stuffed shrimp, homemade pasta festooned with clams, mussels and shrimp, shrimp diana over linguini, and sauteed lobster meat to bouillabaisse and paella for two. A dash of curry sparks the good vinaigrette salad that accompanies. Among starters are broiled clams with garlic, steamed mussels, calamari salad, and oysters on the half shell. Desserts could be Bourbon Street pecan pie, fuzzy navel peach pie, amaretto cheesecake, and chocolate-peanut butter pie. The wine list holds many a bargain.

Lunch, Monday-Friday 11:30 to 2; dinner, Monday-Saturday 5 to 10, Sunday noon to 9.

Sapporo, 520 Sniffen Lane, Stratford. (203) 375-3986.
Japanese. $11.50 to $18.

Taiwan-born Steve Wang and his wife Tomasita have owned the Shell Station since 1979, but you can tell his heart at least is in his new acquisition, built by an American GI who had fallen in love with Japan and recreated a Japanese restaurant where the Housatonic River meets Long Island Sound. Steve bought it in 1988, rechristened it Sapporo, and has made it an enchanting place indeed. The main dining room and lounge take full advantage of the water view, looking across a fabulous Japanese garden onto a bay that's a beehive of activity during oyster season. Inside, a new sushi bar seating ten and six small, private dining rooms with wells for American legs beneath the low tables surround an open atrium with a delightful stone garden around a dry river bed. In the main dining room, a spotlit branch of apple blossoms casts wonderful shadows on the ceiling as you sit on leatherette chairs at black tables, where silk flowers grace mineral-water bottles. In the Japanese tradition, damp towels are served on a little bamboo tray at meal's start. We sampled the sushi, a great assortment notable for California rolls whose rice had been rolled in red caviar roe. Dinners include salad with ginger dressing, miso soup, and steamed or seasoned rice. You can find all kinds of treats: yaki-soba, teriyaki beef or chicken, salmon teriyaki, scallops sauteed in sweet butter, eel kabayaki, sashimi, tempura and more. And you won't find a nicer setting for a Japanese meal in New England.

Lunch, Monday-Friday 11 to 2:30; dinner, Monday-Sunday 4 to 10.

Seascape, 14 Beach Drive, Stratford. (203) 375-2149.
Continental. $12.95 to $16.95.

Here's a typical waterfront restaurant with a great view of Long Island Sound and some locally out-of-the-ordinary fare. The dining rooms are rather too brightly illuminated and the glass coverings over the pink tables are jarring, given such niceties as votive candles in cut-glass containers. But the menu compensates with treats like fettuccine alfredo with crabmeat, Norwegian salmon beurre blanc, seafood primavera al pesto, black rainbow trout with bay scallops and shrimp stuffing on a bed of seafood butter cream, veal marsala, chicken vermouth, and shrimp sauteed with black olives, artichoke hearts, cherry tomatoes, and sherry. Rainbow trout with cracked black peppercorns, lemon and parsley might be a special. For starters, try escargots royale, hot seafood antipasto or one of the hot loaves topped with melted mozzarella, perhaps the shrimp bread or crab bread. Homemade desserts include oreo cheesecake, Bailey's Irish Cream cheesecake, pecan pie, and creme caramel.

Lunch, Monday-Friday 11:30 to 2:30; dinner, Monday-Saturday 5 to 10; Sunday, brunch 10 to 2, dinner 3 to 8:30.

Milford

Maxfields, 314 Bridgeport Ave. (Route 1), Devon. (203) 874-8811.
American/Continental. $11 to $16.

"Spirited dining" is how this pleasing little place refers to itself. We first met up with Maxfields when it was operating up the shoreline in Westbrook and stained-glass artist Kathy Shanley had named it after Maxfield Parrish, whose works were on the walls. Kathy closed and sold it to pursue her art fulltime, so we were pleased to find that her manager and chef had reopened downstate. Jeff Johnson carries on the tradition in Devon and Kathy still comes in to help on Friday nights. Some of her stained-glass pieces enhance the lounge-dining area and a quieter rear dining room, where calico napkins are used as runners on the blond wood tables and a mirrored wall makes the space seem bigger. The menu lists such pleasing entrees as beer batter shrimp, baked stuffed flounder, steak au poivre, and roast duckling laparousse, coated with Swiss cheese, bread crumbs, wine and dijon mustard. Specials could involve shrimp with tomato-basil butter and brie on a bed of angel-hair pasta, salmon in puff pastry on a bed of leeks and asparagus, and veal medallions with tomatoes, artichoke hearts, basil and pine nuts. For starters, try changurro (crabmeat sauteed with sherry, brandy, cayenne pepper and more), a good clam chowder, scallops ceviche, or a sampler of two stuffed mushrooms, two artichoke hearts, seafood phyllo, pesto clams, and fried calamari (which also makes a good luncheon entree with a side salad). Tasty desserts include frozen chocolate mousse, raspberry torte and assorted cheesecakes. The well-chosen wine list is priced primarily in the low teens. Be sure to check out the impressive grapevine twined with dried leaves and tiny white lights over the bar.

Lunch, Monday-Friday 11:30 to 3, Saturday noon to 2:30; dinner, Monday-Saturday 5:30 to 9 or 10.

Scribner's, 31 Village Road, Milford. (203) 878-7019.
Seafood. $14.95 to $25.95.

Impossibly hard to find in the Anchor Beach section of Woodmont, this is worth finding, and devoted fans of chef-owner Scribner Bliss have beaten a path to the door. Here since 1973, it offers two dining rooms full of paneling and exposed rafters, cane and chrome chairs at tables dressed in dusty pink over green, and little pink lalique-style shades over the candles. Upwards of ten daily specials supplement the menu and tend to be more interesting: scrod baked with chopped tomatoes, roasted red onions and gorgonzola cheese, Norwegian salmon broiled with fresh oysters and topped with shallot-basil butter, grilled tuna with etouffee sauce, tilefish baked scampi style, shrimp and scallops fra diavolo, roast duckling with grand marnier-honey glaze, and roasted rack of lamb with espagnole sauce. The broiled dinner includes half a lobster, king crab legs, scallops, and three shrimp. Good starters are roasted oysters with pesto sauce and parmesan cheese, clams casino, and broiled scallops wrapped in bacon with thyme. Among homemade desserts are French silk pie, chocolate decadence, derby pie, and an original (and refreshing) peach freeze that's best of all. The full lunch and dinner menu is served at four booths in the lounge, and people are known to walk down to Anchor Beach for a look-around between courses. One of the state's best wine lists harbors many Californias at affordable prices.

Lunch, Monday-Friday 11:30 to 2:30; dinner nightly from 5.

New Haven Area

New Haven

★ Robert Henry's, 1032 Chapel St., New Haven. (203) 789-1010. New American. $24 to $28.

Well-known Connecticut restaurateur Jo McKenzie offers the city's finest dining amidst the Edwardian formality of the old Union League Club. Tall windows topped by colorful stained glass look out onto Yale University buildings from a luxurious room notable for marble pillars, oak paneling, comfortable banquettes, and high-backed chairs upholstered in off-white. What we think of first here is service, so solicitous that it's too much (almost every time we took a sip of wine, our glass was replenished by the obviously watching staff). Then, of course, we think of the masterful food of French chef Jean-Michel Gammariello, ruling the roost alone now that his two original compatriots have returned to Europe. Dinner is pricey but worth it for triumphs like roasted sweetbreads perfumed with a creamy hazelnut dressing, filet of sea bass in a potato crust, baked red snapper with a tomato coulis and pesto, spit-roasted lamb with goat cheese ravioli, and veal chop served with potato mousseline, wild mushrooms and truffles. Homemade lasagna with scallops, swiss chard and saffron sauce, crab tabouli with citrus mayonnaise, and duck leg confit are among the starters; the tomato salad is a summer treat. Splurge for one of the masterful desserts, perhaps a nougatine of three sorbets, frozen pistachio nougat, apricot brioche or cappuccino torte, or a sampling of five of the most popular. Linger at the table or in the elegant rear lounge over a fine cognac or a fancy liquered coffee.

Dinner, Monday-Saturday 6 to 9:30 or 10.

Serino's, 9 Elm St., New Haven. (203) 562-1287.
Contemporary Continental. $13.50 to $19.95.
This highly regarded establishment moved in 1987 from smaller quarters at Short Beach in suburban Branford into the big time — the downtown space occupied at various times by Scribner's, L'Avventura and Curious Jane's. The young owner and his chef, who trained in Manhattan and at the Homestead Inn in Greenwich, attracted a receptive following and showed signs of staying power. The long, dramatic, high-ceilinged room is stark in black and white, accented by orange lilies in tall vases on each table. Some think Serino's is at its best at lunch, when it has the downtown fine dining scene pretty much to itself. Salads (warm duck, curried chicken), sandwiches, a couple of pastas, and half a dozen entrees like smoked salmon, stuffed eggplant and shrimp francais are the fare. At night, the concise menu (in words as well as offerings) yields such specialties as chicken saute with lemon and garlic, breast of duck with green peppercorn sauce, and filet of beef au poivre. Broiled shrimp comes with wilted greens, veal in three presentations, and angus steaks in two. Four pastas are offered. Appetizers are listed simply as smoked Duck Trap salmon, shiitake mushrooms, escargots, or clams oreganata, but the results are more complex than their names.

Lunch, Monday-Friday noon to 2; dinner, Monday-Saturday 5:30 to 9 or 10.

★ **Azteca's,,** 14 Mechanic St., New Haven. (203) 624-2454.
Mexican/Southwest. $9.25 to $20.50.
You'd never guess it from the outside, along a section of State Street undergoing gentrification and a boom in restaurants. But inside is a gem, undeniably pretty in dusty rose with changing local art and dispensing what many consider the best Mexican food around. Traditional and haute Mexican dishes are the fare, plus an appealing list of Southwest specials that change monthly. How about smoked duck breast and Texas antelope venison scaloppine napped with raspberry sauce nested on wild rice pancakes plated with julienned vegetables or soft-shell crabs with papaya-tequila chutney, haricots vert, carrot strings and rice? You can order any of the traditional Mexican main dishes — from tacos to chili rellenos — but we'd go for such specialties as chicken mole and filet of fresh fish with a green tomato and coriander sauce. And oh those Southwest dishes: perhaps grilled tuna with a melange of chayote, jicama and corn accompanied with garden vegetable rice, or broiled salmon, clams, mussels and shrimp in a light ancho chile broth over angel-hair pasta. Though few, desserts are standouts, too: perhaps pecan toffee

tart, Mexican chocolate mousse, amaretto cheesecake, and fresh papaya with melon sorbet and raspberry sauce.

Dinner, Monday-Saturday 5 to 9 or 10.

Bruxelle's Brasserie & Bar, 220 College St., New Haven. (203) 777-7752.
Regional American. $10.95 to $16.95.
White brick walls, exposed black pipes and black ceilings set the stage for this with-it, many-level eatery. Thin bread sticks stand tall in a brandy glass and crayons are in a glass on each table, the better for doodling across the white butcher paper protecting the white linens as you wait — and perhaps wait and wait, for this is a busy, popular place. The main floor is a convivial bar with tables for eating; upstairs is the main dining room, with windows onto the passing Shubert and Palace theater crowds. Flanking the bar is an array of open rotisseries where the meats are roasted: apple or southwest chicken, duckling glazed with raspberry sauce, roast sirloin of beef provence, and cornish game hen, most served with roasted bliss potatoes and a four-greens salad. Fresh coho salmon and Atlantic swordfish are steamed or chargrilled, and you can get interesting pastas, salads (the grand salon with roast chicken, black forest ham, sun-dried tomatoes and fontina cheese particularly appeals) and thin-crust pizzas, one with roast duck, water chestnuts, scallions, fontina cheese, and hoisin sauce. The totally hazelnut torte, pumpkin-praline mousse pie and frozen lemon mousse are tempting desserts. More salads, sandwiches, pizzas and a couple of roasts, plus a bistro plate, are available at lunch. Interesting wines are pleasantly priced, some by the glass from the wine bar.

Lunch, Monday-Saturday 11:30 to 5; dinner, 5 to 11:30 or 12:30; Sunday, brunch 11:30 to 4, dinner 4 to 11:30.

Scoozzi Trattoria and Wine Bar, 1104 Chapel St., New Haven.
(203) 776-8268.
Contemporary Italian. $10.50 to $18.
This may be the hottest of owner Henry Malone's trendy local restaurants. Take an elevator downstairs to the courtyard level and find a sprightly, L-shaped room and an even sprightlier, evergreened courtyard for outdoor dining. The decor represents something of a departure from the seemingly ubiquitous black and white of New Haven's better restaurants. This is mostly white, with arty accents of displays of bread, garlic ropes and olive oils here, an assortment of salads there. A wine bottle is the centerpiece of each table, again with white butcher paper over linens but no crayons as in Bruxelles, one of the owners' four restaurants. The food is the focus here, from piccoli piatti, an Italian version of Spanish tapas or Japanese sushi, through wafer-thin pizzas and a multitude of delectable pastas to grills and roasts, perhaps swordfish over wilted spinach leaves and pork chop with homemade polenta. Pastas are featured: the Scoozzi is a masterpiece of squid ink pasta, tomato, sweet peppers, mushrooms, garlic, zucchini, pine nuts, fresh fennel, and extra virgin olive oil; spinach fettuccine pugliese combines plump mussels, radicchio and anchovy sauce. Tirami su, Tuscan strudel, tartuffo amaretti, and bittersweet chocolate cake with currants, pine nuts and rum are some of the great desserts. All but three of the well-chosen wines are priced in the teens.

Lunch, Tuesday-Saturday 11:30 to 5; dinner, 5 to 11:30; Sunday, brunch 11:30 to 3, dinner 4 to 11:30.

Gennaro's, 937 State St., New Haven. (203) 777-5490.
Northern Italian. $14.75 to $19.95.
Near-swoon reviews tout this authentic Italian restaurant, simple and charmingly homey in an era of glitz, black and white. Blue is the prevailing color in the

greenhouse, a cozy informal trattoria and a larger dining room where a mirrored wall reflects the clear globes hanging from the ceiling. This is what you'd expect to find in chef-owner Gennaro Aurioso's hometown on the Amalfi coast, photographs of which enhance the restaurant's walls. The cooking is inspired: remarkable pastas like penne with smoked salmon in cream sauce and paglia with prosciutto and peas, no fewer than a dozen veal presentations, and some wonderful fish dishes. Veal saltimbocca, grilled sirloin sauteed with garlic and straw mushrooms, chicken with black olives and mushrooms, and scrod oregano are favorites. At lunch, a more limited menu lists a selection of pastas, meat and fish dishes. Some of the fine pastries are showcased near the entry. The wine list is pricey, except for the basics.

Lunch, Monday-Friday 11:30 to 2; dinner, Monday-Saturday 5:30 to 10.

The Thai Orchid, 1027 State St., New Haven. (203) 624-7173.
Thai. $9.95 to $14.95.

The pink facade of this storefront carries into the intimate interior, where pink cloths (under glass) cover the tables, chairs are black, colorful fans are unfurled on the shelves, and tropical trees soothe. Fresh orchids at each table enhance the fare, to which the New York Times accorded a rare "excellent" rating. The appetizers and soups are so good that you could make a meal of them, especially at lunch. But that would shortchange the entrees, which can be shared Chinese style. Particularly incendiary in the Thai tradition are shrimp or pork with red chile paste, squid or chicken with hot green chile and sweet basil, chicken or sliced beef with bell peppers in a fiery red curry tempered by coconut milk sauce, and beef sauteed with curry, green peppers and peas. Less adventurous palates might be tempted by sizzling seafood or ginger chicken. Pad Thai, the fried noodles dish that is a Thai mainstay, is a good foil to the hotter fare. Desserts are minimal, and Thai beer is the beverage of choice.

Lunch, Monday-Friday 11:45 to 2:30; dinner, Monday-Saturday 5:30 to 9 or 10, Sunday 5:30 to 9:30.

Hatsune, 993 State St., New Haven. (203) 776-3216.
Japanese. $10.75 to $17.75.

The late, lamented Basel's Greek restaurant where lively dinner-dancing used to be the vogue now is home for the serene and venerable Hatsune. It moved from smaller basement quarters near the Yale campus (after surviving a disastrous fire in West Haven a decade ago). The Japanese farmhouse-style restaurant is housed very agreeably indeed, the chopsticks wrapped in blue napkins on bare teakwood tables and Japanese plantings ensconced in recesses in the walls. With black latticework dividers here, some screens there, and haunting music in the background, you feel yourself in rural Japan. That's the way partners Donald Noyes and chef Yoshi Mabuchi would have it. The sushi menu is extensive, the open-hearth steaks, chicken and shrimp are special, and anyone can find a choice from ginger pork to vegetable tempura. If undecided, get a combination plate or, even better, the complete Bento dinner served in a decorative lacquered box. For dessert, try ginger cheesecake or almond cookie cake.

Lunch, Monday-Saturday 11:30 to 2:30; dinner, 5 to 10 or 11, Sunday 4 to 9.

Three Sixty Eight, 60 Audubon St., New Haven. (203) 562-4677.
Steakhouse. $10.95 to $19.95.

This classic Southwestern steakhouse popped up in 1989 at 368 Orange St., with an entrance on the ever-so-upscaling Audubon Street at the edge of downtown. It's the newest venture of Henry Malone's Entertaining Moments Inc., which also owns Bruxelle's, Scoozzi's and Gentree Ltd. Here the theme is steak and chops, presented in a vast expanse of beige evoking the desert Southwest. The sand-colored walls are as barren as much of Arizona, accented by the odd print, wall hanging or cactus. Spacious and well-spaced round tables are flanked by blond-wood upholstered chairs and dressed in white linens over tan, each place setting including the heftiest steak knife we ever saw. The menu comes alive as the server wheels up a cart and shows each plastic-covered cut of top-quality beef, chop, fish, and even vegetables. The a la carte accompaniments run up the bill; be advised that some are big enough to share. Black bean soup, lump crab cocktail, and a helping of sliced tomatoes drizzled with gorgonzola and red onions make good preliminaries. Any of the prime cuts, from lemon-oregano chicken to porterhouse steak, are grilled impeccably. So are the prime "catches," namely thick-cut swordfish and Atlantic tuna. Under "creative selections" you might find Cajun carbonara, sauteed breast of chicken monterey with sliced avocados, cheese and spicy cucumber and tomato salsa, and tournedos of beef with allumella potatoes, caramel-ized onion slices and merlot sauce. Desserts are the grand finale they're purported to be: chocolate and grand marnier souffles for two, creme brulee, poppyseed torte, and white chocolate mousse cake. Linger with a cordial in the front solarium bar.

Lunch, Monday-Friday 11:30 to 4:30; dinner, Monday-Saturday, 5 to 10:30 or 11.

Elm City Diner, 1228 Chapel St., New Haven. (203) 776-5050.
Regional American. $10.95 to $15.95.

The old Mountainview Diner, at this site since 1955, has been transformed into the trendy, theatrical Elm City Diner. Still very much a diner on the outside, it's anything but on the inside — all mirrors and shiny green tables, black and chrome chairs, candles in votive glasses, a mass of flowers atop the grand piano, and 700 small ceiling lights ("we call them golf balls," says the co-owner, "and at night the reflections are magical"). The food is trendy as well. Dinner entrees include an admirable aztec shrimp on a flour tortilla with guacamole that we devoured, wonderful spinach fettuccine with bay scallops and artichoke hearts, cheese tortellini marinara, spicy grilled honey-mustard chicken, and broiled shrimp with a walnut barbecue sauce served over Chinese cabbage. You can get all kinds of appetizers, salads and burgers at dinner as well as on the late-night menu, which is served until 12:30 a.m. or later. The lunch menu is basically salads and sandwiches, plus a few of the dinner entrees. Supplemented by daily specials well worth seeking out, the fare is mighty varied — as it has to be to appeal to the diverse tastes of those who fill its 65 seats plus the bar day and night.

Open daily from 11:30 a.m. to 12:30 or 1:30 a.m.

500 Blake Street, 500 Blake St., New Haven. (203) 387-0500.
Italian. $14.95 to $21.95.

Nestled in the interesting Westville section of the city is this tavern-style place with an immense menu featuring huge portions and highly spiced Italian food. It's also a favorite watering hole with not one but two long bars, plus a piano bar where we hear the singing gets pretty rambunctious at night, and a downstairs rathskellar that serves as a rustic dining room. A recent addition houses a 300-seat ballroom for private parties, as well as an acclaimed $19.95 Sunday brunch featuring a buffet that runs the length of the room. The decor is plain, with scarred oak tables and carpeting that has seen better days. Appetizers include lots of clam, mussel, calamari and scungilli dishes; cherry peppers stuffed with tuna, olives, capers and anchovies are often ordered. Garlic and oil are evident in many of the entrees, which run from baked stuffed shrimp to filet mignon. The house salad and the Italian bread are great.

Open daily from 11:30 to midnight, Sunday noon to 9.

The Rusty Scupper, Long Wharf, New Haven. (203) 777-5711.
American. $11.95 to $19.95.

The harbor view is everything at this large eating and drinking establishment that packs in a young crowd. The circular bar area has two levels of intimate seats by the windows, as well as sofas in the lounge. At night, the lights of New Haven are reflected in the shimmering waters just outside the two contemporary-style dining rooms, and a deck beside the water appeals during warm weather. The lengthy menu is typical of the chain, with everything from prime rib and mesquite-grilled salmon and tuna to shrimp tempura and pastas. Soups, sandwiches, salads and such are featured at lunch. A champagne Sunday buffet brunch is popular.

Lunch, Monday-Friday 11:30 to 2; dinner, Monday-Saturday 5 to 10 or 11; Sunday, brunch 11 to 2, dinner 4 to 9.

Hamden

Valentino, 2987 Whitney Ave., Hamden. (203) 288-7707.
Northern Italian. $14.75 to $21.95.

Chefs and owners have come and gone since we took newspaper colleagues out for a celebratory lunch a decade ago and gasped at the tab. The glamorous pink color scheme we remember has given way to pristine white, with accents of stained glass and modern glass wall sconces. There's a sunken dining area with a grand piano beneath a modern glass chandelier hung from gray fabric billowing from the ceiling. A ballroom dancing mural lurks behind the piano and more dancing scenes hang in the bar. The ambitious dinner menu consists of six beef, nine poultry, eight veal, and eleven seafood dishes, all the familiar Italian favorites and then some. The specialty is chicken stuffed with mozzarella and prosciutto, simmered with mushrooms and peas in sherry wine sauce and served with fettuccine. There are interesting pastas and extravagant desserts like cappuccino dacquoise, hazelnut meringue gateau and black satin cake. The wine list is short and expensive.

Lunch, Monday-Saturday 11:30 to 2:30; dinner, 5:30 to 10:30 or 11.

Wallingford

♥ **Britannia Spoon Company,** 296 Church St. (Route 68 at Route 150)
Yalesville. (203) 265-6199.
American. $9.95 to $19.95.

For atmosphere alone, it's worth the trek to this appealing restaurant with a spectacular setting beside the falls of the Quinnipiac River in the out-of-the-way Yalesville section of Wallingford. On the site where the Yale brothers' factory once manufactured Britannia spoons, you can enjoy a two-level deck beside the falls, a noisy oasis of water amid a forest of green. The inside makes the most of its riverside location as well, particularly the high-ceilinged main dining room with windows on three sides. Tiffany lamps, stained glass in unexpected places (for instance, around the top of the large square bar), barn-type bric-a-brac on the ceiling crossbeams, and little nooks and crannies in which to have a drink abound. Among starters is a combo platter of best-sellers — calamari, potato skins and spare ribs, "enough to share with a friend" — and we liked the tureen of cioppino offered some time ago and the french-fried zucchini with sweet and sour dipping sauce. Best of the entrees are steaks, accompanied by good french fries. Other choices range from baby back ribs and chicken florentine to baked stuffed shrimp and sole oscar. Desserts could be zucchini yogurt cake, taffy apple pie and mud pie.

Lunch, Monday-Saturday 11:30 to 4:30; dinner, 4:30 to 10 or 11; Sunday, brunch 11 to 3, dinner 4:30 to 9.

New Haven Area

Cheshire

The Pavillion, 1721 Highland Ave. (Route 10), Cheshire. (203) 272-3584. Italian/American. $12.50 to $22.50.

"Where the two continents meet" is the theme of this relative oldtimer, lately remodeled to get rid of its enclosed pavilion feeling and made more open with a high ceiling and french doors in the dining room. The two continents are Europe and North America, though chef Bernard Gayraud insists the menu is Italian. The thoroughly French son-in-law of owner Mario Zacco adds some French specials and pastries, however. He's quick to recommend the Italian Mediterranean dinners that are low in fat, perhaps a hot or cold artichoke, pasta with tomato and basil, grilled fish or roasted chicken with rosemary and garlic, and a dish of gelati. You also can select pate, prosciutto with melon, shrimp picanti, and fried calamari from a lengthy list of appetizers. Entrees range from salmon with tarragon sauce and dover sole amandine to osso buco, veal marsala, medallions of sweetbreads, filet mignon, and rack of lamb. The young rooster with woodland mushrooms also appeals. The dessert cart revolves around tarte tatin, bavarian cream cake and chocolate mousse. The renovated room is soothing in beige and white, with a mix of white booths and windsor chairs. The rustic barnwood lounge remains, and food is served there all day long.

Open Monday-Friday noon to 10, Saturday 5:30 to 10.

♥ **Squire House Restaurant & Tavern**, 200 South Main St., Cheshire. (203) 271-1776. Continental. $18 to $24.

No expense was spared in the 1989 restoration of a mid-18th-century white Colonial house and rear barn into this elegant restaurant and tavern. The main-floor dining room in red and white is pretty as can be: reproduction Queen Anne chairs with red seats flank tables set with white linens, red napkins, heavy silver cutlery, and silver candlesticks. A fire blazes in the hearth, white candles shine in the windows, classical music plays, and all's well with the world inside. Chef-owner Richard Zinser's menu is a pricey rendition of the classics, from salmon en croute to three poached fish filets with beurre blanc, shrimp provencale to lobster and shrimp au gratin, veal chasseur to entrecote au poivre. Seafood terrine, lobster gribiche and oysters rockefeller are among starters. Homemade sorbets prime the palate for the main course. Desserts include chocolate charlotte, apple crumb cake with custard, bourbon walnut pie, and lemon mousse cake. There's more dining on the second floor and in the basement **Stone Tavern,** where an appealing menu at half the price is served at lunch and dinner. The tavern is casually elegant with gray woven mats on wood tables, mismatched chairs, a few leather sofas in front of the stone fireplace, and a 26-foot-long mahogany bar.

Lunch, Monday-Friday noon to 2 (also Saturday in the tavern); dinner, 5 to 9 or 10; Sunday, brunch 11:30 to 3, dinner 3 to 8.

Waverly Manor, 286 Maple Ave., Cheshire. (203) 271-2919. American/International. $13.50 to $18.95.

Once one of Connecticut's larger establishments serving up to 4,000 meals a day, the old Waverly Manor outgrew the times. Closed for ten years, it was reopened in 1986 in renovated quarters, and most of the banquet space was turned into medical offices. Only the bar is left from the original Waverly. "We wanted to retain the elegance," said new owner Robert Kashdan, "but we also wanted to keep it small." The result is a hundred seats and casual elegance in brown and hunter green, with bare inlaid tables, napkins resting on the service plates, pink glass Victorian shades over oil lamps, and floral carpeting. Dinner entrees include Cajun snapper, crab patty Creole, shrimp neptune, baked stuffed flounder, chicken polynesian or sicilian, veal marsala, beef stir-fry, and twin medallions of tenderloin with red wine and dijon mustard sauces. Grilled seafood and cioppino are specialties. Starters range from French onion soup to escargots in puff pastry.

Lunch, Monday-Friday 11:30 to 2:30; dinner, Monday-Saturday from 5; Sunday brunch, 11 to 3.

Branford

Jonathan's, 225 Montowese St., Branford. (203) 483-0073.
French/Continental. $13.95 to $19.95.

A long, narrow room with a black and white tiled floor has been something of a revolving door for restaurants, but its latest occupant appears to have staying power. Some of the area's best meals emanate from the kitchen of chef-owner John Catalanotto, a transplanted Long Island restaurateur. The ambience is art deco, from the posters and mirrors on the walls to the lighting fixtures. Music from the 1940s plays on two brightly lit Wurlitzer jukeboxes. Tables are set with white cloths, heavy silver, handsome white china, and black vases sporting deep pink carnations. The lunch menu offers novelties like champagne lobster bisque and an omelet with Canadian bacon and asparagus, amid such classics as French onion soup, fettuccine alfredo, chicken francaise, and veal lemon. At night, fine touches add to such traditional dishes as escargots provencale, veal champignons and fisherman's platter. The beef wellington is sensational, and the frequent special of salmon baked in parchment with shrimp, scallops, lobster and langoustinos is highly rated. There's artistry in the presentation, the classics being prepared tableside (fans rave over the caesar salad) and the plates being garnished with kiwi slices and carved radishes. Favorite desserts include a light cheesecake, mocha raspberry torte and pears helene.

Lunch, Tuesday-Friday noon to 2:30; dinner, Tuesday-Friday 5 to 9:30, Saturday 6 to 10, Sunday 5 to 9.

$ Indulge, 779 East Main St., Branford. (203) 488-9457.
International. $8 to $12.

Hidden in a one-story, shingled house at the rear of Branford Craft Village at Bittersweet Farm is this little eatery, one of the more appealing we've found for an interesting yet unpretentious lunch or weekend dinner. An L-shaped room and an enclosed porch looking onto fields of green are country-pretty in white and mauve. It's a pristine setting for some imaginative cooking by Hermione Mezynski. When we were there, the night's offerings, handwritten on a white board, were roast duckling with blackberry sauce, cornish game hen Hungarian style, rabbit braised in dark beer, chicken in coconut cream and chive sauce, applewood-smoked spare ribs with apple butter, lamb cassoulet, trout with lime butter sauce, and southern fried catfish with a corn and pecan crust. For lunch, you might find gazpacho or cashew-lentil soup, a smoked chicken and pasta salad with red pepper dressing, beef and onion salad, brie with apples and almonds baked in Irish soda bread, vegetarian terrine, Mexican pizza, and salmon patties. Desserts at wallet-pleasing prices could be frozen chocolate rum pie, raspberry cheesecake, maple spice cake, and peach pie. Believe it or not, all wines were priced at $10 a bottle at our visit.

Lunch, Wednesday-Sunday 11 to 3; dinner, Friday and Saturday 6 to 9. No credit cards. Beer and wine only.

Chez Bach, 1070 Main St., Branford. (203) 488-8779.
Vietnamese. $9.50 to $15.95.

Madame Bach Ngo, whose cookbook "The Classic Cuisine of Vietnam" won the prestigious Tastemaker award as the best of the year a while back, runs this well-regarded establishment with staying power in an area where restaurants come and go. After a brief stint with a second Chez Bach in Westport, she's back in Branford repairing the difficulties that two far-flung operations can wrought. Twenty-nine items from soups to entrees are offered on a menu billed as gourmet Vietnamese. Singing chicken, "Good Mother" pork chops, lemon grass beef, and caramelized shrimp are among the entrees. Special dishes, some of which must be ordered a day ahead, are listed at the end of the menu. The choice on the dessert cart is exceptional, as is the sophisticated wine list. The predominantly black color scheme is brightened by white and yellow napkins and maps of Vietnam under glass in the booths.

Lunch, Tuesday-Friday noon to 2:30; dinner, 5 to 9:30, Saturday 6 to 10, Sunday 5 to 9. Closed Monday.

Su Casa, 400 East Main St., Branford. (203) 481-5001.
Mexican. $8.95 to $13.95.

Dark and grotto-like, this ramble of rooms has high booths and Mexican murals. All the standards are available singly and in combinations. Fajitas (beef, chicken or shrimp), chicken mole with a three-pepper and chocolate-based mole sauce, shrimp Acapulco, and fish stuffed with chilies, mushrooms and tomatoes are the real thing. If you like your food extra-hot, try the jalapeno chilies on the table or inquire about the "back-up ammunition" in the kitchen. There are a handful of items for gringos, and the lunch menu yields a varied mix from taco salad to huevos rancheros.

Open Monday-Thursday noon to 10, Friday noon to 11, Saturday 4 to 11, Sunday 4 to 10.

Backwater Tavern, Linden Avenue, Branford. (203) 481-4086.
International. $9.95 to $17.95.

Beside the marshes at Indian Neck and a cut above its peers in decor and culinary style is this cute little place with flowers in Perrier bottles and paper mats on each oilcloth-covered table. The bar is up a few steps to the rear and separated from the dining room by a divider. The blackboard lists interesting specials, perhaps fettuccine with artichokes and mushrooms or another with sun-dried tomatoes and black olives in an alfredo sauce, fish stew, and oysters "backafeller." Garlic shrimp, baked stuffed sole, Cajun swordfish, veal marsala, and chicken and shrimp seville are among the offerings.

Dinner, Monday-Thursday 5 to 10; lunch and dinner, Friday-Sunday; lunch daily in summer.

Chowder Pot, 560 East Main St. (Route 1), Branford. (203) 481-2356.
Seafood. $10.95 to $18.95.

From a seafood shanty, the Chowder Pot has moved and expanded twice, and each time the crowds get larger. Seafood — fresh, fried and lots of it at reasonable prices — is the draw. Regulars tout the surf salad: greens topped with lobster, langoustinos and shrimp, served with cocktail sauce and the house buttermilk ranch dressing. A dozen dinner platters include broiled swordfish, shrimp au gratin, seafood fettuccine, and surf and turf. The decor at the Chowder Pot is dark and nautical in an upscale sort of way, and there's dancing in the lounge. An artistic display of crab legs, huge shrimp and the like is a feature of the raw bar near the entrance; lobsters up to six pounds swim in a glass tank in the wall.

Lunch, Monday-Saturday 11:30 to 3:30; dinner, 3:30 to 10 or 11, Sunday noon to 9.

Guilford

The Dock House, Lower Whitfield Street, Guilford. (203) 453-6854.
Seafood. $12.95 to $26.95.

Seafood with a rare (for this area) water view is the specialty at this long, low fieldstone building with an outdoor patio, captains' tables in the windowed dining room full of hanging greenery, and a sprightly bar with turquoise deck chairs and rose-colored cushions on benches. The menu is fairly standard; dinner entrees run from top sirloin to a fried seafood platter. A section titled "Best of Both" tops off with lobster fra diavolo. There are pasta, chicken, pork, and veal dishes as well.

Lunch daily, 11:30 to 2:30, April-Thanksgiving; dinner nightly, 5 to 9 or 10; Sunday, brunch 11:30 to 2:30, dinner 4 to 9.

La Cuisine, 25 Whitfield St., Guilford. (203) 453-0483.
American. $4.50 to $6.95.

You can have a reasonably priced breakfast or lunch at this small and lively food shop, bakery and cafe facing Guilford's green. Take it out, or sit on bentwood chairs at tables covered with blue and white checked cloths. At lunch there are always a couple of soups (maybe strawberry-melon or wild rice and mushroom), three or four kinds of quiche, sandwiches, and six or seven salads set out on ice. We liked the orange and dill chicken salad and the tuna with summer vegetables and a dill vinaigrette. The combo salad is "a little of each" and worth sampling. Desserts might include a lime mousse pie, white chocolate cheesecake and lemon souffle tart.

Open weekdays, 9 to 4:30; Saturday, 8:30 to 4:30; Sunday, breakfast-brunch, 8:30 to 2.

Madison

Friends & Company, 11 Boston Post Road, Madison. (203) 245-0461.
International. $8.95 to $13.95.

Yes, friends, this is "a restaurant," as the words incorporated into its logo attest. And a good one, although you might not suspect it from its undistinguished dark wood exterior along busy Route 1 at the Madison-Guilford line. It was founded by two friends, and friends helped them open it, thus the name. The main dining room is good-looking with a fireplace, nine intimate booths, bentwood chairs at bare shiny pine tables (except for four covered with linen along one wall), interesting crocheted and lace designs in glass dividers between booths, and dried flowers embedded in the front windows. The limited menu is supplemented by blackboard specials; the problem is, there's only one blackboard and it's at the entrance, so you have to read fast and almost make your selection on the spot as the hostess waits to escort you to your table. The dinner menu offers ten entrees, things like sauteed veal, shrimp scampi and New York strip steak, plus sliced sirloin with sauteed mushrooms, a bargain for two. The blackboard may list the acclaimed Portuguese seafood stew, plus perhaps sauteed scallops, swordfish, or lamb kabob. A platter of the restaurant's special breads (for sale by the loaf — the recipes are secret) and the house salad accompany. The full dinner menu plus sandwiches are served in the bar, which is helpful on weekends when the waits can be long (no reservations accepted). Service at lunch is lightning fast — we were in and out in less than an hour for entrees of flounder stuffed with crabmeat and topped with a dill sauce and curried shrimp in puff pastry, plus a side order of vegetable fritters, a house specialty. Hazelnut cheesecake, chocolate mousse pie and a great ice cream crepe with hot fudge sauce are favored desserts.

Lunch, Monday-Friday 11:30 to 2; dinner 5 to 10, weekends to 11; Sunday, brunch 11:30 to 2:30, dinner 4:30 to 9.

Connecticut River-Shore

The Wharf, Madison Beach Hotel, 94 West Wharf Road, Madison.
(203) 245-0005.
Seafood. $14.95 to $18.95.
About as close to Long Island Sound as you can get, this restored 32-room hotel has a popular Crow's Nest Lounge on the second floor with a large square bar and a narrow canopied outdoor deck with a great view of the water. Many of the lunch items are served nightly upstairs in the Crow's Nest. Downstairs, the menu is a bit more formal in two rustic, barnwood dining rooms appointed in gray and pink. The cuisine is straightforward and familiar, from clam chowder and onion soup to fried shrimp or scallops served with tartar sauce. Among main courses, the seafood casserole, grilled swordfish with basil butter, broiled bluefish, king crab legs, broiled lamb chops with mint jelly, and prime rib are recommended. Start with mussels steamed in garlic and wine, baked oysters with cornbread stuffing or baked artichoke hearts in wine-cheese sauce. Homemade creme caramel, chocolate cake and hazelnut torte are among desserts.
Lunch daily, 11:30 to 3; dinner, Monday-Saturday 5:30 to 9, Sunday to 8:30.

Connecticut River-Shore

Westbrook

♥ **Water's Edge,** 1525 Boston Post Road, Westbrook. (203) 399-3901.
New American. $15.50 to $19.95.
The restaurant and outdoor terrace at this recently renovated inn and resort overlooking Long Island Sound are among the most glamorous around. The three-tiered dining room, with upholstered chairs at tables appointed in peach and gray, is pretty as a picture. So is the food: for lunch, perhaps a wondrous linguini with mussels and garlic, an oriental smoked chicken salad with cashews and honey-ginger dressing, grilled lobster cakes, or lobster and scallop wontons with cilantro cream sauce. Our dessert was an excellent pear-cranberry tart with a strong almond flavoring. At night, the moonlight reflecting off the Sound complements the light from tiny peach-colored, frosted-glass oil lamps on the tables and small brass lanterns on the walls. You might start with poached shrimp with lime cocktail sauce, spiced calamari with lobster, or vol au vent of snails with tomato concasse and pine nuts in pernod. A cranberry sorbet clears the palate for the main course, perhaps baked salmon with sun-dried tomatoes, seared pheasant with hazelnut wild rice, grilled pesto quail on a bed of capellini pasta, grilled loin lamb chops persille, or sirloin steak. The food is inventive and the value received. In summer, the outdoor **Le Grill** with its salutary views offers a luncheon buffet. A limited dinner menu is served outside, and a surf and turf dinner buffet features shrimp and lobster Thursday to Saturday nights.
Lunch, Monday-Saturday 11:30 to 2:30; dinner, 5:30 to 9:30 or 10; Sunday, brunch 10:30 to 3, dinner 6:30 to 9.

Lenny & Joe's Fish Tale Restaurant, 86 Boston Post Road, Westbrook.
(203) 669-0767.
Seafood. $7.50 to $11.95.
Friends who have traveled the world think the best seafood is close to home. They're partial to the Fish Tale, especially the fried platter of clams, shrimp, scallops and scrod, or combinations thereof. We can vouch for the fried clams — with fries and coleslaw, they make a good lunch, though not being fans of things fried, we cannot say whether they're the best in the world. We can say the fried clam roll is a

bargain, overflowing with clams and accompanied by coleslaw. The paper menu is printed daily to list specials like broiled bluefish and broiled sea scallop casserole. Regular dinners range from broiled scrod to charbroiled swordfish and shrimp scampi. The food is served here in a couple of nautical dining rooms, or at the firm's new location: a plain, bare-bones drive-in restaurant with counters, booths and an outdoor porch at 1301 Boston Post Road, Madison.

Open daily from 11 a.m. to 10 or 11 p.m.

Old Saybrook

Wine and Roses, 150 Main St., Old Saybrook. (203) 388-9646. Contemporary French/American. $14 to $19.

From a small start in a former diner gone upscale, chef Martin Cappiello and his wife Karen have parlayed culinary inspiration and hard work into an expanded operation with a new upstairs dining room and a small cocktail lounge. The menu is supplemented by a long list of the night's specials, anything from swordfish nicoise and Connecticut River shad with choice of two sauces to rack of lamb persillade and cassoulet. Oregon red snapper with fresh mint and cherry tomatoes, Norwegian salmon baked with a spinach and mushroom custard and lemon cream, pork curry, and herbed leg of lamb with a zinfandel sauce are among numerous possibilities. The smoked salmon souffle, the house pate laced with garlic and brandy, scotch smoked salmon on rye toast strips, and warm duck and spinach salad are worthy starters. For dessert, seek out the homemade roasted peanut-almond ice cream topped with espresso-fudge sauce or the strawberry croustade. Lunches are pleasantly priced, and as if the energetic Cappiellos weren't busy enough, they serve breakfasts from 8 to 11:30 on weekends.

Lunch, Tuesday-Saturday 11:30 to 2:30; dinner, 5 to 9 or 10. Closed Monday. No credit cards.

Orchid Restaurant, 1315 Boston Post Road, Old Saybrook. (203) 388-6888. Vietnamese. $8.50 to $14.50.

A small sign designates this as a house dating from 1710, and inside the decor hints of old New England. But the cooking is delicate Vietnamese, very creditably so, served amid an incongruous backdrop of beamed ceilings, wide-board floors and white-linened tables, each topped with a hurricane lamp and a single red rose. The sizable menu is categorized under seafood, beef, pork and the like, with simple English translations and numbers for ease of ordering. The poultry dishes are especially intriguing, things like whole cornish hen marinated with five spices and served with tamarind sauce, ginger chicken, or duck breast with orange sauce. We also like the sound of shaking beef on a bed of watercress and shrimp with cashew nuts. Prices add to Orchid's appeal; all but two entrees are under $10.95. The house wine is $1 a glass, and the Chinese beer is a fine accompaniment for Vietnamese food. Desserts are minimal, among them pineapple cake topped with canned pineapple and fresh fruit cup with vanilla cream.

Lunch, Tuesday-Friday 11 to 2; dinner, Tuesday-Sunday 5 to 10.

The Cuckoo's Nest, 1712 Boston Post Road, Old Saybrook. (203) 399-9060. Mexican. $7.25 to $13.95.

An outdoor patio looking as if it's straight out of Mexico with stucco walls and an intricate canopy of branches is a popular addition to this rustic establishment tucked into a small shopping center along Route 1. The food is mainly Tex-Mex with a nod to Cajun and Creole. You can dine outside on aforementioned patio, upstairs on a small porch overlooking the patio, or in any number of crannies and alcoves on two floors filled with Mexican art, sombreros and the like. At lunch, follow a spicy gazpacho with one of the tacos, enchiladas, tamales, tostadas, burritos or empanadas, or the Cuckoo's Nest Mexican hodge-podge. At night, you can get the same things, plus dinners ranging from a small combination plate to Cajun prime rib. Shrimp or catfish Creole, blackened whitefish, delmonico steak, and fajitas are other options. The food is mildly spiced, but hot sauce is provided for those who wish to clear their sinuses. Mexican beers and sangria are the drinks of choice.

Lunch, Monday-Friday, noon to 2:30; dinner, 5 to 10 or 11, Sunday 4 to 10.

Dock & Dine, Saybrook Point, Old Saybrook. (203) 388-4665.
Seafood. $10.95 to $19.95.
This venerable and spacious establishment has perhaps the best water location around, where river meets Sound. Now owned by Jon Kodama, who's forging a chain of coastal restaurants from his base in Mystic, it offers a contemporary menu to appeal to diverse tastes. The seafood nachos and cucumber stuffed with honey lemon shrimp make good appetizers. Entrees run the gamut from fried clams to prime rib and stuffed lobster, with seafood pasta, mixed seafood grill and filet mignon broiled over hickory wood in between. An abbreviated version of the dinner menu is offered at lunchtime. Among the fancy desserts are cappuccino mousse torte, raspberry cream layer cake and grasshopper pie. All this is taken in a spacious windowed dining room, a lively cocktail lounge, or an outdoor terrace with panoramic water views.

Lunch, Monday-Saturday 11:30 to 3; dinner, 4 to 10, Saturday to 11; Sunday, brunch 11 to 2, dinner noon to 10.

Essex/Centerbrook/Ivoryton

✱ Fine Bouche, Main Street, Centerbrook. (203) 767-1277.
French. $17 to $25. Prix-Fixe, $36.
For consistency and creativity, Fine Bouche stands at the head of the list in an area known for fine restaurants. Trained in London and San Francisco before opening his small French restaurant and patisserie in 1979, chef-owner Steve Wilkinson is one of the top chefs in Connecticut. But he remains unassuming and personable, chatting with patrons on a first-name basis and running special wine-tasting and culinary events. As you enter through the patisserie, stop for a look at some of the delectable desserts you might order. As you await your table in a small reception parlor, scan the interesting memorabilia from the owner's career — empty bottles of rare wine, special menus from London and such — discreetly on display in two lighted glass cases. Beyond are two small interior dining rooms seating a total of 45, one with pictures of grapes and vines on cream-colored walls and the other darker with pretty green and flowered wallpaper and old French prints. A pristine, cafe-style wraparound porch is particularly inviting with white, not-quite-sheer full-length curtains, arched lattice-work over the windows, peach-colored walls and rattan chairs, their seats covered by a dark green chintz dotted with exotic lilies. The prix-fixe dinner might start with a choice of smoked salmon with celery root remoulade, galantine of pheasant and duck, poached oysters wrapped in spinach, and snails with an anchovy-walnut sauce. The soup or fish course could be a choice of a delectable mussel soup with fennel and saffron, pheasant soup, coquilles St. Jacques or grilled salmon with fresh oyster mushrooms. After a green salad comes the piece de resistance. How about medallions of veal with onion compote, sliced duck breast with sour cherries and brandy, tournedos of beef with two sauces, rack of lamb with roasted garlic and anise, or breast of pheasant with madeira and truffle sauce? Desserts are superlative, particularly the almond-hazelnut dacquoise and

34

the marjolaine, a heavenly combination of almond praline, hazelnut meringue, creme fraiche and bitter Belgian chocolate. Those with more resistance than we can order a fresh fruit sorbet. The a la carte menu offers a few additional choices, ranging from coquilles St. Jacques to rack of lamb. Although we've been happy dining here on numerous occasions, we'll never forget one dinner of warm duck pate in puff pastry, grilled oysters with fresh herb sauce, sweetbreads, filet of veal with mushrooms, madeira and tarragon, and a rich genoise for dessert. The superb wine list, winner of Wine Spectator's grand award, is especially strong on French but with an interesting selection of Californias, quite reasonably priced.

Dinner, Tuesday-Saturday 6 to 9. Patisserie, 10 to 5.

Daniel's Table, Ivoryton Inn, 115 Main St., Ivoryton. (203) 767-8914.
New American. $16 to $21.

Young Daniel McManamy, who apprenticed at the Old Lyme Inn and Restaurant du Village in Chester, knows how to make the eleven tables sing in his simple, serene dining room, which he leases from the Ivoryton Inn. In an L-shaped room with lace curtains, bare floors, recessed ceiling lights, and stenciling and a few sconces on the plain walls, the white-linened tables are canvases for the chef's artistry. Among appetizers, we're partial to his rabbit pate and crab ravioli, although the duck lasagna with goat cheese appealed at our latest visit. Hot, crusty rolls and a composed salad of tiny lettuces precede the entrees. We liked the salmon on a basil beurre blanc and roast pork loin in a grand marnier sauce with orange and cranberry. Saffron rice with pernod and perfect little haricots verts accompanied. Other choices could be filet of sole filled with crab mousse, filet of beef atop a potato gallette, leg of lamb with anything-but-mundane garlic mashed potatoes, and breast of pheasant with an apple-onion compote. A luscious frozen hazelnut souffle with frangelico and kahlua sauces and a peach crisp with white chocolate and bourbon sauce were among the desserts. The wine list, small but excellent, contains good values. The restaurant lost its lease, and was looking to move nearby in 1990.

Dinner, Tuesday-Thursday 5 to 9:30, Friday-Sunday 5:30 to 9:30.

8 Westbrook Restaurant, 8 Westbrook Road, Centerbrook. (203) 767-7085.
New American. $13.50 to $17.95.

This promising eatery opened in 1989 in a restored barn-red house with a rear view of a mill pond. Its two miniscule dining rooms on two floors are connected by a narrow stairway that has patrons wondering how the staff manages to negotiate. The airy upstairs room, across the hallway from the kitchen, is pristine with pink and white linens, sturdy blond wood chairs with pink seats, and brass lamps and interesting art for sale on the teal-colored walls. Votive candles are in crystal holders, and there's a lovely fireplace. Chef-owner George Tilghman, who formerly ran the eclectic Finest Kind restaurant on Mount Desert Island in Maine, and his wife Polly change their menus seasonally. Appetizers might include baked brie with strawberry chutney, garlicky Thai shrimp, and artichokes and snails in phyllo. Possible entrees are chicken with a black bean sauce, shrimp and scallop curry, crab cakes with lemon butter, and filet mignon with garlic and red wine sauce. Calves liver here might be done with currants and pine nuts as well as onions. Chocolate mousse cake, a rich carrot cake, and homemade pistachio ice cream are favorite desserts.

Dinner, Monday-Saturday 6 to 9 or 10.

Copper Beech Inn, Main Street, Ivoryton. (203) 767-0330.
French. $22.50 to $26.75.

The level of dining at the Copper Beech dropped following the departure of founding innkeepers Jo and Robert McKenzie. It was raised again in 1988 by new innkeepers Sally and Eldon Senner, but the reviews remain mixed. There's no denying the elegant setting: the main Georgian Room has three chandeliers, wall sconces, subdued floral wallpaper, and crisp white napkins standing tall in the water glasses. The dark Comstock Room with beamed ceiling looks a bit like the old billiards parlor that it was. Nearby is a pretty little garden dining porch, its four tables for two spaced well apart amid the plants. Windows in the blue Copper Beech Room afford views of the great tree outside. The menu is printed in French with English translations. Likely starters are lobster bisque, scotch smoked salmon, clams topped with crabmeat and a hazelnut dressing, timbale of sweetbreads and chicken, and escargots in a chervil-garlic cream in puff pastry. Among the more inspired entrees are bouillabaisse, filet of salmon sauteed in a lobster-braised leek cream sauce, sauteed pork loin with potato and leek cakes, tournedos with roasted chestnuts and brandy-cream sauce, sliced loin of lamb in a rosemary glaze with potatoes anna, and beef wellington with a truffle sauce. Desserts include chocolate crepes, sacher torte, white chocolate mousse with strawberries in a pastry tulip, and English trifle. At meal's end, a plate of almond-studded tuiles comes with the coffee.

Dinner, Tuesday-Saturday 6 to 9, Sunday 1 to 9.

♥ **Griswold Inn,** Main Street, Essex. (203) 767-0991.
American. $13.95 to $19.95.

Some things seldom change, and the immensely popular Gris is one of them, going strong since 1776. The always-crowded Tap Room is a happy hubbub of banjo players and singers of sea chanteys, and everyone loves the antique popcorn machine. A meal at the Gris is an experience in Americana. There's much to see in four dining rooms: the important collection of Antonio Jacobsen marine oils in the dark paneled Library, the Currier and Ives steamboat prints in the Covered Bridge Room (actually fashioned from a New Hampshire covered bridge), the riverboat memorabilia in the Steamboat Room, and the musket-filled Gun Room with 55 pieces dating to the 15th century. The menu is a mixed-bag of seafood, meat and game, ranging from fried catfish to medallions of venison. Steak and kidney pie, Irish lamb pie, English mixed grill, seafood gumbo, carpetbagger steak, and barbecued ribs are among the possibilities. The inn's famous 1776 sausages, served with potato salad and sauerkraut, are available to take home and come four ways at lunch, when the fare is lighter and more varied. The traditional Sunday hunt breakfast is as bounteous as ever. Did we say the Gris never changes? It added a new kitchen in 1989. "The old one lasted 213 years," noted innkeeper Bill Winterer. "And we expect the same performance from the new one."

Lunch, Monday-Saturday noon to 2:30, dinner 5:30 to 9 or 10, Sunday 4 to 9; Sunday hunt breakfast, 11 to 2:30.

The Black Seal, Main Street, Essex. (203) 767-0233.
American. $9.95 to $14.95.

The legendary Tumbledown's Cafe gave way in 1988 to the Black Seal, a casual and appealingly nautical place, with so much stuff to look at along the walls of the front tavern and in the rear dining room that it could distract one from the food. Basically the same fare is offered at lunch and dinner, though lunch brings more sandwiches and dinner more entrees. Graze on chile nachos, fire-pot chili, stuffed potato skins, Cajun shrimp, Rhode Island clam chowder, California burgers, and cobb and hunters salad anytime. At night, entrees range from stir-fry vegetables to steak au poivre. "Seal's Delight" is mussels, clams, scallops, shrimp and calamari over pasta. Desserts include white satin torte and Mississippi mud cake.

Lunch, daily 11:30 to 3:30, weekends to 4; dinner, 5 to 10 or 11; Sunday brunch, 11 to 2:30.

Oliver's Taverne, Plains Road (Route 153), Essex. (203) 767-2633.
American. $4.75 to $14.95.

This establishment named for Oliver Cromwell is a casual spot in a breathtakingly high space in the former Hitchcock furniture store. The decor is mostly wood with a massive stone fireplace and a three-story window with large hanging panels of stained glass to catch the light. Upstairs is a long oak and mahogany bar from Cicero, Ill., at which Al Capone once drank, and a suave lounge area with modern sofas and chairs and a fascinating collection of baskets on the wall. Huge sandwiches served with french fries, burgers, salads and a few entrees like quiche or scallops baked in a cheese sauce are available for lunch. Snacky things like nachos, potato skins, fried calamari and such are also offered at night, when entrees include loin of New Zealand lamb and slice-your-own sirloin for two. The barbecued pork ribs are praised by those in the know. Bailey's Irish Cream mousse cake and chocolate chip cookie pie are popular desserts.

Lunch daily, 11:30 to 5; dinner, 5 to 10:30; Sunday brunch, 11:30 to 4.

Chester

* Restaurant du Village, 59 Main St., Chester. (203) 526-5301.
Contemporary French. $21 to $25.

Here's as provincial French a restaurant as you can get, from its canopied blue facade with flowers spilling out of flower boxes to the white-curtained windows and french doors opening onto the side brick entryway. The 40-seat dining room is charming in its simplicity: a few French oil paintings, white linens, carafes of wild flowers and a votive candle on each table, and blue flower-sprigged Laura Ashley-type service plates. Founders Charles van Over and Priscilla Martel, who were looking to pursue a new opportunity in 1990, have attracted a loyal following since opening in 1979. The best French bread we've ever tasted comes with generous cocktails. Among appetizers, the mussels with cream and curry are plump and delicious and the plate of terrines ranges from smooth to hearty. For main courses, we recommend the sweetbreads in a rich sauce of three mushrooms, the filet of salmon on a bed of leeks with salmon caviar, the roasted leg of lamb with thyme and ratatouille-filled ravioli, and the enormous rib-eye of beef with peppercorn, tarragon and whiskey sauce. Accompaniments might be crisp asparagus tied with a red pimento bow and shredded potatoes, roesti style, plus a salad of mixed greens with a vinagrette that packs a wallop. Fabulous desserts vary from a strawberry kirsch cream pudding-like affair served in a goblet and topped with walnuts to bitter chocolate granite with coffee sauce, nested in a fluted pastry shell. The wine list is well chosen and nicely priced.

Dinner, Wednesday-Sunday 6 to 9 or 10.

Fiddler's Seafood Restaurant, 4 Water St., Chester. (203) 526-3210.
Seafood. $10.95 to $14.95.

A cheerful cafe atmosphere prevails in the two blue and white dining rooms seating 60 in this small restaurant with checked cafe curtains, cane and bentwood chairs, pictures of sailing ships on the walls, and tables on pedestals of old gears. Interesting seafood creations are served at fair prices. Three or four kinds of fresh fish can be ordered poached, sauteed or grilled over mesquite. At lunch, look for oyster stew with salad, lobster roll with fries, zuppa di clams, coquilles St. Jacques, and mussels in puff pastry. Dinner entrees include oysters imperial, shrimp casino, scallops with black mushrooms over spinach, bouillabaisse, and lobster with peaches in a peach brandy and cream sauce. Chicken au poivre, New York sirloin and veal of the day are available for those who prefer. Conch fritters and fried calamari are among appetizers, and the garlic bread with an aioli dip is extra-good. Chocolate mousse terrine with lingonberries and a lime mousse are popular desserts.

Lunch, Tuesday-Saturday 11:30 to 2, dinner, 5:30 to 9 or 10, Sunday 4 to 9. Closed Monday.

Moodus

The Salmon River Club, 173 Leesville Road, Moodus. (203) 873-2319.
Regional American. $11.50 to $18.95.

Part of a health club and resort of long tenure along the Salmon River, this fresh new restaurant was opened in 1989 by Philip and Janet Klinck, she a native of Moodus. From the large dining room with pink cloths, ladderback chairs and well-spaced tables, you can look out across the enclosed front porch/reception parlor and down the hill toward the pool and river. It's an appealing setting for lunch: perhaps the Salmon River Club salad of mixed greens with salmon, the grilled chicken breast on an English muffin with pesto mayonnaise and mozzarella, or the Cajun-style shrimp with sun-dried tomatoes in a balsamic garlic cream over linguini. Dinners range from grilled chicken with sweet peppers, leeks and prosciutto to poached salmon with horseradish cream and rack of lamb with a rosemary red wine sauce. Fresh fruits turn up in seasonal entrees like roast duckling with apples and whiskey-peppercorn sauce, and veal medallions with strawberries and shiitake mushrooms. Start with chicken terrine with cranberry relish or asparagus, cucumbers and goat cheese in a sweet vermouth-tomato coulis. Finish with cheesecake, hazelnut-chocolate mousse cake or strawberries romanoff.

Lunch, Monday-Friday 11:30 to 2; dinner, Monday-Saturday 5 to 9; Sunday, brunch 11 to 2, dinner 3:30 to 8.

Old Lyme

★ Old Lyme Inn, Lyme Street, Old Lyme. (203) 434-2600.
New French/American. $18.50 to $26.

Top ratings from the New York Times, desserts on the cover of Bon Appetit magazine, style recognized by the book Restaurant Design, and election to the Master Chefs Institute are among the honors accorded this mecca for traveling gourmets since Diana Field Atwood took it over in 1976. The food is inventive and the setting is formal in three large dining rooms, all regally furnished in gold and blue. Tables in the long, high-ceilinged main dining room are angled in perfect formation, a vase with one pristine rose atop each. Beyond are two more dining rooms, one with an intimate windowed alcove containing a table for four. Chef Chris Hawver, who trained in Paris and Zurich, oversees one of Connecticut's more ambitious menus. Dinner appetizers might range from smoked salmon and new potato timbale or ragout of wild mushrooms to escargots over two pastas and a trilogy of three Italian cheeses in polenta-filled squash boats with a tomato-oregano coulis. Seasonal "interludes" might be truffled brie and a salad of frissee, and shredded smoked chicken and gorgonzola cheese with a sage vinaigrette. Changing entrees include Norwegian salmon filet baked in potato crust and served with braised Belgian endive and shiitake mushrooms, roasted sweetbreads served with blanched spinach leaves and a wild mushroom fettuccine, breast of barbarie duck with grilled foie gras, roast boneless loin of rabbit with braised celery and lovage on a bed of roquefort-enhanced spaetzle noodles, and a game plate of sliced loins of venison and antelope with a sauce of peppercorns, red currant jelly and juniper berries. The inn's raspberry cheesecake Japonnaise was pictured on the cover of Bon Appetit. Other desserts are homemade sorbets and ice creams, cranberry linzer torte, and lemon shortcake tart. At lunchtime, we liked the curried cream of yellow squash soup, the interesting salads (one of venison with a wild mushroom couscous and a currant-brandy vinaigrette), and a special of Niantic scallops. Light suppers are offered in the Victorian grill room amid the inn's notable collection of paintings representing the Old Lyme School of artists who were based at the Florence Griswold House across the street.

Lunch, Tuesday-Saturday noon to 2; dinner, Tuesday-Saturday 6 to 9; Sunday, lunch noon to 4, dinner 4 to 9.

* Bee and Thistle Inn, 100 Lyme St., Old Lyme. (203) 434-1667.
New American. $16.95 to $24.95.

Head chef Francis Brooke-Smith, who trained at the Ritz in London, delights in innovative touches and stylish presentations at this highly regarded dining room. Among them are edible flowers for garnishes and fresh herbs grown hydroponically year-round. Baskets hang from the ceiling and thriving African violets, other plants and knickknacks are all around on the two enclosed, country-stylish dining porches overlooking the lawns. At lunch here, you'll enjoy shrimp salad served on a flaky croissant, a scallop puff, grilled Thai chicken salad, Maryland crab cakes, or cold roasted roulade of veal. Candlelight dinners are also served on the porches or in a small rear dining room, where a guitar-playing couple sings love songs on Friday nights and a harpist plays in a corner on Saturdays. Dinner entrees range from medallions of pork with split pea cakes or grilled breast of chicken served on a bed of white beans to roasted veal chop with semolina gnocchi and rack of lamb with an eggplant charlotte. Sliced breast of pheasant with buckwheat pancakes and loin venison steak served on potato croutons with onion marmalade were on a fall menu. Start with the house-dried gravlax seasoned with green peppercorns and herbs, a three-layered scallop terrine with saffron mayonnaise, a winter sausage stew, or roasted Fishers Island oysters topped with basil and pine nuts. Finish with banana mousse terrine, brandied pear trifle or chocolate mousse torte.

Lunch, daily except Tuesday 11:30 to 2; dinner nightly except Tuesday 6 to 10; Sunday brunch, 11 to 2.

Southeast Connecticut

New London

Ye Olde Tavern, 345 Bank St., New London. (203) 442-0353.
American. $12.75 to $21.75.

An institution since 1918 and now operated by the grandson of the founder, this is the kind of place where the walls are covered with pictures of local celebrities and customers. Not to mention an array of oars, nets, marine artifacts, local memorabilia and the like — enough to keep a browser long entranced. Of great appeal to the regulars in two dark-paneled dining rooms and a "taverna" are broiled steaks, lamb chops, prime rib, chicken oreganato and seafood, prepared and served in the old-school style. The menu bears no surprises, unless it's the dessert baklava, a remnant of the owner's Greek background.

Lunch daily from 11:30, dinner from 5.

Post Victoria, 49 Boston Post Road, Waterford. (203) 442-7953.
Regional American. $14.95 to $21.95.

A brown house with red and yellow gingerbread trim holds some fine stained-glass windows, Tiffany lamps and much brass, copper and marble. It used to be known as Poor Richard's, but the new incarnation under Mystic restaurateur Jon Kodama is more appropriate. Although his other restaurants are fish and steak houses, here he gives free rein to a chef who's into grilling and creative cookery at lofty-for-the-area prices. The eight entrees might include grilled shrimp Creole, veal medallions stuffed with cheese and served over spinach in a sauce of chanterelles, lamb couscous, and peppercorn steak with grilled vegetables and fresh pasta. Even the ubiquitous prime rib is a grilled roast served with popovers and horseradish sauce. Starters could be gravlax over asparagus with chive sauce, fried raviolis stuffed with veal and chicken in a red pepper sauce, or a warm salad of roast duck with avocado and bacon-honey dressing. Chocolate velvet mousse torte and baked fresh fruit in sabayon with raspberry sauce are dessert possibilities. Lunchtime brings with-it salads, grilled pizzas, a few sandwiches, and such entrees as crab cakes and tourtiere.

Lunch, Monday-Friday 11:30 to 4; dinner, 5:30 to 10, weekends, 4 to 10.

Thames Landing Oyster House, 2 Captain's Walk, New London.
(203) 442-3158.
Seafood. $9.95 to $19.95.
A new upstairs dining room yields a view of the Thames River through large windows. While the original Nautical Room on the main floor is so plain as to be austere, this is larger and a bit upscale with framed nautical maps on the wall, windsor chairs and tables set with cream-colored cloths under glass, cut-glass oil lamps, and gray napkins standing tall in water glasses. The menu offers straightforward seafood, generally unadorned, though scrod royale is topped with sliced tomatoes and melted provolone. There are six fried seafood items, including a fisherman's platter, three linguinis, and two non-seafood offerings (not including the French onion soup), sirloin and filet mignon. Three bisques — clam, mussel, and shrimp and mushroom — and conch chowder are among the starters. A short but good wine list has been chosen with an eye to price.

Lunch and dinner daily from 11:30.

Winthrop's, Radisson Hotel-New London, 35 Governor Winthrop Blvd.,
New London. (203) 443-7000.
American. $10.75 to $18.75.
Outfitted in rose and dark green, the dining room at this small new downtown hotel is a mix of windsor and upholstered chairs with a planter-divider separating the two levels. The menu ranges from deep-fried catfish to rack of lamb with a red wine-mint sauce. The chef gets fancy with items like carpetbagger steak with oysters and sauteed medallions of veal with mushrooms and green peppercorns in a light brandy sauce. A section of American heritage specials includes broiled salmon with dill sauce, New England seafood stew over fettuccine, and chicken California sauteed with garlic and white wine and served over a bed of braised lettuce with cherry tomatoes and spiced peppers. For dessert, try the American tipsy pudding, patterned after an English trifle.

Lunch, Monday-Saturday 11:30 to 2:30; dinner, 5 to 10; Sunday, brunch 11:30 to 2:30, dinner 4:30 to 9:30.

Noank

♥ **Abbott's Lobster in the Rough,** 117 Pearl St., Noank. (203) 536-7719.
Seafood. $6.95 to $24.95.
For years we've steered visitors from all over to Abbott's, partly because of the delectable lobsters and partly because of the view of Fisher's Island and Long Island Sound. You order at a counter and get a number — since the wait is often half an hour, bring along drinks and cheese to keep you going. We like to sit outside at the

gaily colored picnic tables placed on ground strewn with mashed-up clam shells and watch a constant parade of interesting craft in and out of Mystic Harbor. Youngsters can look at the lobster tanks or scamper around on the rocks, finding jellyfish and snails. Lobster (about $9 for a 1 1/4-pounder) comes with a bag of potato chips, a small container of coleslaw, melted butter, and a paper bib. Also available are steamers, clam chowder, mussels, and shrimp, lobster or crab rolls.

Open daily, noon to 9, May-October. BYOB.

Mystic

✱ **The Mooring,** Mystic Hilton Hotel, Coogan Boulevard, Mystic. (203) 572-0731. New American. $15.75 to $21.75.

The area's most exciting fare is served in casually elegant surroundings: a comfortable, three-level dining room flanking a courtyard in the center of the quiet, luxurious Mystic Hilton. Crisp linens, upholstered armchairs and banquettes, and much wood and brass give this the look of many a city hotel restaurant, albeit on a far smaller scale. It's rare to find such an inspired menu in a hotel, let alone in the heart of the touristy Mystic area. The Mooring has won rave reviews from food critics, and why not? How often can you start with grilled scallops in their roe with citrus beurre blanc and sevruga caviar, smoked salmon and leek terrine with lemon-thyme cream, or whole wheat and spinach linguini with goat cheese and salmon caviar? For entrees, the seasonal menu might offer steamed halibut with a watercress bouquet, tomato coulis and cactus leaf salad, steamed lobster cakes with sesame miso cream, charred scallops in black bean paste with fried noodles, grilled peppered breast of duck with kumquat relish, and sauteed medallions of beef with stilton ravioli in sauterne cream. We remember fondly a winter's dinner of medallions of venison and rack of lamb, the latter accompanied by roasted new potatoes in their jackets, grilled yellow squash, zucchini and eggplant, and half a broiled tomato garnished with bread crumbs. Dessert was a big almond lace tuile with chocolate mousse and liqueur inside.

Lunch daily, 11:30 to 2; dinner nightly, 6 to 10.

J.P. Daniels, Route 184, Old Mystic. (203) 572-9564. Continental. $12.95 to $18.95.

A restaurant of quiet elegance in an old, high-ceilinged dairy barn, J.P. Daniels has been going strong since 1981. Tables are covered with white linen and centered with fresh flowers. On certain evenings you may hear a harpist or a pianist in the background. Lanterns on the walls and oil lamps on the tables provide a modicum of illumination on two dining levels, as well as in the pleasant lounge where a bar menu is offered nightly except Saturday. Start with the house special, a fresh fruit daiquiri, while you choose from a large menu. Appetizers include grilled mussels, escargots and smoked Long Island duck breast. Among entrees are chicken jardiniere, curried shrimp, blackened sirloin, and three presentations of veal (oscar, francaise and marsala). A specialty is boneless duck stuffed with seasonal fruits and sauced with apricot brandy. For dessert, how about a velvety chocolate mousse laced with curacao, lemon-almond cheesecake or hazelnut pie? The wine list is moderately priced and contains explanations. Check the limerick on chains, a hanging sign depicting the owners, separating the lounge from the dining room.

Lunch, Monday-Friday 11:30 to 2; dinner nightly, 5 to 9:30 or 10; Sunday brunch, 11 to 2.

Flood Tide, Route 1, Mystic. (203) 536-8140. Regional American/Continental. $13.95 to $18.95.

This refined, quiet restaurant at the Inn at Mystic serves some of the area's fanciest food amid elegant Colonial decor. Beyond a new lobby and a club-like lounge is the spacious, two-level dining room with windows onto Pequotsepos Cove and Long Island Sound. The restaurant is known for a lavish Sunday brunch and a bountiful lunch buffet, a far cry from the Mystic norm in terms of fare (interesting) and atmosphere (sedate). We particularly liked the $9.95 lunch buffet, which ran the gamut from ceviche and lumpfish caviar through seafood crepes to kiwi tarts and bread pudding. At night, entrees range from broiled salmon steak au poivre with lime butter and saute of chicken with white asparagus to roast duckling with peach glaze and veal vol-au-vent. Two-tailed Maine lobster stuffed with shrimp is an unusual presentation. Fettuccine alfredo, whole roast chicken, rack of baby lamb, beef wellington, and chateaubriand are served tableside for two. In season, there's an outdoor deck with a view of the water.

Lunch, Monday-Saturday 11:30 to 3; dinner nightly, 5:30 to 9:30; Sunday brunch, 11 to 3.

Captain Daniel Packer Inn, Lower Water Street, Mystic. (203) 536-3555.
American. $12.95 to $18.50.

Once a stagecoach stop on the route from New York to Boston, this 1756 inn was owned by the Packer-Keeler family for all its years until Rhode Islander Richard Kiley turned it into a handsome restaurant. The pub in the basement is especially cozy, with brick and stone walls and a huge fireplace. The two dining rooms on the main floor have working fireplaces as well and floors of wide-board pine and formal mats with sailing ships on the tables. Chowder, salads, sandwiches and entrees are offered at lunch. At night, main courses range from scrod amandine to steak black jack, glazed with Jack Daniels. Lemon-peppered chicken, rack of lamb dijonnaise, veal Sicilian, and scallops Nantucket are among the possibilities.

Lunch, Monday-Friday 11:30 to 2:30 (plus weekends in pub); dinner nightly, 5 to 10 or 10:30, Sunday 4 to 9.

Seaman's Inne, Route 27, Mystic. (203) 536-9649.
American. $12.95 to $19.95.

General manager Charles Baxter and three partners who had been at the Griswold Inn at Essex took over this popular old warhorse next to Mystic Seaport in 1990. It had been upgraded under the ownership of Jon Kodama, who started with the Steak Loft in Mystic and has been developing a small restaurant empire lately. Besides a riverfront terrace for lobster in the rough, there's interior seating in the large riverfront cafe, two properly historic and formal dining rooms, and the taproom, the last a particularly fetching place for lunch with its pressed-tin ceiling, bare wood floors and tables, a greenhouse window full of plants, and a new popcorn machine (a la the Gris). The Griswold influence also shows up in the menu of Ken Tippin, who was its executive chef for sixteen years. We savored a lunch of thick and delicious clam chowder and two appetizers, poached mussels with salsa and an enormous portion of nachos Atlantic. At night, seafood is the specialty, from filet of catfish and shrimp oregano to shrimp and oyster pasta. Other entrees include bavarian-style sausage, steak and kidney pie, roast rack of pork loin, barbecued baby ribs, braised lamb shanks and lentils, grilled veal chop with herbed butter, prime rib, and Yankee pot roast. Favorite desserts include chocolate-butter cream pie, deep-dish apple pie and hot fudge sundae. A country breakfast features a dixieland band on Sundays, and there's live music many evenings in the taproom.

Lunch daily, 11:30 to 2:30; dinner, 5:30 to 9; Sunday, country breakfast, 11:30 to 2:30.

The Steak Loft, Olde Mystick Village, Mystic. (203) 536-2661.
Steaks/Seafood. $9.95 to $19.95.

The first of local restaurant impressario Jon Kodama's restaurants, this is also the most popular, filled day and night with folks who crowd into three dark dining rooms paneled in barn wood around a central salad bar, or what the staff calls "the jungle" because of all its plants and light in a room beyond the soaring bar. Cooks in red baseball caps and young servers in red shirts set a lively pace as they deliver steaks in all guises, seafood and poultry, and nine combinations thereof. Baby back ribs and teriyaki pork chops are listed under steaks, but prime rib is missing. Strangely, the wine list is pricey and stronger on whites than reds, but few notice. They prefer to pig out at the salad bar, enjoy a good steak, and finish with New York cheesecake or creme de menthe parfait.

Lunch, Monday-Saturday 11:30 to 2:30; dinner, 4:30 to 9:30 or 10:30, Sunday 11:30 to 9:30.

* Kitchen Little, Route 27, Mystic. (203) 536-2122.
International. $1.95 to $5.95.

This really is a tiny kitchen (indeed, the whole establishment beside the Mystic River is only nineteen feet square), but it serves up some of the greatest breakfasts anywhere. Chef-owner Florence Brochu's repertoire is extraordinary. Consider the three specials when we stopped: meatloaf and cheese omelet, scrambled eggs with sausage and jalapeno cheese topped with salsa, and a chicken-filled french toast sandwich with cranberry sauce and cheese. We waited our turn outside in the winter chill for a dynamite eye-opener of scrambled eggs with crabmeat and cream cheese, served with raisin toast, and a spicy scrambled egg dish with jalapeno cheese on grilled corned beef hash, accompanied by toasted dill rye. The coffee flows into bright red mugs, and the people at nine tables and five stools at the counter are necessarily convivial. In 1989, the kitchen started serving lunch. The menu was surprisingly pedestrian, given the chef's talents. We were told she couldn't keep up with exotic lunches in the hectic summer, but might experiment in the off-season. Let's hope.

Breakfast daily, 6:30 to noon; lunch, Monday-Friday 11:30 to 1 or 1:30.

Stonington

The Harborview, Water Street at Cannon Square, Stonington. (203) 535-2720.
French. $14.15 to $19.25.

The hurricane candles in the large dining room are lit even at noon in this dark and romantic establishment from which you can glimpse Stonington harbor through small-paned windows. The darkness of wood paneling and the blue-clothed tables is brightened by pink napkins and fresh flowers. Although new owners took over in 1989, the Harborview's large following scarcely knew it. Such is the draw of the atmosphere and the rich French cuisine. Favorites among entrees are a Marseillaise bouillabaisse, sauteed shrimp chinoise with peapods and ginger butter, Jamaican shrimp sauteed with dark rum, kiwi fruit and lime, and veal prepared three ways. We like the veal sweetbreads in a vol-au-vent pastry and the veal scaloppine in a grand marnier cream sauce, a portion large enough for two, served with julienned vegetables and tiny new potatoes, still in their jackets and swimming in butter. Among appetizers we're especially fond of the crevettes remoulade, a dinner plate full of five huge shrimp on a bed of tender lettuce covered with a piquant sauce, and a sensational billi-bi soup, creamy, mussel-filled and redolent with herbs. Many dinner items are available at lunch. The rustic bar with a warming potbelly stove offers daily specials and reasonably priced entrees. The lavish Sunday brunch buffet has unusually interesting hot dishes and enough food to sustain one for a couple of days.

Lunch daily, 11:30 to 3; dinner nightly, 5 to 10; Sunday brunch, 11 to 3. Closed Tuesday in winter.

$ Noah's, 113 Water St., Stonington. (203) 535-3925.
International. $7.25 to $12.95.

The price certainly is right at Noah's, a hip, casual and immensely popular storefront operation that has expanded into a second dining room with a service bar at the rear. When did you last find soups for under $1.50 and desserts like German chocolate pie or tartuffo di chocolate for $2? With a bowl of clam chowder and half a BLT plus a bacon-gouda quiche and a side salad, two of us had a fine lunch for less than $10. The blackboard specials are as appealing as the regular menu (broiled flounder, cod Portuguese, pasta, breast of chicken and such): blackfish stew at lunch, regional and ethnic specialties nightly. The Greek country and sliced breast of chicken salads are masterpieces. Save room for the chocolate yogurt cake, bourbon bread pudding or what one customer volunteered was the best dessert he'd ever had: fresh strawberries in Italian cream made from cream cheese, eggs and kirsch. The colorful decor includes pastel linen tablecloths and fresh flowers beneath a pressed-tin ceiling.

Breakfast, Tuesday-Sunday 7 to 11; lunch, 11:15 to 2:30; dinner, 6 to 9 or 9:30. Closed Monday.

Skipper's Dock, 66 Water St., Stonington. (203) 535-2000.
Seafood. $9.95 to $16.95.

The food is informal and the location salubrious in two paneled dining rooms at this casual spot operated by the Harborview and located behind it right beside the water. Better yet is the canopied deck out over the water, where on a sunny November day we reveled in a lunch of Portuguese fishermen's stew and a tasty linguini with shrimps and clams, studded with black olives, red pimentos, artichokes, and capers. The bloody mary was huge, the loaf of hot bread so good we asked for seconds, and the main portions ample enough that we couldn't face dessert. At night, you might start with fish house chowder, a plate of pickled herring or a bowl of Stonington steamers. Continue with a kettle of that great fishermen's stew, broiled scallops, stuffed shrimps or linguini with clams and shrimp, or specials like grilled tuna with ginger-sesame butter and poached salmon with champagne-tarragon vinaigrette. If you prefer, there are barbecued chicken caribe, london broil and grilled boar ribs. Ice cream puff with mocha ice cream and pina colada cheesecake are among the desserts. The owners opened a second Skipper's Dock with a similar menu in 1989 in an area that needs it — near the beach at Misquamicut, R.I.

Lunch daily, 11:30 to 4; dinner from 4. Open April-December.

♥ Randall's Ordinary, Route 2, North Stonington. (203) 599-4540.
Early American. Prix-Fixe, $25.

Anything but ordinary are the culinary experience and the atmosphere, both of which evoke the Colonial era. Cindy and Bill Clark serve food from the 18th century in three atmospheric but spartan dining rooms in a farmhouse dating to 1685. Up to 40 diners gather at 7 o'clock in a small taproom where they pick up a drink, popcorn, crackers, and cheese. Then they tour the house and watch cooks in Colonial garb preparing their dinners with antique iron pots and utensils in reflector ovens and an immense open hearth in the old keeping room. There's a choice of three entrees, perhaps roast turkey with wild rice stuffing, roast rib-eye beef or Nantucket scallops with scallions and butter. They come with soup (often carrot or clam chowder), whole wheat walnut or spider corn bread, squash pudding, a conserve of red cabbage and apples, and desserts like Vermont gingerbread, pumpkin pie and Indian pudding. It's a memorable experience for everyone, but a one-timer for most.

Lunch daily, noon to 2; dinner nightly at 7.

1 South Broad Cafe, 201 North Main St., Stonington. (203) 535-0418.
International. $9.95 to $14.95.

This successful little cafe in a shopping plaza moved lock, stock and name in 1989 to larger quarters in what formerly was the Village Pub beneath the viaduct in Stonington borough. In the process, it went upscale. The new space is pretty in pink, from glass-covered linens to the ceiling, all that pink nicely set off by dark wood wainscoting. The cafe even got a menu, no longer relying on a blackboard for anything but a few specials. Everything is done from scratch, even the tortilla chips for the nachos, which owner Tricia Shipman claims are the best in the state. House salad and bread accompany such dinner entrees as scrod nicoise, mussels marinara, seafood saute over saffron cappelini, scampi with broccoli and almonds, chicken bolognese, grilled duck with curried mango sauce, and mixed grill, perhaps swordfish, steak and chicken. Salads, sandwiches and international burgers are available all day. Peanut butter pie and gelato are steady desserts. The amiable atmosphere mixes transients at a jolly bar with people dining only a divider away at tables rather close together.

Lunch, Monday-Saturday 11:30 to 3; dinner nightly, 5 to 9:30 or 10.

Pawcatuck

The Nutmeg Crossing, 1 West Broad St., Pawcatuck. (203) 599-3840.
American. $7.50 to $12.95.

The locals give high marks for food and decor to this restaurant that opened in 1989 in a storefront at the bridge straddling the Rhode Island state line and the Pawcatuck River, with swans gathering beneath. A cafe atmosphere is created by pine paneling, big windows with gathered lace curtains, and oak tables with inlaid black formica tops. Owners John and Sheila Fravesi, who cooked earlier at 1 South Broad Cafe, are busy serving three meals a day. Dinner is a mix of four chicken, three veal, ten seafood and four pasta dishes, ranging from the simple (fried fish) to the sublime (scallops provencale). The lunch and breakfast menus are basic and straightforward, except perhaps for chocolate-chip pancakes with whipped cream. Sheila's mother makes the old-fashioned desserts, including grapenut pudding, lemon meringue and banana cream pies. A beer and wine license was pending.

Open Monday-Saturday 7 a.m. to 9 p.m., Sunday 7 to 2:30.

Southwest Connecticut

Bethel

Greenwoods Restaurant, 186 Greenwood Ave., Bethel. (203) 748-3900.
International. $10.95 to $16.95.

Almost everybody's favorite restaurant in Bethel is this informal place on the main floor of an old opera house. For good reason: there's something for every taste on the wide-ranging menu, the prices are reasonable and the portions ample. English food is the underlying theme, from the pub-like fare in the busy pub to the English mixed grill on the dinner menu. Why roast beef with Yorkshire pudding is missing from the "English fare," and why veal sorrentino is included, we don't know. The menu touches bases with French (escargots royale), Italy (homemade pastas and polenta), oriental (San Francisco chicken and shrimp saute), and domestic (grilled andouille sausage and vegetables in an appetizer called "Louisiana lightning," Cajun shrimp and swordfish, corn soup with roasted sweet pepper cream, and cornbread-stuffed baked oysters). The three small dining rooms are notable for ornate black pressed-tin ceilings, brick walls, oak wainscoting and posters of the Nichols Opera

House. At lunch, the menu is on a paper placemat covering the dark green overcloths. Thick sourdough-type rolls and zippy gorgonzola-dressed salads preceded our lunch entrees of angel-hair pasta santa cruz, tossed with an abundance of field mushrooms and bay scallops in a Spanish sherry-butter sauce, and a seafood sampler, including aforementioned cornbread oysters (the small oysters lost under an ocean of stuffing), shrimp, clams and a crock of mussels. For dessert, we were tempted by Dr. Mike's ice cream pie, but instead sidled up the street to the original Dr. Mike's Ice Cream for kid-size cones of heath bar and raspberry crunch.

Open daily, 11:30 to 10 or 11, Sunday 2 to 9.

San Miguel, 8 P.T. Barnum Square, Bethel. (203) 748-2396.
Mexican. $10.95 to $13.95.
We don't know which we like better here, the atmosphere or the food. Not your typical Mexican restaurant, this is true to the land — dark and quiet with candlelight, beams bearing sombreros and baskets, bare and red-clothed tables, and all kinds of nooks and dividers creating a happy mix of intimacy and privacy. A wall of books looms behind one table for six, and there's even a colorful outdoor cantina out back for drinks. Regulars like to sip margaritas in the cozy bar before adjourning to the dining room for starters of guacamole, nachos or quesadillas, the last two served on large platters. Some like the combination platters, but we prefer the spicy chocolate mole poblano, the sizzling red snapper vera cruz and the beef fajitas. The fruit chimichanga and homemade cheesecake are exceptional desserts.

Dinner, Tuesday-Sunday 5 to 9.

Le Tout-Paris, 39 Grassy Plain St. (Route 53), Bethel. (203) 748-6368.
French. $8.95 to $15.95.
A Parisian owner and an Alsatien chef teamed up in this new country French bistro, smartly done up in white linens and captain's chairs, with a pretty floral fabric gathered on one wall and French music wafting in the background. The limited menu is classic French, from escargots to filet of salmon with sorrel sauce and steak au poivre. The house salad is duck, a whole leg and a thigh served alongside lightly dressed ruby lettuce. Broccoli puree, carrots, potato pancakes, and sliced tomato provencale might accompany the entrees. Bay scallops could be sauteed with white wine and leeks, the monkfish with saffron, and the veal liver with shallots. Desserts are standouts, among them creme brulee, an orange tart, orange-scented cheesecake, and floating islands. Although dinners are quite reasonable, the lunch menu is no bargain. The primarily French wine list starts low, but quickly gets pricey.

Lunch, Tuesday-Friday noon to 2:30; dinner, 5:30 to 10, Sunday 3:30 to 9. Closed Monday.

La Fortuna, Route 6, Stony Hill, Bethel. (203) 797-0909.
Northern Italian/Continental. $11.95 to $22.95.
The chef and the maitre-d' from Capriccio in New York opened this tony, New Yorkish place, a picture of elegance in peach and white, with subdued lighting, attractive lattice work and a single flower on each well-spaced table. A mirror on the far wall makes the spacious room seem bigger. Although considered expensive, the food comes highly recommended. The prodigious menu lists twelve veal dishes from saltimbocca to osso buco, sixteen pastas, and enough antipasti, salads, seafood, chicken and grill dishes to make the choice difficult. Beef wellington, steak au poivre, lobster fra diavolo — you name it, and they'll probably serve it, although chateaubriand for some reason requires prior notice. Cannoli, rum cake and tartuffo are among desserts.

Lunch, Monday-Friday 11:30 to 3; dinner, 5 to 10:30 or 11. Closed Sunday.

Pappagallo's, 12 Depot Place, Bethel. (203) 791-0411.
Regional Italian. $7.25 to $14.95.

What do you do when the critics praise your French restaurant but the populace won't support it? If you're Judy and Sal Leo, you close for a couple of weeks, remove the crystal chandeliers and fancy linens, cover the tables with deep rose oilcloths, substitute an Italian menu, and change the name from La Plume to Pappagallo's. Same chef, same owners, same surroundings in an imposing Victorian house; less formal, lower prices and lots of happy patrons. The menu touches all the usual Italian bases, though veal plays second fiddle to chicken in terms of number of offerings, and reasonably priced pastas are clearly the norm. Some of the old French dishes slip onto the night's list of continental specials. Homemade cannoli, chocolate mousse, raspberry cream pie, and souffles are among desserts. The reasonably priced wine list is short and sweet. The same menu is offered at lunch, at lower prices, in three small, hushed dining rooms.

Lunch, Monday-Frdaiy 11:30 to 2:30; dinner nightly from 5:30. Closed Sunday in summer.

Danbury

★ New England Cafe & Catering Company, 4 Liberty St., Danbury.
(203) 798-8122.
New American/International. $9.95 to $16.95.

Charles (Buck) Harris, his wife Kathy and four assistant chefs pack in the lunchtime crowds for inventive food served cafeteria style. They've made their name through catering and their food service for area businesses. But come Friday and Saturday night and the fun begins. "We do what we really like to do," explains Buck, which is to serve innovative, lovingly prepared food at dinners that become special events. Peach-colored screens go up in front of the food cases, floral cloths cover the tables and waitresses serve up to 60 lucky patrons a short menu of exceptionally prepared dishes that change monthly. You might start with chilled sea scallops and shrimp with hot mustard, seafood cakes or lamb with mango chutney. Main courses usually include pecan chicken with sour cream-mustard sauce and poached salmon with lemon mayonnaise, plus specials like sauteed veal chops with mushrooms and spinach pasta, pork loin with peppercorns and apples and, at our visit, rabbit with summer vegetables, a user-friendly (says the chef) dish that has been deboned and enlivened with an array of herbs the Harrises grow at home. Desserts could be chocolate truffle cake or strawberry hazelnut torte. The Harrises are partial to fine wines; their list of unusual Californias is extraordinary and considered an integral part of dinner. The food is of the kind that makes restaurant writers swoon, though some skeptics fault the portions and prices. No one can fault the lunch specials, changing daily at unbelievably low prices, such as cucumber soup and a serving of curried chicken and pasta for $3.50 and salade nicoise ("anchovies optional, but recommended") for $4. Everything is prepared from scratch — "we're fanatic about our breads and pastas," says Buck — and the goal is a simplicity and clarity of natural flavors.

Lunch, Monday-Thursday 9 to 5:30, Friday and Saturday 9 to 3; dinner, Friday and Saturday, 5:30 to 9:30. No credit cards.

Ciao! Cafe, 2-B Ives St., Danbury. (203) 791-0404.
Contemporary Italian. $7 to $14.

Sleek and trendy in white and black. That's this stunner of a place with black tables, black booths and black banquettes. Striking serigraphs and other art on the walls are illuminated by track lights and provide the only color beyond that of the patrons. Here's the yuppies' favorite grazing pad. The lengthy menu obliges with excellent pastas (try the Thai fettuccine with broccoli, shiitake mushrooms, snow peas, baby corn, bamboo shoots, scallions and more in fresh ginger, cilantro and peanut oil) and a handful of other entrees like grilled monkfish, steak aioli, grilled rib-eye steak, and veal orvieto, not all done with equal success, we understand. Garlic, olive oil, mozzarella, fresh parmigiana reggiano, and lots of herbs go into most dishes. Excellent herbed bread sticks come with the meal. Start with grilled pizza with homemade fennel sausage, grilled vegetable skewers or a salad of chicken and arugula. End with flourless chocolate cake with hazelnut sauce, the recipe for which was requested by Gourmet magazine, or apple canoes (spiced apples in puff pastry with hot caramel sauce and whipped cream). Wines are pleasantly priced.

Open daily 11:30 to 10 or 11; Sunday, brunch 11:30 to 3, dinner to 10.

Ondine, 69 Pembroke Road (Route 37), Danbury. (203) 746-4900.
New French. $14.50 to $22.

A cute little stone and stucco house on a hillside near a lake at the Danbury-New Fairfield line harbors an unexpectedly suave interior. A display of cheeses, strawberries, teas, a chocolate confection and a gorgeous flower arrangement greet visitors on a table at the front entry. Gray velvet chairs are at well-spaced tables dressed with white linens, shell cutlery and a small candle in etched glass set into a silver stand. You'd never know the luxurious interior had once been a roadside tavern. Chef-owner Dieter Thiel's menu is as sophisticated as the setting. Among starters, look for a leek terrine with red pepper dressing, scallop and chicken raviolis with artichoke butter, and duck confit with white beans. The fifteen entrees range from grilled monkfish with mustard seeds and sorrel sauce or shrimp with sweet pepper and coriander to sweetbreads sauteed with black currants and green peppercorn sauce, sauteed veal with zucchini and chanterelles, boneless saddle of lamb in pastry, and venison medallions with a celery root puree and juniper berry sauce. Desserts include souffles, creme brulee and chocolate mousse with raspberry sauce. The extensive wine list includes a number of American offerings.

Lunch, weekdays noon to 2:30; dinner, 5:30 to 9:30. Closed Tuesday.

$ Sesame Seed, 68 West Wooster St., Danbury. (203) 743-9850.
Middle Eastern/Vegetarian. $5.50 to $12.

In a town in which restaurants come and go, this has endured for a dozen years. No wonder. On two floors of a turn-of-the-century house that epitomizes the words funky and eclectic, chef Dimitri Chaber (whom we encountered prepping a side of lamb in the walk-in freezer) and his enthusiastic young staff serve innovative meals at bargain prices. The decor has been called purposely unkempt; it's a mishmash of bric-a-brac, fringed lamps, accessories, old photographs and posters amid dark wood floors and walls, with two cluttered dining rooms down and four more up. Service is casual as well. But oh, the food. Everyone raves about the vegetarian dishes, the Mideastern hummus, baba ghanow and tabouli, and the dinner plates of falofel, kibbee, kafta and shish kabob for $5.50 to $7. The night's specials, at slightly higher prices, might be chicken mexicale, veal marsala, Cajun tuna, scallops pesto, and broccoli-cheese pie. Only beef is not included in the Sesame Seed repertoire. Baklava and Mideastern cheesecake head the list of desserts. The good house wines would be at least half again more expensive elsewhere.

Lunch, Monday-Saturday 11:30 to 3; dinner, Monday-Thursday 5:30 to 9:30, Friday and Saturday 5 to 10. No credit cards.

$ Bentley's, 1-C Division St., Danbury. (203) 778-3637.
Regional Italian. $7.95 to $11.50.

When you start a restaurant across the street from Sesame Seed, you've got to be cheap — and good. Richard and Manuela Bentley's cheerful new cafe is both, and doing very well, thank you. They seat 29, count them, patrons at tiny tables covered with wild floral cloths, crimson napkins and vases of fresh daisies. Copper pans, botanical prints, Villeroy & Boch plates on the walls, cactus, and plants provide more color. Richard, who does most of the cooking, credits his Italian wife with the inspiration. They serve dinner three nights a week, offering a changing menu at unbelievable prices. When was the last time you had medallions of veal sauteed in a colorful tomato cream sauce of sweet peppers, onion and basil or shrimp sauteed with zucchini served over spaghetti for under $10? Besides those items, a typical menu might offer an Italian chicken stir-fry, penne with broccoli and cauliflower, and baked marlin with mint and garlic. Soups, salads and a couple of appetizers start the menu; a blackboard might list fruit mousses, plum cake and chocolate cheesecake. Burgers, salads and sandwiches are the fare at lunch, and Sunday brunch brings omelets, frittatas and huevos rancheros.

Lunch, Tuesday-Friday 11:30 to 3; dinner, Thursday-Saturday 5 to 10; Sunday brunch, 8:30 to 2. BYOB. No credit cards.

Bangkok, 72 Newtown Road, Danbury. (203) 791-0640.
Thai. $9.95 to $15.

Vic Horsa traveled frequently to Thailand on business and loved the food, so decided to get himself a Thai partner to be chef (he found her and some of the other kitchen staff in San Antonio, Texas) and open Connecticut's first Thai restaurant. It's in a Super Stop and Shop center, but once inside the door of the pretty little place, you could fancy yourself in the Orient. The hostess is in native dress, Thai parasols hang from the ceiling, Thai posters decorate the walls, and the color scheme of soft orchid, lavender and purple makes the spot inviting. The menu is ambitious, listing no fewer than fifteen seafood dishes, several salads, and many dishes using pork, chicken and beef. A Bangkok sampler is a good way to try a few of the spicy appetizers; the three soups come highly recommended, especially tom yum goong, with fresh shrimp, mushrooms, ginger, green chilies, and lemon grass. Of the seven salads, how about sampling yum pla mouk (sliced squid with lemon grass, lemon sauce, ground green chile and Thai spices)? Four noodle dishes include pad Thai, the ubiquitous dish of rice noodles, shrimp, tofu, onions, and bean sprouts. A house special (and one of the most expensive entrees) is ho mook talay, lobster, shrimp, scallops and squid steamed in a clay pot — you may order it mild or spicy. Ice cream is the way to go after a Thai meal; Bangkok offers homemade coconut ice cream every night and sometimes jack fruit ice cream. Mangos with sticky rice is another typical dessert. The beverage of choice (wine and beer only) is Thai Singha beer.

Lunch, Tuesday-Friday 11:30 to 2:30; dinner, Tuesday-Friday 5 to 9:30 or 10, Saturday and Sunday 4 to 10.

Brookfield

Capers, 265 Federal Road, Brookfield. (203) 775-1625.
Californian. $12.95 to $19.95.

Chef-owner Dick Stokes and his wife, Sandi, returned to their native Connecticut to open a restaurant after a dozen years in California, bringing three assistant chefs with them from their restaurant of the same name at Lake Tahoe. Thus they had a California-style kitchen in place, and it was no time before they had appealed to local palates with what Sandi calls their California cuisine — "fine fresh food, cleanly and simply cooked." Inheriting a mock-Tudor building that housed an earlier restaurant at the side of the Rollingwood Condominiums, they decorated the airy main dining room in crisp California style with limoges cream walls, moss green carpeting, and windsor chairs at blond tables set with peach napkins and little oil lamps. Huge windows look onto the greenery at the rear, and there's a lineup of comfy pillows along the window seat in the lounge. The dinner menu emphasizes grills and sautes, plus entree-size salads, pastas and, most appealing, an insert of the night's specials. The possibilities are endless, but look for Venezuelan red snapper pan-roasted with oregano, Pacific salmon with a lime, honey and mint sauce, albacore tuna grilled with spicy wasabi beurre blanc, lime-ginger chicken, veal marsala, and New York strip steak served with shoestring fries. The entree salads include such typical California extravagances as tuna with snow peas and baby red potatoes, warm sea scallop salad and blackened New York strip salad. Southern pecan pie, raspberry linzer torte, double chocolate-chambord layer caker, and tartuffo could finish this fling with California cuisine. Salads and individual pizzas are featured on the lunch menu, which doubles as the bar menu.

Lunch, Tuesday-Friday 11:30 to 2:30; dinner, Tuesday-Sunday from 5.

Sushi Yoshi, 132 Federal Road (Route 7), Brookfield. (203) 775-1985.
Japanese. $7.50 to $18.95.

Owner Yutaka Yoshida often can be found with two other sushi chefs behind the sushi bar in his large restaurant, which started out French and wisely returned to the chef's land of origin. Every kind of fish imaginable including octopus is on view behind glass counters, and individual pieces are $2 or less. Sea urchin, abalone, flying fish roe, and jumbo clam are a few. Past a display of Japanese artifacts (slippers, shells, fancy sake bottles) on a bed of stones are a large bar, a tatami room, and two dining rooms where the white linens are covered by burgundy mats and koto and samisen music play softly. The miso soup is better than the usual, and for about $1.25 more than the entree, you may have a bowl as well as rice, ice cream or sherbet and tea. Deep-fried soft-shell crabs served with tempura sauce and gyoza (dumplings with vinegar sauce) are among appetizers. Giant shrimp tempura or teriyaki, swordfish teriyaki or broiled, beef kushiyaki (shish kabob, Japanese style), and pork cutlet with tonkatsu sauce are among entrees. Most expensive dinners are the special dinners for two or more; yosenabe incorporates lobster, shrimp, scallops, chicken, fish, and vegetables in a Japanese bouillabaisse, and the shabu-shabu uses prime rib-eye beef. Of course, there are several sashimi and sushi platters. Sake, Sapporo beer or plum wine are the right beverages to go with, but you might want to try a midori daiquiri or a plum sour.

Lunch, Tuesday-Friday noon to 2:30; dinner, Monday-Saturday 6 to 10 or 11, Sunday 5:30 to 9:30.

Pancho's & Gringo's, 777 Federal Road, Brookfield. (203) 775-0096.
Mexican. $9.75 to $12.95.

It's almost too much, a Colonial restaurant all decked out in Mexican paraphernalia. Ditto for the cutesy menu, categorized by "Mexican Meex-up," "zee food" and "Deezurts." Could this be Pedro's South of zee Border? No way, Jose. Although occupying the rear of ye olde New England-style Main Street Marketplace with a large water wheel at the side and an interior of brick and beams, this is the real thing. The hostess said it used to be an American restaurant until her brothers from Mexico took over and made it the huge success that it is, prompting a branch in Southbury. When we stopped early on a Friday evening, both the downstairs and upstairs dining rooms were jammed. That's testimony to the authentic Mexican cuisine, as well as the fair prices. The margaritas are a cut above the norm, and the tortilla chips come with spicy salsa rojo and salsa verde. The kitchen does all the Mexican standards with style, plus gringo steak and five shrimp dishes.

Lunch daily, 11:30 to 3; dinner, 3 to 11, weekends to midnight.

New Milford

★ Carole Peck's Restaurant, 373 Litchfield Road, New Milford. (203) 355-1310.
New American. $14.50 to $23.

"Where European countryside cuisine meets the American bounty" is how one of the first female graduates of the Culinary Institute of America bills her exciting restaurant in a little white house she rents from Skitch and Ruth Henderson, whose famed Silo complex is nearby. Having cooked at many a fancy restaurant, Carole Peck has been called "the Alice Waters of the East Coast," a likeness this diminutive, short-haired woman does not deny. She cooks seasonally, creatively and with only the best ingredients, obtained locally if possible. There are seats for 60 in dining rooms on two floors, notable for tables set with napkins and cloths resembling dish towels, and curtains made of what looks like mattress ticking, pinched in the middle. A collection of salt and pepper shakers and grinders, most obtained at flea markets, adds whimsey, and there are bowls of field flowers, votive candles and chairs covered with a paisley fabric. The walls are hung with the stunning artworks of the chef's French artist-husband. Such is the backdrop for an inspired menu that changes weekly. Starters at our spring visit included fresh asparagus soup with tomatoes and chives, seared sea scallops and corn salad with oriental scallion bread, and veal salad on tropical mango salad. The nine entrees ranged from grilled calves liver on an onion nest with grapes and pancetta to rack of lamb with wild rice and rhubarb chutney. Squab and gnocchi with a sage vermouth sauce, cold rabbit and green beans in tarragon gelee, and roasted salmon in shrimp sauce with a fresh mushroom tart were other offerings from this versatile kitchen. The dessert tray might bear a chocolate anise seed cake with espresso sauce or almond praline crepe with lemon curd and fresh fruits. The wine list is as choice as the rest of the fare. Carole mingles with guests after finishing the night's cooking in this personal gem of a place.

Dinner, Wednesday-Sunday 5 to 10; Sunday brunch, 11:30 to 2:30.

★ The Blue Grotto Restaurant, 33 Danbury Road, New Milford.
(203) 354-9192.
Northern Italian. $10.75 to $17.50.

It looks like a roadhouse, but the interior is glamorous and the food sensational. Fans say they've never found such good food or such spirited camaraderie as that doled out by chef-owner Domenico Chiera, who hails from the Calabria region in the south of Italy and goes three days a week to market in New York, where he had been chef at one of the city's stalwarts, Tre Scalini. A table with a display of exotic fruits, vegetables and wines is at the side of the dining room, richly outfitted with banquettes and velvet and gold chrome chairs, brick walls, intricate chandeliers, and candlelit tables. The menu doesn't change, nor does it need to. We know folks who would walk a mile for the pasta dishes, perhaps penne with a vodka-cheese sauce topped with caviar or egg noodles with a julienne of house-smoked salmon. Both the hot and cold antipasti plates are masterful. Rack of veal stuffed with fontina cheese, prosciutto and mushrooms is tops among six veal dishes. Other standouts are tournedos on a slice of eggplant with chianti wine sauce, sea scallops madagascar with pernod and peppercorns, and lamb chops bearing garlic, peppers, mushrooms, and oregano. Zabaglione, tirami su, homemade pies, and various ice creams are favored desserts. A former takeout shop in front has been converted into an intimate bar.

Lunch, Monday-Friday noon to 3; dinner, Monday-Saturday to 10 or 11, Sunday noon to 11.

Maison LeBlanc, Route 7, New Milford. (203) 354-9931.

French. $14.50 to $21.50

The old Iron Kettle has been transformed into one of the area's better restaurants by Pierre and Rose LeBlanc, he from Montreal by way of the Ritz and the Jockey Club in New York and she a native of nearby Brewster, N.Y. Their 1775 house is pretty as can be, the two dining rooms seating 45 and bearing wide-plank chestnut floors, blue mini-print wallpaper, lace-curtained windows, and tables with white over lace cloths and vases of alstroemeria. The main room can be noisy and a bit stark on a wintry night, but the food is seldom faulted. Pierre's menu echoes his French-Canadian background — "classic country," he calls it, "with a few touches of nouvelle." You might start with a sampling of smoked fish with horseradish sauce, escargots madagascar, or a roulade of spinach and goat cheese with tomato-basil relish. For main courses, how about an ethereal dish of braised sweetbreads and shallots in puff pastry, grilled salmon with chive butter sauce, steak au poivre, or roasted loin of lamb on a bed of arugula? Red snapper sauteed with red and green peppers and grilled rabbit with a sherry ragout were specials the night we were there. Delectable desserts include banana fritters with caramel ice cream and cinnamon sauce, a compote of strawberries and rhubarb served with a cheese mousse, souffle grand marnier, and homemade ice creams (hazelnut and caramel are two) and sorbets. The extensive wine list carries a good selection of American offerings.

Dinner nightly except Monday, 5:30 to 8:30 or 9:30; Saturday and Sunday brunch.

Charles Bistro, 51 Bank St., New Milford. (203) 355-3266.

Country French. $12.50 to $16.95.

In an area of increasingly fancy restaurants, chef-owner Charles Vautaret finds his niche in traditional, no-nonsense French food at affordable prices. The simple downtown storefront has bare floors, calico-type red wallpaper above green wainscoting, and tables topped with mats over rusty red cloths. There's a collection of baskets on one wall, and copper pots hang in the back. Charles arrived in this country from Lyons, via Montreal, and spent ten years as a country club chef in Greenwich before opening his own place, where he "went back to the old cooking, family style." That translates to dinner entrees like coq au vin, baked salmon with hollandaise sauce, veal sauteed with wild mushrooms, and sliced tenderloin with bordelaise, plus such specials as baked monkfish with mustard violette sauce and breast of chicken scapariello with basil sauce. Appetizers are classic, as are desserts like walnut pie, creme brulee and crepes with raspberry sauce. Salade nicoise and a Parisienne meat and cheese plate make zesty lunches. The pleasantly priced wine list is mostly French.

Lunch, Monday-Saturday 11 to 2:30; dinner, Thursday-Saturday 6 to 9.

Poor Henry's Restaurant, 65 Bank St., New Milford. (203) 355-2274.

Eastern European. $13.25 to $14.90.

Czechoslovakian Jan Myslik gave up the old Mayflower Inn to open his own place, a downtown hideaway that you'd likely pass by if you didn't know about it. Looking something like an old hunting lodge inside, it's a hectic hodgepodge of bric-a-brac, mismatched chairs, Christmas ornaments, strings of tiny white lights, and a lit-up tree in the bar, all very dark and foreign feeling. It's also known for fine live jazz and as one of the state's best watering holes, drawing artists and writers. Jan and a Hungarian chef specialize in their native cuisines. The blackboard menu lists things like sauteed fish with avocado and hollandaise sauce, Prague schnitzel, chicken with artichokes and hollandaise, bohemian stew, and garlic-mustard beef with heavy gravy dumplings. Dinner includes soup, salad and a popover. Apple strudel, napoleons, and polimcrika (like crepes suzettes) are specialty desserts. There's live music Friday through Sunday, when your table is yours for the evening.

Dinner nightly, 5 to 10 or 10:30.

Woodbury

The Bistro, 107 Main Street, Woodbury. (203) 263-0466.
Continental. $14.50 to $17.95.

The atmosphere of this restaurant wedged in the corner of a cluster of shops is fairly tea roomish with pale pink walls, lace-edged curtains and tables for 42 set with pink napkins and white cloths. But the food is continental with a French flair at the pleasant family operation run by chef Steven Kopf and his parents, Anne the hostess and Albert the wine consultant, who's partial to interesting wines and prices them to encourage patrons to partake. Red-dot items on the menu denote low-cholesterol fare, like blackened chicken, sea scallops grenoblise and turkey burgers for lunch. Dinnertime brings two menus, one a prix-fixe menu including soup, salad, entree, vegetables and dessert at earlybird prices. The other roams the culinary map, from shrimp martinique and red snapper vera cruz through veal paillard to pork loin madeira, tournedos au poivre and lamb curry. The composed salad is dressed with the house vinaigrette. Desserts include trifle, hazelnut torte, coconut-pineapple cream pie, and chocolate confections.

Lunch, Monday-Saturday noon to 2:30; dinner nightly except Sunday, 6 to 9; Sunday brunch, 11 to 2:30.

Portofino Restaurant, 10 Sherman Hill Road, Woodbury. (203) 263-2371.
Italian. $13.75 to $17.50.

All is light and contemporary in this two-tiered establishment with horizontally striped walls, cane and bentwood armchairs in muted colors, and modern lamps hanging over each glass-topped table. Chef Richie Collette puts out an ambitious menu, including thirteen specialties, ten pasta dishes, and fourteen more labeled "fish" and "from the broiler." We'd go for the veal marsala with the chef's special brown sauce, and perhaps the shrimp fra diavolo or steak diane. A creamy cheesecake, chocolate mousse pie and creme caramel are among desserts. The thick wine list harbors many bargains.

Lunch, Monday-Friday noon to 2:30; dinner nightly, 4:30 to 10.

Southbury

Thatchers, 971 Main St. Extension, Southbury. (203) 264-5688.
American/Continental. $10.95 to $19.95.

Billed as a restaurant and gathering place, this large establishment (lately moved from smaller quarters into a new building) is half restaurant and half bar. Literally. An electric train runs around the top of the horseshoe bar at one end of the lounge, full of comfy seats and perches. The other half of the building is devoted to a high-ceilinged dining room, with two stories worth of windows and a fireplace ablaze on chilly nights. Candles in cut-glass holders flicker on bare tables flanked by windsor chairs. Decor is elegant in an ersatz Williamsburg style. The large menu covers all the bases, from prime rib to grilled loin lamb chops, shrimp florentine to veal oscar. Appetizers tend to nachos, Cajun wings, fried mozzarella sticks and such. Sections of the menu are devoted to pastas, lighter fare and combinations. Desserts include a strawberry fantasy, peach melba, tartuffo, and cheesecake.

Lunch, Monday-Sunday 11:30 to 2:30; dinner nightly, 5 to 9 or 10; Sunday brunch, 11:30 to 2:30.

Newtown

Pasta Fresca, 316 South Main St., Newtown. (203) 426-6789.
Italian. $9.95 to $14.95.

Pastas, of course, are the specialty at this pleasant country tea room of a place in a low red roadhouse behind Hazel's package store in the Bostford section near the Monroe town line. Owner Doreen Scarpetti makes a wide variety of pasta on the premises, along with such seafood and chicken dishes as baked sole pomodoro, shrimp fra diavolo, stuffed chicken angelica, and roasted chicken a la ramone. Pastas vary from simple (with tomato sauce) to more fancy (with basil, garlic, pine nuts and olive oil). There's a full liquor license as well as Italian and domestic wines. Pastas and other items are available for takeout at the Faeto Importing Co. across the way.

Dinner, Tuesday-Saturday 5 to 9:30 or 10:30, Sunday 3 to 9:30.

Oxford

♥ **La Marina,** 162 Coppermine Road (at Route 34), Oxford. (203) 736-2929.
French. $14 to $22.75.

The food and service reviews are decidedly mixed, but no one faults the the setting in a summery, white frame building with black awnings beside the Stevenson Dam and Lake Zoar. A French flag flies out front. Most of the dining is in a broad sun porch, a picture of pristine white: bentwood chairs, double sets of linen on the tables, Royal Doulton china with a floral border, napkins resting in large wine globes, and glass vases, each with two pink roses. Massed flowers atop two pedestals and the sunset across the lake provide color. Owner Marc Saccone offers a changing French menu. You might begin with a country pate made of duck, chicken and quail livers, homemade pork sausage with lyonnaise potatoes, or coquilles St. Jacques. Entrees could include poached salmon with sorrel sauce, grilled tuna with tomatoes and bearnaise sauce, beef bourguignonne, roasted leg of lamb, and prime shell steak with green peppercorns. Cappuccino mousse cake, strawberries chantilly, tarte tatin, and assorted ice creams and sorbets comprise the dessert list. The short, hand-printed wine list is exclusively French in origin.

Lunch daily, noon to 3; dinner nightly, 6 to 10.

Northwest Connecticut

Kent

Kent Station Restaurant, Main Street, Kent. (203) 927-4751.
American/International. $10.95 to $14.95.

Kent's old train depot has been converted into an American bistro by Chuck Phipps. Pretty stenciling, country wreaths, small oil paintings, and lovely flower arrangements in low bowls create a pleasant scene. The French-trained chef's partiality for things Chinese and Cajun are evident in items like daily stir-fries and chicken sauteed with shrimp and andouille sausage. Dinner entrees range from seafood stew over linguini and filet of sole with grapefruit to roast duckling with fig and rum sauce and pork tenderloin with three mustards. At lunchtime, try the Ozark fried chicken on curly lettuce with hot potato salad and Cajun mayonnaise, the pate plate or eggs Gramercy Park, scrambled with smoked salmon and more over herb bread. Tia maria-mocha cheesecake and bourbon-pecan torte are favored desserts.

Lunch, Friday-Tuesday 11:30 to 2; dinner 6 to 9:30, Sunday 5 to 8:30. Closed Wednesday and Thursday.

The Milk Pail, Route 7, Kent. (203) 927-3136.
American. $11.95 to $18.95.

Old milk pails flank the facade of this small brown house with a cozy, Colonial dining room and an airy new solarium beyond. Changing artworks adorn the walls of the beamed, barnwood room with a corner fireplace. You have your choice of traditional or contemporary, in decor as well as on chef-owner Ernie Schmutzler's blackboard menu. Dinner entrees include pastas and specials like striped bass with lemon butter, sweetbreads amandine, veal bearnaise, and three black and white filets (beef, veal and pork). Popular at lunch are things like a western omelet, Ernie's chili in salad, shrimp salad in a star-shaped tomato, and halibut provencale. Desserts run to parfaits, peach cobbler and three-berry pie.

Lunch, Tuesday-Saturday 11:30 to 2:30; dinner, Tuesday-Saturday 5 to 9 or 9:30; Sunday, lunch and brunch, 11:30 to 3.

West Cornwall

Freshfields, Route 128, West Cornwall. (203) 672-6601.
New American. $10.95 to $17.95.

New owners from Troutbeck (a noted restaurant and conference center in nearby Amenia, N.Y.) took over one of our favorite restaurants in 1989, but three of the five chefs stayed on in a spanking new kitchen. The new owners added tables for dining in the upstairs lounge, changed the theme from country bistro to "American restaurant," and toned down one of the state's more exciting menus in length and description, if not in practice. For lunch, try the chunky tomato-basil bisque and curried chicken salad with fresh fruit or a grilled steak sandwich with tomato and ginger chutney. At night, start perhaps with country pate of tongue garnished with pistachios and maple mustard or the smoked salmon with noodles of cucumber. Continue with grilled tuna with Jack Daniels sauce, grilled swordfish with an interesting black bean sauce, or sauteed veal with tomato and braised garlic sauce. End with lemon and blackberry mousse or a fresh fruit tart. An immensely popular Sunday brunch ranges from banana griddle cakes and orange-walnut croissant french toast to crab cakes and ham with tartar sauce and grilled pork tenderloin with spicy peanut cream sauce.

Lunch daily, 11:30 to 2 (weekends to 2:30); dinner, 5:30 to 9 or 10. Closed Tuesday in winter.

Lakeville-Salisbury

Ragamont Inn, Route 44, Salisbury. (203) 435-2372.
Continental. $11.50 to $18.50.

The cooking of Swiss chef-owner Rolf Schenkel has been highly rated for two decades, and the setting could not be nicer for a summer meal. The awning-covered front patio off the main dining room is especially enticing, cool and verdant for lunch or dinner with green cloths and white wooden chairs. The sylvan theme extends inside to the summery main dining room, which has green forests painted on the walls. A more traditional, Colonial-style room has a fireplace for chilly nights. Choose one of the specialities from the blackboard menu, perhaps sauerbraten, scampi, stuffed veal breast, broiled swordfish, or rack of lamb. Rolf supplements his standards with items like lamb curry, paprika goulash, hasenpfeffer, shad roe, soft-shell crabs, and eight presentations of veal. For starters, how about smoked salmon, artichokes stuffed with crabmeat, duck liver terrine, or escargots? Seasonal berry pies and creme brulee are usually on the menu, as is a buttery linzer torte.

Lunch, Tuesday-Saturday noon to 2; dinner, 5:30 to 9 or 10; Sunday brunch. Closed November-April. No credit cards.

White Hart Inn, Route 44 at Route 41, Salisbury. (203) 435-0030.
New American. $12 to $20.

The troubled White Hart Inn, a venerable institution that has had its ups and downs in recent years, was grandly restored for reopening early in 1990 by Terry and Juliet Moore, proprietors of our favorite Old Mill restaurant across the Massachusetts line in South Egremont. Their taste, staff and lots of cash succeeded in bringing back the inn to its original glory, as was their aim. Although the top-to-bottom renovation also involved 26 guest rooms with private baths, the first floor and the dining facilities received top billing. The main dining room has banquettes on three sides, outfitted with Italian tapestries that match the fabrics on the seats of the chairs at the tables in the center. Five chandeliers and brass sconces cast indirect lighting to highlight the tables and a set of eight still-life oil paintings of fruits. Breakfast and lunch are served in the garden room, a sunny place with trellised wallpaper, botanical prints and brass chandeliers. Casual lunches and dinners are offered in the historic tap room. Chef Kevin Schmitz, for five years the sous chef at Chillingsworth on Cape Cod and lately executive chef for the Shearson Lehmann Hutton dining room in New York, planned a small menu that would change frequently. Look for French and oriental touches and local ingredients. Terry Moore promised a wonderful salmon dish, a smoked mushroom salad, and a sophisticated wine list.

Breakfast daily, 7 to 10; lunch, 11:30 to 2; dinner, 5 to 9 or 10.

The Woodland, Route 41, Lakeville. (203) 435-0578.
Regional American. $9.95 to $15.95.

A stylish lounge with slate floor and curved greenhouse windows has been added to this classy looking establishment known for good, reasonably priced food in a wooded area south of Lakeville. Beehive lights hang over the smart red booths in a dining room striking for the artworks on the walls, interesting woven placemats and a profusion of fresh flowers. For lunch, choose from a large variety of sandwiches and salads, or create your own omelet. At night, there are a few salads and sandwiches, plus eight entrees from chicken sesame to sirloin steak. Specials might be swordfish with pistachio beurre blanc or grilled salmon with a key lime-mustard hollandaise. Finish with such delectable homemade desserts as cranberry linzer torte, chocolate fudge cake with kahlua sauce, pear custard cake, or kiwi sorbet.

Lunch, Tuesday-Friday 11:30 to 2:30, Saturday to 2; dinner, Tuesday-Saturday 5:30 to 9 or 10, Sunday to 8:30.

Holley Place, Pocketknife Square, Lakeville. (203) 435-2727.
American. $11.25 to $22.95.

Two historic markers out front signify the site of Holley Place, which occupies the lower floor of the restored brick building that once housed the Holley Manufacturing Co. knife factory. Inside is a tavern with light fare and one of the longest bars in New England and beyond, on two levels, a skylighted dining room. The room is notable for granite walls of huge honey-colored stones, effectively illuminated by track lighting so that the contours show. Outfitted in pink with elegant Villeroy & Boch china and oriental carpets, it's a picture of luxury. The short, straightforward menu ranges from steamed vegetables and rice to New York sirloin, with things like baked shrimp wrapped in bacon and roast quail with walnut-mushroom stuffing in between. We're partial to the grilled calves liver and the veal sauteed in lemon butter, menu fixtures that have stood the test of time. Our country pate was urbanely dotted with pine nuts and served with rough mustard and cornichons. Desserts like grand marnier custard and chocolate souffle are standouts. The tavern menu is good for grazing and light meals.

Dinner, Wednesday-Saturday 5:30 to 9 or 10, Sunday 5 to 9.

Interlaken Inn, Route 112, Lakeville. (203) 435-9878.
Continental. $14.95 to $22.95.

The stylish Vineyard Room in this modern resort and conference center is colorful with purple chairs, orange napkins, large ficus trees strung with tiny white lights, and good local art for sale here as well as in the lobby. Entrees on the extensive menu range from mesquite-grilled chicken with spicy black bean relish, tomato cucumber salsa and lime sour cream sauce to tournedos with peppercorns and cognac cream sauce. Others could be blackened sea scallops over angel-hair pasta, poached salmon with lemon-basil butter, and roasted rack of lamb with grilled tomatoes and fresh mint. Sauteed shrimp sambucca and pan-fried oysters with Cajun cream sauce are possible starters. The signature dessert is chocolate decadence cake with raspberry filling, ganache icing and Bavarian cream; warm apple tart in puff pastry with cheddar and caramel sauce is a close second. Lunch and a light dinner menu are available in the **Circuit Lounge,** which has a rattan-filled dining area and a screened porch overlooking the pool. A life-size stuffed doll looking for all the world like Vladimir Horowitz presides at the player piano.

Lunch daily, noon to 2:30; dinner, 6 to 9 or 10; Sunday, brunch 11:30 to 2:30, dinner 5 to 9.

Peking Restaurant, Main Street, Lakeville. (203) 435-0850.
Chinese. $10.95 to $14.95.

If this modern establishment with plain tables, bentwood chairs and cafe curtains doesn't look Chinese, it's because it began life as the Lakeville Cafe, refashioned at great expense from the old Lakeville Market. The two Chinese partners came from New York to turn it into a restaurant serving an extensive selection of Mandarin, Szechuan and Hunan cuisine. Swordfish with ginger, garlic and oyster sauce, sesame crispy shrimp, Peking pork chops, hot and spicy lamb, and Szechuan smoked duck are among the offerings. Desserts are limited to pineapple chunks, ice cream and stuffed banana for two.

Lunch, Monday-Friday 11:30 to 3, Saturday noon to 3; dinner, 3 to 10 or 11, Sunday 12:30 to 9.

Canaan

★ Cannery Cafe, 85 Main St., Canaan. (203) 824-7333.
American Country. $10.50 to $16.25.

A 1920s stove sits in the front of this dear little cafe, homey as can be, run by Eric and Diane Stevens, an enthusiastic young couple who opened it in 1988. Eric, who trained at Mr. B's in New Orleans, is a chef with a Cajun flair, and Diane makes desserts like warm bread pudding with a whiskey sauce, grand marnier mousse, and a flourless chocolate cake with raspberry sauce that is "like biting into a truffle." Canning jars are the theme here; filled with anything from colored water to dried pastas and beans, they line the shelves and windows. The unmatched china came from flea markets and, says Diane, from people cleaning out their attics. Lemonade, iced tea and cider are served in canning jars (stronger stuff is available), and at both lunch and dinner, a jar of icicle pickles (cucumber, onion and dill) is set upon your table. Eric's Cajun seasoning, packed in (you guessed it) miniature canning jars, is for sale. We've tried it on all kinds of dishes and it packs a wallop. Start your meal with fried catfish remoulade or grilled shrimp and andouille sausage, and feast on such entrees as grilled Wisconsin duckling (from Eric's home state) with raspberry-garlic glaze, peppered pork loin, chicken jambalaya, or summer scallop saute with basil-lemon cream on angel-hair pasta. Lunch brings Cajun chicken fingers, salads, burgers, and entrees like pasta primavera, linguini with white clam sauce, and fish and chips. Diane says the couple wanted to have a place that looked "homemade"

Northwest Connecticut

and would remind people of the twenties, when Canaan was a railroad center and 30 trains a day came through. That it does, although at night when white and yellow linens and blue napkins are brought out and candles are lit, there's a touch of sophistication as well.

Lunch, Tuesday-Saturday 11:30 to 2:30; dinner, Tuesday-Sunday 4 to 8.

Norfolk

Maxfield's, Mountain View Inn, Route 272, Norfolk. (203) 542-5595.
American/Continental. $12.50 to $21.

This big, rustic Victorian inn, built as a private home at the turn of the century, has been upgraded since Michele and Alan Sloane took over in 1987 following a stint as hotel managers in the Caribbean. Maxfield's restaurant, named for artist Maxfield Parrish whose prints are on the walls, consists of a pine-paneled porch with frilly curtains and a more formal inner dining room with brick fireplace and beamed ceiling, nicely outfitted in burgundy and white with fresh flowers. An ambitious dinner menu is served, ranging from chicken citron to beef wellington. Among the entrees are hot scallop salad, shrimp curry, veal saltimbocca, roast duckling and roast pork loin. Appetizers include coho salmon smoked in the inn's back yard, Cajun shrimp and chilled smoked pork with apple chutney sauce. Chocolate grand marnier mousse and derby pie are favorite desserts.

Dinner nightly in season, 6 to 9:30; Sunday brunch, 11 to 2. Closed Tuesday and Wednesday in winter.

New Preston

★ **Doc's,** Route 45 at Flirtation Avenue, New Preston. (203) 868-9415.
Italian. $5 to $12.25.

Don't you love it? A name like Doc's. An address at Flirtation Avenue, across from Lake Waramaug. A roadside stand gone upscale, sort of. Here is where Adam Riess, a Californian fresh out of the University of Pennsylvania and back from a gastronomic tour of Italy, opened an Italian cafe, pizzeria and bakery in 1989 to resounding success. The rustic dining room has 30 chairs painted a pea green, spartan tables bearing butcher paper and big bottles of extra virgin olive oil, and a handful of plants and posters for accents. New-wave pizzas are the specialty, in small and large sizes. Try the capra (goat cheese, bell peppers and olive) or the cipolla (sauteed onion, gorgonzola and rosemary). We hear great things about the breads and pastas (perhaps penne with hot Italian sausage and tomato sauce, handmade noodles with porcini and prosciutto sauce, or tri-colored fusilli with fresh tomato, garlic and oregano). Starters might be fried polenta with gorgonzola, spiedini of fresh mozzarella, or fennel and parmigiana reggiano. Salads are exotic, too. On some nights, that's the extent of the menu. But at peak periods, you may find a few entrees: highly seasoned chicken breasts served with roasted new potatoes, beef and vegetable stew with handmade noodles, and a couple of lasagnas the night we were there. For dessert, indulge in chocolate-prune cake, crostata di ricotta, or ricotta with fresh fruit and honey. Oh, yes, the name? Although he was thinking of calling it Adamo's, which seems appropriate, Adam named it for his grandfather, a doctor who has summered on the lake for 40 years.

Dinner, Monday-Saturday 5 to 9 or 10, Thursday-Sunday in off-season; lunch in summer.

♥ **The Boulders Inn,** Route 45, New Preston. (203) 868-0541.
American/Continental. $15-$23.50.

An intimate inner dining room with walls of boulders, a six-sided outer room with windows onto Lake Waramaug and a couple of tiers of patios for outdoor dining are the setting for some of the area's better food. In season, we like to linger on the patio over a lunch of California salad, smoked chicken and couscous salad, grilled and skewered chicken with a spicy peanut sauce, or a charcuterie plate. At night, the atmosphere turns romantic as subdued light emanates from chandeliers covered with pierced lampshades made by innkeeper Ulla Adema and from hurricane lamps on the white-linened tables. Chef Bruce DeFalco serves up things like striped bass with a white wine-watercress sauce, grilled scallops in saffron, roast duckling with raspberry sauce, chicken mornay, grilled quail, grilled veal chop finished with a smoked tomato sauce, and medallions of lamb with rosemary. Through the years, we've enjoyed dinners of tasty chicken paprikasch and kashmir lamb in a sauce of tomatoes, ground almonds, yogurt, and curry spices. Start with smoked duck with sweet and sour mustard or chilled mussels and scallops with avocado slices. Finish with chocolate souffle cake with creme anglaise or a fresh fruit tart with an international coffee.

Lunch, daily except Tuesday noon to 2, Memorial Day to Labor Day; dinner nightly except Sunday, 6 to 8:30 or 9; Sunday brunch in off-season.

♥ **Hopkins Inn,** Hopkins Road, New Preston. (203) 868-7295.
   Swiss/Continental. $13.25 to $17.25.
   Beautiful Lake Waramaug sparkles below the popular outdoor terrace, with the Litchfield Hills rising all around. You could easily imagine yourself beside one of the lakes in the Alps, and Austrian chef-owner Franz Schober must feel quite at home. Lunch or dinner on the terrace, shaded by a giant horse chestnut tree and distinguished by striking copper and wrought-iron chandeliers and lanterns, is a treat from spring into fall. One dining room is Victorian, while the other is rustic with barnsiding and ship's figureheads. The blackboard menu changes daily, but always includes wiener schnitzel and sweetbreads Viennese, dishes that we remember fondly from years past. Other possibilities might be broiled salmon, trout meuniere, backhendl with lingonberries, chicken cordon bleu, loin lamb chops, and pork filet calvados. The roast pheasant with red cabbage and spaetzle is especially popular in season. For vegetables, you may get something unusual like braised romaine lettuce. Appealing desserts are baba au rhum (rich, moist and very rummy), white chocolate mousse, strawberries romanoff, and grand marnier souffle glace. The varied wine list has half a dozen from Switzerland as well as three from Hopkins Vineyard next door.

Lunch, Tuesday-Saturday noon to 2; dinner, 6 to 9 or 10, Sunday 12:30 to 8:30. Closed Monday and January-March; dinner only in early spring and late fall. No credit cards.

The Inn on Lake Waramaug, North Shore Road, New Preston.
   (203) 868-0563.
   New American. $15 to $21.
   The food here has been upgraded lately, thanks to innkeeper Barbara Kirshner, a former food professional from New York. She describes the cuisine of new chef Paul Dionne, formerly of the Norwich Inn, as "inventive American." Old favorites are made sophisticated, as in grilled breast of chicken on a sauce of roasted peppers and garlic and flavored with brandy, sauteed shrimp and scallops in a roasted pepper and raspberry vinegar-butter sauce, roast duckling with a tart raspberry-plum sauce, broiled tournedos with gorgonzola butter, and grilled lamb chop served on a bed of rosemary and spinach. Appetizers could be grilled shrimp wrapped in bacon and served with a cognac-herb butter or homemade pasta tossed with smoked chicken, crimini mushrooms and parmesan cheese. Salads are dressed with a honey vinaigrette, a specialty that's available in bottles to go. Besides homey desserts, you

might find a lemon cake layered with lemon mousse and topped with lemon curd, garnished with a rosette of whipped cream and a raspberry puree. Dining is in a large, pleasant room with Hitchcock chairs, swagged draperies and pink over burgundy linens, and in an adjacent, more airy room in deep burgundy with a distant view of the lake. There's also an outdoor deck, and barbecue lunches are served by the lake in summer.

Lunch in season; dinner, Monday-Saturday 6 to 9; Sunday, brunch 11:30 to 2:30, dinner 4 to 7 or 8.

Woodville

Le Bon Coin, Route 202, Woodville. (203) 868-7763.
French. $12.75 to $29.

The small white dormered house along the road from Litchfield to New Preston is home for classic French cuisine, lovingly tendered by chef-owner William Janega. The dark, cozy barroom has copies of French Impressionist paintings on the walls and Hitchcock chairs at half a dozen small tables. On the other side of the foyer is a dining room, barely larger but brighter in country French style. Colorful La Fleur china tops the double sets of heavy white linen cloths at each table, and the rooms are most welcoming. The oversize menu is handwritten in French with simple translations and a recent emphasis on dishes from the south of France. Dinners might begin with pate of pork and duck, prosciutto with eggplants and artichokes, a vegetable flan provencale, or Maryland crabmeat cocktail. The dozen entrees range from calves liver with raisins to filet mignon with foie gras and truffles. Others are dover sole, sweetbreads du jour, supreme of chicken with herbs from Provence, pepper steak, duckling with black currants, and pasta du jour, perhaps capellini with shrimp and clams in a heady garlic-herb sauce. Desserts include a plate of ice creams and sorbets, floating island, poached pear with raspberry sauce, frangelico cheesecake, and creme caramel. Chef Janega is proud of his wine list — mostly French — and of his new front entry, decorated with wine casks, spigots and crate labels plus some handsome stained-glass windows.

Lunch, Monday and Thursday-Saturday noon to 2; dinner, 6 to 9 or 10, Sunday 5 to 9. Closed Tuesday.

Litchfield

★ **Toll Gate Hill,** Route 202, Litchfield. (203) 567-4545.
New American. $17 to $24.

This is a wonderful old inn, nicely restored and lately expanded by Fritz Zivic, who founded the late Black Dog Tavern steakhouse chain in the Hartford area in the 1960s. Meals are taken in two small, charming dining rooms on the inn's main floor and upstairs in a ballroom complete with a fiddler's loft for piano or live entertainment. Chef Michael Louchen won the Connecticut Restaurant Association's seafood competition in 1988 with a ragout of Stonington clams and sauteed Long Island Sound bluefish served with grilled polenta and cucumber spaghetti. He features what he calls "updated New England fare" on a varied menu supplemented by nightly specials. Dinner entrees range from grilled pork loin with white beans, escarole and tomatoes to grilled peppered rack of lamb with chevre custard. Our summer dinners of shrimp in beer batter and sauteed sea scallops with sweet butter and braised leeks were outstanding. We've since heard rhapsodic comments about the shellfish pie and the duck breast with maple-vinegar sauce. For starters, look for sauteed soft-shell crayfish with capers and spiced cornbread, smoked salmon tartare with parsnip chips and olive oil, or seafood terrine with roasted red pepper coulis.

Desserts, prepared by a master baker from Europe who teaches at the Culinary Institute of America, are to groan over. They include chocolate bread pudding with pistachio sauce, chocolate-amaretto cheesecake, pumpkin and hazelnut torte, and chocolate pate with grand marnier creme anglaise. The wine list is choice and quite reasonably priced. The lunch menu changes daily, and brunch items are offered on weekends amid piano music in the ballroom.

Lunch daily, noon to 3; dinner, 5:30 to 9:30 or 10:30. Closed Tuesdays from November to July, and most of March.

Mary Dugan's, On the Green, Litchfield. (203) 567-3161.
American. $9.50 to $18.50.

A well-regarded restaurant that closed in 1988 in New Milford, Mary Dugan's popped up again in 1989 on the green in Litchfield to a receptive audience. The long narrow room is flanked by black booths and a row of black formica tables with blond wood edges down the center. One wall is brick; the other has a charming mural of cows and barns. Paper mats top the tables until evening, when white linens come out, the lights are lowered and a gorgeous arrangement of flowers is spotlit. For lunch we enjoyed a cup of split-pea soup, so thick it could hold a spoon at attention, and a generous spinach salad with a yogurt-dill dressing. We felt the polenta with roasted red peppers, mushrooms and cheese could have used more cheese. Other possibilities on the menu that changes daily were clam chowder, henny penny salad, burgers, a philly steak sandwich we heard was the best thing offered, a cold meatloaf sandwich, and a tuna melt. The dinner menu also changes nightly and stretches from chicken pot pie and New England boiled corned beef dinner to grilled albacore tuna with tomatoes and fettuccine and osso buco with roasted vegetables and egg noodles. Half a rack of lamb comes with zucchini casserole and potato cake. Desserts range from apple pie to bread pudding with strawberry sauce. Mary Dugan's is nothing if not eclectic. Our service was of the "so, can I get you guys a drink?" variety. Who is Mary Dugan? Read your paper placemat and you'll find out.

Open Monday-Friday, 6:30 a.m. to 10 p.m.; Saturday, 7:30 to 10; Sunday, breakfast 7:30 to 3, lunch 11:30 to 8, a few dinner specials after 5.

La Tienda Cafe, Sports Village, Route 202, Litchfield. (203) 567-8778.
Mexican. $7.50 to $10.50.

A green neon cactus beckons in the window of this two-room Mexican cafe with a bar in the rear. Glass tops the cloths of wide, bright stripes and a cactus in a small pot is on each table. Colorful prints and rugs adorn the walls. Crispy homemade tortilla chips and a fairly hot salsa are served. Almost too much for one was a lunch of Mexican pizza: a flour tortilla topped with ground beef, cheese, lettuce, tomato, chilies, guacamole, and sour cream. One half had hot peppers, the other mild. Both dinner and lunch menus have "north of the border" dishes, but who would come here for strip steak? Black bean soup, flautas, Arizona-style nachos (topped with ground beef), and quesadillas are some of the appetizers, and there's even a Mexican egg roll. Everything may be ordered mild, medium or hot. Create your own fajitas (chicken or flank steak) at the table and top with a choice of ten items like guacamole, green chilies, refried beans, and Mexican rice. Lime pie is the most requested dessert, but flan and sopaipilla are popular as well. Margaritas, pina coladas and daiquiris are available by the carafe.

Lunch, Monday-Saturday 11:30 to 2:30; dinner, 4:30 to 9 or 10, Sunday 3 to 9.

Wickets, Route 202, Litchfield Commons, Litchfield. (203) 567-8744.
Regional American. $10.50 to $17.50.

Energetic new owner Eric Filkowski, a business type who had run the dining room at Dobber's Den in Washington Depot and then signed on at Wickets part-time, saw an unrealized potential and purchased the place in late 1989. He scored something of a local coup, hiring chef Marty Carlson, long at the Boulders Inn, and two of his assistants. Marty changes the menu frequently, but you might find grilled shrimp with cilantro and andouille sausage, fresh marlin, tortellini primavera, chicken paprikasch, filet mignon with madeira and shiitake mushrooms, and veal with fresh tomatoes, basil and mozzarella. Start with escargots, artichoke hearts or one of his fabulous soups (perhaps black bean, cream of onion with three cheeses, or roast duck and onion potage). Finish with chocolate-chambord cheesecake, chocolate-raspberry torte and locally made ice creams. The wine list offers good values in the teens. There's a new espresso-cappuccino machine, and a light bar menu is available all day. "We're trying to do what everyone dreams of, to be all things to all people," says Eric, and early reports were that they were succeeding. The large, contemporary place at the rear of a shopping complex is named for the American version of cricket, which was first played on these shores at the Tapping Reeve Law School in Litchfield. Prints and cricket paraphernalia adorn the cheerful pink walls. Tables downstairs and in the solarium are left bare with pink inlays; those in the airy upstairs dining room are set with white linens for dinner. The outdoor terrace is popular in season.

Lunch daily, 11:30 to 2:30; dinner nightly, 5:30 to 9 or 10; Sunday brunch, 11:30 to 2:30.

Torrington

Le Rochambeau, 46 East Main St., Torrington. (203) 482-6241.
French. $9.75 to $18.50.

How did veteran chefs Jean Pierre Haffreinque and Georges Dosset, Paris-trained and long at the former Corner House in Farmington, end up in Torrington? "We got lost," quipped Georges. But the Torrington area is the better for it, and the partners couldn't be happier. On one side, there's a long tavern-like bar, and on the other a dark-paneled dining room with booths along one wall and a row of tables flanked by fancy chairs obtained from New York's La Cote Basque. Delacroix prints, white linens and fresh flowers enhance the setting. An even nicer upstairs dining room is used for overflow. The food is traditional, from mussels mariniere to steak au poivre, and served in generous portions with salad and vegetables. Breast of capon cordon bleu, duckling bigarade, veal cardinale, veal kidneys with green peppercorns, and chateaubriand are house specialties. More inspired are some of the nightly specials, perhaps yellowfin tuna sauteed with fresh peppercorns or veal medallions with tri-color mushrooms. In season, roast pheasant, venison, quail and partridge are featured. Desserts are homemade: a mango-chocolate mousse torte, creme caramel and a stellar meringue glace. There's an extensive wine list. Lunch prices are high for the area, but dinner is a steal.

Lunch, Tuesday-Saturday noon to 2; dinner nightly, 5 to 9:30 or 10.

Venetian Restaurant, 52 East Main St., Torrington. (203) 489-8592.
Italian. $13.50 to $16.95.

A fixture locally for more than 60 years, this enduring establishment retains its original black pressed-tin ceiling in the two-story-high front dining room, notable for a decorative red balcony and enormous murals (one of Venetian gondoliers) along the walls. It's a visual time warp, from the 1930s glass-block walls to the 1950s booths and banquettes. The DiLullo family from Abruzzi bought the establishment in 1970 and added their own culinary touches. Seven veal dishes are among the dozen specialties on the menu; otherwise, expect tried-and-true Italian favorites from shrimp or swordfish marinara to sirloin steak pizzaiola, with a few American grill items like filet mignon and pork chops. The pastas are of the old school, as are the antipasti. So are the friendly waitresses, for that matter. Rum zabaglione, Sicilian spumoni and tirami su are dessert favorites.

Lunch weekdays, 11:30 to 2:30; dinner nightly, 5 to 10, Sunday noon to 9. Closed Tuesday.

Pedlar's at the Yankee Pedlar Inn, 93 Main St., Torrington. (203) 439-9226. American. $7.25 to $15.95.

Another Torrington fixture, this 1891 inn has been taken over lately by Classic Inns and is being improved. New manager Stephen Nelson is upgrading the menu as well as taking, thank goodness, the glass off the table tops. But not to worry, oldtimers, you can still order the roast turkey dinner with apple and sausage dressing. New England clam chowder, of course, along with potato skins, deep-fried calamari, Buffalo wings, and a mini raw bar lead off the dinner menu. Seafood fra diavolo, chicken pecan (with a sauce of Kentucky bourbon and cream), baked scrod provencale, beer batter shrimp, baked stuffed pork chop, veal marsala, and broiled swordfish and scallops are some of the entrees. At lunch you can order the same appetizers, plus salads (cobb, oriental, seafood, chef's, or a visit to the salad bar), deli sandwiches or specialty sandwiches like Philly cheese steak and classic club. Chicken pot pie and London broil are other entrees, their price including salad bar. The dining room, down a few stairs in the back of the inn, is paneled in warm wood. Each table holds a lucite pepper grinder, a bottle of balsamic vinegar, and a bottle of olive oil.

Lunch, Monday-Friday 11:30 to 3; dinner nightly, 5:30 to 10 p.m., Sunday 5 to 10.

Winsted

Cafe de Olla, 576 Main St., Winsted. (203) 379-6552. Mexican/American. $8.95 to $15.95.

The various signals in front of this homespun hodgepodge of buildings indicate Mexican fare, steaks/seafood, coffee/dessert, and takeout. That encompasses about everything, except for the Cajun cookery, the marvelous margaritas, the popular patio, the fireplaced room with bookcases full of diverse regional titles, and the side solarium with a balcony on the rear wall suggesting a Mexican house. The solarium has upholstered bentwood chairs at tables with glass over dark green cloths, potted trees, hanging lamps, and walls hung with a few sombreros and artworks. Chef-owner Mark Dodge and partner Kathy Reynolds have a winner of a place with food to match. For starters, try the wings of hell fire (billed as the all-time best recipe for Buffalo chicken wings), the sauteed mussels, and an unusual bean roll — a soft flour shell rolled around a mix of refried beans, cheeses and chilies and enlivened by a smoked jalapeno sauce. Among Mexican dishes are Jeff's shot in the dark (a sampler of several) and seafood enchiladas. There also are three chicken presentations and three of shrimp, including tampico with garlic, scallions, mornay and cheese sauce. The Cajun strip steak, pan-blackened pork tenderloin and chicken Georgia with peaches, schnapps and cream sauce are highly rated. Homemade desserts might include praline meringue torte, kahlua cheesecake and chocolate pecan pie.

Lunch, Monday-Saturday 11:30 to 3; dinner, 5 to 10 or 10:30, Sunday 3 to 10. Closed Wednesday.

Jessie's, 142 Main St., Winsted. (203) 379-0109. Italian. $8.75 to $14.95.

Named after the mother of one of the four partners, this old house is a family establishment in decor and appeal. Pictures tracing the family history of the owners line the walls of the two main dining rooms, where blond wood chairs flank tables with glass tops over beige cloths. A bar has diner-style booths and an enclosed, wraparound porch yields views onto the street or the outdoor courtyard with jaunty umbrella-topped tables and colorful plantings in summer. An upstairs cocktail lounge appeals to those who like to watch sports on TV as they eat or imbibe. The fairly standard menu is supplemented by specials, usually including a spicy clam and sausage soup and, when we were there, cioppino, mussels marinara and veal with white wine, prosciutto, mushrooms and artichoke hearts. About half the entrees are pastas, including homemade lasagnas and cannellonis. The rest range from chicken parmesan to king crab legs. Desserts could be mud pie, banana butterscotch supreme, Swedish almond cheesecake, biscuit tortoni, and homemade pies.

Lunch, weekdays 11 to 4, Saturday 1 to 4; dinner, 5 to 9 or 10, Sunday 1 to 9. Closed Tuesdays.

The Orchid Restaurant, The Shops at Ledgebrook, Route 44, Winsted. (203) 379-8501.
Chinese/American. $8.95 to $16.95.
One of the Chinese chefs who helped make the old Yale Barn in East Canaan a culinary success opened this double-storefront restaurant in a new Winsted shopping center in 1989. It's a large square space in pale pink with minimal decor but for unusual chandeliers, paintings with mother of pearl, and tables set with orchid napkins fanned on glass over white cloths and silk orchids in brandy glasses. The menu is not the usual hodgepodge of Chinese items under categories and inviting sharing. Instead there are such "oriental gourmet delights" as hot and spicy lamb (with red peppers, leeks, ginger and garlic), shrimp and pork Hunan style, shrimp with chili sauce, shrimp and scallops with garlic sauce, and pork with black bean sauce. Non-oriental entrees range from seafood linguini with clam sauce and broiled yellowtail sole to honey roast duckling and veal oscar. Desserts are straightforward cakes, pies and ice cream.

Lunch daily, 11:30 to 2; dinner nightly, 5 to 9:30; Sunday brunch.

New Hartford

Yesterday's Restaurant, Bridge Street, New Hartford. (203) 379-7074.
American. $7.50 to $13.95.
Part of the main floor of the restored New Hartford House, a brick beauty dating to 1737, this casual eatery is a mix of booths and shiny wood tables, high polished wood ceilings and arched windows. All is dark and intimate at night, when votive candles flicker and conversation flows over the something-for-everyone food. Snacky appetizers, burgers, sandwiches, salads, and quiche are the all-day fare. At night, the menu contains a handful of entrees like fried clams or shrimp, chicken parmesan, fettuccine primavera, tenderloin tips, and New York strip steak. Desserts run to mud pie, carrot cake, cheesecake and specials like pecan-praline truffle.

Lunch, Wednesday-Saturday 11:30 to 5; dinner, 5 to 9 or 10, Sunday 11 to 9. Closed Monday and Tuesday.

Central Connecticut

Waterbury

No Fish Today Cafe, 457 West Main St., Waterbury. (203) 574-4483.
Seafood/Italian. $13.95 to $17.95.
When Fred Hall once visited a friend's restaurant in Baltimore, "No fish today" was chalked across the blackboard menu. The words struck Hall as a neat name for a

restaurant, which a decade later he opened just west of the Waterbury green. Chef Tom Santopietro has since taken over, but No Fish Today is still going strong (and planned to open a branch in downtown Hartford in 1990). Don't let the name mislead, for fish is very much the thing here, posted daily on an enormous blackboard that slides along the floor on a wooden stand ("meals on wheels," quipped our waitress). Dinner choices run from blackened redfish, charbroiled tuna and mahi-mahi to clams fra diavolo and scallops rena with artichoke hearts and cheese. A few pasta and meat dishes round out the menu. We remember an incredibly fresh and tasty sole meuniere, served with peas and a rice pilaf, and scampi al parma, four huge shrimp in a zesty red sauce on a mountain of linguini. Start with smelts livornese, escargots provencale, or sausage and spinach saute. End with cappuccino mousse torte, tartuffo, chambord cheesecake, or homemade rice pudding. The cafe is narrow and tiny, seating 36 diners in ten high-backed wooden booths with dark blue leatherette covers on the tables, or at a few comfy seats at the old mahogany bar. A huge mirror on one wall helps prevent claustrophobia.

Lunch, Monday-Friday 11:30 to 2:30; dinner, Monday-Saturday 5 to 9 or 10.

1249 West, 1249 West Main St., Waterbury. (203) 756-4609.
Italian/Continental. $14.75 to $20.50.
An unassuming little black building squashed between houses and an A&P shopping center, Hugo Allegrini's restaurant has been an institution since 1965. Posted at the entrance is an early Connecticut magazine review that called it "probably the best classic Italian restaurant in the state," along with two front pages of the New York Times from the dates of the owner's birthday and the opening of 1249 West. He runs an elegant, clubby place with dark polished walnut walls, framed caricatures overlooking a lavish oak bar, and two dining rooms with deep banquettes and comfortable seats for 60. Pastas are imported from Italy for the fifteen pasta dishes, except for the homemade manicotti and paglia. Veal scaloppine is the house specialty, presented five ways on the not overwhelming menu. Other items under Italian specialties range from saltimbocca to steak diane. "From the Grill" brings classics like calves liver, pork chops and steaks, while seafood offerings range from stuffed shrimp to lobster fra diavolo. Inserted in the menu are a couple of specials, perhaps red snapper florentine and stuffed breast of veal. Portions are huge, and accompanied by potato or pasta, vegetable and salad. So you might be tempted to skip appetizers like the standout mozzarella en carrozza or clams posillipo. But don't overlook such dessert treats as chambord truffle, white chocolate mousse cake, an extravagant zuppa inglese, and mocha ganache.

Lunch, Tuesday-Saturday 11:45 to 2:15; dinner, 5 to 9:15, Sunday noon to 9:15. Closed Monday.

Faces, 702 Highland Ave., Waterbury. (203) 753-1181.
Italian. $15.95 to $17.95.
What do you make of a storefront operation beside Anthony's Pizza Parlor (and with a connecting back hallway) that seats about 36, never advertises, and is jammed all the time? You make it a success, as chef-owner Emmanuel "Sonny" Diorio has done for ten years. Pictures and posters of famous faces line the walls and gaze down upon happy diners in three booths, two curved banquettes and a few close-together tables. It's a happy hubbub, done up in gray and black with pink linens topped by charcoal-dark glass. The very abbreviated menu, whose motto is "The Art of Cuisine," is enhanced by daily specials. Favorite starters are mozzarella en carrozza and a hot antipasto San Francisco combining clams casino, clams oreganata, stuffed mushrooms and more. Among pastas are capellini marinara, linguini with clams, and green noodles with red clam sauce, shrimp, scallops, lobster,

and mushrooms. Main courses range from shrimp florentine and saltimbocca to steak diane. The skimpy wine list is priced in the high twenties.

Lunch, Tuesday-Friday noon to 2; dinner, Tuesday-Saturday 5 to 9.

Westside Lobster House & Raw Bar, 30 West Main St., Waterbury. (203) 573-0122.
Seafood. $13.95 to $19.95.

This attractive restaurant is in the basement of the old Elton Hotel, once considered the most elegant between New York and Boston. Quarry tile floors, a sea of oak paneling and brass rails, large and private booths around the perimeter, and cabinets filled with old pewter pieces in the center of the dining room are a pleasing combination. Stock prices are shown at lunchtime on a big-screen TV in the eat-in lounge beside a square, copper-topped bar. The menu is supplemented by a page of especially tempting daily specials: perhaps monkfish tempura and escargots aioli with broccoli, red bell peppers and water chestnuts for appetizers; broiled corvina with orange-amaretto cream, grilled yellowfin tuna with cilantro and black olive pesto, broiled Norwegian salmon with lime and watercress hollandaise, and grilled mako shark with sun-dried apple and cinnamon butter for entrees. We once tried a special of eel with scallops in puff pastry, lobster savannah and the house cioppino served over linguini. Other possibilities range from fish and chips to lobster and scallop casserole, from chicken grenobloise to porterhouse steak. Desserts include ginger-apricot torte, Bailey's Irish Cream cake and a light lemon cheesecake. The wine list is heavy on Californias. Lunchtime brings seafood quiche, interesting salads, California pizzas, and more fresh seafood specials.

Lunch, Monday-Saturday from 11:30; dinner, 5 to 10 or 11. Closed Sunday.

Across from the Horse, 26 North Main St., Waterbury. (203) 574-0578.
American. $7.95 to $14.95.

A pressed-tin ceiling, brick walls, whirring ceiling fans, and dark wood tables with red napkins are repeated downstairs and up in this popular establishment opposite the landmark horse statue on the Waterbury green. The brass rail along the bar attracts a young crowd, who also turn out for weekend entertainment in the new upstairs dance club. Between bar and club, however, people graze contentedly on a casual all-day menu, lately augmented by a dozen or so entrees. Barbecued ribs, fish and chips, broiled salmon, lemon-pepper chicken, prime rib, New York sirloin, and a combo called hoof 'n fin (sirloin with fried scallops or clams) are featured on the evening menu. But what really draws is the array of casual fare.

Open Monday-Saturday 11:30 to 10, Sunday 2 to 9.

The Hills, Western Hills Golf Course, Park Road, Waterbury. (203) 755-1331.
American Grill. $11.95 to $18.95.

Billed as an authentic grill, this is the creation of Daniel Goggins in the two-level dining room in the clubhouse overlooking a golf course on the western edge of Waterbury. Decor is typical golf club: white-clothed tables and mod blue-upholstered, squat butcher-block chairs against a backdrop of gray walls and outdoor greenery. From swordfish to steaks and chops, entrees are grilled over charcoal and presented with mix-and-match sauces — thirteen all told, among them pesto cream with pine nuts, pineapple sweet and sour, roasted garlic herb, and fresh mint cream. If grills aren't to your liking, you can order cioppino, chicken or veal, along with appetizers like artichoke hearts francais, stuffed mushrooms and smoked fish. Chocolate truffle cake is the favored dessert.

Lunch, Monday-Friday noon to 3; dinner, Tuesday-Saturday 5 to 10, Sunday noon to 8.

San Marino, Thomaston Avenue, Waterbury. (203) 755-1148.
Italian. $11.95 to $18.95.
This expansive establishment in the Colonial Plaza off West Main Street packs in the crowds. Bare tables with seats for 225 are set with white napkins in a front solarium and in the long main dining room, nicely divided into small areas by wood and brass and enhanced by an abundance of hanging plants and potted greenery. Seven presentations of veal, fifteen pastas, and many seafood dishes are featured, most of them straightforward. House specials include quail veneziana with polenta and assorted seafood over linguini for two. Desserts run to carrot cake, mud pie, melbas, and parfaits, with an occasional Italian pastry for good measure.
Open Monday-Saturday 11 to 10 or 11, Sunday noon to 10.

Naugatuck

The Milestone Inn, 18 Neuman St., Naugatuck. (203) 723-6693.
Continental. $12.95 to $15.95.
Dating from the late 1800s, this distinctive red structure with white trim was a private home until lately. Now it's an appealing restaurant on two floors, the downstairs a jolly lounge and the main floor a mix of vaulted ceiling, skylights, a circular window in the roof, unusual brick work, colorful wallpapers, and assorted booths and pine tables set with white paper mats over pink linens. The old milestone marker, spotlit in a corner of the dining room, denotes the distance from the center of Naugatuck, three miles to the east. Chef-partner John Ferrucci prepares classic continental fare with Italian and French overtones. Fettuccine carbonara, baked jumbo shrimp, fresh seafood meuniere, broiled lamb chops, and roast duckling bigarade are house specialties. Other favorites are capon cordon bleu, calves liver, veal saltimbocca, and chateaubriand and rack of lamb persille for two. Billi-bi, chowder, smoked salmon, and clams casino are possible starters. Among desserts are cheesecake, caramel custard, parfaits, and assorted chocolate tortes.
Lunch, Monday-Saturday 11:30 to 2; dinner, 5 to 9 or 10, Sunday noon to 8.

Giovanni's Ristorante, 808 New Haven Road (Route 63), Naugatuck.
(203) 729-4541.
Italian. $11.95 to $28.95.
New in 1988, this is unexpectedly sleek in gray and burgundy. It's an uncluttered space of curved arches, mainly booths and a few well-spaced tables draped with linens. A long oval mirror and wall sconces set in framed squares of burgundy fabric are the only decoration. A tuxedoed staff serves up a variety of pastas with mix-and-match sauces and fish toppings, baked Italian items like lasagna and manicotti, and the usual range of entrees from chicken cacciatore and shrimp scampi to veal marsala and steak pizzaiola. The house specialty is a saute of veal, shrimp and chicken with mushrooms and marsala. By far the most expensive item is cioppino, teaming lobster and king crab with the usual offerings. Scungilli marinara, clams oreganata, fried calamari, and fried mozzarella are among appetizers. For dessert, try tartuffo, rice pudding or spumoni.
Lunch, Tuesday-Friday 11:30 to 4; dinner, Tuesday-Saturday 4 to 9 or 10, Sunday 2 to 8.

Seymour

♥ **Wooster Inn,** 153 North St., Seymour. (203) 888-9008.
Continental. $16 to $23.50.
The blue hilltop mansion that was home in the late 19th century to industrialist William Henry Harrison Wooster was converted in 1989 into a restaurant of

restrained elegance by Bernard Carella. The interior is notable for rich wood paneling, stained glass, embossed wallpapers, an angled bar, an open gazebo-type affair with a grand piano, and abundant space in rooms and foyers. The curving solarium dining room and two smaller rooms harbor well-spaced tables set with pink cloths and white napkins fanned on oversize black octagonal service plates. Written partly in French with English translations, the menu seems a bit pretentious for the area and matches each entree with a recommended wine from the short, fairly priced list on the back cover. The twenty appetizers, salads and soups are predictable, except perhaps for the opening item: fried calamari tomato fondue. More unusual are some of the entrees, including couscous, braised lamb with prunes and Moroccan spices, and paella valenciana. They're interspersed with classics like scallops provencale, grey sole meuniere, veal chanterelles, duckling montmorency, grilled sirloin with three-peppercorn cognac cream sauce, and rack of lamb. Entrees come with seasonal vegetables or pasta. A pianist plays for Sunday brunch and other occasions.

Lunch, Tuesday-Friday noon to 2:30; dinner, Tuesday-Sunday 6 to 11; Sunday brunch, noon to 3.

Derby

Olde Birmingham Restaurant, 285 Main St., Derby. (203) 735-4678.
Continental. $13.50 to $19.75.

Erected in 1893 as one of the finer bank edifices in the state, the old Birmingham National Bank gave way in 1981 to this restaurant run very personally by Leo Mascato. The only obvious signs of the bank are the shiny barred vault, its entrance stacked with wine racks visible from the dining room, and a grotto-like lounge of brick in the basement safe-deposit area. The main floor is handsome as can be, with a big brass Victorian chandelier hanging from the high black ceiling and walls variously of brick, solid oak and wallpaper. Off-white linens, dark brown napkins and stylish silver dress the tables, some flanked by bentwood chairs and a couple by upholstered armchairs. There are mezzanines on three sides, two of them with intimate lineups of deuces having views of the scene below. It's a lovely setting for classic, occasionally inventive fare. For starters, escargots might come with gorgonzola cheese and wild mushrooms, the country pate with pistachio nuts, and fresh mozzarella with roasted sweet peppers. For main courses, filet of sole is pan-fried with macadamia nuts, lobster and mussels are paired with sun-dried tomatoes and cheese over linguini, sea scallops are sauteed with shiitake mushrooms and garlic, and the rack of lamb is seared with dijon. Traditionalists can stick with chicken cordon bleu, calves liver anglaise, or entrecote au poivre. The dessert list yields such treats as chocolate kahlua mousse, fresh fruit tarts, creme caramel, and amaretto cheesecake.

Lunch, Monday-Friday 11:30 to 2; dinner, Monday-Saturday 6 to 9 or 10.

Meriden

Lettuce Pleezue, 480 Chamberlain Hwy. (Route 71), Meriden. (203) 634-4335.
American/International. $8.50 to $15.50.

Taking over an ice-cream parlor in 1977 opposite the Meriden Square mall, chef Kevin Alix and his brother Dan launched a small restaurant featuring gourmet salads. Five years later, the main floor of their building gave way to an Irish lounge and the upstairs became a 100-seat dining room with green and salmon walls, dark walnut wainscoting, a vaulted ceiling, and a shining sea of white tablecloths under glass. The gourmet salads are still incorporated into both lunch and dinner menus and account for 25 percent of the business, lending credence to the restaurant's odd but catchy name. Among the more unusual of the dozen salad offerings are one of oriental pork and pasta and the F.A.T. salad of feta cheese, avocado and tuna tossed in romaine with olives, tomatoes and a spicy vinaigrette. The dinner menu offers plenty of appetizers, from marinated herring to potato skins, and two dozen entrees. Selections include chicken kiev and teriyaki, grilled halibut and tuna, garlic scallops, swordfish au fromage, baked scrod en casserole, turkey parmesan, prime rib, and steak diane. Chambord cheesecake, strawberry mousse and pecan pie are among desserts. There's a pleasant side deck off the upstairs dining room for summer use.

Lunch, Monday-Saturday 11:30 to 2:30; dinner, 5 to 9:30 or 10:30; Sunday, brunch 11 to 2:30, dinner 5 to 8:30.

$ Sadie's, 194 Camp St., Meriden. (203) 634-8139.
French. $11.95 to $15.95.

If ever there were a restaurant find, this is one. It's also hard to find (almost beside but between exits of the crosstown I-691), but once there you'll meet a country charmer of a place, an angled dining room done up in dark green and beige, with white butcher paper over white tablecloths, silk flowers in Saratoga bottles, and balloon curtains, colorful prints and the odd basket enhancing the walls. Former West Hartford caterers Shari and Matthew Kopcza opened in 1989, offering a blackboard menu tailored to fresh ingredients. Dinner the night we were there involved eight choices, including pork tenderloin with garlic sauce, poached salmon with pernod sauce, twin tournedos bearnaise, veal maison (with mozzarella, mushrooms and onions), and leg of lamb with rosemary-mustard-garlic sauce. Starters might be escarole soup, Cajun shrimp (a specialty of chef Michael Russo, who shares kitchen duties with Shari), mozzarella roman style, and tortellini with pesto cream sauce. Black chocolate cake, pineapple pie, creme caramel, and English trifle are worthy endings. Various bobolis (perhaps Cajun sausage with spinach, or crab and scallop) are featured at lunch. The short but select wine list is priced under $21.

Lunch, Monday-Friday 11:30 to 2:30; dinner, Tuesday-Saturday 5 to 8 or 9.

New Britain

East Side Restaurant, 131 Dwight St., New Britain. (203) 223-1188.
German-American. $9.95 to $16.95, Table d'hote.

"Willkommen," greets the small sign between flagpoles bearing American and German flags at the entrance to this dark brown house-turned-restaurant, a local institution. Chef-owner William Bloethe offers full-course meals from appetizer and relishes to dessert. Begin with chicken livers, soup, tomato juice or fruit cup (herring, shrimp cocktail or cherrystone clams for a surcharge). Naturally popular are the German specialties, among them jaeger schnitzel, sauerbraten, roast pork, and pot roast with potato pancakes and red cabbage. Homemade desserts include cream pies, chiffons and rice pudding. German wines are featured on the wine list. The decor is like that you'd find in southern Germany, with wood beams, the restaurant's own placemats on the tables, and a new mural of old Heidelberg on the rear wall of the dining room that bears its name. The adjacent Hunters Lounge is cozy in dark wood and red leather.

Lunch, Tuesday-Friday 11:30 to 2:30; dinner, Tuesday-Friday 4:30 to 10, Saturday noon to 10, Sunday noon to 8.

Banquers, 132 Main St., New Britain. (203) 224-4866.
American/Italian. $9.94 to $15.95.

Ex-banker Jeffrey Stenner's decision to go into the restaurant business made this name a natural. He seats 90 patrons in three dining areas fashioned from an abandoned building with the original high black tin ceiling, birch wainscoting, and salmon walls accented with paintings. White linens, fresh flowers and candles dress the tables. An extensive menu embraces a wide range from potato skins to clams casino, from chicken parmesan to veal pommery, from teriyaki sirloin to filet mignon. Prime rib, veal marsala and stuffed chicken supreme are house specialties. Desserts change weekly, but could include double dutch chocolate cake, amaretto mousse pie, and mandarin orange cake. Downstairs is a comedy club featuring comedians from New York and Boston on weekends.

Lunch, Monday-Friday 11:30 to 4; dinner, Tuesday-Saturday to 9:30 or 10:30.

Berlin

Hawthorne Inn, 2421 Wilbur Cross Highway, Berlin. (203) 828-3571.
American/Continental. $14.95 to $26.95.
This is a restaurant, banquet facility and motor lodge of the old school, but the food is highly regarded locally, and we recall a wonderful special lunch to which we were invited with winemaker Robert Mondavi. The extensive menu holds few surprises, but can scarcely go wrong with chicken cordon bleu, duckling a l'orange, broiled swordfish, Alaskan king crab au gratin, prime rib, or filet mignon. Such appetizers as marinated herring, chopped chicken livers, and fruit cup with sherbet date the place, as do surcharges for the separate list of vegetables. Potato and salad come with the entrees, however, and we've not known anyone to leave hungry. Boston cream pie, cheesecake, strawberry shortcake, and peach melba are desserts of long standing.

Lunch, Monday-Friday 11:30 to 3; dinner nightly, 5 to 10, Sunday to 8.

Middletown

La Boca, 526 Main St., Middletown. (203) 346-4492.
Mexican. $6.25 to $14.95.
Considered one of Connecticut's more authentic Mexican restaurants, this was founded in 1975 by a Smith graduate from Arizona who craved Mexican food done right. She settled upon Middletown, where her husband-to-be was at Wesleyan University, and their LaBoca was an instant success. From one storefront, it expanded into others on either side. When a fourth became available next door in 1988, the owners felt La Boca had reached its optimum size. Now married to an Italian, Sallie Hardin-Bianco believed there was need for a good Italian restaurant, and Ziti's was the happy result. La Boca continues to please with the usual range of Mexican offerings, plus more unusual dishes like two versions of camarones, one with shrimp, onions and tomatoes on a cheese crisp, and the other with shrimp, cheese and hot sauce folded in a flour tortilla. One of Sallie's favorites is the chimifrijole — beans and cheese in a deep-fried burrito with rice. The New York strip steak with rice or fries, tomatoes and scallions is available for those who prefer. There are a variety of margaritas, including orange-mango and one with cointreau. Mexican flan is the dessert of choice. Hanging baskets of fake geraniums add color to two dark dining rooms, a mix of booths and tables where candles flicker even at noon. Murals and three arched, covered booths enhance the cantina bar.

Lunch, Monday-Friday 11:30 to 2:30; dinner, 5 to 10, Saturday noon to 10, Sunday 4 to 9.

Ziti's, 528 Main St., Middletown. (203) 346-3217.
Northern Italian. $7.50 to $14.95.
Operating side by side with La Boca (but with a separate kitchen and chef) is this

little winner. The narrow room has high black booths (for four or two) along the walls, inlaid tables of dusty rose down the center, long black hanging lamps, and a marble-counter bar at the rear. It's a simple, casual setting (bare tables with pink paper napkins) for well-prepared fare. The spicy seasonings from next door have permeated Ziti's in such appetizers as the changing ravioli del giorno, Ziti's special dumplings that might be stuffed with pine nuts in a fiery jalapeno pesto and a marinara sauce that's not for the faint of palate. Fried calamari with basil mayonnaise and pan-blackened scallops are other good starters. Standouts among entrees are chicken marsala over fettuccine, linguini with scallops and shiitake mushrooms with Italian salsa, and shrimp fra diavolo. Five pizzas, here called stone pies, also are available. Best of the desserts is the cappuccino-chocolate cake.

Dinner nightly, 5 to 9 or 10.

Middlesex Opera House Restaurant, 600 Plaza Middlesex (College Street), Middletown. (203) 344-9439.
American. $9.95 to $19.95.
The curtain has dropped on Middletown's old opera house, but the showbills live on in display cases in the colorful bar at the entry. Ahead lies a gorgeous, two-story-plus expanse in pale yellow with green and pink accents. A massive crystal chandelier hangs over the curving staircase, while two smaller ones light the mezzanine. Bentwood chairs flank tables dressed in peach cloths and gold-rimmed white china. The extensive menu embraces chicken in six guises, shrimp and sole in three each, plus Norwegian salmon maltaise, New York sirloin, prime rib, rack of lamb, and veal oscar. Roast clams with hazelnuts is the specialty appetizer. For dessert, enjoy chef Dennis Welch's chocolate decadence or sacher torte, which won ribbons in the annual Chocolate Expo in Hartford.

Lunch, weekdays 11:30 to 2:30; dinner nightly, 5 to 10; Sunday brunch. Closed Tuesday.

Harbor Park, 80 Harbor Drive, Middletown. (203) 347-9999.
American. $10.95 to $19.95.
The sign outside this large, nautical establishment in blue and white at a bend of the Connecticut River proclaims "a restaurant and gathering." It's more the latter than the former, particularly in the enormous main-floor lounge. Upstairs is a soaring, two-level dining room around an open space in which resides the mast and boom of a sailboat with a neon sail. The view of the river here is everything. From the outdoor decks and enclosed porches off the modern dining room, you think you're dining right on the water. What you're eating may be irrelevant, whether it's baked scrod or scampi in puff pastry. The choices range from snapper en papillotte, grilled swordfish, fried seafood platter, and baked stuffed shrimp to veal and chicken piccata, chicken teriyaki and prime rib. Popular appetizers are oysters with sour cream and caviar and a chilled glass of pepper vodka, escargots in puff pastry, and sauteed provolone. The dessert tray brings a changing selection like California mud slide, Boston chocolate cheesecake, and mocha ganache.

Lunch daily, 11:30 to 3; dinner, 5 to 9 or 11; Sunday brunch, 11 to 3.

Hartford Area

Hartford

* Max on Main, 205 Main St., Hartford. (203) 522-2530.
Contemporary American. $9.95 to $18.95.

A neon sign identifies this as a "city bistro," and a very snazzy one it is indeed, all decked out in black, white and gray with spots of color from striking artworks. The floors are bare, the white cloths are covered with white paper, and the black chairs are lacquered. It's trendy enough to have an oyster bar, a long list of wines by the taste or glass, and pizzas dubbed "stone pies," with toppings like Italian plum tomatoes with three cheeses or California escargots with roasted leeks. At various lunches here we've enjoyed the mussels steamed with cilantro, cumin and tomato, and a salad of radicchio, watercress, arugula and Belgian endive with black pepper goat cheese. The arugula and meat ravioli with a sauce of tomatoes, fennel and leeks was grand, as was the dish of grilled homemade sausages with fried new potatoes and cucumber salad. At night, you might go for the phenomenal tequila-lime marinated grilled shrimp with black bean sauce and papaya-tomato-mint salsa, grilled bluefish on sesame bok choy with an orange-wasabi butter sauce, mustard-grilled pork chops with pan-fried new potatoes, or grilled duck breast and leg with (and this was autumn) fresh strawberries and rhubarb with wild rice and pecans. The white chocolate mousse tart over raspberry puree, blueberry-ginger tart, and key lime mousse cake are worthy endings, but we'd opt for the creme brulee that a globe-trotting friend says is the best this side of Paris.

Lunch, Monday-Friday 11:30 to 2:30; dinner, Monday-Saturday, 5 to 10 or 11.

* L'Americain, 2 Hartford Square West, Hartford. (203) 522-6500.
New American. $22 to $28.

Bring a fat billfold to dine at what many consider the city's best (and most expensive) restaurant. Chef Chris Pardue changes his menu seasonally for patrons in two luxurious, restful dining rooms. We prefer the smaller Gray Room, with spotlit oil paintings, brass chandeliers, tall windows with rose draperies, reproduction Queen Anne chairs, and two striking stained-glass windows with intricate and colorful depictions of vegetables and herbs. The other dining room is in a former car wash, but you'd never know it, so complete is the renovation. Chris cherishes the artistry in food, and his cuisine is in the vanguard: lately, roast buffalo with a sauce of tequila, sage and cactus pears served with blue cornmeal polenta; Norwegian salmon with almonds, garlic-tarragon butter and sauteed Belgian endive; cinnamon-smoked duck with a baked black walnut peach, and a dish called black beer lamb (garlic-seared medallions with a mustard seed crust and a black beer sabayon). You might start with jasmine-smoked scallops fanned out with a salad of mini bok choy and oranges with a gingered star anise dressing, duck and black currant pate with a millet salad, and artichoke and smoked pheasant with juniper foie gras mousse. Finish with a chocolate concoction called la bete noir, passion fruit bavarian, or a tart filled with kiwi, strawberries and pineapple. Food like this is meant for celebratory occasions.

Lunch, Monday-Friday 11:30 to 2; dinner, Monday-Saturday 6 to 10.

* Peppercorns Grill,, 357 Main St., Hartford. (203) 547-1714.
Contemporary Italian. $12.95 to $18.95.

We liked the food here so much at a birthday lunch shortly after it opened that we went back for a birthday dinner the same day. The California menu has been

72

dropped lately in favor of what new chef-owners Dino and Salvatore Cialfi, just back from running a restaurant in Rome, call cucina fresca. That translates to entrees like a fork-tender osso buco with grilled polenta and saute of fresh spinach, grilled red snapper with an herbed tomato sauce, a couple of dollops of arugula pesto and three large mussels on the side, and an exceptional spiedini di pesce, a huge plateful of grilled scallops, shrimp and calamari over arborio rice. Pastas include a house-made ravioli stuffed with ricotta, spinach and orange rind, a robust fettuccine with a rich sauce of braised lamb and porcini mushrooms, and lobster ravioli with a luscious lobster bisque sauce. An oversize appetizer of carpaccio is one of the best anywhere. Chocolate bread pudding with bourbon-custard sauce is the signature dessert, but we also like the bittersweet chocolate torte and the raspberry noisette. The somewhat deco dining room is noisy and distracting, but the food more than compensates.

Lunch, Monday-Friday 11:30 to 2; dinner, Monday-Saturday 5:30 to 9 or 10.

Pierpont's, 1 Haynes St., Hartford. (203) 246-7500.
New American. $18.50 to $26.

This new restaurant in the J.P. Morgan Hotel at Goodwin Square opened at the turn of the decade, 1990. Named for Hartford financier John Pierpont Morgan, who maintained an apartment in the now restored 1881 Goodwin Building, it aspired to the stars — like those of the Seasons restaurant at the Bostonian Hotel in Boston, opened earlier by J.P. Morgan's manager and the Fisher Hotel Group, which runs both hotels. Executive chef Gary Hoffman was lured from Boston's Meridien Hotel to oversee an ambitious, pricey menu. Possible starters are parsnip and potato soup with chives, a fine North Atlantic scallop pie, a skimpy portion of seared sirloin with olive oil and greens, and a tasty spinach salad with goat-cheese dressing. A tart lemon granite cleared the palate for the main courses, salmon steak that lacked the punch of the pepper sauce and candied ginger that supposedly accompanied it, a mixed grill of lamb chop with veal sausage and bacon, and sauteed chicken breast with wild mushrooms and pancetta. In the early going, the kitchen only half fulfilled the creativity and assertiveness that its menu promised, and the service was unpolished, to say the least. But the setting positively shone. The 100-seat dining room is notable for rich redwood burl walls, vases of ferns and irises spotlit on each table, and upholstered chairs and banquettes. The striking and colorful Jaguar Jungle service plates were custom-designed for the hotel by a Ridgefield artist.

Lunch, Monday-Saturday 11:30 to 2, Sunday to 3; dinner nightly, 5:30 to 10:30.

Hot Tomato's, 1 Union Place, Hartford. (203) 249-5100.
Italian. $7.25 to $14.50.

You like an assortment of pastas and crowds? You'll get both in the best of the new Union Station eateries, a cavernous place smashingly done up with striking red chairs with triangular backs, green booths, black carpeting, and amusing posters of tomatoes on the walls. Only three of the twenty-seven items on the dinner menu do not contain pasta: veal milanese, tenderloin al ferro and baked eggplant mascarpone. Otherwise, from fettuccine marinara to lobster lasagna, the pastas are fresh, interesting and go well with a loaf of the great garlic bread and one of the reasonably priced Italian wines. Even the cioppino comes on a bed of linguini. Look for the farfalle cinque verdure, bow-tie pasta tossed with asparagus, broccoli, red peppers, mushrooms and carrots in a light alfredo sauce, or the fusili pomodoro fresco, a heady mix of plum tomatoes, fresh basil, garlic, olive oil and corkscrew pasta. This place is hot; no reservations are taken, so expect a wait of up to an hour at dinner.

Lunch, Tuesday-Friday 11:30 to 2:30; dinner, 5:30 to 10 or 11, Sunday to 9:30.

Lewis Street Bistro, 36 Lewis St., Hartford. (203) 247-2300.
Country French/Italian. $12 to $20.75.

Local restorationist Tom Tramont and chef Tim Smith teamed up in 1990 to reopen the Greek Revival townhouse that was the site of the old 36 Lewis St. restaurant. Former habituees hardly recognize their casual downtown bistro, now subtly done up in rose and aubergine colors with rag-rolled walls, marbelized columns and stylish place settings in two dining rooms and a sunken lounge. Chef Tim, who opened our favorite Panache restaurant before it became Peppercorns, offers an intriguing menu. The dozen entrees include four pastas from salmon alfredo to toulouse, sauteed shrimp with diced sweet peppers and dijon cream sauce, mixed grill of shellfish, sauteed veal with roasted peppers and mushrooms in a parmesan cream sauce, and roast leg of lamb with goat cheese-spinach ravioli. Start with crab and cheddar bisque with jalapenos, a duck confit salad, or chilled terrine of sea scallops and shrimp with a tomato-ginger chutney. For dessert, how about casino cake (layers of raspberries and genoise filled with white chocolate bavarian and served with raspberry puree), marquis au chocolat, or fresh fruits with creme anglaise? A few esoteric choices are on the affordable wine list, and a cafe menu is available all day in the bar.

Lunch, Monday-Friday 11:30 to 3; dinner, Monday-Saturday 5 to 10.

Shenanigans, 1 Gold St., Hartford. (203) 522-4117.
Contemporary American. $12 to $17.

This neat city cafe with a vintage diner in the middle has become upscale under new ownership. Gone is most of the endearing diner food; in its place is fresh, contemporary fare in the manner of Freshfields restaurant in West Cornwall, owner Charles Wilfong's former venue. The menu varies daily, but you might find roast duckling with sweet and sour sauce, oddly topped with deep-fried pasta strips and slathered with grapes, pineapple and chives; sweet pepper fettuccine tossed with chicken in ginger-cashew butter; a superb venison scaloppine doused in a mush-room game sauce, and veal jerusalem with a rich madeira sauce, chunky with mushrooms, black olives and artichokes. Start with a bowl of steamed mussels with mustard-vermouth sauce, a salad of bibb lettuce with poached chicken and lemon-lime vinaigrette, or roast loin of rabbit over cranberry game sauce. Desserts are a Shenanigans strong suit, traditionally the Hartford cream pie and lately a masterful toasted walnut cheesecake, light and chilled and served with creme anglaise, and a goblet of ethereal white chocolate mousse with strawberry puree. There's live music nightly and at Sunday brunch at this revived local institution on the way up.

Breakfast, Monday-Friday 7 to 10:30; lunch, 11:30 to 2:30; dinner nightly, 5 to 10; Sunday, brunch 11 to 3, dinner 5 to 9.

Congress Rotisserie, 7 Maple Ave., Hartford. (203) 560-1965.
Contemporary. $9.95 to $16.95.

The front bar at this with-it restaurant is crowded at happy hour, when the addictive homemade no-salt potato chips are gratis, and we're glad the music gets turned down after HH is over. Wonderful aromas emanate from the ever-turning rotisserie, where the cooks wear black berets. A hip crowd dines on two levels amid a plain black-and-white decor. Lunch choices include a rotisserie club sandwich with roasted meats, red peppers, cheese and tomatoes, a chicken caesar salad, and sauteed chicken livers with bacon and leeks on toast points. At dinner you might start with salmon cakes on sauteed Chinese spinach with tartar sauce. The roasted half chicken with shoestring potatoes, carrots, fennel, and a three-green salad is the best around. Other choices include sauteed veal with sun-dried tomatoes and grilled sirloin with caramelized onions and blue cheese butter. Fresh yogurt of the day with fruit topping and peach mousse are among desserts. An adjacent carry-out sells interesting sandwiches, many of the dishes offered in the rotisserie, and those delicious potato chips.

Lunch, Monday-Saturday 11 to 5; dinner nightly, 5 to midnight or 1.

Gaetano's, Hartford Civic Center, Hartford. (203) 249-1629.
Northern Italian. $16.25 to $19.50.
Opened with the Civic Center as the Signature, then Hartford's best and most glamorous restaurant, this is still glamorous. But it's no longer number one, despite its operation by the Carbone family, whose Carbone's restaurant in the South End is a 50-year tradition. The kitchen features familiar offerings, competently prepared and generously served. The six veal dishes (especially the saltimbocca and the scaloppine stuffed with fontina, pine nuts and mushrooms) are stalwarts. You also can choose cioppino over capellini, shrimp and scallops with amaretto-cream sauce in puff pastry, marinated chicken inglese broiled with mustard, filetto catalone with grilled vegetables and bearnaise sauce, and grilled baby New Zealand rack of lamb.

Lunch, Monday-Saturday 11:30 to 2:30; dinner nightly, 5 to 10:30.

Brown, Thomson & Co., 942 Main St., Hartford. (203) 525-1600.
International. $7.50 to $14.50.
Built around an atrium on several levels filled with antiques and memorabilia from an old department store in the historic Richardson Building, BT is worth a visit just to look — that is, if you can get past the mob scene at the bar. The oversize menu is huge in scope as well as size and covers all the trendy bases, from fajitas and coconut shrimp to Thai chicken and Cajun blackened fish. Dinner entrees, available all day long, run from steak and mushrooms with mozzarella to blackened swordfish. Mud pie and chocolate chip cookie pie are house favorites, but Lisa's pie with coconut ice cream and almond praline is a must for coconut addicts. BT is billed as "the most fun place in Hartford — period." Could be.

Open daily, 11:30 to midnight or 1, Sunday to 10.

State Street Grill, 30 State House Square, Hartford. (203) 549-1377.
American. $9.75 to $15.95.
Until lately this space housed Arne's of Boston seafood fame. Its new-in-1989 incarnation got off to a shaky start, despite the ownership of David Canter, who earlier rescued the Hearthstone restaurant. Seafood is still the star in this sleek, contemporary place with lots of glass, brass, turquoise and coral. Most fish is available grilled, broiled, poached, sauteed or blackened. "Signatures" like calamari provencale, pecan-breaded scrod, and shrimp saganaki with brandied tomato sauce and feta cheese are more elaborate, as are the pastas and meat dishes.

Lunch, Monday-Saturday 11:30 to 3:30; dinner, 5 to 10 or 11. Closed Sunday.

The Hearthstone, 678 Maple Ave., Hartford. (203) 246-8814.
Continental. $16 to $25.
Once Hartford's leading restaurant and the place to see and be seen, the Hearthstone has been reborn by David Canter with a clubby atmosphere, a classic menu and much tableside preparation. Fancy wood paneling, etched-glass panels with hunting scenes, spacious marble-like tables with gray runners under the plates, comfortable chairs, and red-fabric booths are a pleasant setting for tucking into a hearty steak or chop. Through a rear window you can spot the chefs at work on the open hearth, possibly preparing carpetbagger steak, grilled salmon, veal chop with wild mushroom sauce, grilled lobster, and sirloin steak. Duck bigarade, steak diane,

veal with lobster, and dover sole (fileted tableside) are other entrees, and chateaubriand and rack of lamb are carved tableside for two. Escargots in puff pastry with brie, oysters rockefeller and lobster ravioli are among appetizers. Cakes and tortes are displayed on a dessert cart.

Lunch, Monday-Friday 11:30 to 2:30; dinner, Monday-Saturday 5 to 9 or 10.

Capitol Fish House, 391 Main St., Hartford. (203) 724-3370.
Seafood. $16.95 to $19.95.

If it's seafood you're after in a comfortable setting done up in brick and green, you can't do better than here. Upwards of fifteen daily specials supplement the small menu of traditional dishes, adhering to the rule that fresher is better. The night's list of broiled, poached or sauteed fish is the most rewarding, perhaps red snapper sauteed with grapes and almonds, grouper baked with basil and dill glaze, pan-fried catfish with Creole sauce, and broiled mahi-mahi with maltese sauce. Start with broiled sea scallops wrapped in bacon with water chestnuts or smoked baby trout with horseradish sauce. For dessert, standbys like cheesecake and carrot cake are supplemented by nightly specials.

Lunch, Monday-Friday 11:30 to 2:30; dinner, Monday-Saturday, 5 to 10:30 or 11.

DiFiore of Hartford, 395 Franklin Ave., Hartford. (203) 522-2123.
Northern Italian. $10.50 to $16.

Good Italian restaurants are a dime a dozen in Hartford's South End, and they run the gamut from pizza to pricey. Arguably the best (and reservations are made weeks in advance) is this spot beside chef-owner Don DiFiore's renowned family pasta shop. Seating is comfortable at fabric-covered booths and handsome, sturdy chairs in a fairly large room with brass chandeliers, columns that are painted to look like marble, and gray and white embossed wallpaper. The extensive menu lists fourteen pasta dishes, including linguini with clams, tortellini primavera, and fusilli con pesto genovese. Veal is prepared nine ways, from parmigiana to piccata, and there is a good choice of meat and fish dishes. At lunch, try the salad of fresh mozzarella, sun-dried tomatoes and basil, with a dressing of extra-virgin olive oil and balsamic vinegar. Strawberry crepes are among the good desserts.

Lunch, Tuesday-Friday 11:30 to 2; dinner, Tuesday-Saturday 5:30 to 10, Sunday 4 to 9. BYOB.

Carbone's Ristorante, 588 Franklin Ave., Hartford. (203) 249-9646.
Italian. $13 to $20.50.

Just how far has Hartford's dining scene progressed? Time was when Carbone's and the Hearthstone were the only games in town. Carbone's is still plugging along, doing things its way in a showy, luxurious setting. You'll find a lengthy list of entrees like garlicked shrimp topped with sharp Italian cheese, scallops sauteed with spinach and tomatoes, beef filets sauteed in cognac and mustard, and marinated chicken polenta with mustard sauce. There are many tableside flourishes, but regulars stick to the homey Italian standards — especially the veal dishes — on the ambitious menu. They also know to order the orange salad that isn't on the menu at all. Or start with the fabulous caesar salad for two. Finish with bocce balls (chocolate-covered ice cream flamed in orange liqueur) or a seasonal zabaglione.

Lunch, Monday-Friday 11:30 to 2; dinner, Monday-Saturday 5 to 10.

Bellini, 438 Franklin Ave., Hartford. (203) 527-2100.
Northern Italian/French. $16.50 to $22.50.

This new culinary star is a picture of elegance and glamour behind its modest storefront facade. A blend of art deco and classic Italian style, the small dining room fairly shimmers with its gray moire walls, deeper gray draperies, gray upholstered chairs edged with chrome, and multo marble. Chef-owner Gianpaolo DiGrazia oversees a changing menu. Osso buco with risotto, navarin of braised lamb, and skate on a bed of spinach with a sea urchin sauce are among the standout entrees, and one of the surprising appetizers is poached eggs in a red wine and black chanterelle sauce. Try the passion fruit mousse cake for dessert.

Lunch, Tuesday-Friday 11:30 to 2; dinner, Monday-Saturday 5:30 to 9:30.

Costa del Sol, 901 Wethersfield Ave., Hartford. (203) 560-1714.
Spanish. $11.95 to $21.95.

Go for one of the classic versions of paella for two at this personal, unpretentious place run by two families from the Galicia region of northwest Spain. The treats begin long before you sample the masterful paellas, however. For starters, try the octopus Galician style or empanada Gallega, both unique to the family's home region. Steamed mussels are dressed with a remoulade-like sauce so good that we asked for the recipe. Other house specialties are such entrees as shrimp sauteed in olive oil and garlic, baked filet of sole in lemon and white wine sauce, and broiled boneless chicken with garlic and mushroom sauce, all accompanied by a melange of vegetables and Spanish rice spiced with imported saffron that chef Emilio Feijoo calls "red gold." Raising desserts in Spanish restaurants to a new level are a classic flan, rice pudding and a key lime mousse pie that puts most in Florida to shame. Two small, comfortable dining rooms sport paintings of Spain on white stucco walls.

Lunch, Tuesday-Friday noon to 2:30; dinner, Tuesday-Saturday 5 to 10, Sunday 4 to 9.

Truc Orient Express, 735 Wethersfield Ave., Hartford. (203) 249-2818.
Vietnamese. $9.50 to $13.

With a pretty greenhouse out front and a suave interior that's a cut above those of most Vietnamese restaurants, this is where Trai Thi Buong of Truc Orient Express in the Berkshires got her start. A third Truc Orient Express in Springfield lamentably closed in 1989. Here, chef-owner Bing Buong, Trai's brother, offers dishes like Vietnamese egg rolls, pork with cashews, sauteed squid with bamboo shoots, and a Mongolian hotpot for two. Our favorite dish is happy pancake, with many vegetables inside a rice batter crepe. Bing concocts a dynamite lemon mousse for dessert.

Lunch, Tuesday-Saturday 11:30 to 2; dinner, Tuesday-Saturday 5 to 10 or 11, Sunday-Monday, 4 to 9.

Windsor

Madeleines, 1530 Palisado Ave., Windsor. (203) 688-0150.
French. $17 to $23.

Deriving its name from the French pound cake molded into the shape of a seashell, this is the aspiring new establishment of chef-proprietor Warren Leigh, former chef at the Eatery in East Windsor. It occupies an expansive space with windows onto the Connecticut River, but more impressive than the setting and the so-so decor is the ambition of the haute-cuisine menu. Dinner starts with a complimentary appetizer, in our case a plate with tasty slivers of prosciutto, sliced sausage, oil-cured olives and lavasche, the Mideastern flatbread. You can pick and choose from the a la carte menu to develop your own six-course, prix-fixe meal for $35, a welcome touch and good value. Among appetizers, the silken duck foie gras and the lobster ravioli rests on a rich saffron cream sauce. Salads contain exotic greens and edible flowers, with dressings so assertive that you welcome the "intermezzo" course, perhaps a papaya-mint sorbet. Winning entrees include roast rack of lamb topped

topped with garlic hollandaise, duckling McIntosh served with apple marmalade and laced with applejack brandy, and sweetwater prawns glazed with lobster truffle cream. The chef prides himself on his special desserts: apple and cranberry strudel with applejack creme anglaise and berries au gratin, usually raspberries in sabayon with eau-de-vie. Two wrapped chocolates and two damp, warm towels arrive with the bill. The promised madeleine that every diner is supposed to receive never came, nor did the bread basket that it supposedly comes in — such lapses in service marring what the kitchen aims to deliver. Appetizers and light entrees are available on a haute-bistro menu in the lounge, and you can sample a nine-course menu gastronomique for $55.

Dinner, Monday-Saturday 5 to 9 or 10; bistro menu, 4 to 10 or 11; lunch, Friday only, 11:30 to 2:30.

East Windsor

The Eatery, 297 South Main St. (Route 5), East Windsor. (203) 627-7094.
Continental. $16 to $23.

Who'd ever guess that this expanding restaurant and entertainment center started as a hot-dog stand, and its energetic proprietor as one of the first rolling lunch-truck entrepreneurs in downtown Hartford? Paul J. Ianni has come a long way, and so has his restaurant, which sprouted from P.J.'s Drive-In and later P.J.'s Eatery. In fact, the day we were there, he was breaking ground for a 150-seat cabaret and entertainment center joined to the main restaurant by a gazebo with a courtyard for outdoor lunches. Despite its unassuming name, the Eatery is surprisingly impressive in decor and in food. The elegant table appointments are the same throughout, but the enclosed front porch is in summery white, the parlor (in the old hot-dog stand) looks Victorian with lace curtains, wood paneling and a fireplace flanked by bookshelves at the far end, and the main dining room is sleek in white and black with black lacquered chairs and accents of pink and teal. A small dining room beyond is called "The House." It is part of his original house that has been swallowed up by the restaurant. Family photographs and fresh flowers grace the dining rooms, and everything comes together with taste and elan. P.J. was the original chef, but now employs seven who prepare a dozen entrees, plus weekly specials. Although the menu is a la carte, the best value is to order the six-course, prix-fixe dinner for $35, allowing a choice of appetizer, salad, entree and dessert off the menu. You might start with shrimp ravioli, leek turnover or clams rockefeller. Continue with Louisiana redfish with a horseradish bechamel, swordfish en papillote, veal au poivre, broiled duckling with grapefruit and currant compote, or New Zealand rack of lamb carved tableside. Cream cheese pie with raspberry sauce is the specialty dessert, but you could choose seasonal fruit tarts or crepes suzette. The extensive wine list is affordably priced. If you've made a reservation, when you arrive at your table you'll find a matchbook engraved with your name, a dated though endearing touch.

Dinner, Tuesday-Saturday 5 to 9 or 10; Sunday, brunch 11 to 3, dinner 4 to 9.

Jonathan Pasco's, 31 South Main St., East Windsor. (203) 627-7709.
American/Continental. $12.95 to $22.95.

The 1784 home of a local Revolutionary War hero named Jonathan Pasco had been abandoned for 44 years until chef Brian Mozzer grandly restored it for reopening as a restaurant in 1988. The place oozes atmosphere in small downstairs dining rooms with working fireplaces, wide-board floors, stenciling and spare Colonial decor, and upstairs in a large, contemporary addition with Palladian windows, skylights and a loft dining area over the lounge. Runners of colors matching the various rooms cross the center of the mismatched antique tables. A second-story rear deck is popular in season. Entree choices vary from Norwegian salmon rolled in puff pastry with raspberry beurre blanc and breast of chicken with roasted pecans and walnuts to tournedos marsala, Long Island duck with an orange-caramel sauce, and grilled rack of lamb with mint relish. Barbecued scallops, pizza bianca, vegetable custard pie and lamb cubes with artichokes are possible starters. Desserts include apple dumplings, cheesecake and chocolate mousse.

Lunch, Tuesday-Friday 11:30 to 2; dinner, Monday-Saturday 5 to 9 or 10; Sunday, brunch 11:30 to 2:30, dinner 4 to 8.

Manchester

* **Cavey's,** 45 East Center St., Manchester. (203) 643-2751.
French/Northern Italian. Upstairs, $13.95 to $18.75. Downstairs, Prix-Fixe, $49.
Behind the huge carved wooden doors admitting you to Cavey's, long considered to be one of the most — if not *the* most — elegant restaurants in the Hartford area, lie two worlds. One is country Italian, Riviera style, upstairs. The other is expense-account French, downstairs. Quarry tile floors interspersed with flowered tiles and paintings in the foyer hint of the delights to come. Arched windows and striking paintings give the high-ceilinged upstairs rooms a rare serenity. Chef-owner Steve Cavagnaro, whose grandparents started the restaurant in 1936, has taken a special interest in the upstairs menu, overseeing its transformation from southern to northern Italian. Lunch brings such delicacies as a salad of warmed greens with bacon, potato and mushrooms; fettuccine garnished with fresh vegetables, and shrimp and sea scallops sauteed with pancetta and brandy. The menu is considerably enlarged at night, with abundant antipasti choices and seafood and meat entrees like capellini with shrimp and sun-dried tomatoes, grilled swordfish with goat cheese, and rack of pork with spicy pasta and greens. Downstairs is sheer luxury with parquet floors, a two-tone raised beige fabric covering chairs and walls, candles inside crystal lamps, paneling (some black walnut) from an Upstate New York mansion that was being dismantled, and black-clad waiters attending to one's every need. The large potted palms give this two-level room an Edwardian feel as in the Upstairs of "Upstairs, Downstairs," but the service and food are definitely classic French. The prix-fixe dinner takes about three hours and is comprised of five courses (although you may order just the entree for $24). Au courant and written in French, the menu changes often but every item we've tried has been a triumph. After hors d'oeuvres come a fish course and the meat course, perhaps entrecote of beef, rack of lamb with garlic and couscous, or veal forestiere. Desserts include an espresso flan, the recipe for which Gourmet magazine requested, and interesting "combos" — pear sorbet with pear gratin zabaglione and pear tart in almond pastry cream, or white chocolate ice cream with cognac and warm bananas. The watermelon sorbet, suitably shaped with rinds of kiwi and seeds of currants, is to die for. Cavey's has one of Connecticut's most extensive wine lists with many rare vintages, and its "educational kitchen" has been a training ground for many a chef.

Upstairs, lunch, Monday-Saturday 11:30 to 2:30; dinner, 5:30 to 9:30 or 10:30; closed Sunday. Downstairs, dinner, Tuesday-Saturday 6 to 10.

Glastonbury

The Parson's Daughter, 2 Hopewell Road at Route 17, South Glastonbury. (203) 633-8698.
American. $14.95 to $19.95.
A dear little cream-colored structure with small-paned windows dating back to 1753 houses this charming, country-style restaurant that reminds us of an English

tea room, a pub and a French country inn all wrapped up into one. Chef-owner Karl Schaefer oversees the kitchen and his wife Bonnie the front of the house. The dinner menu ranges from chicken Creole to veal saltimbocca and surf and turf. Salmon braised in champagne with a lime-ginger cream sauce and roast pork with a currant-apricot glaze are interesting choices. We particularly liked the mushrooms stuffed with crabmeat, the honey-mustard vinaigrette on the salads and, among desserts, a strawberry-rhubarb crunch. Lunch items include salads, sandwiches, quiche and entrees like grilled duck and shrimp and scallop scampi. The Sunday country brunch is a Glastonbury tradition.

Lunch, Tuesday-Saturday 11:30 to 2; dinner 5:30 to 9 or 10; Sunday brunch, 11:30 to 2.

The Blacksmith's Tavern, 230 Main St., Glastonbury. (203) 659-0366.
Continental. $11.95 to $19.95.

A blacksmith shop was once attached to this sprawling house, part of which is thought to date from around 1700, in the center of Glastonbury. One can dine in a well-proportioned main dining room, in one of the seven small dining rooms named after local historical figures or, at lunchtime, in the spacious upstairs bar and lounge and in season on a small outdoor roof garden. For lunch, try the clam chowder, a local favorite, very thick and laced with thyme. The shrimp salad platter is also a winner — generous with the shrimp and garnished with hard-boiled eggs, olives, coleslaw and tomatoes. At night, entrees include chicken moutarde, veal oscar and marsala, seafood mixed grill, and shrimp genevieve. A small loaf of warm bread served on a wooden paddle and a salad topped with sprouts with a good sweet and sour house dressing accompany. For dessert, everyone loves the buttercrunch pie, the recipe for which has been published in the Ford Times.

Lunch daily, 11 to 4; dinner, 5 to 9:30 or 10; Sunday, brunch 11 to 2:30, dinner 4 to 9.

♥ **The Great American Cafe,** Somerset Square, Glastonbury. (203) 657-8057.
American. $6.95 to $15.25.

If you like Disney World, you'll love this cafe, which opened in 1989. Smack in the middle of the suave shops of Somerset Square, it has a bakery, a huge disco and bar upstairs called the Pacific Beach Club and, on the main floor, a mind-boggling series of small dining rooms, each decorated for a different part of the country. Peter and Paula Tripp of the Blacksmith's Tavern created this incredible place, and the artifacts they have assembled are awesome. The menu is casual and varied, from salads and pizzas to burgers and New York-style deli sandwiches. You could start with Mount St. Helens onion rings, Narragansett Bay calamari, Texas taco salad or Senate bean soup, and go on to Arizona black jack ribs, Georgia pecan scallops, Santa Fe fajitas or campfire tenderloin. For dessert, how about Granny's apple pie, Mom's homemade chocolate cake, a Vermont maple moose (yes, moose) or a banana split? Kids young and old dig this place, but serious diners find the merry-go-round of food no match for the decor.

Lunch and dinner from 11:30 a.m. to 11 p.m., Sunday to 10.

Wethersfield

Standish House, 222 Main St., Wethersfield, (203) 721-1113.
Regional American. $15.50 to $24.95.

One of the grandest homes in Old Wethersfield when it was built in 1790, this took on a new life as a restaurant under the aegis of the Wethersfield Historical Society, which owns the building. It has been carefully restored with soft Williamsburg colors and Axminster woven carpets. Two small dining rooms downstairs (one with Queen Anne chairs) and larger ones upstairs seat 100 people for lunch and dinner. Chef

Laureen Arno's seasonal menu is short but sweet. For dinner, you might start with a super assortment of smoked fish with horseradish and apple mayonnaise, a game terrine and cumberland sauce, or a winter sweet potato and sausage soup. For main courses, we liked sweetbreads with cepes, loin of veal stuffed with goat cheese with mousse of leeks, breast of chicken with pears and walnuts, and breast of duck with kiwis and grand marnier. The changing dessert menu might harbor a dacquoise with hazelnut meringue and coffee buttercream, amaretto chocolate cheesecake, sweet potato-pecan pie, and poached pears in zinfandel with macaroon stuffing.

Lunch, Tuesday-Sturday noon to 1; dinner, Tuesday-Saturday 6 to 9, Sunday 5 to 8; Sunday brunch, noon to 2:30.

Newington

Ruth's Chris Steak House, 2513 Berlin Tpke., Newington. (203) 666-2202.
Steakhouse. $15.50 to $22.50.
This is New England's only outlet for the "home of serious steaks," founded by Ruth Fertel in New Orleans. Specially aged beef, hand-cut on the premises, is supposed to be exceptionally good. We can't say, for after we had made reservations for a birthday dinner for a college-age son on a slow night, we were promptly seated in a back room and forever forgotten. Between that and what we felt were close to rip-off prices, we left for a more appropriate place in which to celebrate. There's no denying the attractiveness of the three rooms, handsome in white and black with crisp linens, well-spaced booths and tables, and a steak knife at every setting. Nor is there any denying the quality of the steaks, served sizzling in butter, or of the lamb, pork and veal chops, or of the lobster and salmon. All are presented simply, and everything, including hollandaise and bearnaise sauces, costs substantially extra. That includes potatoes, from baked and julienne to lyonnaise and au gratin, and vegetables, plain, creamed or au gratin. Among desserts are fresh fruits in sweet cream sauce, bread pudding, cheesecakes, and ice cream freezes. A shrimp cocktail, salad, garlic bread, steak, vegetable, potato and dessert will set you back $45, excluding beverages, tax or tip.

Dinner nightly, 5 to 10, Sunday to 9.

West Hartford

Assaggio, 904 Farmington Ave., West Hartford.
New Italian. $9.95 to $18.95.
This establishment sandwiched between a motor inn and a funeral home has had many incarnations. The latest, a sleek, contemporary place, is perhaps the one that will endure. It's a vast space, made more intimate by well-placed dividers. From a wood-burning oven come four versions of pizzas with a crisp, crackling crust; we liked the one of seasonal vegetables smothered with four Italian cheeses. Other good starters are spiedini romano, a skewer of shrimps and pancetta-wrapped oysters, and a delicate soup blending black beans and sweet red peppers. Eleven variations of pasta, made in house with semolina flour, include a zesty angel-hair campagnia topped with shrimp, sun-dried tomatoes, pine nuts, and a multitude of calamata olives. Assaggio prepares certain dishes on an open grill, and here it shines. We liked grilled catfish with a garlicky tomato-pesto aioli and a grilled veal chop with a delicate sweet red pepper and pesto cream sauce. For dessert, we'd choose the white chocolate mousse dotted with strawberries or the chocolate hazelnut cake rather than a ricotta cheesecake that was cakier than any in our experience.

Lunch, Monday-Friday 11:45 to 2:30; dinner, Monday-Saturday 5:30 to 10.

Hartford Area

Panda Inn, 964 Farmington Ave., West Hartford. (203) 233-5384.
Chinese. $9.95 to $15.95.

The latest in the Panda chain that's so popular in Massachusetts arrived in 1989 in West Hartford Center at the site of the former South Seas, to which it bears no resemblance. All is airy and contemporary with wood accents and nary a trickling fountain in sight. Clay-pot dishes from southern China are featured on the dinner menu, including sizzling beef or lamb with mushrooms, bamboo shoots and onions, and bean curd with slices of beef, chicken, shrimp, and roast pork with vegetables. Other specialties include chicken with scorched red peppers in a tangy sauce, lamb with leeks and garlic in a black pepper sauce, and baby shrimps with chicken, black mushrooms and snow peas in a red sauce. The extensive menu also offers a broad selection of standard Chinese fare.

Open Monday-Saturday, 11:30 to 10 or 11, Sunday 2 to 10.

Farmington

♥ **Apricots,** 1593 Farmington Ave. (Route 4), Farmington. (203) 673-5405.
Regional American. $15.50 to $28.

An old trolley barn beside the Farmington River houses one of the area's more versatile restaurants. You can dine outside on a jaunty terrace beside the river, inside on an enclosed porch, its windows taking full advantage of the view and its white walls painted whimsically with apricots, in a more formal inner dining room of brick and oak, or downstairs in a cozy pub with exposed pipes painted with more apricots. The food is usually equal to the setting, thanks to the inspiration of Ann Howard, a local resident known for her cooking lessons and later the Ann Howard Cookery before opening Apricots, "a juicy pub." We know folks who eat dinner at least once a week in the cozy pub, but we prefer the upstairs porch with its view. For lunch, we've enjoyed the spinach and strawberrry as well as the cobb salads, pizza a la mexicaine, the specialty chicken pot pie, fettuccine with crab and mushrooms, grilled lime chicken, and wonderful mussels. At night, you might find poached sea scallops in a champagne-watercress cream sauce, sauteed veal with sweetbreads, roast quail paired with roast pork loin in a calvados sauce, and roast rack of lamb with a mustard hollandaise. Start with a multi-layer terrine of scallops or lobster and brie in phyllo. Finish with apricot gelato, frozen nougat glace or one of the heavenly cakes, marquise au chocolat, charlotte russe, lemon roulade, or New York cheesecake with strawberry puree.

Lunch, Monday-Saturday 11:30 to 2:30; dinner, 6 to 10; Sunday brunch, 11:30 to 3, dinner 5:30 to 9. Pub, daily 2:30 to 10, Sunday 4 to 9.

Avon

Cafe Chanticleer, Riverdale Farms, Route 10, Avon. (203) 677-6026.
American. $10.95 to $17.95.

A standing sheep, attired in black vest and white gloves, holds the blackboard specials at this restaurant in the middle of the shops of Riverdale Farms, where one of us has enjoyed many a good lunch and shopping spree with "the girls." Lately it has expanded and serves dinners. The original dining room (now with a small bar and serving a blackboard pub menu at night) has tile floors, bare tables, ladderback chairs, and lace curtains. Adjacent is a popular outdoor dining porch. The newer dining room has similar tables and chairs amid spotlit paintings, carpeting and a rounded wood ceiling. The lunch menu is basic, because the list of specials is extensive. The chantiburger with bacon, cheese, onions and green pepper is terrific. We're fond of the croissant filled with spinach souffle, and the spinach and mandarin orange salad with almonds and a sweet and sour dressing. Soups here are outstanding and could include seafood bisque or curried chicken. At night, sample such entrees as black cherry-cognac-glazed chicken, grilled shrimp in an orange-ginger glaze, scallops dijonnaise, baked sole stuffed with shrimp and broccoli, or New York sirloin with cracked pepper in a burgundy sauce. Renowned desserts include chocolate truffle cake, hot apple spice cake with whipped cream, raspberry charlotte russe, and chocolate triple torte.

Lunch, Monday-Saturday 11:30 to 3; dinner, Tuesday-Saturday 5 to 9. Beer and wine only.

Avon Old Farms Inn, Routes 44 & 10, Avon. (203) 677-2818.
American/Continental. $16.95 to $21.95.
Established in 1757, this is one of the twenty oldest inns in the United States, although now it's strictly a restaurant. Seven dining rooms sprawl through a series of additions and are usually filled. Our favorite Forge Room has a splendid tavern atmosphere, with rough dark stone walls, flagstone floors, cozy booths made from old horse stalls, and lots of equestrian accessories hanging from dark beams. Up to 700 people may partake of the Sunday champagne brunch, which has been voted best in the state for ten years by Connecticut magazine. The extensive dinner menu goes from liver pate and herring in sour cream through baked onion soup, a salad of mozzarella and sun-dried tomatoes, to seafood rockefeller and chateaubriand. Veal sentino, a house specialty, combines tender medallions with layers of Danish cheese, asparagus and mushrooms. Other entrees include chicken with peaches and grapes, broiled salmon bearnaise, roast duckling bigarade, and tournedos with two sauces. The English trifle is a masterpiece among desserts.

Lunch, Tuesday-Saturday noon to 2:30; dinner, 5:30 to 9:30 or 10; Sunday, brunch 11:30 to 3:30, dinner 5:30 to 8:30.

Simsbury

Hop Brook, 77 West St., Simsbury. (203) 651-0267.
Regional American. $10.95 to $24.95.
This expansive restaurant in an old sawmill and grist mill complex is on several levels beside a roaring waterfall. Handsome service plates bearing the restaurant's logo on the antique table tops, old photos and a decor of brick, copper, beams and plants are eye-catching enough to compensate if you get a table without a view. Several fresh seafood choices may be ordered hardwood-grilled, pan-blackened, poached, baked or sauteed, and with a choice of sauces. Entrees range in price from sesame chicken stir-fry, turkey pot pie and excellent sauteed calves liver with applejack to oversize black angus steaks served on sizzling platters with duchess potatoes. The hardwood-grilled lamb skewered with roasted new potatoes and roast duckling with local maple syrup, cranberry glaze and apple jack are good choices. Maryland crab cakes with homemade ketchup, Cajun shrimp in a spiced beer sauce, and escargots sauteed with pesto and served with linguini are among appetizers. Favored desserts are chocolate bread pudding, rum-pecan pie, and toll house cookie pie. Ample salads (the grister's platter combines chicken tarragon and tuna salads with fresh fruit, vegetables and smoked cheese) and sandwiches are the fare at lunch. There's an appealing outdoor deck in season.

Lunch, Monday-Friday 11:30 to 2:30, Saturday noon to 3; dinner, Monday-Saturday 5 to 10 or 11; Sunday, brunch 10 to 2:30, dinner 4 to 9.

Simsbury 1820 House, 751 Hopmeadow St., Simsbury. (203) 658-7658.
New American. $14.95 to $24.95.
The dark and intimate lower floor of the Simsbury House provides a refined setting

for some of the Farmington Valley's better meals. Brick archways, deep green walls and carpeting, reproduction Chippendale chairs, hunting prints, and deep green-rimmed china service plates on white linens are the backdrop for three cozy dining rooms and a small bar. A single rose graces each table. At dinner, we liked the grilled bluepoint oysters served chilled with a splash of pernod and a rather diminutive trio of smoked fish with lime-horseradish sauce. The ten entrees might include grilled Norwegian salmon with a swiss chard, fennel and red onion cream sauce, roast leg of veal with crimati mushrooms and fresh herb cream sauce served with spinach fettuccine, and sauteed tournedos of beef with roasted garlic and balsamic vinegar. We can vouch for the roast duckling sauced with black currants, porcini mushrooms and madeira, and the sliced loin of lamb with two sauces, one of basil and curry and the other a rosemary brown sauce garnished with wild mushrooms and Holland peppers. Likely desserts are chocolate terrine on a raspberry puree, peach torte, and French chocolate cake with vanilla sauce.

Lunch, Monday-Friday, 11:30 to 2; dinner nightly, 6 to 9 or 10, Sunday 5 to 9; Sunday brunch, 11:30 to 2.

Evergreens, Simsbury Inn, 397 Hopmeadow St., Simsbury. (203) 651-5700.
New American. $17.95 to $25.95.

The gracious main dining room at this new inn has wood pillars, brass sconces, lace draperies, and a mural of 18th-century Simsbury. Tables are set with English bone china, crystal and sterling silver. Dinners begin with the plunking of a lemon slice in each water glass and end with the presentation of warm, scented towels. Following a complimentary cheese ball with croutons, you might order a lobster turnover, escargots in phyllo, eggplant gateaux, or black peppercorn pasta prepared tableside with smoked goose and chanterelles. Among entrees are roast free-range chicken with sausage cornbread stuffing, poached halibut, salmon with a scallop mousseline, veal chop on a tomato fondue, roast rib of beef with a Vermont cheddar popover, medallions of venison, beef wellington, and pheasant with a pumpkin-fran-gelico sauce. Most of the house-made desserts ($3.50) are triumphs, among them key lime pie, white chocolate mousse and pumpkin cheesecake. Wines come from a cellar visible off the entry hall.

Lunch, Tuesday-Friday 11:30 to 2; dinner, Tuesday-Saturday 5:30 to 9:30; Sunday brunch, 11 to 3.

Canton

★ **Lily's,** 160 Albany Turnpike (Route 44), Canton. (203) 693-8558.
Continental. $9.95 to $18.95.

Named in memory of co-owner Barbara McCarthy's mother, Lily's is a tiny bistro in a little white house where the front porch is painted pink and the picture window is outlined in white lights. Barbara and her husband Robert, the extraordinary chef, put the place together in 1988 with a shoestring budget and a lot of sweat. They expanded a bit in 1989 to seat 42 at fifteen tables topped with paper mats and votive candles in etched glasses. Bentwood chairs, bare floors, and funky old cans and packages — remember Duz? — are the decor. An old flexible flyer sled belonging to Barbara's mother hangs on the wall of the addition. Classical music plays in the background, and the atmosphere is friendly and unpretentious. Bob cooks impec-cably fresh food in a down-home manner (roast loin of pork with pan gravy and mashed potatoes is one popular dish) but with elegant touches. Along with a thick and hearty lentil soup, we sampled escargots in mushroom caps in an ethereal sauce. The blackboard usually lists six entrees (one of them nearly always duckling with a fruit sauce). We were delighted with a perfectly cooked salmon filet with dill-lemon butter sauce, sea scallops sauteed with mushrooms and garlic butter, and linguini with clams, scallops and shrimp. The McCarthys seem to love bananas, and you might find banana chocolate mousse, chocolate-banana bread pudding or grilled banana bread for dessert. Chocolate-pecan torte, Swedish apple cake and warm gingerbread with whipped cream are others. At lunch, Lily's serves hot sandwiches like sauteed breast of chicken with bacon and cheddar on a bun, cold ones like egg salad made with caramelized onions, and salads.

Breakfast, Saturday 8 to 11:30, Sunday 8 to 2; lunch, Tuesday-Saturday 11:30 to 3; dinner, Tuesday-Saturday, 5:30 to 9. BYOB. No credit cards. No reservations.

Eastern Connecticut

Somers

Somers Inn, 585 Main St., Somers. (203) 749-2256.
American. $10.95 to $16.95.

The first stagecoach between Boston and Hartford stopped at this white-pillared inn more than two centuries ago, and for locals this has been the old reliable for family celebrations ever since. You'll likely spot several generations at tables in dining rooms dressed in white linens or on an enclosed porch, darker and more intimate with hanging plants and woven placemats. The food is good old American, and lots of it, with vegetables served family style. Prime rib is the entree of note, a huge slab whether ordered in regular or large size. Broiled scrod, broiled scallops, veal cordon bleu, veal parmigiana, broiled lamb chops, roast duckling with orange sauce, and three versions of surf and turf are other choices on the all-too-familiar menu. The cellophane-wrapped crackers with salty cheddar spread that precede may be enough to forego such appetizers as stuffed mushrooms, stuffed grape leaves, cherrystone clams, and escargots. Homemade desserts run to hot fudge sundaes, strawberry shortcake and pies a la mode.

Lunch, Tuesday-Friday 11:30 to 2:30; dinner, Tuesday-Saturday 5 to 9 or 10, Sunday noon to 8.

Stafford Springs

Chez Pierre, 179 West Main St. (Route 190), Stafford Springs. (203) 684-5826.
French. $21 to $23; Weekends, Fixe-Price, $32.

The old-fashioned atmosphere of a bourgeois country inn pervades the restaurant that Pierre and Marie Courrieu established in a white Victorian house astride a hill in 1972. Several small dining rooms have tables decked out in brown and white, dark beams on the ceilings, ornate wallpaper, and white and gold draperies around the windows. A gas fire flickers above artificial logs in the front parlor dining room, and some of the flowers turn out to be fake. There's nothing fake or pretentious about the fare, however. Chef Pierre, who left La Provence in New York where he was sous chef for fourteen years after arriving from France, set up this eastern Connecticut outpost to showcase his vision of country French cooking. Meals are a la carte on weekdays and prix-fixe for three courses and beverage on weekends. You might start, as we did, with such classic appetizers as mussels normande, marinated mushrooms, and a country pate of pork and duck liver seasoned with brandy, or perhaps smoked scallops and shrimp with a creamy horseradish sauce, coquilles St. Jacques and escargots in puff pastry. Our entrees — a seafood crepe with riesling wine sauce, filet with green peppercorn sauce and escalloped veal with a peppery bercy sauce — were good but unmemorable. Other possibilities are filet of sole braised with vegetables, rack of lamb persillade, roast duck in a calvados sauce, and Pierre's famed cassoulet, a dish requiring advance notice and melding

Eastern Connecticut

chunks of pork, lamb, sausage, duck, navy beans and more. The dessert cart harbors treats like orange chantilly, creme caramel, rum cake, and cheesecake with lingonberries. Pierre is at his best during his annual August seafood festival when he and the chef from La Grenouille in New York prepare fish more than twenty ways.

Dinner, Tuesday-Saturday 5 to 9 or 10 in summer; rest of year, Wednesday-Saturday 5 to 9 or 10, Sunday 3 to 8. Reservations and jackets required.

Mansfield

Mansfield Depot, Route 44A, Mansfield Depot. (203) 429-3663.
American/Continental. $8.95 to 19.95.
Here's a restaurant whose cuisine defies categorization and whose unusual blend of formality and informality makes things interesting. Blue-jeaned patrons from the University of Connecticut campus have earnest discussions over expensive wines while strains of Vivaldi fill the air in this restored railroad depot. The busy bar on the entrance level has a few tables for dining, as does the front caboose. But most of the dining action is up a few stairs in a room with high beamed ceilings, bare floors, mismatched chairs, and a collection of old railway posters. Best of all are the handful of tables in a renovated railway car off to the far side, with green and white linens and fabric banquettes. Mussels are a feature on both the lunch and dinner menus. Big and tender, they come with a good broth for soaking up the sourdough bread that is hot, dense and crusty. The house filet mignon flamed in brandy and served atop a pate-covered crouton with madeira sauce heads the lengthy list of dinner entrees. We've enjoyed stuffed pork tenderloin rolled around apples, prunes and raisins with a savory sauce; chicken with toasted mustard seed sauce, and a special of grilled halibut with citrus butter. Appetizers include duck pate, gravlax and a boboli (thick gourmet pizza with unusual toppings), also available as a main course. Among appealing desserts are Russian cream with raspberry puree, a light cheesecake, Mississippi mud cake, and apple torte. Owner Larry Ross prides himself on the wine list, which includes good values under $10 among much pricier offerings.

Lunch, Monday-Friday 11:30 to 2; dinner, Monday-Saturday 5 to 9:30 or 10; Sunday, brunch 11 to 2:30, dinner 5 to 9.

The Homestead Restaurant, 50 Higgins Hwy. (Route 31), Mansfield.
456-2240.
American/Italian. $9.95 to $15.95.
This newly built restaurant at Perkins Corner is not an old homestead, although it might as well be for all its down-home country decor, including wreaths on the walls, dried flowers, paper placemats, and baskets of crackers. Chef-owner Michael Kapsch sticks to a straightforward menu with an Italian accent. Four presentations of veal, three of linguini and five steaks are among the offerings, but almost everyone goes here for the prime rib. Other possibilities are baked stuffed shrimp, broiled or fried scallops or sole, chicken cordon bleu, and surf and turf. Appetizers range from fried mozzarella and fried calamari to shrimp scampi and escargots in mushroom caps. Desserts like Belgian waffle, chocolate truffle cake and cheesecake "topped with your favorite cordial" win plaudits. Meals also are served in the tap room.

Lunch, Tuesday-Friday 11 to 4; dinner, Tuesday-Saturday 5 to 9 or 10, Sunday 3 to 9.

Storrs

Altnaveigh Inn, 957 Storrs Road (Route 195), Storrs. (203) 429-4490.
Continental/American. $12.95 to $20.95.
The stone walls indigenous to the area surround this rambling 1734 Colonial

farmhouse atop Spring Hall south of the University of Connecticut campus, marked out front by a striking sign centered with a pineapple logo. The pineapple is the symbol of the homey hospitality that owners William and Victoria Gaudette try to convey, and they also convey a considerably spiffed-up image to a long-established restaurant. They have refurbished the original dining room and added another centered with a striking four-sided brick fireplace of their own design, and turned a small front dining room into a cozy parlor and bar. Dusty rose and white linens, lace curtains and delicate wallpapers convey a fresh country feeling. Bill Gaudette, who does the cooking, offers an array of classic dinner favorites, among them salmon stuffed with sole and salmon mousse, roast duckling with a citron glaze, lobster newburg, veal oscar, beef wellington, and steak au poivre. They're served with a choice of green or spinach salad and potato or vegetable. Lunch is lighter and more casual: quiches, sandwiches, fettuccine primavera, and a few entrees like baked scrod and stuffed filet of sole. On nice days, it can be served outside on a side patio.

Lunch, Monday-Friday 11:30 to 2:30; dinner, 5 to 9 or 10; Sunday, brunch 11 to 2, dinner 2 to 8.

$ Cup-o-Sun Restaurant, 1254 Storrs Road, Storrs. (203) 429-3440.
Natural Foods. $4.95 to $8.95.

Formerly a vegetarian restaurant, this somewhat cavernous establishment with oilcloth-covered tables and a cafeteria counter was taken over by Hartford chef Carl Cozza and two partners in 1988 and became "a whole foods restaurant." You still can get wonderful soups, salads and breads, but also excellent fish (halibut steak with orange-basil butter, brown rice and vegetable saute), chicken (honey-mustard) and meat (beef liver with onions and bacon) at our visit. Also tempting were the Indian spiced vegetarian dinner (broccoli and yams, lentils and brown rice, curry-toasted nuts and yogurt) and the spiral pasta toss with spinach, mushrooms, roasted peppers, olive oil, herbs, garlic and parmesan cheese. Prices are as humble as the ambience — a Spanish omelet, soup and salad bar, and a pastry case full of enticing desserts are half what they'd cost elsewhere. No wonder it's a favorite of UConn professors and students. A changing buffet is offered cafeteria-style at lunch.

Lunch, Monday-Friday 11 to 4; dinner, Monday-Friday 4:30 to 8; weekends, breakfast 7 to 2.

Willimantic

Victorian Lady, 877 Main St., Willimantic. (203) 456-4137.
Regional American. $12.95 to $16.95.

Listed on the National Register of Historic Places, the unassuming red brick exterior with green trim makes a colorful cover for the menu of this casual establishment. Having upscaled itself from its early billing as "a dining saloon," it now emphasizes American cuisine with a Louisiana and Southwest accent. Lots of old signs and a sled adorn the exposed brick walls. Tiffany-style stained glass tops the long, L-shaped bar, which also has its share of stuffed animal heads. One alcove has musical instruments on the walls; old white Victorian lights are on the ceiling and at some tables. Dining is in two rooms on two levels. Part of the menu lists Southwest platters like chile burritos and grilled quesadillas, and the Louisiana section offers blackened specialties, rock shrimp etouffee and barbecued shrimp. American dinner entrees range from sage-roasted chicken stuffed with Granny Smith breading and finished with cider sauce to grilled filet mignon with armagnac-shallot butter. The Boston scrod is baked with shrimp and spinach in parchment; the chicken oriental is stir-fried with a raspberry-oyster sauce. The dining saloon atmosphere remains, as do snacks like super nachos and stuffed potato skins, but the Lady is aiming to change the taste preferences of people hereabouts.

Lunch daily, 11:30 to 4; dinner nightly, 4 to 11:30.

The Clark's, 28 North St., Willimantic. (203) 423-1631.
American. $9.95 to $15.95.

Very popular locally, the Clark's has been owned by one family for 40 years — first in a ramshackle red wooden building, more recently in a large modern structure next door. The decor is vaguely Colonial with pine paneling and lots of red. Dinners range from chicken pie ("a perennial favorite here for more than 30 years," according to the menu) to filet mignon with a peppercorn bordelaise. Atlantic seafood saute, baked stuffed shrimp, medallions of pork with mustard and red currant sauce, and veal normandy are among the possibilities. Appetizers are old-hat, except perhaps for the local deep-fried farm mushrooms, but the three pasta dishes appeal. There also are nightly specials like scallop pie and roast stuffed pork. At lunch, you can get sandwiches, salad plates and such entrees as corned-beef hash and chicken livers with mushrooms and marsala. The dessert tray features New England desserts like Indian pudding.

Lunch, Monday-Friday 11:30 to 3; dinner 5 to 8:30, later on weekends, Sunday noon to 8.

Norwich

* Norwich Inn & Spa, Route 32, Norwich. (203) 886-2401.
Regional American. $12.95 to $21.95.

The stately, red-brick Norwich Inn was refurbished and reopened by Edward J. Safdie, author of the book, "Spa Food," and founder of the luxury Sonoma Mission Inn and Spa in California. The guest rooms are filled primarily by those coming for the spa, but the Prince of Wales dining room attracts those into luxury dining, including spa cuisine. Pale red silk on the walls and green wainscoting create a pleasant backdrop for white-linened tables flanked by high-back chairs of light pine with cane seats. The menu changes seasonally and the spa selections nightly. Entrees could be grilled swordfish in a pepper-vodka marinade, medallions of pork sauteed with shiitake mushrooms and honey, loin of veal roasted with dijon and herbed bread crumbs, and roast rack of lamb with red wine sauce. Our family enjoyed a navarin of seafood garnished with fresh vegetables, grilled salmon with bearnaise, roast cornish game hen with thyme and mushrooms, and the New York strip steak with morels. Excellent breads, mixed green salads and seasonal vegetables accompanied. The emphasis among starters now is less on appetizers and more on salads. For dieters, resolve dissolves with desserts like hazelnut torte, chocolate roulade and pumpkin cheesecake. The dining room lately has been expanded to 75 seats with the addition of a Pub Room to the rear. In season, there are twice that many seats outside on a lovely terrace overlooking the golf course, an especially beguiling setting for lunch.

Lunch, Monday-Saturday noon to 2:30; dinner nightly, 6 to 10 or 11; Sunday brunch, noon to 3.

River Cafe, 1 American Wharf, Norwich. (203) 886-5666.
American/Italian. $6.95 to $9.95.

Billed as a waterside bistro, it's like none we ever saw — a contemporary square building surrounded on four sides by decks, and with a separate kitchen building a quick sprint away. An impressive square bar in the center is the focal point, along with a soaring ceiling topped by a skylit cupola. It's airy and trendy, and there's no denying its role as a fortuitous spot for an outdoor lunch along the Thames River in the midst of the new, nicely landscaped American Wharf and marina. There's lots of snacky food for those who hang out here, including three appetizer platters, seven salads and, a new one on us, onion loaf (sweet Bermuda onions dipped in buttermilk batter and golden fried). The all-day menu lists a dozen entrees, from linguini with clams and eggplant rollatini to Cajun chicken and steak teriyaki. A Sunday brunch buffet offers everything from soup to nuts, and there's live entertainment at night.

Open daily, 11:30 to 10, March-November.

Brooklyn

♥ **The Golden Lamb Buttery,** Hillandale Farm, Bush, Hill Road, Brooklyn. (203) 774-4423
American. Prix-Fixe, $50.

For more years than we care to remember, the Golden Lamb has been our favorite restaurant. We love it for summer lunches, when the surrounding fields and hills look like a Constable painting. We love it for summer evenings, when we have cocktails on a hay wagon driven by a tractor through the fields and listen to Susan Smith's pure voice as she sings and plays guitar. We love the picnic suppers and plays put on in the barn on occasional Thursday nights. We love fall lunches and dinners ensconced beside the glowing fireplace. And everyone loves Jimmie and Bob Booth, the remarkable owners of the farm on which the restaurant stands — she the wonderful chef and he the affable host. You can tell as you enter through the barn, where a 1953 Jaguar convertible is displayed among such varied items as a totem pole and a telephone booth, that you are in for an unusual treat. Step out on the back deck and gaze over the picturesque scene as waitresses in long pink gingham show the blackboard menu and take your dinner order. After you are seated following the hayride, the table is yours for the evening. Appetizers consist mostly of soups, and Jimmie makes some knockouts. Using herbs from her garden — especially lovage, her favorite — she might concoct country cottage, minestrone mother earth, cabbage soup made with duck stock or, in summer, a cold soup like raspberry puree or cucumber. There is usually a choice of four entrees, always duck, often chateaubriand and lamb, and lately smoked salmon florentine in puff pastry with mornay sauce. These are accompanied by six to eight vegetables, served family style and to us almost the best part of the meal. Marinated mushrooms are forever among them and, depending on the season, you might find celery braised with fennel, carrots with orange rind and raisins, tomatoes with basil and lime juice, or a casserole of zucchini and summer squash with mornay sauce. Jimmie cooks without preservatives or salt, and believes strongly in fresh and healthful food. Desserts might be chocolate roll made with Belgian chocolate, lemon or grand marnier mousse, and butter cake with fresh berries. This unfoldment takes place in dining rooms in the barn or the attached building with a loft that was once a studio used by writers. The old wood of the walls and raftered ceilings glows with the patina of age, as do the polished wood tables in the flickering candlelight. Colored glass bottles shine in the windows, and the whole place is filled with country things like decoys, deacons' benches, pillows, bowls of apples, and rag rugs. Add classical music on tape or Susan Smith's folksongs and a bottle of wine from Bob's well-chosen wine list, and you will find yourself part of a midsummer night's dream. The a la carte lunches lack the theatrics, but are wonderful nonetheless and you probably can get in (dinners may be booked months in advance). Entrees in the $8 to $13 range could include pasta parmesan, seafood crepes, red salmon quiche, Hillandale hash, and Londonderry pork stew.

Lunch, Tuesday-Saturday noon to 3; dinner by reservation, Friday and Saturday, one seating from 7. Closed January-May. No credit cards.

Pomfret

The Inn at Gwyn Careg, Route 44, Pomfret. (203) 928-7768.
New French. $16 to $26.

One of the potentially great small inns of the East is emerging on the exotic estate upon which the Marquis and Marquessa de Talleyrand entertained guests from across the world in the 1940s and 1950s. The dining room has had its ups and downs since its opening in 1988, with various chefs offering entrees ranging from chicken piccata to poached salmon and tenderloin of beef roquefort with port wine sauce. We enjoyed sauteed pork medallions finished with calvados, cream and sliced apples, accompanied by a melange of winter vegetables and tiny potatoes. We were disappointed with the grilled noisettes of lamb with fresh goat cheese raviolis and orange-basil sauce, which weren't at all as the menu had promised. Owner George Flonnes, a carpenter by trade from Hartford, said better things were ahead as he was about to hire a four-star chef for the spring of 1990. Details were sketchy, but he envisioned sophisticated meals "worthy of a world-class restaurant." He planned refurbishing to make the setting match the meal, particularly in the banquet facility. The small main dining room, lit almost entirely by candles, already was elegant with parquet floors, Victorian parlor chairs upholstered in green velvet, pink cloths, and built-in shelves full of china.

Dinner, Wednesday-Saturday 5:30 to 9; Sunday, brunch 11 to 2, dinner 5 to 7.

$ **The Vanilla Bean Cafe,** Junction of Routes 44, 169 and 97, Pomfret.
(203) 928-1562.
American. $3.50 to $4.85.

Home cooking and incredible values are offered by Eileen (Bean) Jessurun and brothers Brian and Barry in part of a 150-year-old barn they renovated for opening in 1989 near the campuses of the Pomfret and Rectory schools. Oversize sandwiches with house-smoked meats (perhaps smoked turkey with gruyere on a croissant) and hearty soups (ham and bean, tomato, and cream of broccoli) are the fare. The short all-day menu is supplemented by blackboard specials — chili with jalapeno cheddar corn muffins, gumbos, venison or beef stews, and quiches (lorraine or spinach and mushroom) proving popular with the academic community for supper. The three Jessuruns do the cooking, assisted by three employees who bake pies and cakes to embellish the regular dessert fare of cookies and brownies. Bagels, muffins (carrot-raisin, blueberry bran, and cranberry-nut), cappuccino, and espresso go fast in the morning. Beneath an eighteen-foot ceiling with exposed beams, diners partake at seven round wood tables amid lots of plants and a 75-gallon fish tank in the middle, or seasonally on an outdoor patio. The Jessuruns applied for a beer and wine license and planned to open an Irish pub serving bistro fare in another section of the barn in 1990.

Open daily, 7 a.m. to 8 p.m.

Woodstock

* **The Harvest at Bald Hill,** Route 169 and 171, South Woodstock.
(203) 974-2240.
Contemporary Continental. $11.95 to $22.95.

Two chefs who had upgraded the Brown University Faculty Club in Providence teamed up in 1988 to buy this cozy barn of a restaurant that museum curator Wylie Cumbie had put on the gastronomic map a decade earlier. Peter Cooper and Carol Twardowski take turns in the kitchen and out front, and change their menu with the seasons to reflect the restaurant's name. The porch is great for summer dining. The decor is comforting: peach linens in summer, dark green in winter; Dudson china, flickering oil candles, comfortable cane armchairs, and dark wood walls and ceiling. At lunch, we've enjoyed an appetizer of gyoza (tasty Japanese dumplings), sauteed scrod with winter vegetables, and two excellent and abundant salads, oriental seafood and tuna nicoise. These were so filling we couldn't begin to think of such desserts as truffle cake, linzer torte, baked bread custard with a calvados sauce, and a classic marjolaine. Dinner entrees range from pasta with spinach, cheese and spiced sausage to veal with shrimp and bearnaise sauce. Other tempters include grilled salmon with a mustard-dill hollandaise, roast duckling with black currant sauce, sirloin steak bearnaise, and "gentlemen's grill" of filet mignon and lamb chop. Wine Spectator has honored the wine list, which is affordably priced.

Lunch, Tuesday-Friday 11:30 to 2; dinner, Tuesday-Saturday 5:30 to 9 or 10; Sunday, brunch 11 to 2, dinner 2 to 8.

The Inn at Woodstock Hill, Plaine Hill Road, Woodstock. (203) 928-0528. Regional American. $13.50 to $19.

This promising new inn has had many a chef, the latest being Richard Naumann, newly hired as co-innkeeper with Sheila Becks. Off to the side of the inn in a carriage house, the restaurant is luxurious with crystal chandeliers, banquettes draped in chintz, and blue armchairs. Well-spaced tables are set with Villeroy & Boch china and pink napkins stashed in large wine glasses. There's an outdoor deck for dining in summer. The dinner menu offers ten entrees, among them grilled swordfish with Mississippi wild rice, sauteed monkfish with lobster cream sauce and fettuccine, grilled scampi in garlic butter on linguini with tomato concasse and parmesan cheese, sauteed pork steak with a hearty leek sauce and au gratin potatoes, and grilled filet mignon with green peppercorn sauce and baked potato stuffed with chives, bacon and cheese. Start with the house pate (duck, veal and pork with lingonberry relish), smoked trout with horseradish sauce or escargots. Dessert could be Dutch hazelnut cake, white amaretto mousse or chocolate-almond torte laced with grand marnier. A good wine list is fairly priced. An abbreviated version of the dinner menu is offered at lunch, when you might also order a tri-salad plate or the grilled Woodstock whopper.

Lunch, Tuesday-Saturday 11 to 2; dinner, Tuesday-Saturday 6 to 9:30; Sunday brunch, 11 to 2.

Thompson

Vernon Stiles Inn Restaurant, Route 193, Thompson Hill. (203) 923-9571. Continental. $10.50 to $17.25.

Built in 1814, this venerable stagecoach tavern is what a New England restaurant should look like: a homey old place with a fire blazing in the pub, three dining rooms and a great picture of the inn made with what look to be pieces of tiles. The place was named for one of its more colorful landlords, who claimed "more stage passengers dined there every day than at any other house in New England." Owner Joseph Silbermann and new chef Steven Tokarz oversee an extensive menu that is well regarded locally. Dinner entrees include two pastas, four chicken dishes, five versions of veal, and various sizes of broiled steak or filet mignon. Other choices include seafood saute, broiled scallops, roast duckling, and beef diane. A winter tradition that is always sold out is the weekly Stew and Story sessions on Wednesday evenings. Cocktails and a supper of stew (perhaps lamb or beef) precede a fireside story told by local actors or professors in the reading room.

Dinner, Monday-Saturday 4:30 to 8:30 or 9; Sunday brunch, 11 to 2:30.

Southern Berkshires

Lenox

Church Street Cafe, 69 Church St., Lenox. (413) 637-2745.
International. $12.95 to $16.95.
Billed as an American bistro, this is the casual, creative kind of restaurant we like, the one we keep returning to for a quick but interesting lunch whenever we're in Lenox. We're not alone, for it's No. 1 on most lists of favorite eateries in town. Co-owners Linda Forman and Clayton Hendrick offer fresh, light cafe food inside amid changing artworks or by the ficus tree, and outside on pleasant decks. Clayton, who once was chef for Ethel Kennedy, supplements the seasonal menus with blackboard specials. Lunch items include black bean tostada, Thai beef salad, tabouli salad with pita bread, and Louisiana gumbo. The dinner menu is slightly larger and more ambitious. You might start with southwestern bean nachos with two salsas and sour cream, grilled garlic sausage with croutons and cornichons, spicy Thai chicken with peanut sauce, or smoked Maine trout with horseradish cream. Entrees range from eggplant rolatini to grilled Szechuan sirloin sliced on a bed of greens with ginger vinaigrette. Entrees change frequently to encompass such diversity as pork medallions with Mexican mole sauce, Chesapeake Bay crab cakes, and grilled lamb chops with pear-ginger chutney. We've enjoyed every dish we've tried. The chocolate espresso torte with cappuccino ice cream and lemon chiffon cake with fresh blackberries and custard sauce are worthy endings.
Lunch, Monday-Saturday 11:30 to 2:30; dinner nightly, 5:30 to 9; Sunday brunch in summer and fall.

✱ Wheatleigh, West Hawthorne Road, Lenox. (413) 637-0610.
New American. Prix-fixe, $58.
Regal and perfect, say those who adore it. Pretentious and overpriced, say those who don't. Its detractors tend to outnumber its fans, but Wheatleigh remains at the cutting edge of the culinary world — "as good as anything in New York," in the eyes of New Yorkers and some of the international press. Even with the departure in 1989 of chef Bill Holbert, who raised it to its elevated stature, Wheatleigh didn't miss a beat. Sous chef Peter Platt took the helm, offering inspired fare at what mere mortals consider an outrageous tariff. Several items carry surcharges, so if price is an object — and it shouldn't be, if you eat here — you might want to try the menu degustation for $80, which requires the participation of the entire table. A typical menu involves seven choices for each of the three courses. The winter night we visited, we could have started with a warm salad of grilled shrimp, lobster, scallops and endives; scallops in sorrel cream sauce with tomato and mache; consomme of pheasant and squab with poached quail egg, or butternut squash soup with prosciutto and fig quenelles. Among main courses were halibut enrobed in crisped potato with oysters and a caviar butter sauce, grilled tuna on a bed of wilted spinach with ginger and leeks, roast squab with foie gras, potatoes anna and black truffle sauce, and roasted loin of venison with wild black huckleberries. Desserts included a gateau of chocolate and hazelnuts with praline creme anglaise, spiced black mission figs with iced anisette souffle and a tasting of house sorbets: cranberry-quince, pear and passion fruit. The prize-winning wine list bears piratical prices from $30 ("that's the level that begins to fit in with our food," the maitre-de told us) to $1,500. One big-spender had ordered three $750 bordeaux a few nights earlier, we were informed. Are you impressed yet? An eighteen percent gratuity is added to the bill.
Dinner nightly by reservation, 6 to 9 or 9:30; Sunday lunch, 11:30 to 1:30. Closed Tuesday in off-season.

Lenox 218, 218 Main St., Lenox. (413) 637-4218.
American/Continental. $12.95 to $18.95.

Even unflappable Lenox residents were agog in 1989 with the opening of this strikingly contemporary, New Yorkish restaurant in the old Log Cabin. Vastly expanded, it now contains a state-of-the-art kitchen, an inviting lounge, and two airy dining rooms (one the Fireplace Room, one the Sunroom) with soaring cathedral ceilings. Decor is mostly black and white with black lacquered chairs, gray striped wallpaper coordinated with black and gray carpeting with stripes on the diagonal, mod posters and handsome black-rimmed Shaunwald china from Germany. Peripatetic local restaurateurs Jim and Lynne DeMayo sold their Painted Lady in Great Barrington not long after its opening to concentrate on their largest venture yet, and a grand place it is indeed. Its with-it menu ranges from grilled spring chicken with lime, garlic and cilantro to grilled American lamb chops with mint conserve. Jimmy DeMayo makes the pastas, and desserts like French apple tart, banana cream pie and cappuccino-chocolate custard. The atmosphere surpasses the food, according to some, although we've heard more raves than brickbats. For lunch there are sandwiches, salads and entrees like chicken pot pie and roast beef hash with a poached egg. At little round black tables in the bar, with its black and white tiled floor, you can snack on shrimps, oysters and clams, or maybe a taco salad.

Lunch, Monday-Saturday 11:30 to 2:30; dinner nightly, 5 to 10; Sunday brunch, 10:30 to 2:30.

Gateways Inn and Restaurant, 71 Walker St., Lenox. (413) 637-2532.
French/American. All Entrees, $27.

Noted chef Gerhard Schmid turned over the reins to his sous chef of four years, Jeffrey Niedeck, a Culinary Institute grad, when he sold the inn in 1988. Jeff kept the menu the same and the restaurant's coterie of regulars didn't detect a change. One of the formal dining rooms is the small and intimate Rockwell Room, named for the late artist Norman Rockwell, who dined here regularly. The Orleton Room, elaborately refurbished, has a sofa and chairs in the center, surrounded by five tables for dining. It leads to the new Procter Room in back. Fresh flowers grace the tables, set with white linens and fanned pink napkins. The menu rarely changes but is supplemented by fresh seafood and game in season. All entrees are $27, including salad, rolls and vegetables, regardless of whether you order chicken, pheasant or dover sole. House specialties are shrimp stuffed with crabmeat and flavored with cognac, rack of lamb, medallions of beef tenderloin, and Norwegian salmon topped with shrimp and lobster meat and finished in a dill-champagne sauce, garnished with hollandaise and toasted almonds. Appetizers include herring with sour cream, escargots, and warm duck salad with raspberry vinaigrette. Viennese apple strudel, sabayon torte and praline-pecan ice cream truffle are favorite desserts. The wine list contains an interesting mix of Massachusetts, California, New York, Pacific Northwest, French, German and Italian wines in that order, most priced in the teens and twenties.

Dinner nightly, 5:30 to 9 or 9:30. Closed Sunday in winter.

Blantyre, Route 20 and East St., Lenox. (413) 637-3556.
Contemporary French/Mediterranean. Prix-fixe, $65.

The Blantyre dining experience — which is likened to eating in a castle — was opened to the public in 1989. The luxury inn in a 1902 Tudor-style brick manor patterned after the Hall of Blantyre in Scotland served lunch to upwards of twenty people a day in summer on the outdoor terrace, and offered dinners for about 40 in the formal, oak-paneled dining room or a couple of smaller private rooms. Investing heavily in the kitchen, Blantyre put in a barbecue for grilling purposes and offered an alternative menu for the health-conscious. Chef Stephen Taub cooks in the the style of Provence, with a light hand on the sauces. A typical five-course dinner starts with a choice of cucumber vichyssoise with shellfish butter, veloute of avocado, or seafood minestrone perfumed with lemon balm. Next comes perhaps a confit of duck salad with Belgian endive and pears, ravioli of wild mushrooms with white truffles or a duo of oysters in spinach pillows with caviar butter sauce. A sorbet precedes the main course, perhaps steamed sea bass over red spinach with two caviars, Maine lobster with Thai herbs and tomato, medallions of veal with madeira and chanterelles, or grilled filet of beef with foie gras and zinfandel-butter sauce. Desserts could be Viennese chocolate-walnut torte with chocolate ganache, cognac parfait with raspberry coulis and pistachio anglaise, or terrine of two chocolates. Most guests retire to the Music Room, where a harpist and pianist play on weekends.

Lunch, July and August; dinner by reservation, Tuesday-Sunday in season. Jackets required.

Cafe Lucia, 90 Church St., Lenox. (413) 637-2640.
Northern Italian. $13.95 to $17.95.

Authentic northern Italian cuisine is served up with flair by Jim and Dianne Lucie in this former gallery transformed into a restaurant that shows and sells art. Working from an open kitchen, Jim dishes up food that is much favored by locals, who praise his pasta creations, baked polenta with homemade sausage and Italian codfish stew. The osso buco con risotto is so good that it draws New Yorkers back regularly, and Jim reports he received so many complaints when he took the shrimp alla medici off the menu, it was promptly restored. Among desserts are cold chocolate souffle cake with almonds and amaretto, frangelico and hazelnut cheesecake, gorgonzola and fresh pears, and a sauteed apple, cinnamon and sour cream pie. Those desserts, a fine port or brandy, and cappuccino can be taken on the flower-bedecked patio on warm summer evenings.

Dinner nightly from 5; off-season, Tuesday-Saturday from 5:30.

Apple Tree Inn, 224 West St., Lenox. (413) 637-1477.
Continental. $14.50 to $18.

The circular dining room still has the spectacular panoramic view and carousel ceiling with ribs of bulb lights that it had when it was Alice's at Avaloch — Alice's upscale restaurant after she moved from Housatonic to the inn across from Tanglewood. It is all pink and white, with Austrian curtains. In cooler months, meals are served in the **McIntosh Tavern**, a cheery haunt, with red and white checked curtains, red tablecloths, paneled walls, booths and a big fireplace. Of the five pasta dishes offered at dinner, linguini al gustav sounds wonderful: jumbo shrimp in a sauce of tomato, basil, garlic, olive oil and wine. Other entrees include three presentations each of veal and chicken, as well as broiled salmon, blackened fish with Cajun remoulade sauce and roast Long Island duckling. Sauteed langoustinos, smoked trout and pate of the day are among appetizers. There are sometimes as many as fourteen desserts ("you'd think you were in a Viennese pastry shop," says owner Greg Smith), with fresh fruit tarts, profiteroles and chocolate mousse cake always popular, along with more exotic specials like Kentucky bourbon pound cake with buttered bourbon sauce and frozen white chocolate-frangelico mousse.

Lunch daily during Tanglewood season, noon to 2; dinner nightly, 5:30 to 9:30. No smoking in dining room.

The Village Inn, 16 Church St., Lenox. (413) 637-0020.
Regional American. $12.95 to $17.95.

Afternoon tea and well-regarded dinners are served in this recently restored inn, which was built in 1771 and carries its age well. Villeroy & Boch china, pistol-handled knives and fresh flowers enhance the white-clothed tables in the Harvest Room. An enclosed side porch was converted into a dining area in 1989 to accommodate summer patrons. Chef John Clapper's dinner entrees run from pecan-breaded chicken to veal and crabmeat casserole over pasta or roasted breast of pheasant served with braised red cabbage and Kentucky bourbon sauce. Shaker chicken, poached salmon with brandy and dill cream sauce, and pork medallions with a pear and clove coulis are other possibilities. You might find a novel pasta — tenderloin tips and jumbo shrimp in creamy herbed bordelaise sauce — on the winter menu. Scallop and shrimp chardonnay, venison pate and smoked breast of duckling with ginger root and grand marnier glaze are typical starters. Creme brulee, apple and raisin crisp, cranberry sherbet and ginger ice cream are among seasonal desserts. English tea is served every afternoon from 2:30 to 4:30, and light fare is offered at night in the **Village Tavern.**

Dinner, Tuesday-Sunday 5:30 to 9:30. No smoking.

Dakota, Route 7, Lenox. (413) 499-7900.
Steaks/Seafood. $8.95 to $16.95.
   Rebuilt and expanded following a fire in 1988, this immensely popular steakhouse near the Pittsfield-Lenox line is part of the Sirloin Saloon group from Vermont. It looks like a ski chalet with rustic, hunting-lodge decor — a far cry from its heritage as a Howard Johnson's. Patrons wait for up to two hours on busy weekends to get a table in the restaurant, which seats 250 in a variety of rooms. The focal area contains two enormous salad bars (with a spectacular selection), an open grill, a lobster tank, a display case containing slabs of beef, and a table where huge loaves of Buffalo bread are displayed (and are for sale to take home). Western grain-fed beef is featured, ranging from teriyaki sirloin to prime rib. Mesquite-grilled chicken, swordfish, shrimp, and sirloin are offered separately or in a variety of combinations. Among the day's specials when we were there were Norwegian salmon with lime-coriander butter, wood-grilled yellowtail tuna or rainbow trout, and baked scrod. Light entrees, including homemade whole-grain bread and salad bar, go for $7.95 to $10.95 — little wonder the place is packed. The wine list has similar values, and New York cheesecake and mud pie are the obligatory desserts.

Dinner nightly, 5 to 10 or 11.

Stockbridge/West Stockbridge

♥ **Red Lion Inn,** Main Street, Stockbridge. (413) 298-5545.
American. $16 to $25.
   Whenever one of our brothers from Montreal is on his not-infrequent business trips to the Berkshires, he stays and dines at the Red Lion Inn. So do a lot of travelers from around the world, it seems. Such is the draw and the name of the Red Lion, the quintessential New England inn that since 1773 has dominated the Main Street made famous by Norman Rockwell. The feeling is formal in the spacious main dining room, where entrees run from stuffed chicken breast to prime rib or double lamb chops. Oyster pie, grilled swordfish, and lobster baked, stuffed or steamed also are listed. Desserts range from rice, bread and Indian puddings to pecan ball with butterscotch sauce, parfaits and sundaes. At noon, you can get anything from a peanut butter and jelly sandwich to smoked salmon on a bagel, or from a crock of Boston baked beans with brown bread to roast beef hash with poached eggs. For a tete-a-tete meal, the dark-paneled Widow Bingham Tavern is just the ticket. In warm weather, canvas deck chairs dot the popular outdoor courtyard lined with spectacular impaties, one bed with a statue of a lion in the middle. It's a colorful

and cool spot for lunch, dinner or drinks. The same menu is served inside and out. During Tanglewood season, a light menu is available between meals in the tavern or on the courtyard.

Lunch daily, noon to 2; dinner 6 to 9, Sunday noon to 4 and 5 to 8:30, summer to 9:30.

La Fete Chez Vous, off Main Street, Stockbridge. (413) 298-4278.
French. Expensive.

Down a little alley between the market and an art gallery is this tiny takeout and sitdown establishment in the space formerly occupied by Alice's Restaurant (the original one of Arlo Guthrie fame), all "updated for the '80s," as an International Herald Tribune article says. Make that the '90s, for Chez Vous is nothing if not trendy. Clouds are painted on the high ceiling, topiary trees are by the french doors, the floor is a striking black and white tile, and it's all ever so European looking. Partners Joseph Wheaton and Bernard Mallon have been known for their catering in the area for several years. Display cases are full of such dishes as chicken with lemon and caper berries, filet of beef with peppercorns, celeriac remoulade, curried lamb, stuffed grape leaves, lemon sole wrapped in lettuce, stuffed with boursin and poached in champagne, and the like. You can order soup and a salad platter, a filet of beef sandwich with asparagus, or a baby linzer torte. If you want to eat in at one of the four tiny round black tables, you may BYOB.

Open daily except Tuesday from 10 to 8, Sunday to 4.

♥ **Truc Orient Express,** off Main Street, West Stockbridge. (413) 232-8565.
Vietnamese. $11.50 to $17.

Who wouldn't like this sleek yet charming Vietnamese restaurant that stays open all day year round, whether any patrons are there or not? In the dead of winter, sometimes they're not; in summer, the place can be packed. It's such a success that it was greatly expanded in 1988 with 120 more seats on two floors of an adjacent building, linked to the original by an umbrellaed outdoor deck. Here there are lacquered burgundy chairs on polished wide-board floors with beautiful oriental rugs scattered about, and some gorgeous screens and huge black vases inlaid with mother of pearl. Vietnamese music plays in the background and wonderful aromas based on garlic waft from the kitchens. The occasional communications gap with the Vietnamese family that runs this wonderful place is bridged by pointing to the numbers of the 66 items on the exotic menu. The perfectly prepared dishes are as spicy as you ask for. The "singing chicken" and Mongolian hotpot are great, but one of us can never order anything but the happy pancake.

Open daily from 11 to 9 or 10.

Williamsville Inn, Route 41, West Stockbridge. (413) 274-6118.
Country French/American. $18 to $25.

This quiet, remote country inn was built in 1797, but feels considerably newer. Dining is in four country-pretty, candlelit rooms. One, the library, has walls of books and tables on old sewing-machine bases. Nine choices are offered for entrees, among them chicken paupiette with spinach, tomatoes and goat cheese, pan-seared loin veal chop with a sauce of exotic mushrooms, roast duck with a poached pear and port wine sauce, and tournedos au poivre. Seasonal vegetables, popovers and salads of Belgian endive and mixed greens dressed with a basil-shallot vinaigrette come with the meal. For starters, try smoked trout and salmon with vodka creme fraiche, veal and pork pate, goat cheese raviolis with a wild mushroom sauce, or mussels provencale. End with raspberry sorbet or a flourless Belgian chocolate cake served with raspberries and whipped cream.

Dinner nightly, 6 to 9 in summer and fall, Thursday-Sunday rest of year.

Shaker Mill Tavern, Route 102 and 41, West Stockbridge. (413) 232-8565.
American/Italian. $4.50 to $19.95.

A spacious and recently expanded outdoor deck is especially popular at this large, two-story affair with several dining rooms and a greenhouse section filled with plants at one end. The menu is a casual mix of burgers (one has sour cream and mushrooms; another guacamole and salsa), spa food, salads, nachos, chicken wings, stuffed potato skins and "stix," the house answer to kabobs. Pizzas, pastas and Italian specialties from veal parmesan to chicken oreganato are available all day. Everything is under $13.50 except for a twenty-ounce T-bone steak. The beer list is extensive and the wines reasonable, and live entertainment is featured frequently. In the works for 1990 behind the restaurant was the first phase of a large new Inn at the Shaker Mill, with another restaurant and 155 guest rooms.

Open daily from 11:30.

Ghinga, Route 7, Stockbridge. (413) 298-4490.
Macrobiotic Japanese. $7.50 to $18.25.

The sushi bar is the main attraction at this unusual restaurant housed in the former Stockbridge railroad station, a fairly expansive space with bare shiny tables, bare floors and lots of rich wood. Specialties include tempura and noodle dishes, oshitashi, katsu and a variety of vegetarian selections. No sugar or MSG is used. Start with deep fried tofu with ginger-tamari sauce or steamed watercress with soy sauce, go on to fish or shrimp katsu or try salmon teriyaki or a nigiri sushi platter. The sashimi dinner is the most expensive dish on the menu. Sample the rice dream or other all-natural desserts. Wine and beer are served.

Dinner, Tuesday-Sunday 5 to 9.

Lee/South Lee

★ Federal House, Route 102, South Lee. (413) 243-1824.
Contemporary European. $21.95 to $25.95.

The handsome red brick and white-pillared house built in 1824 was an ordinary bed-and-breakfast operation until Robin and Ken Almgren took over in 1982. They have upgraded the guest rooms, but it is food for which the Almgrens are particularly known. Three small, pristine dining rooms, two with working fireplaces, have white lace curtains on high windows, heavy silver, white linens and masses of fresh flowers, and — if they're not filled — the kind of hushed feeling that makes you whisper. The menu combines classic French with a bit of nouvelle. Among appetizers, we loved the shrimp in beer batter, a dish that harkens back to chef Ken's days at Stonehenge in Connecticut, and the smooth pate of fresh salmon and flounder with sorrel sauce. Among entrees, the roast duckling with pear and lingonberries and vegetables like roesti potatoes and braised fennel with parmesan cheese were superb. Other options might be quenelles of chicken with cognac and fresh basil, stuffed filet of flounder with herb beurre blanc, sweetbreads with mousseline sauce, veal scaloppine with tarragon and grand marnier, and roast rack of lamb provencale for two. Desserts are sensational, especially the frozen cappucino pie and apple fritters in kirsch. The mostly French wine list is distinguished and fairly priced.

Dinner nightly, 6 to 9; Sunday brunch, noon to 2:30. Closed Tuesday in winter. No smoking.

$ Hoplands, Route 102, South Lee. (413) 243-4414.
American. $4.95 to $15.95.

The folks from Federal House opened this casual American bistro across the street in 1987 and sold a couple of years later to Sheila Nickerson and her father Ronald, a contractor, who made few changes to a going concern. Decor is fairly minimal but the ambience is lively, downstairs by the bar and upstairs in a rather plain dining room. The all-day menu is traditional country American, from a Hopdog and a Hopburger to chicken pie, pasta Hopfredo, stir-fry and broiled sirloin — the last the most expensive of the Hopplates. The Joshua Slocum is fried fish in a special batter, served on a hard roll, and Hoplands' eggplant comes fried on a hard roll with mozzarella, tomato sauce and mayonnaise. Specials might be a hot meatloaf sandwich or broiled scrod. Homemade apple pie, chocolate cake and a fried tortilla topped with cinnamon and sugar are dessert favorites.

Lunch daily, 11:30 to 5; dinner nightly, 5 to 9. Closed Monday and Tuesday in winter.

The Place, 51 Park St., Lee. (413) 243-4465.
Regional American. $9.95 to $15.95.
Co-owner Richard Rice, who arrived in the Berkshires from his native Mississippi via New York, used to call his granddaddy's property "the place." So when he finally got his own place, the name was a natural. He and partner Charles Petrie took over the former Inn at Lee, redid every wall, floor and ceiling (not to mention stripping eight coats of gold paint from a slate dining-room fireplace), and opened a restaurant and B&B in October 1989. Theirs is a beautiful place, with a collection of African art in the foyer, gorgeous backlit stained glass in one dining room, and a spacious bar that accommodates overflow. Two intimate dining rooms in teal are outfitted with substantial ceiling fans, chintz curtains, bentwood chairs, and a handful of tables set with beige linens and oil lamps. Reports were mixed in the early going, but the menu held great promise. Entrees ranged from sauteed tiger shrimp with piquant sauce to sauteed rainbow trout with spinach florentine, from grilled cornish game hen with tarragon butter to duck with dark molasses, lingonberries and brandy. Who wouldn't be impressed with an offering of prime Canadian goose with choice of sauce, prepared for four? Appetizers might be sweet potato and apple fritters or Malpeque oysters on the half shell. Key lime mousse, sweet potato pie and Mississippi apple cake (made from apples sent by Richard's mother) were among desserts.

Lunch, Monday-Saturday 11:30 to 2; dinner nightly, 5:30 to 10 or 11.

Black Swan Inn, Route 20, Lee. (413) 243-2700.
Continental. $12 to $19.
With a new atrium addition overlooking Laurel Lake, the dining room at this inn-motel has gone glamorous indeed. The expanded room is a picture of pink, with double damask linens, handsome white and gold china, silver candlesticks, crystal salt and pepper shakers with silver tops, and vases of fresh flowers. Chef David Renner prepares a short but wide-ranging menu that retains specialties of one of the owners, who was a Hungarian freedom fighter. Entrees include shrimp and scallops cilantro over angel-hair pasta, Norwegian salmon, poached chicken Ester-hazy, pork tenderloin Zurich, authentic Hungarian gulyas, and grilled rack of lamb. Start with the house pate or cerapcici (spicy handmade grilled sausages). Finish with creme caramel, chilled lemon torte with rhubarb sauce, or chestnut puree chantilly. The hearty Egri Bikaver from Hungary is a steal on the wine list.

Lunch daily, 11:30 or noon to 2; dinner, 5:30 to 9:30, Sunday 5 to 9. Closed Tuesday.

Great Barrington

★ **Castle Street Cafe,** 10 Castle St., Great Barrington. (413) 528-5244.
Contemporary. $7 to $16.
Michael Ballon, who cooked at the Williamsville Inn in West Stockbridge in its

heydey and then for several years at upscale restaurants in New York City, returned to the Berkshires to open his own cafe in 1989. Other restaurants have not had much luck in this space beside the movie theater, but Michael's bistro has been packing in the locals. With appetizers like grilled shiitake mushrooms, grilled homemade veal sausage, and warm salad of chicory, bacon and croutons, and entrees like a Castle burger, there is something for everyone. Other possibilities include grilled cornish game hen, coho salmon stuffed with mushroom mousse topped with a cucumber-dill sauce, eggplant roulade stuffed with three cheeses, calves liver with onion marmalade, steak au poivre, and cassoulet of lamb. There are accompaniments like homemade onion rings, straw potatoes and zucchini fritters. The world's best chocolate mousse cake (according to Newsday), creme brulee, warm bread pudding with sour mash whiskey sauce, and homemade ice cream (maybe espresso or mint-chocolate chip) top off a satisfying meal. Michael makes a point of using Berkshire farmers and purveyors for everything from maple syrup and goat cheese to the flowers on the tables. The long narrow room with its windsor chairs and white-linened tables has a brick wall hung with artworks. The bar at the back (where Michael puts out goodies like pate and cheese) is the only place where smoking is allowed.

Lunch weekdays; dinner nightly, 5 to 10 or 11; Sunday brunch. Closed Tuesday in winter.

The Painted Lady, 785 South Main St., Great Barrington. (413) 528-1662.
Northern Italian/Continental. $12.95 to $17.95.
Peripatetic chef Jimmy DeMayo, formerly of the Candlelight Inn and Restaurant in Lenox, opened this nifty little Victorian restaurant in 1986 and left it in good hands, those of sous chef Daniel Harris, when he returned to Lenox to launch Lenox 218. Long and narrow and painted green with pumpkin trim, it looks like one of its San Francisco namesakes pictured inside the entry. Two small dining rooms containing about a dozen tables are sleekly modern. Regulars are partial to entrees like angel-hair pasta with marinara and meat sauce, shrimp scampi and veal saltimbocca. Baked clams is the appetizer of choice. Among desserts, deep-dish apple pie with ice cream is the house favorite, with creme caramel close behind.

Dinner nightly except Wednesday, 5 to 10, Sunday to 9:30.

Whole Wheat & Wild Berrys, 293 Main St., Great Barrington. (413) 528-1586.
Natural Foods. $7.95 to $14.50.
A simple natural foods restaurant (the owners run another on West 10th in New York City), this is, one restaurateur told us, the best place for lunch around. The menu changes daily but you might find zucchini bisque, steamed vegetables with homemade pesto, pita pizza, or turkey-avocado club sandwich. On a wintry day, we liked the basket of breads, hearty mushroom-barley soup and the vegetable pancakes with a choice of mushroom or cucumber-yogurt dressings (we asked to try both) as well as the nutburger, served on an English muffin topped with melted cheese and sprouts. At dinner, the short menu might harbor a savory vegetable cheesecake, mushroom-tofu stroganoff, brook trout with maple-apple marinade, and swordfish Italian. Desserts like chocolate-walnut pie, peanut butter-rice dream pie, and apple crisp are sweetened by honey. The only meats used are sausage and bacon for the Saturday breakfast and Sunday brunch, when you can order cheese blintzes, waldorf salad or poppyseed pancakes. Every Friday night a different ethnic cuisine is featured. There's live music Friday and Saturday from 7 to 9, as well as a full bar. The two long and narrow rooms full of blond wood are lit by track lighting and tiny votive candles.

Lunch, Tuesday-Saturday from 11:30; dinner, 5 to 9 or 10; breakfast, Saturday 9:30 to 11:30; brunch, Sunday 9:30 to 3. Closed Monday. No credit cards.

Southern Berkshires

$ 20 Railroad Street, 20 Railroad St., Great Barrington. (413) 528-9345.
American. $3.95 to $10.95.

Great for children as well as adults (both babies and grandmothers abounded when we lunched there) is this little place with its stunning old mahogany bar. Soups, salads, sandwiches and burgers are the all-day fare. We had a "hap hazard," pita bread full of chili and bacon and topped with melted cheese, filling and really delicious. A perfect broccoli and cheese omelet was accompanied by a decent little salad. Another time we had a chicken salad vinaigrette and a crabmeat puff, each accompanied by enough slices of fresh melon, strawberries and grapes that we skipped dessert. Nightly dinner specials are under $11, be they hot roast beef platter with mashed potatoes, herb-roasted chicken, prime rib or New York sirloin with a baked potato. Desserts include an outrageous chocolate cake, coconut custard pie, and apple crisp with ice cream. The tables are covered with collages of old pictures, walls are brick or barn red, and overhead fans add to a casual, relaxed feeling.

Open daily, 11:30 to 10; Sunday brunch, 11:30 to 2.

Noodles, 12 Railroad St., Great Barrington. (413) 528-3003.
American/Italian. $5.50 to $13.50.

The name indicates the theme — pasta and informality — at this place founded by the original chef at 20 Railroad Street and now under new ownership. Pasta dishes like fettuccine with smoked salmon and dill cream, scallops with snow peas and vodka, and goat cheese with sun-dried tomatoes and walnuts particularly appeal. Other dinner choices include chicken tarragon, broiled swordfish, a sauteed seafood platter, Danish baby back ribs, veal merlino, and New York strip steak. For starters, how about country pate or smoked salmon with black bread? Some of the same dishes are offered at lunch, plus a more extensive selection of salads and sandwiches. Creamy carrot cake and several kinds of cheesecake are featured desserts. Lamps illuminate the artworks on the walls and oriental rugs dot the floors, but the tables are covered with paper.

Open daily, 11:30 to 10.

$ Martin's Restaurant, 49 Railroad St., Great Barrington. (413) 528-5455.
International. $7 to $11.

"Breakfast served all day," proclaims the sign in the window of this intimate, L-shaped storefront with black and white linoleum floors, crayons and paper mats on the tables, and a corner bar. And with good reason. Martin Lewis, formerly a chef at the Waldorf and the Regency in New York, whips up incredible omelets (with potatoes and toast) that draw in the locals for lunch as well as breakfast. Lately, he started serving weekend dinners followed by live music. He offered a changing selection of leg of lamb, chicken curry and scrod one night, roast loin of pork, shrimp provencale and entrecote steak the next at prices that New Yorkers expect to pay for breakfast. Eight salad plates, a dozen sandwiches (from peanut butter with banana and honey to seafood salad) and all those breakfast items are the everyday fare. But it is the "tower of bagel" with smoked salmon, cream cheese, tomato and bermuda onion that's the big hit, our waitress said.

Breakfast daily from 6 (weekends from 7); lunch, 11:30 to 3; dinner, Friday and Saturday (Saturday only in winter), 6 to 9. No credit cards or checks.

South County

* The Old Mill, Route 23, South Egremont, (413) 528-1421.
Regional American. $12 to $22.

This restored 18th-century grist mill, which opened as a restaurant in 1979, is one of our favorites anywhere. The atmosphere is a cross between a simple Colonial tavern and a European country inn — homespun and friendly, yet sophisticated — a happy combination created by owners Terry and Juliet Moore, he an English chef who trained on the Cunard Line ships. Entrees are bargain-priced for specialties like smoked pork chops with apple chutney, grilled spring chicken with fresh herbs, and shrimp and scallop curry. Filet of salmon au poivre with lime butter, black angus steak with red wine-shallot butter, and rack of lamb are at the higher end of the price range. The sauteed calves liver with Irish bacon is a masterpiece. If black bean soup is on the menu, try it, but save room for the mocha torte, the apricot charlotte or truffle loaf with vanilla and raspberry sauce. The house salad is better than most. The interesting wine list, reasonably priced, is evenly split in origin between California and France, with nods to Italy and Australia. An addition to the smaller of two dining rooms provides large windows looking over Hubbard Brook in back. No reservations are accepted except for large parties, so arrive before 7 on weekends if you don't want to wait; the creative food and exceptional value make the Old Mill very popular.

Lunch, Saturday and Sunday 11:30 to 2; dinner nightly, 5:30 to 9:30 or 10:30. Closed one or two weekdays in off-season.

Embree's, Main Street, Housatonic. (413) 274-3476.
Nouvelle International. $9.75 to $22.50.
Former New York theater scenery painter Jay Embree owns this funky, creative restaurant, which explains its theatrical air. Hand-carved wooden trees bearing tropical fruits brighten the prevailing expanse of wood floors and tables in the old, high-ceilinged hardware store, still with open shelves at either end. The place is noisy, laid-back and utterly without pretension, the better to enjoy the food, which is primarily seafood, pasta and vegetarian dishes. We've enjoyed a tender breast of chicken coated with a crisp batter and topped with lemon sauce, a sensational grilled bluefish spiced with ginger and strands of scallions, and — one of the more interesting dishes we've had in ages — baboutie, spicy balls of ground lamb and curry, atop a delicate custard and accented with chutney. With Embree's renowned, melt-in-the-mouth mashed potatoes plus crisp carrots, this was a meal fit for a rajah. Other entrees might be Mediterranean fish soup, blackened Cajun catfish, grilled butterfly shrimp with saffron, and pasta creations containing everything from rock shrimp to chicken livers, with an emphasis on olive oil, garlic and spices. Good starters are nachos with salsa verde, mushrooms stuffed with a pungent mix of chevre, garlic and herbs, and vegetarian egg rolls served with chutney and hot dijon sauce. Lemon pound cake with orange sherbet makes a cooling end to an assertive meal. The wine list is small but serviceable.

Dinner, Wednesday-Sunday 6 to 10 or 11.

♥ **The Old Inn on the Green,** Route 57, New Marlborough. (413) 229-7924.
Regional American. Prix-Fixe, $40.
People come from near and far for the weekend dinners in this abandoned 1760 inn restored over a ten-year period by Bradford Wagstaff. His wife, Leslie Miller, a baker who used to supply area restaurants, oversees gourmet dinners served totally by candlelight in as historic a setting as can be imagined. About 50 people may be seated in the tavern room, a formal parlor, or at the harvest table in the dining room. In each, the original wainscoting, stenciling, antiques, and windows draped in velvet are shown to great advantage. The large mural of cows grazing on the New Marlborough green is wonderful to see, and it's easy to imagine yourself transported back a couple of centuries for the evening. Chef David Lawson's fare is thoroughly up to date, however. The prix-fixe dinners have a set menu except for two choices

of desserts, and the selection is arranged three months in advance for a mailing to regulars. Chevre and almond puff-pastry sticks accompany drinks, served in delicate stemmed glasses. From a mushroom and herb soup that is the essence of mushroom to the final cappuccino with shredded chocolate on top, things go from great to greater. A typical winter meal might bring a ramekin of burgundy snails with tomato and garlic, roast loin of veal with artichokes and shallot cream, fried parsnips with parsley, wilted greens and fennel, and a choice of black and white chocolate mousse or apple-cinnamon feuillete. Brad oversees the extensive wine list, periodic wine-tasting dinners and the candlelit bar at the rear.

Dinner by reservation, Friday-Sunday 6 to 9:30. No credit cards.

✱ Boiler Room Cafe, Buggy Whip Factory, Norfolk Road, Southfield.
(413) 229-3105.
International. $13 to $22.

Caterer Michele Miller, once a chef at Alice's Restaurant of Arlo Guthrie fame and founder of Suchelle Bakers, opened this little cafe with a handful of tables inside and out in the rear of the Southfield Outlet and Craft Center in 1987. Her kitchen caters some of the Berkshires' best parties, but also puts out a limited dinner menu of things like salmon in parchment with lime sauce, roast duckling with cider sauce and garlic mashed potatoes, and potato enoki al forno with spicy tomato sauce. Creamy Boston clam and halibut chowder, chevre souffle, warm lentil salad with duck confit, crab cakes, and Michelle's antipasto plate make good starters. For dessert we'd choose her superb dacquoise, although the rich and creamy cheesecake, nectarine pie, creme caramel, and ginger-pear tart sound good, too. At lunch, soups, pates, salads and such are featured.

Lunch, Thursday-Monday 11:30 to 3:30; dinner, Thursday-Saturday 6 to 9:30. Winter, lunch Saturday-Monday, dinner Friday and Saturday.

Northern Berkshires

Williamstown

✱ The Orchards, 222 Adams Road, Williamstown. (413) 458-9611.
Regional American/Continental. $13.50 to $19.75.

Upholstered reproduction Queen Anne chairs, rose and green carpeting, forest green walls, and well-spaced tables set with soft rose linen, ribbed glassware, flowered German china, silver baskets for the rolls and antique teapots — what could be more elegant than the L-shaped, two-part dining room at the Orchards? We enjoyed a Saturday lunch, settled in comfy high-back rose velveteen chairs in an airy, two-story greenhouse-like area at one end, looking onto the courtyard used for summer dining under striped umbrellas. Swordfish soup with vegetables was an interesting starter, as was the excellent chilled apple-curry soup. The chicken salad with papaya slices, apples and pecans was a winner, and a beef bourguignonne special was fine. Not so wonderful was the strawberry-almond cake that tasted like a jelly roll; next time we'll try the peanut butter cheesecake or the homemade sorbet. The dinner menu changes nightly and is respected by area chefs because of its scope. Entrees could be sauteed soft-shell crabs with lime-cilantro butter, grilled swordfish with poivrade sauce, sauteed veal liver with port and shiitake mushrooms, broiled veal chop with chanterelle demi-glace, and grilled quails with wild mushrooms. Start with sauteed sweetbreads nantua or chilled duck breast with salsa fresca. Finish with a good-looking apple tart with crumb crust or chocolate roulades from the pastry cart.

Lunch daily, noon to 2; dinner, 6 to 8:30 or 9.

Le Country Restaurant, 101 North St., Williamstown. (413) 458-4000.
French. $12.95 to $19.95.

A warm, country atmosphere and the personalities of chef-owner Raymond Canales, his wife Beverly, and son Gregory pervade this long-established restaurant in the continental tradition. The rustic main dining room is done up in beige and brown, with a beamed ceiling, a mix of shaded lamps and candles on the tables, and a Franklin stove to ward off the chill in winter. A striking antique sideboard from Brittany is decked out with wines, glasses and grapes. The extensive menu is supplemented by nightly specials, prime rib and veal curry the night we were there. Entrees include chicken prepared four ways, veal three, and such classics as duckling bigarade, coquilles St. Jacques, broiled lamb chops, and tournedos bordelaise. Southern pecan pie and baba au rhum are featured desserts. Many of the appetizers and desserts are available at lunch, along with sandwiches, salad plates, and entrees like chicken fricassee on toast, Spanish omelet and shrimp curry. There are extraordinary values among the wines.

Lunch, Tuesday-Friday 11:30 to 1:30; dinner, Tuesday-Sunday 5 to 9.

Le Jardin, 777 Cold Spring Road, Williamstown. (413) 458-8032.
French. $12 to $20.

The two partitioned dining rooms are country French and quite elegant, with velvet striped seats, white linens and dark napkins placed sideways, hanging lamps with pierced-tin panels, white draperies, and plants in every window. German chef Walter Hayn shares honors with Raymond Canales of Le Country (twenty years) for the longest tenure in town. His menu is classic French, from the onion soup to the herring in sour cream and escargots bourguignonne. Dinner entrees range in price from chicken Henry IV to filet mignon bearnaise. They include Long Island duckling and pepper steak flambe, all nicely prepared with fine cream sauces. Desserts tend to be rich — chocolate truffle mousse cake, double fudge chocolate layer cake, hazelnut torte, kahlua cheesecake, and pecan pie.

Dinner nightly, 5 to 10; Sunday brunch, 10:30 to 1:30. Closed mid-November into winter.

$ Hobson's Choice, 159 Water St., Williamstown. (413) 458-9101.
American. $8.95 to $12.95.

This cozy little place is a favorite of the locals. Old tools hang on its wood walls, paper mats are on bare tables with Tiffany-type lamps above and mismatched chairs around, and there are a few stools at the bar in back of the room. Around the front door are wonderful panes of stained glass with flowers and birds therein. The large menus offer something for everyone. Lunchtime favorites are a crock of onion soup, tempura onion rings, Buffalo wings, sandwiches and burgers. Fish and chips are served the British way, with vinegar. The same appetizers, sandwiches and burgers are listed for dinner, with ten or so entrees ranging from chicken piccata to seafood fettuccine and Cajun catfish. Mud pie, carrot cake, chocolate mousse and cheesecake are some of the desserts. The wine list is skimpy but cheap.

Open Monday-Saturday, 11:30 to 9 or 10.

North Adams

Freight Yard Restaurant & Pub, Western Gateway Heritage State Park, Route 8, North Adams. (413) 663-6547.
American. $7.95 to $14.95.

There are a pub-like atmosphere in the main-floor tavern and a "unique restaurant upstairs," according to advertising. That translates to an airy room with bare tables, red upholstered windsor chairs, exposed beams and posts, pink curtains on the tall windows, and wreaths and plants here and there. Unique? Perhaps for the area. Certainly the prices aren't the Berkshires norm. Nor is the menu — an extensive listing from fried clams to seafood mornay, chicken parmigiana to cordon bleu, barbecued pork ribs to filet bearnaise. Basics are covered in potato skins, chicken wings, nachos, Cajun tips, mud pies (the signature dessert) and such, and there's an all-you-can-eat salad bar. Broiled scrod is the priciest item on the pub menu, and it's not pricey.

Open daily from 11:30 to 9, Sunday from noon.

LaCocina, 850 State Road (Route 2), North Adams. (413) 664-4757.
Mexican. $8.75 to $11.75.
We've always gotten a kick out of the funky original of this two-restaurant "chain," located off the beaten path at 140 Wahconah St., Pittsfield. So we had to stop at the newer LaCocina, which looks for all the world like a diner, inside and out, in North Adams. There's nary a bit of Mexican decor — just a lineup of booths, tables and a tiled bar with a counter looking into the kitchen. But from that kitchen come some good Mexican dishes in the familiar style — tacos, enchiladas, flautas, quesadillas, tostadas, burritos, chimichangas, fajitas, arroz con pollo, and a couple of "grande dinners," one with shrimp, scallops, crabmeat, and pollock served with rice on a flour tortilla). All dinners come with tortilla chips, LaCo sauce, tossed salad, and a choice of refried beans, Mexican rice, chili or gazpacho. A zesty jalapeno bean dip is served with tortilla chips for starters. Among desserts are sopapillas, fried bananas with kahlua, and hot apple-raisin burrito. There's live entertainment at night, when things can get noisy.

Open daily from 11:30, Sunday 4 to 10.

Hancock-New Ashford

★ **The Mill on the Floss,** Route 7, New Ashford. (413) 458-9123.
French. $17 to $25.
Genial Maurice Champagne, originally from Montreal, is the chef-owner at this established and well-regarded restaurant. And, good news for his coterie of regulars, he's back in the kitchen year-round after a few years of closing in winter so he could handle the executive chef's duties at Drummonds, the more formal of two restaurants at the new Country Inn at Jiminy Peak ski resort in nearby Hancock. He loves to socialize, and one reason he designed the open, blue and white tiled kitchen was so that patrons could come up and talk with him as he cooked. The dark brown wood building, pleasantly landscaped, was once a mill. Inside it is cozy, with beamed ceilings, paneled walls, a hutch filled with Quimper pottery, white linens, and many hanging copper pots. Before dinner, complimentary cheese and crackers, chicken liver pate, radishes and olives are served. Among starters are duck pate with plum wine, prosciutto and melon, and soups like cold cucumber or black bean. Entrees range in price from chicken amandine to rack of lamb. Sweetbreads in black butter, veal kidneys with mustard sauce, calves liver with bacon, and sliced tenderloin with bordelaise sauce are some, and the fish of the day could be halibut meuniere or swordfish. To finish, you might sample a nut torte or a chocolate roll cake filled with grand marnier souffle, or try cafe diablo for two.

Dinner nightly, 5 to 9:30 or 10 in summer, to 9 or 9:30 in winter. Closed Monday from November to mid-May.

Hancock Inn, Route 43, Hancock. (413) 738-5873.
Continental. $14 to $19.
Hidden in an old house at the edge of Hancock is this small inn with an acclaimed

restaurant on the main floor and six guest rooms upstairs. The two dining rooms are cheery with white linen and old wood stoves. One has crystal glassware, fringed curtains and bare floors; the other has a piano, deep rose walls, candles in old colored glass candlesticks, and a doll on a plush rocking horse. The service plates are mismatched and it's all rather charming. The menu is limited but intriguing: appetizers like duck liver pate stuffed in mushroom caps, Polish sausage with beet horseradish, smoked salmon on a dill blini with sour cream and caviar, and shrimp sauteed in pernod; billi-bi or escargot soups, and entrees like veal and shrimp dijonnaise, duckling braised in port wine with grapes, cheddar cheese and walnut raviolini in pesto, and baked stuffed leg of lamb. Dessert might be a pear with chocolate sauce or strawberries and cream.

Dinner, Wednesday-Sunday from 5.

Pittsfield

★ Wendell House Bistro, 17 Wendell Avenue Ext., Pittsfield. (413) 499-0025.
Regional American. $12.95 to $17.95.

Billed as "the culinary melting pot of the Berkshires," this new-in-1988 restaurant in downtown Pittsfield is a fascinating mix of New Orleans cuisine and local personality. The personality is that of chef-owner Dennis Powell, who returned to his native Pittsfield after a career with the Culinary Institute of America. In what used to be a men's bar in a downtown hotel, he upgraded the decor with a bit of a New Orleans feeling: wood paneling, lots of booths, etched-glass fixtures and partitions between the booths, and artifacts collected from local antiques stores. Much tableside cooking and new treatments of old standards — like rolling escargots in phyllo and serving oysters rockefeller in a ramekin — are featured. Start with a Cajun martini, spiced with his own pickled okra and jalapeno vermouth. Try catfish beignets, oxtail bistro, oyster stew or wilted spinach salad. Continue with seafood gumbo, shrimp etouffee, grilled marinated quail (served with sweet potato gaufrette and roasted garlic), or seafood platter en papillote. Finish with homemade sweet potato pie, bread pudding with Wild Turkey hard sauce, rice pudding, banana mousse or bananas foster. Here is a master at work; the sweet potatoes that are Dennis's signature turn up as french fries or baked with meats. At lunch, you can order things like oyster loaf New Orleans, minted chicken and pineapple salad, or a Cajun sausage boboli.

Lunch, weekdays 11:30 to 2; dinner, 5:30 to 9 or 10, Sunday 3 to 8. Closed Tuesday.

★ Truffles & Such, Allendale Shopping Center, Route 9, Pittsfield.
(413) 442-0151.
New American. $9.75 to $16.25.

Interesting meals, desserts and afternoon tea are served by Irene and Michael Maston, she a Culinary Institute of America grad, in this crisp, contemporary restaurant that opened in 1985 and moved to a space triple its size at the dawn of 1990. The expanded quarters have a patisserie and a sit-down bar in front, and one wall of mirrors, the other with artworks. Black lacquered chairs are at glossy black lacquered tables with inlays that resemble stone, left uncovered — the better to display the food. Classical music plays as patrons lunch on wild mushroom stew, smoked duck breast, gingered chicken salad, spinach and walnut tortellini tossed with sun-dried tomatoes, chevre cheesecake, Mediterranean torte and the like. At night, the possibilities include a pasta of triple cheese and herb raviolis with pine nuts, grilled lamb chops with mint pesto, chicken truffles, filet mignon with wild mushrooms, and turban of sole with lump crabmeat and green peppercorn stuffing in a lime beurre blanc. Pick one of the sensational looking desserts in the case for a happy ending, perhaps hot apple dumpling or peach pie. Everything is made on premises and available to take out. Look for the distinctive black and glass-block facade in the plaza's center.

Open Monday-Saturday, 11 to 9 or 10, Sunday, 5 to 10.

The Dragon, 1231 West Housatonic St., Pittsfield. (413) 442-5594.
Vietnamese/Oriental. $7.25 to $12.50.

Kim Van Huynh, who once owned a restaurant in Saigon and whose escape from Vietnam is a fascinating and moving tale, expanded from a teeny diner into a larger restaurant, where he serves up exceptional Vietnamese and oriental food. Dusty pink booths with oilcloths on the tables are in two small dining rooms on either side of a service bar (beer and wine only — there are some exotic beers one seldom encounters). Vietnamese spring rolls (more crisp and delicate than Chinese egg rolls) make good starters. Chicken with lemon grass, ginger chicken, spicy pork with broccoli, shaking beef, and scrod crisped with fresh tomatoes and onion sauce are among the standbys. Top off your meal with lychee nuts, longan berries or ice cream, and a pot of the excellent Vietnamese coffee, done in French cafe-filtre style.

Dinner nightly, 4 to 10.

Giovanni's Ristorante, 1331 North St., Pittsfield. (413) 443-2441.
Italian/American. $6.95 to $13.95.

The decorating touch of the member of the family who owns an interior-design shop is evident in this beautifully restored brick building, newly expanded with an addition allowing seating for 150 on the main floor. The homemade pastas are considered the city's best; served with salad and Italian bread, they range from spaghetti with meatballs to linguini with shrimp or clam sauce. There are an assortment of veal dishes, as well as fresh seafood like broiled swordfish, filet mignon, and combination plates.

Pioneer Valley

Greenfield

Brickers, Intersection of Route 2 and I-91, Greenfield. (413) 774-2857.
American. $8.95 to $16.95.

There are thousands of red bricks inside and out at this aptly named place in the old Turnbull's Green Mountain Ice Cream factory. To the left as you enter is a sunken lounge with many couches and upholstered chairs in dark blue, Laura Ashley-like fabric. A stunning iron chandelier has a twin in owner Herm Maniatty's restaurant in the middle of town, Herm's. On the right is the dining area, filled with handsome booths and bare wood tables, and an airy dining solarium in front. Apricot fabric hanging from polished brass rails separates some of the spaces. Dinner entrees run the gamut from liver and onions to sirloin steak, and prices include the salad bar. Baked stuffed sole, garden scrod, shrimp scampi, Cajun chicken, roast duck, and veal castelli romano (with mushrooms, Italian sausage and madeira sauce) are a few. Among light dinners are an eggplant casserole and turkey pot pie; sandwiches, burgers and tacos also are available at night. The wine list is fairly extensive and reasonable.

Open daily, 11:30 to 9:30 or 10:30.

Famous Bill's, 30 Federal St., Greenfield. (413) 773-9230.
American. $6.95 to $14.95.

Famous by virtue of longevity (and an early article in the Ford Times, from which it is said to have derived its fame) is this crowded establishment of the old school. The sign outside the unimposing exterior proclaims jumbo shrimps, lamb chops and lobster. The three family-style dining rooms with booths and tables are congested and noisy, but the throngs don't seem to mind. The lunch menu is simple, offering several salads in small and large portions and sandwiches of all kinds. Specials might be shepherd's pie with coleslaw or ham steak with pineapple ring, whipped potatoes and squash. We sampled a toasted tuna salad sandwich and a seafood roll that came with french fries and coleslaw, quite a bargain for $3.75, even if it was composed of those fake sea legs. Earlybird dinner specials like fried sea scallops, chicken parmesan and sirloin tips for $7.95 (including soup and salad) draw weekday crowds. The no-nonsense dinner menu offers everything tried and true, and we hear the prime rib is the best around.

Open daily except Monday from 11 a.m. to 11 p.m.

Herm's, 91 Main St., Greenfield. (413) 772-6300.
American. $7.95 to $14.95.
Turn-of-the-century memorabilia and a casual all-day menu are featured in this small, tavern-like establishment owned by Herm Maniatty, who also owns the new Bricker's and the old Corner Cupboard hereabouts. Soups, salads, sandwiches and light meals are served all day, with fancier entrees ranging from filet of sole amandine to Herm's prime rib au jus available at night. Check out the old gasoline station pump lights (remember Richfield and Tydol?) and tire signs over the bar and the walls laden with old posters and thermometers. There's lots more memorabilia among the booths partitioned by red curtains in the dining room.

Open daily, 11 to 9:30 or 10:30.

Taylor's Tavern, 238 Main St., Greenfield. (413) 773-8313.
American. $5.95 to $13.95.
A tavern in the contemporary idiom, this downstairs place has nicely private booths separated by glass dividers, lots of wood and hanging lights in two rooms. Snacks, salads, a couple of pastas, seafood, and entrees are featured on the all-day menu, which is supplemented by daily specials like chicken a la king and barbecue dinner at old-fashioned prices. Starting with breakfast at 6 a.m., you can order almost anything from nachos and potato skins to spaghetti with meat sauce, fried seafood platter and Cajun blackened prime rib.

Open daily, 6 a.m. to 1 a.m.

Deerfield

♥ **Deerfield Inn,** Main Street, Deerfield. (413) 774-2359.
Continental. $17 to $21.95.
Seemingly light years away from busy Interstate 91 barely a mile away, the serenely elegant dining room of the inn, built in 1884 and rebuilt after a disastrous fire in 1979, is an oasis of graciousness in a bustling world. The spacious main dining room seems like that of a private club with its muted oriental-type carpets, chintz curtains, gleaming brass chandeliers, striking Colonial cutlery and heavy glassware on white linens, and reproduction Chippendale and Duncan Phyfe chairs. The dinner menu includes such specialties as saddle of venison in a wild mushroom sauce, local brook trout stuffed with fresh sea scallops served with walnut butter, sauteed breast of chicken with lobster medallions in a brandied cream sauce, and rack of lamb with garlic, tomatoes and sweet basil. Appetizer choices could be hickory-smoked trout with horseradish sauce, gravlax with a honey-mustard and dill sauce, and breast of duck with a spiced wild plum sauce. At noon the menu is more informal:

a warm chicken salad comes with cashews and a honey-mustard sauce; smoked sea scallops are served with spinach, scallions, julienned red peppers, and a hot sesame seed dressing. One of us made an entire lunch out of the appetizer of country veal and chicken liver pate and a hearty French onion soup, almost a meal in itself with plenty of onions, sealed with a thick layer of cheese. The other had scallops florentine, a delicate dish accented with garlic. From the dessert list, you won't go wrong ordering the apple crisp just like your mother used to make. Indian pudding, cheesecake with strawberries, chocolate truffle cake, and chocolate indulgence are other choices.

Lunch daily, noon to 2; dinner, 6 to 9.

Amherst

Cafe DiCarlo, 71 North Pleasant St., Amherst. (413) 253-9300.
Northern Italian. $12.25 to $21.
A pizza parlor took on a stylish new life in 1988 with the opening by Bonni DiCarlo of this appealing place, all arches and brick and fine paintings by a local artist. Set with black mats and red napkins, most tables are in booths, and there's a screened patio in back. A new chef from Italy came aboard for 1990, adapting an extensive menu that already was ambitious: ten pastas, vodka scallops, cioppino, sauteed duck with garlic in a creamy brie sauce, and osso buco. We'd start with the roasted garlic with sun-dried tomatoes and black olive sauce, or calamari stuffed with shrimp and cheeses. The rack of lamb roasted with garlic and basil also tempted. Who could resist a dark chocolate-hazelnut gelato mousse cake? Similar fare is pleasantly priced at lunch, and a cup of espresso is a modest $1.25.

Open daily, 11:30 to 11.

Marcie's Place, 30 Boltwood Walk, Amherst. (413) 256-0036.
International/Vegetarian. $6.95 to $13.95.
After the closing of Plumbley's Off the Common, Marcie Abramson transformed its large kitchen into an inviting cross between an American diner and a European cafe. A lunch counter with red swivel seats facing the kitchen and a long table are for communal dining. Privacy is afforded by tables with checkered cloths around the perimeter facing the walk in front and lovely gardens to the rear. The menu, billed as hearty homestyle cooking, changes every two weeks. Lunches are healthful and reasonable: hummus platter, salade nicoise, falofel or roasted eggplant sandwiches, Indian curry of cauliflower and peas or zucchini and feta cheese pancakes. Bouillabaisse is featured at both lunch and dinner, when many of the noontime offerings become appetizers and main courses could be Italian-style polenta, enchiladas and spinach crepes with mushroom-sherry sauce and roasted yams. The chef's complete meal might be carrot salad, coquilles St. Jacques en papillote and a pear crisp. The wines, beers and Italian aperitifs are most affordable.

Open Tuesday and Wednesday 11 to 8, Thursday-Saturday 11 to 10.

The Lord Jeffery Inn, On the Common, Amherst. (413) 253-2576.
American. $16 to $22.
Chefs seem to come and go at this venerable inn, but those in 1989 raised the culinary standards of an institution never particularly known for its food. In spring, Jonathan Marohn from New York took over the kitchen (and his wife the dining room). His ideas and his menu were exciting — too much so, apparently, to last. The vacuum following his departure was filled in October by Dan Mattoon, a Culinary Institute grad who trained in Vail and at the Ritz-Carlton in Naples, Fla. He expanded the menu and toned down the prices. Among entrees are brook trout with cranberries

and toasted almonds, roast duckling with mandarin-cranberry sauce, Swiss-style veal cutlet with dill-havarti sauce, breast of pheasant with roasted corn and wild rice pancakes, and tournedos of beef with mushroom ragout in puff pastry. Smoked trout and caviar ravioli, and duck rilette with orange-caper mayonnaise are likely starters. Dan considers his desserts more basic: cheesecake with grand marnier sauce and white chocolate mousse. The large square room is pretty in peach and white, each table set with floral china and a vase with one perfect salmon rose.

Lunch, Monday-Saturday 11:30 to 2:30; dinner, 6 to 9 or 10; Sunday, brunch 11:30 to 2:30, dinner 5 to 8.

Judie's, 51 North Pleasant St., Amherst. (413) 253-3491.
American. $9.95 to $15.25.

A trendy establishment with a glassed-in front opening onto the main street, a gray and pink color scheme, track lighting and colorful kites suspended from the ceiling, Judie's is theatrical in its menu as well as its decor. Billed "Hot Pops Now in Concert on Center Stage," it opens into a fanfold array of munchies ("first act"), burgers and so on through "center stage" to "grand finale." For all the cutesy nomenclature, the kitchen offers some ambitious fare, from curried chicken and Italian sausage salads to paella, scallops and shrimp alfredo, coq au vin with petite sirloin steak, and seven dishes listed under "now that's a garlic." The double croissant napoleon sundae is a popular dessert. There's something for everyone, and that's why most of Amherst seems to be here.

Open daily, 11:30 to 11 or midnight.

Seasons, 529 Belchertown Road (Route 9), Amherst. (413) 253-9909.
American. $9.95 to $15.95.

Two miles southeast of town in a large barn formerly occupied by the Rusty Scupper is this renovated place with new windows and an upscale decor (dark green banquettes, rose-colored mats and comfortable seating upstairs and down). The rear windows opening onto a deck give a fine view of the hilly countryside toward the Amherst College campus. A large menu covers all the bases, from seafood to prime rib to changing veal dishes. Shrimp and scallop scampi, salmon en croute, and steak diane are among the more unusual. There's an abundant salad bar, and the fresh rolls are studded with caraway seeds. The wine list is more varied and more reasonable than many, and desserts like triple layer chocolate cake and chocolate mousse are displayed on a cart. The young servers are outfitted in black pants, aprons and bow ties. A new light menu is served upstairs in the loft.

Dinner nightly, 5 to 10; Sunday buffet brunch, 10:30 to 3.

Northampton

★ Beardsley's Cafe-Restaurant, 140 Main St., Northampton. (413) 586-2699.
French, $15.95 to $19.95.

Harkening back to Edwardian London is this oak-paneled haven. It's a smallish place dedicated to the memory of Aubrey Beardsley, the father of art nouveau, and the entry is lined with many of his elegant works. Light filters onto the booths and solid oak tables through beautiful stained-glass windows, rescued by owner Nick Doherty from a salvage yard in Springfield. Here you'll find the best formal food in town. We enjoyed the chicken crepe, a succulent portion of osso buco and a lemony-flavored, super-moist cheesecake from an appealing, reasonably priced lunch menu. At night, Beardsley's dons heavy white linens and changes from cafe to restaurant. The house pate and mussels stuffed with garlic butter and bread crumbs make good openers. Coquilles St. Jacques with saffron, steak au poivre, and duck with honey and Spanish vinegar are among entrees. For dessert, the white chocolate mousse cups and a flourless chocolate and bourbon layer cake come highly recommended. The wine list has more than 300 selections.

Lunch, Monday-Saturday 11:30 to 2:30; dinner, 5:30 to 10; Sunday brunch, 10:30 to 3.

Eastside Grill, 19 Strong Ave., Northampton. (413) 586-3347.
Regional American. $8.95 to $13.95.

A relative newcomer at the east edge of downtown, this is considered the trendiest place in town, so trendy that Cajun was about to be back-burnered after its day in the flame. The look is contemporary in the multi-level dining room with chairs and booths, the bar and in the newly enclosed porch, which started as an outdoor cafe and now is spiffy with blue and white deck chairs. As for the menu, there's still popcorn chicken, blackened steak salad, Cajun burgers, Creole chicken, shrimp etouffee, paneed catfish and praline sundae, along with the newer sauteed duck salad, pastas, and grilled ginger shrimp and scallops, and the standard broiled scrod and mud pie. Enjoy a Philly steak sandwich for lunch, the seafood piquant or grilled pork chops with fruit chutney for dinner. There's a wide range of mix-and-match, both for palates and pocketbooks.

Lunch, Monday-Saturday 11:30 to 3; dinner nightly, 5 to 10 or 11.

Spoleto, 12 Crafts Ave., Northampton. (413) 586-6313.
Northern Italian, $7.95 to $11.50.

This downtown space opposite City Hall has been occupied by a succession of Italian restaurants, among them Hot Tomato's and Andiamo. In its latest incarnation it's named for the Italian festival, and keeps the previous configuration in two dining rooms, a take-out display case and a with-it menu. The only jarring notes were the unattractive green banquet chairs and the deuces lined up cheek to jowl alongside tables for four. We've heard tales of two-hour waits for tables on weekends, yet those who waited did not regret it. The freshly made pastas are sensational, as are the veal dishes, the fish, and the chicken rollatini with fresh spinach and fennel sausage. There are people who'd travel miles for the mozzarella appetizer garnished with sun-dried tomatoes and basil vinaigrette. Chef Claudio Guerra, who worked in Europe, is partial to desserts like Italian cheesecake and chocolate-hazelnut cake. The wine list bears a number of bargains. At lunch, you can't do better than the grilled chicken caesar salad or brodetto, hearty fish soup flavored with tomato.

Lunch, Monday-Saturday 11:30 to 3; dinner, 5 to 10 or 11; Sunday, brunch 11:30 to 4, dinner 4 to 10.

La Cazuela, 7 Old South St., Northampton. (413) 586-0400.
Mexican. $6.50 to $9.50.

The old Rahar's that one of us remembers fondly from his college beer-drinking days on forays to Smith has turned into perhaps the best ethnic eatery in an area of many. Proprietors Barry Steeves and Rosemary Schmidt, formerly of Kansas City, grew up on Mexican food and make sure it's served right. Among their authentic winners are chilaquiles, chilies rellenos, fajitas, and enchiladas de mole poblano, the house version of the national dish of Mexico blending chicken and bitter chocolate. The tortilla chips are fried daily. Most dishes contain zesty chilies, and come with both mild and hot sauces; for the ultimate in fire, ask for the Pequin chile sauce. The menu is one of the more sophisticated you'll find this side of the Southwest. The margaritas are knockouts, and five brands of Mexican beer go well with the fare. Sunday brunch brings a panoply of interesting Mexican egg dishes. The decor is contemporary with soft adobe colors and striking Southwestern art.

Dinner, weekdays 5 to 9 or 10; weekends, brunch 11 to 3, dinner 3 to 9 or 10.

Sze's, 50 Main St., Northampton. (413) 586-5708.
Chinese. $7.95 to $13.95.
There are those who think Sze's has slipped under new chefs, playing second fiddle for food to the Panda Garden (part of a popular area chain) around the corner. But we like our food with a semblance of decor, and Sze's has it: an elegant and contemporary space in pink and burgundy, with sleek chairs and wood floors. Harry and Kathryn Sze offer Szechuan and Mandarin favorites by the numbers, 86 at last count. Peruse the menu and share such delights as yung-yung shrimp, ginger duck, stir-fried lamb, governor's chicken with hot peppers and peanuts, sweet and pungent fish, or sliced veal with bamboo shoots and more. If you don't like to make choices, come for the Sunday brunch buffet. The restaurant's success has spawned a similar venture at 456 Sumner Ave., Springfield.
Lunch, Monday-Saturday 11:30 to 3; dinner nightly to 9:15 or 10:45; Sunday brunch, 11:30 to 3.

Paul & Elizabeth's, 150 Main St., Northampton. (413) 584-4832.
Natural Foods. $5.95 to $11.95.
Thorne's Marketplace, a warren of shops in a recycled department store, is the locale for this well-respected natural foods restaurant, basically vegetarian but offering fish as well. It's a large room with exposed pipes, Japanese-style paper globe lights and daisies on the tables, with an old cast-iron stove as a focal point. At lunch you could try a hummus or tabouli salad, an omelet, or vegetables tempura. Whole grain noodles are the main ingredient in some of the evening dishes — with fried tofu and fish or vegetables tempura. Scallop and shrimp tempuras are the most expensive dinner items. The antipasto platter for two with marinated fresh fish and vegetables is an appealing starter. Indian pudding, mocha custard and fresh fruit crunches are some of the desserts. Herb tea by the pot is available; so are wine and beer.
Open Monday-Saturday, 11:30 to 9:30.

North Star, 25 West St., Northampton. (413) 586-9409.
Seafood. $8.75 to $15.95.
Front windows filled with sand and fake sea creatures (a glass lobster, for one) tell you that this has got to be a seafood restaurant. The Chinese god of the North Star is the god of higher education for women, a meaningful coincidence when you realize that Smith College is nearby. Enter through a large bar with a prominent new dance floor where disco reigns after 10; choose either the colorful outdoor terrace or two serene, Orient-inspired dining rooms with blue cloths, a tulip in a white vase on each table, and comfortable cane and chrome chairs. The sushi here is outstanding; several kinds are available as a platter or a la carte. Dinner entrees embrace everything from shabu shabu, swordfish and poached Norwegian salmon to eight shrimp concoctions, one of them Indian. A few vegetarian and meat dishes appeal to those who don't want seafood, and international coffees become prominent as the deejay warms up and the dance club takes over.
Dinner, Tuesday-Sunday 5 to 10.

Brewster Court Bar & Grill, 11 Brewster Court, Northampton. (413) 584-9903.
American. $8.95 to $13.95.
Come for a smooth golden or amber beer or a hearty stout, brewed here in the oil-company-turned-Northampton Brewery. Sit on the outdoor deck (try not to face the hulking parking garage behind Thorne's Market) or inside around a semi-circular bar or a round balcony overlooking all. There's plenty of snack food (pan-blackened Easthampton kielbasa and fiery chicken wings), Greek salad, many sandwiches,

Pioneer Valley

burgers, pizzas and, after 4 p.m., pasta, fish of the day, and grilled chicken and steak. The beer goes down ever so smoothly in pints, twelve ounces or "shorts" (seven ounces), and it's available only here.

Open Monday-Saturday 11:30 a.m. to 1 a.m., Sunday 1 to 1.

Plainfield

The Restaurant at Cummington Farm Village, South Street, Plainfield. (413) 634-5551.
New American. $11 to $18.

Part of a cross-country ski resort with a new inn whose guest rooms were fashioned from lofts and stalls that once housed cows and horses, this restaurant opened in the fall of 1989 on the lower floor of an old dairy barn. Inside, you'd hardly guess its heritage, given the room's elegant decor: rounded oak chairs, burgundy tablecloths, candlelight and fresh flowers. A large fireplace takes away any chill. An all-you-can-eat weekend brunch and all-you-can-eat theme buffets highlighting a different cuisine each Thursday night are featured. The regular dinner menu might include pan-fried trout with toasted pecans and riesling sauce, salmon stuffed with shrimp and halibut mousse, smoked roasted pork loin with a sauce of three-colored peppercorns and cranberry relish, grilled duck breast and leg with a black currant sauce, and grilled filet mignon with mushroom-cabernet sauce. Favored starters are Vermont cheddar cheese soup, crisp apple and potato pancakes with smoked salmon and chive creme fraiche, and grilled leeks and goat cheese served on field greens dressed with walnut oil.

Dinner nightly, 6 to 9:30; Saturday and Sunday brunch, 11 to 2:30.

South Hadley

Windows on the Common, 25 College St., South Hadley. (413) 534-8222.
American/Continental. $9.95 to $15.95.

The centerpiece of the sprightly new Village Commons complex across from the Mount Holyoke College campus produced this badly needed restaurant in 1988. The folks who own the locally popular Depot restaurant in Northampton are responsible for Windows, the eclectic Fedora's Tavern frequented by collegians downstairs, and the Cream of the Crop ice cream parlor at the side. The formal dining room is bright and cheery in cherry with curved banquettes and willowware china; its casual companion is lovely in teal and polyurethaned rattan and wicker, with decorative baskets all over the walls. The menu runs from scallops casino and veal italiano to duck teriyaki and prime rib, a house specialty. Shrimp primavera, halibut New Orleans and porterhouse steak are other possibilities. Can't decide? Go for the sirloin with shrimp and scallops provencale combo, or the prime rib with lobster en croute. The appealing wine list contains a page of chardonnays, some new to us and nicely priced. Pub fare and ice cream drinks are among the offerings of **Fedora's Tavern,** a stylish addition enlivening a stylish establishment.

Lunch, 11:30 to 2; dinner, 5 to 9 or 10; Sunday brunch.

Holyoke

The Delaney House, Route 5 at Smith's Ferry, Holyoke. (413) 532-1800.
American/Continental. $11.50 to $17.25.

This landmark alongside the Connecticut River and visible from I-91 was totally refurbished to the tune of several million dollars for a grand reopening in 1989. No expense was spared by owners George Page Jr. (of Page's Loft at the Northampton

Hilton) and chef Edward Klinger. Guests arrive through a wide doorway of beveled glass into a reception hall with an oriental rug and a sign noting jackets are required in the dining room. Ahead is a clubby lounge with upholstered chairs and a curving bar, to the left a directory showing the night's functions, and to the right four dining rooms seating up to 225. Typical is the Library, where swagged draperies cover the windows and tables are appointed with oversize, maroon-rimmed service plates with the Delaney logo at the top, swirled matching napkins, shaded oil lamps, heavy silver, and leather and upholstered chairs. The elegant theme is the same but the colors change in the Solarium with a fireplace, the Living Room, and the chandeliered Verandah. Could the food possibly match the setting? The kitchen certainly tries, with a wide range of options, from gourmet meatloaf to roast rack of lamb, from roast pheasant to veal forestiere, from baked scrod to lobster regale (a 2 1/2-pounder surrounded by mussels, clams, shrimp, scallops and onion rings for $29.95). "Delaney's Dilemma" gives a choice of any two of nine petite portions for $15.95. Still undecided? Choose any three appetizers as a full meal for $14.95 and get a house salad as well. Among desserts are poached pear frangipane, frozen lemon mousse, English trifle, chocolate mocha charlotte, and tirami su.

Dinner, Tuesday-Saturday 5 to 10, Sunday 4 to 9:30.

Yankee Pedlar Inn,1866 Northampton St., Holyoke. (413) 532-9494.
Continental/American. $11.95 to $17.95.

There's an incredible ramble of rooms in this local institution that's run by the Banks family, as you're reminded at every turn. There's piano music in the Gilded Cage Lounge, next to the dark and beamed Ye Tavern dining room built in 1785, where pewter service plates bear the Banks family's inn symbol. To the side is an enormous enclosed porch in pink and green, full of garden furniture. Downstairs is **Simone's**, a country French restaurant serving weekend prix-fixe dinners, and somewhere is the **Oyster Bar** that is open from 7 a.m. to midnight. The food is a blend of continental and traditional New England, from chateaubriand to lobster pie, tortellini alfredo to roast duckling with cranberry chutney. Relishes, salad and French bread come with. Deep-dish apple pie heads the dessert list, though you may be so well fed you won't have room. Oh, yes, an old-fashioned New England breakfast buffet is served Sundays from 11 to 2 in the **Opera House**.

Open daily, 7 a.m. to 10 p.m.

The Log Cabin, Easthampton Road (Route 141), Holyoke. (413) 536-7700.
New England. $9 to $21.

From the cocktail terrace outside this sprawling log building atop Mount Tom, you can see much of the Pioneer Valley. Besides the view, the home-cooked food — and lots of it — are the draws in an area partial to both. Five dining rooms seat 400, fresh flowers and greenery are everywhere, and the atmosphere is cozy if at times hectic. Starting with assorted relishes and breads, there is so much food one wonders how the average person can eat it all. When we dined en famille, we were offered a choice of both appetizers and soups, included in the price of the entrees, and found that a finger bowl followed the sauteed frog's legs. The extensive dinner menu, printed daily, offers such comfort food as calves liver, finnan haddie, broiled scrod, lobster and roast beef, plus more exotic items like langoustinos thermidor and lobster savannah. Family-style vegetables accompany. You can start with smoked salmon, chicken rice soup or tomato juice, and finish with Indian pudding or strawberry Jell-O. The food and the atmosphere are perfect for a family's Sunday dinner.

Lunch daily, 11:30 to 3; dinner, 5 to 10, Sunday noon to 10.

Chicopee

★ Michael's Restaurant, 85 Montcalm St., Chicopee. (413) 532-2100.
New French. $13.95 to $21.95.

Robert Provost and family had run a banquet house called Chateau Provost before son Michael opened an aspiring French restaurant in 1984 in a front addition at the edge of Chicopee (which edge we're not really sure, for we got hopelessly lost coming and going, but we think we were closer to downtown Holyoke and Mount Tom than to Chicopee Center). The new digs are stylish: a two-level dining room appointed with subdued wallpaper above rich wood wainscoting and well-spaced tables dressed in white and burgundy, each with a bud vase holding a couple of roses and carnations. A pianist plays on weekends, the enthusiastic young staff is in formal black and white, and the atmosphere is altogether appealing. New chef-partner Michael Beriau, a Culinary Institute grad who helped the New England team win a gold medal in the 1988 Winter Culinary Olympics, oversees an inspired menu of original dishes, artfully presented. The ten entrees include filet of sole stuffed with salmon mousse and garnished with lobster sauce, grilled salmon and swordfish with a warm smoked shellfish salad, breast of chicken pancetta, pork medallions with tri-colored peppercorns and poached apples, and twin tournedos filled with lobster mousse. Pay special attention to the night's specials — when we were there, one was slices of roast lamb loin interspersed with brunoise of red peppers and centered by a four-inch-high custard-baked potato garnished with rosemary. A slice of broccoli and shredded zucchini, carrots and summer squash fanned out from a wedge of acorn squash accompanied the night's entrees. Shrimp and crabmeat bouchees flamed in brandy, Tuscan scallops flamed in anisette, and duck liver pate are worthy openers. Finish with a flourish: bananas flambe, strawberries romanoff or crepes suzette, prepared tableside. The wine list harbors good values. Fans wonder how they can offer so much for the price. The energetic Provost family was planning to add a patisserie-cafe in 1990.

Lunch, Tuesday-Friday 11:30 to 2; dinner, Wednesday-Saturday 5:30 to 9:30 or 10.

Springfield

★ Johann's, 73 Market St., Springfield. (413) 737-7978.
European/Indonesian. $8.25 to $17.75.

This has been the hottest ticket on the Springfield dining scene since Dutch-born chef Johann DeVries and his wife Leslie left the Student Prince, where he had been in the kitchen for 26 years, to open a place of their own. Little wonder that tables are hard to come by. The prices are low, the standards high, the atmosphere on the elegant side, and much of the menu is exotic. A wide wall of mirrors facing the arriving patron makes this downtown retreat appear twice the size that it is. There are seats for 120 or so in a lineup of booths against the mirrors and at white-linened tables (every other one covered, inexplicably, with a glass top). Four large brass chandeliers, beige floral-print wallpaper, blue plates on the walls, and a prominent reception desk dressed in tiles complete the scene. The oversize menu is staggering: 49 entrees at last count, plus nightly specials, with new ones added after every one of the restaurant's theme festivals (St. Nicholas Night in December, gouda cheese in February, tulips in April). The Student Prince's Teutonic heritage has been embellished here with French, Dutch and Indonesian accents. The house specialty appetizer (also available as a main course) is sambal oedang, an Indonesian hot and spicy shrimp dish prepared tableside, as are the spinach and caesar salads. Warm gouda bread stuffed with cheese, Malaysian shrimp and spinach soup, homemade pate, shrimp or beef bitterballen, sauerkraut balls, and home-cured gravlax are other trademark starters. As for entrees, suffice to say there are seven veal presentations, from wiener schnitzel to gypsy veal goulash; eight of pork, including a Dutch platter combining smoked sausage, Johann's homemade sausage, and smoked pork chop; seven Indonesian specialties, and a mix of tradition and exotica like coquilles St. Jacques and calves liver sauteed with Dutch bell peppers and chile powder. Much of the wine list charts unfamiliar territory, at wallet-pleasing prices. The dessert domain is Leslie's. You might find chocolate brownie cheesecake, cinnamon date-nut strudel, apple flappen, pears helene, and amstel-ginger cake.

Lunch, Monday-Friday 11 to 4; dinner, Monday-Saturday 4 to 10 or 11. Reservations advised.

The Student Prince and The Fort, 8 Fort St., Springfield. (413) 734-7475.
German/American. $8 to $17.

A downtown institution for 55 years, this is beloved for its ambience, its endearing service, and prices from yesteryear. A fascinating collection of beer steins, plates and clocks adorns the bar where wooden booths stand tall, the main dining room with tables close together, and the Heidelberg room for overflow. All told, 300 can be accommodated at once, and the tables turn over constantly. Third- and fourth-generation regulars were occupying them the crowded night we were there. Owner Rudy Scherff oversees a tight ship that rarely changes. The menu runs the gamut from such European dishes as hasenpfeffer, jaeger schnitzel, bratwurst, Hungarian beef goulash and broiled tripe to lobster newburg, baked stuffed shrimp, stuffed veal steak and filet mignon rossini, delivered variously with sides of red cabbage, buttered noodles, potato dumplings, sauerkraut and the like. Salads and continental-style vegetables are extra. German beers and wines head the beverage list. German pancakes and crepe suzettes are flamed tableside; otherwise the desserts are standard, like parfaits, sundaes and Indian pudding.

Open daily, 11 to 11.

Springfield's on the Park, 232 Worthington St., Springfield. (413) 787-1522.
Continental/American. $10.95 to $15.95.

Former Hartford restaurateur Walter O'Halloran commissioned a large, striking mural of downtown Springfield, as viewed from across the river, for the long wall of this venture he opened in 1988. The main floor, part of it two stories high, is a quiet lounge. Dining is on a mezzanine, which affords a view of the mural as well as Duryea Way and the tiny park outside. The mezzanine is pleasant with subdued lighting, white linens, gray napkins and posters on the brick wall. The limited menu includes changing stir-fries, pastas and fish dishes, as well as seafood flamed in brandy and served over tri-colored pasta, pork tenderloin normandy, veal oscar, and filet mignon. Homemade avocado-buttermilk and honey-mustard dressings grace the house salad. Start with a trio of fried cheeses, fried calamari or Cajun shrimp cocktail. Likely desserts are chocolate-amaretto cake, Boston Irish mint cake, raspberry torte and oreo ice cream pie.

Lunch, Monday-Saturday 11:30 to 3:30; dinner, 5 to 10 or 11. Closed Sunday.

T.D. Smith's, 57 Taylor St., Springfield. (413) 737-5317.
Seafood Grill/Caribbean. $6.95 to $14.95.

A big neon "diner" sign and green palmetto trees stenciled on the path point the way to this, "the finer diner," renovated and re-themed in 1989. The Donald Watroba family, who run three area seafood houses, acquired the building in 1984 as a nightclub, then turned it into a 1950s diner before going upscale with a tropical bar, grilled seafood and a Caribbean theme. The menu features diner fare with a twist

Pioneer Valley

— meatloaf that is chargrilled and roast turkey with garlic mashed potatoes and gravy. The open grill at the rear produces barbecued shrimp and scallops, Caribbean swordfish, mesquite chicken with raspberry sauce, porterhouse steak, and grilled lobster tails. Burgers, sandwiches, pockets, grilled vegetables, and fried seafood are also on the all-day docket. The entire menu is available to go, though you'd likely not be able to go far after partaking of the T.D. Shipwreck, an island punch served for two in a shallow, beached boat with mast ablaze. The casual, contemporary decor is a mix of booths and bare gray tables, tiled floor, votive candles, and lots of neon portraying waves, stars and palms. A 550-pound aquarium helps separate the dining room from the greenhouse bar alive with palm trees, mirrors and twinkling lights, and what the manager called foreground music.

Open daily, 11:30 to 11:30.

Grill Room, Springfield Marriott Hotel, Vernon and Columbus Streets, Springfield. (413) 781-7111.
American. $11.95 to $21.

The downtown Marriott upgraded its restaurant in 1989, creating a typical hotel dining setting with nautical and sea life prints, upholstered chairs, and well-spaced tables, each topped with white cloths, dusty-rose fanned napkins and oil lamps with pink shell shades. The menu runs from grilled chicken, duck, swordfish and rack of lamb to chicken oscar, steak diane, and veal chop stuffed with fontina cheese and mushroom ragout and served with framboise sauce. The grill stick with marinated beef, chicken and vegetables, and seafood cocktail are favored appetizers. The dessert cart at the serving pedestal in the center of the room yields strawberries in grand marnier in a pastry tulip, chocolate chambord cake, marble cheesecake, and chocolate mousse pie. Light fare is available in the adjacent **Oyster Bar**.

Lunch, Monday-Friday 11:30 to 2; dinner nightly, 5 to 10 or 11; Sunday brunch, 11 to 2.

West Springfield

Hofbrauhaus, 1105 Main St., West Springfield. (413) 737-4905.
Bavarian/Continental. $10 to $23.

Established in 1935, the same year as the better known Student Prince just across the Connecticut River, this has as loyal a following and more style, both in the cooking and the surroundings. The interesting menu features kassler rippchen (pork chops with German fried potatoes), chicken paprika, wiener schnitzel, veal shank with red cabbage and spaetzle, veal cordon bleu, beer batter shrimp, roast goose with chestnuts and lingonberries, and, the most expensive dish, rack of spring lamb carved tableside. Goulash soup, marinated herring, herbed clams, Austrian pasta with Black Forest mushrooms and smoked bacon in a cream sauce, and a combination plate stand out on the lengthy list of appetizers. For dessert, how about homemade apple strudel, black forest cake, sacher torte, or bavarian cheesecake? The nicely priced wine list is mainly German. Beer tankards in cases and shelves, plates and paintings decorate three dark-walled dining rooms, very European looking with beamed ceilings, solid red leather chairs and well-spaced, white-linened tables.

Lunch, Tuesday-Friday 11:30 to 2:30; dinner, 5:30 to 9, Saturday 5 to 10. Closed Sunday and Monday.

The Gathering, 1068 Riverdale St., West Springfield. (413) 781-0234.
Steaks/Seafood. $10.75 to $15.75.

The epitome of its kind, this decade-old steakhouse packs in the crowds (particularly the younger set) for prime steaks and roast beef prepared by a meatcutter in house, standard seafood dishes, and light fare like chicken barbecue and sirloin teriyaki. A new menu lists fried seafood, singly or in combination, and the night's specials might add fettuccine primavera with scallops, porterhouse steak and green beans amandine. Homemade breads are among items at the enormous salad bar, which is divided into sections for regular, caesar and spinach. Desserts run to mud pie, creamy cheesecake, deep-dish apple pie, and chocolate decadence. Walls, stained glass and plants help divide the 200-seat space into more intimate groupings of dark booths and shiny wood tables with green napkins.

Dinner nightly, 4:30 to 10 or 10:30, Sunday to 9.

Agawam

Federal Hill Club, 135 Cooper St., Agawam. (413) 789-1267.
Continental. Table d'hote, $22.75 to $35.75.

Run by the Moretti family for 53 years, this stately, porticoed establishment that looks like an antebellum mansion shed its private-club status in the early 1970s and has been quietly open to the public since. It retains its clubby grace and feel, however. There's no menu, and no prices are mentioned. The courtly maitre-d simply joins each table briefly, recites the day's rather lengthy menu (which fortunately, under the circumstances, is straightforward and familiar to most), and makes note of the party's selections. A team of waiters then serves up a five-course dinner, starting with the "first course," a choice perhaps of clams or oysters on the half shell, shrimp cocktail, fresh fruit cup with sherbet, marinated artichokes, or filet of herring with sour cream. The "second course" is a soup, New England clam chowder, minestrone or chicken consomme, or a pasta, perhaps lasagna, linguini a la marinara, homemade cannelloni or a house specialty, tagiatelle verde with sauce bolognese. Following salad, the entrees could be chicken breast, roast duckling a l'orange, broiled lamb chops, rib roast, filet mignon, veal in four guises (parmigiana to marsala), lemon sole in five versions, scallops, swordfish with bearnaise, and oysters mornay, accompanied by a choice of three vegetables. The dessert cart may yield pecan or apple pie, cheese or lemon tarts, chocolate mousse, assorted cookies, or strawberry parfait. The wine list is one of the area's best, priced from $10 into the hundreds. The long main dining room is properly club-like in an old-fashioned way, with upholstered, curved-back chairs at well-spaced tables bearing heavy white linens, service plates emblazoned with the club's logo, and small oil lamps. Subdued floral draperies and a few paintings, hung slightly askew at our visit, accent the walls.

Dinner by reservation, Tuesday-Saturday 4:30 to 9:30.

Longmeadow

The Glass Lily, 674 Bliss Road, Longmeadow. (413) 567-2080.
Continental. $9.95 to $17.95.

The founder of the Friendly Ice Cream chain has attracted a succession of high-end restaurateurs in an effort to complement Friendly's at the other end of his tony Longmeadow Shops mall. The latest is this, named for the etchings in the window of the front door. The setting is elegant: upholstered Louis XVI chairs at well-spaced tables on two levels, beige linens and fresh flowers, mirrored walls with tiny lamps in sconces, and niches filled with flowers. Chef-owner Joseph C. Stevens of Boston's Cafe Marliave family stumbled across the empty restaurant, reopened it and offers continental fare at appealing prices. Interestingly, the menu is the same as he produced a decade earlier as executive chef at Newton's famed Mill Falls restaurant; he finds local palates and prices ten years behind those in Boston. Dinner entrees start with broiled scrod maitre d'hotel and rise in price to rack of lamb, roasted in a mild curry-mustard marinade and served with mint jelly. Beef wellington, tournedos diane, baked stuffed shrimp with pistachio nut stuffing, veal marsala, and chicken kiev are among the offerings that have drawn acclaim locally. An inordinate number of burgers, sandwiches, salads and omelets comprise the bulk of the lunch menu. The wine list is unusual in that it groups its offerings by price — ten for $12, thirteen for $17, and so on up to $45.

Lunch, Tuesday-Friday 11:30 to 3; dinner, Tuesday-Saturday 5 to 10 or 11, Sunday 11 to 9. Closed Sunday in summer.

East-Central Massachusetts

West Brookfield

♥ **Salem Cross Inn,** Route 9, West Brookfield. (508) 867-2345.
American. $10.95 to $18.95.

Listed on the National Register of Historic Places, this gem among old country inns contains an attractive downstairs taproom, several dining rooms, interesting planters and tables fashioned from massive tree trunks, and enough memorabilia to warrant the offering of guided tours. Dating to 1720, it's run by the Salem brothers, originally from Syria. A crossed witch mark, emanating from Salem to protect inhabitants against the evils of witchcraft and found on the front door latch of the main house, gave the inn its name. For atmosphere, try to dine in one of the intimate rooms of the main house, where you'll find beautiful walls of wide-plank boards, some horizontal and some vertical, and a huge fireplace. A low, rough-plastered ceiling with dark beams enhances the large main dining room, its windows revealing a peaceful panorama of green lawns, trees and white fences. A basket of hot rolls and gooey sticky buns, followed by a relish tray with cottage cheese and three kinds of spicy relishes, arrives with the dinner menu. Appetizers are standard, except for a Middle Eastern specialty, a zesty hummus b'taheenie. Entrees include such specialties as sauteed pork tenderloin, calves liver and bacon, baked stuffed filet of sole ambassador, and fried scallops. With our dinners of broiled scrod and baked stuffed scallops came an herbed pilaf of Mediterranean rice, and a choice of steamed zucchini, peas, sliced tomatoes or boiled onions. Salad was a large bowl of crisp greens with the house dressing, a tart creamy Italian. A waitress went from table to table offering steaming hot ears of corn to anyone with room left to try. We refrained in order to sample the pie of the day, a mouth-watering bavarian cream, and the old-fashioned pecan bread pudding with fruited sauce. Worth a special trip in summer are the monthly outdoor drovers roasts featuring cauldrons of chowder and 300-pound beef roasts skewered in a fieldstone pit. From late fall through spring, hearthside dinners on most Friday evenings (prix fixe, $39.95) include a hay or sleigh ride, roasts cooked on the nation's only operating roasting jack, and breads from a beehive oven.

Lunch, Tuesday-Friday noon to 2:30; dinner, 5 to 9 or 10, Sunday and holidays noon to 8. Closed Mondays except holidays.

Sturbridge

Le Bearn Restaurant Francaise, 12 Cedar St., Sturbridge. (508) 347-5800.
French. $13.95 to $22.95.

In a refurbished Cape Cod house on a side street just off the main drag, this is a true and personal French restaurant, the unassuming kind you'd expect to find in the Gallic region of Le Bearn, where Rose Marty grew up. Inside is the handiwork of her family, who started Le Languedoc restaurants in Boston and Nantucket. Rose is the hostess and her husband Leon the chef, assisted by son Jean-Louis. The two small dining rooms are utterly charming with delicate stenciling and nicely spaced tables set in the French style with heavy silver on either side of a napkin folded horizontally, candles flickering in fluted glass holders inside gleaming brass containers, and a vase bearing three red roses. The menu is unabashedly old-country French; "I've been cooking since 1935 and am too old to change," said Leon in his French accent. The 30 entrees range from haddock meuniere to steak au poivre. The roast duckling finished tableside and other flaming dishes are most popular and patrons enjoy the show. A special might be cassoulet from the region where it originated. The Martys bake the baguettes that accompany the meal, as well as the dessert pastries, apple mousse and baked Alaska. The family points with pride to comments in their guest book, including one in their first year (1988) by Arlo Guthrie, who has a home in nearby Brimfield: "Great food, good time." What better tribute for a promising new restaurant run by old hands who care?

Dinner nightly, 5 to 9:30.

The Whistling Swan, 502 Main St., Sturbridge. (508) 347-2321.
Continental. $12.95 to $23.95.

This imposing white Greek Revival house built in 1855 has been restored by Rita and Carl Lofgren, who added to it an old barn to which they gave wonderful fanlight windows, enhancing the facade. Three fairly formal dining rooms occupy the original house; the barn holds the **Ugly Duckling Loft** upstairs. Outdoor dining on a brick patio under black and white umbrellas is offered in summer. The varied menus offer something for everyone: at lunch, omelets, salads (one of our favorites was marinated mussels and potatoes on spinach), sandwiches on various kinds of breads or croissants, stuffed potato skins, and many daily specials. The lobster bisque was heartier than most; combined with an appetizer of four huge shrimp in beer batter, served with two sauces, it made a fine lunch. The pasta primavera salad was more than one person could handle, with shrimp, scallops, peas, broccoli, spinach and more, on top of a mound of fettuccine and with a delicious basil cream dressing. Daughter Kim Lofgren makes the wonderful desserts: white chocolate mousse, macadamia nut pie, bread pudding with whiskey sauce, chocolate-almond pie, and creme brulee. At night, entrees range from Szechuan shrimp, swordfish au poivre and mixed seafood grill with a garlic flan to chicken madeira, veal with apples and calvados, and rack of lamb with fried artichokes and broiled tomato. An extensive menu from snacks and sandwiches to dinner specialties is offered in the airy upstairs loft.

Lunch, Tuesday-Saturday 11:30 to 2:30; dinner nightly, 5:30 to 9:30, Sunday noon to 8; Loft, II:30 to 11. Closed Monday.

Crabapple's, Haynes Street, Sturbridge. (508) 347-9555.
American. $7.25 to $12.25.

Located in the former Orchard Inn and opened in 1983 to accommodate the overflow from the historic Publick House, this is popular with families and singles — we encountered a lineup at 6:15 on a rainy spring Tuesday. Apples are the theme (down to bright red cloths and green and white checkered napkins). Scores of baskets (some bushel) and even a bicycle hang from the ceiling, Tiffany-type lamps brighten the booths, and a small area has booths separated by chicken wire and is decorated to look like a chicken coop. A covered outdoor terrace offers lunch, snacks and cocktails in season. Steaks, swordfish, coho salmon and burgers are grilled with mesquite. Dinner entrees range from southern fried chicken to stuffed shrimp. At lunch, you'll find many of the same items plus croissants, omelets, salads and such, including tourtiere, the hearty French-Canadian meat pie. Wines are pleasantly priced, and cranberry-apple wine is available by carafe or glass.

Lunch, Monday-Saturday 11:30 to 5; dinner, 5 to 9 or 10; Sunday, brunch 11 to 2:30, dinner 3 to 9.

Leicester

★ The Castle, 1230 Main St. (Route 9), Leicester. (508) 892-9090.
Continental. $20.50 to $33.95.

This highly regarded restaurant really is a castle — a gray stone fortress that you'd never guess evolved from a dairy bar. There's a moat at the entrance, enough armor and medieval paraphernalia to fill a castle, a great outdoor patio beside Lake Sargent, and food and wine fit for area royalty. Run by Stanley and Helen Nicas and their offspring for 40 years, it now seats 400 in the deluxe Camelot Room (with pewter service plates and hand-carved, high-back chairs that look as if they came from a castle) and various public and function rooms that carry out the theme. Stones and beams for the additions came from the old library, YWCA and Elks Home in Worcester, while carved plaques and iron gates on the patio came from Newport estates. Head chef John Nicas and a trained kitchen brigade of seven offer a short a la carte menu and three prix-fixe dinners, one of them low-cholesterol for $37. The regular prix-fixe dinner ($41) might include fettuccine with prosciutto, sun-dried tomatoes and fresh mozzarella, a granite, a main course of salmi of duckling with pears, currants and rosemary, a salad of grilled duck leg on greens with raspberry vinaigrette, and a sabayon Creole. The $57 prix-fixe game dinner adds lobster and mushrooms baked in pastry and a mixed grill of venison, pheasant and wild boar sausage. The regular menu starts with a hearty lobster-mussel bisque and the mille feuille of the day, in our case fresh warm blinis with salmon, trout, caviar and anise yogurt. Possible entrees are sauteed scallops with leeks and ginger, sweetbreads with mushroom duxelle, filet of veal mixed grill, steak au poivre, and roast rack of lamb persillade. Among fancy desserts are strawberry mille feuille, eggnog pie, English trifle, sabayon torte, and charlotte russe. The award-winning wine list is categorized by year, includes 109 cabernets, and totals 135,000 bottles. The patio beside the lake in back is positively Camelot on a summer's day.

Open Tuesday-Saturday 11:30 to 9:30, Sunday 2 to 9. Open weekends only in July.

Worcester

★ Struck Cafe, 415 Chandler St., Worcester. (508) 792-5660.
New American. $17 to $20.

This small, ten-year-old storefront cafe is considered the most innovative restaurant in the city. The walls are covered with works of local artists, and a huge and colorful rainbow climbs the side wall from the entrance and meanders over the ceiling and down the far wall at the rear. Table appointments are white cloths and blue napkins, votive candles, and fresh flowers in crystal vases. Jeff Cotter serves a mean martini in an oversize martini glass, and his wife Barbara oversees a kitchen with broad reach. "Soups from scratch" are hearty, Portuguese kale and roasted garlic and potato at our latest visit. The cooking is assertive, as in the night's three appetizers: three-cheese ravioli with a port wine and mandarin orange sauce, grilled quail stuffed with wild rice and figs and served with a pumpkin seed sauce, and a wonderful smoked seafood plate (trout, oysters and scallops served on a bed of greens with remoulade sauce and grilled breads). For entrees, how about sauteed medallions of veal layered with mushrooms, sweet red peppers and leeks; chicken caribbean served with papaya wedges, or sea scallops with a tarragon-pernod sauce? These come with such varied accompaniments as potato-zucchini cake and spicy red pepper relish, black bean and chile torta, or baked double-stuffed potatoes and a peach-lime chutney, all garnished with fruit. For dessert, we succumbed to amaretto mousse served in a flaky pastry shell topped with a big strawberry; you might try the chocolate mousse pie, rhubarb torte, or Bailey's Irish Cream chocolate-chip cheesecake. Every item on the lunch menu appeals.

Lunch, Tuesday-Friday 11:30 to 3; dinner, Tuesday-Saturday 5 to 9 or 10.

✱ Beechwood Inn, 363 Plantation St., Worcester. (508) 754-5789.
New American. $16.50 to $24.

This odd-looking, round red-brick structure looks like an oversize silo with windows but is an inn of distinction with 58 guest rooms. On the lower level is a new restaurant, which attracted the highest possible ratings from local newspaper reviewers upon its opening in 1989. The long, narrow dining room is light and airy with mirrors and windows onto a pleasant, black-umbrellaed terrace, where lamp-like heaters allow outdoor dining from March into November. While soothing, the room is rather nondescript: a mix of banquettes and upholstered chairs for 75, well-spaced tables with heavy white linens, black-stemmed glassware, black vases, black pedestal lamps, and a black and pale yellow color scheme. There's nothing nondescript about the fare offered by chef Chris Mohr, who came here after successful stints at the Simsbury 1820 House and the Norwich Inn in Connecticut. The dinner menu is reminiscent of those during his tenure at his former establishments. Printed daily, it might offer grilled swordfish with tarragon-horseradish butter, sauteed sea scallops with citrus-vodka cream, poached Florida striped bass with smoked salmon and lobster cream, roasted pheasant with shallots and tomatoes, roast duckling with raspberry-plum sauce, and medallions of venison with cassis and fresh huckleberries. Start with his signature soup, a butternut-crabmeat bisque, or the black bean soup with sour cream, sherry and red onion. Save room for dessert, perhaps Chris's favorite chocolate crepe filled with white chocolate mousse on a raspberry puree. The pricey wine list is sophisticated and service is flawless.

Lunch daily, 11:30 to 2:30; dinner nightly, 6 to 10, Sunday 1 to 8.

✱ Arturo's Ristorante, 411 Chandler St., Worcester. (508) 755-5640.
Northern Italian. $11.75 to $17.95.

We met this understated winner when it was thriving in a shopping center in West Boylston. It was preparing to move in 1990 to larger quarters at Chandler Square, but Arturo and Dianne Cartagenova assured us everything would remain the same. From Genoa, he "cooks light," stressing vegetables, herbs, light sauces and pastas. A lunch of grilled sausage with an inspired tomato and scallion sauce served on tri-color pasta and an assertive pasta genovese, accompanied by crusty breads and good salads, showed that he and his kitchen crew knew what they were doing. At dinner, try any of the wondrous homemade pastas made with semolina flour and brown eggs. Specials like salmon alla griglia and bistecca of the night supplement highly regarded entrees like veal marsala and sauteed shrimp in garlic. The dessert tray bears such delectables as hazelnut torte, lemon poppyseed cake, white and dark chocolate mousse and, our choice at lunch, an ultra-rich tirami su that cost more than the pasta special that preceded. The change in location allowed Arturo to expand his menu, adding more seafood, pizzas and grills, as well as seating capacity. At the end of a shopping center, the new Arturo's has seating for 90 in a quiet, understated room of warm woods, skylights, modern cushioned chairs, white tablecloths, and fresco colors of peach and dark green.

Lunch, Monday-Friday 11:30 to 3; dinner, Monday-Saturday 5 to 10 or 11; Sunday, brunch 11 to 3, dinner 3 to 9.

East-Central Massachusetts

El Morocco, 100 Wall St., Worcester. (508) 756-7117.
Lebanese/American. $7.95 to $15.95.

"If you cook with love, you can't miss," the late Helen Aboody used to say. The Aboody family has been cooking with love since 1945, first in a tiny place with two tables and two booths, and, since 1977, in a sprawling, palace-like structure poised on a hillside just east of downtown. The founders' eight grown children run a hugely successful operation that serves up to 700 people on a Saturday night in a luxurious two-level dining room overlooking the city. The Aboodys lavish as much attention on their Lebanese and American food as they do their customers, at prices so low as to be unbelievable. The traditional shish kabob is excellent. You can pick and choose among seven Lebanese dishes, or combine them in a "variety platter." Start with lamb soup and finish with baklava for a meal to remember. An outdoor terrace is popular in season, and the sunsets as dusk settles over the city are spectacular any time of year.

Open daily except major holidays, 11:30 to 10.

Tiano's, 108 Grove St., Worcester. (508) 752-8901.
Italian. $7.95 to $14.95.

An expansive place occupying the third floor of the restored Northworks complex, this was opened in early 1990 by Mitch Terricciano and partners from Cape Cod. There are marble floors in the entry, brick walls, upholstered chairs at well-spaced tables dressed in beige over white, abundant plants, exposed pipes beneath the high ceiling, statues here and there, and tall windows with a view of a pond. The opening menu included standard pastas and entrees like chicken with artichokes, capers and mushrooms, four veal dishes, and tournedos Tiano, with pate, madeira, oyster mushrooms, and eggplant croutons. Baked shrimp stuffed with spinach, prosciutto and two cheeses was the most expensive dinner item. Phyllo pecan pie, baba au rhum, and chocolate bags filled with white chocolate mousse were among desserts.

Lunch, Monday-Saturday 11:30 to 3; dinner nightly, 4:30 to 10 or 11.

Maxwell Silverman's Toolhouse, 25 Union St., Worcester. (508) 755-1200.
American/Continental. $12.95 to $19.95.

The first Worcester restaurant in a restored building, Robert Giordano's award-winner emerged in 1976 from the screw machine department of an old factory. Some of the machines could not be moved, so the dining room was built around them, and very nicely, too. More luxurious than most of its ilk, this has comfortable chairs at generally well-spaced tables, white linens, hurricane lamps, and fresh flowers in old beer bottles. A tool and die box contains the menu, which ranges from fried catfish and prime rib to sauteed rabbit au poivre and veal francaise. Carpetbagger steak, smoked duckling with a plum sauce, crawfish etouffee, turtle soup, and an appetizer of baked oysters are among the appealing dishes. The beer and wine lists are impressive, and there's entertainment and dancing after dinner.

Lunch, Monday-Saturday 11:30 to 2:30; dinner 5 to 9:30, Sunday 4 to 9:30.

Legal Sea Foods, 1 Exchange Place, Worcester. (508) 792-1600.
Seafood. $9.95 to $18.95.

This smart-looking, two-story establishment fashioned from the former police garage across from the Centrum is perhaps the nicest of the Boston chain. Downstairs is informal in blue and white, while the expanded upstairs is elegant and sedate, full of neat nooks and crannies in windowed alcoves overlooking a courtyard or the street. The huge menu offers the freshest seafood (delivered twice daily) —

the normal fare plus more exotic items like king salmon, shad roe, mako shark, soft-shell crabs, whole sea bass and such. Cioppino, lobster by the pound, blackened Cajun dishes and pastas are among the offerings. One steak and four chicken items are available for those who prefer, but we can't imagine coming here for anything but fish, the more exotic the better. The ever-changing wine list offers good specials. In season, the outdoor courtyard shared by the Legal and neighboring restaurants is packed for cocktails, appetizers and raw-bar goodies.

Open Monday-Friday 11 to 10. Saturday noon to 11, Sunday 1 to 10.

The Windsir, 7 Boylston St., Worcester. (508) 853-7713.
American/Continental. $11.95 to $16.95.

A cavernous place of elegance and diversity, this bears little resemblance to its earlier incarnation as Nick's Bar & Grill. All is serene with a vaguely oriental feeling in two large dining rooms with many booths, cane armchairs and striking china. The fare runs the gamut from wiener schnitzel cordon bleu and duckling a l'orange to baked stuffed shrimp and prime rib. Beyond the main dining room is a contemporary pub called **McDundee,** where bowls of popcorn are on glass-covered tables flanked by high-back booths or wicker chairs. Opened in 1989, it serves salads, sandwiches and entrees like chicken Eugenie, beef brochette, sausage cacciatore, and seafood and vegetable bouquetiere. All these items plus more are available at lunch, both in the pub and in the main dining room.

Open Monday-Friday 11:30 to 10, Saturday 4 to 10.

Thai Orchid, 144 Commercial St., Worcester. (508) 792-9701.
Thai. $5.95 to $12.50.

A large square room punctuated by columns and Thai statues, this is another of the restaurants across from the Centrum. It's also newer and more elegant than its companions, and more sedate since it's less crowded, Thai food not appealing to every taste (although we can't imagine why). The setting is occidental with a long western-style bar, but the decor is authentic, especially the "tea table" on a raised platform in the center, where one may dine, legs folded underneath, at low, intricately carved tables. The platform occasionally serves as a site for Thai dancing. All the standard Thai dishes are marked with asterisks from spicy to hot and spicy to *very* hot and spicy. You can experiment with conunk squid and curries, or settle for lemon chicken and vegetable stir-fries. The hot and sour salads intrigue. Prices are modest, ranging from pad Thai tofu to jumbo shrimp in a pot; most are under $10. A sampling of the Orchid's specialties is offered at lunch.

Lunch, Monday-Friday 11:30 to 3; dinner, 5 to 10, Saturday 12:30 to 10:30, Sunday 4 to 10.

The Sole Proprietor, 118 Highland St., Worcester. (508) 798-3474.
Seafood. $8.99 to $19.99.

Deliveries come twice a day from the Cape, Gloucester and Boston to its adjacent fish market, so you know the fish here is impeccably fresh. With its rousing bar, raw bar and couple of dining rooms packed, even at 5 p.m., its large menu, augmented by almost as many blackboard specials, and its reasonable prices, it has appeal to many. The decor is brick walls, bare tables, captain's chairs and stained-glass lamps. There are some chicken and beef choices in a cutesy section of the menu and, of course, hamburgers for children, but 95 percent of the customers order seafood, say the owners. At lunch, from the mesquite grill come things like swordfish on a skewer, baby coho salmon, monkfish, and tuna steak. At night, fish and seafood are mesquite-grilled, broiled, fried, steamed, stuffed or served in casseroles. A deluxe seafood platter and "a fine kettle of fish" both contain lobster. Smoked Irish salmon and smoked Cape bluefish were blackboard appetizers at our visit. Everything on the menu is available for takeout at the pricey seafood market.

Lunch, Monday-Friday 11:30 to 4,; dinner, Monday-Saturday 4:30 to 10, Sunday 1 to 9.

Firehouse Cafe, 1 Exchange Place, Worcester. (508) 753-7899.
American. $7.50 to $15.95.

The old firehouse was turned into a popular pub in 1984, but much fire memorabilia remains. The hostess station is in a fire truck cab, the large bar evolves out of the rear of a fire engine, the phone is in a red call box, and a fake dalmatian is perched atop a piano. The main dining room looks out onto a courtyard, where the full menu is served in season. The drink list is more elaborate than the menu, which lists appetizers, sandwiches and salads plus eleven dinner entrees, including three chicken, three pasta, two steak, and two seafood dishes. The greenboard specials may contain a few surprises like escarole soup, scallops and pea pods on rice, and chicken, broccoli and pesto with pasta.

Lunch, Monday-Saturday from 11:30; dinner from 4:30, Sunday from 5.

Whitinsville

The Victorian, 583 Linwood Ave., Whitinsville. (508) 234-2500.
New American. All Entrees, $22.50.

In a lavish house that Mark Twain would have admired, you can dine in the elaborate Victorian manner, surrounded by fancy furnishings and literature. There's the main library dining room, with faded oriental rugs, lacy white curtains, dark wood paneling, a fireplace, crystal sconces and red leather chairs. Off it is an enclosed sun porch, while at the other side of the grand entrance hall is a small dining room in blue and gold. This is the elaborate setting for hushed, candlelit dining at prices that are rather extravagant for the area — all entrees, from baked chicken stuffed with apricots, figs and cashews to lobster in puff pastry are $22.50; all appetzers, $7.50. You might start with smoked salmon raviolis or scallops and pesto on angel-hair pasta. Main courses could be grilled swordfish with a lemon-thyme beurre blanc, sauteed veal topped with goat cheese in a tomato-basil sauce, roasted duck with a sauce of dried Michigan cherries, and filet au poivre. Desserts run to chocolate grand marnier mousse layered with whipped cream, strawberry cassis over vanilla ice cream, blueberry brown betty, and apricot sherbet. Like the menu, the short wine list is priced for special-occasion splurges, for this is "destination dining," in the words of innkeeper Rick Clark. It has to be, for no roads on the map lead directly to Whitinsville. You're advised to call for precise directions.

Dinner, Wednesday-Sunday 5:30 to 9:30.

West Boylston

Nancy Chang, Routes 12 & 110, West Boylston. (508) 835-3663.
Chinese. $7.50 to $16.95.

When first-timers arrive at this stunning contemporary restaurant built in 1989, the hostess likes to tell them to head upstairs and look out the front window. What they see is a view of the Wachusett Reservoir through large windows from a chic dining room full of etched glass and brass, linened tables bearing delicate oriental vases and service plates emblazoned with the name Nancy Chang, and carved dark wood chairs upholstered in deep teal velvet. A grand piano occupies a niche at the top of the stairway. More dining tables and a good-looking lounge are on the main floor. Who is Nancy Chang? The name was made up by owners Ignatius and Theresa Chang, who run a jewelery store in Worcester. The food is Mandarin-Szechuan, and the menu warns that "those little dry red peppers in some of our dishes are very hot — so eat them with caution." The lengthy menu by the numbers covers the usual bases, from spring rolls to peking duck. A gourmet royal dinner is $24.95 per person.

Lunch daily, 11:30 to 3; dinner, 3 to 9:30.

Fitchburg

* One Cottage Square, 740 Main St., Fitchburg. (508) 343-4444. French/Continental. $12.95 to $18.95.

Don't be put off by the dingy storefront or the side entrance at the west end of Main Street near City Hall. Inside is a perfectly charming French-style bistro that started as a family operation. Now that his parents have retired, Christopher Gagnon runs the show. The long narrow room with striped awnings along the sides is intriguing. One side has four booths with a wall of mirrors; the other has wood tables with ornate white chairs. And upstairs, where windows look onto a landscaped mini-park, is a smashingly decorated cocktail lounge with small rugs adorning the walls and beige-cushioned rattan chairs and sofas that you can really sink into. By local standards, the menu is exotic: chicken with an extremely hot curry sauce, veal in lime sauce, scampi provencale, four kinds of baked fish with a cracker crumb topping, and renowned rack of lamb and steak diane. Among desserts are a seasonal concord grape pie that every year draws people from as far as Maine to take home for Thanksgiving and a bread pudding topped with bourbon sauce. The wine list is pleasantly priced. Special touches abound; we were impressed with the mass of carnations in a silver ice bucket on its stand one winter's day. A violinist plays during dinner on weekends.

Lunch, Tuesday-Friday 11:30 to 2:30; dinner, Tuesday-Saturday 5 to 9 or 10.

Ashburnham

* The Victorian House, 16 Maple Ave., Ashburnham. (508) 827-5646. Continental. $11.95 to $17.95.

There's no sign and the owners do no advertising. Yet customers are drawn by word of mouth from near and far to this treasury of Victoriana and good eating just south of the New Hampshire line. Prompted by their clientele, Fitchburg caterers Bob and Florence Saccone decided to open a restaurant. They scouted around and found a red-brick, mansard-roof house that was the payroll-reception office for the old Boston Chair Manufacturing Company down a side street in tiny Ashburnham. Since 1987, they've been pleasing patrons in two downstairs dining rooms with working fireplaces and in a larger room that runs the length of the second floor. The latter is especially pretty, all nooks and crannies with deep mulberry wallpaper, recessed windows, spotlit paintings of flowers, and tables dressed in white with fanned napkins. It's a lovely setting for the fare offered by chef Bob and his son Robert. You might start with the house pate of veal, pork and duck liver, a three-cheese terrine chiffonade, oysters rockefeller, or the cold or hot seafood samplers. The dozen main courses include seafood patisserie (in phyllo), scallops provencale, grilled skewered pork tenderloin Cajun style, medallions of tenderloin oriental, noisettes of lamb scampi, and roast duckling with a currant-citrus sauce laced with grand marnier. Daughter Lori Saccone does the desserts, perhaps fresh fruit trifle, mocha-caramel chocolate mousse pie, banana-praline parfait, or linzer torte with raspberry cream. The wine list is unusually affordable, with many priced in the low teens. Besides catering, Bob teaches cooking at the area vocational school, which accounts for the restaurant's limited hours of operation.

Dinner, Wednesday-Saturday 5 to 9:30.

Merrimack Valley

Chelmsford/North Chelmsford

Vincenzo's, 170 Concord Road, Chelmsford. (508) 256-1250.
Northern Italian. $10.95 to $19.25.

Occupying a large portion of an unassuming strip shopping plaza is Vincent Ciccerchia's highly regarded restaurant seating 120 in a variety of small rooms done up in brick, stucco and tile. His chef of Sicilian extraction was born in Brazil, which accounts for what he calls his "gourmet Italian, mix-and-match" fare. Veal is featured, especially the medallions sauteed with scallops and shrimp and finished with a sun-dried tomato butter. Another favorite is veal stuffed with roasted red peppers, prosciutto, spinach, cheeses and more, served in a zesty bordelaise sauce. If it's seafood you want, go for the scallops sauteed with basil, mushrooms and orange zest and flamed with grand marnier. Mussels over linguini and cheese-stuffed tortellini tossed with broccoli and prosciutto make meals in themselves. From the artichoke hearts stuffed with seafood to the cappuccino cake for desserts, this is a class act.

Lunch, Tuesday-Thursday 11 to 2; dinner, Monday-Saturday 5 to 10, Sunday to 9.

Bainbridge's, 75 Princeton St., North Chelmsford. (508) 251-8670.
American. $9.95 to $19.95.

In a restored woolen mill beside a narrow canal, this long, oval structure with six-foot-high windows on all sides is contemporary as can be. Whirring fans on the ceiling are reflected in the glass tops over the tables, a sight we find dizzying. But the mix of banquettes and tables, green and burgundy napkins, and etched-glass lamps is quite attractive, and the banners flying from the beams are colorful. The all-day menu offers everything from quesadillas to warm pecan duck salad, from oysters from the raw bar to Philly cheese steak sandwich. Entrees include smokehouse chicken with barbecue sauce, veal oscar, prime rib, and shrimp in diverse guises, from deep-fried to coconut, baked stuffed to oriental. Jambalaya and eggplant parmesan are listed among specialties. The cracked wheat bread with cinnamon-honey butter is baked fresh every day. Desserts include heath bar crunch pie and raspberry bash, a heavy chocolate cake with a layer of raspberry preserves and whipped-cream frosting.

Open Monday-Saturday 11:30 to 11, Sunday 10:30 to 9.

Tyngsboro

★ Silks, 160 Pawtucket Blvd., Tyngsboro. (508) 649-4400.
Nouvelle French. $17 to $27.50.

Named for the jackets and caps worn by jockeys, this is the glamorous restaurant in local developer Gilbert Campbell's new $10 million, 30-suite Stonehedge Inn, a self-styled grand (and showy) hotel modeled after an English lodge. Its owner breeds horses in Florida, and inn guests here may see horses grazing beyond the condos in the pastures on his 40-acre farm out back. In the expansive dining room with a greenhouse on two sides, all is elegant, from the pitched ceiling with wood paneling to the comfortable armchairs upholstered in striped fabric. Spacious tables are set with white linens, subtly patterned china, heavy silver, and hurricane lamps. European-trained chef Serge Wechseler oversees an ambitious, pricey-for-the-area menu. You might start with seafood and avocado ceviche, sauteed snails with garlic and hazelnut butter, or seafood ravioli with two sauces. Main courses are grouped "en sauces" or "les grillades." Among them are Norwegian salmon en croute with wild mushrooms, watercress and caviar sauce, veal medallions with morel sauce, roast rack of lamb with ratatouille, pork tenderloin with lime and ginger sauce, a mixed grill with three sauces, and chateaubriand for two. Nearly 200 selections are offered from a 7,000-bottle wine cellar. The changing desserts might include cappuccino mousse, bavarian cream made with seasonal fruits, and Silks' ice cream truffle — half chocolate, half pistachio, covered with whipped cream and topped with raspberry sauce. At lunch in such a pretty setting, the salad nicoise and tortellini with seafood are downright reasonable.

Lunch, Monday-Saturday 11:30 to 2:30; dinner nightly, 6 to 9 or 10. Jackets required at night.

Lowell

* La Boniche, 110 Gorham St., Lowell. (508) 458-9473.
French Country, $12 to $17.50.

Were we surprised to find this little gem in downtown Lowell? You bet we were, though Lowell is hardly a dining wasteland. Once this was a bar called Nicky's, which native son Jack Kerouac frequented. Now it's the creation of Anna Jabar and her original partner who was born in France. Boniche is an old slang word for maid. One of the two rooms is occupied by a long and handsome bar, at which we enjoyed a mouth-watering lunch. The soup of the day, white bean, tomato and escarole, was dotted with whole cloves of tender cooked garlic, and the pate (pork and veal with pistachios and raisins) came with apple chutney. The black pepper fettuccine tossed with garlic, tomato and mushrooms in a fresh basil cream sauce was merely sensational. The three-onion quiche of the day contained white and yellow onions and scallions, and the pizza provencale had a thick French bread crust topped with plum tomatoes, garlic, black olives and grated cheese. At night, you could begin with shrimp en croute or escargots in a dijon-tarragon cream sauce atop toasted French bread. Entrees include hot and spicy pan-fried shrimp on a bed of crisp vegetables, broiled sirloin with a ripe tomato, garlic and fresh basil sauce, and pork loin stuffed with mushrooms, zucchini and roasted red peppers on a sauce of garlic and sage. The wine list contains all French vintages. Chocolate-almond fudge cake and Anna's tarts like honey-almond, lemon or raspberry silk are among desserts. The long and narrow, high-ceilinged dining room has oak tables, pressed-tin walls, huge arrangements of flowers, etched-glass lights that look like saucers, and a handsome quilt hanging on the wall.

Lunch, Tuesday-Friday 11:30 to 2:30; dinner, Tuesday-Saturday 5 to 9:30 or 10.

A.G. Pollards & Sons, 98 Middle St., Lowell. (508) 459-4632.
American/Continental. $9.95 to $13.95.

In an area not known for trendy restaurants, Pollards was ahead of its time. It emerged in 1971 in a downtown building, with brick walls, bare pitted wood floors, niches filled with book shelves, beamed ceilings, and all the plants and bric-a-brac that one could imagine. Through on-and-off lunch service and salad bars, Pollards has endured. At our latest visit, there was no more salad bar that helped our kids stave off hunger some years back, nor was lunch available. The dinner menu is wisely limited, offering just over a dozen entrees from chicken teriyaki and veal piccata to shrimp scampi and steak au poivre. Pasta dishes include two with chicken or veal parmesan; among the combos are sirloin paired with, of all things, Boston scrod. Pollards keeps up with the times by offering starters like nachos and potato skins, burgers, and a hot chicken salad "right off the grill." For dessert, there are a multitude of cakes: white chocolate, amaretto, chambord, and chocolate mousse. The wine list is quite good and bargain-priced.

Dinner, Monday-Saturday 5 to 10 or 11.

Prince Grotto, 10 Prince Ave., Lowell. (508) 458-0621.
Italian/Continental. $9.95 to $18.95.
When locals refer to this as the spaghetti factory, they're not far off the mark. It's in an area called Spaghettiville, next to (and part of) the Prince spaghetti company, the largest pasta plant in this country and second largest in the world. The restaurant, too, is huge, having expanded over the years to seat 500 in a variety of rooms full of brick walls, wine racks, splashing fountains, niches and arches filled with statuary and urns, and pink-linened tables. It's all rather grotto-like, though far from dingy. Chef Adriano Orrao proudly showed off the vast kitchens, and paused to restart the enormous ice-cream machine. The leather-bound menu has been scaled down a bit of late, featuring veal, seafood, "Italian dishes" and, of course, pastas, most of them from the old school. You can stick to basics like spaghetti and meatballs or eggplant parmigiana, or splurge on veal oscar, rack of lamb and steak diane. Twelve flavors of gelati, spumoni with claret sauce, peach melba, and cheese cannoli are favored desserts.
Lunch, Tuesday-Friday 11:30 to 2:30; dinner, Tuesday-Saturday 5 to 10, Sunday 4 to 9.

Banners, 201 Cabot St., Lowell. (508) 441-3001.
American. $7.95 to $11.95.
Trendiness, 1990s style, arrived in Lowell with the 1989 opening of this establishment in the vast old Dye House mill tucked amid (and behind) a series of brick mills. They were going to name it the Dye House Restaurant and so advertised in the Yellow Pages, until marketing types prevailed and renamed it for the colorful banners that divide some of its booths and banquettes — or is it for the college pennants hanging above the bar? All is up-to-date with soaring ceilings, exposed pipes and lots of brick, rich wood, glass, and bare tables. The all-day menu caters to contemporary tastes. The Banners platter is a combination of potato skins, mozzarella sticks, broccoli bites and tempura mushrooms. The "three-vote chowder" took second place in the Lowell Chowder Festival before the restaurant opened; "we lost by three votes — wait til next year," the menu proclaims. Salads, sandwiches and burgers give way at dinnertime to a parade of seafood, pastas, chicken dishes, fajitas, Texas ribs, and oriental stir-fry. Fine casual, grazing food is this.
Open daily, 11:30 to midnight or 12:30.

Hugh Cummiskey's Restaurant & Oyster Bar, 26 Andover St., Lowell.
(508) 459-6765.
American. $8.50 to $18.95.
Trendiness also is evident in the renovation of this establishment, sleek in gray and mauve with pictures of fish on the walls, sconces in the form of shells, a raw bar at the entry, and a ficus tree in the center. It's named for the city's leading Irishman of the 19th century, whose spirit continues in the lounge. The oyster bar serves up shrimp, littlenecks and oysters Baltimore or Belon. You might also start with oyster stew, smoked gouda and tomatoes with pesto, or baked brie in phyllo with almonds. There are three pasta dishes, blackened chicken and roast of the day. House specialties — equal in number to the rest of the menu — include swordfish with soy and ginger, blackened tuna with pesto, seafood stew and those staples, baked scrod and fish and chips.
Lunch, 11:30 to 4:30; dinner, 5:30 to 10. Closed Sunday.

$ **Athenian Corner,** 207 Market St., Lowell. (508) 458-7052.
Greek. $4.75 to $14.95.
You want Greek food? This institution across the street from the Lowell National Historical Park & Heritage State Park complex claims the largest variety of Greek

food in New England. Locals and tourists alike head here for the $4.50 luncheon special, including soup, entree, and Greek salad or rice pilaf. The long, narrow room outfitted in white and blue has copper plates, dark beams and photos of Greece in a dapper atmosphere. All the Greek classics are offered, from spanakopita to baklava. The lamb shish kabob is the house specialty; it and the broiled kidney lamb chops are about the only items over $10, and the former just barely. Greek wines are featured on the wine list, and the live entertainment on weekends prompts some patrons to get up and dance.

Open daily, 11 to 11, Thursday-Sunday 11 to 2 a.m.

Himalaya, 45 Middle St., Lowell. (508) 937-9355.
Indian. $7.25 to $14.50.

In a city in which small ethnic restaurants are prized, this is a standout. Indian music plays in a fairly plain room with carved screens, native art and a turquoise color scheme. Vegetarian specials cover the gamut, up to a complete Thali dinner. Curries at lunch come at wallet-pleasing prices; one can order, for $2, five vegetable pakoras. At night try the fish masala or chicken biriyani, with saffron-flavored long-grain rice, nuts, boiled eggs, and exotic spices. Wash it all down with mango juice and end with kulfi, a creamy dessert studded with nuts.

Lunch, 11 to 3; dinner, 5 to 10:30.

The Speare House, 525 Pawtucket Blvd., Lowell. (508) 452-8903.
American/Continental. $9.95 to $16.95.

A wall of photos of local celebrity-owner Zenny Speronis with other celebrities greets patrons in the foyer of this institution furnished in ersatz medieval decor. Dining is in one vast, castle-like room in beige and red with a salad table in the center and walls of murals and stone. The lengthy menu bears traces of the owner's Greek heritage: stuffed grape leaves here, souvlakia there. But most items are predictable and comforting, like shrimp scampi, veal piccata, chicken cordon bleu, prime rib, and chateaubriand for two. Special vegetables and sauces are a la carte. The Speare House now offers swordfish and halibut grilled or Cajun style, but the rest of the fare harkens back to its beginnings 35 years ago.

Lunch, Tuesday-Friday 11:30 to 2:30; dinner, 4 to 10, Saturday 5 to 11, Sunday 3:30 to 9.

Andover

Rembrandt's, 18 Elm St., Andover. (508) 470-1606.
International/Mexican. $9.50 to $19.50.

A portrait of Rembrandt is in the foyer of this large, two-story restaurant run by Frans van Berkhout, who also owns Le Bellecoeur in Lexington. Reproductions by the Dutch masters and etchings by a Portuguese man hang on the walls of the upstairs dining room, sleek with cane and chrome chairs. The original 1808 ceiling beams, outlined in tiny white lights, bear all kinds of china and wooden ducks. The Dutch owner was in the process of adding Mexican dishes and more casual fare to his continental menu, which listed such specialties as shrimp, scallops and monkfish in a saffron-leek sauce over fettuccine, veal oscar, beef tenderloin wrapped in bacon, and roast duckling with a changing sauce. New England seafood hot pot, sauteed Idaho trout with an orange-basil butter, Indonesian chicken, lamb kabobs, and Szechuan stir-fry are other possibilities. Starters include Portuguese seafood chowder, escargots and Louisiana chicken fingers. Featured desserts are creme caramel, coupe Lydia made with coffee ice cream, brandy sauce, chocolate bits and whipped cream, and Swiss chocolate and grand marnier fondue.

Lunch, Monday-Friday 11 to 2; dinner, Monday-Saturday 5:30 to 10.

Merrimack Valley

Andover Inn, Chapel Avenue, Andover. (508) 475-5903.
Continental. $16.50 to $22.50.
This venerable inn in the thick of the Phillips Academy campus appears and feels very much like a private club. The dining room beckons the public with its elaborately draped high windows, lofty ceiling, huge mirrors, and crystal chandeliers. Not as foreboding as it sounds, the room is terribly suave in peach and green, each table set with Villeroy & Boch china, heavy silver, two wine glasses and a crystal water glass, a silver candlestick bearing a single tall white taper, and pretty bouquets in clear glass vases. The menu wastes no words in listing salmon oscar, tuna steak provencale, wiener schnitzel, veal scallops with apple cider and walnuts, roast duckling with orange sauce, pan-fried dover sole, loin of lamb with madeira rosemary sauce, and something called simply tumis. Appetizers vary from scallops with pesto fettuccine and mushrooms en croute with corn relish to shrimp cocktail and fresh fruit cup. Among desserts are Indian pudding, "pure fruit sorbet," apples devonshire, peach melba, and selections from the pastry tray. A traditional Indonesian rijsttafel feast ($21.50) is served Sundays by reservation.
Lunch, Monday-Friday 11:30 to 2:45; dinner, Monday-Saturday 5:30 to 9:30; Sunday, buffet brunch 11 to 2:45, rijsttafel 5 to 9.

Backstreet, 19 Essex St., Andover. (508) 475-4411.
American/Continental. $11.95 to $19.50.
Very popular locally is this small restaurant, dark and rich looking with brick walls on one side and a ceiling of cedar slats in a decorative pattern. Entertainment is featured in the lounge, but the adjacent dining room with tables topped with glass over pink over gray offers a variety of fare, from casual to complex. The menu ranges from prime rib to beef wellington, broiled lamb chops to chateaubriand. Five veal dishes and three each of shrimp and scallops are featured. Grasshopper pie, chocolate chip-pecan pie and chocolate grand marnier cup are favorite desserts.
Lunch, Monday-Saturday 11:30 to 2:30; dinner nightly, 5 to 11; Sunday brunch, 11 to 3.

Lawrence

Metamorphosis, 291 Essex St., Lawrence. (508) 689-0404.
International. $12.95 to $21.95.
From something of a hole in the wall in downtown Lawrence, this little-known but highly regarded eatery moved down the street in 1989 to new quarters. It's nicely ensconced upstairs in an airy old room with brick walls, dark wood, white linens, all kinds of lilies in clear vases, and windows onto the main street. A big butterfly over the bar and smaller ones on the aprons of the staff testify to the name. Interestingly, there's no silverware on the tables; that's served when the waiter takes the order. The opening menu was short but sweet: chilled strawberry soup, bacon-wrapped scallops, and mussels marinara among appetizers; medallions of veal with avocado and almonds, tempura shrimp, grilled rack of lamb on couscous with a side of dijon-red pepper sauce, seafood lasagna, and lobster, scallops, snow peas and mushrooms in puff pastry among entrees. Specials like oysters baked in garlic and topped with prosciutto supplement the menu. For dessert, try rice pudding with whipped cream, black forest cake, macadamia nut cream pie or ice cream crepe with strawberries in a warm grand marnier sauce. Downstairs under the same management is **Morin's,** a Lawrence institution. A more casual, diner-style restaurant and old-fashioned soda fountain, it serves breakfast all day and bargain lunch and dinner specials.
Open Monday-Friday 11:30 to 10, Saturday and Sunday 4 to 10.

Bishop's, 99 Hampshire St., Lawrence. (508) 683-7143.
Middle Eastern/American. $8 to $20.25.
It looks something like a mosque from the outside, which surprises those who don't know its Mideastern background and role in town as a special-occasion place of abundant food at reasonable prices. Bishop's was founded in 1938 by a Lebanese woman, who has run it with four of her children ever since. It moved in 1968 to its present site, where it seats 500 in one enormous dining room in black and white with black leather booths along the sides and a vaguely Mideastern feel afforded by spool dividers and hanging lights. Founder Sadie Bashara is still in the kitchen, overseeing the preparation of such Arabic specialties as hummus dip, tabouli salad, raw kibbee, and rolled grape leaves. We'd try the combination plates, available in various sizes, but the less adventurous would be quite content with prime rib, lamb kabob, baked stuffed shrimp, or sirloin steak. There's an extensive wine list of all countries and price ranges. After dessert (perhaps bilawee, sundaes, or baked alaska with strawberries), adjourn to the new downstairs odah (lounge) for music and dancing.
Open 11:30 to 10 or 11, Saturday and Sunday from 4.

The L.A. Grill, 2 Amesbury St., Lawrence. (508) 685-7055.
American. $8.95 to $16.95.
No, it's not Los Angeles. The L.A. stands for Lawrence-Andover, where Bostonians Jay Fallon and James Pagonis decided in 1989 to open their first restaurant. Once a 19th-century boarding house, the long, narrow building has been nicely renovated into three small, cheerful dining rooms with handmade tables topped with black vases of alstroemeria and pepper grinders, rattan chairs with comfy seats, hardwood floors, balloon curtains, and brick walls at the front and back. Grilled seafood is the specialty, from mahi-mahi and mako shark to marlin and swordfish. Co-owner Pagonis, who was voted Boston's best bartender in a magazine poll, touts the nachos topped with chicken or ground beef and the prosciutto with seasonal melon as starters. Pastas and sandwiches are available all day. Desserts are simple: ice cream, oreo cookie pie and New York cheesecake. The nice little wine list is better than many, probably because of Jim's background as a liquor distributor.
Lunch, Monday-Saturday 11:30 to 3:30; dinner, Monday-Saturday 5 to 9:30 or 10; Sunday brunch in winter, noon to 4.

Haverhill

Bayberry's, 1 Washington St., Haverhill. (508) 372-3110.
American. $7.50 to $11.95.
Transformed from the bar of an old hotel, this started in 1987 as a gourmet restaurant of some elegance on the main floor of Whittier Place in downtown Haverhill. In 1989, the menu was "redirected" to prevailing local tastes, according to manager Paul Gene Dion, who promised the same food quality at lower prices and casual dress amid the same elegance. The main dining room in pink and green retains the hotel look; more intimate are the Grill with butcher-block tables inlaid with tiles, etched-glass dividers between booths and an open grill, and the Gallery with spotlit artworks, more butcher-block inlaid tables and booths, and colored glass panes in the window. Twinkling white lights in the windows beckon passersby into the appealing, pubby lounge with a piano bar and entertainment. The dinner menu ranges from chicken teriyaki and baked haddock to garlicked shrimp and scallops over linguini, veal with asparagus and bearnaise, and filet mignon at prices so low as to make one blink. Along with such appetizers as nachos, fried mozzarella sticks

and potato skins, you might find tahini, a blend of chick peas, olive oil and garlic served with raw onion and Syrian bread.

Lunch, Monday-Friday 11:30 to 3:30; dinner, Monday-Saturday 3:30 to 9 or 10.

Bradford

Roma, 19 Middlesex St., Bradford. (508) 374-8001.
Italian-American. $7.95 to $14.50.

Rebuilt in 1989 after a fire, this has occupied a riverfront site facing downtown Haverhill for fifteen years, and is said to be the area's oldest restaurant. Long windows take full advantage of the river view in several dining rooms full of booths, a peach and green motif, and a vaguely Howard Johnson's look. More stylish is the lounge, where tables are set for casual dining. The Schena family oversees the whole operation. The menu lists "olde Roma favorites" and specialties, plus sandwiches Italian style, seafood and beef dishes. Veal saltimbocca, chicken florentine, pasta primavera with chicken, eggplant parmigiana, and chicken piccata are examples. These plus "waist-watcher specials" are available at lunch.

Open daily, 11 to 9 or 10.

North Shore

Winchester

Le Neuchatel, 14 Thompson St., Winchester. (617) 729-2008.
Continental/American. $12.95 to $19.95.

A Swiss theme prevails at this contemporary spot that formerly housed the Dover Grill. Helene Paquin, who hails from the Lucerne area, redecorated the once austere, three-tiered dining rooms in pretty pink and green. It's an expansive space, enhanced by lots of wood, plants and the stunning photos of Winchester photographer Arthur Griffin. Swiss tapes occasionally offer yodeling, and Helene's recipes inspired the menu, which she oversees with chef Stephen James. Six veal dishes lead the list of entrees, including the namesake medallions with morels in cream sauce. Other choices range from rainbow trout with fresh mushrooms and artichokes to poached Norwegian salmon with dill sauce, from sauerbraten with spaetzli to tournedos rossini. Start with the Grison delight (bunderfleisch with gruyere and cornichons), herring with mustard and dill, or clams casino. Finish with wonderful desserts like lemon sponge cake, white chocolate mousse, bread pudding with bourbon sauce, and a legendary torta from St. Moritz. The wine list is more reasonable than many in the area, and the list of international coffees is exotic. A half papaya filled with seafood salad, bratwurst with roesti potatoes, a mandarin chicken and pineapple salad, and a crabby shrimp sandwich are among offerings from the extensive lunch menu.

Lunch, Tuesday-Saturday 11:30 to 2; dinner, 5:30 to 9:30 or 10, Sunday 11:30 to 8. Closed Monday.

Ristorante Lucia, 5-13 Mt. Vernon St., Winchester. (617) 729-0515.
Italian. $14 to $33.

Really two restaurants in one, this offshoot of a Boston establishment must be seen to be believed. The main floor is a showplace in peach and white, with chairs trimmed in metallic gold, marble floors, hand-painted murals of the Sistine Chapel (though in this version everyone is clothed) and the Last Judgment, a lifesize statue of Michelangelo up on a platform painting the ceiling, a perfect rose on each table, and mirrors everywhere. Downstairs is **Pizza in Piazza,** a gourmet pizzeria and wine library described as a cross between an amusement park and a mirage. Here are more marble floors, marble tables covered with white runners, stars on the ceiling, and a wine cellar all around, with spotlit murals of Italy behind the shelves of bottles interspersed with statues. Wood-fired ovens cook pizzas from owner Filippo Frattaroli's native Abruzzi as well as from the nineteen other regions of Italy — a staggering 42 varieties in all, and each worth trying, according to those in the know. Big-spenders can go for the Torino from Piemonte, topped with mozzarella and truffles, but there are plenty of down-to-earth offerings as well. There's nothing earthy about the upstairs, where the prices match the reach of the oversize, twelve-page menu with a shiny cover that looks like marble and bears sketches of ingredients used in the food. Symbols of water pitchers from Abruzzi denote the house specialties, making the choice among fifteen veal dishes, for instance, a mite easier. The regional dishes are best, and unless you're shooting the works, you can probably skip the sides of broccoli or the radicchio and endive salads that would set you back a cool $9.50 each. The Italian ice creams and cakes are made in the Winchester kitchen.

Dinner, Monday-Thursday 4:30 to 11, Friday and Saturday 11:45 to 11, Sunday 2 to 10.

Maximilian's Cafe, 17 Converse St., Winchester. (617) 729-6035.
Regional American. $8.95 to $12.95.
Some serious restaurateurs scoff, but this large, mod-looking place and its sister in Needham are packed at all hours. And why not? The food is abundant and priced to move. Formica and oak tables, paper napkins, oil lamps, and lots of brass and plants mark the angled dining rooms. The all-day menu of salads, sandwiches, snacks, pizzas and the like is supplemented by the day's specials. They might range from New Orleans crab pie and catfish Creole to Savannah citrus sole, Hawaiian marinated steak and smoked Chicago ribs. Chocolate seduction, key lime pie, almond cheesecake, and brandied pecan pie are favorite desserts. It's not for serious diners, but then most people aren't.

Open daily, 11:30 to 10 or 11.

Danvers

Flash in the Pan Diner, 181 Newbury St. (Route 1), Danvers. (508) 774-9367.
New American/International. $13.95 to $16.95.
Hidden far back from the highway in a vintage 1940s diner (one that surely has seen better days on the outside) is this intimate winner with ten tables and a counter pressed into service on weekends. Mirrors make the place seem bigger and darkness helps, but the mauve and gray decor with white napkins is still updated diner-ish, with diner accoutrements stacked on shelves behind the counter. Chef-owner Patrick Belanger, formerly of Seasons and Restaurant Jasper in Boston, works wonders with a short, changing menu. From his small kitchen come entrees like poached salmon in champagne with tomato-basil-orange sauce, sauteed beef loin with parmesan and capers, a mixed grill of lamb chop, smoked pork loin and livers served with a spicy mustard, and Patrick's favorite, duckling marinated in soy and ginger with a homemade egg roll. Appetizers might include another favorite, scampi pie (shrimp, garlic, mushrooms and tomato in puff pastry), garlic custard with basil sauce, escargots over pasta with garlic and mushrooms, and stuffed grape leaves with an egg-lemon sauce. For dessert there likely will be variations on bread pudding, chocolate mousse cake, lemon tart with raspberry sauce, and chocolate torte with hazelnuts. The two dozen wine selections are nicely priced in the teens and twenties.

Dinner, Tuesday-Saturday 5 to 9:30.

North Shore

Ponte Vecchio, 435 Newbury St., Danvers. (508) 777-9188.
Northern Italian. $16.95 to $26.

Stylish as all get-out and with food to match is this family-owned newcomer in a shopping plaza. The hostess, the maitre-d and most of the staff speak Italian, so you know the place is authentic. What you may not expect is the subdued elegance, the dusty rose walls over pale green wainscoting enhanced by artworks, the mirrors, a divider here topped by magnums of wine, a pillar there to separate tables done up in white over mauve, and white lights twinkling in a couple of ficus trees. Tuxedoed waiters serve some inspired creations, perhaps medallions of veal sauteed in riesling wine with blackberries, poached salmon in vermouth sauce with pink grapefruit, beef tenderloin in barolo wine with polenta, and loin veal chop with garlic, rosemary and shiitake mushrooms in cognac sauce. Among antipasti are baked clams breaded with Japanese rice bread, garlic and oregano, a stellar carpaccio with shaved parmigiano, and Italian cured beef with Belgian endive. Pastas come in full or half portions and include ravioli stuffed with lobster, and gnocchi made of beets with sage and cream. Desserts are to groan over, especially a fresh lime tart, a flourless hazelnut torte, white chocolate cake with a raspberry mousse center, and the house specialty, tirami su. The extensive Italian wine list from various regions is priced up to $950.

Lunch, Monday-Friday 11:30 to 2:30; dinner, Monday-Saturday 5 to 11, Sunday 4 to 10.

Salem

★ Courtyard Cafe, 7 Summer St., Salem. (508) 741-4086.
New American. $15.95 to $23.

The basement of the Salem Inn is a fortuitous spot for two dining rooms with exposed brick and stone walls, a homey little waiting area near the bar, and an attractive brick-walled outdoor courtyard with many rose bushes and a zinc bathtub from 1880 planted with herbs. Stunning art by local artists — we coveted one of seashells for a cool five grand — creates a gallery feeling. Votive candles flicker in brandy glasses, classical music plays, and the setting is the match for some exciting cuisine. Veteran Boston chef-owner Anthony Young is in the kitchen and his wife Cynthia is out front. Anthony, who prepares everything himself, is into grilling: at our latest visit, all but one of the eight entrees on the menu that changes monthly were grilled, from breast of duck with a maple-pecan demi-glaze and fresh strawberries to rack of lamb with a warm tomato and rosemary concasse served over a nest of fresh butternut noodles. He adds European, Italian, Japanese and California touches, as in appetizers of grilled Szechuan sausage with sweet and sour cabbage or Japanese barbecued eel with wasabi and pickled ginger. His amaretto gelato mousse cake, chocolate torte with candied Turkish apricots, and heath bar rum truffle are to die for, and the exclusively West Coast wine list is superb. Anthony's diversity can be sampled at lunch, perhaps in a Greek salad with black olives stuffed individually with feta cheese or linguini with artichokes, sun-dried tomatoes and fresh oregano, which we savored on our last visit.

Lunch, Tuesday-Saturday 11:30 to 2:30; dinner, 6 to 10.

★ The Grapevine, 26 Congress St., Salem. (508) 745-9335.
Regional American. $10.50 to $15.50.

Some of Salem's more interesting fare is served in this restaurant that opened in 1988 in a former garage across from Pickering Wharf. Walk past the sleek bar, where there are a few tables and an espresso machine, to the rear dining room with a soaring ceiling, striking rows of bare light bulbs on the beams, and sturdy wood chairs at tables dressed in paisley prints. Beyond is a small garden for outdoor dining. There are some heavenly light pastas, but chef-owner Kate Hammond's specialties are dinner entrees like veal V.S.O.P., grilled salmon with fresh tomato salsa, grilled duckling on a bed of wilted spinach with grand marnier sauce, and local spearfish that, she says, "I can't get enough of to keep up with demand." Start with leek, potato and pesto soup, grilled oysters or grilled shiitake mushrooms served with garlic butter. Finish with cannoli stuffed with an amaretto-ricotta mixture or fresh raspberry and strawberry or kiwi sorbet. Interesting wines are offered by the glass.

Lunch, Monday-Saturday 11:30 to 2:30; dinner nightly, 5:30 to 10.

Nathaniel's, Hawthorne Hotel, On the Common, Salem. (508) 744-4080. American/Continental. $13.95 to $19.95.

Salem gourmands sing the praises of this elegantly restored dining room in the renovated Hawthorne Hotel. The setting is pretty in peach and green, with upholstered banquettes and chairs and brass chandeliers. Chef Steve Nelson is known for his grilled salmon with dill-hollandaise sauce, grilled veal chop with chanterelles, grilled breast of duck with cranberry-orange and bourbon sauce, and a fine bouillabaisse. Other entree possibilities are sauteed breast of chicken stuffed with chevre and herbs, baked scrod with lobster butter, and shrimp monte carlo. Strawberry-horseradish sauce accompanies the smoked trout appetizer; there are also a cassoulet of mushrooms with chevre and sauteed shrimp in almond cream, and a sampling of three soups. The pastry chef fills a mean chocolate cake with strawberry mousse and offers such treats as linzer torte and cappuccino cheesecake. We hear wonderful things about the elegant Sunday brunch buffet when a jazz trio entertains.

Lunch, Monday-Saturday 11:30 to 2:30; dinner nightly, 5 to 9 or 9:30; Sunday brunch, 10 to 2.

The Lyceum, 43 Church St., Salem. (508) 745-7665. New American. $9.95 to $14.95.

Founded in 1830, the Salem Lyceum hosted some formidable Americans, and history was made here in 1877 when Alexander Graham Bell demonstrated the first telephone, talking to Thomas Watson, eighteen miles away in Boston. In 1989, it closed for renovations and a change in menu under new owner George Harrington, formerly of Rosalie's in Marblehead. He upscaled the decor, restoring the original windows and adding carpeting and tablecloths to create a softer, warmer feeling in the pub, the main bar-dining room, and the rear enclosed patio with brick walls, large windows and skylights. The once-extensive menu has been scaled down and lightened up in presentation and price. The dozen dinner entrees might include grilled turkey cutlet with sauteed red onions and vinegar, broiled coho salmon with fried Sicilian capers, pork cutlet sauteed with cornbread crust and a spicy green tomatillo sauce, peppered grilled swordfish with diced tomatoes and lemon, black angus sirloin steak with cabernet sauce, and what George calls "my semi-famous London broil." Starters could be baked oysters with garlic butter and prosciutto, grilled scallops with pesto, smoked Irish salmon, and nicoise salad with fresh tuna kabobs. Regular desserts are caramelized bread pudding and raspberry-chocolate cake, supplemented by specials like cheesecake with kiwi sauce. The all-California wine list is priced mainly in the $12 to $15 range.

Lunch, Monday-Saturday 11:30 to 2:30; dinner nightly, 5:30 to 10; Sunday brunch, 11:30 to 2:30.

Soup du Jour, 7 Central St., Salem. (508) 744-9608. International. $8.95 to $16.95.

Creative soups, quiches, breads and specials are the fare at this rather spare, informal spot with brick walls and hanging plants. Patrons in two dining rooms can make their own salads, sample special soups like French onion, baked bean and tomato, potato-cheddar or New England clam chowder and three kinds of quiche, or luncheon specials like Mexican crepe or broccoli strudel. The gentle lunchtime prices rise for dinner, when you might find fresh haddock over a bed of julienned steamed vegetables or beef wellington. Interesting wines and beers are available; liquor seasonally, April-January. Classical music plays in the background, and dinner is by candlelight.

Open Monday-Saturday, 11 to 9 or 10.

Marblehead

Rosalie's, 10 Sewall St., Marblehead. (617) 631-5353 or (508) 744-5858.
Continental/Italian. $13.95 to $20.95.
Other Marblehead restaurants come and go, but Rosalie's has been catering to local gourmets since 1973. Housed in an 1890 box factory, the restaurant on three floors is a family operation — that of Rosalie Harrington and her four children — and reflects the personality of its namesake, who also teaches cooking classes upstairs. The main-floor dining room is notable for its three cozy canopied booths in the bar area, a dogwood tree lit with white lights, and striking balloon curtains on the windows. The menu lists ten entrees like haddock francesca, broiled swordfish with pesto butter, veal chop with a brandy-mushroom demi-glaze, and filet florentine. Oysters danielle, baked with garlic butter and prosciutto, is a popular appetizer, as is the lobster ravioli with seafood cream sauce. The creamy seafood chowder harbors scallops, clams, fennel, and red peppers. Cappuccino or espresso make fine endings to what many locals consider the town's fanciest meals.

Dinner nightly from 5:30; Sunday brunch, 10:30 to 2:30.

Tien's Restaurant, 12 School St., Marblehead. (617) 639-1334.
Thai/Vietnamese. $8.25 to $11.95.
Eat here and you'll help along a touching success story as well as savor piquant Thai and Vietnamese cuisine. The newspaper clippings posted in the window tell how Tien Truong escaped from Vietnam in a refugee boat in 1981 and eventually landed in Boston. Working two jobs and attending night school, over three years she saved $50,000, enough to open her restaurant in 1988 to quick acclaim. The spacious place is often packed and rather brightly lit; inlaid mother-of-pearl paintings and classical music on tape help soften the atmosphere. At lunch, erratically-paced though willing service was too fast when the entrees arrived as we were still eating soup, too slow when we asked for the bill. Such lapses failed to mar the famous pad Thai noodle dish with shrimp and chicken or the rice plate with shrimp and cashews. The hot and sour shrimp soup was a triumph and the chicken broth okay, but we missed the happy pancakes we associate with other Vietnamese restaurants. At night, we'd try the Nha-Trang sea specialty, a variety of seafood and vegetables in oyster sauce on a bed of fried potatoes that resembles a bird's nest.

Lunch daily, 11 to 3; dinner, 5 to 10:30.

Giancarlo's Ristorante, 261 Washington St., Marblehead. (617) 639-2156.
Northern Italian. $15 to $23.
Since 1986, this newcomer has attracted a strong following of those partial to exciting pastas and an ambitious menu ranging from saltimbocca to rack of lamb persille. The carpaccio, penne with hot pepper and garlic, and beef tenderloin with green peppercorn sauce sound super. The filet mignon is topped with goose pate, mushroom caps and madeira. Among seafood specialties are seafood stew, grilled

shrimps, and whole dover sole sauteed with lemon and wine. Hanging pierced-tin lamps cast a nighttime glow on booths fashioned from church pews and separated by lattice work, and Italian music plays. Four tables in the front window look onto the street, or is it vice-versa? Here's the real thing, an intimate yet elegant trattoria. Success has spawned a second Giancarlo's at 100 Warrenton St., Boston.

Dinner nightly, 5 to 10; Sunday brunch, 11:30 to 3.

Michael's House, 26 Atlantic Ave., Marblehead. (617) 631-1255.
Continental/American. $9.95 to $15.95.

Built about 1685, this brown clapboard house became a restaurant in 1973 and still thrives amid a competing array of casual, trendy newcomers like Jacob Marley's, Horsefeathers and the Sand-Bar & Grille. The ceilings are beamed and portraits line the walls of the main dining room. The leather-bound menu details fare from shrimp curry and veal piccata to shrimp etouffee, Cajun chicken with peaches, lobster grand marnier and, "by popular demand," chicken livers decatur, sauteed with walnuts, bacon and mushrooms in a wine sauce. A more casual room by the bar is popular for lunch. Sunday brunch includes a "seaside Mary," a bloody mary with two shrimps.

Lunch, Monday-Saturday 11:30 to 2; dinner nightly, 5:30 to 10:30; Sunday brunch.

The Barnacle, Front Street, Marblehead. (617) 631-4236.
American. $9.95 to $14.95.

The best water view in historic Marblehead — a town seemingly surrounded by the sea and full of small restaurants — is at this crowded, no-nonsense restaurant on the harbor. In fact, you can sit at a narrow counter running the width of the restaurant smack dab against the windows at the rear and feast on the view as you eat. The typewritten menu lists New England seafood basics, from haddock and sole to baked stuffed shrimp, scallops, "jumbo shrimp scampi" and such for dinner. All entrees are served with salad, potatoes, rolls and butter — "no substitutions." No credit cards or checks are accepted either. The tables are almost on top of each other, the nondescript decor is vaguely nautical and the small, crowded bar in front also has a good view.

Lunch and dinner daily from 11:30. No credit cards.

Swampscott

Palmers Restaurant, 408 Humphrey St., Swampscott. (617) 596-1820.
American/Italian. $9.95 to $14.95

From the front door, gaze across the harbor at the Boston skyline rising out of the mist at sunset, and you'd almost think you were in Sausalito, looking off at San Francisco. The similarity ends inside, where you find a typical North Shore restaurant in red and white with nautical prints on the wall. Proprietor Jim Ingalls opened here in 1988 after cooking at Locke-Ober Cafe in Boston. It bears his middle name, an appropriate indulgence for the great-great-great-grandson of one of Swampscott's founders. The presentation is nouvelle — an entree will typically have five vegetables arranged around it — but the food is New England with an Italian accent. The seafood is rich: sole stuffed with crabmeat and topped with breadcrumbs, the shrimp sauteed in egg batter, the haddock topped with havarti cheese. Chicken comes four ways and veal three. Desserts like a pastry horn filled with amaretto cream topped with raspberries and almonds, and a white chocolate bag filled with a dark chocolate-sambucca mousse, are works of art. The mostly California wine list is pleasantly priced.

Dinner, Tuesday-Sunday 5 to 9 or 10.

Beverly

$ Union Grill, 208 Rantoul St., Beverly. (508) 927-2028.
New American. $9.95 to $14.95.

Ribbed turquoise rubber placemats, cutlery rolled up in napkins, and a black and white linoleum floor set the theme at this cute and funky place opened to immediate acclaim in 1989 by Bob and Christine Granese. Jazz plays in the background as you sit on upholstered stools at the bar for casual dining or choose a couple of informal dining areas in peach and aqua or, in season, a large rear deck with a raw bar and a glimpse of the Bass River. The menu is a creative mix of appetizers and pizzas, soups and salads, pastas and skewers, sandwiches and entrees like veal medallions sauteed with avocado, jack cheese and sherry-tomato sauce, stuffed chicken breast with mushroom duxelles and goat cheese-cream sauce, and the "Union grill:" swordfish, scallops, shrimp, catfish and monkfish. Entrees come with a choice of fried potatoes or rice, steamed vegetables flavored with ginger, and perhaps a dynamite jalapeno bread or a garlicky flatbread. The chef gets even more creative with daily specials like sauteed breast of duck with golden raisin pear and port wine sauce, grilled swordfish and mussels with tequila and lime sauce, and grilled medallions of beef with green peppercorn and oyster mushroom sauce. Lunch is every bit as innovative, from the fresh scallop and lobster salad with fusili and tarragon mayo to the sauteed trout with crabmeat and jalapeno garlic. The all-American wine and beer selections are as nicely priced as the rest of the menu. Desserts aren't quite as interesting, though who could resist the three-berry shortcake or the American bread pudding with strawberries and apples?

Lunch, Tuesday-Saturday 11:30 to 2:30; dinner, 5 to 10 or 11; Sunday, brunch noon to 3, dinner 3 to 9.

The Beverly Depot, 10 Park St., Beverly. (508) 927-5402.
Steaks/Seafood. $10.50 to $19.95.

"Look before crossing," warns the sign near the entrance. That's because you must cross the railroad tracks to get from the parking lot to the restaurant in the abandoned Boston & Maine depot, now a stop for North Shore commuters to Boston. Once described by a newspaper as "a barny affair," the 1839 depot has been transformed into a dining room of some elegance, still cavernous but enhanced by stained-glass windows, hanging plants and lots of dark wood. Bare wood tables are set with blue napkins and oil lamps. The fare is representative of other restaurants owned by the Barnsider group: typical steakhouse plus chicken teriyaki, lamb chops, seafood and combinations thereof. Besides a salad bar, there are the genre's obligatory desserts: chocolate-walnut pie, oreo cookie ice cream pie, grapenut-custard pudding, deep-fried ice cream and such.

Dinner nightly, 5 to 10 or 11, Sunday 4 to 9.

Manchester

* Ben Sprague's, 40 Beach St., Manchester. (508) 526-7168.
Contemporary/International. $10.95 to $15.95.

In an area where seafood and tradition reign, it's rare to come across a place or a menu like Ben Sprague's. Housed in a shopping plaza with its own **La Groceria** next door and a sidewalk cafe out front, it's a casual yet sophisticated cafe in peach and deep green with delightful accents like striking prints, pottery, vases of alstroemeria, and clay baskets filled with bullrushes and other dried plants. The decorators know what they're doing, and so does the kitchen: lots of with-it appetizers with a salsa theme as in Mexican crab cakes with fried chile fettuccine, salads (oriental duck, ceviche with cilantro and red peppers), pizzettas and pizzas, unusual pastas (shredded duck, ginger, snow peas, scallions and more over fettuccine), a few sandwiches and entrees for lunch, more for dinner. The basically all-day menu is supplemented at night with things like fresh drumfish with sun-dried tomatoes, basil and roasted garlic, Jamaican curried chicken with a tropical fruit salsa, barbecued duck breast with grilled cornbread and Southwestern barbecue sauce, grilled beef tenderloin with fried artichoke hearts and red onion rings, and a couple of mixed grills (one with marinated sirloin, curried chicken and spicy sausage). Desserts range from chocolate swirled cheesecake and fruit crisps to maple-walnut bread pudding.

Lunch daily, 11:30 to 4:30; dinner, 4:30 to 10:30; Sunday brunch.

Seven Central Publick House, 7 Central St., Manchester. (508) 526-7494. American. $10.95 to $17.95.

Billed as an old, warm seaside tavern, this lives up to its name in the historic, beamed front rooms with shiny dark wood tables, benches and booths and a nautical atmosphere. Out back beyond the copper bar is a contemporary addition in burgundy and green with skylights, copper tables, lovely lamps and expansive windows onto a rear deck overlooking a mill pond. The large, cutesy menu (sandwiches are listed under "Cheese'd to Meat You") is all-encompassing, catering to the baked stuffed scrod as well as to the chicken burrito crowd. It covers all the bases, from chicken McCentrals ("our own version" with sweet and sour sauce), Mexican potato skins and Cajun popcorn to escargots, veal oscar and steak au poivre. Prime rib is featured alone and in various combinations. The day's specials might run from gourmet pizzas to beef wellington. Enough said.

Lunch daily from 11:30; dinner, 4 to 10:45.

Gloucester

The White Rainbow, 65 Main St., Gloucester. (508) 281-0017. Regional American. $18.95 to $29.95.

What could be more intimate than the downstairs beamed grotto, dim and romantic with walls of stone and brick and tables dressed with white cloths and cranberry napkins standing tall in dark-stemmed wine glasses? Service is friendly and professional, and the menu intrigues. We dined on an interesting appetizer of buffalo mozzarella, tomato and maui onions dressed with walnut oil and cracked pepper, followed by roast duckling with apricot-honey sauce and glazed Australian apricots and grilled Australian lamb on a zinfandel sauce blended with ginger jam, garnished with kiwi. We liked the piping hot Italian bread and the salsify and herbed potatoes that came on side plates. The excellent salad of three greens served after the entrees was topped with a mandarin orange. We passed on the Swiss chocolate-almond tort, Kentucky derby pie with fresh raspberries and white chocolate mousse, feeling we had spent quite enough already. Next time we'll try the adjacent cafe and wine bar, where we would order grilled pork medallions on a green chile and garlic-mustard sauce, garnished with tomato salsa, for $13.95.

Dinner nightly, 5:30 to 9:30, Saturday 6 to 10. Closed Monday, also no dinner Sunday in off-season; instead, brunch, 11:30 to 3.

The Rhumb Line, 40 Railroad Ave., Gloucester. (508) 283-9732. American. $9.95 to $16.95.

The upstairs dining room in this otherwise undistinguished yellow stucco building across from the railroad tracks is beautifully restored to look like the deck of an old

North Shore

Gloucester schooner. The handsome bar is made from mahogany and teak; dining is at tables with inlaid nautical charts or booths of pine and leather beneath a mast and rigging atop the high ceiling. The chef shines with such blackboard specials as charbroiled salmon, tuna teriyaki and sauteed pork dijonnaise along with such menu standards as seafood casserole, lobster pie, rack of lamb, and roast duck glazed with grand marnier and honey-marmalade sauce. The appetizers, desserts and wine list are fairly standard; the garlic and tarragon dressing with the spinach and crouton salad is not. Downstairs, you can get a fine and filling lunch or supper in a casual room with deck chairs and a large bar.

Dinner upstairs, Tuesday-Saturday 6 to 10, Sunday 5:30 to 9:30. Downstairs, open daily 11:30 to 10, Sunday 4 to 10.

The Raven, 197 East Main St., Gloucester. (508) 281-3951.
Continental. $11.95 to $14.95.

With its intimate atmosphere of pink linens, roses and green plants, this is a longtime Gloucester favorite. Lately the "imaginative European menu" has been downscaled. Gone is the more creative fare of recent years; in its place are standards like baked stuffed shrimp, scallop casserole and roast duckling a l'orange. Veal chesterfield turns out to be sauteed with parsley, garlic and tomato sauce, and served in a casserole with a blend of cheeses, peppers and mushrooms. Even the scallop and shrimp stir-fry and the steak au poivre seem a bit old hat. But if you tire of the ubiquitous Gloucester seafood emporia you should like the pink and black decor here and the white lights twinkling on jade plants in the floor-to-ceiling bay window.

Dinner nightly, 5 to 10. Closed Monday and Tuesday in winter.

Rockport

Hungry Wolf Restaurant, 43 South St., Rockport. (508) 283-8194.
American. $9.95 to $13.95.

The best restaurant in town lately has been a newcomer, relocated in 1988 from its old haunt in Gloucester's Rocky Neck. Locals had high hopes for owners Charlie and Laura Wolf to succeed year-round in a spot where others had failed. Off the tourist path, the Hungry Wolf looks a bit like a country bistro, thanks to Laura's decorating talents: pink, white and deep blue linens, gathered lace curtains, the works of a Rocky Neck artist on the walls, and votive candles and bouquets of fresh flowers on each table. A picture of a wolf in a dinner jacket, with knife and fork in hand, adorns both the entrance and the menu and sets a whimsical theme. Charlie specializes in fresh fish, vegetables and produce, for which he shops each morning. The deceptively simple menu lists a dozen entrees from chicken teriyaki and two versions of pork chops to four of sirloin steak (plain, teriyaki, dijon or with garlic butter). Grilled Norwegian salmon with dilled hollandaise sauce might be a special. Start with scallops wrapped in bacon, Italian fish soup or ratatouille au gratin. Homemade croutons dress the complimentary caesar and garden salads. Laura makes the desserts, including amaretto bread pudding, peanut-butter fudge brownie pie, apple crisp, and pecan pie. Rockport is dry, but as with other restaurants in town, you may bring your own spirits.

Dinner, Monday-Saturday 5 to 9:30. BYOB.

♥ **My Place,** 72 Bearskin Neck, Rockport. (508) 546-9667.
American. $10.50 to $18.

When Cristull and Robert Sheath decided to open a restaurant in 1982 in an old black and yellow tea house at the very end of Bearskin Neck, they didn't know what to call it, Cristull said, "so we called it My Place." Now taken over by their chef, Charles Kreis, My Place seems to be missing Cristull's feminine touch and attention to detail. You can't argue with the ambience, blessed with an unbelievable location on the rocks at water's edge and decidedly romantic with an un-Rockport-like rose and aqua color scheme and, at night, flaming torches and pink and blue spotlights on the rocks. As flute music plays while the sun sets, the setting is magical for diners on the two flower-lined outdoor decks and, indeed, for people across Sandy Bay who admire the sight as well. The lunch menu is unexciting and expensive (a peanut butter sandwich for $4, "with jelly" for $4.50). Our BLT was a tiny sandwich made with wooden winter tomatoes, in August, mind you. The chef's salad was a mass of slivers of ham, roast beef, chicken and cheese heaped on a bed of iceberg lettuce, with a side of dressing and garnished with a slice of watermelon. Things are better at dinner, we understand, when entrees range from baked scrod or sole in lemon butter to scallops of the day, seafood fettuccine, prime rib, and steak au poivre. Lobster comes in several variations. The setting remains one of the best for a restaurant anywhere.

Lunch, noon to 3; dinner, 5 to 9:30. Closed Wednesday, and November to mid-May. BYOB.

The Greenery, 15 Dock Square, Rockport. (508) 546-9593.
American/International. $8.95 to $14.50.
The name bespeaks the theme of this casual place, but nothing could be more picturesque than the view of Motif No. 1 across the harbor, from the butcherblock tables at the rear of the L-shaped dining room. Seafood and salads are featured, as are a salad bar and an ice cream and pastry bar out front. Otherwise the fare runs from what the owners call gourmet sandwiches to dinner entrees like seafood casserole, seafood linguini, chicken milano, pesto pizza, stuffed shells, and mussels in tomato herb sauce. For sandwiches, how about the Sproutwich — muenster and cheddar cheeses, mushrooms and sunflower seeds, crammed with sprouts and served with choice of dressing? Apple pie with cheddar-streusel topping and cheesecake with fresh strawberries are popular desserts. The chocolate-chambord and amaretto cheesecakes are available here or to go.

Open daily, weekdays 10 to 9, weekends 9 to 10. Closed November-April. BYOB.

Essex

Tom Shea's, 122 Main St. (Route 133), Essex. (508) 768-6931.
Seafood. $11.95 to $18.95.
After an aborted attempt at opening a new restaurant in Sudbury, Tom Shea's is concentrating again on what it does best: serving fresh seafood to its legion of North Shore fans. The properly nautical dining room with votive candles, plenty of dark wood and prolific plants takes full advantage of the view of the Essex River and surrounding wetlands. The menu is a bit more adventurous than those of many competitors, as in shrimp in coconut beer batter (available both as appetizer and entree). Cajun barbecue shrimp, smoked Irish salmon and shrimp remoulade are other appetizers; grilled teriyaki shrimp, shrimp scampi (my, how they like shrimp), scallop-stuffed sole, and baked scrod with blue cheese are among main courses. Beef kabob, steak au poivre and roast duckling with orange sauce are available for landlubbers.

Dinner, Monday-Friday from 5, Saturday and Sunday from 11; weekend brunch, 11 to 2.

$ **Woodman's,** Main Street, Essex. (508) 768-6451.
Seafood in the Rough. $7.25 to $10.50.
What's a trip to the shore without fried clams? Some of the best we've tasted are

served at this glorified clam shack without a single frill, making Tom Shea's across the street look positively tony. A local institution for 70 years, it's famed for its clambakes, on your site or theirs. When we last stopped, the special of all the specials was fried (that's right, fried) lobster with the usual trimmings for $10.50. You can get onion rings cooked in the Woodman family's secret batter, steamed clams, fresh fish dinners, and combination plates of clams, shrimp, scallops, fish and the like in rustic (make that very) surroundings. Take a number, place your order, and wait with a wine spritzer or Samuel Adams beer.

Open daily in summer, 11 to 10, to 9 from Labor Day through winter.

Ipswich

★ La Tavernetta, 24 Essex Road, Ipswich. (508) 356-5969.
  Northern Italian. $12.95 to $19.95.

New owner Stephen Cole has earned a winning reputation for this unlikely looking establishment in a corner of Bruni's Farm Marketplace. The kitchen sings with appetizers like onions stuffed with porcini mushrooms, spinach and ricotta in a roasted red pepper sauce; escargot ravioli in a sauce of garlic, chopped tomato and parsley, and oyster stew with julienned vegetables, sherry and leeks. There are five pasta dishes, and main courses range from salmon filet stuffed with smoked oysters and mascarpone cheese to veal medallions sauteed with wild mushrooms, pine nuts, oregano and cognac. Grilled chicken on polenta in a vegetable ragout, roast duck with a honey-mustard sauce, and grilled lamb chops flavored with rosemary and garnished with tomato and leeks are other possibilities. Desserts could be strawberry or walnut-praline genoise, grapes with fresh cream in Italian brandy, and homemade ice creams and sorbets. An abundant supply of Italian red and white wines is supplemented by a fine reserve list. A pedestal divider topped with plants gives color to a pristine dining room with paneled wainscoting, interesting art on the walls and stenciled chairs at well-spaced, white-linened tables.

Lunch, Tuesday-Thursday 11:30 to 2:30; dinner, Tuesday-Saturday 5 to 10:30 or 11; Sunday, brunch noon to 4:30, dinner 5 to 10:30.

Chipper's River Cafe, Caldwell's Block, Ipswich. (508) 356-7956.
  International. $8.95 to $11.95.

An unassuming little place hidden in a walkout basement beside a river in downtown Ipswich, this is popular for interesting food in a casual setting. There's a long counter at the rear, a Wurlitzer jukebox at the entrance, and bare wood tables scattered throughout. The food is the thing, perhaps mulligatawny soup or a scallop, broccoli and leek quiche with salad for lunch. At night, the selection is short but sweet: items like bacon-wrapped scallops with a horseradish dipping sauce, a chicken and Canadian bacon sandwich, Santa Fe salad, and such entrees as mustard-lemon chicken, shrimp and avocado saute, curried leg of lamb over rice, and grilled tuna with garlic mayonnaise. The baked goods come from Chipper's Brick Alley Bakery next door.

Open daily from 7 a.m. to 10 or 11 p.m., Sunday to 9.

Newburyport

★ Joseph's Winter Street Cafe, 22 Winter St., Newburyport. (508) 462-1188.
  Northern Italian/Continental. $9.95 to $17.50.

You remember Joseph? He used to have Joseph's Rye on the Rocks, an institution up the coast in Rye, N.H., and also Joseph's Riversmere in Portsmouth. Well, they went the way of so many restaurants. Joseph Pignato tried his hand at teaching and turned up again in Newburyport, opening this New York-style bistro in 1987 in a good-looking gray shingled building that was part of a train station. Illuminated outside by white lights on trees and inside by candles, it is intimate and romantic at night, with a dark-beamed ceiling, a pianist playing, and gleaming silver dishes and knickknacks reflecting pink lights on the bar. We enjoyed an appetizer of oysters san remo and one of the better salads we've had in a long time, a mix of greens, red cabbage and shredded mozzarella cheese dressed with a dijon vinaigrette. The rack of lamb was one of the best ever, and we also liked the skewer of lamb a la grecque, served with sauteed small red potatoes. Scampi, grilled prawns, scallops provencale, pasta with seafood, mixed grill, filet mignon, and Sicilian sausages with roasted peppers are other favorites. Creme brulee smothered with fresh raspberries and creme fraiche was a fitting finale to a fine meal. Joseph's also offers an acclaimed jazz brunch on Sundays.

Dinner nightly except Monday, 5 to midnight; Sunday, brunch noon to 4, dinner 4 to 8.

Scandia, 25 State St., Newburyport. (508) 462-6271.
Continental. $13.75 to $17.75.
The reason for the name eludes us, but there's no denying the romance of this dark, intimate storefront restaurant with candles lit even at noontime. The ambience is Edwardian, and chandeliers set an elegant theme. At dinner, likely appetizers are seafood sausage, veal pate and baked oysters brie. The ten entrees range from chicken prosciutto to steak diane and rack of lamb with mustard-mint sauce. Shrimp and scallop curry, stuffed yellowtail sole, and salmon en croute are seafood standbys. Meals include a salad with a choice of five dressings. Many of the evening items (as well as salads, sandwiches and entrees like Moroccan chicken) are available at lunch, but we find the candlelight and formal atmosphere more appealing at night.

Lunch, Monday-Saturday 11:30 to 3; dinner, Monday-Thursday 5 to 10, Friday and Saturday 6 to 10; Sunday, brunch noon to 4, dinner 5 to 10.

Ten Center St., 10 Center St., Newburyport. (508) 462-6652.
Continental. $11.95 to $22.50.
Built in 1790 as the home and shop of a baker, this restaurant was much expanded in 1987 following a kitchen fire. The original tavern and a Colonial dining room upstairs remain, but the building was tripled in size with a reception area, two more upstairs dining rooms, and an outdoor deck. Seating varies from formal and elegant in the brick-walled Colonial room to light and airy in the contemporary, skylit addition. Dinner in the dark and intimate downstairs pub is obviously very popular. The extensive dinner menu devotes two pages to appetizers, soups and salads, from chilled gazpacho to fettuccine alfredo and smoked salmon. More than two dozen entrees range from sherried chicken livers to lobster Newbury. Sole with bananas, Brazilian shrimp, Irish veal with smoked salmon, and veal and oysters are some out-of-the-ordinary dishes. A house favorite is chicken breasts garnished with prosciutto, mushrooms, artichoke hearts, and parmesan cheese. The pub menu served nightly in the pleasant bar is a bargain.

Lunch, Monday-Saturday 11:30 to 3; dinner, 5:30 to 10:30; Sunday, brunch 10:30 to 3, dinner 4:30 to 10.

Boston

Downtown

* Le Marquis de Lafayette, Lafayette Hotel, 1 Avenue de Lafayette, Boston. (617) 451-2600.

New French. $24 to $36.50.

Since it opened in 1985, the Lafayette's signature dining room has earned a reputation as a palace of plenitude on the New England gastronomic scene. Supervising chef Louis Outhier, owner of the Michelin three-star L'Oasis on the French Riviera, plans extraordinary menus of great range and delicacy for the Swiss-owned hotel's restaurant. The windowless, 96-seat dining room seems larger than the number of seats suggests, the silver and gray expanse accentuated by lights from four enormous crystal chandeliers and dainty crystal wall sconces reflected in discreetly placed mirrors. Comfortable banquettes provide many a private dining space. White-linened tables are set with floral-patterned white china atop octagonal silver service plates, tiny vases bearing two rose buds each, cut crystal stemware, and heavy silverware that changes with each course. You can order a la carte, but three prix-fixe menus (one based on mushrooms for every course) are better values for those who like to sample chef Pierre Schutz's creations. Here are exotic works of art: cream of partridge soup, terrine of foie gras, and frog's legs timbale with confit of tomatoes and tumeric, for starters. Entrees could be grouper with fried lotus root, lobster medallions with garlic and potatoes, salmon roulade with savoy cabbage in juniper vinaigrette, haunch of venison roasted with pepper sauce, breast of pheasant with potato and pheasant hash, saddle of veal with green apple juice, and — a new one on us, poached foie gras in lentils. Our December meal, a variety of courses chosen by the chef, was an extraordinary, three-hour-long feast. It began with a masterful salad of three shrimp and a sweetbread, crossed with strips of black truffles in a vinaigrette on a bed of at least ten kinds of baby lettuce. An ethereal truffle consomme preceded two fish courses, one of lobster in a sauterne and ginger sauce, the other salmon with a fresh mint sauce. One entree was filet of venison atop toast slices; the other, veal medallions with potatoes anna, julienned fennel and roasted peppers of many colors. Three plates of coffee parfait, amaretto truffle and a banana mille feuille, the last an especially transcendental sweet, were followed by a couple of wedges of mousses from the dessert cart, hazelnut with coconut and apple with calvados. As if we needed it, a tray of petits fours came with the bill. The distinguished wine list starts at $30.

Lunch, Monday-Friday noon to 2:30; dinner, Monday-Saturday 6 to 10.

* Seasons, Bostonian Hotel, North Street, Boston. (617) 523-4119.

New American. $25 to $33.

The place that Jasper White and Lydia Shire put on the map, Seasons is the culinary gem of the Bostonian Hotel, its curved, windowed dining room on the fourth floor looking out over Faneuil Hall Marketplace. Silver-rimmed service plates, heavy cutlery and a pristine freesia in a bud vase on each well-spaced table add to the feeling of warm, contemporary elegance. Chef Bill Poirier's seasonal menu is American, regional and international — witness such starters as lobster and finnan haddie chowder, terrine of venison with red pear jelly, pheasant boudin with cabbages and hard cider, or tuna spiedini with calamari and capers. An appetizer of smoked fish — red sturgeon with scallops and salmon in a horseradish-champagne vinaigrette, with a side presentation of cucumbers, watercress and capers — was superb, as was a smooth and spicy onion and oxtail soup. Among main courses, we cottoned to a masterful duckling with ginger and scallions, surrounded by Chinese vegetables, and seared quail with soft polenta and little sausages. A sensational array of sorbets — papaya, pear, apple and raspberry — was a refreshing ending. The bill came with chocolate truffles and a pastry with crushed macadamia nuts on a doily. The choice all-American wine list is enormous, with 53 chardonnays, 22 sauvignon blancs, and 41 special-reserve cabernets at last count. Seasons also serves a more typical hotel breakfast, a fancy weekend brunch with what is considered to be the best hash in Boston, and a pricey lunch that mirrors the dinner menu.

Breakfast daily, 7 to 10:30; lunch, Monday-Friday 11:30 to 2:30; weekend brunch, noon to 2 or 3; dinner nightly, 6 to 10 or 11.

＊ Julien, Hotel Meridien, 250 Franklin St., Boston. (617) 451-1900.
New French. $23 to $33.
The setting is historic, the former Members Court of the stately Federal Reserve Building built in 1922 and patterned after a Renaissance palace in Rome, across from the site of Boston's first French restaurant, opened in 1793 by French-emigre Jean-Baptiste Julien. But its spirit is highly contemporary, with the chef taking his cue from the Meridien's new consulting chef Olivier Roellinger, owner of a Michelin-rated Brittany restaurant. Some of Boston's fanciest food is served in this formal room with towering gilded ceiling, three crystal chandeliers, and lattice work on the walls with lights behind. Mushroom velour banquettes or Queen Anne chairs flank tables set with unusually heavy silverware, Wedgwood china, tiny shaded brass lamps, and Peruvian lilies. If you're not up to appetizers like leeks and quail eggs with ossetra caviar sauce or pheasant and squab with sweet and sour squash, splurge on a masterful soup, perhaps consomme of game birds with cauliflower and truffles or a cream of wild mushroom soup with belon oysters. Among entrees are roulade of salmon with walnuts and hazelnuts, roasted Maine lobster with mushrooms and an autumn salad, tenderloin of venison with pepper and chutney, veal medallions with clementines, cloves and dates, and lamb filet with napoleon of potato and parsley. We'll never forget the lobster ravioli, the lobster reconstructed from its head and tail, the body made from ravioli filled with lobster mousse, the legs and feelers represented by green beans and asparagus or snow peas, and the whole topped with tomatoes and truffles — presentation personified. For dessert, we enjoyed a delicious almond ice-cream cookie and two mille feuilles, pastries layered with whipped cream and peaches in one case and strawberries and raspberries in the other. A plate of homemade candies and cookies sweetens the bill's arrival.

Lunch, Monday-Friday noon to 2; dinner nightly, 6 to 10 or 10:30.

Cornucopia, 15 West St., Boston. (617) 338-4600.
New American. $14 to $22.
Once the gathering spot for the area's 19th-century literati, the former Peabody home is now a dramatic, contemporary restaurant on a somewhat rundown street across from Lafayette Place. Snack with a drink in the main-floor bar or head up to the cheery mezzanine, where parasols hang from skylights, or to the second floor, art deco and very comfortable, all in moss green, purple and blue with backlit, stained-glass affairs descending the walls to each table. The menu changes monthly. For a December lunch, we had a wonderful oyster and fennel soup and a roasted rabbit and chicory salad for starters, followed by a chicken breast grilled with Indian spices, served with crisp carrots and vegetables and a cucumber salad, and egg fettuccine with a spicy tomato, herb and clam sauce. Beautifully presented, the portions were small, but we asked for seconds of the good French bread and

our formally attired waiter obliged with thirds as well. At dinner, entrees range widely from pan-fried catfish with avocado salsa and jalapeno-buttermilk biscuit or roast chicken with sage and sausage stuffing to grilled tuna with capellini pasta and citrus-soy sauce or roast lamb chops with asparagus and chive spaetzle. The menu lists a recommended wine with each entree and appetizer, by the bottle or glass.

Lunch, Monday-Friday noon to 2; dinner, Tuesday-Saturday 5:30 to 9:30.

Zuma, 7 North Market, Faneuil Hall Marketplace, Boston. (6l7) 367-9114.
Cuisine of the Sun. $8.95 to $13.95.

Stephen Immel, owner of this peppy new (late 1989) cafe in the basement space that used to be Romagnoli's Table, calls his cuisine the "food of the sun." We call it dynamite, as in a delectable corn chowder, heavily herbed and filled with chunks of potato and sun-dried tomatoes. A sandwich of the day, tangy roast duck salad on crusty Italian bread with jicama slaw and watermelon, was no slouch in the spice department, either. The Thai shrimp salad with spicy cabbage was a generous platter with four huge shrimp and more vegetables than one person could deal with, although we couldn't detect any of the lemon grass flavoring the menu promised. Good crusty bread and a couple of beers from the sophisticated selection added to the festivity of a Christmas lunch. And the key lime pie, a proper yellow, was one of the best we've had. Zuma, named for a beach in Malibu, offers pasta dishes like grilled chicken and sun-dried tomatoes on fettuccine, and shrimp, scallops, baby clams and mussels on linguini, and main courses like a roasted and grilled half duck with grilled banana and a guava-molasses glaze and a spit-roasted pork loin with fresh thyme, apple cider and black rum. Zuma "grills" (a choice of chicken breast, shrimp, sausages or top round steak) are served with fresh tortillas, three salsas, jicama slaw, dirty rice, and black beans. Salads (jicama with sweet red onion, navel oranges and raspberry vinaigrette, grilled tuna with dry cured olives, marinated mushrooms, jalapenos and fresh pico de gallo) and sandwiches (maybe avocado, tomato and smoked slab bacon) round out the menu, along with a few appetizers. We like the name of one: roasted peppers and expensive mushrooms on fresh greens. We also like the chairs painted turquoise, the sponged canary yellow walls in the main dining room (a smaller room is painted an intense purple with neon strips along the walls), the brick floor, and the handpainted boxes (done by Steve's daughter and son-in-law) on the tables, each containing tabasco, towelettes, a vase of fresh flowers and, purchased from the East Coast Grill in Cambridge, Inner Beauty sauce made from Scotch bonnet peppers. Taste it if you dare!

Open daily, 11:30 to 10 or 11.

Maison Robert, 45 School St., Boston. (617) 227-3370.
French. $24 to $33.

Formal and a tad forbidding, this has been a bastion of classic French cuisine since chef-owner Lucien Robert opened it in 1972 in the Old City Hall. The Empire-style Bonhomme Richard dining room with its lofty molded ceiling, three majestic crystal chandeliers and twenty-foot-high draperies is elegant and expensive. Ben's Cafe downstairs is less so. The familiar French standards of the upstairs menu have not changed since we dined regally fifteen years ago as guests of an entertaining businessman. But there are innovations: a warm rabbit sausage with carrot sauce, roulade of shrimp and sole with fennel sauce, fresh stuffed quail with pistachio pasta, and venison filet with green peppercorns. The ambitious menu has thirteen appetizers, including a remarkable pate de foie gras, and sixteen desserts from creme brulee to crepes suzette for two. **Ben's Cafe,** bright and cheery, is now the domain of M. Robert's 30-year-old daughter Andree, who is doing some highly rated cooking. Her menu changes monthly and, with things like California salads and shrimp with black pepper pasta, is a bit more up to date than that upstairs.

Lunch, Monday-Friday noon to 2:30; dinner, 6 to 10 or 10:30; Sunday brunch, 11 to 1.

Locke-Ober Cafe, 3 Winter Place, Boston. (617) 542-1340.
Continental/American. $17.50 to $39.50.

Traditionalists love this institution dating to 1875. It's a calm refuge of power lunches and sedate dinners in a clubby atmosphere. Women are now allowed into the Men's Bar and Cafe, a treasury of hand-carved mahogany, gleaming metal steam dishes along a room-length mirrored bar, tables covered with crisp white linens, chairs with burgundy leather seats and, oh yes, the famous painting of the nude Mademoiselle Yvonne. Upstairs, dining in the Ober room is like being in a Newport mansion, some of the furnishings having been obtained from one (Locke's owner, David Ray, also owns the Clarke Cooke House in Newport). Except for the prices, the menu has changed little over the years. Veteran waiters in black jackets and long white aprons serve up patrons' favorites, such as finnan haddie, shad roe, calves liver with bacon, dover sole meuniere, and wiener schnitzel with butter noodles. One of us dined on lobster savannah here at age 18 with her father; it's still the priciest item on the lengthy menu, which lists ten kinds of salad (yes, one is au courant with arugula, endive and radicchio), ten vegetables (from spinach in cream to sauteed snow peas), and five versions of potato. Pistachio nuts lace the country duck pate and remoulade sauce accompanies the fried oysters. But Locke-Ober is best with its simpler, traditional basics. The Indian pudding and English trifle are without peer.

Lunch, Monday-Saturday 11 to 3; dinner nightly, 3 to 10 or 10:30, Sunday 5 to 10.

Dakota's, 34 Summer St., Boston. (617) 737-1777.
American Grill. $11.95 to $23.

Opened in 1989, this offshoot of a Dallas grill of the same name occupies part of the second floor of the restored 101 Arch Building. A pleasant expanse with big windows overlooking the street, it has well-spaced tables and banquettes, a striking floor of squares in rust and black, and a shelf with newspapers to read as in a European coffeehouse. The white-linened tables are set with wine glasses upside down and multi-colored peppercorns in lucite grinders. The menu is ambitious, from coho salmon with soy-ginger butter and crispy fried leeks to New York strip steak with fried cayenne onion crisps and papaya-avocado salsa, from breast of turkey with winter pear and plum compote and horseradish mashed potatoes to double lamb chops with roasted garlic, minted tomatoes and feta cheese vinaigrette. House specialties include changing pastas, smoked venison chili with jalapeno corn cakes, roasted veal chop, and confit of duck. Start with carpaccio, "hill country" venison sausage quesadillas or warm goat cheese salad. Finish with sweet potato-pecan pie, peach and pear bread pudding with Jack Daniels sauce, or the day's sorbet.

Lunch, Monday-Saturday 11:30 to 3; dinner nightly, 5 to 11.

Brasserie Les Halles, 301 North Market, Faneuil Hall Marketplace, Boston.
(617) 227-1272.
French. $12.95 to $19.95.

A sleek restaurant in white and black, this occupies the upstairs Faneuil Hall Marketplace space of the former Wild Goose Grill & Rotisserie. Most of the game dishes are gone, but now you can get salads of arugula and endive with grilled duck sausage or plum tomatoes with grilled blue cheese, as well as entrees of grilled salmon with roast pepper confiture or lamb chops grilled with garlic, herbs and caramelized onion flan. Try a salad of grilled salmon and spinach with coarse mustard dressing, or a dish of roast monkfish filet with thyme and red wine sauce. Among desserts are fresh fruits and berries grilled with creme anglaise and chocolate pate with a nut pastry cream.

Lunch, Monday-Saturday 11:30 to 3; dinner, 5:30 to 11 or midnight. Closed Sunday.

$ Durgin-Park, North Market, Faneuil Hall Marketplace, Boston. (617) 227-2038. American/Seafood. $3.95 to $15.95.

What can you say about an institution that's been around, in one form or another, since 1742 and is as well-known as the Freedom Trail? But for a new facade and a downstairs oyster bar when it was incorporated into Faneuil Hall's North Market, Durgin-Park remains its own solid self amid the trendy marketplace. Everyone ought to eat here at least once. Yes, the decor is plainer than plain — the ceiling is tin, the light bulbs are bare, and you often share tables with strangers after waiting in line. But the line moves fast, you may luck out and get a table of your own, the reputedly snippy waitresses can be delightfully droll, and the prices and portions are amazing. For less than five bucks, you can devour chicken pot pie or poor man's roast beef, a platter of fried smelts, short ribs with Creole sauce, or franks and beans (these beans are proper Bostonians; those who love them may purchase a pint or two in Quincy Market). The legendary prime rib is a huge slab that spills off the plate. Most entrees come with mashed potatoes or french fries; vegetables are extra, but at these prices, who cares? Nearly half the 47 entrees are under $8.25, including broiled salmon and roast turkey. For dessert, most folks choose Indian pudding or fresh strawberry shortcake.

Open daily from 11:30 to 10, Sunday noon to 9. No credit cards, no checks and no reservations.

Ye Olde Union Oyster House, 41 Union St., Boston. (617) 227-2750. Seafood. $11.75 to $24.95.

Just around the corner from Faneuil Hall Marketplace but eons removed from much of it in spirit is the nation's oldest restaurant in continuous service, a time warp dating to the early 1700s. Beyond the simple crescent raw bar at the entrance is a warren of rooms with creaky floors, booths, bare wood tables, and walls of memorabilia. Above the oyster bar ringed with tall stools is a sign claiming that frequent customer Daniel Webster downed a half dozen plates of shucked oysters at a sitting, each washed down with a tumbler of brandy and water. The custom today is for a half dozen oysters or clams to be paired with a beer or two. We remember the clam chowder from years ago as the best in Boston. The menu stresses seafood, of course, with oyster stew, broiled scrod, baked stuffed shrimp, seafood newburg, lobster thermidor, and others of a kind that appeals to tourists. Locals find the historic surroundings more interesting than the food.

Open daily, 11 to 9:30 or 10.

Theater District

★ Biba, 272 Boylston St., Boston. (617) 426-7878. Contemporary. $15 to $28.

Lydia Shire is back where she belongs. Boston's culinary star, who was enticed away from Seasons at the Bostonian Hotel in 1986 to launch the Four Seasons Hotel in Beverly Hills, returned to town in 1989 to open a restaurant of her own. And it's one like no other, which is not surprising to those who know Lydia. The two-story emporium in the tony Heritage on the Garden shopping-residential complex seats 50 in a main-floor bar serving tapas and such, and 150 in a wildly colorful dining room up a curving staircase. The bar features a Winston Churchill-style smoking couch, a mural of chubby, well-fed people, a lineup of photos taken by Lydia on her various travels, and framed shopping bags from the late Biba, her favorite London store. The Biba Food Hall upstairs is notable for a glassed-in wine cellar along the stairwell, an open space with a tandoori oven, pale yellow walls, ceilings with patterns taken from Albanian carpets, warm woods, and white-clothed tables covered with butcher paper and placed rather close together. Lydia refutes those who classify the decor as Southwest; "if anything, it's Mediterranean in feeling," she counters. Her menu defies classification as well. Instead of appetizers and entrees it's categorized according to fish, offal, meat, starch, legumina and sweets. Full of surprises, it's hard to follow (and figure) but delightfully quirky, as in "pressed rare tuna sandwich in paper bag," calves liver with flaky turnip pastry "and sort of burnt maui onions," "venison with pipian sauce, sweet and sour pumpkin," and "crackling frizzy salad" with roasted chestnuts. Fun stuff, and oh-so-good, if you're into new twists and tastes that make food reviewers swoon. The public is not universally charmed; some complain of a high decibel level and slow service. Lydia has the audacity to offer not one but two dishes of brains, to add lobster to a finnan haddie chowder, to accompany main dishes with beet chips or pickled squash salad, and to offer a luncheon dish of squash orechiette with hickory nuts and little venison meatballs. But from the basket of breads (the naan cooked in the tandoori oven is spectacular) to the concord grape, cantaloupe and ginger bombe for dessert, Biba provides a novel dining sensation.

Lunch, Monday-Friday 11:30 to 2:30 (Saturday in bar only); dinner nightly, 5:30 to 10 or 11; Sunday brunch, 11:30 to 3.

Aujourd'hui, Four Seasons Hotel, 200 Boylston St., Boston. (617) 338-4400.
New American. $19.75 to $37.

A window table at Aujourd'hui is a prospect on the finer things in Boston life, among them a view of the swan boats plying the pond of the Public Garden and the extraordinary cooking of Boston-born chef Mark Baker. The second-floor restaurant's setting is serene: floral-fabric banquettes, rich oak paneling, Royal Doulton china atop white damask cloths, nicely spaced tables, and a solicitous staff. At lunch, we enjoyed the subtle cream of fennel soup and smoked duck pieces encased in tiny herbed rice pancakes with a sesame-flavored dipping sauce. Entrees were a tasty peppered chicken breast with roasted artichokes and chives and a special of medallions of wild boar with pearl onions and madeira, accompanied by tiny beans, baby carrots and small roasted potatoes. The fruit tart that we'd admired in the lavish pastry display near the entry was perfection, filled with oversize blackberries, blueberries and strawberries in a pastry cream with a shortbread-like crust. The sorbet lover among us freaked out on the day's trio — pear, mixed berry and mango. At dinner, you might try grilled Atlantic monkfish with broccoli rabe, braised salsify and caramelized onion; Chinese barbecued salmon with black radish turnip cakes; herb-roasted saddle of lamb with black olives and sunchoke ravioli, or a hunter's plate of pheasant, mountain squab and axis deer with juniper, ginger and lime. The wine list, one of Boston's best, includes a full page of wines by the glass.

Lunch, Monday-Friday 11:30 to 2:30; dinner nightly, 6 to 10:30; Sunday brunch, 11 to 2:30.

Rocco's, 5 Charles St. South, Boston. (617) 723-6800.
Eclectic/International. $5 to $25.

Amazing Grace was playing on tape as we gazed up at the satyrs and nymphs on the ceiling mural, two stories high. Amazing space, we thought. Owner Patrick Bowe, former manager of Harvest in Cambridge, wanted a place that was "playful and colorful," and that it is, along with a bit of the bizarre. Huge windows are framed with incredible draperies, gigantic bronze chandeliers hang from the ceiling, and avant-garde sculptures (from changing displays) decorate the bar and environs. Chef Danny Wisel (of the late Devon at the World Trade Center) cooks in an open kitchen. The polished bare wood tables are ringed with comfortable bow-back chairs and topped with dishtowel-size napkins. Each table sports a decoration (perhaps a carousel horse, a marble urn or a pewter fish pitcher) that is for sale, the prices listed on the back of the menu. This is definitely not a conventional place, nor is the menu. On a day that was raining cats and dogs, we took refuge for a heart-warming lunch of fettuccine tossed with mushrooms, scallions and pieces of game hen, and a fabulous version of chili (pork, beef, chicken and black beans, very spicy and garnished with raw red onion, guacamole, and both blue corn and regular tortilla chips). A "country" salad sported several kinds of exotic lettuces, barley, dates, goat cheese spread on croutons, and a truffle vinaigrette. Comfort food can't get more comforting than the warm pumpkin Indian pudding, fragrant with spices, accompanied by hard sauce and bourbon-vanilla ice cream. A couple of glasses of the house Coviro wine and we were ready to face the soaking streets again. At dinner, mix and match things like the acclaimed Maryland crab cake (crisp with its coating of cornflakes and accompanied by a delicious pureed fresh corn sauce), fried raviolis with Dungeness crab and parmesan stuffing, stir-fried Thai shrimp and scallops with glass noodles to wrap in Chinese pancakes, and stuffed breast of guinea hen. A traditional paella, a roasted half chicken with mashed-potato gratin and a southern BBQ trio are other choices, and grazing on a couple of appetizers is not frowned upon. The fruit pastry of the day could be a pear and raspberry strudel and you might find banana-walnut ice cream layered with fresh bananas and raspberries. Add a cup of cappuccino, lean back and look at the incredible ceiling, and appreciate one of Boston's more original restaurants.

Lunch daily, 11:30 to 2:30; dinner nightly, 5:30 to 11:30.

Restaurant Suntory, 212 Stuart St., Boston. (617) 338-2111.
Japanese. $14 to $24.
Not at all a typical Japanese restaurant, this is a three-story, top-of-the-line showcase for food run by Japan's largest liquor company (check out the main-floor lounge with its display cases of exotic liquors, including whiskey in bottles shaped like a violin and a grand piano). Here, in the chain's first of several American restaurants, is the kind of sophisticated style and cuisine you might expect to find in Tokyo, amid priceless Japanese art and rock gardens made of Japanese stones. Besides the lounge, the first floor contains Boston's best sushi bar. The second floor has the Shabu-Shabu Room, where food is boiled, broiled or stir-fried in hot pots on a heated stone at your table. The third-floor Teppan-Yaki Room is where meats, seafoods and vegetables are cooked Benihana style — without the showmanship, we're told — at tables for twelve, with empty chairs left between groups for a semblance of privacy. Here, among other selections, you can get a seven-course imperial dinner. Although Suntory seats 126, it seems much bigger and includes a number of private or small-group rooms, some of which require removal of shoes (but the bases of the seating areas are discreetly hollowed out for the comfort of American legs).

Lunch, Monday-Friday 11:30 to 2; dinner, nightly 6 to 10 or 10:30, Sunday 5:30 to 9:30.

Bnu, 123 Stuart St., Boston. (617) 367-8405.
American/Italian. $9 to $16.50.
A Broadway set designer did the Roman-style decor in this spare but striking little restaurant taking the nickname of owner Linda Criniti. Housed in CityPlace between Bennigan's and Joyce Chen's huge new Chinese restaurant, it specializes in pizzettas, pastas and salads as well as a few entrees. Stars from a midnight-blue

ceiling flicker down on bare wood tables and cement floors as happy patrons dine on some of the city's best pizzas: sun-dried tomato pesto with chicken, basil and mozzarella, or roasted peppers with chives and gorgonzola. Grilled shrimp with oranges, olives, citrus and olive oil on Italian greens is a standout among salads. Add grilled shrimp to the fettuccine with cream, parmesan, pine nuts and basil for a winner of a pasta dish. Other entree possibilities are (again) grilled shrimp with gorgonzola polenta and grilled chicory, grilled chicken breast with wild mushrooms, and grilled lamb chops with romesco sauce and caponata. Dessert choices could be an incredibly airy cannoli, chocolate zabaglione, bread pudding, and polenta cake. Italian and California wines are featured at wallet-pleasing prices.

Lunch, Monday-Friday 11:30 to 2:30; dinner, Monday-Wednesday 5 to 9:30, Thursday-Saturday to 10:30, Sunday to 9.

Back Bay

★ L'Espalier, 30 Gloucester St., Boston. (617) 262-3023.
Contemporary French. Prix-Fixe $56.

For ten years, consensus anointed this formal restaurant in a Back Bay townhouse as the best in town. Then founding owner Moncef Meddeb sold it in 1988 to his former sous chef, Frank McClelland, who had made quite a name for himself at the former Country Inn at Princeton, and consensus is that it's as good as ever, but with far more competition than previously. Frank patrols the new-cuisine frontier, tinkering tirelessly with his menu and adding exotica like squab and fig salad with wild mushroom quenelles and foie gras vinaigrette or soup of crayfish and frog's legs with green garlic and chanterelles, souffled corn and smoked salmon pancakes. And those are just for starters. His entrees might be grilled partridge with chartreuse of cabbage, foie gras and cepes with a champagne, huckleberry and sage sauce; fricassee of Maine lobster and lotte with fennel, favas and saffron piperade, and stuffed roast veal rib-eye with sweetbreads and swiss chard, sauced with black truffles, port and tarragon. Some items carry surcharges on the prix-fixe menu of three courses. Available on weekdays is a more expensive menu degustation, for which the chef chooses your meal. We'll never forget ours that started with an intense soup of three game meats, a pheasant salad with truffles and foie gras, and a fish course of scotch salmon and sea scallops with truffles in a champagne sauce. A sorbet of champagne with ossetra caviar cleared the palate for the main course, a canon of tender, rare lamb resting on a cream of red bell pepper sauce with an eggplant charlotte, wrapped in thin slices of zucchini. Desserts are as stunning as the rest of the meal. You might find a chocolate bete noir with coffee creme anglaise and chocolate espresso beans, pumpkin and mascarpone cheese custard with brandied chestnuts and scotch creme anglaise, or a trio of raspberry, pear and imperial grape sorbets. Two chocolate truffles and coconut macaroons might gild the bill. The setting is the upstairs of an elegant townhouse, where you ring a doorbell to gain entry. Dining is in high-ceilinged rooms on the second and third floors, full of carved moldings, antique art and beautiful flower arrangements in niches. Pin spotlights illuminate tables enhanced by damask linen and comfortable lacquered chairs with curved arms. The wine list is extensive, expensive and notable for fine bordeaux.

Dinner, Monday-Saturday 6 to 10.

★ The Colony, 384 Boylston St., Boston. (617) 536-8500.
Contemporary New England. $28 to $38.

In this land of bean and cod, the Colony's goal is to create a sophisticated regional cuisine based on traditional New England foods and recipes. With co-owner Bruce

Frankel moving back to oversee his original Panache in Cambridge in 1989, partner David Kantrowitz is in the kitchen, and reports are that the Colony remains as good as ever. Yankee cooking is elevated to high art in starters like corn "oysters" (fritters of sweet corn in the shape of fried oysters) with a spicy tartar sauce, littleneck clams with grated ginger and cider vinegar, and sauteed New York foie gras with local apples and hard cider. For main courses, how about wood-grilled lobster with fresh herbs and hot pepper, roast chicken with garlic and cornmeal cakes, and aged rack of lamb with succotash, smokehouse bacon and crisp potatoes? There are other surprises: veal steak comes with a macaroni and cheese casserole made of pasta and goat cheese. The cheese tray of fine New England farm cheeses with Vermont crackers is not to be missed. Nor are the chocolate bread and butter pudding made with sliced brioche, deep-dish fruit cobbler with homemade vanilla ice cream, and traditional Indian pudding with maple-glazed apples. The regional theme extends to the wine list, where a page of selections from New England wineries vies with California and French vintages. The elegant room is decorated in turn-of-the-century Brahmin style: soft yellow walls with gray wainscoting and molding, polished brass chandeliers and wall sconces, thick carpets and Chinese Chippendale chairs with leather seats at well-spaced tables set with white cloths, burgundy-rimmed china and heavy silver.

Dinner, Tuesday-Saturday 6 to 10 or 10:30.

♥ The Cafe Budapest, 90 Exeter St., Boston. (617) 734-3388.
Hungarian/Continental. $19 to $33.

If you have any romance in your soul, you'll love the Cafe Budapest. From the main dining room, all in red and white and dark woods, with old Hungarian flasks, walking sticks, wine jugs and decorated plates on the walls, to the small blue dining room used at night, with handsome stenciling done by a Provincetown artist and glazed ceramic della robbia all around the arched entry, to the dining room off the lounge all in pink except for some green chairs, it's almost too pretty for words. The late Edith Ban's formula for romance and fine dining now is being carried on by her sister, Dr. Rev Kurey. Our first memorable lunch began with a hearty peasant soup topped with fried noodles and exquisite chicken paprikas crepes, continued with gypsy baron rice pilaf and the authentic beef goulash that an Austrian friend who manages a fine hotel thinks is the greatest, and a sensational Hungarian strudel, accompanied by fragrant Viennese coffee, made from beans ground fresh hourly and served in glass cups. Most of the 25 dinner entrees are Middle European, although chateaubriand for one with salad mimosa and broiled lemon sole vie with things like sweetbreads a la Hongroise sous cloche, sauerbraten and wiener schnitzel. One night, our party declared spectacular the veal served with rice, string beans and carrots, tied in a bundle, and a special salad of grapes and endive arranged like a star. The desserts are unusual, from a champagne torte to crepes with farm cheese and raisins.

Lunch, Monday-Saturday noon to 3; dinner by reservation, 5 to 10:30, Friday and Saturday to midnight, Sunday 1 to 10:30.

Papa-Razzi, 271 Dartmouth St., Boston. (617) 536-6560.
California-Style Italian. $6.75 to $19.95.

In its incarnation as Dartmouth Street, this expansive basement restaurant with a woodburning pizza oven set into the rear wall drew the trendies for a few years. With a new chef from Prego in Beverly Hills, it reopened in late 1989 with a new name and what management says is a "lighter, healthier, more California-style concept." That translates to fourteen versions of pizza, from del mare (tomatoes, shrimp, garlic, mozzarella, and basil) to California (fresh tomatoes, sun-dried tomatoes and goat cheese). An equal number of pasta dishes includes linguinette al pesto and farfalle al salmone (bowtie pasta with smoked salmon, peas and light cream). The most expensive dish on the menu is lambata di vitello, a large veal chop done in brown butter and rosemary. Most of the pizzas and pastas are listed on the lunch menu at a dollar or so less than dinner, along with salads like grilled chicken breast on mixed greens with balsamic vinaigrette. Start with minestrone and end with fresh strawberries and zabaglione or bomba Papa-Razzi, a large pastry puff filled with gelato and topped with chocolate and berry sauce. Wines start in the low teens. Each table sports a bottle of olive oil infused with hot peppers, and in a rack near the door are European and American magazines to read. Prints of Italy are on the walls of three dining areas flanking a marble bar, and the atmosphere is definitely European.

Lunch, Monday-Friday 11:30 to 3:30; dinner nightly, 5:30 to 11:30 or 12:30; brunch Saturday-Sunday, 11:30 to 3:30.

Cactus Club, 939 Boylston St., Boston. (617) 236-0200.
Southwestern. $7.25 to $11.95.

Allegro on Boylston gave way in 1989 to this trendy place, furnished in Santa Fe style. Although co-owner Jimmy Burke is still involved at Allegro in Waltham, this is his fun spot. About the biggest stuffed buffalo you ever saw stands guard over the bar, which is popular with the young crowd. There are horns, skulls, saddles, and bunches of hot peppers and cactus everywhere. Windows are trimmed in deep pink and turquoise, and the chairs and tables are an attractive blond wood with a pickled finish. Very good tortilla chips and salsa spiked with cilantro start the meal. At lunch we savored the fabulous corn and chili chowder and black bean soup with jalapeno sour cream, the chicken fiesta with spicy lime dressing, and the roasted vegetable salad with black bean aioli. The spinach and avocado salad is served with cornbread croutons and a creamy salsa dressing; the barbecued Texas beef ribs with grilled potato salad and ranch beans. At dinner you could begin with cold smoked pork loin with coriander pesto or a black bean and chevre tostada and move on to grilled yellowfin tuna with aztec butter and roasted corn relish or grilled salmon with serano chilies and honey glaze. Try an adobe mud pie or chocolate-caramel pignon torte for dessert. There are all kinds of beers and, of course, several versions of margaritas. The bloody maria is made with jalapeno tequila and the coyote killer is just that, harboring light and dark rum, ginger beer, pineapple and cranberry juice and triple sec, with a peach schnapps float.

Open daily from 11:30 to midnight; Sunday brunch, 11 to 3.

Mr. Leung, 545 Boylston St., Boston. (617) 236-4040.
Chinese. $16 to $22.

Hong Kong-born Bernard Leung, who had been manager at Sally Ling's, opened his own urbane place in a Copley Square basement in 1987. It's hardly your typical Chinese restaurant. It couldn't be with black ceilings dotted with hundreds of tiny spotlights zeroing in on the lavish flowers on each table in three glamorous, mod dining rooms and an eat-in solarium bar. And the menu is not the usual mix-and-pass smorgasbord; it's "Hong Kong style," the host advised. Among the Cantonese and Mandarin treats are crispy whole fish Hunan style, pan-fried veal with oyster sauce, sliced chicken with young ginger root, steak kew with onion and black bean sauce, and leg of lamb sauteed with Szechuan spicy sauce and macadamia nuts. The Peking duck is served in two courses: crispy duck skin wrapped in pancakes, and duck meat slices sauteed with fresh vegetables in brown sauce. Fetching starters include chicken velvet corn soup, Szechuan wontons in spicy oil, and crispy shrimp balls. Ginger ice cream and sesame fried banana with ice cream are the desserts of choice. A tasting dinner of eleven courses and a Boston seafood dinner of ten courses are available for two or more. The last page of the menu includes eleven "combination" dishes for those who prefer.

Lunch, Monday-Friday 11:30 to 3; dinner nightly, 6 to 11.

Ritz-Carlton Dining Room, Ritz-Carlton Hotel, 15 Arlington St., Boston.
(617) 536-5700.
Continental. $25 to $60.

The Ritz is not just a hotel. It's an institution — *the* place where proper Bostonians put up visitors or go themselves for lunch in the cafe, tea in the lounge, or drinks and dinner in the Ritz Bar and Dining Room. What could be more traditional than a meal in the airy second-floor Dining Room (no fancy name here) with its gold-trimmed ceiling, cobalt blue water glasses and chandeliers, and its sedate view over (and above) the hubbub of the Boston Public Garden? What could be higher than the prices — appetizers to $65 (for caviar), salads to $32, vegetables for $5? You might start with avocado filled with lobster, try the breast of pheasant sauteed with truffles or chateaubriand ceremoniously carved tableside for two, and finish with a dessert souffle. The menu is standard Ritz — which is to say classic, continental and a bit old hat, but the presentation and service are straight out of Europe. The martinis in the Ritz Bar are legendary, as are power breakfasts in the sidewalk Ritz Cafe and English tea in the Victorian parlor-lounge.

Lunch, daily noon to 2:30; dinner, 6 to 10 or 11; Sunday brunch, 11 to 2:30.

St. Botolph Restaurant, 99 St. Botolph St., Boston. (617) 266-3030.
Regional American. $14.50 to $24.50.

This architectural gem of a restaurant hidden behind the Colonnade Hotel in a brick townhouse has had its ups and downs while we've been dining there during convention breaks since its opening in 1975. In the vanguard of Boston's early restaurant revival, it dipped and then rose with a change of chefs. At our latest visit, everything was up with a pleasant, contemporary menu served in pleasant, comfortable surroundings. Try for a table at one of the turreted windows, looking onto a quintessential Back Bay townhouse scene. Walls are brick, chairs are cane and chrome, and nicely spaced tables on two floors are draped with crisp white linens. Dinner entrees embrace the traditional broiled Boston scrod with red and white grape beurre blanc and roast breast of turkey with cranberry horseradish, as well as sea scallops with pear-ginger cream and grilled tenderloin of pork with green peppercorn chutney. Start with a wild mushroom and sage sausage set on an herbed demi-glace or warm smoked salmon mousse with chive butter. Finish with a chocolate-hazelnut torte, deep-dish pecan pie or a fruit tart.

Lunch, Monday-Friday noon to 2:30; dinner, nightly 6 to 10:30, Friday and Saturday to midnight; Sunday brunch, noon to 3.

Back Bay Bistro, 565 Boylston St., Boston. (617) 536-4477.
Contemporary. $13.95 to $17.95.

Here's a classic uptown American bistro: a long and narrow high-ceilinged room, noisy and cheerful, with a menu posted daily to tempt with the freshest ingredients. It's also a place for dinner in a hurry; we arrived at 7:30 on a Saturday night to beat the crowds (no reservations taken), and then felt rushed as patrons waited at the bar and the busy staff did their best to turn our tiny table. But not until we had shared a good appetizer of salmon and mussel mousse, followed by a creamy though rather bland pasta with scallops, smoked shrimp and cod cheeks, and two noisettes of veal on a sauce of balsamic vinegar and sun-dried tomatoes, accompanied by small red potatoes, brussels sprouts and summer squash. The menu also offers cheese and fruit platters, creative salads and interesting sandwiches. Some surprises are carrot-ginger soup, warm chicken liver salad, loup de mer (breaded and baked with a sauce of roasted red pepper and pernod), and poached trout stuffed with fish mousse and served with watercress beurre blanc. Desserts are of the strawberry-almond bread pudding, double chocolate cake with raspberries and frangelica brownie ilk. Even the wine offerings change daily on the small but select wine list, with a second and lengthier list available by the glass..

Lunch, Monday-Saturday 11:30 to 2:30; dinner nightly, 5:30 to 10:30.

Echo Restaurant & Cafe, 279A Newbury St., Boston. (617) 236-4488.
Regional American. $10.50 to $19.50.

This new establishment has a large outdoor dining area, a downstairs cafe and an upstairs dining room in black and white, with color provided by the works of local artists and the passing Newbury Street scene. The menu is limited but serviceable. Dinner entrees range from sauteed chicken livers with mustard cream sauce to sauteed veal with fresh morels. Grilled duck with tarragon and grapes, jalapeno fettuccine with black beans and creme fraiche, and baked trout stuffed with shiitake mushrooms are winners. For lunch, try the salade nicoise, whiskey-grilled shrimp, brandade (cod with croutons and nicoise olives), pissaladiere (provencale onion pie with tomato and olives), or cold braised veal with tuna-caper mayonnaise. Scotch eggs with salad and French bread is a hit at brunch.

Dinner, Monday-Saturday 6 to 10 or 11; cafe, 11:30 to 10 or 11; Sunday brunch, 11:30 to 4.

Grill 23 & Bar, 161 Berkeley St., Boston. (617) 542-2255.
Steakhouse. $15 to $27.50.

What can we say about a steakhouse? This one is fancy, pricey and sometimes unbearably noisy. Antiques and oriental rugs, rich wood paneling, polished brass rails and marble columns enhance the masculine, high-ceilinged dining room in the historic Salada Tea Building. This is Boston's quintessential steakhouse, crowded and animated to a deafening pitch. The uncomplicated fare includes well-aged steaks (the eighteen-ounce New York sirloin is renowned), thick veal and lamb chops, and grilled seafood, especially swordfish and salmon, deftly broiled in an open kitchen. Potatoes and vegetables are a la carte. Appetizers are straightforward, from oysters to smoked salmon tartare. Considered best of the desserts is Indian pudding.

Lunch, Monday-Friday noon to 2:30; dinner nightly, 6 to 10 or 11; Sunday brunch, 11:30 to 3.

Turner Fisheries, 10 Huntington Ave., Boston. (617) 424-7425.
Seafood. $9.95 to $18.95.

The Boston seafood house of the same name supplies all the fish to the Westin Hotel's large restaurant with its many-boothed dining room, greenhouse dining area and several raw bars. Paintings of underwater marine life dominate the dining room walls, fans whir overhead, and brass hooks between the booths are for hanging coats on. At lunch, you can get an award-winning clam chowder (also available to take home), a bucket of mussels, cobb salad and soup, or cold poached salmon on dill-cucumber sauce. Only what is fresh that day is served; we had monkfish broiled to perfection, served with crisp carrots, cauliflower, broccoli, and red-skinned potatoes. Bouillabaisse is a house specialty, and a seafood salad special was an interesting mixture of green and white pasta with salmon, shrimp, mussels and scallops. For dessert, choose from the many pastries and cakes of the day. The almond slice pastry is commendable, and the mile-high ice cream pie is a tradition.

Lunch, Monday-Saturday 11 to 4; dinner nightly, to 11:30; Sunday brunch, 10:30 to 2:30.

South End

* Hamersley's Bistro, 578 Tremont St., Boston. (617) 267-6068.
Contemporary American. $16.50 to $26.

Two redheads, Gordon and Fiona Hamersley, run this fun and friendly place whose 50 seats are as crowded as the Fenway Park bleachers when the Red Sox are hot. Hot most of the time is chef Gordon, once apprentice to Wolfgang Puck at Ma Maison in Los Angeles and then executive sous chef to Lydia Shire at Seasons. Bobbing around in red baseball caps in an open kitchen, he and two assistants show a refreshing lack of pretense as they prepare what he calls rustic, peasant food. We call it gutsy. Our dinner began with a memorable grilled mushroom and garlic "sandwich" (two toasted bread slices flanking an abundance of mushrooms and watercress) and a tasty but messy whole braised artichoke stuffed with olives and mint. Roasted pumpkin soup with cabbage and curried lentils, duck confit with sweet and sour prunes, and sweetbread, tasso and pepper hash are other recommended starters. Among "roasts, braises and main courses," we loved the duckling with turnips, endive and apple slices — an enormous portion, including an entire leg and crisp slices grilled and blackened at the edges. The roast chicken with garlic, lemon and parsley is a menu fixture. Seared scallops with ginger and scallions, seared veal chop with pears and baked roquefort cheese, and grilled pork with toasted pumpkin seeds, pickled pumpkin and rice are other seasonal possibilities. Desserts are earthy: perhaps spiced gingerbread with grilled pears and creme fraiche or cranberry-mincemeat pie. Fiona Hamersley, former New England director of the American Institute of Food and Wine, has put together an interesting if pricey wine list. The decor is typical bistro: white paper over the tablecloths, silverware rolled inside white napkins, track lighting that is rather too bright, and tables rather too close. But oh, what food.

Dinner, Monday-Saturday 6 to 10:30.

Icarus, 3 Appleton St., Boston. (617) 426-1790.
New American. $18.50 to $28.

A statue of the mythological Icarus looming above tree branches lit with tiny white lights high on the rear wall oversees this stylish spot that reopened in 1987 after a move from Tremont Street. It's a sunken, split-level room full of rich dark wood and a mix of booths and round mission oak tables left bare except for dusty pink napkins folded sideways between fluted silverware. Recessed aqua lighting outlines the perimeter of the ceiling. The menu is short but sweet: entrees like salmon steamed in romaine with scallops, ginger and soy, grilled chicken with roast garlic and garlic mashed potatoes, duck with cider and a wild rice pudding, and roasted beef tenderloin with shiitake mushrooms and brandy. For openers, how about pear and leek soup, poppyseed and onion crepes with smoked trout and golden caviar, grilled quail with smoked bacon and wilted greens, or a pizzetta of red pepper, eggplant, goat cheese and sage? Many of the starters turn up on the interesting brunch menu. Chocolate is the dessert specialty, from a dense black and white pate on raspberry sauce to a chocolate-cherry truffle torte.

Dinner, Monday-Saturday 5:30 to 10:30; Sunday, brunch 11 to 4, supper 4 to 9.

St. Cloud, 557 Tremont St., Boston. (617) 353-0202.
New American. $16 to $26.

Tres chic and ever-so-trendy is this newcomer with a crowded bar and a small, sleek dining room, its floor-to-ceiling windows filled with views of the passing street scene and the John Hancock Tower between clay planters. Purple upholstered chairs, eggplant-colored banquettes, track lighting from the black latticed ceiling, gray formica tables, and gray carpeting set the scene. This is the latest showplace for the considerable culinary talents of owner Rebecca Caras of Rebecca's on Charles Street. Appetizers are diverse: grilled squid stuffed with shrimp, ginger and coriander in a sesame vinaigrette, hummus and baba ghanoush, chicken and corn tortillas with mole sauce, and terrine of foie gras, port jelly and truffle vinaigrette. Main courses range from sauteed salmon with corn and oyster fritters to rack of lamb with goat cheese and ratatouille ravioli, from pumpkin ravioli filled with ricotta cheese and prosciutto to grilled duck breast with crackling salad, fresh figs and port wine sauce. A section of the menu offers eight lighter items. Desserts range from several chocolate pastries to a deep-dish pear tart with dates and an Italian cheesecake of ricotta topped with a brandied date puree. Most wines are Californias.

Open Tuesday-Saturday, 11:30 to midnight; Sunday and Monday, 11:30 to 10.

Beacon Hill

Another Season, 97 Mount Vernon St., Boston. (617) 367-0880.
International. $14 to $23.
The tables in this romantic refuge with three small dining rooms, though tiny and close, are decked out in white napery and fresh flowers. The colorful French murals on the walls make you think you're eating in a small and intimate art gallery. The meals combine the artistic and culinary talents of English-born chef-owner Odette Bery. Her changing menu is eclectic: appetizers like shrimp sausage with grilled fennel and tomatoes, venison pate with grilled pears, cumberland sauce and watercress, and goat cheese salad with arugula, grilled eggplant, onions, and olives with a balsamic dressing. Likely entrees include beef bourbon with roasted onions and puree of celery root, chicken chevre with grilled squash, and swordfish Mexican style with black bean stew and avocados. Odette Bery melds continental, Mediterranean, Latin American and Asian influences into a cuisine that is hers alone. We have fond memories of a winter dinner that began with shrimp aioli with a great garlicky sauce and a fantastic watercress mousse with prosciutto. Entrees were a beef tenderloin sauteed with red peppers and juniper berries, and chicken breast with a sauce of brie and fresh thyme. The dessert list yielded a super marjolaine and apricot cheesecake with a shortbread crust garnished with kiwi.

Lunch, Tuesday-Friday noon to 2; dinner, Monday-Saturday 6 to 10.

Ristorante Toscano, 41 Charles St., Boston. (617) 723-4090.
Northern Italian. $14.50 to $21.
A table of antipasti, hams, cheeses, oils and vinegars near the entry greets diners at this charming Tuscan restaurant in Beacon Hill. A dining room with a quarry tile floor and windows onto the street has pale peach walls bearing posters of Florence and a brick wall hung with old pans and tools. Sturdy rush chairs flank tables set with white linens and heavy cutlery. Specials supplement the permanent menu, which offers interesting pastas and entrees like veal with porcini mushrooms and cream, grilled cornish hen marinated in olive oil, roasted pork loin with rosemary and garlic, and steak flambeed with black pepper, cognac and cream. Carpaccio presented in an overlapping geometric pattern is a stalwart starter. Signature desserts are tirami su and creme caramel. The wine list is mostly Italian.

Lunch, Monday-Saturday 11:30 to 2:30; dinner nightly, 5:30 to 10 or 10:30.

Hungry I, 71½ Charles St., Boston. (617) 227-3524.
Contemporary French/International. $13.95 to $23.
"Ouch," says the hand-painted word on the arch above the doorway to the

Boston

subterranean quarters of this intimate charmer. Once past the head-basher, you'll find yourself in a long, narrow basement room reminiscent of a country inn in France. Copperware and a shelf of antique plates decorate a brick wall, and close-together tables are appointed with white over red cloths, white china and white napkins standing tall in the water glasses. It's a cozy, romantic setting for chef Peter Ballarin's changing fare. The short but sweet menu might list red snapper grenoble, New Zealand venison sauteed with cognac and concord grapes, bracioli, poussin tarragon with almond-cranberry farcie and port wine sauce, and saddle of rabbit braised with sausage and fennel in dark beer. Starter possibilities range from chilled Alaskan crabmeat to Syrian lentil salad with feta bread. Brunch and lunch are served outside in summer.

Dinner nightly by reservation, 6 to 10; Sunday brunch.

Waterfront

★ Jasper's, 240 Commercial St., Boston. (617) 523-1126.
Contemporary American. $18 to $35.

Jasper White, who teamed with Lydia Shire at Seasons before opening his own restaurant in 1983 in an old molasses warehouse near the waterfront, is considered the crown prince of Boston's culinary kingdom. In 1989, he branched out with the publication of a cookbook, "Jasper White's Cooking from New England," and is producing a fish and clam fry mix, an all-natural, stone-ground meal made at Gray's Mill in Adamsville, R.I. One look at Jasper and you can tell he loves food; one look at his menu and you know he knows what to do with it. To basic New England cooking he adds an international flourish, as in the Portuguese pork rib-eye with clams and garlic sauce, Alentejo style, or the mixed grill of marinated quail and spicy duck sausage with johnnycake polenta. Rare bluefin tuna comes with olives and saffron noodles and pan-roasted lobster with chervil and chives. All is not highfalutin': there are salt cod cakes with warm greens and country bacon, and Yankee pot roast with root vegetables. We liked the breast of squab with poached oysters in zinfandel sauce, served with wild rice pilaf and a side salad of arugula, mache and radicchio topped with two tiny squab legs. Jasper is at his most inventive with starters: chunky lobster stew with tomalley toasts, warm terrine of rabbit with cranberry onion jam, sauteed moulard foie gras with warm beet and crackling salad, and remarkable salads like one of grilled duck with papaya and spiced pecans. Desserts are more limited, perhaps a pear upside-down cake, chocolate-walnut tart or a selection of homemade ice creams and sorbets — kiwi, coconut and champagne, intense and refreshing. Jasper doesn't skimp on the wine list and charges dearly for it; you'll find only a few under $30. Service is professional and dining is calm, relaxed and not at all intimidating. The brick interior has been painted in pretty pastels, with organdy curtains at the windows, spectacular floral arrangements, and striking art on the walls of three small dining rooms.

Dinner, Monday-Saturday 6 to 10 or 11.

Anthony's Pier 4, 140 Northern Ave., Boston. (617) 423-6363.
Seafood. $9.95 to $29.95.

Many famous people (Richard Burton and Elizabeth Taylor, to name two) have dined in Boston's most famous restaurant. You can see them in the hundreds of pictures on the walls of the largest of Anthony Athanas's restaurants beside Boston Harbor, where 600 diners can be seated on the main floor. Extravagance is his byword, with lots of seafood, lots of dining rooms, lots of plants and ferns, lots of nautical mementoes — in fact, lots of everything, including food and value. It's all a bit overwhelming but fun, and the views of the Boston skyline, the planes landing and taking off at nearby Logan Airport, and the passing ships help take your mind off the occasionally lackluster fare. From baked finnan haddie to shrimp rockefeller, bouillabaisse to lobster savannah, prime rib to grand marnier souffle, Anthony's has it all and packs in the crowds. The outdoor patio by the water is good for cocktails and, for the first lucky 75 or so, dinner.

Open from 11:30 a.m. to 11 p.m., Saturday from noon, Sunday 12:30 to 10:30.

$ No Name Restaurant, 15½ Fish Pier, Boston. (617) 338-7530.

Seafood. $5.95 to $9.95.

Not only is there no name but no sign or identifying reference other than a makeshift winter storm entrance. You need to know where this is, halfway down Fish Pier, not far past the Super Snooty Seafood Co., but almost any Bostonian can tell you. Fish (broiled or fried) is impeccably fresh if rather unseasoned and the price is right. Specials of the day's catch (salmon, bluefish, swordfish, mussels with garlic) are offered, and the seafood chowder has many fans. The homemade pies are also good. No Name is very plain with lineups of tables, each topped with a knife and fork on a paper napkin, a ketchup bottle and plastic cups, and you'll probably have to wait in line unless you go at an off hour. Owner Nick Contos is especially proud of the new upstairs dining room, which is surprisingly spacious. Try to sit in the rear, where there's a water view. After years without a license, beer and wine are now available.

Open Monday-Saturday from 11 to 10.

Charlestown

$ Olives, 67 Main St., Charlestown. (617) 242-1999.

New American. $10.50 to $16.50.

One of two hot new restaurants in the Boston area in 1989 (Biba was the other), this is not really in Boston proper. It's a brief hop from downtown, but a world apart in historic Charlestown. Paul Revere, whose house was nearby, would have been happy here with a hearty supper before his famous ride — if he could have gotten in. The 50 seats in the intimate restaurant are hard to come by. The reasons: the celebrated chef-owner is young Todd English, who left Michela's in Cambridge to do his own thing with wife Olivia (hence the name); the food is abundant and ranges from simple to exciting, and the prices are about half what they'd be across the Charles River in Boston. Olives takes no reservations. With the place filled most nights by 6, hostess Olivia takes names and sends would-be diners up the street to the Warren Tavern for drinks. Once seated, you'll find a spare black and pale yellow decor, bentwood chairs and tapestry banquettes, and clothless black tables bearing tiny dishes of salt and pepper and colorful Spanish plates. A big jar on the bar, "Olio de Oliva," is filled with grapevines and berries. Also on the bar are a plate of home-cured olives and a basket full of loaves of bread from the wood-fired oven. There are six stools at the bar, the least noisy and most spacious place to eat in the restaurant, and a good vantage spot for watching the goings-on in the open kitchen. Here, Todd and crew whip up starters like Olives tart (marinated olives, anchovies, onions and goat cheese), chargrilled octopus and squid in garlic and olive oil, Tuscan bean soup with cabbage-wrapped salmon, and wood-grilled prosciutto salad with shallot vinaigrette, green beans and walnut sticks. Brick-oven baked rabbit lasagna and new potato-sausage pizzetta with basil and garlic are among pastas and pizzas. Entrees might be brick-oven cassoulet, grilled filet of pork with fennel and honey-vinegar glaze and white bean puree, osso buco Sicilian style with olives and semolina dumplings, salmon cakes with creamy lentils and aioli, whole sea bass with fennel and hen of the woods, and grilled leg of lamb sandwich with roasted red pepper salad and chive toast. The cheapest item on the menu, spit-roasted chicken with watercress salad and fried mashed-potato cake, is considered the best chicken in town. Desserts could be candied ginger creme brulee, pear and date upside-down cake, banana cream pie, and the night's souffle. The wine list is reasonably priced.

Dinner, Tuesday-Saturday 5:30 to 10. Beer and wine only. No smoking.

Cambridge Area

Cambridge

* Michela's, 245 First St., Cambridge. (617) 494-5419.
New Italian. $19 to $28.

Mention Michela's and start a spirited debate among Cambridge foodies. Better than ever, say fans of Michela Larson; lost its touch, say those disenchanted since original chef Todd English left to open his own restaurant in Charlestown. The space in the hard-to-get-to Carter Ink building is a stunner. The elegant square cavern of a room is vaguely art deco and painted in terra cotta. Prim white tables are set with square water glasses and heavy silver beneath exposed pipes on the salmon-colored ceiling. There's also a sidewalk cafe in the building's high-tech atrium, where light and casual Italian soul food is available, all dishes for under $10, and no reservations are taken (they're usually essential in the dining room). Spattered pink and green menus detail the limited but ambitious fare, from antipasti, salads and pizzettas through exotic pastas and main courses like grilled tuna with escarole, a red pepper and olive pizzetta, pan-roasted salmon with potato focaccia, and pan-fried veal chop with roasted tomatoes, eggplant and polenta. La cucina nuova never had it so good as in our lunch of mozzarella salad with fresh tomatoes, basil, black olives and pepper; goat-cheese ravioli with spinach pasta in a sauce of wild mushrooms, and a pasta with a ragout of veal, grilled quail and artichokes served on a tomato coulis, followed by a honeydew sorbet almost as creamy as ice cream. Other desserts to surrender to are poached pears baked in a pistachio tart with cinnamon cream and cranberry compote, and a frozen praline ice cream cake with hazelnuts. The crusty Italian bread, made with olive oil, is served minus bread plates and minus butter. The wine list mixes fine offerings from Italy with those from France, California and Oregon.

Lunch, Monday-Friday noon to 2:30; dinner, Monday-Saturday 6 to 10 or 10:30. Cafe, Monday-Friday 5:30 to 10:30.

* Upstairs at the Pudding, 10 Holyoke St., Cambridge. (617) 864-1933.
New Italian. Prix-fixe, $42.

Founding chef-owner Michael Silver is gone, but partner Mary-Catherine Deibel and chef Deborah Hughes remain at the helm of this unexpected treasure on the top floor of Harvard's famed Hasty Pudding Club building. The beamed cathedral ceiling of the Pudding's venerable refectory is hung with brass chandeliers and its soaring green walls are decorated with posters from Pudding shows of yore. In prevailing pink and green, it's a beautiful setting for the serving of beautiful food at the cutting edge. The three-course prix-fixe dinner changes nightly. For the first course, try any of the tagliatelles (said to be as good as those in Bologna), especially the version with sun-dried tomatoes, artichoke hearts, Moroccan lemons, and goat cheese. The parsnip and celeriac chowder with chervil butter and the fresh fig, feta cheese and thyme pizza also are recommended. Main courses range from swordfish with sweet red pepper relish to rack of lamb with roasted red peppers, anchovies and parsley. The plate overflows with interesting accompaniments, perhaps fresh young asparagus, a spoonful of yam puree, braised leeks, salsify, wild Italian mushrooms,and shallots stewed in wine-vinegar broth. The final course is a choice of salad or dessert, perhaps charlotte au chocolat, citrus almond cake, macadamia nut torte, or mocha ice.

Dinner, Tuesday-Saturday 6 to 10.

★ 798 Main, 798 Main St., Cambridge. (617) 876-8444.
Contemporary New England. $13 to $17.

Bruce Frankel, one of Boston's better chefs, returned in 1989 to his original Cambridge restaurant, Panache, after several years in the kitchen at the Colony, the Boston restaurant he founded with David Kantrowitz to showcase updated New England cuisine. What he found back on the homefront was a restaurant and a menu that needed updating — his words, not ours (we always loved it). So he closed at Thanksgiving, renovated and reopened in December with pristine quarters and a changing menu of contemporary New England fare. A typical night's entrees might be sauteed skate with herbed oil and garlic potatoes, native crab casserole, maple-barbecued baby chicken with white cornbread, grilled venison steak with cranberries, and braised lamb with winter vegetables and herbs. Start with garnished Hubbardston chevre with grilled flatbread, wild mushroom stew with corn pasta, or grilled quail and garlic salad. Finish with hard apple cider sorbet and raspberries or goat's milk custard with maple. Transplanted New Yorker Bruce believes in rooting for the home team, so is on something of a crusade to promote the oft-overlooked New England cuisine. Although some found the Colony too pure and straightlaced, he's having fun here in an updated New England tavern atmosphere: black chairs and bare floors, a forest green chair rail along the walls hung with quilts, and white-linened tables set with hand-painted wooden plates in Colonial colors and oversize silverware. In place of the mirrored niches at the rear he planned to install a playful trompe-l'oeil mural of his kitchen.

Dinner, Tuesday-Saturday 6 to 10.

★ Chez Nous, 147 Huron Ave., Cambridge. (617) 864-6670.
New French. $18 to $25.

An unassuming storefront on Cambridge's West Side houses a 31-seat restaurant that is pure and beloved by neighborhood connoisseurs. Chef-owner Elizabeth Fischer hails from Germany and grew up with Austrian influences. She prefers "good cooking, basic and simple," lacking nouvelle conceits but contemporary as can be. Her short menu changes weekly. When we were there, starters included butternut squash soup with curry butter, duck liver pate with cassis-onion relish, Nantucket scallops with grapefruit and lillet, and smoked American sturgeon with mustard-dill sauce. Typical main courses are seared tuna steak with roasted yellow peppers and garlic, Norwegian salmon with ginger and scallions, loin lamb chops provencale, and filet of beef with horseradish sauce. Cauliflower, spinach, fennel, and a blend of sauteed potato and sweet potato might accompany. For dessert, try Elizabeth's torte (we're told it's better than a sacher torte), an exceptional creme brulee or meringue with strawberries. The space that housed Le Bocage before it moved to Watertown remains pristine: walls are sponged a midnight blue, there's a trellised ceiling, and white linens and pepper grinders are on each table. The small wine list is as well chosen as the menu.

Dinner, Tuesday-Saturday 6 to 9:30. Reservations required. No smoking.

Rarities, Charles Hotel, 1 Bennett St., Cambridge. (617) 864-1200.
New American. $26 to $31.25.

Cambridge's highest-style dining room, Rarities derives its name from a 1672 botany treatise, "New England Rarities Discovered," a chronicle of the region's flora and fauna, much of which the kitchen uses in its cooking. The menu is full of rarities as well. Seasonal appetizers could be crisp risotto cakes with lamb sausage, roast skate with black beans and radish, parsnip ribbons with lobster and trumpet mushrooms, white truffles on homemade egg noodles, grappa-cured tuna with artichoke pancakes and ossetra caviar with, what next, animal crackers. What next also might be a soup of roasted hubbard squash with hard cider or another called seafood operetta (at $10.45, it had better sing). For entrees, how about salmon in a potato shell with caviar, duckling with ginger and oak mushrooms, pan-roasted lobster with sour cream and sweet potato, and venison with savoy cabbage and juniper? The pastry chef composes ethereal desserts at an open station behind a buffet table groaning with the night's array. The wine recommendations on the menu are piratically priced, but some are available by the half bottle. Ask to see the more extensive "cellar book" if you dare. The dining room seats 70 at white-clothed tables flanked by black lacquered chairs upholstered in gray flannel. The only spot of color is a spray of orchids on each table. After dinner, tarry for a drink outside Rarities in the romantic **Quiet Bar,** all loveseats and plush chairs, or go on to the **Regattabar,** which is known for top jazz.

Dinner nightly, 6 to 10 or 11.

Harvest, 44 Brattle St., Cambridge. (617) 492-1115.
  New American. $23 to $28.
  The earliest (1975) of the new Cambridge restaurant breed and trendy before its time, Harvest has had its culinary ups and downs while always remaining *the* place to see and be seen. Hidden behind the Crate & Barrel store, it's furnished in Marimekko, bentwood, stoneware, tiles, zippy prints, and one entire wall of tiny colored lights — all very high-tech, as is typical of designer-owner Jane Thompson and her architect-husband Ben. You can sit in the main dining room, **Ben's Cafe** or the bar (and, seasonally, in an outdoor garden where the trees are strung with white lights). For a spring lunch, we chose a pillowed banquette near the bar and enjoyed hearing classical guitar and excerpts from "The Messiah" on tape. The terrine was a great rough country pate, and we thoroughly enjoyed a huge artichoke served with a mayonnaise and tomato sauce, ringed by crisp vegetables chilled in a vinaigrette, and an entree of sauteed salmon sprigged with fresh dill and served with hot mashed avocado and crisp carrots. The colorful dinner menu, with geese and vegetables painted by Milton Glazer, changes daily. Among appetizers you might find smoked eel and Norwegian salmon with red onion and a spicy cilantro flan, or seared roulade of beef tenderloin with saga blue cheese and pecans. Main courses could be grilled yellowfin tuna with ginger-lime flan, medallions of venison with juniper-port sauce, and a roasted trio of native quail with balsamic-pancetta sauce. An interesting cafe menu changes every six weeks. It's pleasantly priced and contains such surprises as grilled Georgia prawns and Sri Lanka fish curry. For dessert, try bourbon-chocolate mousse cake with macadamia nut dacquoise or sweet potato flan with a champagne genoise. **Harvest Express** is a tiny new takeout with three stools at the counter.

Lunch, Monday-Friday 11:30 to 2:30; dinner nightly, 6 to 10 or 10:30; Saturday and Sunday brunch, noon to 3.

East Coast Grill, 1271 Cambridge St., Cambridge. (617) 491-6568.
  Barbecue/Equatorial. $11.25 to $13.75.
  "Grills just want to have fun" is the motto on the menu and the T-shirts of the staff at this former Inman Square luncheonette that's hot, hot, hot. The hottest dish in New England is an appetizer called ravioli from hell, stuffed with sausage and fired

by the house-bottled Inner Beauty sauce — the label cautions: "This is not a toy. This is serious." So it is. The mustard-colored liquid fire derives its wallop from scotch bonnet chilies, which make jalapenos taste like tofu. Those with less incendiary tastes can start with grilled shrimp and sweetbreads or a roast duck salad. Chef-owner Chris Schlesinger, grandson of the late Harvard historian Arthur Schlesinger, bases his changing menu on equatorial cuisine — food from hot places. He always offers three kinds of barbecue: Memphis spare ribs, authentic and succulent; North Carolina shredded pork flavored with vinegar, and Texas beef brisket. The uninitiated can try a sampler of all three. Grilled dishes include fish of the day, steak with a ginger-peanut sauce and sweet and hot cucumber relish, duck breast and grilled ham with tangerine-cranberry glaze and sweet potato pancakes, and chicken breast with fennel-celeriac slaw and lemon-herb vinaigrette. Cool off with a dessert like Mexican flan with tia maria, chocolate pudding cake or apple crisp. A dozen wines start in the low teens, but frozen margaritas and boutique beers are the beverages of choice. The newly redecorated place is a funky melange of geometric shapes in earthy colors on the walls, splashes of neon, crazy lights, a marble-topped bar, and a rear wall of stainless steel that reflects the flames from the open-pit barbecue. The 48 seats are packed nightly. If you can't get in, take out from **Jake and Earl's Dixie Barbecue,** which Chris and partner Cary Wheaton run next door. Open daily from 11:30 to 11, it's named for his pet Labrador and her father, and looks as if it would be quite at home in his native South.

Dinner nightly, 5:30 to 10 or 10:30.

Cajun Yankee, 1193 Cambridge St., Cambridge. (617) 576-1971.
  Cajun. $9.95 to $17.95.
  The Cajun Yankee is John Silberman, a New Yorker who developed a taste for Cajun food while a student at Tulane University a decade ago and stayed in New Orleans to train with Paul Prudhomme. Evidence that Cajun cookery not only can transfer but endure is provided in this rustic storefront with a linoleum floor, pine wainscoting, high-back carved chairs and bare tables, with strings of red peppers dotted about and a few New Orleans posters and Mardi Gras masks on the walls. From shrimp remoulade and seafood gumbo to praline parfait and sweet potato pecan pie, the food is authentic (the chef flies in his seafood from New Orleans). Start with Cajun popcorn, an avocado stuffed with deep-fried cheese and chipotle salsa, or crab claws in a honey-mustard vinaigrette. Main courses could be blackened almost anything — redfish or tuna, chicken with orange-sour cream sauce, prime rib with brown butter-garlic sauce, pork loins with apple-ginger-raisin compote, or lamb chops with red wine-rosemary sauce. John leavens the blackening with five different seasonings — you know there's something spicy, but you won't lose your tastebuds. Or try chicken and sausage jambalaya, seafood-stuffed trout, pan-fried catfish with pecan mousseline, or roast duckling with orange-chipotle sauce. Finish with the signature bread pudding, sauced with lemon and brandy-chantilly cream.

Dinner, Tuesday-Saturday 6 to 10.

Cottonwood Cafe, The Porter Exchange, 1815 Massachusetts Ave.,
  Cambridge. (617) 661-7440.
  Southwestern. $13.50 to $19.50.
  With its color scheme of aquas and purples, its mod tweed upholstered chairs with green arms, hanging ropes of red peppers and napkins of varied colors on bare washed-paint tables, this is the epitome of a chic Southwestern cafe. Paintings of the Southwest and thick water tumblers edged in aqua add more color. The food is colorful as well: at lunch, a wonderfully thick and spicy minestrone combining every kind of squash, corn and olives you could imagine, a mixed grill sampler that includes

tender strips of chicken and beef served over caramelized onions and peppers, along with purple slaw and a corn pudding served inside a tamale, and grange chicken with a fresh tomato salsa and black bean salad dotted with tomatoes and corn. These dishes were served with thin warm flour tortillas in which to wrap the meat and were delicious. A honeydew margarita was a smooth lead-in to the meal. At night, start with blue mesa shrimp, grilled and smoked and served cold with cilantro mayonnaise and blue corn tortilla strips, or an O'Keeffe salad combining flowering kale, endive, watercress, bell peppers, shiitake mushrooms, and avocado. Entrees include pork loin stuffed with chorizo, apricots and pine nuts, topped with pumpkin-peanut sauce, and seafood posole, a stew of New Mexican corn and chile verde, blended with wine, garlic, shrimp, scallops, fish, and mussels. We like the sound of popcorn chicken roman, sauteed breasts coated with popcorn and served with roasted red pepper sauce and cilantro mayonnaise. End with a raspberry-cranberry hot cobbler or pumpkin cheesecake with bourbon-rum sauce. Sangria comes in the flavor of the week, and fresh fruit margaritas are available by the pitcher.

Lunch daily, 11:30 to 4; dinner, 5:30 to 10 or 11.

Changsho, 1712 Massachusetts Ave., Cambridge. (617) 547-6565.
Chinese. $8.95 to $30.

So stylish is this reincarnation of a modest operation moved from next door that some call it the Frank Lloyd Wright of Chinese restaurants. Its dramatic expanse, partitioned into intimate areas by lattice-work dividers and columns, has spacious tables, high-back upholstered chairs, abundant mahogany and brass, ornamental decorations, and an enormous urn full of flowers. Owner Lily Yu oversees an extensive menu of Szechuan and Mandarin treats. The Peking duck comes highly recommended; always on the menu, it need not be ordered in advance. Chicken is served in fourteen versions, from the house specialty with vegetables, topped with pine nuts and cellophane noodles, and served with lettuce leaves for wrapping, to spicy chicken with five colored vegetables. We'd start with the sampler of five appetizers for two, move on to the sizzling platter of prawns, beef and chicken with broccoli, bamboo shoots and snow pea pods, and be content to finish with a dish of ginger ice cream or honey apple fritters.

Lunch, Monday-Friday 11:30 to 3; dinner nightly, 3 to 10:30 or 11:30, Saturday 11:30 to 11:30; Sunday, dim sum buffet, 11:30 to 3.

Border Cafe, 32 Church St., Cambridge. (617) 864-6100.
Tex-Mex/Cajun. $4.79 to $10.95.

The folks at this popular cafe just off Harvard Square have a sense of humor, and so should their customers. Not for the faint of heart or palate, the atmosphere is lively and downright funky, something of a cross between Durgin-Park and Tiajuana Charlie's, with sturdy wood tables and chairs, walls covered with amusing murals and signs, and Corona beer in a bathtub. On each bare table is an army-size bottle of tabasco sauce, a big container of sea salt, and a beer bottle full of pepper, the better to add spice to the fare. The fajitas are great, especially the Cadillac version with filet mignon. Mesquite-broiled redfish heads the list of Mexican specialties, while blackened redfish does the same among Cajun favorites. Redfish royale, covered with a shrimp and sargento parmesan cheese cream sauce, is the house specialty. You'll find oysters en brochette, catfish saute, Creole chicken, blackened tuna and all the usual Mexican dishes, as well as Cajun popcorn, Mexican ceviche, and blackened chicken pasta and redfish salads. Iced tea is served in quart jars, and the frozen margaritas have been voted the best in Boston.

Open Monday-Saturday, 11 to 11, weekends to 2 a.m., Sunday noon to 11.

Somerville

♥ **Dali Restaurant and Tapas Bar,** 415 Washington St., Somerville.
(617) 661-3254.
Spanish. $10 to $17.

"We are proud to be a real Spanish restaurant," says courtly owner Mario Leon Iriarte, born in Bilbao and raised in Argentina. He opened in 1989 and does no advertising, yet word has gotten around. His restaurant near the Cambridge border packs in people at the tapas bar with its copper plate tiles made in Seville and the crooked picture of Dali on the wall behind. Hanging over the bar is an incredible assortment of items: serrano hams, wine skins, salt cod, dried flowers, ropes of garlic, baskets of corks, and copper dishes. Eleven cold and thirteen hot tapas ($2 to $5) are on the regular menu, and every day twelve or thirteen more are on an "inspiraciones" menu. Served in natural clay bowls, they vary from eggplant flan to skate in paprika sauce to beer-batter prawns to lentil and pork sausage stew to garlic soup to white asparagus with shrimp dressing. To go with, there are more than 25 kinds of sherry and 60 wines, many under $15 and all Spanish. That's not all — two dining rooms with tiled tables are beyond the tapas bar, and the decor must be seen to be believed: curved rails here, Daumier reproductions of Don Quixote there, a wonderful mural of a bacchanal by Mark Steel, walls the color of "blood of the bulls," a plaster arch that makes one think of the Alhambra — it's wild and wonderful, and quite charming. A favorite entree is pescado a la sal, Dali's signature dish: red snapper baked in a crust of salt that is broken when the dish comes to the table, leaving the fish, pure and simple, smelling of the ocean. Also popular is gambas con salsa romesco (shrimp in a sauce of Barcelona origin that includes pimento, almonds, spices, onions and garlic and is like pink velvet, according to the owner). Rabbit is braised in juniper berries, cinnamon, serrano chilies, sherry vinegar and red wine, and could be accompanied by mashed potato rosettes and red cabbage and apples. Of course, there's paella in three versions, valencia, del oceano and de la huerta (for vegetarians). End with flan, crepes filled with fruit and topped with chocolate sauce and orange liqueur, or a dish of quince paste and manchego cheese. "I've been in the business 57 years and 9 months," says Mario with a wink. "My mother was cooking when I was born."

Dinner, Monday-Saturday 5 to midnight.

Watertown

✱ **Le Bocage,** 72 Bigelow Ave., Watertown. (617) 923-1210.
French. Prix-Fixe, $34 to $36.

The name means "a meadow in the woods," and that describes this pristine jewel in a transitional neighborhood. Tall windows in the rear dining room yield a view of a tiny garden with white lights twinkling in espaliered trees, a soothing sight against the urban backdrop. The restaurant has been a culinary oasis since it opened in 1974 in a Cambridge storefront; it moved across the town line two years later for more room and a liquor license. Founder Enzo Danesi died in 1986, but his family carries on, especially son Marc, who had worked with his father since he was 16 and now is head chef and occasional maitre-d. The short, prix-fixe menu varies slightly each night, offering a choice of six appetizers, four entrees, salad, and four desserts. You might start with seafood mousse, country pate or artichokes provencale. Main courses at our visit were salmon with a dill-butter sauce, roast tenderloin of beef with a dark beer and black peppercorn sauce, rack of lamb with vinegar and garlic sauce, and grilled veal chop with a tarragon beurre blanc, accompanied by snow peas and roasted new potatoes or risotto milanese — the last a sign of the chef's Italian heritage. A salad of greens, dressed with a tarragon vinaigrette and bearing a slice of brie in the middle, precedes dessert: perhaps creme brulee, hazelnut tart or a napoleon with strawberries. The 120 selections on the wine list are priced from the high teens to $180. The tables in the two small dining rooms are dressed with white linens and there are modern black lacquered and rose chairs with round backs. Unusual paintings of vegetables and painted faux columns adorn the pinkish walls. No wonder so many regulars are devoted to this welcoming, unpretentious place.

Dinner, Monday-Saturday 6 to 10.

West of Boston

Brookline

* Harvard Street Grill, 398 Harvard St., Brookline. (617) 734-9834.
Contemporary/International. $13.25 to $22.95.

John Vyhnanek, who was executive chef at the Ritz-Carlton in his 20s, decided he was spending too much time in meetings and not enough time cooking. So in 1988, he and his wife Bess bought this little storefront restaurant with its open kitchen, and now he cooks in front of a loyal clientele. Pretty posters on peach walls, white linens, and vases of alstroemeria comprise the minimal decor. The modern chrome-framed chairs are comfortable, and there's a nice, neighborhood air about the place. John grew up on a farm in upstate New York and tries to cook "the way our grandparents did, from scratch." He likes melting-pot cooking but is not "weird and trendy." His menu changes often, although you will always find rack of lamb, maybe with hoisin sauce and scallions, and salmon, which on our visit was topped with spinach, basil and oyster mushrooms. Grilled sea scallops with a citron sauce, vermicelli with Maine crabmeat, fresh tomato and black mushrooms, and aged sirloin steak with crispy onions and pink peppercorn butter were other choices. Rosemary and garlic mashed potatoes and a medley of green beans, parsnips and mushrooms accompanied. You might start with a salmon and dill terrine in aspic with a fresh herb sauce, or spinach salad with Coach Farm goat cheese, sugared walnuts and apple vinaigrette. For dessert, try a pear linzer torte, a chocolate ganache flan with caramel sauce, or pecan bread pudding chantilly. For such a small restaurant, the wine list is extensive and complex, with no fewer than twelve cabernet sauvignons ($18 to $87) and seven chardonnays.

Dinner, Monday-Saturday 5:30 to 10 or 11. Beer and wine only.

The Dover Sea Grille, 1223 Beacon St., Brookline. (617) 566-7000.
Seafood. $10.95 to $18.95.

Housed for five years in the lobby of the former Hampton Court hotel, this is the fortunate survivor of a once-promising group that included at various times the Dover Grill, Devon on the Common, and Devon at the World Trade Center. The building's origin shows in the marble columns, brass chandeliers, paneled walls, and coffered ceiling. They provide an elegant setting for marble tables set with aqua napkins in lucite rings, flickering oil lamps and round-back Victorian chairs. Fresh seafood, imaginatively prepared and sauced, is the hallmark here. The printed menu is supplemented by nightly specials like an appetizer of empanadas stuffed with rock shrimp, rice, potato and more, served with a sweet vinegar and jalapeno sauce, and entrees of sauteed red snapper with a tangerine-jalapeno sauce and grilled wahoo served on a pear-ginger puree with cilantro-hot pepper pesto and pomegranate seeds. Ten items are available from the grill, including salmon with spinach-hazelnut pesto and swordfish with green sauce. House specialties include Brazilian seafood stew, mako shark caribbean with a fruit chutney, rainbow trout with red peppers, capers and pine nuts, and, of course, dover sole. Exotic touches elevate such appetizers as fish cakes with black bean salsa, oysters or clams with lemon-horseradish vinaigrette, and a Japanese seafood plate. White downey cake layered with raspberry-grand marnier buttercream is one of the changing desserts.

Dinner nightly, 5 to 9:30 or 10:30.

Chestnut Hill

Legal Sea Foods, 43 Boylston St., Chestnut Hill. (617) 277-7300. Seafood. $10.99 to $21.99.

Occupying the front section of a shopping mall near Bloomingdale's, this and the downtown Park Plaza restaurant are the largest of a uniquely Boston operation that has many imitators but no equals. A pink neon fish and squiggly aqua waves top the new oyster bar, part of an expansion that nearly doubled the size and added a grill with lighter fare. The "new" Legal has gone upscale since the time we first ate here, sitting cheek-by-jowl with who knew whom at tables for twelve, serving our own coffee and tea, and foregoing desserts because there were none. Now Legal has truly arrived, opening in 1990 in Boston's fashionable Copley Place, taking over the space opened by the late Arne's Fine Seafood. At all Legal establishments, expect the freshest of fish (including such seldom seen kinds as sturgeon, sea bass, tile and cusk). Legal's fish chowder was served at the 1981 Presidential inaugural, its clam chowder at the 1985 inaugural. There's an enormous variety of grilled, Cajun, steamed, baked, sauteed and fried seafood, including lobster in many sizes and versions. One steak and a few chicken dishes are offered for those who prefer. The menu at the new grill and oyster bar is quite up to date, and now you can get desserts at Legal: a blackboard listed ice cream bonbons, profiteroles, apple crunch, homemade grapenut custard pudding, and cheesecake with raspberry melba sauce the day we were there. The wine list is extensive, sophisticated and pleasantly priced.

Lunch, Monday-Saturday 11 to 4; dinner, 4 to 9:30 or 10, Sunday 1 to 10.

Newton

♥ **The Mill Falls,** 383 Eliot St., Newton Upper Falls. (617) 244-3080. New American. $17 to $28.

Take one of Greater Boston's more picturesque restaurant locations, in the nation's first silk mill beside a waterfall on the Charles River. Add executive chef Walter Zuromski from Rarities in Cambridge and general manager Pietro Valentini, who opened three hotel dining rooms (Julien, the Marquis de Lafayette and Rowes Wharf) in Boston. The result in late 1989 was new life for an old (25 years) establishment, one that Pietro pledged to make the best in the suburbs. The main dining room, glamorous in pink with Queen Anne chairs, affords a superb view of the falls and the famous Echo Bridge spanning the gorge, spotlit at night for maximum effect. There are also a lush lounge with more views and an outdoor deck beside the water. Lately the atmosphere has been upstaged by the food, an inventive mix that troubles some oldtimers. For them, a line at the bottom of the menu notes that all entrees are "also available in our traditional style," meaning straightforward continental. The new Mill Falls yields paupiettes of sole and crab with a tomato cream coulis, pan-broiled scrod with curry, gewurtztraminer and carrots, and grilled swordfish in chardonnay with olives, sun-dried tomatoes and mussels. Meat-eaters can choose rack of lamb in crumbled roquefort with a mushroom turnover, paillards

West of Boston

of veal in lemon grass with blue prawns, and cobb-smoked prime rib with foie gras popover and merlot. Starters could be smoky clam chowder with turnips and sweet potatoes, cured venison on turnip slaw with a peppered pear compote, and southern fried rabbit with hominy grits, kale and bourbon sauce. Finish with chocolate-raspberry velvet mousse cake or chocolate-pistachio pie with cinnamon ice cream. Similar treats are available at lunch at reasonable-for-Boston prices.

Lunch, Monday-Friday 11:45 to 2:30; dinner, Monday-Saturday 5:30 to 10 or 11.

The Pillar House, 26 Quinobequin Road (Route 16 at I-95),
Newton Lower Falls. (617) 969-6500.
American. $15 to $23.

In a gracious, pillared mansion built in 1828 and since surrounded by highways, this beautiful restaurant is jammed every weekday for lunch and dinner but, astonishingly, is so successful it can close on Saturdays and Sundays. Unexpectedly elegant in a hotel dining room kind of way, it's a complex of several rooms with seating for 150, luxurious parlors to wait in, and a huge upstairs lounge. The menu is fancy American, with an occasional touch of continental and contemporary, as in classic Irish smoked salmon or native crab ravioli with sweet red pepper cream. The eighteen entrees run from broiled scallops, poached salmon with cucumber-hollandaise sauce, and chilled seafood and avocado salad to chicken with lobster and spinach stuffing, rack of lamb with rosemary-mustard sauce, roast duckling with strawberries and port, prime rib, and chateaubriand for two. Pecan tart with warm bourbon sauce, strawberries romanoff, and assorted sorbets and homemade ice creams are favored desserts. The entire establishment is non-smoking.

Open Monday-Thursday, 11:30 to 9:30, Friday to 10. Closed Saturday and Sunday. No smoking.

Waltham

★ Allegro, 313 Moody St., Waltham. (617) 891-5486.
Contemporary Italian. $17.95 to $24.

Chef-owner Jim Burke is always in Boston's culinary vanguard (his latest venture is the Cactus Club on Boylston Street). But this is his bellwether, a high-ceilinged place of mod simplicity a couple of blocks removed from his 1979 original in downtown Waltham. Beyond a small bar and waiting area, track lights illuminate a few artworks on the expansive, light blue walls of the airy dining room. Light oak chairs flank white-linened tables. There's nothing to detract from the food on the plate, which traditionally has been among the the Boston area's best. The hand-written menu changes every three weeks. At our visit, you could start with grilled calamari salad, risotto with littleneck clams and parmesan, salads or pasta of the day, or crostini with grilled chicken, peppers and fontina. The half-dozen entrees included osso buco with saffron gnocchi, sauteed breast of chicken with roasted garlic ravioli, roast rack of lamb with gorgonzola and walnut turnover, and sauteed duck with mission figs, shallots, balsamic vinegar and thyme. Desserts were a pear tartlet with almond creme brulee, chocolate-raspberry truffle cake, and a trio of sorbets (blackberry, raspberry-cranberry and lemon-lime). Many prefer the tasting menu ($43, available Tuesday-Thursday), a six-course meal sampling highlights from the day's fare. The short but select wine list is on the pricey side.

Dinner, Tuesday-Saturday 6 to 9 or 9:30.

★ Il Capriccio, 53 Prospect St., Waltham. (617) 894-2234.
Contemporary Italian. $17.50 to $25.

Tucked between a gasoline station and a sub shop on a Waltham side street is this storefront that most passersby would pass by. Behind its unlikely facade lies an intimate, 38-seat dining room in which the knowing feast on some of the area's most imaginative fare, including what a rival chef calls the best homemade pasta in Boston. Maurie Warren, former sous chef at Le Bocage, opened in 1981; his longtime chef, Rich Barron, lately bought him out and changed to an innovative, a la carte menu. The prices may stagger (corn and clam chowder with leeks for $7), but splurge for an antipasto of pork, venison and bresaola with three relishes; a salad of scallops, shrimp and squid, or an unusual dish of escargots mixed with raisins, chili pepper and sweet figs, rolled in a crepe and served with a mild ginger sauce. Don't miss the pastas, perhaps fettuccine with pancetta, ricotta and garlic, cannelloni with snails, or sweet potato ravioli with curry, raisins and pine nuts. On to the main course: perhaps grilled red snapper with plum tomatoes and extra-virgin olive oil, roast chicken with spinach, garlic and pistachios, grilled veal chop with malt scotch and wild mushroom sauce, or roast rack of lamb with balsamic vinegar and tarragon. A fine mixed green salad with a light vinaigrette and parmesan is available after the meal, but most of the antipasti contain enough salad items to carry one through. Desserts could be frozen fudge cake, apple cheesecake, lemon mousse with candied rinds, walnut tart, and roasted almond-chocolate chip ice cream. All these treats come in a convivial, somewhat cramped room with changing art on the peach walls, a ficus tree in a corner, tables set with white plates and linens, and quasi-garden chairs with rust cushions and backs. A good wine list is strongest on Italian reds and French whites.

Dinner nightly, 6 to 10. Beer and wine only. No smoking.

Lexington

Le Bellecoeur, 10 Muzzey St., Lexington. (617) 861-9400.
French. $14.95 to $21.95.

Inside this pretty room of pink linens and butcher-block cane chairs with velvet burgundy seats, you'd hardly know you were in the center of historic Lexington. Dutch owner Frans van Berkhout's influence sometimes shows up in Indonesian dishes like skewered chicken satay. Otherwise, all is continental, with such entrees as grilled Norwegian salmon with orange-basil butter, garlic-roasted chicken with watercress salad, roast duckling with changing sauces, veal medallions with apples and calvados, and beef medallions with blue cheese. Start with escargots in puff pastry or an unusual combination of smoked catfish and smoked salmon with sour cream and caviar. Enticing desserts include a hazelnut-macaroon mousse laced with frangelico, hot ricotta dumpling sprinkled with honey and powdered sugar, and a New England sweet potato cake with spiced pears and vanilla ice cream.

Lunch, Monday-Friday 11:30 to 2; dinner, Monday-Saturday 6 to 10.

The Hartwell House, 94 Hartwell Ave., Lexington. (617) 862-5111.
Continental/American. $13.95 to $26.95.

Built from scratch in 1985 in a developing commercial zone west of Route 128, this imposing white Colonial establishment is elegant indeed. What the literature describes as the foyer of a French Renaissance castle leads into a sunken, two-story dining room appointed in blue and white, with a huge crystal chandelier overhead, a few spotlit paintings on the walls, and a small oil lamp and bud vase on each well-spaced table. At one side is the more casual "island room," decked out in rattan furniture. Out of the way upstairs are a lounge and bistro, and there's a terraced patio outside. The setting is perhaps fancier than the food, which ranges from broiled scrod and shrimp scampi to roast duckling with a cranberry-lime glaze, prime rib and veal milanese. Featured specialties at top-of-the-line prices are tournedos

West of Boston

neptune (with lobster, asparagus and artichokes), rack of lamb persille, swordfish piccata, and veal with lobster, asparagus and bearnaise sauce. The goose liver pate with apricot mustard and escargots bourguignonne are billed as award-winning appetizers. Desserts include Swiss chocolate mousse, Indian pudding, caramel custard, and Florida key lime tart.

Lunch, Monday-Friday 11:30 to 2:30; dinner, Monday-Saturday 5:30 to 10.

Concord

Walden Station, 24 Walden St., Concord. (508) 371-2233.
Regional American. $8.95 to $16.95.
The old Concord fire station has been converted into a long, narrow restaurant full of wood, brick and hanging lamps, and a lot of railroad memorabilia. The food from the all-day menu has flair that packs in the crowds for noisy lunches and jovial dinners. Under appetizers and lighter fare, you can mix and match, from cold melon soup to lobster ravioli, from jalapeno and cheese boboli to shrimp orzo plate. The grilled chicken breast salad, tossed with walnuts and grapes and a raspberry dressing, comes in a tortilla shell. Entrees range from vegetable stir-fry to filet mignon from the wood grill. Stuffed roast pork loin with blackberry-sage sauce, blackened Atlantic catfish with a Kentucky peach chutney, chicken Santa Fe with a pear and fig chutney, and scallops fettuccine are interesting choices. The limited wine list is priced in the teens; the menu has two pages of exotic drinks. Hot fruit crisps with ice cream, Vienna layer cake and bread pudding are among desserts.

Open daily, 11:30 to 10.

A Different Drummer, 86 Thoreau St., Concord. (508) 369-8700.
Continental. $8.95 to $15.95.
A menu so extensive that some wonder how they can do it from so small a kitchen is offered upstairs in the Concord Depot building. Good-looking dried flowers decorate the walls of the two dining rooms, one a non-smoking area with cane and chrome chairs overlooking a nifty gift shop below. Popular at lunch are any of the five salads served in large glass bowls. We liked our choices of spinach with egg, bacon, mushrooms, and a sweet and sour dressing, and tuna, egg and olive with creamy Italian. There are four kinds of burgers, and entrees from basque chicken saute to curried shrimp and scallops. At night, there are again sumptuous salads (available as a starter or a meal) and more than two dozen entrees from vegetarian casserole to sauteed soft-shell crabs, baked stuffed shrimp, coquilles St. Jacques, sole florentine, medallions of veal genevieve, and sirloin with bearnaise sauce. The five stir-fry dishes are especially popular. The Different Drummer's "different drinks list" offers numerous frozen concoctions.

Lunch, Monday-Saturday 11:30 to 3; dinner 5 to 9; Sunday, brunch 11:30 to 3, dinner 4 to 8.

Acton

Chez Claude, 5 Strawberry Hill Road, Acton. (508) 263-3325.
Country French. $13.50 to $19.
The charming little red house up the hillside just off Route 2A is 150 or perhaps 200 years old, no one knows for sure. Since 1977, Chef-owner Claude Miquel from Paris and his French-Canadian wife Trudy have run an appealing place of unassuming durability. In the original house, they offer three small dining rooms full of interesting touches like exposed beams, hanging copper pans and large lanterns over the fireplace. Paper placemats protect the white linens here and in a new, larger

dining addition to the rear. The menu rarely changes except for the prices, and those not all that much. We can vouch for the chef's pate, an artful combination of pork and chicken liver, the French onion soup, and the salad of bibb lettuce tossed with a masterful vinaigrette. We also liked the veal marengo and a house specialty, roast duck with orange sauce, both accompanied by potatoes anna, carrots, parsley, and onions. Other entrees include rack of lamb with mustard and garlic coating, trout amandine, coq au vin, and frog's legs in garlic butter. Desserts are fairly standard (chocolate mousse, creme caramel, pear helene, and strawberries romanoff), but for an extraordinary almond pie with apricots and a crumb crust.

Dinner, Monday-Saturday 6 to 9:30.

Ciao, 452 Great Road (Route 2A), Acton. (508) 263-6161.
Northern Italian. $14.95 to $17.95.

A cozy, crowded and rather grotto-like restaurant at the rear of the small Collage Mall, Ciao is acclaimed both for its regular menu and its "molto speciale" blackboard offerings of the day. One example is the torta rustica, a layered country pie of eggplant, three cheeses, two kinds of sausage, and five herbs and spices. The onion soup is served inside a loaf of bread, there are three kinds of antipasti, the garlic bread is extra good, and the pasta dishes always interesting. Entrees include rib-eye steak with tomatoes, garlic and black olives; veal piccata, and filet of sole baked with mushrooms, chives, parsley, and onions. A cinnamon powder puff torte is the signature dessert. The wine list is all Italian. The decor is made special by the stained-glass windows, taken from churches being dismantled, and especially by a large one that owner Jim Bailey had copied from the famous Tiffany wisteria window at the Metropolitan Museum — but with grapes instead of wisteria. A copper sculpture of an Italian town is also striking.

Lunch, Monday-Friday 11:30 to 2:30; dinner, Monday-Saturday 6 to 9:30; Sunday, brunch 10 to 2, dinner 5:30 to 8.

Maynard

★ La Grange, 4 Waltham St., Maynard. (508) 897-2850.
French. $17.95 to $22.95.

Avain and Josette Fraysse Vincent, from Lyons by way of Chilmark and Lexington, run a country French restaurant of distinction in Maynard. Inside the white stucco building with brown shutters are two dining rooms full of dark brown beams, copper pots and twinkling white Christmas lights that were left up from one holiday season and quickly became a year-round fixture. "When we took them off it looked so dull we put them back up," explained Josette. "They make the copper shine." They are a pleasant backdrop for the renowned cuisine, which is classic French with a bit of updating. At lunch you can try the specialty scallop bisque and crepe florentine, beef bourguignonne, chicken livers provencale, or cassoulet. Dinner brings a fancier menu. Start with snails in puff pastry with goat cheese or rolled pasta with ricotta and ham. Main courses range from pork chops normande to medallions of beef or rack of lamb marinated with thyme. Quail in a bordelaise and mustard sauce, monkfish in pastry with cream and mussels, and breast of duck with black cherries are other possibilities. For dessert, try white chocolate mousse with raspberry sauce, apricot sabayon, or fresh strawberries flambeed over ice cream with grand marnier.

Lunch, Monday-Friday 11:30 to 2; dinner nightly, 5 to 10, Sunday to 9.

Grille 62, 20 Powdermill Road, Maynard. (508) 897-7111.
American. $6.95 to $14.95.

The rear windows at this casual new establishment face the Assabet River, giving

West of Boston

most diners in the back room a view of the goings-on at a couple of popular bird feeders on the far bank. Wood tables with burgundy mats, windsor chairs, blue speckled china, plants, and interesting art comprise the decor. The all-day menu offers plenty of mix and match. Start perhaps with quesadillas, beef and chili nachos, seafood sampler, Peking raviolis, or sashimi. The sandwiches and burgers are hefty, and the chicken fajitas at lunch so abundant that we took half home in a doggy bag for an encore the next day. The grilled chicken salad was laden with walnuts and grapes. Fourteen items, from yellowfin tuna with orange-walnut butter to coconut beer shrimp and baby back ribs, are available from the grill. Six more are listed under "saute." Fruit trifles, lemon chiffon roll, white chocolate mousse pie, and chocolate-grand marnier layer cake are among desserts.

Open daily, 11 to 10 ro 11; Sunday brunch, 11 to 3.

Sudbury-Framingham

Longfellow's Wayside Inn, Route 20, South Sudbury. (508) 443-8846.
American. Table d'hote, $12 to $27.

Ghosts of the past seem to hover over the Wayside Inn, extolled by Henry Wadsworth Longfellow in *Tales of a Wayside Inn.* From the Old Barroom, a delightfully warm room with glowing fireplace and wide-plank floors dating to 1702, to the Longfellow Parlor, furnished with pieces mentioned in *Tales,* the entire establishment exudes authenticity. The oldest operating inn in the United States draws tourists from afar, both for dining (up to 800 on a busy night) and for tours of a 5,000-acre preserve that includes a gift shop and a sylvan chapel. The menu changes daily, featuring tried-and-true Yankee favorites like grandmother used to make. After snacking on complimentary cheese and crackers followed by fresh and marinated vegetables, you may not need an appetizer like fresh cider, cranberry juice, marinated herring, French onion soup, or fresh fruit cup with sherbet, but they come with the meal. Among main courses, fresh scrod is a specialty, ours baked with a floury cheese sauce that detracted from the fish, but we managed to scrape most of it off. We found the baked stuffed shrimp delicious and the filet of sole with crabmeat stuffing and lobster sauce adequate. Other possibilities range from Yankee pot roast and chicken pie to prime rib and roast duckling. Dessert selections include baked Indian pudding, deep-dish apple pie with a spiced whipped cream, pecan pie and custard pudding. The food is predictable, and people return time and again to enjoy it in historic surroundings. The large Colonial Dining Room where most eat has an air of simplicity from bygone days: shiny wood floors, gold cloths and napkins, pretty flowered china, floral draperies, and sconces on the walls.

Lunch, Monday-Saturday 11:30 to 3:30; dinner, 5 to 9, Sunday noon to 8.

Spinazzola's, 1138 Worcester Road (Route 9), Framingham. (508) 872-1200.
Contemporary Italian. $13.50 to $21.50.

The Boston Globe's first restaurant critic dreamed of opening his own restaurant, and this is the result. Barely nine whirlwind months after Anthony Spinazzola's untimely death in 1985, his wife Dorothy, their two sons, two daughters and a couple of their spouses opened and have been going strong ever since. It's a larger place than you might expect, done up in handsome Americana — pink and white linens, chintz curtains, gray carpeting, comfortable chairs, Impressionist paintings, and brass chandeliers suspended from the high ceiling. The menu is all that Tony Spinazzola would have wished: a fabulous clam chowder, interesting pastas, and prime meat and seafood with seasonal presentations. You might find grilled tiger shrimp with a spicy sauce and mushroom-vegetable egg roll; veal scaloppine with polenta and a sauce made from plum tomatoes, pancetta and peppers; grilled salmon with a red wine-butter sauce and a spinach potato tart; grilled pheasant with smoked bacon, apples and thyme; Long Island duck with risotto and raisins, served with mixed beans and grapefruit-lime sauce, and pan-roasted veal chop with sweet potato fries. The beautiful white chocolate mousse in a caramel cage is the signature dessert. The bulk of the 55 wine offerings are in the $20 range. Many of the evening specialties are available at lunch, at wallet-pleasing prices.

Lunch, Monday-Friday 11:30 to 2:30; dinner, Monday-Saturday 5 to 10.

Ashland

John Stone's Inn, 179 Main St., Ashland. (508) 881-2268.
Regional American. $12.95 to $17.95.

We heard that people in the Boston suburbs trek out here to get the feeling of dining in a small Vermont inn. And when we saw John Stone's Inn, we could understand why, In the heart of Ashland Center, this red brick three-story inn, built in 1832, looks like the New England inn of one's dreams. The interior is rather more deluxe than many: a lovely beamed, fireplaced, candlelit dining room with swagged draperies, antique furniture, old-fashioned wallpaper and sconces, and bunches of candles hanging from the beams. There are two other dining rooms, one the Library upstairs, as well as a cozy bar with wing chairs and a fireplace. The inn is said to be inhabited by a ghost who tips bartenders with $10 bills. The menu is fairly contemporary: Seattle-style grilled salmon with clams and bell pepper sauce, veal San Francisco with lobster and leek raviolis, southern grilled chicken with ham and corn fritters and a pecan-butter sauce, New England sweet seared duck with wild onion-herb relish, and garlic-grilled shrimp over pasta. Likely appetizers are escargots ravioli, beer-steamed littlenecks, crab and corn cakes with jalapeno pepper mayonnaise, and cold roasted lamb salad. Featured desserts are chocolate pate with grand marnier creme anglaise and shortbread, Irish whiskey cake, and fresh fruit cobbler. The mostly American wine list is excellent and starts in the low teens.

Lunch, Monday-Saturday 11:30 to 3; dinner nightly, 5 to 10 or 11; Sunday brunch, 11 to 3.

Sherborn

✱ Sherborn Inn, Route 27, Sherborn. (508) 655-9521.
New American. $16.50 to $22.75.

Grandly restored and expanded in 1988 from the 18th-century residence of Col. Samuel Bullard, this gleaming white structure houses four dining rooms, an 1827 tavern and four luxurious overnight guest rooms. The food is the main attraction, along with the elegant country atmosphere at this seemingly remote outpost southwest of Wellesley. Dinner could begin with sugar pumpkin soup with toasted pumpkin seeds, a goat cheese tart with red and green peppers, carpaccio with homemade sauerkraut and garlic croutons, seafood terrine with whole grain mustard sauce, or escargots with spinach, garlic and bel paese cheese in puff pastry. For entrees, how about a tranche of salmon with parmesan crust and pesto provencale sauce, chicken stuffed with foie gras, beef wellington, or veal medallions with three kinds of apples, frangelico, hazelnuts, and roesti potatoes? Dessert could be flourless chocolate cake filled with white chocolate mousse and raspberry sauce. An appealing tavern menu is served all day in as luxurious a tavern as you'll ever see; it has a cathedral ceiling, tall windows, chandeliers, huge fireplace, and a long bar with seats for eating.

Lunch, Tuesday-Saturday 11:30 to 2:30; dinner, Tuesday-Sunday 5 to 9:30 or 10; Sunday, brunch 11 to 3; Monday, lunch and dinner in tavern only.

Dedham

$ Thai Emerald, 79 East St., Dedham. (617) 326-8824.
Thai. $4.25 to $12.75.

We spent more than half an hour searching for Le Bourgignon, a French restaurant that was supposed to be among the best in suburban Boston. When we finally found the location, you guessed it: the sign said "Thai Emerald." Le Bourgignon's owner had retired and sold to a Thai family in November 1989. Such are the hazards of restaurant reporting. However, the search was salvaged by an excellent lunch of tom yum goong, the hauntingly good Thai hot and sour prawn soup spiced with chilies, lemon grass, mushrooms, lime juice, and coriander; todmun, deep-fried shrimp and codfish patties with cucumber sauce, and shredded chicken basil, spicy and delicious. The four little spring rolls were super, too. All this is served in a large, refined room with peach-colored draperies and linens, Thai statues, intricately carved screens and pictures (some interesting ones of Bangkok's floating market) scattered about. The charming Sopchockchai family (a mother and five grown children) operate Thai Emerald — one son, a physician who heads a local clinic, waits tables on weekends to help out. At night choose between six appetizers, four soups and four noodle dishes, four rice dishes and many, many entrees. House specialties include tamarind duck, seafood hot pot, crisp fried fish with chile sauce (one of the hottest dishes, marked with two peppers), and duck choo chee. Finish with tapioca pudding, ginger ice cream, or what the owners call their best dessert, fried banana on ice cream. There's a full bar, and the house wine is served in generous glasses.

Open Monday-Saturday, 11:30 to 11; Sunday, 5 to 11.

South Shore

Hull

* Saporito's Florence Club Cafe, 11 Rockland Circle, Hull. (617) 925-3023.
Regional Italian. $12.95 to $15.95.

Pair a chef from Allegro in Waltham with a chef from Bnu in Boston. The result is a marriage and the opening in 1988 of Saporito's, a down-home cafe with trendy cuisine at the entrance to the Naponsket Beach section of Hull. Andy Boothroyd of Allegro and MaryAnn Saporito Boothroyd, who also was at Harvest in Cambridge, share kitchen duties in this unpretentious blue house known since 1941 as the Florence Club; hence its incorporation into the name of the couple's new cafe. It's a rustic place, with booths painted white with green seats beside little shuttered windows, some tables with kitchen chairs painted green, cloths of ivy covered with paper, and a tiny bar in the rear. The chefs' reputations preceded them to the South Shore, where area foodies were quick to pick up on the contemporary regional Italian fare. Helpings of marinated Sicilian olives and lusty foccacia bread start the meal. Andy says the grilled pizzetta is the most popular opener, the preparation changing daily but typically including goat cheese, Sicilian olives and marinated tomatoes. Other favorites are porcini mushroom tart with grilled shrimp, a hearty vegetable-bean soup with sausage and pesto croutons, and a salad of spinach and romaine with parmesan, pancetta and black olives. Likely pastas are grilled vegetable lasagna with ricotta, chevre and rosemary, and noodles with savoy cabbage, potato, fontina, and garlic butter. Main dishes could be grilled salmon with tomato, saffron and garlic cream; veal scaloppine with hazelnuts and caramelized onion; lamb ragout with artichokes, pork chop with chestnuts and dried fruits, and grilled steak with mushrooms and marsala. Roasted vegetables and a stuffed tomato might accompany. Featured desserts include an intense chocolate-espresso torte, cranberry or peach bread pudding made with Italian bread, and ricotta and rice pie. The short but select list of Italian and California wines is affordably priced.

Dinner, Tuesday-Sunday 5 to 9 or 10. Also closed Tuesday in winter.

Hingham

♥ **Navona,** 415 Whiting St., Hingham. (617) 337-0757.
Northern Italian. $14.95 to $23.95.
Beautiful. What more can you say for the setting and the main dining room at this restaurant that emerged in 1986 in the Old Pilgrim Quarry, from which came much of the stone for Boston College and Yale University. Tapestries hung on the walls of stone, glass-enclosed cathedral ceilings, lighted ficus trees, and trickling fountains make an incomparable backdrop, with views onto the quarry pond outside. Add white linens, curved black chairs, pink napkins, white china rimmed in gray, and flickering oil lamps, and you have a magical atmosphere that almost outshines the food. Start with a foccacia pizzetta, country pate with crostini and assorted mustards, or escargots on a bed of spinach with puff pastry and ricotta cheese. Five pastas are on the menu, as are two dozen entrees from chicken frangelico and grilled swordfish with pesto to osso buco, saltimbocca, four steaks, and rack of lamb dijonnaise. The signature dessert is a chocolate hazelnut torte, the recipe for which appeared in Gourmet magazine. There's a curving bar in the sunken lounge.

Lunch, Tuesday-Friday 11:30 to 2:30; dinner, 5 to 10 or 11; Sunday brunch, noon to 3. Closed Monday.

Amontea's, 14 North St., Hingham. (617) 749-8988.
Italian. $11.50 to $17.95.
Small on the outside, this 1910 grainery building keeps opening up to the rear, yielding a melange of dining areas with brick walls, exposed pipes, brass rails and red-curtain dividers, stained-glass windows high up the walls, and assorted glass-topped and bare tables. Rip and Sheila Amontea are known for hearty fare. You might start with escargots in mushroom caps, fried cheese and fried squid. Among entrees are nine veal dishes (from cutlet to marsala), eleven seafood dishes (from cioppino to shrimp fra diavolo), nine chicken dishes, and six steaks. The menu lists only two pastas, eggplant parmigiana and fettucine alfredo, though others come as sides with most of the entrees. An Austrian baker does the desserts, including rum raisin mousse and hazelnut cheesecake.

Lunch, Tuesday-Friday 11:30 to 3; dinner, Tuesday-Saturday 4:30 to 9:30 or 10:30; Sunday, brunch 10:30 to 2, dinner 3 to 9.

Scituate

♥ **Barker Tavern,** 21 Barker Road, Scituate. (617) 545-6533.
Continental/Greek/American. $13.95 to $22.
One of the two oldest wood buildings in the country, this 1634 beauty has been expanded to accommodate its growing clientele since it became a restaurant in 1978. The exterior looks more like a big white mansion than a tavern, but the inside is historic as all get-out. Barker's is the favorite of many in the area, and it's not hard to understand why: a location near Scituate Harbor, good food, and a rustic yet elegant decor with sloping ceilings, wood wainscoting, striking pierced-tin hanging lamps casting wondrous shadows, lots of stenciling, patterned rugs, folk art on the walls, and a mural over the fireplace in the main dining room. Classical music plays

as patrons dine, many of them on the lamb dishes for which Barker's is known. There are shish kabob and shashlick, as well as specials like baron of lamb or loin lamb chops. The Greek heritage of the owner is reflected in such appetizers as spanakopita, baked kibbie, borek, and stuffed grape leaves, which are listed alongside mussels bordelaise, smoked Scotch salmon and marinated herring. An assorted appetizer platter for two combines many of the favorites. Besides lamb, entrees range from shrimp New Orleans to seafood newburg, from prime rib to beef stroganoff and veal cordon bleu. Among desserts are Indian pudding, fruit pies, fudge brownies, and orange-flavored creme caramel.

Dinner, Tuesday-Saturday 6 to 10, Sunday 1 to 9 or 10.

P.J.'s Country House, Route 3A, Scituate. (617) 545-1340.
Continental. $11.95 to $19.95.
Started in 1935 as an ice-cream stand, this elegant establishment belies its heritage. Run now by the third-generation of the O'Brien family, it's a pleasant mix of rooms — a library full of books on one side, a lounge with a pub menu and piano entertainment, and a main dining room with a solarium harboring four coveted tables for two overlooking the lighted rear gardens. Queen Anne chairs, booths, blue willow china on pink linens, shiny brass candlesticks, and duck prints comprise the decor. Seafood is the specialty, from catch of the day and shrimp curry to baked finnan haddie, lobster newburg and lobster thermidor. Wiener schnitzel, roast duckling with fruit sauce, veal marsala and filet mignon are other possibilities. Appetizers are predictable; not so are such desserts as hazelnut layer cake laced with triple sec and frangelico, amaretto mousse torte, and mocha-macaroon ice cream pie.

Lunch, Tuesday-Saturday 11:30 to 4; dinner, 5 to 10, Sunday from 12:30. Closed Monday.

♥ **Mill Wharf Restaurant,** 150R Front St., Scituate. (617) 545-3999.
American/Continental. $8.95 to $18.95.
Go here for the waterfront setting, one of the best of any restaurant anywhere. Fashioned in 1984 from an old lumber mill, it's a two-story masterpiece with wraparound windows taking full advantage of the view of Scituate Harbor, from tables on two levels of the main-floor dining room or upstairs in a lounge with more windows and a greenhouse strung with strands of tiny white lights. The only better view is from the outdoor patio and raw bar in summer. Entrees, served with soup or salad, run from mussels marinara and chicken parmesan to boiled lobster, prime rib and veal francaise. Nachos, potato skins and stuffed mushrooms are appetizers of choice. Desserts include oreo ice cream pie, apple crisp, carrot cake, and German chocolate cake. The shiny wood tables are left bare to expose the inlaid saw blades and old invoices taken from the lumber mill. Buoys hang from the beams, walls bear sheet music of old songs and signs from London shops, votive candles flicker, and the nighttime atmosphere is dark and intimate.

Lunch, Monday-Saturday 11:30 to 3; dinner, Monday-Saturday 5 to 9 or 10; Sunday, brunch 10:30 to 2:30, dinner 4 to 9.

North Abington

Vin & Eddie's Ristorante and Wine Bar, 1400 Bedford St. (Route 18),
North Abington. (617) 871-1469.
Northern Italian. $12.95 to $26.
The best wine list on the South Shore is one claim to fame of this long-running (1955) establishment. Five typewritten pages list more than a hundred Italian reds from $15 to $250, for instance, along with a not inconsiderable number of French and American reds. Many are available by the glass. The reds are far more

numerous than the whites, which surprises some, given the menu's strength in seafoods and pastas. Another claim to fame are the seasonal game dishes, which turn up as entrees like rabbit in woodland sauce with baked polenta, and specials like pan-braised venison steak with venison sausage and wild mushroom sauce, and braised pheasant with prosciutto, white grapes and asti spumonte. Grilled veal chop with polenta, osso buco, and braised duck with apples head the regular menu offerings. More exotic might be specials like tripe and hot sausage marinara stew with penne, baked coho salmon with crabmeat-polenta stuffing, pheasant and spinach ravioli with gorgonzola cream sauce, and braised lamb tenderloins with sun-dried tomatoes and scallions. Start with carpaccio with mushrooms and par-migiano cheese or wild mushroom tagliatelle with black truffles. Finish with tartuffo, mascarponetti, creamy cheesecakes or mousses, and perhaps a rare armagnac (one from 1893 is $150 a glass). Chianti bottles in baskets hang from the beams of the three fairly bright dining rooms, simply but effectively outfitted with white linens, fresh flowers and one wall of murals. No reservations are taken, and there's usually a long wait at peak periods.

Open Tuesday-Saturday, 11:30 to 10 or 10:30, Sunday 1 to 9.

Southeast Massachusetts

Duxbury

Milepost Tavern Restaurant, Route 3A, Duxbury. (617) 934-6801.
Seafood/International. $9.95 to $14.95.
The owners call the decor of their unprepossessing little restaurant "country charming." That it is, from the beamed peaked ceiling to the quilted mats on dark polished-wood tables. The locals call the restaurant "popular," turning over its 60 or so seats four times on a Saturday night. The cooking is generally straightforward, as in baked scrod au gratin, golden fried shrimp and shrimp scampi, although the chef adds some twists to the six chicken and four veal dishes — veal maximilian is sauteed with orange slices and mushrooms and finished with orange brandy, for instance. The menu covers most of the bases from sauteed liver with onions to steak dijonnaise and bouillabaisse. The signature dessert is a "sinful sundae," with a macaroon base and laden with toasted almonds and amaretto. A light menu is served in the tavern. The wine list is limited and, strangely, fails to mention the vineyards of origin.

Lunch, Monday-Saturday 11:30 to 3; dinner nightly, 5 to 10; Sunday, lunch-brunch.

The Winsor House Inn, 390 Washington St., Duxbury. (617) 934-0991.
American. $10.95 to $19.95.
In an imposing 1803 mansion in the heart of historic Duxbury, this needs to be a destination restaurant to succeed. New owners Myles Maguire and chef Bob Driscoll and their wives are aiming for that. The front dining rooms are Colonial and elegant with oriental rugs dotting wide-board floors, beamed ceilings, delicate wall sconces, and crisp white linens on well-spaced tables. Beyond a pubby tavern that oozes history is a newly opened carriage house serving light fare beside a patio for outdoor dining. The cuisine is billed as traditional New England. The dozen dinner entrees range from grilled salmon steak with a creamy cucumber-dill sauce and shrimp scampi to twin tournedos au poivre, rack of lamb, and roast loin of veal stuffed with fresh spinach pesto and served with a roasted red bell pepper sauce. The shrimp casablanca in a fresh citrus and white wine marinade is a refreshing variation of the standard shrimp cocktail. Among desserts, obtained commercially, the seasonal

cranberry mousse pie is a standout. Hefty salads and sandwiches like a swordfish club as well as entrees are served all day in the carriage house.

Lunch daily, 11:30 to 5; dinner, 5 to 9:30.

Deckers, Depot Street, Duxbury. (617) 934-7368.
American. $8.95 to $13.95.

There are no Deckers involved in this bright and airy establishment transformed in 1989 from a pizza parlor in the Duxbury Marketplace. Instead, the host informed, it takes its name from the back deck. The menu was in transition the summer Saturday we visited. A blackboard listed ten straightforward entrees from baked scrod to grilled filet mignon. Crostini, saucisson and vegetable strudel were tempting offerings among appetizers. Fans who praised its food and its stylish yet casual peach and green decor were saying Deckers was Duxbury's answer to the New Yorkish Star Lunch in nearby Plymouth.

Lunch, 11:30 to 3; dinner, 5 to 9. Closed Monday.

Plymouth

★ The Star Restaurant, Standish Avenue at Savery Lane, North Plymouth. (508) 746-4001.
New American. $10.95 to $16.50.

Did this little gem known as Star Lunch drop from the sky? Here five years, we had never encountered it nor heard of it on our travels, until a knowing gent in a Duxbury bookstore tipped us off. Formerly a bar and diner, the modest gray-shingled roadhouse with petunias in its window boxes and "Star Lunch" for a sign hides an interior that's art deco to the max. It's a melange of barnwood painted deep green, black and white faux marble panels, a black and white checked floor, and tiny white lights strung over fake dogwood branches everywhere. Most seating is in booths. Here loyal customers feast on, perhaps, Mediterranean tomato bisque or salmon cream pie topped with American caviar and served with crudites, going on to entrees like lamb regina, skewered with artichoke hearts and marinated in many fresh herbs, or lobster en croute. The two chef-owners, former school teachers, change the menu every two weeks, but you could find Ballymaloe pork flamed with brandy and glazed with apricot and rosemary, or bluefish heaven, baked with sherry, ginger, shallots, garlic, lemon, tomatoes, and soy sauce. At lunch, along with the grilled reuben and tuna melt, you might encounter mussels ceviche, grilled chicken with aioli and wedge-cut french fries, and deep fried ravioli. For dessert, how about peanut butter-fudge pie, mudslide parfait or, our choice, midsummer ambrosia, a lemon custard shortbread tart topped with summer berries and whipped cream? The wine list is reasonable, mellow jazz plays softly in the background, and the only thing we'd change is the glass over the black and white printed tablecloths.

Lunch, Monday-Friday 11:30 to 3:30; dinner, Wednesday-Saturday from 5.

Marina Landing, Plymouth Marina, 14 Union St., Plymouth. (508) 746-5570.
American. $12.95 to $16.95.

Pity the hordes confined to the lineup of other harborfront restaurants. They could be enjoying the view at the Marina Landing, which has by far the most appealing location in town. The harborside deck and raw bar are jaunty and casual for outdoor meals. The upstairs dining room is more formal with white tablecloths, upholstered chairs, a bar in the middle, and windows on three sides. Dinner entrees run from halibut with scallops, leeks and cream or prime rib to sole stuffed with crabmeat in basil gravy, and sirloin steak stuffed with crabmeat, scallops and shrimp and a mushroom burgundy sauce, which sounds like culinary overkill. The deck's all-day menu is a bit pricey. Skip the quarter-pounder hot dog in favor of a mix-and-match deli sandwich piled high on Portuguese bread.

Lunch daily, 11:30 to 4; dinner, 4 to 10 or 11.

Station One, 51 Main St., Plymouth. (508) 746-6001.
American/Cajun. $11.25 to $16.95.

Once a working firehouse, this casual, with-it restaurant has dining on several levels as well as a sidewalk cafe smack up against the main street. Chandeliers with fluted globes, hanging plants and brick walls make an attractive backdrop. The veal sauteed with shrimp, mushrooms and lemon and flambeed in marsala wine comes highly recommended. The Cajun specialties are old-hat, but the kitchen gets adventurous with things like veal thermidor, grilled chicken with vegetables sauteed in raspberry vinegar, and duckling in a black raspberry glaze. Lobster benedict draws the tourists for Sunday brunch.

Lunch, Monday-Saturday 11:30 to 3:45; dinner, from 4:45; Sunday brunch, 10:30 to 3.

320 Court Street, 320 Court St., North Plymouth. (508) 747-4226.
Continental/American. $10.95 to $15.95.

The late, lamented Sante, which drew rave reviews for new American cuisine, gave way in 1989 to this less ambitious, more casual establishment that the owners felt would be more in keeping with the local market. The two small dining rooms remain about the same. The chef's specials lean to the classic French, but the menu cops out to the common denominator craving potato skins, prime rib, and London broil with mushroom gravy. The kitchen knows (and shows) its stuff in items like veal normandy and a garden spice cake (carrot with zucchini and what-not). And everything is homemade, which is more than can be said at many local eateries.

Dinner, Tuesday-Saturday 4 to 10.

South Carver

♥ **Crane Brook Tea Room,** Tremont Street, South Carver. (508) 866-3235.
New American. $16 to $25.

Mary Cunningham bought an old iron foundry-turned-cranberry-screening-house in 1979 for her antiques business. Her sister suggested she serve tea and pastries, and within a few years the antiques gave way to an innovative restaurant that draws knowing diners out to the middle of nowhere. A gazebo on a rear deck overlooking a lily pond and, beyond, larger Sampson Pond was an idyllic setting for a leisurely lunch that lasted well into the afternoon. The tomato soup with buffalo mozzarella topping a crouton was superb, as was a smoked salmon sandwich served open-faced on grilled French bread. Although a diminutive portion, the grilled duck breast salad with four slices of rare duck over greens with raspberries and blueberries was a work of art. An ethereal cheesecake with hazelnut crust and blueberries capped a memorable meal. Dinner in cozy dining rooms that reveal their antiques heritage is a treat as well. Self-taught chef Myles Huntington offers such changing entrees as Portuguese-style pork loin, roulade of range-fed chicken, grilled duckling with pineapple and tamari-rum glaze, potato-crusted Norwegian salmon with lemon-leek coulis, and grilled leg and rack of lamb with port wine sauce. Start with grilled spiced shrimp with roasted red pepper sabayon; finish with one of the wondrous desserts prepared by the chef's sister, Martha Huntington. Owner Cunningham maintains high standards and provides a restful setting. "It's good for people to pause and take a deep breath here," she says. Formal tea is served Wednesdays by reservation.

Lunch, Tuesday-Friday 11:30 to 2:30; dinner by reservation, Wednesday-Sunday 5:30 to 9; Sunday brunch, September-May.

New Bedford

The Candleworks Restaurant, 72 North Water St., New Bedford, Mass.
(508) 992-1635.
French/Regional American. $11.95 to $18.95.
It took ten years for Maurice Jospe, the courtly Belgian who founded Candleworks, to put his restaurant on the culinary map. Once he did, he decided to retire and sold it in late 1989 to Marcel Godbout, a French-Canadian chef who came from the Sheraton-Bradley and the old Signature restaurant in Hartford. Marcel kept the appealing decor, but redid the menu. It now features such appetizers as ceviche, Maine crab cakes, Cajun shrimp, roasted oysters with herbs and pepper butter, and clams and mussels Portuguese style. An unusual winter soup was fresh fruit gazpacho, made of green and red tomatoes, cantaloupe and grapes, and finished with hard cider. Seafood and the local Portuguese influence figure prominently in the entrees: New England cioppino, shrimp a la grecque, poached salmon with sorrel sauce, tournedos of beef, chicken with Portuguese sausage, and sauteed veal with shrimps, capers and olives. Desserts include caramel custard, creme brulee, and specialty crepes with liqueur cream fillings. At the edge of New Bedford's Historic District, the restaurant occupies the lower floor of a handsomely restored gray stone building that once housed the Rodman Candleworks. The original gray stone walls and beams enhance the interior dining room, which is a cross between a cozy tavern and a clubby lounge. The walls are hung with the fascinating artworks of the former owner, who paints as a hobby and left them on consignment. We prefer the more open feeling afforded by the enclosed terrace at the side of the building, with its large windows, striped canvas ceiling, and abundance of plants.
Lunch, Monday-Friday 11:30 to 2:30; dinner, Monday-Saturday 5:30 to 10.

Freestone's, 41 William St., New Bedford. (508) 993-7477.
American. $8.95 to $11.95.
A brass monkey from Pavo Real Gallery hangs over the crowded bar at Freestone's, a "casual dining and socializing" spot in the Citizen's National Bank Building, erected in 1883 and part of the renovation of New Bedford's historic district. It's almost impossible to get in on a Friday night since this is a popular gathering place for singles. The front rooms are fairly noisy; a quieter room is tucked away in back. The all-day menu includes chowders, appetizers like chicken wings, stuffed potato skins and Syrian nachos, as well as salads and sandwiches (one sandwich is a taco pocket). Entrees include vegetable lasagna, grilled scallops, chicken teriyaki, Cajun tips, and barbecued ribs.
Open daily from 11 a.m. to 11 p.m.

Cafe Restaurant Mimo, 1528 Acushnet Ave., New Bedford. (508) 996-9443.
Portuguese. $5 to $8.25.
Three men from the Azores run this unprepossessing place that's the real thing and considered the best in an area of nondescript Portuguese restaurants. The aromas are a delight, the portions hefty and the prices right. If you visit the bar, you'll overhear Portuguese chatter as men drink standing up. The all-day menu includes caldo verde, the Portuguese soup, and quite a selection of Portuguese specialties from pork and clams and boiled codfish to daily specials like roast octopus and roast mackerel. Grilled or fried quails, barbecued sardines and small steak with eggs are priced at the low end, and come with big baskets of Portuguese rolls and "your choice of rice or potatoes, or both." Chocolate mousse and flan pudding are favored

desserts. That good Sagres beer and bottles of Dao and vinho verde are featured. We guarantee you won't leave hungry.

Open daily, 11 to 10.

Muldoon's Saloon, 17 Mechanics Lane, New Bedford. (508) 999-1010.
Irish/American. $4.50 to $9.95.

A green and white color scheme and Irish flavor prevail year-round at this bar and dining room with full-length windows opening onto Pleasant Street downtown (there's a suburban Muldoon's at 1309 Phillips Road, Exit 5 off Route 140). The menu is heavy on nibbles, soups, salads and sandwiches, plus a French meat pie, Irish quiche of the day, and a few entrees like steak, chicken, barbecued ribs and fish items. The wine selection is mediocre (Coke seems to be the drink of choice at lunch). A special children's menu leads off with linguica sandwich. The decor is ladderback chairs, butcherblock tables, hanging plants and fans.

Open daily from 11 a.m.

South Dartmouth

★ Le Rivage, 7 Water St., South Dartmouth. (508) 999-4505.
French. $14 to $19.50.

What's a fine French restaurant doing in the picturesque hamlet of Padanarum in South Dartmouth? Treating local palates to excellent food at bargain prices, that's what. Margaret and Jean-Claude Galan came here from the Pyrenees by way of the Jockey Club in Washington, D.C. Their new restaurant's name means river bank, and the harbor view is interesting from the window tables of this larger-than-expected establishment with soft blue and polished woodwork, charming country curtains, white linens, and flowers in clear vases. At lunch, excellent hot crusty rolls and perfect salads dressed with creamy dijon preceded entrees of Norwegian salmon with a delicate spinach sauce and calves liver with bacon and shallot sauce and properly al dente vegetables. Washed down with a bottle of the house Entre Deux Mers from a reasonably priced wine list, it was a meal to remember and so filling that we couldn't even think of trying the apricot mousse, the chocolate truffle cake, or the key lime pie. Dinnertime brings more of the same, from broiled swordfish with whole grain mustard sauce and bouillabaisse to medallions of veal with mustard and shiitake mushrooms, roast Wisconsin duckling with wild rice and lingonberries, and broiled lamb chops with fresh thyme. To start, sample the lobster bisque, the terrine of duck with sweetbreads and pistachio, or oysters on the half shell with caviar.

Lunch, Monday-Friday noon to 2; dinner nightly, 6 to 9:30; Sunday brunch in off-season, 11 to 2. Closed Monday and Tuesday in winter.

Bridge Street Cafe, 10A Bridge St., South Dartmouth. (508) 994-7200.
Continental/American. $10.95 to $17.95.

Greg and Sally Morton have turned a former coffee shop into a larger, sparkling restaurant with a rooftop deck that gives a glimpse of the harbor in Padanarum. The regular menu is supplemented by printed menus that change daily and give Greg Morton a chance to experiment. At lunch, try the smoked trout and salmon sampler, ground lamb in a pita pocket or salad in a pouch. Dinner entrees might include chicken grilled with ginger and garlic, shrimp en brochette, grilled Norwegian salmon, grey sole sauteed with crab legs, and delmonico steak with mushrooms and brandy. Sally Morton has been told that her key lime pie is better than the real thing from Florida. Nautical photos from the family scrapbook adorn the rather spartan, tile-and-slate-floored main dining room; the open kitchen takes up about half the space in the adjacent barroom. On warm days and nights, snacking or dining on the canopied roof is popular.

Lunch, Monday-Saturday 11:30 to 3; dinner nightly, 5:30 to 9 or 9:30; Sunday brunch, 11:30 to 3. Closed Sunday evening and Monday in winter.

Westport

Kate Cory's, 438 Main Road, Westport. (508) 636-5559.
American. $10.95 to $20.95.

Known as Bittersweet Farm, a grand, soaring barn with huge windows and three floors has become the favorite restaurant of vacationers in this low-key area near the ocean. The lovely interior is notable for wide-board floors, ladderback chairs at tables graced with white cloths, pink carnations and candles in hurricane lamps, beneath a wraparound balcony with more tables and a high ceiling. Lanterns on the walls and baskets of dried flowers hanging from the beams contribute to a sophisticated country feeling. Downstairs is a pleasant lounge with wing chairs grouped around small tables; a munchie menu offers spicy chicken wings, spinach boboli and nachos. The food upstairs is fine, if uninspired: typical area fare listed under pasta, seafood, veal and poultry, beef and lamb, ranging from baked chicken with herb and sausage stuffing to mixed grill of shrimp, lamb chops and filet mignon. The prime rib is a weekend favorite, as are such standbys as steak au poivre and steak diane, baked stuffed shrimp and veal marsala.

Lunch, Tuesday-Friday 11:30 to 2:30; dinner, Tuesday-Saturday 5 to 9 or 10, Sunday noon to 9.

Fall River

Leone's, Davol Street, Battleship Cove, Fall River. (508) 679-8158.
American/Italian. $8.95 to $13.95.

A nautical place beside the river, the old Gangplank restaurant gave way a few years back to Leone's. Owner Dominick Leone said the locals had deserted him, thinking the Gangplank had been sold for condominiums. A name change and refurbishing brought them back to a two-level dining room, which takes full advantage of the river view. One reviewer waxed ecstatic over a menu described as a "culinary League of Nations." That translates these days to chicken fingers and potato skins, escargots, antipasto salad, veal cacciatore, baked stuffed sole, and steak au poivre. The white and peach linens are obscured by darkened glass covers. A few seafaring murals, potted palms and an aquarium comprise the decor. Nightly entertainment is offered in the enormous lounge, and a new outdoor bar and grill serves light food beside a marina.

Open daily, 11 to 10.

$ T.A. Restaurant, 408 South Main St., Fall River. (508) 673-5890.
Portuguese. $5.75 to $11.50.

This is an authentic Portuguese restaurant, but it's a less likely looking one than most we've seen this side of Lisbon. After a fire, the building was renovated and the result is unexpectedly light and airy: a mix of stucco and paneling, carpeting and tiled floors, rattan chairs and hanging plants. Tables covered with paper mats over blue cloths under glass add to a colorful scene. The all-day menu offers all the Portuguese standards and then some, like fried ling and shish kabob of octopus. You can dine very well here at prices from yesteryear, which must explain its appeal to the downtown business crowd.

Open daily, 11 to 11.

Lizzie's, 122 Third St., Fall River. (508) 672-7688.
American. $6.95 to $11.95.

Even the least upscale of cities seems to have a fern bar, and Fall River's occupies one of the best examples of Victorian commercial architecture left in town, a hard-to-get-to downtown building beside the interstate highway. It takes its name from Lizzie Borden, the socialite who was accused and later acquitted of the infamous axe murders of her parents a block away in 1892. A greenboard at the entrance supplements the all-day menu. It offered salmon pie with salad, an open veggie pocket, a crab salad pocket, and a lobster meat plate the lunchtime we visited. Steaks are the dinner specialty. A mix of bentwood chairs and church pews are at white-linened tables between pressed-tin walls of brown and green.

Open Monday-Saturday 11:30 to 9, 10 or 11 (no lunch Saturday in summer).

Seekonk

★ Cafe in the Barn, Route 6, Seekonk. (617) 336-6330.
Regional American. $11.50 to $23.50.

This rustic but sophisticated restaurant — attractive by day, enchanting by night — features innovative cuisine and many special touches. The flower arrangements are fantastic: on our spring visit, colorful tulips on the tables and extravagant clay pots filled with dozens of branches and blooms. The bar sports comfortable sofas and brown directors' chairs; if you have a drink here before dinner, you may find a tray of cheese and fruit to nibble from. A small charcuterie with takeout foods and a good selection of preserves, mustards and the like is just off the foyer. A huge tree in the middle of the high-ceilinged dining room is festooned with tiny white lights in the winter and spotlit at other times, and two flickering votive candles are on each table. Classical music plays, and bread sticks stand tall in a wine glass to tide you over as you study the menu. You might start, as we did, with buffalo pate, studded with macadamia nuts and served with an orange-cranberry relish, and a California chevre custard tart with scallions and apple. Or try conch fritters with key lime sauce, Maine mahogany clams with grilled leek and thyme butter, or smoked turkey croquettes with green chile pesto. Go on to broiled salmon with shrimp tapenade and spaetzle, Louisiana shrimp stuffed with artichoke hearts and feta cheese wrapped in phyllo, sauteed veal with poppyseed vinaigrette, or roasted red pheasant with sauteed cranberries and apple brown betty. These were accompanied, on a winter visit, with crisp snow peas and asparagus. The reasonably priced wine list begins with New England vintages, and we found a freesia blossom in our ice bucket. Finish with one of the splendid desserts, like the lemon and cassis charlotte. Lunch and Sunday brunch menus are equally inventive, with things like roasted hazelnut pancakes, coconut chicken with sweet and sour ginger sauce, and warm Texas lobster salad with flour tortillas. What will owner Guy Abelson dream up next?

Lunch, Monday-Saturday noon to 3; dinner 6 to 10; Sunday brunch, noon to 3.

Audrey's, Routes 114A & 44, Seekonk. (508) 336-4636.
American/Continental. $11.95 to $17.95.

The fancy restaurant in the Johnson & Wales Inn could be a typical hotel dining room, but with a difference: it's staffed by students in the culinary program at Johnson & Wales University. One of three Johnson & Wales restaurants in the Providence area, this is the most sophisticated, presenting a mix of traditional and trendy. Among main courses, you might order veal oscar or chateaubriand for two, salmon athena in puff pastry or seafood lasagna with a tomato-basil sauce. Appetizers are a bit more au courant: terrine of duck with pistachios, pecans and pine nuts on toast points, timbales of salmon trout with an herbed creme fraiche,

Cape Cod

whole wheat fettuccine with grilled venison, and quail in peppered puff pastry. Other good starters are the sampling of two homemade soups served with sea toast and conch salad. Much of the dinner menu is available at lunch, and there are real values in twilight specials and lunchtime promotions. The decor is urbane with much dark wood and etched glass, spotlit paintings, and upholstered booths and wing chairs.

Lunch, Monday-Saturday 11:30 to 2:30; dinner, Sunday-Friday 5 to 10, Saturday 6 to 11; Sunday brunch, 10:30 to 2:30.

Taunton

Benjamin's, 698 Bay St., Taunton. (508) 824-6313.
Continental. $10.95 to $16.95.
This hard-to-find place must be seen to be believed. Starting with a Victorian manor in 1968, it has grown upward and outward to the point where its white and gray facade looks something like a large alpine ski lodge. Inside, the main dining room is ensconced in the original house, though you'd never know it today. Around it are a soaring Library Lounge with tall shelves of books and evening entertainment, the balcony dining room with a view of the lounge, the Terrace garden room with greenery and a fountain, the Master Suite, and the Grand Chamber. All told, they seat 650 with an intimacy that eludes other places its size. This is considered a special-occasion restaurant, and all of Taunton seemed to be there the Saturday night we were. George Benjamin and his four offspring attend to every detail and lend their individual recommendations to the menu: escargots florentine, Nantucket scallops, baked stuffed sole, roast duckling with orange sauce, and tournedos in perigourdine sauce. Oysters bienville, clams casino, and goose liver pate with truffles are among the fancy appetizers; caesar and crab louis are favored salads.

Lunch, Monday-Friday 11:30 to 3; dinner nightly, 5 to 10.

Cape Cod

Barnstable

The Barnstable Tavern & Restaurant, 3180 Route 6A, Barnstable.
(508) 362-2355.
Regional American. $13.95 to $19.95
Built to look old in a small Colonial shopping center opened in 1985, this has outdoor dining in summer as well as formal dining in a large, properly historic-looking room accented with prints of birds and decoys. Many seem to congregate in the tavern and its adjacent smaller dining room. For lunch, we've enjoyed an ever-so-smooth cream of garlic soup, spinach salad and a pasta assertive with littlenecks, olive oil and garlic. The dinner menu changes nightly, offering entrees like blackened red snapper with dill-mustard cream, sauteed shrimp and halibut with red pepper coulis, grilled breast of chicken with peaches and raisins, Long Island duckling with spicy tangerine, and mixed grill of quail, tenderloin and shrimp. Desserts could be Nantucket spice cake with coconut icing and grand marnier creme caramel.

Lunch, Monday-Friday 11:30 to 2:30, Sunday noon to 2:30; dinner nightly, 5 to 9 or 10.

Yarmouth Port

The Cranberry Moose, 43 Main St. (Route 6A), Yarmouth Port.
(508) 896-3501.
Contemporary/Italian. $17.50 to $25.
Veteran Cape restaurateurs Marietta and Robert Hickey have taken over this with-it establishment, which evolved whimsically and with artistic flair out of the old

184

Cranberry Goose. For the Hickeys it's a homecoming of sorts: he got his culinary start at the Goose and she was founder of the nearby La Cipollina. Creative young chef Brett Lancaster oversees a changing menu of classical fish dishes with Italian influences, including seafood in parchment, bouillabaisse, poached or braised salmon, veal scaloppine, and pasta with shellfish. The seafood terrine is a specialty, as are cold and hot dishes of mixed shellfish and changing raviolis. The salad of eight wild greens from California with edible flowers on a bed of radicchio is a work of art. Desserts run the gamut from chocolate terrine with raspberry sauce to creme caramel. The new Rosenthal china and seafoam colors are a foil for changing art exhibitions in four small dining rooms, one appropriately called the Gallery.

Dinner nightly from 5:30 in summer; fewer nights and lunch, Thursday-Sunday in off-season.

Chanterelle, Route 6A at Kings Way, Yarmouth Port. (508) 362-8195.
New American. $15 to $25.

Ensconced for eight years in a hideway at the rear of a small shopping center, Chanterelle up and moved in 1989 to much-expanded quarters, front and center in the golf clubhouse of the vast Kings Way development. Here you'll find an elegant, English-style dining room with high ceilings and windows onto the golf course, a smaller Tavern on the Green for lighter fare of interest to golfers, and a sunny outdoor patio. Partners Tracey Gordon and Avi Camchi serve up a wide-ranging menu with an emphasis on health-conscious items. At a spring lunch, a tasty but tepid cream of broccoli soup was followed by a classic cobb salad. The fixed-price luncheon ($10) included a light house pate and a zesty shrimp with oregano over pasta, ample enough that we had to forego the roasted banana crepes, almond grand marnier cake and key lime pie. At night, good starters are chilled shrimp wrapped with smoked salmon and crab cakes with mustard remoulade. Entrees ($15 to $25) include chicken stuffed with crabmeat, poached salmon splashed with cranberry vinegar and pink peppercorns, baked stuffed shrimp with crab and oyster dressing, grilled loin veal chop with apple chutney and onion relish, and roast rack of lamb with goat cheese and pesto. The wild mushrooms for which the restaurant is named turn up in some of the appetizers and entrees.

Lunch daily, 11:30 to 2:30; dinner from 5:30.

Dennis

The Red Pheasant Inn, 905 Main St. (Route 6A), Dennis. (508) 385-2133.
Regional American. $18 to $24.

The exterior is strictly old New England — a rambling, red 200-year-old saltbox house and barn. Inside is a new reception area-living room (used for wine tastings), a couple of dining rooms and a porch, a mix of bentwood chairs and white linens, barnwood and walls with painted flowers, hanging plants and flickering oil lamps. The creative hand in the kitchen and at the Cape's first hickory wood grill belongs to chef Bill Atwood Jr., whose family has been involved in the Red Pheasant since 1977. His entrees are inspired: perhaps pan-fried tuna with shallots and red wine sauce, sauteed scallops with caramelized grapefruit, grilled salmon with tomato fondue and saffron butter sauce, grilled veal chop with Craigston camembert sauce, and pan-roasted pheasant with a sauce of five wild berries. Tuna tartare with marinated European cucumbers and tomato concasse and sweetbreads with wild mushroom ragout are possible starters. The warm confit of duck with field greens and goat cheese is a good summer salad. Among desserts are praline torte and white chocolate mousse. The wine list has been honored by Wine Spectator.

Dinner nightly from 5:30, closed two nights in winter; Sunday brunch, 11 to 2.

Cape Cod

Gina's By the Sea, 134 Taunton Ave., Dennis. (508) 385-3213.

Northern Italian. $11.95 to $13.95.

You can't really see the sea from Gina's House, which started years ago as a restaurant for her cottage renters and has become a favorite for those seeking northern Italian cuisine. Patrons wait up to two hours for a table in the pine-paneled sun porch or fireplaced rear dining room. Accents are parrots of all shapes and sizes, which also adorn the staff's T-shirts. The blackboard menu features things like mussels nicoise on linguini, chicken genovese, roasted vegetables primavera over fettuccine in warm balsamic vinaigrette, and veal stuffed with artichokes, Italian ham and asiago cheese. Scampi a la Gina's and sauteed chicken on a bed of spinach and mushrooms are house specialties. Lunches for beachgoers are served on summer weekdays.

Dinner nightly in summer, 5 to 10; spring and fall, Thursday-Sunday.

Brewster

★♥ Chillingsworth, Route 6A, Brewster. (508) 896-3640.

New French/American. Prix-Fixe, $37.50 to $49.

For years, this rambling Cape Cod house full of period antiques has been known for the finest dining on the Cape — perhaps the finest of any resort area in New England. A harpist plays in the background as you study the menu, a mix of complex choices composed daily by chef-owner Robert (Nitzi) Rabin. The formerly classic French fare has evolved into new French-American cuisine, with appetizers like snails with pistachios and garlic cream and entrees like loin of veal with truffle sauce, asparagus and potato pie. The seven-course, prix-fixe dinner ($37.50 to $49, depending upon choice of entree) starts with such treats as a crab cake with creme fraiche and sorrel, chilled plum soup, excellent breads, a classic green salad and a palate-cleansing sorbet (perhaps grapefruit with a sprig of mint) in a Waterford sherry glass. Then comes the piece de resistance: grilled striped bass with tomatoes, leeks and truffle vinaigrette; breast of pheasant with marjoram, snow peas, sweet potato and corn, or rack and loin of lamb with pepper mousse and saffron risotto. The choices are legion and invariably stunning. Desserts, which follow a plate of varied cookies called "amusements," are ambrosial. We enjoyed the raspberry tuile and a grand marnier custard on a bed of strawberries. Intense chocolate truffles accompanying the bill ease the moment of reckoning. Nitzi and his wife Pat offer lunch in the greenhouse lounge area in summer, and are converting their former quarters upstairs into two rooms and suites for overnight guests.

Lunch, Wednesday-Saturday 11:30 to 2:30 in summer; dinner by reservation, nightly except Monday at two seatings, 6 to 9:30; Sunday brunch. Weekend dinners, spring and fall. Closed November to Memorial Day.

★ The Bramble Inn & Restaurant, Route 6A, Brewster. (508) 896-7644.

New American. Prix-Fixe, $35 to $42.

A profusion of flowers, Queen Anne chairs, and peacocks on deep blue wallpaper grace the four small dining rooms in this well-regarded inn. Ruth and Cliff Manchester, who got their start at her parents' nearby Old Manse Inn, have a devoted following. The price for the four-course dinner varies with the choice of entree. Start perhaps with Bermuda fish chowder, lobster quesadilla with salsa and guacamole, or grilled quail with Cajun spices and potato salad. Eight main-course choices range from farm-raised Atlantic salmon with three caviars and harbor stew (Ruth's version of bouillabaisse) to rack of lamb with garlic and thyme, roast tenderloin of beef with roquefort and white wine sauce, and tenderloin of veal with shiitake mushrooms, whole-grain mustard and vermouth. An exotic seafood curry (cod, lobster, shrimp, scallops and squid paired with banana, chutney, almonds and toasted coconut) attests to the inspiration in the kitchen. Chambord truffle tart, white chocolate coeur a la creme, and flourless chocolate terrine with coffee cream sauce are among renowned desserts.

Dinner nightly in season, 5:30 to 9:30; weekends, October-May.

High Brewster, 964 Satucket Road, Brewster. (508) 896-3636.
New American. Prix-Fixe, $28.50 to $33.

This rambling Colonial house on a hill overlooking Lower Mill Pond was run for 25 years by two gentlemen of the old school as a low-key restaurant in their home. New owners took over in 1987 and chef Martin Murphy executes a short menu that celebrates new and classic American cuisine. Because of its rural, residential setting, the owners' attempts for a liquor license have been blocked, but you may bring your own spirits. Crisp white linens, Blue Willow china, and fine paintings and antiques are displayed to good advantage amid rustic beams, paneling and barn boards. The tab for the four-course, prix-fixe dinner varies, depending on choice of entree. Dinner begins with an hors d'oeuvre like spicy corn relish with fresh vegetables and a blue cheese sauce. The appetizer, perhaps angel-hair pasta with mussels and smoked bacon or pan-fried cod cheeks with homemade remoulade, is followed by a green salad dressed with a raspberry-herb vinaigrette. Interesting vegetables (saute of swiss chard and smoked bacon, fried onion rings with corn meal) accompany the entrees, which could be roasted filet of salmon with pesto butter, grilled pork chops with chile butter, smoked breast of duck with maple glaze, or grilled loin lamb chops with smoky port wine sauce. Seasonal fruits turn up in desserts like deep-dish apple pie and strawberry-rhubarb crisp.

Dinner nightly except Monday in season, 6 to 9:30; weekends from 6 to 8 in winter. BYOB.

Orleans

Captain Linnell House, 137 Skaket Beach Road, Orleans. (508) 255-3400.
Regional American. $12.50 to $19.75.

From the outside, you'd think you were looking at a stately Southern plantation dropped incongruously beside a Cape Cod forest. From the inside of the main dining room looking out onto a formal rear garden shaded by a huge, gnarled European linden, you might think you were in a palace. In a sense, you'd be right on both counts. This rambling, white-pillared mansion is, in fact, a replica of a French neoclassic villa that Cape Cod sea captain Eben Linnell saw on a sailing trip to Marseilles in 1850 and had built for his bride. New owners took over in 1988 to mixed reviews, the majority positive. The menu features grills, roasts and sautes, as in grilled swordfish with a tomato, red onion and basil relish, sauteed veal with crab, and roast duckling with a raspberry-honey glaze. Scallops and shrimp are sauteed with a tarragon-lobster sauce, and rack of lamb roasted with an herbed mustard crust and a pinot noir sauce. Bourbon-lobster bisque and Wellfleet oysters with julienned vegetables and champagne-ginger sauce are favored starters.

Lunch, Monday-Friday 11:30 to 2; dinner nightly except Tuesday, 6 to 10; Sunday brunch, 11 to 2.

The Arbor, Route 28 at Route 6A, Orleans. (508) 255-4847.
International. $12.95 to $16.95.

Funky as all get-out, but charming as well, are the several dining rooms (one on a tilted porch, one in a paneled room with a fireplace, one in a quiet back room with four tables for two) in this old sea captain's house with attached barn. They're full of the owners' unusual collections acquired from flea markets. The food is creative and gutsy, from the complimentary tray of pickled peppers and crudites with a dip and large buttermilk biscuits to a heavenly dessert of a meringue shell filled with coffee ice cream and praline sauce. The choice embraces a staggering 53 items, from seven pastas and seven veal dishes to six Cajun-style offerings and five of "the Arbor's best" — two preparations of lobster and one each of pasta, veal and sole. One of us had bouillabaisse, which came in a huge crock — it was crammed with so much seafood she could eat only about a quarter of it, and was given a doggy bag (make that a Stop & Shop container) to take home. The other had scallops stephen in a cream sauce on pasta and loved it. Prices are so low you wonder how they can do it, as well as how they can succeed so handsomely with so extensive a repertoire.

Dinner nightly, 5 to 10. Closed Tuesday and Wednesday in winter.

Nauset Beach Club, 221 Main St., East Orleans. (508) 255-8547.
Northern Italian. $9.50 to $15.
A small white house with red awnings, a new outdoor deck and three intimate rooms in a casual red and white decor is the setting for reasonably priced Italian fare. Six pastas are available as appetizers or entrees; we liked the sound of festonati sauced with Italian sausage, sun-dried tomatoes and cheese. Spiedini, squid salad, steamed shrimp with a red pepper mayonnaise, and mussels glazed with mozzarella are fetching appetizers. Main courses range in price from sausage and potatoes to grilled shrimp scampi over pasta. Gnocchi and scallops, grilled shrimp with ginger-mango sauce, swordfish cacciatore, and strip steak with gorgonzola cheese are other possibilities. The Nauset Beach club sandwich is lobster meat, pancetta and arugula served on a toasted Portuguese muffin. Finish with creme caramel, white chocolate mousse with strawberry puree, or cranberry cobbler with ginger ice cream.

Dinner nightly, 5:30 to 10:30.

Wellfleet

Aesop's Tables, Main Street, Wellfleet. (508) 349-6450.
New American. $14.75 to $19.75.
Creative cuisine with nightly variations is featured in this highly rated restaurant in a large white house built about 1805 in the heart of Wellfleet. A warren of small dining rooms and an appealing porch display some of the charming collages of artist Kim Kettler, co-owner with her husband Bryan. Upstairs is a tavern outfitted with plush sofas and offering light meals. Arty touches accent the menu, as in Monet's garden salad of exotic greens, sun-dried tomatoes and montrachet, and the poulet d'art (an artful variation of a classic chicken dish, changing daily). Aesop's Wellfleet oysters, chilled or hot, are excellent appetizers; they may come in a sauce of soy and balsamic vinegar, topped with all colors of peppers including jalapeno. Among main courses are scallops framboise, uptown duck (herb-roasted, from Wisconsin), and grilled lamb chops with pommery, fresh rosemary and garlic. Desserts include an acclaimed hazelnut fruit torte, chocolate-kahlua-pecan pie, and key lime pie.

Dinner, nightly from 6; Sunday brunch, 10 to 1. Open mid-May to mid-October.

Truro

Adrian's, Route 6A, North Truro. (508) 487-4360.
Light Italian. $4.95 to $14.95.
This is a favorite of Provincetown chefs on their nights off, as well as other foodies

seeking gourmet pizzas and pastas in a casual setting full of local character. Adrian Cyr and his wife, Annette, have a homespun, summery place with bare wood tables, cathedral ceiling, striking paintings, lacy curtains, and fresh flowers. In the off-season, Adrian is an instructor at the culinary school that he attended in Cambridge. Pastas and pizzas come in small and large sizes, the better to mix and match — which is good, since every one appeals. Sliced potatoes, pesto, pine nuts and parmesan go into one pizza; grilled chicken with jalapeno peppers, salsa and cilantro, another. The pasta al pesto with fresh basil, pine nuts, parmesan cheese and more on linguini is correctly billed as "summer's glory." The creativity extends to the breakfast menu as well.

Breakfast 8 to 1, dinner 5:30 to 10. Closed Tuesday and Wednesday. Seasonal.

Provincetown

♥ **Franco's By the Sea,** 442 Commercial St., Provincetown. (508) 487-3178.
Continental. $10.95 to $20.95.
What started as the tiny Franco's Hideaway down a somewhat shabby alley has moved and expanded into a dramatic, two-level establishment with windows right onto the beach. It's theatrical and camp, done up in pink and black with gleaming lacquered black tables and booths, each booth named for a flamboyant star like Hedda Hopper, Dorothy Lamour, Tallulah Bankhead and Delores del Rio. Round mirrors and pictures of these women — even letters they wrote — hang above the booths. A collection of silver cocktail shakers is displayed. It's all very Noel Coward-ish; in fact, the menu contains one of his quotes, "Cocktails and laughter, but what comes after?" Chef-owner Franco Palumbo is proud of his "outrageous number of specials," among them tournedos Franco topped with lobster or blackened shrimp, and boneless lamb loin with madeira and truffle sauce. Cold curried mussels, Cajun sausage and Maine crab claws are a few of the appetizers. Exciting pastas, four presentations of veal, and grilled Indonesian chicken with peanut sauce are favorite entrees. "Brownie all the way" (with ice cream and nuts) and a meringue with coffee ice cream and praline sauce are best-selling desserts. An all-day menu of snacks and appetizers is served in summer on the Promenade Deck off Tallulah's Lounge.

Dinner nightly, 5:30 to 11.

Napi's, 7 Freeman St., Provincetown. (508) 487-1145.
International. $9.95 to $18.95.
Run by Helen and Napi Van Dereck, this venerable restaurant with an eclectic menu is a favorite of local artists and musicians. On two floors of a veritable art gallery, it's a showcase of local art, from cartoons by Howie Snyder to a freeform brick wall sculpted by Conrad Malicoat. The lampshades are made of scallop shells, a couple of colorful carousel horses prance atop a room divider, and the amount of antique stained glass is awesome. So is the variety on the menu: page after page of beef, chicken and seafood dishes, plus categories for shrimp and scallops, fresh catch, mussels, stir-fries, vegetarian dishes and pastas. There's everything from Moroccan shrimp feta to Japanese sushi rolls and Portuguese bouillabaisse. Half a loaf of Helen's whole wheat bread comes with dinner. Save room for the "double fudge madness," a chocolate-glazed rum custard cake, or the apricot mousse.

Dinner nightly from 5:30.

Front Street, 230 Commercial St., Provincetown. (508) 487-9715.
New American. $14.95 to $21.95.
Chef Donna Aliperti took over this highly rated restaurant in 1986, and has added her creative touch to a perennial winner. Her menu changes weekly, and features

game in fall. Favorite items include such starters as lobster and leek bisque, smoked seafood lasagna, and mandarin scallop seviche. Main courses could be grilled Norwegian salmon, tea-smoked duck, lobster-stuffed tenderloin, and herb-crusted rack of lamb. The praline cheesecake and strawberry-pine nut tarte are to groan over. The basement room with brick walls is dark and intimate. Striking tables made by a local artist are topped with tiny pieces of cut-up wood under a layer of polyurethane. Wines are showcased in back-lit storage shelves along one wall.

Dinner nightly, 6 to 11. Closed January-March.

Anna Anna Anna, 149 Commercial St., Provincetown. (508) 487-2900. Regional American. $6.75 to $25.75.

"The world's best food," says the sign outside Anna Annunziata's new restaurant in a shingled bungalow spiffed up with a trellised white and aqua dining room. On opening day, Anna was in the kitchen readying the evening's specials, among them chimney-smoked lobster, shrimp in a walnut sauce over black pasta, a 22-ounce tuna steak, and saddle of lamb. You can order a roasted globe of garlic, and lobster up to fifteen pounds. Anna is from Atlanta, which she says helps explain her blend of New England and regional American cuisines. Among desserts are peanut butter pie and chocolate cake.

Brunch daily 8 to 1; dinner nightly, 6 to 11. Closed Thanksgiving to April.

The Lobster Pot, 321 Commercial St., Provincetown. (508) 487-0842. Seafood. $11.95 to $15.95.

Tourists rub elbows with locals at this institution known for consistent, abundant seafood. There's the typical lobster-pot decor, but not its typical menu. Some fairly sophisticated fare comes out of the rows of kitchens opening off the long corridor on the way to the rear dining room beside the water. We certainly liked the prize-winning clam chowder, rich and creamy, and the mussels marinara with the plumpest mollusks ever. The shrimp chantilly tossed with spinach fettuccine is a lunchtime classic. Shellfish algarve, bouillabaisse and cioppino are among the litany of seafood offerings at dinner. The Lobster Pot also has a fish market, raw bar and bakery.

Lunch daily, noon to 5; dinner from 5.

Chatham

★ Christian's, 443 Main St., Chatham. (508) 945-3362. American. $15 to $20.50.

With an abiding interest in cooking and a degree from the Culinary Institute of America, all Christian Schultz needed was a restaurant. In 1981, his father Walter provided it, purchasing the old Chatham Arms. Christian's mother did the pretty decorating and his younger brother became the maitre-d. The family project has since grown from something of a summer lark into an expanding, longer-than-seasonal venture with **Upstairs at Christian's,** a classic English bar serving a tavern menu, and an outdoor upper deck for drinks or light eating. The complimentary liver pate is thick and robust, the French bread crusty, and the salad enhanced by a zesty herb and cheese dressing. Entrees, which change every three weeks, range from baked scrod with orange hollandaise to poached salmon topped with lobster in a champagne sauce. Roast duck with a fresh fruit sauce (once raspberry, the next time pear and pink peppercorns) is a house specialty. We liked both the fresh halibut topped with asparagus hollandaise and the veal medallions sauteed with shrimp, garlic, lemon and white wine. A grand marnier torte topped with a chocolate shell filled with grand marnier is a special dessert. After dinner in one of the two main-floor dining rooms, it's fun to adjourn upstairs to enjoy Spanish coffee while listening to a fellow singing folk songs and playing several different instruments — a most pleasant way to end an evening.

Dinner nightly, 6 to 10. Closed Thanksgiving-March.

Wequassett Inn, Pleasant Bay, Chatham. (508) 432-5400.
New American. $16.50 to $22.50.

The centerpiece of this luxurious inn is the lovely old Eben Ryder "Square Top" with its wedgwood blue shutters against white clapboard. Here, inn guests and the public may dine, indoors and out, facing what we consider the most alluring water view of any Cape restaurant. The terrace, covered with a yellow and white awning, has blue deck chairs; boxes of vivid pink geraniums frame Pleasant Bay with its scores of sailboats. Indoors the two dining rooms are more formal, yet serene and simple so as not to detract from the view. Service is friendly and chef Frank McMullen's cuisine is considered the best of the Cape's large resorts. Lunch can be as casual as an open-face clam roll or fish and chips, or you could have swordfish and shrimp kabob. At night, we enjoyed the salmon and scallop terrine garnished with blood oranges so much we ordered it the next night, this time with beurre blanc and burnet. The escargots with pine nuts in phyllo dough and barbecued clams with caramelized onion were winners, too. Among entrees, we're partial to the grilled swordfish with sun-dried tomato butter, shrimp sauteed with apples, and the twin beef tenderloins sauteed with roasted garlic and fresh rosemary. The chocolate truffle cake and the cranberry mousse in an almond tuile are delectable desserts.

Lunch daily, 11:30 to 2; dinner 6 to 10. Open mid-May to mid-October.

The Impudent Oyster, 115 Chatham Bars Ave., Chatham. (508) 945-3545.
International. $14 to $21.

With a name like the Impudent Oyster, this small restaurant down a side street in Chatham was destined for success. An avid local following jams together at small glass-covered tables under a skylit cathedral ceiling, beneath plants in straw baskets balancing overhead on the beams. The changing international menu, based on local seafoods, blends regional, French, Mexican, Chinese, Indian and Italian cuisines, among others. We couldn't resist starting with the drunken mussels, shelled and served in an intense marinade of tamari, fresh ginger, Szechuan peppercorns and sake. The Mexican chicken, chile and lime soup, spicy and full of interesting flavors, was one of the best we've tasted. Entrees range from chicken saltimbocca to filet mignon with roquefort and horseradish sauce. A house specialty is bouillabaisse. On one visit we liked the feta and fennel scrod, a Greek dish touched with ouzo, and the swordfish broiled with orange and pepper butter. This is the kind of fare of which we never tire, although we might prefer to have it in a more tranquil and less crowded setting.

Lunch, daily 11:30 to 3; dinner, 5:30 to 10.

The Queen Anne Inn, 70 Queen Anne Road, Chatham. (508) 945-0394.
New American. $25 to $28.50.

Pretty, posh and with prices to match, the Queen Anne is a 30-room inn with a small, pink-linened dining room favored by well-heeled inn guests. The hand-written menu offered by a team of European chefs changes frequently. The food is exquisite: starters like cream of butternut squash with diced sweetbreads or homemade ravioli with confit of duck, sauteed foie gras and black currant sauce. Among entrees, the veal chop might be endowed with lobster and spinach, and the sole and scallops with lobster cream sauce and fettuccine. Loin of lamb might come with garlic-thyme sauce, and the medallions of venison with creme de cassis. Innkeeper Guenther

Cape Cod

Weinkopf compares the delectable desserts with those of the finest pastry shops in Europe. We've heard great things about the sacher torte, the fresh fruit mousses and homemade sorbets.

Dinner nightly except Tuesday, 6:30 to 9, late spring through December.

Harwich Port

★ Cafe Elizabeth, 31 Sea St., Harwich Port. (508) 432-1147.
French $18.50 to $32.

Marguerite and Paul Nebbia, formerly of the esteemed Rive Gauche in Washington, D.C., run this charming country-French restaurant in a former sea captain's house. Edith Piaf music played in the background as we sampled an elegant appetizer, the signature blinis a la Russe, whole wheat pancakes stuffed with sour cream and fresh salmon caviar, served with a glass of homemade frozen cranberry vodka. Main courses of breast of duck with cranberry sauce and breast of chicken in a curry sauce with raisins, almonds and apples were colorfully garnished with baby corn, carrots and teeny beans wrapped in red pepper strips. Other entree possibilities might be sauteed Louisiana crawfish with tomato and oregano, roasted quails and a filet of wild boar with cranberry sauce, four baby lamb chops with tarragon sauce, and a mixed grill of shrimp with sauce bonifacio, veal with wild mushrooms, lamb with fresh tarragon, and filet with bearnaise. Pastry chef Marguerite's dessert specialty is homemade chocolate truffles served on a bed of fresh whipped cream with chocolate sauce and roasted almonds.

Dinner nightly, 6 to 9 or 10. Open May-October.

Hyannis

The Paddock, West Main Street Rotary, Hyannis. (508) 775-7677.
Continental. $14.25 to $22.95.

This city restaurant is what you'd expect in Cape Cod's big city. The menu is fancy and the setting urbane in a richly paneled, Victorian dining room with well-spaced tables in brown and beige linens and an airy, enclosed green and white courtyard called the Garden & Grill, where a luncheon fashion show was in progress when we visited. For nearly twenty years, owners Maxine and John Zartarian have been known for such fare as poached Cape scallops, baked New England grey sole, prime rib, steak au poivre, rack of lamb persille, and tournedos bearnaise. The menu is extensive, the portions ample, and the wine list honored by the Wine Spectator.

Lunch daily, noon to 2:30; dinner, 5 to 10, Sunday noon to 9. Open April to mid-November.

Penguins Go Pasta, 331 Main St., Hyannis. (508) 775-2023.
Northern Italian. $10 to $18.50.

They've got to be kidding with this whimsical name (the place is also known as Three Thirty-One Main, for obvious reasons). But there's no doubting the popularity of chef-owner Robert Gold's specialties, especially the pastas. No reservations are taken and on the spring weekend night we tried to eat, there was a two-hour wait — which, for us, was two hours too long. If you get in, you'll find an extensive menu with pastas from $10 to $12, seafood, beef and veal (ten presentations, from marsala to osso buco). Prices top off at rack of lamb. You may even find rabbit huntsman style.

Dinner nightly from 5.

Cotuit

✳ The Regatta of Cotuit, 4631 Falmouth Road (Route 28), Cotuit.
(508) 428-5715.
Regional American. $10.50 to $25.

The Crocker House, a short-lived restaurant in a handsome 1790 Federal-style house, was acquired in 1987 by Wendy and Brantz Bryan of the Regatta in Falmouth. In contrast to their summery, New Yorkish waterfront establishment, the new venture features regional Americana on a year-round basis in seven elegantly appointed small dining rooms, one with only two tables. Chef Gilbert Pepin's menu is a mix of tavern-type grill fare and fine dining, from grilled seafood sausage to lobster and Cotuit Bay oysters with fresh herb cream, from grilled calves liver with balsamic vinaigrette to a trilogy of grilled lamb (chop, medallion and kidney) with a pinot noir sauce. Start with corn and codfish chowder or Maine crabmeat raviolis with chardonnay cream sauce. Finish with a couple of the best desserts we've tasted: chocolate seduction on a lovely patterned raspberry sauce and creme brulee garnished with red and gold raspberries and blackberries. Berries, herbs and edible flowers come from the garden out back.
Dinner nightly from 5:30.

Falmouth

♥ The Regatta, Scranton Avenue, Falmouth. (508) 548-5400.
New American. $16 to $26.

A waterfront location, a cheerful pink and white decor, inventive food, and a smashing wine list — it's little wonder that Falmouth folks rate this restaurant right up with Chillingsworth and keep it consistently crowded and lively. Many of the 100 seats take advantage of the harbor view, while those in the back room focus on colorful murals and an aquarium full of exotic fish. Salty and skinny homemade breadsticks stand tall in a champagne flute on each table. Seafood is the specialty, from appetizers like carpaccio of tuna with ginger and soy or oyster fritters to a sensational lobster bisque with red pepper rouille and lobster concasse or a warm salad of monkfish with edible flowers. Entrees are a treat for the eye as well as the palate: grilled scallops with a lime and chive butter sauce, grilled shrimp with a sauce of three mustards, soft-shell crabs with roasted red pepper and opal basil, and palette of two fish, each with its own sauce. Nightly specials that might include buffalo and rabbit supplement the printed menu. Desserts are triumphs; splurge on the trilogy of three favorite desserts (ours was a chocolate truffle cake, almond torte with framboise sauce, and hand-dipped chocolate strawberries). Owners Wendy and Brantz Bryan, very personable hosts, maintain the highest standards.
Dinner nightly from 5:30, Memorial Day to Columbus Day.

Coonamessett Inn, Gifford Street at Jones Road, Falmouth. (508) 548-2300.
American. $14.95 to $19.95.

Landscaped grounds backing up to hidden Jones Pond enhance the view from the main dining room of this large, barn-red, traditional New England establishment. The view is grand from the Ralph Cahoon Room, hung with his paintings. You'll miss it if you're seated in the fireplaced Vineyard Room strung with white lights in grape vines along the beams, or the casual Eli's Lounge in front, where a tavern menu is served. Try for the Cahoon Room or the rear Garden Room and enjoy New England specialties like Cape Cod lobster pie, broiled scrod, grilled swordfish, chicken piquante, and seafood newburg. The lobster bisque has won awards. About the only nouvelle touches are a leek and apple tart and Maryland crab cake with tomato coulis on the list of appetizers and, oh yes, the spinach salad with goat cheese.

Lunch, 11:30 to 2:30; dinner, 5:30 to 9:30; closed two weeks in January.

Martha's Vineyard

Edgartown

★ Warriners, Post Office Square, Edgartown. (508) 627-4488.
Regional American. Prix-Fixe, $36; Sam's, $7.75 to $12.25.

Tops on everyone's list of favorite restaurants in Edgartown, this is actually "two concepts under one roof," as owner Sam Warriner advertises it. Changing prix-fixe menus, fine wines and an elegant, home-like setting amid fine china and antiques combine for luxurious dining in the **Library.** The new, adjacent **Sam's** is billed as casual elegance (with the emphasis more on elegance, since this was, after all, part of the original Warriners), but the menu is informal, the prices moderate and the ambience spirited. Striking Dudson china (with everything matching, even vases and salt and pepper shakers) and heavy print mats adorn the English reproduction mahogany tables in the dark-paneled main dining room that lives up to its Library name. Our prix-fixe dinner began with a pate of duck accompanied by a beach plum chutney and grilled quail with honey-poppyseed mustard, followed by a house salad with a strawberry vinaigrette. Entrees range from medallions of salmon with watercress and lillet to tournedos diane. We liked the peppered duck steak mousseline with zinfandel sauce and the roulade of lamb brunoise with prosciutto, nicely presented with an array of brussels sprouts, cherry tomatoes and small red potatoes, garnished with a bunch of small wild grapes. The dessert tray yielded a tasty kiwi cake, a grand passion genoise with liqueur, butter cream and kiwi, chocolate pate with creme celeste, a dish of four kinds of chocolate truffles, and Sam's favorite raspberry mousse with chocolate sauce. Honored with the 1989 award of excellence by Wine Spectator magazine, the magnificent wine list contains more than its share of bargains among pricier offerings. At our latest visit, we thoroughly enjoyed Sam's, where you can pick and taste from an inspired menu. We shared a seafood terrine before digging into a generous dish of fettuccine with shrimp in basil, garlic and tomato butter sauce and an equally hefty plate of curried chicken India. A frozen blueberry mousse with the consistency of ice cream was a refreshing dessert.

Dinner nightly in season, 6 to 9 in Library by reservation, to 10 in Sam's. Open Wednesday-Sunday in winter.

★ L'Etoile, South Summer Street, Edgartown. (508) 627-5187.
Regional American. Prix-Fixe, $48.

Handsomely outfitted with brick walls, skylights, paintings, lush ferns, and a blooming hibiscus tree is this bow-windowed conservatory dining room, ensconced at the rear of the exquisite Charlotte Inn. Chef-owner Michael Brisson and his wife, Joan Parzanese, overcome what could be a chilly environment with exquisite food and artistic presentation. The 30-year-old chef, who cooked for four years at the acclaimed L'Espalier in Boston, takes special pride in his treatment of game, lamb and native seafood. He also is partial to the understated place settings of white, gold-edged Villeroy & Boch china, the Reed & Barton silverplate, and fluted crystal wine glasses at white-linened tables seating 45 inside. Another twenty or so can be accommodated on a patio beside a trickling fountain outside. Leisurely dinners start with a choice of five appetizers: perhaps basil ravioli with pine nut and chive cream sauce and tomato concasse or a confit of game birds, rabbit and baby vegetables with tomatillo chutney and honey mustard. Or you can sample a soup of island shellfish, a salad of marinated goat cheese, or sauteed fresh foie gras with leeks and cognac-soaked golden raisins. A homemade champagne sorbet or a salad precedes the main course, which could be a saute of lobster and scallops with ancho chilies and corn, lobster bourbon and cilantro sauce, roasted pheasant with warm figs and a cognac and thyme sauce, or grilled filet mignon with oyster and chive butter and a roasted tomato stuffed with spinach and cheese. Among desserts are creme brulee, warm apple tarte tatin, almond cream peach tart with bourbon chantilly cream, and white chocolate grand marnier ice cream. The wine list starts with many champagnes, since for most this is special-occasion dining.

Dinner nightly in summer, 6:30 to 9:30; Wednesday-Sunday in spring and fall, Friday-Sunday from November-April; Sunday brunch, 10:30 to 1. Closed January and first two weeks of February.

Savoir Fare, Post Office Square, Edgartown. (508) 627-9864.
Regional American. $14.50 to $19.50.

What began as basically a gourmet takeout shop has expanded into a small but full-fledged restaurant known for the best lunches in town. Lately, owners Scott and Charlotte Caskey added dinners as well. Chef Scott, who used to cook in Vail, works in an open kitchen at one end of the small restaurant, which is a picture of pristine white from its glass-covered linened tables to the lights on a ficus tree. For lunch, you order from a blackboard menu and the staff brings your choices to the table. We savored a caesar salad topped with grilled chicken and a small combination plate of curried chicken and pesto-pasta salads, accompanied by good French bread and a glass of the house Spanish wine. The dinner menu changes frequently. Typical summer appetizers might be Vineyard bay scallops ceviche, antipasto of sliced prosciutto and fresh figs, and goat cheese tart with sun-dried tomatoes and roasted garlic. Lobster in brioche and smoked-duck salad are offered as light dinners. Cioppino heads the list of main courses, which could include grilled tuna steak with mango-chile salsa, fettuccine with bacon, feta cheese and pine nuts, and sauteed tournedos of beef with wild mushroom ragout. Chocolate mousse cake with pecan crust, baked apples in pastry, and hot fudge pudding are delectable desserts.

Lunch, Monday-Saturday 11 to 3; dinner, Tuesday-Saturday 6 to 10; slightly shorter hours in off-season. Closed Christmas to March.

Shiretown Inn, North Water Street, Edgartown. (508) 627-3353.
Seafood. $17 to $22.

The large indoor-outdoor dining room and covered terrace at the rear of the Shiretown Inn is one of the more popular spots in Edgartown. A pink and green color scheme, well-spaced tables, soft candlelight, and quiet music provide a glamorous backdrop for the widely acclaimed fare of chef Jack Hakes, one of the island's veterans. Seafood is the specialty, particularly among appetizers (shrimp and raspberry compote with haricots verts, baked littlenecks and garlic), and the inn claims the best clam chowder on the island. Three kinds of breads in a basket and salads with caesar dressing and pine nuts preceded our entrees of four jumbo shrimp in a rich garlic sauce, accompanied by baby vegetables, and an enormous helping of baked Norwegian salmon in puff pastry. Other entrees might be yellowtail tuna, sauteed shrimp romana, seafood brochette, rack of lamb dijon, veal martini-quaise, and tournedos sauteed with crabmeat and brandy, served with avocado pate and bearnaise sauce. Fancy ice creams are the dessert specialty, among them the Shiretown wonder: ice cream with hot fudge sauce, creme de menthe and shredded coconut. We decided instead on a slice of tangy key lime pie, smothered with whipped cream, from the pastry cart.

Dinner nightly except Wednesday, 6 to 9 or 10, spring to mid-fall.

Andrea's, Upper Main Street, Edgartown. (508) 627-5850.
Northern Italian. $14.95 to $26.95.

This northern Italian restaurant is one of those places that locals seem to love or dislike. The setting is a large white house, built in 1890, with a wide front porch, a side garden patio, and a downstairs bar-lounge and wine cellar. The airy dining rooms have bare wood floors and large windows framed by lacy white curtains. Deep green tablecloths contrast with the white walls. The fare is about what you'd expect: hot and cold appetizers of melon and prosciutto, clams casino and mozzarella in carozza, a dozen pastas, four salads, and the usual array of veal, seafood, chicken and beef dishes. The late Boston food critic Anthony Spinazzola raved about "the best linguini and white clam sauce I ever experienced." Another standout is the veal Andrea, sauteed in white wine and baked on a bed of fresh spinach and herbs before being topped with prosciutto and imported cheese.

Dinner nightly except Sunday, 6 to 11.

Martha's, 71 Main St., Edgartown. (508) 627-8316.
International. $15 to $25.

What could be more New Yorkish than Martha's, the arty, unbelievably colorful and crowded downstairs restaurant and the upstairs nightspot with a glassed-in waterfall behind the bar, tiny theater lights that flash on and off, and a small front porch where patrons vie in warm weather for the few tables overlooking the Main Street goings-on? It seems an unlikely spot for the busloads of elderly tourists who jam it every lunchtime we're in town, but it turns out, they're the ones who will, most locals having been turned off lately. Quiches, omelets and salads are featured at lunch. Dinners are more international and pricey, with entrees from vegetable stir-fry with Japanese tofu to bouillabaisse and rack of lamb bouquetiere. Seafood is baked, grilled or blackened, and comes with choice of eight sauces, including cashew-ginger and mustard-peppercorn. A sushi bar, a raw bar, cafe menu, Sunday brunch, afternoon snacks — you name it, Martha's offers it.

Open daily from 11 to 10:30.

The Square-Rigger Restaurant, Upper Main Street at West Tisbury Road, Edgartown. (508) 627-9968.
American. Table d'hote, $16.50 to $28.

The folks who run the immensely popular Home Port seafood restaurant in Menemsha acquired this 1800 house and turned it into a restaurant of deceptively large size, specializing in grilled American fare. The theme is nautical at tables set with woven blue mats and surrounded by captain's chairs. From an open hearth come a variety of charbroiled entrees, ranging from bluefish and swordfish to sirloin steaks and lamb chops. There are also prime rib, roast duck, lobster newburg, and bouillabaisse. At first glance the prices seem steep, but they include appetizer — anything from house pate to shrimp cocktail — salad, beverage and dessert (from parfaits and sorbets to chocolate truffles). No wonder it's a favorite with families.

Dinner nightly from 5:30.

The Seafood Shanty, 31 Dock St., Edgartown. (508) 627-8622.
Seafood. $15.95 to $18.95.

This contemporary, three-level spot is anything but a shanty. Edgartown's best harbor view for dining is from the upstairs deck with a raw bar above a glass-enclosed porch with water on three sides. Unusual plastic chairs with deep blue mesh frames, bare tables with blue and white mats, and bare wood walls add up to an attractive nautical setting. You pay for the location. Our lunch for two came to $30 for a cup of clam chowder and a spinach salad, plus a pasta salad loaded with seafood; the sunny Indian summer setting was such, we admit, that we lingered over a second beer. The seafood dinner entrees are fairly traditional, ranging from broiled scrod or bluefish to swordfish or a fried seafood platter; rolls and salad or coleslaw, baked potato or french fries accompany. After all this, who needs the desserts, which are standard anyway? But you might want to adjourn upstairs to the **Shanty Cabaret,** where singers (most from Yale) perform show tunes in summer.

Lunch daily, 11:45 to 3; dinner, 5 to 10:30. Open May-October.

Vineyard Haven

∗ The Black Dog Tavern, Beach Street Extension, Vineyard Haven.
(508) 693-9223.
Regional American. $14.95 to $19.95.

Vineyard Haven's only restaurant on the water, this weathered old shanty happens to have some of the island's most creative food at prices that are tough to beat (made even lighter because it's BYOB). As you enter you might think you were in a cafeteria, because of the open kitchen along the side wall and the menu that changes daily, and the decor is practically nil (a dark beamed ceiling and a few boat signs). Proceed if you can get a table to the long and narrow screened porch over the water. There is no linen and the flowers are in juice glasses, but as dusk falls, the candles are lit, the ferry arrives and departs nearby, and it's all quite enchanting. Our smoked bluefish with dill sauce was the fastest appetizer ever served (no reservations are taken, and this staff knows how to turn the tables). It came with two side plates for sharing, and was garnished with apples, Greek olives and cherry tomatoes. Then came a loaf of hot bread and excellent house salads in large glass bowls, dressed with Russian or vinaigrette. Among entrees, we chose wisely: fresh tuna with lime and green peppercorns, and sauteed oysters with tamari, snow peas and red peppers. Sauteed scallops with shiitake mushrooms and sun-dried tomatoes, grilled swordfish with avocado salsa, chicken stuffed with spinach and cheese, and grilled loin lamb chops with braised vidalia onions and sage — these are the stuff of which culinary dreams are made. Appetizers are so appealing that we could order them all, and you can even get sides of vegetables like sauteed baby bok choy with shallots and oyster sauce or sauteed wax beans and black-eyed peas with tamari and pine nuts. Now those are interesting! Portions were so ample we had no room for dessert, although the sour cream apple and fudge bottom pies appealed. Breakfast and lunch could never top that candlelight dinner by the water.

Open daily except mid-winter, breakfast 7 to 11, lunch 11:30 to 2:30, dinner 5 to 9 or 10; Sunday, brunch 7 to 1, dinner 5 to 9:30. BYOB.

Le Grenier, Upper Main Street, Vineyard Haven. (508) 693-4906.
French. $14.95 to $24.95.

Charming and colorful is this European-looking restaurant run by French chef Jean Dupon of Lyon above La Patisserie. White molded chairs are at green tables topped with peach napkins, and walls are painted a soft green and graced with white birds and flowers. An artist obviously has been at work here, what with the tulips painted up the stairs and the morning glories painted on posts on the porch, which is the place to dine if you can. An artist also is at work in the kitchen, turning out entrees like poached salmon with cream of leeks, scallops flambeed with vodka, cream and red caviar, tunafish nicoise with mirepoix of fresh vegetable, veal oscar, steak au poivre, filet mignon wellington, and venison with raspberry demi-glaze. Appetizers are more traditional, like onion soup gratinee, vichyssoise, escargots bourguig-nonne, and oysters rockefeller. Dessert treats come from the bakery below.

Dinner nightly from 6. BYOB.

Martha's Vineyard

Oak Bluffs

The Oyster Bar, 162 Circuit Ave., Oak Bluffs. (508) 693-3300.
New American. $14.95 to $24.95.
Looking quite polished amidst all the gingerbread of this Victorian time warp of a town, the Oyster Bar calls itself an American bistro. Most people think it's straight from SoHo, and find it fun, kicky and sophisticated. Jaime and Raymond Schilcher, who once owned the celebrated Feasts in Chilmark, made this a congenial space with high tin ceilings, painted columns, striking paintings, cane and chrome chairs, white-linened tables rather close together, and an open kitchen. The lengthy menu is the kind of which we never tire. From the raw bar you can get five kinds of oysters, plus things like peppered bluefish gravlax, petrossian smoked wild scotch salmon, sashimi napoleons with tuna, halibut and salmon, and oysters with caviar. Specialty appetizers include lobster and crab cakes with Cajun red sauce, roasted elephant garlic with goat cheese and bruschetta, charred carpaccio rolls with Japanese dipping sauce, and torta of smoked salmon, mascarpone and caviar. There are four soups, including saffron and tomato seafood stew and lobster pan roasts, four salads, four gourmet pizzas, and five pastas. Then the real fun begins: fifteen kinds of seafood, from red snapper to bonita and soft-shell crabs, and a dozen entree specialties, from lobster and crayfish pot pie to roast veal loin with armagnac and morels, marinated paillard of chicken with mango salsa, and charred Chinese mustard glazed rack of lamb. Save room for one of the delectable desserts, say grand marnier-lemon mousse cake, hot chocolate mousse with espresso cream, choclate pate with white and dark chocolate sauces, or homemade sorbets.
Dinner nightly from 5.

Up Island

Feasts, Beetlebung Corner, Chilmark. (508) 645-3553.
American. $15.95 to $22.95.
This trendy, two-level restaurant with a market and catering service has its ups and downs, depending upon who's cooking. But most like the barn-like atmosphere of the interior, which has vaulted ceilings, white walls, high-tech lights, and cane-back chairs at tables covered with pale pink oilcloth squares over white cloths. There's an art gallery on the mezzanine, where seats afford a view of the whole scene. The extensive menu covers the gamut. Consider the range of starters: smoked scotch salmon, clams with pesto, Maryland crab cakes, boboli pizzas, mesquite-grilled veggies, and chicken wings, most with Feasts' own twist. Entrees range from bluefish with Cajun remoulade sauce, grilled tuna with spicy peanut sauce, and jumbo shrimp and fajita to loin lamb chops with mint salsa, breast of duck with local beach plum sauce, and North Carolina barbecued ribs and chicken. Among desserts are "outrageous, obscene" items like chocolate mousse cake, bittersweet chocolate bread pudding, cheesecake, and ice cream.
Dinner nightly in summer, 6 to 10:45; weekend brunch, 11 to 2. Closed mid-October to Memorial Day. BYOB.

The Home Port, Menemsha. (508) 645-2679.
Seafood. Table d'hote, $16 to $26.50.
A long nondescript building with shiny wood tables overlooking Menemsha Creek, this is a destination for tour buses and locals alike. They're attracted by the quaint harbor view (enhanced by a BYOB cocktail on the jetty or beach beforehand) and an enormous selection of fresh seafood, served in no-nonsense style by a young

staff in blue and white. The dinner price includes appetizer (juice, fruit cup, stuffed quahog or quahog chowder — go for the last), entree, beverage and dessert (homemade pies, ice cream and sherbet). Lobster comes in eight variations; the shore dinner includes steamed clams or mussels and corn on the cob. If you can't choose between broiled Menemsha swordfish, baked stuffed Vineyard scallops or fried Vineyard oysters, order the Home Port fish platter that combines them all. Among desserts are homemade pies and ice cream.

Dinner seasonally, 4:30 to 10; reservations required in summer. BYOB. Closed mid-October to early May.

Nantucket

Siasconset

⁺♥ Chantecleer Inn, New Street, Siasconset. (508) 257-6231.
French. Prix-Fixe, $52.

Lunch in the rose garden is a local tradition, as is an after-dinner drink in the Chantey Bar. But the four-course dinners and the extraordinary wine cellar are what draw the knowing from hither and yon to the world-class restaurant run since 1969 by Jean-Charles Berruet. Prix-fixe dinners are $52 "and worth every penny," all kinds of fans told us. The setting, the service and the food could not be more perfect, which is exactly the way Jean-Charles wants it. Seating is in the sought-after, formal main-floor dining room with a fireplace at the end and a greenhouse on one side, an upstairs dining room serene in peach and white, and an informal bar. The complicated French menu and the endless wine list are so staggering that both first-timers and knowing regulars put themselves in the hands of a solicitous, knowledgeable staff to help with their selections. Our experience began with a tiny spinach blini, "compliments of the chef." For starters, we enjoyed Nantucket oysters served in a warm mussel broth topped with American sturgeon caviar and lobster and sole sausage poached with a puree of sweet red peppers. We would have gladly ordered any of the sixteen entrees, but finally decided on the Nantucket-raised pheasant, stuffed with mushrooms, herbs and ricotta, and the roasted tenderloin of lamb with a venison sauce. A triangle of potato pancake, spinach, and ratatouille nicoise accompanied, and a salad of greens with two kinds of cheeses followed. For dessert, small dollops of assorted sorbets were interspersed with fresh fruit on a raspberry sauce. Creole-style lime meringue pie was an ethereal second choice. Over demitasses of decaf and espresso, we savored an experience that ranks with the ultimate in fine dining. If you can't get in for dinner (tables are booked far in advance), splurge for lunch in the garden beneath trellised canopies of roses and surrounded by manicured hedges.

Lunch, noon to 2 in summer; dinner, 6:30 to 10. Closed Wednesdays and mid-October to late May. Reservations required.

Wauwinet

★ Topper's at the Wauwinet, Wauwinet Road, Nantucket. (508) 228-0145.
Regional American. $22 to $31.

Named for their dog, whose portrait is in one of the dining rooms, Topper's succeeded beyond the dreams of owners Stephen and Jill Karp in its initial season in 1988. A kitchen designed to serve 100 dinners and frequently called upon to put out half again that many was expanded, and chef Keith Mahoney, who was imported from Stuart, Fla., was on board year-round to oversee the culinary realm. Dining is leisurely in two elegantly appointed, side-by-side rooms with large windows.

Nantucket

Upholstered chairs in blue and white are comfortable, tables are well-spaced (or screened from their neighbors), and flowers are massed all around. The menu is a testament to the trendy and exotic. We liked such appetizers as lobster and crab cakes with smoked corn and a wonderful mustard sauce, grilled shrimp with buffalo mozzarella and grilled pizza, and quail with truffles on a toasted brioche. Inspired main courses are things like grilled rack and leg of lamb with a tomato-eggplant timbale and grilled veal chop with Texas ham, fresh mozzarella, red pepper sauce and eggplant cookies, both accompanied by baby vegetables (tiny pattypan squash and carrots about as big as a fingernail) and a wedge of potatoes. Seafood dishes like salmon with spicy black beans and striped bass with a hot vegetable relish proved the chef likes to leave a fiery after-taste. That can be cooled with dessert, perhaps a refreshing pineapple-papaya sorbet or peach-blackberry crisp with ginger ice cream, although the selection is heavy on pastries like macadamia tuiles with ice cream and rum sauce or triple chocolate terrine with mocha sauce. The water comes with a lemon slice, the bread is crusty, salt and pepper are served only on request, and the wine list is strong on California cabernets and chardonnays.

Brunch daily, 8 to 2:30; dinner nightly, 6 to 9:30. Closed December-March.

Nantucket

★ 21 Federal, 21 Federal St., Nantucket. (508) 228-2121.
New American. $21 to $27.

This is Nantucket dining at its best, not as pretentious (though just as pricey) as some and more exciting than many. Celebrated founding chef Robert Kinkead has left to open another Twenty-One Federal in Washington, D.C., but partner Chick Walsh and chef Carl Keller are continuing their tradition of American grill cuisine in Nantucket. The restaurant occupies two floors of a sand-colored house with white trim, designated by a brass plaque and elegantly decorated in Williamsburg style. There are six dining rooms, some with their white-linened tables rather too close for privacy. Our latest lunch in a small room next to the jolly bar produced a smashing pasta — spaghettini with two sauces, one thyme-saffron and one smoked tomato, topped with crabmeat-stuffed shrimp — and a grilled shrimp salad with Greek olives, feta cheese, pine nuts, and spinach. Three varieties of breads came with, and a tropical fruit sorbet was a refreshing ending. Even more memorable was a summer lunch in the courtyard, served on large wicker trays: the pheasant and wild rice soup of the day and a linguini salad with shrimp and pine nuts were out of this world. At dinner, entrees include the likes of roasted poussin with pine nut risotto, tenderloin of veal with risotto and oyster mushrooms, and a trio of grilled lobster tail, ravioli and lobster cake, supplemented by such specials as salmon with lobster-tomato-cream sauce and crab fritters. Start with grilled oysters with pancetta, seared raw tuna with nori rolls and smoked salmon, or zarzuela, a Southwest seafood stew. Finish with a palette of chocolate, pumpkin creme brulee, or one of the great homemade ice creams and sorbets.

Lunch daily, 11:30 to 2:30; dinner, 6 to 10. Closed March and Sundays in off-season.

Le Languedoc, 24 Broad St., Nantucket. (508) 228-2552.
New French/International. $24 to $28.

Longtime chef-owner Neal Grennan is back in the kitchen of this family-owned restaurant, where he produced one of our best meals in Nantucket a few years back. Downstairs is a cafe with checkered cloths. Upstairs are four small dining rooms with peach walls and white trim, windows covered with peach draperies and valances, and prints and posters framed in chrome. Windsor chairs are at nicely spaced tables bearing hurricane lamps with thick candles and vases, each containing one lovely salmon rose. Among appetizers, smoked Nantucket pheasant with cranberry relish was very good and very colorful with red cabbage and slices of apples and oranges on a bed of lettuce. One of us sampled noisettes of lamb with artichokes in a rosemary sauce. The other had sauteed sweetbreads and lobster in puff pastry, in a sauce that included shiitake mushrooms, cognac and shallots. Nicely presented on piping hot oval white plates, they were accompanied by snow peas, broccoli, pureed turnips, yellow peppers, sweet potato and peach slices. Other interesting choices were wok-seared halibut with papaya and lime, roast duckling with Jamaican caramelized lemon sauce, and veal chinoise with garlic and ginger. Dessert was strawberry pie and a dense chocolate hazelnut torte spiked with grand marnier. You can dine lightly but well in the cafe, where some of the upstairs appetizers and salads are available and there are always fish and pasta specials. Lunch is available on a canopied sidewalk terrace.

Lunch in season, daily except Monday and Tuesday 11:30 to 2:30; dinner nightly except Monday, 6 to 10. Closed in winter.

The Second Story, 1 South Beach St., Nantucket. (508) 228-3471.
  Contemporary/International. $23 to $30.

The second floor of a building across from the harbor is done up in pink walls and linens, pink and green floral overcloths, and green napkins. An alcove area beside the window onto the harbor is awash with comfy pillows. At night, the place is illuminated entirely by candles, and the setting could not be more glamorous. The fare served up by chef-proprietors Patricia Tyler and David Toole is a mix of Mexican-Spanish, French, Cajun, and lately Thai. Their hand-written dinner menu changes monthly and is sufficiently obscure as to require explanation by the servers. Appetizers could be littlenecks Sesimbra, squid sauteed in Cambodian saffron and caraway cream, oysters and soft-shell crayfish Bayou Teche, or spicy Thai sesame shrimps with lemon-paprika sauce. We sampled the hot country pate, a huge slab of goose, duck, chicken and sausage, piping hot and bathed in a creamy green peppercorn sauce. The scallops au gratin (with avocado, tomato, garlic and cream) was an ample entree. The Thai shrimp with black bean and coriander sauce was super spicy and left the mouth smoldering long into the night. Other entree possibilities include grilled sweetbreads with truffles and mushroom sauce, breast of duck and shrimp in Thai masaman curry, and lobster and avocado enchilada with goat cheese, jalapeno and cumin sauce, and spicy red pepper salsa. Desserts include amaretto souffle, coeur a la creme with raspberry sauce, and pears in puff pastry with caramel sauce.

Dinner nightly, seatings at 7 and 9:15. Open April to mid-December.

Straight Wharf Restaurant, Straight Wharf, Nantucket. (508) 228-4499.
  Regional American. $23 to $28.

Marian Morash of television and cookbook fame was the original force behind this summery restaurant on the waterfront. She wrote the encyclopedic Victory Garden Cookbook in 1982 with inspiration from her husband Russell, a television producer and weekend gardener, plus Jim Crockett and Julia Child, and finally left the restaurant in 1987 to finish a second cookbook. Seafood is featured in this popular spot that is the height of chic and priced to match. The complex includes a fish market, a gourmet shop, and a contemporary restaurant consisting of a large room with soaring, shingled walls topped by billowing banners made by owner Elaine Gifford, a canopied and rib-lit harborfront deck, and a popular bar where appetizers, light entrees and desserts are served. The short menu changes weekly. Appetizers could be lobster and fish cakes with tomato-basil beurre blanc, tuna sashimi and fish soup with rouille. Entrees run the gamut from poached salmon and scallops with champagne-ginger sauce, sole paupiettes with leeks and sun-dried tomato beurre blanc, and grilled swordfish with ancho chili butter to roast rack of Australian lamb with ratatouille. We enjoyed a complimentary bluefish pate that came with drinks, some first-rate lobster crepes and grilled salmon with tarragon-mustard sauce, and the peach bavarian laden with raspberry sauce. We were not impressed with the much-heralded vegetables, which turned out to be plainly cooked broccoli and carrots. Regulars rave about the bar menu, where you can sample some of the Straight Wharf specialties like spicy shrimp with sesame-spinach salad, bluefish with pesto-potato salad, and pork chops with black bean salad and cornbread.

Dinner nightly except Monday, 6:45 to 10; bar menu, 7 to 10:30. Closed Mondays and October through mid-June.

The Club Car, 1 Main St., Nantucket. (508) 228-1101.
New American/International. $24 to $33.50.

The red train car at the side of this luxurious establishment with the profuse window boxes is a lounge that's open from noon daily and enlivened by a piano bar nightly. Beyond, the elegant dining room has cane-backed chairs with rose-colored velvet cushions at crisp, white-linened tables. Large artworks and a shelf of copper pans add color. This is where chef Michael Shannon serves up some of the island's priciest food to a loyal clientele. The formerly French menu lately has been Americanized, but many items remain the same. Appetizers start with squid in the style of Bangkok and rise rapidly in price through duck foie gras with raspberry vinegar to beluga caviar with Stolichnaya vodka at a tab that many would consider exorbitant for an entire dinner. The preparation of most of the nine entrees, from Irish salmon and grey sole to Indian curry, veal sweetbreads and rack of Vermont lamb, varies daily. The wine list and desserts are in keeping with the rest of the menu.

Dinner nightly, 6 to 10; weekends only in off-season. Closed mid-December to late May.

Boarding House, 12 Federal St., Nantucket. (508) 228-9622.
New American. $24 to $27.

The Boarding House provided our most memorable meal when we first visited Nantucket in 1972. It had just opened in the downstairs of a former boarding house on India Street and was the culinary hit of the summer. The restaurant since has moved to larger quarters around the corner at Federal and India streets, but the food continues to be highly regarded. A sidewalk courtyard and the cathedral-ceilinged Victorian lounge with small marble tables are popular for lunch, perhaps an excellent carrot and dill soup followed by a spicy pizza with andouille sausage or the day's pasta special, in our case beet linguini with scallops and a rich lobster sauce. Dinner is serene downstairs in a sunken room that has an Italian feel, curved arches and along the far wall a striking mural of asparagus stalks and small crabs on a sandy beach. The concise menu might begin with sauteed sweetbreads with ham and wild mushrooms, sauteed shrimp in oriental marinade, smoked salmon with tarragon-lemon creme fraiche, and Javanese barbecued chicken. Entrees could be grilled swordfish with macadamia nut butter, steamed salmon with tomato pistou, and grilled loin lamb chops with rosemary-garlic sauce. Among desserts are a bourbon-flavored bread pudding and a frozen brandy mousse with crushed praline.

Lunch daily, noon to 2:30; dinner, 6:30 to 10. Closed January and February.

American Seasons, 80 Centre St., Nantucket. (508) 228-7111.
Regional American. $12 to $22.

A simple square room with Southwestern decor, eclectic American food, and moderate prices have made this off-the-beaten-path newcomer a hit since 1988.

Brothers Stuart and Everett G. Reid III, both Culinary Institute of America grads, do all the cooking. They turn out such entrees as pan-fried Louisiana catfish with hot and sweet pepper tartar sauce, grilled Pacific salmon with artichoke pancakes and crayfish-coriander butter, grilled South Carolina quail with dirty rice, Idaho trout with jalapeno-peach chutney, and grilled bluefin tuna with an Arizona cactus relish. Start with raviolis of smoked duck and crayfish or a grilled artichoke and fried oyster salad. End with bourbon-banana cream pie, strawberry shortcake with blood oranges, fresh blueberry and peach crisp, or honey-cinnamon pecan pie with maple ice cream. With one of the reasonably priced bottles from the all-American wine list, you'll get out for what would be considered normal mainland prices. Seating 52, the dining room is simple yet pretty with Southwestern red and deep green wood trim, paint-spattered floors, and white-linened tables topped with hurricane lamps and pots of cactus. An outdoor patio is popular in summer.

Dinner nightly except Wednesday, 6 to 10. Closed in winter.

Company of the Cauldron, 7 India St., Nantucket. (508) 228-4016.
Regional American. Prix-Fixe, $40.

The former quarters of the Boarding House lately have been occupied by this intimate little restaurant, where the day's prix-fixe dinner menu is posted outside the door in the morning. Patrons crowd in for the nightly seatings and take what's served, which is reputed to be excellent. Behind a wrought-iron shelf divider laden with flowers and breads at the entry are a number of small tables rather close together, colorful with a mix of pink and green floral mats and overcloths atop white linens or bare wood. Copper pots, cauldrons and ship's models hang from the stucco walls, and it's all very dark and romantic. A typical dinner brings wild mushroom soup with St. Andre cheese, tomato and hearts of palm salad, veal chop with port wine and roasted garlic sauce, potatoes au gratin and farm vegetables, and a fruit crisp with vanilla ice cream. Another could be shrimp and scallop bisque, green salad with a lemon-pepper dressing, grilled tenderloin of beef with tomato-shallot beurre blanc, roasted garlic thyme potatoes and buttered broccoli, and a lemon sorbet with raspberry sauce. The small but select wine list is rationally priced by local standards.

Dinner nightly except Monday; seatings at 8, or at 7 and 9:15 on busy nights. Closed mid-October to spring.

The Morning Glory Cafe, Old South Wharf, Nantucket. (508) 228-2212.
International. $12.50 to $15.95.

Although not in the luxury category, this is listed as a perennial favorite by most Nantucketers, who gather on the wharf patio at breakfast to wake up with strong coffee and morning glory muffins as they trade gossip from the night before. An impressive variety of breakfast, lunch and dinner fare is put out by owner Liz Gracia from an open kitchen inside the small cafe, which has stunning trompe l'oeil paintings on the walls and a handful of tables. At lunch there are interesting salads, sandwiches and pizzas. Dinnertime brings a handful of appetizers, five pastas and four entrees, ranging from tarragon chicken to roast pork tenderloin with fresh peach chutney and sauteed veal cutlet with spinach and capers. Save room for one of the delectable desserts.

Breakfast, daily 7 to 11:30; lunch, noon to 3:30; dinner, 6 to 9:30. BYOB. Open Memorial Day to mid-September.

South County

Westerly

★ Shelter Harbor Inn, Route 1, Westerly. (401) 322-8883.
American. $12.95 to $16.95.

The highly regarded restaurant in this inn has two country-pretty dining rooms, one a relatively recent, two-level affair with rough wood beams and posts, brick walls, comfortable chairs with curved backs, and white linens, all overlooking a flagstone terrace with white furniture. At Sunday brunch, we liked two of the day's specials, baked oysters and lamb shanks with rice pilaf. Although the former was smallish and the latter too large, we managed by sharing the two as well as feasting on the "surprise salad" of greens, radicchio, orange slices, cantaloupe, kiwi, and strawberries with a creamy poppyseed dressing (the salad and champagne no longer are included in the price, but brunch is still a bargain). At dinner, be sure to try the Rhode Island johnny cakes with maple butter and, among appetizers, the duck liver pate with roasted corn relish or the smoked bluefish with apple horseradish. Entrees range from hazelnut chicken with orange-thyme cream to double lamb chops with mint pesto and sauteed veal with grilled shiitake mushrooms and creme fraiche. Highly rated are the seafood pot pie chock full of shrimp, scallops and lobster, and gingered duck breasts with raspberries and honey. You can even get finnan haddie poached in milk with bacon. Desserts include genoise, chocolate raspberry cake, lemon-custard tart, blueberry crisp, and Rhode Island Indian pudding.

Lunch daily, 11:30 to 2:30; dinner, 5 to 10; Sunday, brunch 11 to 3, dinner 4 to 9.

Weekapaug

Weekapaug Inn, Weekapaug. (401) 322-0301.
American. Prix-fixe, $27.

Meals in this venerable inn of the old school are available to the public by reservation. Be advised, however, that the dining room has a clubby air (most of the guests are old-timers), you must bring your own bottle for cocktails in the Pond Room, and jackets and ties are required at night. The six-course menu changes daily. Following a chilled juice, there's a choice of two appetizers, perhaps steamed mussels and smoked salmon pate. Then come lobster bisque, chilled melon or jellied madrilene and a salad with choice of dressings. The six main-course offerings could be grilled pigeon breasts, sauteed rainbow trout with almonds, grilled tuna with grapefruit beurre blanc, sauteed sea scallops with garlic and tomatoes, sauteed calves liver, and grilled sirloin with hazelnut butter. Buttered carrots, rice with walnuts and corn on the cob might accompany. Desserts could be hazelnut dacquoise, white chocolate mousse, banana rum cake, fresh berries, or ice cream and cookies. No one leaves the table hungry here.

Dinner nightly, 6:30 to 8. BYOB. No credit cards. Open mid-June to Labor Day.

Charlestown

Wilcox Tavern, Route 1, Charlestown. (401) 322-1829.
Seafood/Continental. $10.95 to $16.95.

An enormous stuffed rabbit lies on an 1820 sofa in the waiting room at this surprisingly large restaurant. As owner Rudy Sculco tells it, his wife Eva bought it because she caught him napping there one afternoon and didn't want anyone to sit on her prized antique. He credits Eva with the decor, the fresh flowers and many of the niceties in a quirky establishment dating to 1730. The original rooms with wide-board floors and beamed ceilings are pretty in white and black; the Sarah Jane Room that the Sculcos added after moving from Rudy's Charlestown Room down the road is more formal in pink and burgundy with upholstered chairs and balloon window treatments. The extensive menu ranges from broiled scrod to deep-fried oysters, crab cakes to shrimp martinique. Yankee pot roast, veal marsala, broiled lamb chops with mint jelly, and pork chops with apple sauce are other entrees, and four pastas are available. Lots of specials pack in the locals: a roast turkey dinner on Sunday and a prime rib dinner with lobster bisque on Tuesday and Wednesday. Twinkling white lights on the tall trees out front point the way. As Rudy tells it, "you'll never get lost coming here if you look for all those lights."

Lunch, Monday-Friday from noon, October-June; dinner nightly, 4:30 to 9:30 or 10, Sunday from noon.

The Charlestown Lobster Pot, Route 1, Charlestown. (401) 322-7686.
Seafood/Continental. $10.95 to $18.95.

If you expect a lobster pound here, think again. A small house holds four small rooms with a mix of mismatched chairs and tables, some covered with pink cloths and some bare with woven mats. The food is a cut above: seafood specialties like lobster newburg, broiled Block Island swordfish, fried oysters, and baked stuffed flounder, and entrees like coq au vin, roast duckling with a beach plum sauce, veal marsala, and filet mignon. The wine list is an interesting mix of French, Italian and California offerings, plus some from Rhode Island's Sakonnet Vineyards. The place is billed as being across from Charlestown Pond, but unless you're on the enclosed porch you'd never know.

Dinner nightly from 5, Sunday from 4. Fewer hours in off-season.

Wakefield

✱ South Shore Grille, 110 Salt Pond Road, Wakefield. (401) 782-4780.
California/American. $15.95 to $19.95.

"Like dinner at Le Cirque for a fraction of the price." That's what Rhode Island food critics were saying following the opening in 1989 of this small, with-it restaurant beside a marina overlooking Great Salt Pond. Chefs Geoffrey Zakarian, who was sous chef at New York's Le Cirque and chef de cuisine at 21 Club, and Nancy Carr from the Meridien and Four Seasons restaurants in California, make a dynamite team. In a modest, shingled building, they seat 65, inside on captain's chairs at copper-topped tables along a wall of windows and outside on a waterside deck. We came without reservations for a weekend lunch that had been advertised a few weeks before, only to find it had been discontinued, so had to settle for a deck menu that was abbreviated and pricey. The grilled chicken on peasant bread with a hearty potato salad was a standout; the caesar salad was small and uninspired, but the meal was salvaged by extra peasant bread. We'll return for dinner, perhaps Norwegian salmon steak with bacon-perfumed cabbage, grilled gingered scallops served with a dish of sliced zucchini, tomatoes and yellow squash baked on a bed of sweet onions, crispy free-range chicken with wild mushrooms and potato puree, or black angus tenderloin with scalloped potatoes and roasted garlic. One diner pronounced the South Shore bisque made with Rhode Island rock crabs the best she'd ever had; another raved over the appetizer of grilled duck breast piquant with coriander and served on a potato puree with roasted rosemary apples. For dessert, how about "butternut amber" (cheesecake flan served with a lime-butterscotch sauce) or chocolate marquise with a light mocha custard sauce? The wine list is carefully chosen with an eye to rarely seen vintages from California and Australia,

South County

priced from the mid-teens to the mid-twenties. Sandwiches (maybe grilled salmon with homemade tartar sauce), salads and pasta are included on the dinner menu.

Deck, Friday-Sunday noon to dusk; dinner, Tuesday-Sunday 5:30 to 9:30.

Center Cafe, 552 Kingstown Road, Wakefield, (401) 789-3070.
Seafood. $6.75 to $15.95.

White cloths, maroon paper mats and fresh flowers give a sparkle to this small cafe adjacent to its own fish market in a shopping center. The most interesting items are the blackboard specials listing things like Cajun tuna or salmon, mako shark au poivre citron, shrimp Creole, and whole crispy sea bass Szechuan style. Pastas include spinach fettuccine with a scallop-pesto cream sauce and red pepper fettuccine with lobster-sherry cream sauce. More standard fare is available on the regular and takeout menu. Desserts here are exceptional: Italian rum cake, chocolate truffle cake, chocolate-chambord cake, and Bailey's Irish Cream mousse cake. You can BYOB from a package store nearby.

Lunch, Tuesday-Saturday 11:30 to 3; dinner, 5 to 9 or 10. Closed Sunday and Monday.

South Kingstown

The Pump House, 1464 Kingstown Road, Peace Dale. (401) 789-4944.
American/Continental. $7.95 to $19.95.

The stone facade with arched windows and porte cochere make you think you're entering a ritzy lodge or club. But this is the former pumping station for the local water system, now an elegant restaurant full of atmosphere, both in the pub and dining room with low beamed ceiling and a huge fireplace. The menu is standard, from chicken cordon bleu or parmigiana to five sole dishes, baked stuffed shrimp, duck a l'orange, filet mignon, and surf and turf. The baked seafood platter brings stuffed filet of sole, jumbo shrimp and scallops. Stuffed potato skins and chicken fingers vie with escargots and clams casino as appetizers.

Lunch, Tuesday-Friday 11:45 to 4:30; dinner, Tuesday-Saturday from 5, Sunday 2 to 10.

Narragansett

★ Basil's, 22 Kingstown Road, Narragansett. (401) 789-3743.
French/Continental. $13.95 to $19.95.

Consistently good and consistently crowded is this small establishment in quarters formerly occupied by Le Petite Bistro. Basil Kourakas, who had been a chef in Vail, Colo., took it over in 1984 to be closer to Europe, he said. Here he does all the cooking himself, offering an ambitious menu that lists six veal dishes, including his specialty with a cream and mushroom sauce. Among other entrees are sole meuniere, soft-shell crab amandine, coq au vin, duck a l'orange, beef stroganoff, pepper steak, and steak diane. Start with steamed mussels brunoise, ceviche or herring lucas. Finish with a French chocolate mousse, coupe Basil, a parfait, or strawberries romanoff. The wine list is good, and the dining room intimate and lovely with striking wallpaper and ornately framed paintings.

Dinner nightly, 5:30 to 10.

Spain Restaurant, 1 Beach St., Narragansett. (401) 783-9770.
Spanish/Portuguese. $9.50 to $17.50.

The airy, circular dining room of the contemporary Village Inn is the unlikely location for a Spanish restaurant of elegance, owned by two men from Spain. This has cane chairs with upholstered backs, blue tablecloths and a multitude of plants, plus an appealing outdoor deck looking onto the water. Spanish music plays in the background as diners sample typical Spanish appetizers, from mussels in green sauce to clams marinara and shrimp in garlic. Gazpacho and garlic are among the soups. The two dozen entrees include two versions of paella and two of shellfish casserole, plus red snapper pastelera, garlic chicken, veal in almond sauce, and filet mignon. Flan and chocolate truffle mousse cake are favored desserts.

Lunch, Monday-Saturday noon to 3; dinner nightly, 3 to 10 or 11.

Coast Guard House Restaurant, 40 Ocean Road, Narragansett.
(401) 789-0700.
Continental. $9.95 to $15.95.

We always enjoy lunch on the upstairs deck beside the ocean here, watching the swimmers in the distance on the Narragansett beach and the windsurfers riding the waves. In fact, one of us had his first lobster dinner here as a child and gave it short shrift to go outside onto the rocks to watch the pounding surf. The setting in the National Register-listed landmark beside the Towers is more interesting than the fare. We enjoyed a seafood kabob and a sausage, pepper and onion sandwich for lunch, and admired the snail salad and items from the raw bar. The large dinner menu starts with escargots bourguignonne and oysters rockefeller, includes pastas and continental items like chicken cordon bleu and veal marsala, steaks and a dozen seafood dishes, and finishes with parfaits and international coffees. A fireplace warms the large cocktail lounge filled with velvet sofas and Victorian chairs.

Lunch, Monday-Saturday 11:30 to 3; dinner nightly, 5 to 10 or 11; Sunday brunch, 11 to 2.

Mercedes Ocean House, Mariner Square, 120 Point Judith Road,
Narragansett. (401) 789-3380.
Seafood. $8.95 to $15.95.

The fifteen nightly seafood specials chalked on the blackboard are reasons enough for visiting this good-looking restaurant in a shopping center. The chef gets creative with things like Cajun saute, sole Carlsburg, blackened tuna, and lobster Mercedes, the last a specialty in which lobster meat is sauteed with garlic and relishes and served over angel hair pasta. The regular menu ranges from broiled sole to bouillabaisse, and there are three dishes for those who don't want fish. The excellent wine list is reasonably priced. Dark paneled and cathedral ceilinged, the dining room and bar are outfitted with dark wood tables, Tiffany lamps, comfortable chairs and booths, and etched-glass drawings of Mercedes automobiles, as well as of a single Ford.

Lunch and dinner, Monday-Saturday 11:30 to 10, Sunday 1 to 10.

Casa Rossi, 90 Point Judith Road, Narragansett. (401) 789-6385.
Italian. $6.95 to $15.95.

Chef-owner Peter Rossi converted a house into a pleasant restaurant with orange walls, brown linen, and beige and brown sheer curtains. Local people rave about the food, based on family recipes passed down through the generations: homemade pastas and Italian breads and seven veal specialties. You also can get fettuccine alfredo, shrimp fra diavolo, Sicilian flounder and steak zingarella. Zabaglione cake, cannoli and ice cream pies are favored desserts. The wine list is a mixed bag of Italian, French and California vintages.

Dinner nightly, 4 to 9 or 10, Sunday 1 to 9.

Antipasto, Mariner Square, 140 Point Judith Road, Narragansett.
(401) 789-5300.
Italian. $9.50 to $15.95.

Would you believe there are six shrimp and scallop dishes among the blackboard

West Bay

specials at this small shopping-center cafe, which has a "super salad bar" in the rear corner, complete with turkey, ham and cheese. The regular menu has a good selection of chicken, veal, beef and seafood dishes in interesting sauces, plus pastas, lasagna and baked eggplant topped with mozzarella cheese. The locally popular Buffalo wings are favorite starters. Dessert specials include cannoli and raspberry cheesecake. The tables are covered with blue cloths and white napkins. A tavern menu with light entrees, appetizers and individual pizzas is served in the upstairs lounge.

Open Monday-Friday 11:30 to 10; Saturday 4 to 10, Sunday 3 to 9.

Wickford

Wickford Gourmet Foods, 21 W. Main St., Wickford. (401) 295-8190.
Deli. $2.95 to $4.95.

Wickford folks think the best place to eat in town is at this specialty food shop with a deli, one of the nicest we've ever seen. You can get sandwiches, a ploughman's platter or a pasta salad, and an individual pizza is the most expensive item except for dinner entrees to go. "Berserk desserts" include killer brownies, sadistic scones and galloping ganache. Take it all outside to tables out back or to a secluded spot along the harbor and enjoy.

Open daily from 9 to 6:30, Sunday to 5 and Friday to 7.

West Bay

Cranston

Haruki, 1096 Park Ave., Cranston. (401) 943-5668.
Japanese. $7.25 to $12.50.

Small and plain, this Japanese restaurant is an oasis in an undistinguished, strung-out commercial strip. There are a few photos of Japan, the odd rice paper screen and lineups of butcherblock tables, but the authenticity comes from the sushi bar — which seems to be something of a local hangout — and from the kitchen. At lunch, we enjoyed the chicken teriyaki that came with miso soup, salad, a pork dumpling and rice, and an excellent deluxe sushi platter that was the equal of any in New York. Deep-fried tempura ice cream in three flavors (vanilla, ginger and green tea) made a refreshing ending. The dinner menu adds a few dishes to the midday fare, like salmon, broiled eel and halibut. Sushi comes in many combinations or a la carte; those undecided can spring for "sushi heaven," the chef's choice and a large portion. The service and the management are American (the only Japanese we saw was the sushi chef), and yet the place rings true.

Lunch Monday-Friday, noon to 2; dinner, Monday-Saturday 5 to 9:30 or 10.

Warwick

♥ **Down Under,** One Masthead Drive, Warwick. (401) 884-1850.
International. $14.95 to $22.95.

This contemporary restaurant with decks and dining on two levels offers the best water view around. That the decor is so stylish and the menu so appealing is a bonus. A view out East Greenwich Bay into the broad Narragansett is afforded from the jaunty decks and window seats in the dining room. Beige and pale green walls, white linens and aqua napkins provide a soothing setting at a mix of booths and tables with sleek black upholstered chairs. Water is poured into tall glass cylinders and bread served on striking black shell side plates. Although the place can accommodate 200 inside and out, it's arranged for intimacy. A young staff in formal white and black serves a wide-ranging menu from scrod stuffed with scallops and baby shrimp topped with a snow crab hollandaise to carpetbagger steak stuffed with oysters. Shrimp and vegetable tempura, Jamaican sole garnished with kiwi and banana, chicken frangelico, veal medallions sauteed with roasted peppers and red seedless grapes, and Szechuan beef are among the choices. Start with clams Cajun style, Japanese tempura vegetables, or littlenecks steamed with Portuguese sausage and garlic. Finish with lemon mousse cake, double fudge torte, sour cream apple pie, ice cream or gelato. Then adjourn upstairs for entertainment at **Moonlighting,** a terraced nightclub that serves appetizers, sandwiches and entrees at tables around an enormous center bar area draped with twinkling white lights.

Lunch, Monday-Friday in summer; dinner nightly, 5 to 10 or 11.

Bank Cafe, 40 Post Road, Warwick. (401) 467-4747.
American. $7.50 to $14.95.

Listed on the National Register, this 1814 red-brick building that once housed a bank in the heart of the old seaport village of Pawtuxet offers casual dining upstairs and down. Bare wood tables are set with blue mats, votive candles and slender vases of fresh flowers. Wainscoting, lace curtains and wide-board floors round out the decor. The menu starts with Buffalo wings, potato skins and nachos, but you also can get snail salad, grilled tenderloin of lamb and veal marsala. Entrees are served with soup, salad or fruit cup. Sandwiches are available day and night and are accorded regular and deluxe status (the latter with fresh fruit cup or french fries).

Lunch, daily 11:30 to 3:30; dinner, Monday-Saturday 4:30 to 10;30, Sunday from 11:30.

East Greenwich

Walter's, 5600 Post Road, East Greenwich. (401) 885-2010.
Northern Italian. $11 to $21.

Anchoring one end of the new East Greenwich Marketplace is this stylish restaurant with some of the most creative Italian dishes we've encountered. The owner is from the Abruzzi, but the influences of California cuisine show in dishes like risotto alla fragole (arborio rice, saffron, mozzarella cream, fresh strawberries, and pine nuts) and chicken with dried figs, asparagus and vermouth in cheese sauce. The three veal dishes on the short but sweet menu are anything but traditional: one comes with smoked prosciutto, pesto, mozzarella, and salsa gremolata; another has vodka, smoked salmon, artichoke hearts, and pine nuts. The steak bears fresh crimini mushrooms and sliced chestnuts in a salsa spagnola. One of the pasta dishes, pennette al salmone, blends quill-shaped pasta with smoked salmon, ginger, basil, cream, tomato concasse, and parmigiana. Among interesting appetizers is grilled leg of lamb, marinated with rosemary and garlic. All this is nicely presented in a luxurious room distinguished by curves, dividers and posts, with upholstered chairs at white-linened tables and balloon draperies over the windows. The black-stemmed wine glasses match the black rims of the china.

Dinner, Monday-Saturday 5 to 10. Reservations required.

Twenty Water Street, 20 Water St., East Greenwich. (401) 885-3700.
Continental. $12.95 to $22.95.

America, the ship that initiated the America's Cup Race, is incorporated into the motif of this elegant waterside restaurant with a large outside deck and a view of the crowded harbor. The boat is replicated on both the water and wine glasses atop white-linened tables on four dining levels, including a couple of small sunken dining rooms perched right beside the water. The menu covers all the bases from Cajun

Providence Area

barbecued shrimp over fettuccine and shrimp oriental to chicken tarragon, veal forestiere and rack of lamb garnished with mint and fresh vegetables. Minced quahogs is an award-winning appetizer. The dessert tray might yield espresso mousse torte, carrot cake and berries romanoff.

Lunch, Monday-Friday noon to 2:30; dinner nightly, 5 to 9:30.

Providence Area

Providence

* Lucky's, 577 South Main St., Providence. (401) 272-7980.
Country French. $15.95 to $21.95.

Food at its gutsiest is served in this comfortable and casual, bistro-style restaurant that garners national publicity of the sort given Alice Waters of Chez Panisse in Berkeley. Johanne Killeen and George Germon call Lucky's cooking French country. We, who count ourselves lucky to have eaten here twice in its first two years, call it more California-style. In any event, we had two of our more memorable meals in a long time. In the kitchen, with a window into the bar, are a wood-burning oven and wood grill, where the most delectable dishes are turned out. Pizza done over the grill is Lucky's signature dish, as it is at the couple's original restaurant, Al Forno. With a crackly thin crust and different toppings every day (ours had onion, gorgonzola, chicken, tarragon, and tomato coulis), it is sensational. We also loved a starter of cool vermicelli with five little salads (cucumber, jicama, carrot, red pepper, and Egyptian beans). The menu changes daily, but you might find grilled chicken breast with fiery curry martinique and pancetta, grilled pork chops with braised lentils and garlic mashed potatoes, or composed warm and cool grilled and roasted vegetables. The choucroute garni includes three of the fattest sausages you ever saw topping mild and unsalty sauerkraut, accompanied by wide noodles sparked with fresh coriander. The skirt steak is seared right on the coals and served with wilted watercress and a green chile sauce. Portions are huge and we saw many others leave, as we did, with doggy bags (lately, Lucky's has added smaller dishes on a bistro menu for $8.95 to $14.95). Dessert is the icing on the cake. We'd order one of Johanne's special tarts; the lemon souffle version is ethereal. Another masterpiece is warm crepes with apricot puree and creme anglaise. In contrast to the food, the decor is simple: short lace curtains hang from the high beams, tables are covered with sheets of paper, the wine is poured into stemless glasses like those used for vin ordinaire in France, and the atmosphere is jolly and just right.

Dinner, Tuesday-Saturday 5:30 to 10. No reservations. No smoking.

* Al Forno, 577 South Main St., Providence. (401) 273-9760.
Contemporary Italian. $17.95 to $24.95.

Celebrated local restaurateurs Johanne Killeen and George Germon began their culinary adventures in a miniscule space on Steeple Street, which became a mecca for those who love innovative Italian food. In 1989, they moved Al Forno to the upstairs of the renovated stable that houses their newer restaurant, Lucky's. Designed in a classic and sophisticated European style by George, using lots of dark slate and bluestone marble, the room is more elegant than Lucky's, with a big fireplace at one end and, at the other, an interesting wall piece with cutout mirrors in various shapes. The couple traveled to Italy for many of their accessories, including cutlery from Florence in the trattoria style, with long-tined pasta forks and pasta spoons. The larger kitchen allowed them to expand their menu, and a new fryolater meant they could serve such things as fried zucchini blossoms and dessert fritters. Their signature pizzas grilled over an open fire remain, of course — perhaps

210

with fresh herbs, prosciutto, tomato, and two cheeses, or tomato, garlic, gorgonzola, eggplant puree, and olive puree. Lasagna, made with light sheets of pasta folded over freestyle, might contain sliced grilled chicken breast with fresh tomato salad or turkey, bechamel sauce and diced vegetables. A delmonico steak is served with great mashed potatoes and homemade ketchup. The wine list, featuring many Italian vintages, starts reasonably and goes sky high. Tartuffo, tirami su and wonderful tarts for two are among desserts. Since its move, Al Forno has created a new section of the menu: plates for small appetites ($7.95 to $12.95). The remaining plates for Al Forno appetites, Johanne concedes, "are ample for two people."

Dinner, Tuesday-Saturday 5:30 to 10. No reservations. No smoking.

* Pot au Feu, 44 Custom House St., Providence. (401) 273-8953.
French. $14 to $19.25.

This split-level restaurant (a bistro in the basement; a glamorous French salon upstairs) has long been one of our favorites, thanks to the loving care tendered by owners Ann and Bob Burke. In the Bistro, with its ancient stone and brick walls and zinc bar, you may order typical bistro food — omelets, onion soup, pate, escargots, quiche, fruit and cheese plates, and salade nicoise, all at reasonable prices. The hazelnut tart is not to be missed. The eighteen or so dinner specials that change nightly might include fresh tuna with raspberry and chive butter, roasted chicken Japonnaise and flank steak au poivre. Upstairs, amid crisp white linens, lacquered black chairs and wall panels with a striking peach, white and foam green print, you may order the same bistro items for lunch or choose again from daily specials. But we'd rather save up to have dinner here; it's a special-occasion place with perfect lighting, service and classical music. You can order a la carte, but we prefer the five-course dinners, an astounding value. Start with snails in garlic butter on mushroom caps, go on to soup and a watercress salad with sieved egg, enjoy duckling flambed with cognac and sauced with strawberry liqueur and fresh berries, and end with an ethereal lemon mousse.

Salon: lunch, Monday-Friday noon to 1:30; dinner, Tuesday-Saturday 6 to 9 or 9:30. Bistro: lunch, Monday-Friday 11:30 to 2; dinner, Monday-Saturday 5 to 10 or 11, Sunday 4 to 9.

* Angels, 125 North Main St., Providence. (401) 273-0310.
International. $13.95 to $21.95.

One of the hottest new restaurants in a city with more than its share, this is the creation of Jaime D'Oliveira, who left the chef's post at the celebrated Al Forno to open his own place down the street in 1988. The space, formerly occupied by Panache, is tight and handsome in black and white. Rich dark wood, mirrors and close-together tables convey intimacy, and a few angels from the owner's collection adorn the walls. Growing up with a mother of French and a father of Portuguese extraction, Jaime learned to cook in the European manner, goes to the market daily, and prepares everything from scratch and to order. The limited and appealing menu, beautifully handwritten, mixes "French, Italian, Spanish, American — a little bit of everything," says Jaime. Among entrees, you might find Portuguese-style cioppino, grilled trout with sweet red onion sauce, grilled chicken on a bed of Georgia corn with mint and lime, or grilled lamb chops with apricot-jalapeno-mint relish, grilled asparagus and potato gratin. Start with smoked salmon with lentil-vegetable salad or grilled chicory salad with endive, frisse and radicchio. Save money and room for one of the great desserts, perhaps apple-rhubarb crisp with homemade rose-petal ice cream or strawberry-raspberry crepe with creme fraiche. The good-looking place settings are notable for twenty-ounce water glasses, the tallest we've seen, with reliefs of naked men and women on the sides. "They're there to show I haven't lost my sense of humor," says Jaime, who professes to be fairly purist and simple despite what appears to be a complex cooking style.

Dinner, Monday-Saturday 5:30 to 11.

Troye's, 404 Wickenden St., Providence. (401) 861-1430.
  Southwest. $12.95 to $16.95.

In a two-level room with high ceiling, aqua brick walls, chairs covered with what look like pony skins and cactus all around, the former chef from Rue de L'Espoir runs a highly rated southwestern grill. Troye Mackie, a Colorado native, opened in 1989 to raves from a clientele that appreciated her version of the latest culinary rage. Lunch and brunch bring things like eggs Troye (two poached on herbed scones with pesto hollandaise, grilled ham and roasted red peppers), layered tortilla frittata with shrimp and pesto, and tart of tomatoes, smoked provolone and basil. She's at her gutsiest at dinner: reddened fish du jour with herbed lemon aioli, grilled veal chop with cilantro and tequila butter, crab cakes with two salsas, and grilled chicken with cantaloupe sauce over pasta garnished with prosciutto and roasted green chilies. Zippy salads, tortilla pizzas, duck tacos with tropical fruit, and goat cheese and sun-dried tomato rellenos are delicious starters. Tempting desserts include sweet potato flan, oreo cookie cheesecake, grapefruit-campari sorbet, and cappuccino ice cream deep-fried in a flour tortilla shell with caramel sauce and dusted with cinnamon sugar.

Lunch, Tuesday-Friday (except summer), noon to 3; dinner nightly except Monday, 5:30 to 9 or 10; Sunday brunch, 10 to 3. BYOB.

Adesso, 161 Cushing St., Providence. (401) 521-0770.
  Californian/Italian. $10.75 to $18.95.

Best of the new wave of eateries proliferating on College Hill is this chic California cafe in a converted garage, founded by Anthony Michilitti, owner of Anthony's restaurant downtown. Adesso means "now" in Italian, and this is a now place. Noisy and fun, it has gray oilcloths on the tables, heavy European cutlery rolled up inside white linen napkins, and neon signs on the walls. Skylights and huge windows make the rear room an oversize greenhouse. From the open mesquite grill and wood oven come interesting pizzas; eggplant with garlic, barbecued chicken with cilantro, and shrimp with pesto are some. We lunched on a marvelous pizza with lamb sausage, roasted red and yellow peppers, wild mushrooms, and madeira mustard, plus grilled squid with a salsa of red peppers, onions and black olives, accompanied by excellent grilled zucchini, potatoes and snap peas. Dessert was pear bread pudding with bourbon sauce. The mesquite grill yields such dinner entrees as Norwegian salmon with watercress sauce and pork chops with red pepper jelly glaze. Many like to mix and match the appetizers, pizzas and pastas. Finish with tirami su or imported white peaches with champagne sabayon, orange sorbet, raspberry sauce, and crushed amaretti cookie. Strong coffee is served in stainless-steel cups, and the sleek chrome and glass salt and pepper grinders are so handsome that we bought a pair to take home.

Open daily from noon to 10:30, weekends to midnight.

Rue de L'Espoir, 99 Hope St., Providence. (401) 751-8890.
  French/International. $5.95 to $15.95.

When it opened nearly fifteen years ago, this Left Bank-style bistro was far and away the city's most interesting eatery. With the proliferation of restaurants of late, it has lost that distinction, but remains an authentic cafe that could have been lifted from the streets of Paris. Tables of quarry tile, leather seats and booths, hanging pots, a wall of artistically arranged copper molds and cooking utensils, framed

212

Toulouse-Lautrec posters, and two huge baskets laden with greenery hanging from the pressed-tin ceiling decorate the interior dining room on several levels. The menu was totally revamped in 1989, and ads proclaimed "smokin' shrimp tempura, rockin' rack of lamb, sassy sesame chicken and roarin' rasta pasta." You can still get plates of pates, onion soup, crepes, quiche and a cheeseboard (served with choice of two cheeses, fruit, French bread, wafers and a house salad — "a meal in itself"). But you'll also find chicken and cashew spring rolls, Thai crab cakes with cilantro and ginger, goat cheese lasagna, and grilled duck with lingonberries. The Rue Rue platter, a sampler of any five small dishes, is a good way to go. The artichoke and mushroom salad has a nippy curry dressing, and the charlotte malakoff is a masterful dessert.

Lunch, Tuesday-Sunday 11:30 to 2:30; dinner, 5 to 10. Closed Monday.

Bluepoint, 99 North Main St., Providence. (401) 272-6145.
Seafood. $17.95 to $23.95.

In summer you can dine al fresco on little desk-like tables on the sidewalk in front of this storefront, which could pass for a dive on the outside and is funky inside as well. Swinging doors, a few fish on the walls, lights that look like shells beside blue booths, wildly painted orange chairs and a standup bar make up the decor. As longtime chef Maureen Pothier would have it, the food is the thing — some of the best seafood in Providence, especially the appetizers. The lengthy blackboard menu against the back wall changes daily and the writing is so small that we had to stand up and confront the list head-on. Homemade seafood sausage, clams oreganata, native conch salad, fried oysters with spicy caper mayonnaise, and oysters broiled in champagne cream with fresh salmon roe might be starters. Entrees could be grilled halibut with picholine olive butter and grilled fennel, local brook trout with bing cherry and almond dressing, and grilled lobster on a bed of greens with grapefruit, avocado and raspberries. Grilled rib-eye steak was the only non-seafood item when we were there. End with pineapple and macadamia nut cheesecake or strawberry-rhubarb trifle with vanilla cream and toasted pecans. The Wine Spectator gave its 1988 Grand Award to the Bluepoint's wine cellar.

Dinner nightly, 5 to 11 or 11:30.

La France, 960 Hope St., Providence. (401) 331-9223.
French. $11.50 to $19.50

Grandly rebuilt after a fire, this elaborate restaurant, looking like Paris in the Belle Epoque era, is run by chef-owner David Gaudet. It occupies a long narrow room with pressed-tin ceiling, handsome brass chandeliers and gray velvet banquettes against deep red wallpaper. The tiny bar area at the entry is a joy, with its velvet sofas and poufs. The menu is classic French and reasonably priced. At night when the oil paintings on the walls are softly spotlit and candles flicker, entrees run from lemon chicken and roast duckling with raspberry and cognac sauce to steak au poivre and chateaubriand of veal. For lunch, we tried an unusual and excellent soup, cream of persimmon with orange and almond. Entrees are mostly smaller versions of the evening fare. Desserts include pear helene and bananas foster and something called decadence, "our ultimate chocolate experience." The wine list bears lots of bargains.

Lunch, Tuesday-Friday 11:30 to 2:30; dinner, Tuesday-Saturday 5:30 to 9:30 or 10.

New Rivers, 7 Steeple St., Providence.
Contemporary International. $12 to $20.

Providence's newest restaurant, opened in February 1990 and without a phone listing as this book went to press, was being touted by no less a food connoisseur than Johanne Killeen. Of course, she's not exactly impartial — the venture occupies the space where her Al Forno got its start and it's run by friends, Bruce and Patricia Tillinghast. Both Tillinghasts had been chefs in executive dining rooms in Boston after training with Madeleine Kamman, and were looking forward to their own operation in his hometown. They planned a limited menu that would change frequently. Typical offerings might be warm oysters marinated with fennel and sweet and hot red peppers, and a soup combining chicken stock with carrots, parsnips, turnips and dill for starters. Entrees could be grilled rack of lamb, grilled salmon with seasonal sauce, an alsatien choucroute with pork chops and German wieners, and a Moroccan dish of grilled chicken with sweet potatoes and saffron. Food for the health-conscious might be emphasized, but the couple won't stint on desserts like chocolate-hazelnut torte with warm chocolate sauce and a sun-dried cherry tart with almond cream. They were lightening up the former black decor in the tiny space to a deep blue-green background with orange and yellow accents and seating for 30.

Dinner, Tuesday-Saturday 5 to 10.

Hemenway's, 1 Old Stone Square, Providence. (401) 351-8570.
Seafood. $11.95 to $18.95.

With a pleasant view of the Providence River from its sleek glass quarters on the main floor of a newish downtown bank building, Hemenway's is the archtypical upscale seafood house. The tables bear huge bottles of tabasco sauce, and neon fish hang from from the ceiling amid the clubby decor of dark greens, etched glass, brass lamps, bare tables and dark wood booths. An extensive, eight-page menu with colorful fish swimming all over it, printed every other day, starts with seventeen entries from Hemenway's oyster bar; five varieties were offered in the non-R month we were there, including Malpeque, Sakonnet and Chincoteague. Crab and shrimp potato skins, and oysters Hemenway (grilled with herb butter, lime juice and Absolut vodka) are favorite appetizers. Every kind of fish you've heard of — and probably some you haven't, including seven "fresh from Hawaii" — are listed for main courses. Baked flounder topped with hazelnut cream, blackened tilefish with Creole sauce and English plaice with a spicy pepper coulis were among the evening's specials. There are a few steak and chicken items for landlubbers, and quiche and croissants join the seafood parade at lunch. The house salad that comes with every entree is topped with baby shrimp. Desserts are ho-hum, except perhaps for the apple crumb pie a la mode.

Lunch, Monday-Saturday 11:30 to 3; dinner, Monday-Saturday 4:30 or 5 to 10 or 11, Sunday 11:30 to 10.

In-Prov, 50 Kennedy Plaza, Providence. (401) 351-8700.
American/International. $4.95 to $17.95.

This contemporary American bistro opening into the atrium of the Fleet Center is just the ticket for those into tapas and rotisserie foods. Started by Guy Abelson, owner of Cafe in the Barn in suburban Seekonk, it's now run by his longtime chef, John Elkhay. Frozen flavored vodka is one of the bar specialties, and 30 wines are available by the glass. Faux marbled walls and marble floors are the backdrop for tables with rattan chairs in the lounge, the small dining room and out in the atrium. The menu lists a dozen tapas and appetizers, from fried squid rings with a chipolte pepper mayonnaise and scotch smoked salmon with grilled bread and chive chauce to lo mein hung lo, a prize-winning stir-fry with swordfish, broccoli, wood ear mushrooms, snow peas and peppers, and a bento box sampler of grilled shrimp, seared red pepper tenderloin, tempura vegetables, and sweet and sour cucumber noodles. If these aren't enough, there's a limited list of entrees: perhaps roast chicken with Jack Daniels gravy, hickory-grilled leg of lamb with rosemary and cranberry-mint jelly, baked stuffed shrimp wrapped in phyllo dough with mixed greens and feta cheese, and baked pasta. Peanut butter-chocolate chip cheesecake and chocolate-pistachio cake with three fruit sauces are among desserts. There's a large takeout counter where we picked up apricot-glazed chicken and delicious salads for a late dinner at home.

Lunch, Monday-Friday 11:30 to 3; dinner, Monday-Saturday 5:30 to midnight or 1.

Raphael's, 207 Pine St., Providence. (401) 421-4646.
Italian. $12.50 to $18.50.

This stylish restaurant is in the boiler room of one of Providence's many old jewelry factories. Pizzas from the brick oven and salads are the rage at lunch; the latter include arugula and mushroom or spinach, walnut and soft cheese. The dinner menu is extensive, embracing almost every classic Italian dish you could think of, plus some you might not — perhaps sweetbreads with macadamia nuts. The pastas are outstanding. In the high-ceilinged room, exposed pipes are painted in soft pastels, pretty peach chintz covers the chairs, Italian jazz plays, oil lamps float in little vases and fancy desserts like baked apples in puff pastry or zuppa inglese are displayed on a flower-bedecked stand. Light snacks and a raw bar are available in the large bar-lounge, and in summer there is outdoor dining on a brick courtyard.

Lunch, Monday-Friday 11:30 to 2:30; dinner, Monday-Saturday 5:30 to 10 or 11.

Anthony's, 70 Washington St., Providence. (401) 273-2350.
Italian. $14.50 to $21.50.

Anthony's is dark and formal and we would rather have dinner than lunch here, but it appears to be a good place for a power lunch or an intimate rendezvous. Done up in restful beiges and browns, the small restaurant with stuccoed walls, little grottoes and comfortable armchairs is considered one of Providence's best for Italian cuisine. Pasta comes seven ways and veal eight, but with modern European touches and California influences, as in lasagna with scallops and a lobster bechamel sauce or broiled veal chop with Roman mushrooms, pine nuts, and red and orange peppers in a whole-grain mustard and veal sauce. A dessert tray includes chocolate mousse on a cookie crust and tirami su.

Lunch, Monday-Friday 11:30 to 2:30; dinner, Monday-Saturday 5 to 10 or 11.

New Japan, 145 Washington St., Providence. (401) 351-0300.
Japanese. $7.95 to $14.95.

Very popular with other restaurateurs is this plain little place with hanging lamps in wooden boxes, extremely small booths and Japanese music playing in the background. We lunched on a combination plate of impeccably fresh sashimi, delicate shrimp and vegetable tempura, and rare beef teriyaki, before which came a bowl of soup with cubes of tofu and mushrooms cut into thin threads. At night, a special dinner for two yields sashimi or tempura, soup, salad, entree and ice cream. Grilled fish steaks include mackerel and salmon. A yaki dinner wraps fish, chicken and vegetables in foil with mushrooms, zucchini, lemon and butter. You can cook shabu shabu in broth at your table. There's no sushi, except on Sunday.

Lunch, Monday-Friday 11:30 to 2:30; dinner, Monday-Saturday 5:30 to 9:30 or 10, Sunday (sushi and sashimi only) 5:30 to 10.

Leon's on the West Side, 500 Broadway, Providence. (401) 273-1055.
Contemporary American/Italian. $10.95 to $22.95.

Off the beaten path, this funky little place is a find for its wide-ranging (and delectable) food and gentle prices. It's the restaurant portion of Catering on Broadway. Knowing locals pack its faux marble tables for three meals a day, amid a cafe-diner atmosphere of friendly waitresses, bare wood floors, and green hanging lamps and fans. Start your day with a raspberry-almond croissant or salmon benedict served on a crumpet. Lunchtime brings gorgeous-looking salads like a wood-grilled vegetable platter with aioli sauce, pesto chicken and a fantastic antipasto, as well as frittatas, six versions of chicken cutlet sandwiches, burgers, and daily specials like falofel and clam zuppa. Dinner entrees range from salmon in dill cream sauce over black and green fettuccine and veal saltimbocca to shepherd's pie and an extravagant but pricey mixed grill garnished with marinated salads and chutney. You might start with deep-fried squid or wood-grilled pizza. In the display cases are incredible desserts, among them a chocolate-strawberry shortcake topped with chocolate-dipped strawberries, and a chocolate-concord crepe cake, with layers of crepes, pistachio paste and prune paste, topped with exotic fruit in a glaze and whipped cream.

Breakfast, Tuesday-Friday 7 to 11; lunch, 11:30 to 2:30; dinner, Wednesday-Saturday 5 to 10.

Wes Brewton's Original BBQ, 103 Richmond St., Providence.
(401) 272-5006.
Barbecue/Southern. $5.95 to $14.95.
Local investors have staked Wes Brewton, who brought finger-licking Southern barbecue to Rhode Island in 1976, to his airy new upstairs barbecue emporium done up in yellow, red and black at the edge of downtown. In front of a 22-foot-long wood-fired barbecue pit that's New England's biggest are baskets of onions and watermelons and barrels full of bottles of root beer on ice. The heat is on for choice ribs, chops and steaks, cooked over a native hardwood fire and basted with the Brewton family vinegar and spice. "Served with sauce on the side, the way it's supposed to be," says Wes. "Just like you'd be served any Sunday afternoon in Blackjack, Missouri." Now he's into "nouvelle barbecue," things like Mississippi freshwater catfish, halibut and swordfish, along with Cajun prime rib, bayou gumbo and pork rinds. The classics remain: real chunk-beef chili served with jalapeno peppers and crackers, and sweet potato pie. Regulars say the best introduction (as well as the best deal) is the Southern sampler, a variety of meats with veggie, potato, chili and corn bread, listed under appetizers for $12.95 but enough for two to share. Bowls of peanuts in their shells are ready on each table to stave off hunger. Wash it all down with a couple of beers and you'll have a feast, here or to go.

Open Monday-Thursday 11:30 to 10, Friday 11:30 to 1 a.m., Saturday 3 to 1, Sunday 3 to 10.

Kabob-n-Curry, 261 Thayer St., Providence. (401) 273-8844.
Northern Indian. $7.50 to $10.95.
Providence's Indian restaurants come and go. The latest rage is this small eatery with a greenhouse at one end overlooking a busy street scene. Glass covers woven tablecloths, and Indian art is on the walls. Here most of the dishes are in the style of northern India, everything is fresh, and you may order anything mildly or highly spiced. Start with one of the nine breads, maybe onion nan or khasta roti cooked in the tandoori oven. Chicken chat, vegetable pakoras and nargisi kabob (deep-fried minced lamb patties) are a few of the good appetizers. Basmati rice and onion chutney (which you have to ask for specially) come with the 22 curry dishes, but maybe you'd rather have tandoori shrimp, marinated in spices and yogurt and baked on skewers in the tandoori oven. A pistachio or coconut ice cream would be a cooling end to the meal, or perhaps a mango milkshake would hit the spot.

Open daily, 11 a.m. to 11 p.m.

East Providence

The Culling House, 28 Water St., East Providence. (401) 431-0300.
Seafood. $9.95 to $14.95.
The former home of the Stratford Oyster Company is one of the few places in this area where you can dine right by the water. The big gray shingled building is at the edge of the Seekonk River in the shadow of the Washington Street bridge. In the large square dining room where tables have paper mats over glass, three walls are floor-to-ceiling windows and doors to outdoor decks and greenhouse additions. For lunch there are four versions of cobb salad, many sandwiches and mostly fishy entrees like shrimp oriental and baked stuffed filet of sole. The dinner menu covers the usual bases from baked scrod to grilled swordfish. You also may order veal, chicken, beef or pasta. A lighter menu is available in the busy bar.

Lunch, Monday-Friday 11:30 to 2:30; dinner nightly, 5 to 10 or 11, Sunday 1 to 9.

Pawtucket

China Inn, 285 Main St., Pawtucket. (401) 723-3960.
Chinese. $5.50 to $13.
One of the larger and more striking landmarks in downtown Pawtucket is the stylish new home of what many consider to be Rhode Island's best Chinese restaurant. The China Inn moved in 1986 from cramped, dark quarters into a bright and airy building with a contemporary oriental motif, topped by a pyramid ceiling with light from skylights bathing tall ficus trees. Comfortable rattan chairs, booths and banquettes encircle an atrium of sorts; walls are hung with original oriental art. This is the backdrop for a broad range of Chinese fare, done in the Szechuan, Hunan and Mandarin styles as well as the specialty Cantonese. Szechuan and Peking duck can be ordered half or whole, and one section of the vast menu lists six vegetarian dishes like Buddha's delight and bean cake with black mushrooms. The Happy Family Bird's Nest mixes roast pork, chicken, lobster meat and shrimp with bamboo shoots, water chestnuts, snow peas and such over an edible nest of potato noodles. Special family dinners with a variety of combinations are listed for two to eight people.

Open daily from 11 a.m. to 11 p.m., weekends to midnight.

2 George St., 2 George St., Pawtucket. (401) 724-5522.
American. $6.95 to $12.95.
The orange roof of a former Howard Johnson's restaurant beside I-95 has been raised (and painted light green), the walls paneled in oak and pine, and a twelve-foot-scale model of the Statue of Liberty added to oversee the goings-on. The decor and the menu are trendy, Pawtucket style, one reviewer cooing that she thought she was in California at Mustard's Grill or Spago. Hardly, though Howard wouldn't recognize the place. The menu has something for everyone, from grilled three-mustard chicken to barbecued ribs, pastas and fajitas. Since the initial trendiness of grilled pizzas and french-fried sweet potatoes, the menu has been toned down a bit, offering (like HoJo's 28 flavors) something for everyone. Most of the dinner entrees are available at lunch. Burgers, sandwiches (a club with grilled chicken, BLT and guacamole), salads, pastas, and omelets are among the fare. Carrot cake, New York cheesecake and ice cream are popular desserts, and the well-chosen wine list is nicely priced in the teens.

Lunch daily, 11:30 to 4; dinner, 4 to 10 or 11.

Providence Area

$ Modern Diner, 364 East Ave., Pawtucket. (401) 726-8390.
Old-fashioned American. $2.55 to $5.95.

Here is the antithesis of trendy (although diners are said to have originated in Providence in 1872). The Modern is a Sterling Streamliner, one of a line of "modernistic" diners manufactured circa 1940 and moved from a downtown site to the East Side in 1986. It's the first diner to be accepted on the National Register of Historic Places. A rear addition was under construction in 1989 (the inside to "look like a train station, we hope"), according to one of the longtime owners. But the diner is where nostalgia buffs congregate, on shiny chrome stools, at booths and intimate shelf-tables for two, amid mirrored walls and linoleum floors. It's the real thing, and so is the food: the day's specials when we visited were chicken pot pie with salad, a gyro sandwich with french fries, and pasta salad ("spaghetti and vegetables"). The menu lists meatloaf with mashed potatoes, vegetable and salad, delmonico steak, chicken amandine, corned beef and cabbage, swordfish steak and more at bygone prices. A hot dog is still a hot dog and still 95 cents; ditto for the fried egg sandwich and the hamburger. Beer and wine are available.

Open Monday-Friday 7 a.m. to 8 p.m., Saturday 7 to 4, Sunday 8 to 2 (breakfast only).

Woonsocket

The Mill House, 153 Hamlet Ave., Woonsocket. (401) 766-1500.
American/Italian. $9.95 to $14.95.

A stylish dining room emerged in 1986 from the office section of an old mill in a rundown section of town. There's a solarium-bar at the side with a number of raw-bar specialties, but the candlelit inner sanctum appeals, nicely divided into sections and with tables dressed in white and green linens. A shelf encircling the room just beneath the lofty ceiling harbors copper pots and plants amidst a background of hunter green wallpaper, green-shaded lamps and brass railings. The staff in tux shirts and bow ties is solicitous, serving an ambitious menu that goes beyond cliches. No nachos or potato skins here. Instead there are sauteed calamari and fried smelts, both in a spicy cherry pepper and black olive sauce, stuffed hot cherry peppers, stuffed mushrooms, and broccoli cheese balls. Veal comes in six guises, from steak to saltimbocca, and chicken in seven, including nicoise. Some of the seafood and beef offerings have Cajun accents, as in blackened swordfish and sirloin, but you'll also find seafood casserole, bay scallops with mushrooms and mozzarella, scampi Sicilian, and steak fra diavolo. Seven pasta dishes are served as entrees with soup or salad. Desserts include chocolate cake, cheesecake, grapenut pudding, and Jamaican parfait, made with rum, tia maria and coffee ice cream.

Lunch, Monday-Friday 11:30 to 3; dinner, 3 to 9, Saturday 4 to 10; Sunday, brunch 10 to 2, dinner 2 to 8.

Chan's, 267 Main St., Woonsocket. (401) 765-1900.
Chinese. $4.50 to $13.50.

Although dating to 1905, this was rechristened Chan's Fine Oriental Dining in 1974 and doubled in size in 1986. It's known for an enormous menu featuring the four main cuisines of China, along with Polynesian and American fare, and for excellent jazz in the new Four Seasons banquet room, fashioned from an old bank and with the vault used as an intimate (and different) private dining room. The room takes its name from the stunning Chinese porcelain vases bearing floral arrangements depicting the seasons along its perimeter; the periodic jazz concerts turn it into a veritable supper club. Owner John Chan, a jazz afficionado, horticulturalist and photographer, designed the restaurant and gave it an unusually oriental feeling (his award-winning photos of guest artists line the corridor and make something of a hall of fame for jazz buffs). The main room in vivid red and gold is a medley of booths and leather chairs, oriental art and bronzes, and a horseshoe-shaped bar made of vibrant tiles is at one end. The food selection is so broad that you'll have a tough time deciding, but the waiters can steer you to special treats. Worth a special trip are the See Gyp littlenecks cooked in oriental spices and black bean sauce with a touch of garlic and scallions. A luncheon buffet is $4.50 for all you can eat.

Lunch, Monday-Saturday 11:30 to 3; dinner nightly, 3 to midnight or 1.

Johnston

The Little Inn, 103 Putnam Ave. (Route 44), Johnston. (401) 231-0570.
Italian/American. $8.95 to $14.50.

It's not little and it's not an inn, but this traditional establishment in the Graniteville section is welcoming, family-run and considered a treasure by folks at a more sophisticated restaurant across town. Harold and Yolanda Russo and their married daughters do things you expect in fancier places, such as their signature entree of broiled veal steak stuffed with eggplant, mozzarella and a wine-flavored mushroom sauce. All of the veal dishes are good, but you might go for the sirloin with artichoke hearts and garlic, the scrod florentine, the jumbo scampi, or the chicken neapolitan. The menu is supplemented by a lengthy list of specials, including updated New England seafood and meats (like roast loin of pork with apple-walnut dressing, glazed carrots and new potatoes) and ethereal pastas (perciatelli with scallops, broccoli and sun-dried tomatoes). Hot chocolate-walnut pie with ice cream and creme de cacao, deep-dish apple pie fresh from North Scituate, bread and butter custard pudding topped with fresh fruit, and chocolate-fudge cake are exceptional desserts. Candles, a fire in the hearth and a homey decor of brick, paneling and captain's chairs make this a favorite, especially in winter. Check out Yolanda Russo's antiques collection in the foyer, and the paintings done by a member of the family, a tailor by trade who lived on Providence's Federal Hill. Harold Russo, who started in the kitchen and is a wine connoisseur, oversees the wine selections, some offered at exceptionally low prices.

Lunch, Monday-Friday 11:30 to 4; dinner, Monday-Saturday 4 to 10, also Sunday in winter.

Newport County

Newport

♥ **The Black Pearl,** Bannister's Wharf, Newport. (401) 846-5264.
New American/Continental. $13 to $21.

Our favorite all-around restaurant in Newport — and that of many others, judging from the crowds day and night — is the informal tavern, the fancy Commodore's Room and the deck with umbrella-topped tables that comprise the Black Pearl. You can sit outside under the Cinzano umbrellas and watch half the world go by while sampling Newport's best clam chowder (creamy, chock full of clams and amply herbed, served with a huge soda cracker). Inside is the hectic and historic tavern, offering the outdoor fare as well as heartier items that can serve as lunch or dinner. We thoroughly enjoyed wintertime lunches of eggs Copenhagen (smoked salmon instead of ham) and the famed pearlburger with mint salad in pita bread and good fries. Dessert standouts are a delectable brandy cream cake, a dish of golden grand marnier ice cream and an apple-raisin bread pudding. Candlelight dinners in the formal Commodore's Room are lovely, the lights of the waterfront twinkling through small-paned windows. Shrimp, scallops and lobster in a light sauce americaine, soft-shell crabs meuniere, duckling sauteed with brandied raisin sauce, noisettes of veal with a watercress-cream sauce, and roast loin of lamb with thyme and truffle sauce are among the offerings.

Tavern and outdoor cafe open daily from 11; dinner in Commodore Room, 6 to 11. Closed January or February.

* La Petite Auberge, 19 Charles St., Newport. (401) 849-6669.
French. $16 to $23.

On two floors in the historic Stephen Decatur House, Roger Putier serves classic French fare from an extensive menu in five small and elegant dining rooms where lace tablecloths are layered over pale blue or gold linen. Some consider this among the best traditional French restaurants in New England. Chef Putier's hand-written French menu is so extensive and his specials so numerous that the choice is difficult. His sauces are heavenly — from the escargots with cepes, a house specialty (its heavily garlicked sauce demanding to be soaked up by the hot and crusty French bread), to our entrees of veal with morels and cream sauce and two tender pink lamb chops, also with cepes and an intense brown sauce. Starters include a fine Marseilles-style fish soup and a mousse of chicken livers with truffles. Entrees run from frog's legs provencale to lobster americaine and saddle of lamb with garlic sauce, and include classic meat and poultry dishes. The excellent wine list is reasonably priced. Desserts are mostly classics like crepes suzette and cherries jubilee.

Dinner, Monday-Saturday 6 to 10, Sunday 5 to 9.

The Clarke Cooke House, Bannister's Wharf, Newport. (401) 849-2900.
French Nouvelle. $18.75 to $23.50.

The setting is a 1790-vintage Colonial house with dining on several levels and a couple of breezy upper decks. The **Candy Store Cafe** downstairs serves an informal menu in a bistro-like bar with marble tables and bentwood chairs. The all-day menu ranges from a hamburger with addictive french fries to broiled sirloin. Grilled shrimp and andouille sausage on pasta, fried oysters on a warm spinach salad, and cassoulet of lamb, duck and sausage are some of the unusual offerings. Upstairs in Colonial dining rooms and on the canopied deck with a great view of the harbor, the setting is elegant and the prices more expensive. But the food is inspired: grilled monkfish with scallion and red pepper coulis, nage of shrimp, red snapper and sea bass with orange sauce, veal in puff pastry with shiitake mushrooms, and filet mignon with port and truffle sauce. Even the lowly chicken here is stuffed with lobster meat. Start with a terrine of salmon and pompano on tomato coulis or pate of duck with pistachios and pearl onion marmalade. Finish with Indian pudding from Locke-Ober, the Boston restaurant that proprietor David Ray also owns.

Cafe, 11:30 to 11; dinner nightly, 6 to 10 or 10:30, weekends only in off-season.

Le Bistro, Bowen's Wharf, Newport. (401) 849-7778.
Contemporary French. $15.50 to $29.95.

Creative cuisine and an elegant decor in the second- and third-floor dining rooms with glimpses of the harbor commend this French bistro, which is chef-owned by John and Mary Philcox. We've enjoyed a fine salade nicoise and a classic bouillabaisse from a luncheon menu on which everything looks good. Dinner entrees run the gamut from breast of chicken with lemon, thyme and onions to steamed lobster beurre blanc. We can vouch for the veal kidneys in port and the roast duck in a red cream sauce with endives. The feuillete of asparagus and morels and the hazelnut foie gras salad make good starters. We liked the dessert tart of green grapes in a puff pastry with whipped cream and the Creole-style bread pudding with bourbon sauce. The amiable third-floor bar serves a tavern menu and is crowded all day and evening.

Lunch daily, 11:30 to 2; dinner nightly from 6; Sunday brunch, 11:30 to 2; bar fare, 11:30 to 11.

White Horse Tavern, Marlborough and Farewell Streets, Newport.
(401) 846-3600.
Continental. $18 to $31.

Established in 1673, this imposing burgundy structure is the oldest operating tavern in the country. It has elegant Colonial decor in a cocktail lounge and dining rooms on two floors. The tuxedoed staff offers a fancy menu and prices to match. The historic charms of this place are particularly welcoming in the off-season, when we've enjoyed a lunch of halibut with grapefruit sauce and chicken salad in half an avocado. The lunch menu ranges from a tavern burger and club sandwich to grilled duckling salad and shrimp and scallops en brochette over pasta. At night, the menu has higher aspirations and prices soar: things like grilled veal steak on a red and yellow pepper coulis, medallions of veal with sweetbreads, sauteed lamb rib-eye, individual beef wellington, and de-shelled lobster sauteed in brandy and cream. A triple silk torte on a bed of raspberry melba sauce is a fitting ending.

Lunch, Monday-Saturday noon to 3; dinner nightly, 6 to 10; Sunday brunch, noon to 3.

♥ The Inn at Castle Hill, Ocean Drive, Newport. (401) 849-3800.
American/Continental. $18 to $25.

The most sumptuous bar in Newport is tucked away in the front corner of this elegant Victorian inn, its tall windows taking in the grand views of bay and sunset as you sip a drink and snack on crackers with a zippy spread. Beyond is a three-sided dining porch with rounded walls that juts out toward the water, all very inviting with white tables and chairs and flowered seats. Also available are a fancy small room and a large formal dining room, richly paneled but for one wall of deep blue and rose wallpaper. Dinners could begin with escargots, sweetbreads in pastry, raw Cajun tenderloin, or lamb noisettes provencale. Entrees include halibut paupiette, veal with chanterelles, dover sole, and sliced duck with raspberry and peppercorn sauce. From meals past, we can vouch for a fine filet of sole stuffed with scallop mousse and an excellent tournedos au poivre. There's nightly piano music, and jazz is played on the lawn during Sunday brunch.

Lunch in season, Tuesday-Saturday noon to 2:30; dinner, Monday-Saturday 6 to 9; Sunday brunch, noon to 4. Restaurant closed November to mid-April. Jackets required at dinner.

Amsterdam's Bar & Rotisserie, 509 Thames St., Newport. (401) 847-0550.
Contemporary American. $7.95 to $14.95.

A branch of a Manhattan restaurant, Amsterdam's opened in a small storefront in 1987 and moved down the street to the larger quarters of the old Southern Cross in 1988. A casual place with red and white woven cloths and black chairs, it still specializes in roast chicken, which we found delectable with fresh green herb sauce, three-green salad and super fried potatoes. Lunch also brings gravlax, Amsterdam's grand salad with roasted meats and vegetables, and chicken sandwich with green herb mayonnaise and sun-dried tomatoes. At dinnertime, you might start with smoked trout with freshwater caviar sauce, cucumber and watercress, have a grilled shell steak with herb butter and french fries, and end with key lime pie. A few egg dishes are added at brunch.

Lunch daily, noon to 4:30 (Saturday only in winter); dinner, 5 to 11; Sunday brunch, 11 to 2:30.

Scales and Shells, 527 Thames St., Newport. (401) 846-3474.
Seafood. $9.75 to $14.95.

Almost as fast as seafood can be unloaded from the docks out back, retired sea captain Andy Ackerman cooks up a storm in an open kitchen near the door of this casual restaurant, an instant success following its 1988 opening. Plain and exotic seafood, simply prepared but presented with style, comes in many guises. The delicious aromas almost overpowered as we studied the blackboard menu on the wall listing the offerings. There's an enormous range, from calamari salad and Sicilian mussels to mesquite-grilled mahi-mahi and shrimp marsala, but nary a meat item in sight. Recent additions are grilled clam pizza and crab fra diavolo. Entrees come with a simple green salad or pasta. A raw bar offers fresh goodies near the entry, and there's a small wine list.

Dinner, Monday-Saturday 5 to 9 or 10, Sunday 4 to 9.

$ Puerini's, 24 Memorial Blvd. West, Newport. (401) 847-5506.
Italian. $5.95 to $12.95.

Dan Puerini's tiny, cafe-like Italian restaurant is a favorite of the locals. They squeeze together at perhaps twenty tables in two narrow, side-by-side dining rooms with tile floors, lacy curtains and not much else in the way of decor. The tables are covered with strips of paper, the lighting is bright, prices are gentle, and the food is true. The menu seldom changes (it doesn't need to), and among antipasti you can always find spinach pie, pepperoni and cheese calzone, and hot cherry peppers stuffed with prosciutto and provolone. The spinach salad with a creamy pesto dressing includes gorgonzola cheese and walnuts and is out of this world. All the pasta is made fresh daily. It comes in sixteen versions, from spaghetti with meatballs to five presentations with chicken. The linguini with pesto and pine nuts was voted the best in the state. Shrimp scampi and fish of the day (perhaps sole stuffed with lobster, pine nuts, brie, and sun-dried tomatoes) are other entrees, most served in huge portions. Desserts include tartuffo, gelato, rice pie with custard and raisins, and apple strudel.

Dinner nightly, 4 to 10 or 11. BYOB. No smoking. No credit cards.

The Mooring, Sayer's Wharf, Newport. (401) 846-2260.
Seafood. $14.25 to $23.95.

Our favorite outdoor spot by the water is this casual place with dining on a brick patio under blue umbrellas or an upper deck covered by a green and blue canopy and brightened by colorful geraniums. The lines for meals can get long, but you can wait on stools overlooking the water in the canopied outdoor bar and nurse spicy bloody marys. For a late lunch on a summer Saturday, we only had to wait ten minutes for a table on the breezy patio as we eyed the abundant seafood salads and a monstrous one called simply "The Salad" ($5.90, to feed one to four) passing by. Our party of four sampled the seafood quiche with coleslaw, steamed mussels with garlic bread, half a dozen littlenecks and a bulky tuna sandwich, and a terrific scallop chowder (deemed even better than the award-winning clam chowder) with half a lobster salad sandwich. The all-day menu includes typical steak and seafood entrees from baked scallops to hot seafood platter or surf and turf. The inside is blue and nautical (the building used to belong to the New York Yacht Club) and is warmed by a large fireplace in winter.

Open daily, 11:30 to 10 or 11. Closed in January.

Dave & Eddie's, Brick Market Place, Newport. (401) 849-5241.
Seafood. $9.95 to $23.95.

A blackboard at the entrance of this modern and airy seafood grill and raw bar lists where the fish is from on a particular day (lobster, local; mussels, local; clams on the half shell, Block Island). On two levels, it has large photographs of boats on the walls, a raw bar and shiny wooden floors, and an outdoor sidewalk cafe. All kinds of seafood — baked, fried, broiled — and several pasta dishes, plus some more expensive dinner specials (lobster thermidor, tournedos with lobster meat and steak au poivre, among them) are offered. Lunch brings a variety of quiches and salads as well as sandwiches. Desserts are standard, but the California-based wine list is interesting and reasonably priced.

Open daily from 11:30 to 9:30 or 10:30. Closed Tuesday in winter.

Pronto, 464 Thames St., Newport. (401) 847-5251.
Italian. $5.95 to $10.50.

When Amsterdam's Rotisserie moved to larger quarters in 1988, one of its chefs, Nora Forbes, stayed behind to cook in the open kitchen at the rear of this small bistro. Black chairs, wild floral cloths, bare floors, and pressed-tin walls and ceiling set a colorful backdrop for a limited menu of Italian specialties. Mix-and-match pastas with the sauce of your choice (the one with olives, prosciutto, anchovies, garlic, and olive oil sounds terrific) are featured. That's about it, except for a few appetizers like wild mushroom crostini, antipasto, and mozzarella salad, chicken and steak of the day, and a couple of fish specials — broiled swordfish with aioli and broiled bonita with a spicy ginger and sesame mayonnaise the night we were there. Three desserts are offered: chocolate mousse, cheesecake and a changing seasonal fruit like poached pears.

Dinner nightly, 5 to 10 or 11. No reservations. No credit cards.

Pezzoli's, 673 Thames St., Newport. (401) 846-5830.
Contemporary Italian. $16 to $17.50.

As if Newport needed more good restaurants. There must be safety in numbers, for this little gem up and moved in 1989 from a small house in out-of-the-way Jamestown into the thick of things in Newport. Well, not exactly the thick — it's at the far end of lower Thames Street — but the site was made famous by local restaurateur Volker Frick. Frick's eventually gave way to Recorder's, a small French restaurant of note. When we last were in town, we called to reserve a table at Recorder's, only to learn that it had been replaced by Pezzulli's — "a really good, authentic Italian restaurant," the hostess cajoled. And so it is. The two small dining rooms look about the same, somewhat cramped and intimate in white and black, with a black folder containing the menu serving as a temporary placemat at each setting. The handwritten offerings are primarily pastas: chicken penne with rosemary and bel paese cheese, grilled shrimp and scallops with black pepper linguini, shrimp in ginger-cream sauce with snow peas on ginger fettuccine, veal stuffed with spinach and mozzarella on spinach fettuccine, sauteed calves liver and onions with grilled radicchio and anchovy-mustard sauce, and farfalle with pesto and grilled chicken. All dishes come with Evian water, fresh baguettes and house salad. Scallop stew or calamari and kiwi make good openers.

Dinner nightly, 5 to 11.

Muriel's, Corner of Spring and Touro streets, Newport. (401) 849-7780.
International. $6.50 to $13.95.

Life-like mannequins make visitors do a double-take at the entrance to this funky restaurant, and the "water closet" turns out to be unisex. The tables, covered with glass over lace over green, are rather close together. Lace curtains shield the windows, the floors are bare, and ceiling fans and globe lamps hang from the ceiling. Muriel Barclay-deTolley, something of a Newport institution, makes the soups, including an award-winning but overly thick seafood chowder. We loved the luncheon crepe of spinach, mushrooms, cheese, and tomatoes with an extraordinary side salad of greens with slivers of cheddar cheese dressed with creamy dill, and a hefty bowl of spinach salad topped with apple slices, a new one to us, and lots of crisp bacon. Crepes and salads also are available at dinner, when you can get appetizers like escargots, pate and baked brie. Entrees range from vegetable stir-fry and lasagna to filet mignon with bearnaise sauce. Bananas foster and raisin bread pudding with butter-rum sauce are good desserts. For breakfast, there's huevos rancheros, and Muriel's french toast is grilled and topped with walnuts.

Breakfast, Monday-Saturday 8 to 11:30; lunch, II:30 to 2; dinner 5 to 10; Sunday brunch, 9 to 2. BYOB.

Cafe Zelda, 528 Thames St., Newport. (401) 849-4002.
American. $10 to $15.

A bit removed from the often overwhelming hustle and bustle of the wharf, this ever-crowded neighborhood bistro is named after Zelda Fitzgerald. It was among the first of the burgeoning restaurants on lower Thames Street, and was expanded in 1988. The etched-glass doors, brass handles, lace curtains, and high ceilings give it quite a Parisian quality. The same menu is served all day, supplemented by specials at night. Creative appetizers include calamari aioli and smoked mussels dijon. Crab Zelda, with mornay sauce over crab on an English muffin with cheese, is popular, as are pastas, vegetarian specialties, and such standards as filet mignon and fish and chips. The food is good, if you don't mind loud music and lots of cigarette smoke.

Lunch daily, 11:30 to 2:30; dinner, 5:30 to 10; weekend brunch, 11 to 4.

Brick Alley Pub & Restaurant, 140 Thames St., Newport. (401) 849-6334.
American. $9.95 to $14.95.

We don't know which is more dizzying: the bar with its mirrors and memorabilia, or the twenty-page menu, which blows the mind. No matter. Ralph and Pat Plumb's venerable establishment with a neat rear courtyard is locally esteemed for good food at pleasant prices. We can't begin to detail the fare encompassing more than 200 items. Suffice to say that the menu contains a page for Tex-Mex appetizers, another for potato skins, another for soup and salad buffet, two for sandwiches, and two for dinner specials (from pastas to steak au poivre). Other dinner choices include eight chicken dishes, four of scallops, sole stuffed with scallops and crabmeat, barbecued beef ribs, and steak teriyaki. Despite all this, heaping nachos are the best-seller.

Open daily from 11 to 10 or 11; Sunday brunch.

The Rhumbline, 62 Bridge St., Newport. (401) 849-6950.
American. $12.95 to $17.95.

Off the tourists' path and hidden away in the historic Point section, this bistro-type place is favored by locals, and appeals particularly in the fall and winter. Old-fashioned lamps and woven tablecloths, an old piano in one corner and a wood stove in another, and oriental rugs scattered about the wide-board floors create a cozy feeling. Salads, burgers and sandwiches are great at lunch. The "Nurse Roberta" combines sliced turkey breast, melted cheddar with cranberry sauce and spinach on a split french roll. Among dinner entrees are curried chicken, wiener schnitzel, steaks, and scallops provencale. Nana's chocolate bread pudding, assorted tortes, and Bucks ice creams and sherbets are favored desserts.

Lunch, Monday-Friday 11:30 to 2:30, Saturday-Sunday to 5; dinner, 5 to 10 or 11; Sunday brunch, noon to 4.

Sardella's, 30 Memorial Blvd. West, Newport. (401) 849-6312.
  Italian. $10.50 to $15.50.

Formerly known as Barclay's, this restaurant changed names and cuisines in 1987. Fine, European-style Italian dining is advertised, and translates into two serene dining rooms, one with red woven tablecloths and the other all in white, against a backdrop of European paintings on exhibit and for sale. A heady aroma of garlic greets patrons as they enter, and turns up in mussels, chicken and other dishes. Escarole and bean soup, two versions of mussels, fried mozzarella with tomato sauce, snail salad, and caesar salad are popular starters. Eight pastas are offered, plus fifteen entrees from baked fish with a marinara sauce to grilled sirloin with garlic butter. The specialty is veal, served five ways. The wine list is all Italian. In the rear of the large establishment is a pub with TV and pool tables, an outdoor patio, and a regulation bocce court.

  Lunch in summer, Monday-Saturday 11 to 2:30; dinner nightly, 5 to 10 or 10:30.

Las Tapas, 190-A Thames St., Newport. (401) 846-7060.
  Spanish. $8.95 to $14.95.

Newport always sports a new restaurant or two, and one of the latest to attract our attention is this basement storefront featuring Spanish cuisine. A couple of dozen tapas are offered, including one of baby octopus. We eyed two: chicken sate with peanut sauce, and meatballs in tomato and cumin sauce. Entrees range from baked chicken with garlic to sirloin steak with garlic butter. They come with fries and salad. The paella valencia with salad makes a bargain dinner. Coupe alaska and Spanish flan are worthy endings, and there are live flamenco shows on weekends.

  Open Wednesday-Sunday, 11:30 to 10.

Portsmouth

★ Sea Fare Inn, 3352 East Main Road, Portsmouth. (401) 683-0577.
  Contemporary/Continental. $12.95 to $23.95.

From a fifteen-table family restaurant in nearby Bristol to this imposing mansion seating 400 in the lap of luxury, George and Anna Karousos must be doing something right. And they have the food-service industry's Ivy Award to show for it. Set on ten acres, theirs is a magnificent, tasteful Victorian mansion full of grand dining rooms on two floors, each seemingly more elegant than the last. Our favorite is the new upstairs front room with a handsome chandelier, arched windows, skylights, lovely antiques, oriental rugs, art pieces from Florence, and bentwood armchairs at round tables set with white linens, floral china and two wine glasses at each place. "We sleep elsewhere but live here," says Anna, the ebullient hostess. She then calls for "the chef," husband George, who appears from the kitchen to tell about his Archestratios cuisine. It takes its name from the ancient Greek pioneer of gastronomy and, we learn, is basically "light cuisine over a sauce so you can see the quality of what you're eating." It's also basically what Americans call nouvelle and when we visited, the chef was going to press with a coffee-table book, "The Sea Fare's Culinary Treasures." The fare is worthy of the setting. George is known for his seafood (six presentations of lobster, seven of crab and a few, unexpectedly, "from our good old backyard grill," according to the menu). We like the sound of the nightly Archestratios specials: when we were there, chargrilled swordfish with lobster and caviar and finished with a lobster-rosemary sauce, triple loin lamb chop or chargrilled veal rib chop, both with honey-mustard sauce, and filet of sole rosette, shaped like a flower and finished with a tomato-clam sauce. Dishes are garnished with flowers and herbs from the gardens in back and come with fresh breads and hot popovers, mixed salad, and three to five vegetables. Desserts could be galliano torte, white chocolate mousse, strawberries romanoff, and cherries jubilee, with much flambeeing at tableside. The nicely priced wine list contains 350 selections. With their three offspring, George and Anna travel to Europe every winter to keep up with matters culinary.

Lunch, Tuesday-Friday noon to 2; dinner nightly, 5 to 9 or 9:30.

Jamestown

The Bay Voyage, 150 Conanicut Ave., Jamestown. (401) 423-2100.
Continental. $13 to $21.

This century-old hotel was totally renovated in 1986, and it's a beauty, particularly the formal dining rooom with aqua velvet chairs and floral china on white linens. The Bay Room with the original stained-glass windows is where most people ask for tables, but the porch with black wrought-iron furniture is the place to be on a nice day. The menu lives up to the elegant setting. The dozen entrees range from honey-mustard braised salmon with baby shrimp and scallions and seafood sauteed with pink peppercorns and cognac to grilled breast of duck served in a framboise sauce with fresh strawberries and roast rack of lamb provencale. Veal steak with a watercress dijonnaise and tournedos au poivre are other possibilities. The appetizers strike us as overpriced (Belgian endive, apples and gorgonzola cheese in a vinaigrette for $7, for instance). Save money and room instead for key lime pie or amaretto ice cream pie. Sunday brings an excellent brunch and a champagne supper with a choice of four entrees for $14.95.

Lunch, Tuesday-Saturday, 11:30 to 2; dinner nightly except Monday, 6 to 10; Sunday brunch, 11 to 2.

East Bay

Bristol

The Lobster Pot, 119 Hope St. (Route 114), Bristol. (401) 253-9100.
American. $9.50 to $18.95.

Although it's been around since 1929, the Lobster Pot has never been better than since Jeff Hirsh took it over and upgraded both decor and cuisine. A vast place with equally vast windows onto the harbor, it has one of the nicest water views of any restaurant — you almost feel as if you're on a boat. A tiled fireplace, photos from Mystic Seaport, and white linens and china on the tables add to the setting. Dining is by candlelight on traditional Yankee fare — lobster, of course, but also all kinds of fresh seafood, steaks, poultry and veal, including veal oscar. Lobster comes in stew, newburg, saute, salad, fried and in a clambake, as well as in sizes up to three pounds. There's little unusual, although in this area bouillabaisse and shrimp tempura with coconut might qualify. More of the same is available at lunch, as well as seven salads and lunchy things from welsh rarebit to eggs oscar. The wines are mostly French and pleasantly priced. Desserts tend to liqueur parfaits, ice cream puffs and Indian pudding.

Open Tuesday-Saturday 11:30 to 10, Sunday noon to 9.

S.S. Dion, 520 Thames St., Bristol. (401) 253-2884.
Italian. $9.95 to $15.95.

Sue and Steve Dion combined their names for this restaurant with a clamshell logo, a nautical setting and a water view across the street. Japanese carp entertain in a large aquarium as classical music plays and candles flicker in hurricane lamps at well-spaced tables that are colorful with pink and green paper mats. There's outside dining under an awning in summer. Steve is the host and Sue the head chef, preparing stylish seafood and pasta fare — things like scrod pizziaola, sole stuffed with lobster, pollo primavera and seafood scampi with pasta. Veal and poultry come seven different ways; there are steaks and lobsters as well. A spread of fresh dill and cream cheese and crackers awaits diners at each table. Pecan pie is a favorite dessert.

Dinner nightly except Tuesday, 5 to 10, Sunday to 9.

Warren

Nathaniel Porter Inn, 125 Water St., Warren. (401) 245-6622.
New American. $10.95 to $18.95.

Here is an 18th-century sea captain's home, an authentic restoration of yesteryear from the dramatic stenciling to the Colonial uniforms scattered about. The food is highly rated in the three properly historic dining rooms, two small and cozy and one larger and tavern-like. Updates on Colonial favorites include whiskey cream scallops and shrimp in puff pastry, chicken breast with apricots and grand marnier sauce, filet mignon flambeed with cognac and roasted hazelnuts, and pheasant veronique. A house specialty is the chicken filled with oysters and spinach and served with Mary Washington's oyster sauce. Appetizers range from calamari flambeed in drambuie to venison sauteed with prunes, apricots and mushrooms. Among desserts are a white chocolate torte, ice cream cake and strawberry mousse.

Dinner, Monday-Saturday 6 to 10, Sunday 4 to 8.

Bullock's, 50 Miller St., Warren. (401) 245-6502.
American/Continental. $7.25 to $13.95.

Owner Paul Bullock, a native Rhode Islander, tries to feature wines from Sakonnet, beer from Cranston and seafood, of course, from Narragansett Bay — a chauvinistic idea that works. His is a pert, modern place with good-looking pale wooden chairs, bare tables and rondelles created by a professor at Rhode Island School of Design. In winter, a potbelly stove takes the chill out of the air; in summer, a small outdoor dining area with striped canvas deck chairs faces a Water Street scene that can be busy. The all-day menu leans to light fare like steamed mussels, seafood salad roll, seafood antipasto and marsala burger. Among appetizers are conch salad and clam zuppa. The seven entrees range from spinach lasagna with no noodles to charbroiled delmonico steak. The chili and seafood chowder here are good, and prices are gentle.

Lunch, Tuesday-Sunday noon to 2:30; dinner and light fare, Tuesday-Saturday 5 to 10, Sunday and Monday 5 to 9.

Tav Vino, 267 Water St., Warren. (401) 245-0231.
Italian/Seafood. $8.50 to $15.95.

Paul Bullock has renovated this older place in a strange-looking shingled house beside the water into a tavern and restaurant with interesting angles, bare wood floors and beams, and an upstairs with tablecloth dining for special occasions. The main floor is called **The Blue Collar.** Why, we don't know, for the food is anything but. When we were there, the blackboard menu listed dandelion and endive salad with fennel dressing, and salmon and lobster in pesto cream over pasta. Fresh produce and fish are displayed in glass cases, and everything looks spiffy as can be: grilled swordfish, sole florentine and baked scallops. The printed menu is more casual and more Italian, from burgers and clams zuppa to mussels capellini and veal piccata. There's a covered open-air deck beside the water for dining in summer.

Dinner nightly except Monday (also Tuesday in winter), 5 to 10.

Adamsville

$ Abraham Manchester Restaurant and Tavern, Adamsville. (401) 635-2700.
Italian/Seafood. $3.95 to $13.95.

In the center of tiny Adamsville (home of our favorite Stone Bridge Dishes store and a funky general store where we buy aged cheddar called, simply, Adamsville cheese) is this rather large place with a cheerfully rustic atmosphere. It has a divider of glass bottles and twinkling white lights brightening the beamed inner room, a yellow garden room and a large menu categorized by seafood, Italian and American. Although the place and the prices are straight out of the past, the eight-page menu has something for everyone; appetizers vary from tomato juice and fruit cup to chicken wings and clams casino "with bacon." You can get broiled "fish" with Creole sauce, baked stuffed "fish" with newburg sauce, ham steak or hot roast turkey plate, veal cutlet and filet mignon. Mud pie is the dessert specialty. Gourmet it's not, but popular it is. As if they weren't already keeping the local folks well fed, Manchester's opened **Breakfast in the Barn** at the rear, where boosters praise the thick toast, home fries, fruit garnishes and best eggs benedict around.

Breakfast daily, 6:30 to 11:30, weekends to 12:30; lunch and dinner daily, 11:30 to 10.

Tiverton

Provender, 3883 Main Road (Route 77), Tiverton Four Corners.
(401) 624-8084.
American. $4.50 to $6.95.

This is a special food shop and bakery that could have been lifted straight out of the Big Apple. It also has a handful of small tables at which you can sample interesting salads and sandwiches, entrees to go, exotic cheeses, pates, the most divine breads (we always take home a loaf of whole wheat French), coffees and cookies. Owner Cindy Burns wants her food to be remembered for being spicy rather than boring, so you'll find salads like curried chicken with cilantro and golden raisins, fresh corn salad with peppercorns and thyme, and Thai pasta with changing vegetables. Soups could be chili, black bean, tortilla, bleu cheese, and potato-turnip. This is a popular spot for snacking or picking up the makings for a gourmet picnic.

Open daily 9 to 6 in summer, 9 to 5 in fall, Thursday-Sunday in winter. Closed in January.

Block Island

Old Harbor

Winfield's, Corn Neck Road, Old Harbor. (401) 466-5856.
New American. $13 to $18.

As romantic a dining setting as you can get here, this is next door to one of the island's more popular nightspots and operated by the same management. White stucco walls, dark wood wainscoting and beams, stained-glass windows, and a few plants judiciously hung from the rafters make it dark and intimate. An unusual centerpiece on each table is a small bowl of water with flowers and a candle floating in it. Among entrees are Winfield's shrimp, marinated in dark rum and served with a grape and onion chutney, and sirloin umbriago, sauced with red wine, garlic and parsley. The night's specials might include sea scallops sauteed with shrimp and brandy mustard or a tuna steak broiled with herbed mayonnaise. The extensive wine list offers a couple of Australian varieties.

Dinner nightly in season, 6 to 10; reduced schedule through New Year's Eve.

Hotel Manisses, Spring Street, Old Harbor. (401) 466-2421.
New American. $14.50 to $26.

The three dining areas at this nicely refurbished Victorian hotel are highly regarded. Inside near a paneled oak, 23-foot-long bar that once graced a Boston waterfront restaurant is a dining room with floral wallpaper, rattan chairs, and pink-over-burgundy cloths on the tables. Sliding doors lead to a glassed-in garden terrace with ornate white wrought-iron furniture around a fountained garden, and beyond is a half-circle deck with umbrella-topped tables. Fresh vegetables and herbs from the hotel's large garden show up in the soups (often turnip or broccoli) and in many of the main dishes. The dozen entrees include grilled tuna with a red pepper coulis, scallops sauteed with herbs and leeks, chicken breast stuffed with chevre and roasted garlic, roasted duckling with a boysenberry sauce, tournedos with a mustard sauce on eggplant croutons, and bouillabaisse. A whole wheat pizza and a pasta of linguini with concasse of tomatoes and clams are offered under light fare. Baked oysters with slivered almonds and garlic butter, seasonal pate and mussels cataplana are favorite appetizers. Afterward, adjourn to the Upstairs Bar for a cordial or flaming coffee.

Late lunch daily in summer, 2 to 5; dinner nightly, 6 to 10, weekends April to Memorial Day.

The Atlantic Inn, High Street, Old Harbor. (401) 466-5883.
Contemporary. $13.50 to $19.50.

Perched on a grassy hilltop where it catches the best of the island's breezes and views, this large Victorian hotel is popular for breakfast, taken in a multi-windowed room with white cloths and burgundy napkins on the tables and mismatched chairs. But it's also the site for some of the island's more wide-ranging dinners. The hand-written menu might list such main courses as grilled yellowfin tuna teriyaki style, scallop stew with shiitake mushrooms and vegetables in a tomato-based broth, deep-fried chicken breast rolled with spinach and swiss cheese and served with a light ginger sauce, prime rib, and grilled duck breast served with potato-pear salad and grilled vidalia onions. Starters range from New England gazpacho and smoked local fish sampler to Szechuan noodles and a hummus plate. Regional wines are featured on the wine list.

Dinner nightly, 6 to 9 or 10.

New Harbor

Harborside Inn, Water Street at the Ferry Landing, New Harbor.
(401) 466-5504.
American/Continental. $12.95 to $18.95.

Across from the ferry landing, this century-old inn listed on the National Register offers a cheery welcome with its red and white striped umbrellas and colorful window boxes. Dine outside amid geraniums on the terrace and watch the local world go by, or inside in refurbished dining rooms recreating 19th-century nostalgia. The menu is predictable, from baked scrod to sole amandine, except perhaps for the house specialty, scallops giovanni, sauteed in garlic butter and earning a place in posterity with a mention in the New York Times. Chicken primavera, varying veal selections, sirloin steak, and filet mignon are other possibilities, all accompanied by salad bar and baked potato or fries. Clams figure in all but one of the appetizers (chowder, casino, baked stuffed and on the half shell). The other is stuffed mushrooms. Desserts are limited to cheesecake, carrot cake, sundaes, and ice cream.

Lunch daily, 11:30 to 4; dinner nightly, 5 to 10. Open May-September.

Dead Eye Dick's, Payne's Dock, New Harbor. (401) 466-2654.
Seafood. $18 to $25.

"You can't get fresher seafood without getting wet," claims this rustic, no-nonsense establishment, now under the ownership of John Kodama of the restaurant chain based in Mystic. The one-story clapboard building near the Great Salt Pond is particularly favored by boaters, who crowd the outdoor deck as well as the interior. The dinner menu offers entrees like a fried seafood platter, stuffed shrimp, scallops primavera, roast duck, several versions of veal, tournedos, and surf and turf. Smoked mussels is a popular appetizer.

Lunch daily, 11 to 5; dinner, 5 to 11. Open Memorial Day to mid-September.

Smuggler's Cove, Payne's Dock, New Harbor. (401) 466-2828.
American. $11.95 to $20.95.

A long bar and two outdoor decks for lunch and cocktails distinguish Smuggler's from Dead-Eye Dick's, its next-door neighbor. So do dinner specials using shiitake mushrooms, sun-dried tomatoes and goat cheese for a touch of new American cuisine amid the prevailing standard fare. The menu runs the gamut from seafood casserole, grilled swordfish with pesto cream and tomato and linguini clam vongole (billed as the chef's favorite) to prime rib, pan-blackened sirloin steak, and chicken or shrimp fajitas. Escargots in phyllo, sausage quesadilla, and a soup of gazpacho and lobster are good starters. Desserts include cakes, pies and parfaits.

Lunch daily, 11 to 5; dinner, 5 to 11. Open Memorial Day to mid-September.

Block Island Broiler, Water Street, New Harbor. (401) 466-5811.
New American. $15 to $25.

Sprightly red geraniums in window boxes mark this casual storefront piano bar and restaurant, which is known for sophisticated presentation of local seafood and produce. Enlargements of antique postcards of early Block Island scenes grace the walls and evoke local nostalgia. Chef Donna Insalaco, who came from New York's Hubert's and Arizona 206, revealed Southwestern influences in her spirited cooking for the 1989 season. The menu changes, but you could find grilled salmon with lemon-sage sauce, fried soft-shell crabs crusted with blue cornmeal and topped with roasted red pepper sauce, grilled marinated chicken with soy sauce and lemon grass, and rack of lamb with roasted potatoes and fennel salad. A light menu is available in the **Broiler Bar,** where a guitarist entertains on weekends and friends join in on the piano. Connecticut wines are among those on the well-chosen wine list.

Dinner nightly, 6 to 10:30.

What the symbols mean:
Three symbols are used throughout this book to point out places of exceptional merit:

✱ exceptional food.
♥ exceptional atmosphere.
$ exceptional value.

Southwest Vermont

Bennington

* The Four Chimneys Inn and Restaurant, 21 West Road (Route 9), Old Bennington. (802) 447-3500.
French Nouvelle. $13.50 to $21.50.

Thanks to Alex Koks, one of Southern Vermont's premier chefs, the Four Chimneys has been restored to its heyday of the 1950s and 1960s. Two spacious dining rooms on either side of a luxurious lounge are beautifully appointed in shades of pale mauve, pink and rose, from the velvet seats of the chairs to the brocade draperies and matching panels on the walls. Along with an enclosed porch and an outdoor patio, it's considerably bigger than Alex's former hostelry, the Village Auberge in Dorset. But he proved at a weekday lunch he's equal to the challenge: creamed spinach soup and an order of home-cured gravlax were simple and superb, while the roast quail came with a complex brown game sauce, wild rice and a side dish of asparagus scented with nutmeg. Hazelnut praline in a chocolate shell and a trio of refreshing sorbets (raspberry, blueberry and strawberry) ended a memorable meal. Dinner entrees could be sauteed lotte and grilled shrimp in a strong garlic sauce, cornish hen flamed with calvados, sweetbreads and smoked tongue in a madeira sauce, veal steak with glazed onions and beaujolais, filet mignon with foie gras and truffles, and the house specialty, rack of lamb. Good sourdough bread and salad with a champagne vinaigrette come with. Creamed fennel and celery root with rice or a creamy swirl of pureed and rebaked potato might accompany. Dinner is preceded by complimentary cheese fritters, a Koks trademark. To begin, go for Alex's oft-requested cream of mustard soup, a hot country pate with vidalia onions and green peppers, galantine of goose liver mousse, or mushrooms in puff pastry. A chocolate marquise with raspberry sauce, peach cheesecake, apple-almond torte, Bailey's Irish Cream cake, creme caramel, and those sparkling sorbets are among desserts.

Lunch, Monday-Saturday noon to 2; dinner, 5:30 to 9; Sunday brunch, 11:30 to 3. Closed Monday.

* Alldays & Onions, 519 Main St., Bennington. (802) 447-0032.
Regional American. $9.95 to $18.50.

Matthew and Maureen Forlenza named their new restaurant-deli-fish store for an obscure manufacturer of British cars early in the century. Style they have: from the racks of choice specialty foods (including those wonderful chocolates from Mother Myrick's in Manchester) to the lucite pepper grinders with colored peppercorns on the tables, which are set with unusual black octagonal plates and coordinated white octagonal cups. And, oh, what food. A weekday lunch produced a delicate cream of golden squash soup and a delightful dish of nachos made with organic blue corn chips, all kinds of chopped vegetables (but, thank goodness, no refried beans), spicy salsa and melted jack cheese. Another winner was a trio of salads, fettuccine with smoked chicken, tortellini with basil, and red potato, all distinctive. An oversize glass of the house concha y toro white wine for a bargain $2 accompanied. At dinner, when black, white and pink linens dress the tables and tall black halogen lamps are brought out for soft lighting, the room is transformed, and chef Matthew's experience at the Village Auberge and the Barrows House in Dorset shows in a wide-ranging menu. One week's offerings included calves liver with fresh sage and madeira, sauteed sweetbreads with shiitake sauce, grilled tuna with ginger-lime butter, grilled New Zealand venison chop with rosemary sauce, and rack of lamb with honey-thyme sauce. Start with roasted eggplant and red pepper terrine with herbed mayonnaise or smoked salmon and brie with honey cup mustard. Finish with double diablo, a chocolate-lover's dream with a warm bittersweet ganache, or fresh peach pie. There's an interesting wine list with exceptional values. If you find something you really like, buy a bottle to take home at the couple's wine store (in the same room, but entered through a different door — in compliance with Vermont liquor laws). Patrons dine cafe-style amid the specialty-food shelves or outside on a covered patio.

Deli-cafe, Monday-Saturday 7 to 5; dinner, Thursday-Saturday 6 to 8.

✱ Main Street Cafe, 1 Prospect St., North Bennington. (802) 442-3210.
Northern Italian. $9.75 to $17.95.

This tiny storefront cafe (the building was a general store from the 1880s) has had several incarnations, but never as successfully as since it reopened in 1989 as Main Street. Gussied up with sponged peach walls under the deep burgundy pressed-tin ceiling, it is charming with its cafe lights, one hanging over each table, casting a flattering glow. Co-owner Jeff Ben-David, who used to be at the famous Sam's Diner in Saratoga, does most of the cooking, assisted by Lorenzo Daliana, and says "we'll make up any dish you want if we have the ingredients here." His sister, Roberta, takes care of the stunning dried flower arrangements and the fabulous array of antipasto dishes on the bar. Tuxedo-clad waiters serve, each table sports bottles of red and white house wine that you may open and pour as much or as little of as you want into the delicate pink-stemmed wine glasses (and be charged only for what you drink), and it's all quite jolly and "like coming to our home," says Jeff. If you don't choose antipasto, you might try sauteed calamari or a spinach ricotta souffle for two. Pastas, which may be split for appetizers, include rigatoni with romano and parmesan cheeses with broccoli and sausage, and filetto al pomodoro, fettuccine topped with prosciutto, basil, onion, tomato, and garlic. Entrees might be veal nina, a stew with tri-colored peppers over fusili, seafood fra diavolo, bracciola (rolled beef stuffed with cheese, raisins and pine nuts and topped with marsala sauce) or grilled chicken with a basil-lime butter served over pasta. Cannoli, creme caramel, fresh berry tarts with pastry cream, and tirami su with tia maria and Myers's dark rum are among the yummy desserts. There are some good bargains on the wine list.

Dinner, Wednesday-Sunday from 6. Wine and beer only.

Brasserie, 324 County St., Bennington. (802) 447-7922.
French. $3.95 to $9.95.

A cafe with quite a European flair and an expansive outdoor terrace paved in marble, Brasserie was opened in the 1960s by the late great chef, Dionne Lucas, and still bears her mark under Sheela Harden, who took over in the early 1970s. Airy and bright except for a small dark paneled area in the rear, the restaurant has quarry tiles on the floors and plain white walls and ceilings (even the old rough beams have been painted white). Tables are set with Bennington pottery from the Potter's Yard next door. The all-day menu is fairly simple but was innovative ahead of its time. Open-face Danish sandwiches bring a choice of smoked ham, roast beef or herring and sour cream. Our favorite item — something we seldom see in New England — is pissaladiere, a Provence snack of sweet onions cooked until they are almost like jam, topping thick French bread, with anchovies and calamata olives forming a pattern on top. Another fine lunch is the Yard special, a crock of Danish pate sealed with clarified butter, with French bread and a salad of delicate Boston lettuce with a fabulous dressing of olive oil, tarragon vinegar, garlic, lemon juice, dijon mustard and a pinch of salt, bound with eggs. A friend thinks the onion soup gratinee is the best anywhere. We liked the cream of watercress and potato soup, as well as the house quiches, lorraine and spinach, both of the melt-in-the-mouth variety. Thirteen omelets, salads, pate and antipasto plates are offered daily, as are changing specials for heartier appetites, among them chicken livers, the "big soup" of black bean chili, veal stew over rice, and crabmeat pasta. The roulade leontine and Austrian nut roll make magnificent desserts. The wine list is limited but the teas are numerous and properly served in china pots.

Open daily except Tuesday, 11:30 to 8, Sunday from 10:30.

The Villager Restaurant, Main Street, North Bennington. (802) 447-0998. Regional American. $8.95 to $13.95.

Its name and a spare setting of windsor chairs at white-clothed tables not withstanding, this establishment has been serving interesting food to good notices lately. The short menu ranges from fettuccine alfredo and vegetable lasagna to veal sweetbreads with caper-butter sauce and grilled leg of lamb. Spicy citrus chicken and pork tenderloin sauteed with a marsala and black mushroom sauce could be nightly specials. For starters, how about baked brie with fresh herbs, escargots in garlic butter or carpaccio? Desserts are a big deal: perhaps a three-layer moist chocolate cake with mocha frosting, coeur a la creme with framboise sauce or cranberry crisp with fresh whipped cream. The tavern side offers an appealing bistro menu.

Dinner nightly except Monday, 6 to 9. Bistro, 5 to midnight.

Publyck House, Harwood Hill, Route 7A, Bennington. (802) 442-8301. Steaks/Seafood. $6.95 to $18.95.

A popular steak and seafood house in a remodeled barn full of dark wood, stained glass and the warmth of a roaring fire on chilly nights, this local institution has a salad bar that everyone seems to love. Choice Western beef is featured and prime rib is the specialty. A blackboard menu adds things like broiled salmon, roast duckling and lamb chops dijon. Desserts include key lime pie and kahlua cheesecake made by the nuns of New Skete. The new greenhouse at the back is like an indoor garden, with fine views of adjacent apple orchards, the Bennington Monument, and the town and mountains.

Lunch, Monday-Friday 11:30 to 2:30; dinner nightly, 5 to 9 or 10.

Arlington

★ The Arlington Inn, Route 7A, Arlington. (802) 375-6532. Regional American. $13.95 to $18.95.

A pillared, cream-colored Greek Revival mansion with dark red shutters houses the reborn Arlington Inn, expanded by Paul and Madeline Kruzel, he a chef of great acclaim. A fire blazes in the fireplace of the main parlor. On the other side of the grand entry hall are a couple of pretty dining rooms plus an appealing wraparound solarium, all pink and green against a marble floor. Blue willow plates, candles ringed with bobeche roses and mulberry walls create an elegant setting in the interior rooms for Paul's innovative fare, which seems to win awards annually in Taste of Vermont competitions. Maine lobster and corn chowder is the house specialty soup; other starters include lobster cannelloni filled with ricotta and lobster meat, smoked salmon filled with crabmeat and topped with caviar, chicken and plum pate with a plum and orange sauce, and two phyllo triangles, one filled with wild mushrooms and the other with curried chicken and walnuts. Among main courses, consider filet of trout coated with corn flour and topped with pecan sauce, salmon cooked on oak planks with a shrimp-caper butter, scaloppine of veal with fresh strawberries, grilled pork chop with zinfandel-plum barbecue sauce, and T-bone steak with a Kentucky bourbon and mushroom sauce. Inspired desserts could be fresh pumpkin mousse with Myers's rum-eggnog sauce, blackberry bavarian with raspberry coulis, and chocolate truffle cake with maple creme anglaise. The wine list is superb, but horrendously expensive.

Lunch, Wednesday-Saturday 11:30 to 2:30 in season; dinner nightly, 5:30 to 9; Sunday brunch, noon to 2:30.

Manchester

★ Mistral's at Tollgate, Toll Gate Road, Manchester Center. (802) 362-1779. New French. $13.75 to $19.

This is a French restaurant with a difference. Gone is the haute demeanor of the old Toll Gate Lodge with its award-winning, oversize continental menu and sky-high prices. In its place is a less intimidating dining room, a simpler menu and the hospitality of young chef-owners Dana and Cheryl Markey. Both local, they met as kids at the Sirloin Saloon, worked their way through area restaurants and ended up here, living upstairs in a rustic structure that looks like Grandmother's cottage in the woods. The dining room is country pretty with dark woods, lace curtains, blue and white linens, gold-edged white china, and huge picture windows looking onto the flume of Bromley Brook below (one table for two is almost right over the falls). At night the scene is magical, the river and woods illuminated and accented by purple petunias and brilliant impatiens. The menu offers a choice of about a dozen appetizers and an equal number of entrees, most classic French with some nouvelle and northern Italian touches. Smoked trout with Beefeater sauce, grilled game sausage with wild mushrooms, and smoked salmon crepes with caviar are tempting starters. Main courses range from salmon stuffed with scallop mousse and champagne sauce and grilled swordfish with tomato grenobloise to sweetbreads dijonnaise, roast duckling with framboise, veal chanterelles, noisettes of lamb, and chateaubriand for two. Homemade bread, house salad with a choice of dressings and vegetables come with. Dessert could be chocolate tart with raspberry sauce, coupe mistral (coffee ice cream rolled in hazelnuts with hot fudge sauce and frangelico), hot souffles, and fresh fruit sorbets.

Dinner nightly except Wednesday from 6.

♥ The Garden Cafe, Southern Vermont Art Center, Manchester. (802) 362-4220. American. $4.95 to $9.75.

This nifty cafe, halfway up a mountain, has been run for years by people associated with noted restaurateur Alex Koks — first his daughter Marianne, then Alex and lately Arjan VandenHoek, who works at Alex's new Four Chimneys Inn and Restaurant in Old Bennington in the winter. A dining room and outdoor terrace at the back of the Art Center is the setting, with sculptures all around in the sloping gardens, and a view of distant mountains through the birch trees. On a nice day it could not be a more idyllic site for lunch or Sunday brunch. Soups, open sandwiches and salads, with a few daily specials, are the fare, but everything has special touches. The tomato-orange soup, served in a glass bowl with a slice of orange and whipped cream on top, was delicate yet tangy, and the cream of mustard soup superb. Almost everyone we saw was ordering the chicken pot pie with croissant crust, but we tried an open-face sandwich of chicken salad and snow peas and a pasta salad with parmesan cheese and mushrooms. On another occasion, the ragout of herbed mushroom with chicken on rye served with a hearty salad was a hefty plateful and the chef's salad was good but smallish. A duck breast sandwich with olives and gherkins, a skewer of shrimp and scallops with pepper pasta, and sauteed sweetbreads with puff pastry were other interesting choices. Desserts include a wonderful raspberry-strawberry-blueberry mousse, a fruit tart of the same berries plus grapes and a thin layer of chocolate, and ice creams.

Open Tuesday-Sunday, 11:30 to 3, Sunday noon to 3, Memorial Day to mid-October. No credit cards.

The Black Swan, Route 7A, Manchester. (802) 362-3807.
Continental.$14.50 to $19.50.

Richard Whisenhunt, a classically trained French chef who acquired a California touch in Sausalito, and his wife Kathy opened their first restaurant in 1986 in an 18th-century farmhouse almost in front of the Jelly Mill complex. Beamed ceilings and brass chandeliers, windsor chairs and pink linens enhance the country look of the three small dining rooms. A glass of the house Sichel white wine and warm crusty bread preceded a lunch (since discontinued) of wild mushroom soup, an ample and tasty curried chicken salad, and a small pasta carbonara with pancetta and asiago cheese, served with a green salad. The dinner menu is ambitious, starting with chilled strawberry soup, the chef's special pates, oriental duck with Belgian endive, and homemade lobster and chive ravioli. Entrees include grilled chicken with a fresh cilantro salsa, oriental stir-fried shrimp, poached salmon with a roasted red pepper sauce, veal marsala, and sauteed pork loin sauced with triple sec, oranges and toasted almonds. The dessert selection might be white chocolate mousse with raspberry melba sauce, walnut torte, and poached pear in brandy and triple sec with cinnamon.

Dinner from 5:30. Closed Wednesday except in peak season, also Tuesday in winter.

Wilburton Inn, River Road, Manchester. (802) 362-2500.
Regional American. $15 to $18.50.

A gracious inn with an air of grandeur, this baronial red-brick mansion is away from the hubbub on a hilltop overlooking the Battenkill Valley. The rich, dark decor of carved mahogany paneling, moldings, beamed ceilings, carved brass doorknobs, and leaded windows is enhanced by oriental rugs and fine art. The main dining room has a clubby feel with its green leather chairs and dark paneling; the smaller has a tiled fireplace and cabbage rose wallpaper. Dinner might begin with chilled shrimp with salsa verde or remoulade sauce, angel-hair pasta tossed with seafood in romano cheese cream, or three homemade raviolis with seasonal sauces. Main courses could be grilled Atlantic tuna with sweet red pepper butter, shrimp and scallops en brochette, red snapper poached with artichoke hearts, sauteed sweetbreads, rack of lamb with mint-onion confiture, and grilled venison chops with blueberry vinegar-butter sauce. Baked alaska is among the fancy desserts.

Dinner nightly except Tuesday, 6 to 9. Jackets required.

Dina's, Route 7, Manchester Center. (802) 362-4982.
Contemporary American. $14 to $21.

The 1780s farmhouse, part of the Inn at Willow Pond north of town, is a lovely setting for the up-to-date fare of chef-owners Henry and Dina Bronson. Rustic elegance best describes the decor, with much wood and nicely appointed tables. Among the dozen entrees are grilled brook trout with oriental black bean sauce, sea scallops baked in Vermont cider, grilled salmon with wasabi butter, grilled veal chop with sage butter, warm chicken salad with walnut vinaigrette, and rack of lamb flavored with thyme. Starters include French onion soup with apple brandy, wild mushrooms and goat cheese in phyllo, chilled veal and spinach roulade, sweetbread pot pie, and polenta with tomato, grilled eggplant and tapenade.

Breakfast daily, 7:30 to 10:30; dinner, 5:30 to 9 or 10.

Dorset

★ Dorset Inn, Church and Main Streets, Dorset. (802) 867-5500.
New American. $14 to $19.50.

Interesting, creative food has been emanating from the kitchen of this venerable inn in recent years. Fresh flowers, classical music and candlelight enhance the mood of the pleasant main dining room, outfitted predominantly in blue with frilly white curtains screening the windows and folk-art paintings on the walls. Chef Sissy Hicks, co-innkeeper with Gretchen Schmidt, changes her menu seasonally. Pre-dinner drinks are served with a basketful of french-fry-size cheese sticks. Sauteed oysters with balsamic vinaigrette, crabmeat mousse with a cucumber-mustard dill sauce, and warm Vermont goat cheese with radicchio and endive make fine appetizers. Crusty French bread and green salads with excellent stilton or basil-vinaigrette dressings accompany. The calves liver, served rare with crisp bacon and slightly underdone slices of onion, is superb. Fresh trout, deboned but served with its skin still on, is laden with sauteed leeks and mushrooms. These come with an assemblage of vegetables, including red-skin potatoes with a dollop of sour cream, and crisp cauliflower, broccoli and yellow squash. Other entrees could be chicken stuffed with brie and coriander in pear and cider sauce, veal medallions with a lime-ginger sauce, grilled duck breast with brown raspberry sauce, roast boneless quail stuffed with chicken and veal farci on wild rice, and broiled shrimp and scallops with aioli sauce. Pies, wild rice pudding and chocolate terrine with raspberry sauce are on the dessert menu. A favorite fall dessert is Sissy's cider sorbet with spiced wine sauce. For lighter fare, all the locals head for the inn's taproom. Among the intriguing selections: warm chicken tenderloin salad, crisp garlic potato skins filled with avocado sauce, baked eggplant crepes, sauteed chicken livers on puff pastry with madeira tomato sauce, and a chilled goat cheese and walnut fettuccine.

Lunch daily in summer and fall, noon to 2; dinner nightly, 6 to 9. Taproom menu, Sunday-Thursday 5:30 to 10.

★ Village Auberge, Main Street, Dorset. (802) 867-5715.
French Nouvelle. $16.50 to $21.

Former chef-owner Alex Koks was a tough act to follow, but chef Richard Schafer is tailoring the inn's traditional French menu to his own style, and the clientele is responding. Striking built-in cabinets displaying china are a focal point in the attractive, restful dining room with a large bay window at the far end. Tables are covered with moss green linens and topped with pretty botanical service plates. A piping-hot cheese fritter is brought to each diner along with the menu. Among appetizers, the rabbit terrine comes with hazelnuts, pine nuts and pistachios, the cold poached salmon with two mayonnaises, and the snails and mussels in puff pastry. Excellent sourdough bread and mixed green salad with zesty roquefort or vinaigrette dressings precede the main course. We savored the veal medallions with wild mushrooms and the sauteed sweetbreads with morels and cream, both accompanied by broccoli, tomatoes, spinach with nutmeg, and duchess potatoes. Other possibilities are two or three seafood dishes, game in season, roasted rabbit with endive and cream, and grilled filet of beef with lemon-ginger sauce. Desserts include a fancy assortment of sorbets and ice creams, a dense chocolate-orange almond torte made with ground almonds instead of flour, a fruit tart on a cheesecake base, and an apple spice cake. The newly expanded bar with dark green wainscoting and beams offers a limited tavern menu with appealing choices.

Dinner nightly except Monday, 6 to 8:30 or 9, Saturday only in winter. Tavern, nightly except Saturday in summer, Wednesday-Friday in winter.

Barrows House, Main Street, Dorset. (802) 867-4455.
Regional American. $11.95 to $19.50.

With the attractive grounds outside (flowers in summer, snow in winter), the setting is enchanting in the new greenhouse dining room here. The larger main room with ruffled curtains, floral china, and dark green flowered and ferned wallpaper is more traditional. The menu, which changes seasonally, is augmented by nightly specials. We started with smoked tuna with caper and red onion creme fraiche and a tartlette of smoked scallops and mussels with scallions and red peppers. A small loaf of bread and a garden salad with a honey-mustard dressing came next. The sirloin of beef with four-peppercorn sauce and calves liver with caramelized onions and smoked bacon, both delicious, were accompanied by a platter of vegetables served family style, vegetables being a perennial Barrows House strong point. On this night they were spaghetti squash Creole, lemon-scented broccoli, carrot puree with maple, and risotto with fennel and red peppers. Other entrees might be drunken chicken (sober version also available), grilled swordfish on bell pepper purees, rack of lamb with rosemary sauce on a bed of ratatouille, and sauteed escalopes of veal and rock shrimp with tomatoes and raclette. A huckleberry tart and cappuccino ice cream appealed from the dessert list.

Dinner nightly, 6 to 9; weekends only in November. No smoking.

* Chantecleer, Route 7, East Dorset. (802) 362-1616.
Swiss/French Provincial. $15.95 to $25.

The food is consistent and the atmosphere rustically elegant, though service has been a problem lately at what has been considered the best restaurant around. Swiss chef-owner Michel Baumann acquired the contemporary-style restaurant fashioned from an old dairy barn in 1981. Appetizers include a highly rated Danish pate with lingonberries, bunderfleisch (Swiss air-dried beef), stuffed veal breast with raspberry sauce, crab and shrimp with chilled pasta, and grilled seafood sausage with saffron sauce. Entrees are strong on veal dishes, the four running from wiener schnitzel to zurichoise. Others could be braised pork and sweetbreads, frog's legs with garlic butter, medallions of turkey wrapped in sausage and sun-dried tomatoes, roast quail madras, roast duckling with apricot-walnut sauce, or rack of lamb coated with herbs and garlic. Favored desserts are chocolate fondue, coupe matterhorn, bananas foster, and Swiss Tobler chocolate cake. A number of Swiss wines are included on the reasonably priced wine list, and Swiss yodeling music may be heard on tape as background music.

Dinner, Wednesday-Sunday 6 to 10.

Londonderry/South Londonderry

$ Three Clock Inn, Middletown Road, South Londonderry. (802) 824-6327.
Continental. Table d'hote, $13.25 to $18.50.

Heinrich Tschernitz and his wife Frances have been running the Three Clock Inn for more than 22 years. They haven't changed much about the decor or the menu over the years, nor do they need to. Their inn in the little white house with black shutters, up a steep hill from the center of South Londonderry, remains the favorite of many. Two centuries old, the house harbors a cozy parlor where guests can relax near the hearth with a drink before dinner, and three small dining rooms seating 50 people (plus three tables on the porch in summer). All through the house and kitchen are hippopotomi in many guises, most brought by local customers to reinforce the painting of the hippopotomus in the living room ("I put it there so people would be amused," explains the chef). The meal price includes most appetizers and desserts — surely a bargain for a carefully prepared four-course meal these days. Among appetizers are pate maison, herring in sour cream, eggplant caponata, peppers with anchovy filets, and soup du jour, which could be anything from black bean in winter to onion gratinee or vichyssoise in summer. Add surcharges for escargots, scampi or smoked Irish salmon. The ten entrees range from capon valdostana (stuffed with ham and cheese) to lamb chops or filet mignon au poivre. Others are three veal dishes, duckling a l'orange, sirloin steak, frog's legs, and scampi. Heinrich makes a couple of specials like venison ragout with pasta or sauteed baby pheasant every night. Salad follows the main course, and different vegetables are prepared nightly. For dessert you can have strawberries romanoff, peach melba, pear helene, cassata, or cheese. By the way, the only time you see prices is on the menu posted at the door; if paying an extra $6.75 for a special appetizer throws you for a loop, check it carefully. Otherwise, enjoy fine food at prices out of the past.

Dinner by reservation, Tuesday-Sunday 6 to 9:30. No credit cards. Open Memorial Day to mid-October and Dec. 20-March.

The Swiss Inn, Route 11, Londonderry. (802) 824-3442.
Swiss. $13.25 to $20.

Very popular locally is the recently renovated dining room in this Alpine-style motel run most personally by Hans and Lisa Gegenschatz. Lisa and another Swiss chef do the cooking, which is classic Swiss from the geschnetzeltes (veal a la Swiss) to beef stroganoff made from filet mignon. The salmon mousse appetizer is a steal, as is the homemade fettuccine with rich creamy gruyere sauce. Entrees run the gamut from chicken lugano, a specialty of the Italian side of Switzerland, to shrimp with pernod. Beef fondue with four sauces is offered in winter, roast duck in the fall, and wiener schnitzel at least once a week. Everyone loves the homemade spaetzle, and many have tried to copy Lisa's vinaigrette (made from honey and lime) that dresses the salad. Chocolate truffle cake, harvest cheesecake and meringue glace are favored desserts.

Dinner, Thursday-Tuesday 6 to 8:30. Closed mid-October to mid-December and April to mid-June.

Landgrove

Nordic Inn, Route 11, Landgrove. (802) 824-6444.
Continental/Scandinavian. $10.95 to $18.95.

The striking solarium dining room has a soaring cathedral ceiling and skylights, brick floor, two dining levels, and huge windows looking onto the lawns and birch-filled forests. Cane and bentwood chairs flank tables with pink linens; appointments have that clean Scandinavian look. Chef Peter Cassan, son of a chef in France, has added French dishes while keeping a few Swedish specialties. Recorded classical music played during Sunday brunch as we enjoyed hot French bread, an olive, tomato and celery soup, a special shrimp and crab souffle, and Swedish hash with a fried egg, pickled beets and a distinct bite. On another occasion we found Peter's country pate of pork and calves liver and a duck liver pate phenomenal. Some of the Scandinavian brunch items are available as appetizers at dinner. The entrees are mostly classic French: sauteed salmon slices with a sorrel sauce, medallions of veal with a brandy sauce, lamb chops with mint hollandaise in an artichoke bottom, and pepper steak flambeed with cognac. A frozen hazelnut souffle with raspberry coulis, white chocolate mousse, profiteroles, and cheesecake with kiwi are among the delectable desserts.

Dinner nightly, 6 to 10; Sunday brunch, 11 to 3.

Weston

The Inn at Weston, Route 100, Weston. (802) 824-5804.
Regional American. $13.50 to $22.50.

Innkeepers Jeanne and Bob Wilder have expanded the dining room of this much-admired inn fashioned from an 1848 farmhouse. A Culinary Institute-trained chef, Jay McCoy, is responsible for the fare in the airy new dining room, quite chic with small hurricane lamps, floral wallpaper and beige over white linens, as well as in the older dining room with barn siding and an amiable pub with a fireplace. Among entrees are grilled chicken on a cilantro-accented black bean sauce, shrimp stuffed with crabmeat and sweet peppers, roast duckling with a port wine and raspberry sauce, medallions of lamb with shiitake mushrooms, steak au poivre, and changing preparations of veal and fresh seafood. Start with the acclaimed duck soup with Chinese cabbage, oriental pasta salad or pate maison. The dessert tray offers cheesecakes, fruit-filled cakes and tarts, and an abundance of chocolate items. Tuesday is Vermont Night, when four-course dinners with a local twist are available for $12.95.

Dinner nightly from 5:30.

Southeast Vermont

Brattleboro

∗ T.J. Buckley's, 132 Elliot St., Brattleboro. (802) 257-4922.
Regional American. All Entrees, $20.

Chef-owner Michael Fuller bills his as "uptown dining" in a black, red and silver diner with tables for up to twenty lucky patrons. The setting is charming, the food creative and, amazingly, this city slicker from Cleveland who came to Vermont fifteen years ago to apprentice with Rene Chardain does everything himself, except for some of the prep work and serving. He offers four entrees nightly at a fixed price of $20, which he's quick to point out includes rolls, vegetable, and a zippy salad of four lettuces including endive, radicchio and marinated peppers dressed with the house vinaigrette. At our visit, the choice was roasted chicken coated with goat cheese and sun-dried tomatoes on a bed of fennel and Italian sausage, pine nut-coated swordfish with roasted garlic and mashed potato with local feather turnips, poached Norwegian salmon topped with a puree of Maine rock shrimp and coriander, and sliced tenderloin of beef simmered in red wine with domestic and shiitake mushrooms and cracked peppercorns. Appetizers might include a country pate of veal and pork, and a four-cheese tart that resembles a pizza. For dessert, there might be a lime macadamia tart that's very tart and a rich but not terribly sweet chocolate-hazelnut torte. The wine list is priced from $17 to $42. Red roses in profusion grace the tables in wintertime, and other flowers the rest of the year, adding to this very special place.

Dinner, Tuesday-Sunday 6 to 10. Beer and wine only.

Peter Havens, 32 Elliot St., Brattleboro. (802) 257-3333.
Continental. $9.75 to $16.25.

"Established 1989," says the logo of this sprightly dining room opened by chef Gregg Van Iderstine and Thom Dahlen, who opened Taft's up the street seven years earlier. The new venture borrows the first and middle names of Gregg's father. Theirs is a handsome white room with high ceilings, cane and chrome chairs, beige-clothed tables with pottery lamps crafted in Marlborough, and track lights aimed at stunning artworks by an artist-friend of Thom's. A large plant hangs from a recessed skylight. The short menu emphasizes fresh seafood, perhaps poached grouper with lemon-cilantro bechamel sauce, baked red snapper beurre blanc, and trout amandine. Other possibilities include two pastas, lemon chicken with capers and pine nuts, veal saltimbocca, tournedo and quail with choron sauce, and grilled loin lamb chops with mushrooms, shallots and cream. Pan-fried wontons, mussels mariniere and smoked trout with horseradish sauce are good starters. Among desserts are caramel custard, strawberry-rhubarb pie, and assorted cheesecakes made by Thom's mother. The chocolate-butternut sauce that tops the ice cream proved so popular that the owners bottled it and sold 300 jars at Christmas.

Dinner, Monday-Saturday 6 to 10.

$ The Common Ground, 25 Elliot St., Brattleboro. (802) 257-0855.
Natural Foods. $2.35 to $12.

Call it funky, beatnik, hip, whatever. This enduring meeting ground that's a collectively run workers' cooperative dating to 1971 attracts a laid-back crowd and is not for the faint of heart. For one thing, it's a long climb up to the high-ceilinged second floor of an old factory building. For another, once there you're apt to be on your own. It's seat yourself, mostly help yourself, relax, and enjoy. Beyond the entry room where you place your order from the extensive list of daily specials is an airy dining room with pictures askew on the walls and a solarium with views onto the street. For lunch, we much enjoyed a vegetable stir-fry over brown rice and topped with tamari-ginger sauce and something called haba a la catalana, a concoction of white beans with pepper, onions, pimento, pine nuts, olive oil, and who knows what-all on saffron rice with sauteed tofu, peppers, onions, peas, lemon, and tomatoes. The possibilities are exotic and endless: perhaps aduki pate and crackers, sea vegetable salad (made with Maine seaweed and tossed with vegetables), burritos, cashew burger, avocado meltdown, and grilled tofu sandwich. The dinner menu adds vegetarian, fresh fish and scallops specials, and more vegetable stir-fries. There's a self-service bar for salads, soups, cider, coffee, mineral water and the like. Soy milk shakes, ginger frappes and banana yogurt shakes are more in evidence than beer and wine.

Lunch, Wednesday-Monday 11:30 to 2:30, Sunday 10:30 to 1:30; dinner, 5:30 to 9. Closed Tuesday.

$ Shin La, 57 Main St., Brattleboro. (802) 257-5226.
Korean. $6 to $8.

This is a family operation through and through, one cherished by locals who are into exotic food. They've supported the restaurant run by Yisoon Kim and her husband, Taemo, through three name changes and moves into larger quarters in town over the last ten years. Interesting Korean vegetarian items are the specialty. The Kims say the yakimandoo, a pan-fried dumpling, is the single most popular item. We've also heard good things about the noodle salad with egg, cucumber, turkey, and crabmeat on top of noodles with mustard sauce. On the all-day menu you'll also find bool ko ki, marinated sirloin sliced thin, seared and served with cucumber salad, kim chi and rice. The Kims present a Tuesday night special of Japanese sushi, using fresh tuna, shrimp, octopus, vegetables and the like. Have some ginseng tea or a Kirin beer with. Those who would rather eat deli style will find sandwiches (dagwoods, reubens, hot pastrami, ham and swiss), grinders, and spaghetti with meatballs. Mr. Kim made up the restaurant's name, derived from one of the three sections of Korea from a thousand years ago. The place seats 50 at a mix of wood and copper booths and tables, including three in a little raised balcony in the window.

Open Monday-Saturday, 11 to 9. Beer and wine only.

Jolly Butcher's, Route 9, West Brattleboro. (802) 254-6043.
Steaks/Seafood. $6.25 to $25.95.

Many is the time we have stopped with family in tow on the way home from a day's skiing at this lively and casual steakhouse with an open hearth. The ravenous eaters like the salad bar and array of slice-your-own breads. Everyone likes the pleasantly priced steaks, chicken, seafood and teriyaki dishes, alone or in combinations (the mixed grill is shrimp, chicken and small steak kabob). Mud pie and the locally made Page's ice creams are the desserts of choice.

Lunch, daily 11:30 to 2:30; dinner, 5 to 10, Sunday noon to 9.

Newfane

★ The Four Columns Inn, 250 West St., Newfane. (802) 365-7713.
French Nouvelle. $19 to $24.

The culinary tradition launched here by Rene Chardain is continued — even enhanced — by Jacques Allembert and his head chef, Gregory Parks, who was sous chef under Rene. Beamed timbers from the original barn, a huge fireplace, antiques on shelves and walls, and tiny white lights aflickering make the dining area at the rear of the inn a charming setting. Add the magnifcent old French pewter bar decorated with country things like calico hens and an inventive menu, and you have one of the premier dining experiences in southern Vermont. Blackboard specials supplement the seasonal dinner menu. Appetizers seem to get more interesting with every visit: lately, wild boar pate, carrot and spinach mousse with shrimp, and spinach fettuccine with mozzarella, shiitake mushrooms, roasted peppers, and cream. It's hard to choose among such entrees as broiled salmon with poblano chili sauce, baked rabbit with sage and chardonnay cream, grilled pheasant with pears and cream, medallions of pork with mustard and chestnuts, and loin of venison with juniper and cranberries. The chicken is likely to be stuffed with basmati rice, mozzarella, hazelnuts, and sun-dried tomatoes. Desserts change nightly (perhaps raspberry cream tart, tirami su or homemade ice creams like calvados with butternut or chocolate macadamia sauce). You can stop in the lounge to pick one from the cart, even if you haven't dined at the inn.

Dinner nightly except Tuesday, 6 to 9. Closed April and November.

The Old Newfane Inn, Route 30, Newfane. (802) 365-4427.
Swiss/Continental. $14.75 to $25.50.

Chef-owner Eric Weindl, who trained in a Swiss hotel, cooks at this classic New England inn dating to 1787. The food is as predictable as when we first went out of our way to dine here nearly two decades ago during a ski trip to Mount Snow. A few daily specials spark up the enormous printed menu, which remains virtually unchanged over the years and lists most of the standards, starting with a slice of melon through marinated herring and escargots bourguignonne to Nova Scotia salmon. Capon florentine, duckling a l'orange or with peppercorns, veal marsala, brochette of beef bordelaise, frog's legs provencale, shrimp scampi, and pepper steak flamed in brandy are a few of the entrees, accompanied by seasonal vegetables and salad. Chateaubriand "served the proper way" and rack of lamb bouquetiere are offered for two. Featured desserts include peach melba, Bavarian chocolate cream pie, cherries jubilee, and pear helene. The decor matches the vision of what people think a New England inn dining room should look like. Narrow and beamed with a wall of windows onto the green, it has white lace curtains, pink and white linens, lamps on the window tables, shiny dark wood floors, floral wallpaper, and a massive fireplace.

Dinner nightly except Monday, 6 to 9, Sunday 5 to 8 or 8:30. Closed November to mid-December and most of May.

South Newfane

★ The Inn at South Newfane, South Newfane. (802) 348-7191.
New American. $16.95 to $19.95.

Lisa Borst, who loves to cook, reigns over the big kitchen at her parents' inn. Always looking for that extra oomph, she gets drenched picking blackberries early in the morning from her extensive vegetable, herb and fruit garden out back, and she makes preserves, purees and sauces (even watermelon pickles) from her produce to carry over to winter. Her summer menu might feature shanks of spring lamb with tomatoes, onion and lots of garlic, California duckling served with a ginger oriental sauce, Pacific coho salmon with bearnaise sauce, and a loin veal chop with sorrel sauce. We began with a country pate of game, veal and pork and a dish of escargots, leeks and mushrooms in a garlic cream with Cajun tasso. The roast breast of pheasant with lavender-garlic sauce and the oven-roasted poussin on a coulis of red pepper were unforgettable. A light grand marnier cheesecake and ginger-peach ice cream were refreshing desserts. In other seasons you might find prime rib of buffalo, rack of lamb with red wine vinegar and rosemary, an apple-walnut salad with a mint-strawberry vinaigrette, and a fig and cinnamon sorbet. From the French bread at the meal's beginning to the chocolate truffle at the end, everything is homemade and served in a serene, candlelit dining room with comfortable bow or Queen Anne wingback chairs, beige linens, crystal water glasses, and proper large wine glasses. The Mikasa china is rose colored, and the wallpaper features big tulips in beiges and mauves, with matching valances and draperies.

Dinner nightly except Monday, 5:30 to 9 or 9:30. Reservations required by 4. No credit cards.

Wilmington

The Hermitage, Coldbrook Road, Wilmington. (802) 464-3511.
Continental. $13 to $21.45.

Although the Hermitage has greatly expanded its dining facility with a smashing rear addition, its menu rarely changes — it doesn't have to. Innkeeper Jim McGovern, one of whose many talents is cooking, specializes in game birds that he raises on the inn's property. He also is a connoisseur of wines. Combine the three interests and he has a going concern indeed. From the relatively small dinner menu you can get filet of sole, boneless trout, frog's legs provencale, veal marsala, wiener schnitzel, or filet mignon. But who wouldn't opt for the nightly game specials — perhaps pheasant, quail, duck, goose or partridge? For such a feast you should try something special from the prize-winning wine cellar containing 40,000 bottles, remarkable for their quality and variety. At one memorable lunch we sampled the mushroom soup with a rich game pate on toast triangles plus a house specialty, four mushroom caps stuffed with caviar and garnished with a pimento slice and chopped raw onion on a bed of ruby lettuce. Chicken salad was a winner: an ample plateful colorfully surrounded by sliced oranges, apples, green melon, strawberries, grapes, and tomatoes on a bed of bibb lettuce. The portions were large enough that we could not be tempted by such desserts as hot Indian pudding, maple parfait made with Hermitage syrup or fresh strawberries on homemade shortcake. Meals may be served outside on a marble patio, inside on an intimate sun porch or in one of the two small, elegant dining rooms, or in the rear addition with its collection of Delacroix prints, upholstered chairs at widely spaced tables, huge windows looking onto the grounds, a grand piano, and hand-carved decoys everywhere.

Lunch weekdays in season, noon to 2; brunch weekends and holidays, 11 to 3; dinner nightly, 5 to 11, Sunday noon to 11.

Le Petit Chef, Route 100, Wilmington. (802) 464-8437.
French/International. $13 to $21.50.

This low white 1850 farmhouse smack up against the road to Mount Snow harbors three intimate dining rooms, a spacious lobby abloom with spring flowers in midwinter, and an inviting lounge. Tables are set with white cloths, blue napkins, handsome white china, and oil lamps. Chef-owner Betty Hillman, whose mother Libby is the cookbook author, studied in France. Her appetizers might include marinated goat cheese en croute, home smoked beef with maple-mustard sauce, orange-scented sea scallop salad, lemon linguini with smoked salmon and black caviar, and crabmeat imperial in pasta shells. Among entrees you might find fish of the day poached Mediterranean style, duckling with juniper-honey sauce and cranberry chutney, two versions of veal (cream or herbs), filet of beef with a five-pepper sauce, and noisettes of venison with red currant sauce and chutney. Fresh fruit tarts, chocolate torte, and special ice creams and sorbets are among the homemade desserts.

Dinner nightly except Tuesday, 6 to 9 or 10.

Mainstreets, West Main Street, Wilmington. (802) 464-3183.
American/Italian. $8.25 to $17.95.

A casual menu featuring soups, salads, quiches, special entrees, and desserts is served all day in a striking rear dining room with skylights and colorful wallpaper, beamed ceiling, fans, and hanging plants. The dinner menu adds charbroiled swordfish, shrimp scampi, veal piccata, and steak au poivre. But things like three-alarm chili, Viennese escargots (served in a warm roll with a creamy garlic sauce), neptune salad, barbecued ribs and, of course, burgers are de rigeur here. Dark wood tables with white napkins lend an informal air, as do the front bar and open lounge area. Mainstreets is popular with skiers and others seeking a middle ground between fast food and gourmet dining.

Lunch, Monday-Friday 11:30 to 3, Saturday and Sunday to 4; dinner nightly, 5 to 9 or 10.

The White House, Route 9, Wilmington. (802) 464-2135.
Continental. $12.50 to $17.95.

Looking something like a Southern plantation atop a hill, the White House takes full advantage of its commanding view for dining. Its devotees have a tough time deciding whether they enjoy more the Sunday brunch or a sunset dinner. You can dine in one of several paneled Colonial rooms, the large windowed lounge, or outside on a patio. The setting is perhaps more inspired than the menu — omelets and eggs benedict for brunch; coquilles St. Jacques, wiener schnitzel, duck a l'orange, frog's legs provencale, veal piccata, and saltimbocca for dinner. If the food strikes some as unexciting, who cares? The Boston Herald once called the White House "one of the most romantic places in the world."

Dinner nightly, 6 to 9; Sunday brunch, 11 to 2:30.

West Dover

✶ The Inn at Sawmill Farm, Route 100, West Dover. (802) 464-8131.
Regional American/Continental. $19.50 to $28.

One of New England's finest inns also has one of its finest dining rooms, thanks to engineer-turned-chef Brill Williams, who has joined his parents as innkeepers. The three candlelit dining rooms are as smashing as the rest of the inn and display the owners' collection of folk art. Tables are set with white linens, heavy silver and pretty flowered china. And, for the ultimate in decor coordination, the waitresses wear long peasant-style dresses made of the same print as the rose and ivory wallpaper in the main dining room. We like best the Greenhouse Room, a colorful plant-filled oasis. The menu is rather larger and more ambitious than one might expect, comprising a dozen appetizers and twenty entrees, many of the favorites remaining on the list year after year. For starters, we were tempted by salmon mousse with black American caviar, sauteed quail, and shrimp in beer batter, but chose the thinly sliced raw prime sirloin with a shallot and mustard sauce and a dry cured smoked salmon. Delicate green salads and a basket of good hot rolls and crisp, homemade melba toast followed. Entrees range from Indonesian curried chicken breasts to steak au poivre flambe. Duck is prepared two ways and frog's legs come with sliced truffles. Pork is sauced with cognac, cream and walnuts, and veal loin steak with morels and calvados sauce. We found outstanding both the rabbit stew and the sweetbreads chasseur garnished with french-fried parsley. Desserts are masterful, especially chocolate-whiskey cake with grand marnier sauce and bananas romanoff. The espresso is strong, and better-than-usual decaffeinated coffee is served in a silver pot. The inn's wine cellar has been ranked one of the top 100 in America by Wine Spectator.

Dinner nightly by reservation, 6 to 9. Jackets required. No credit cards.

Two Tannery Road, 2 Tannery Road, West Dover. (802) 464-2707.
American/Continental. $14.50 to $22.

Once the home of Theodore Roosevelt's son and used by the president as a retreat, this historic house-turned-restaurant has been renovated to perfection. A dark oak and mahogany bar from the original Waldorf-Astoria Hotel is the focus of the bar-lounge, where a jukebox plays oldies like Glenn Miller. The Garden Room in back, with a wall of windows looking onto it from the beamed and stenciled Fireplace Room, has large windows on three sides onto the spotlit lawn and trees. Copper pans and pots glow on the brick fireplace, and folk art is everywhere. The menu includes such appetizers as smoked seafood medley, baked artichoke hearts and Acadian pepper shrimp. Soup of the day could be tomato-basil or salmon bisque; the cold cucumber with dill is particularly good. Entrees run the gamut from three versions of chicken (including one stuffed with four cheeses and a leek cream sauce) to grilled lamb chops with mint jelly. Stuffed shrimp, veal kiev, roast Long Island duck, grilled medallions of veal with homemade garlic mayonnaise, and steak au poivre are other choices. We can vouch for a couple of the specialty veal dishes from past visits. Favorite desserts include apple crisp, chocolate mousse cake and homemade peanut-butter chocolate-chip ice cream.

Dinner, Tuesday-Sunday 6 to 10. Open Monday of holiday weeks. Closed mid-April to Memorial Day and first three weeks of November.

Elsa's European Deli & Cafe, Route 100, West Dover. (802) 464-8425.
Continental. $6.95 to $10.95.

This sprightly little place offers a few chairs facing a right-angle counter, tables beside the food shelves and in an airy front room, and outdoor decks in front by the road and in back by the stream. The open kitchen where copper pots hang is bordered by a multi-colored awning. Posters, lots of tile, a wood stove, and shelves with pastas, pickles and such for sale add to the cafe feeling. A blackboard lists many specials to supplement the menu, which is comprised mostly of sandwiches, burgers, omelets, and salads. Bratwurst with potato salad, barbecued ribs, chili, and cream of mushroom soup might be specials. For a winter lunch we enjoyed a cup of wild rice florentine soup, duck liver pate with a delicious cumberland sauce served with crusty warm French bread, and an unusually bountiful salade nicoise. Desserts could be tollhouse cookie pie and chocolate-chip cheesecake. Chef Mark Longo's blackboard dinner specials the day we were there included fried flounder, veal marsala and beef brochettes.

Open daily except Tuesday, 11:30 to 9. No credit cards.

Doveberry Inn, Route 100, West Dover. (802) 464-5652.
Regional American. $15 to $21.

The sign outside the inn says "Home cooking and old-fashioned charm," but when did you last make duck confit on mixed greens or salmon tartare, fresh and smoked salmon with capers, onion and egg? Chef Kathleen Snyder is a graduate of the New England Culinary Institute, and her repertoire is ever-changing. Soups might be cream of carrot, bean with bacon, or mushroom and wild rice; appetizers, rumaki, baked brie with seasonal fresh fruit, or fettuccine alfredo. Dinner entrees include New York strip steak with a choice of sauces, pork chops with apples and calvados, grilled duck with honey-mustard sauce, scampi in a pungent pesto sauce, and grilled tuna with fresh salsa and avocado. The house salad of many greens, including radicchio and spinach, is served with a choice of house dressings. With a cup of the good Green Mountain coffee, try a Doveberry devil (a fudge nut brownie with Ben and Jerry's ice cream, hot fudge sauce and whipped cream) or an apple pocket with caramel sauce. A collection of pink depression glass is on the shelves and the red hurricane lamps and green napkins pick up the colors in the tartan carpet covering the floors of the two beamed, country-style dining rooms.

Lunch, Saturday and Sunday during foliage season; dinner, Wednesday-Sunday 6 to 9:30 or 10.

West Wardsboro

* Brush Hill, Route 100, West Wardsboro. (802) 896-6100.
Contemporary American. $16.75 to $21.95.

Michael Sylva, who trained with Jasper White in his famed Boston restaurant, opened his own restaurant with wife Lee in 1989 in a rural, rustic place that used to be the Old Barn restaurant. It's so small one wonders how they can make a go of it, Michael having to work in what Lee calls "a kitchen the size of a shoebox." An open, twelve-foot-wide brick fireplace is the central feature of the candlelit dining room, which seats 25 at pink-over-white clothed tables amid a backdrop of artworks and oriental rugs on old pine floors. Lee handwrites the night's menu in her distinctive cursive. A gutsy starter is new wave antipasto (a selection of roasted and grilled items, like artichoke, asiago cheese and a small open-face sandwich on sourdough farmhouse bread doused with freshly pressed olive oil topped with a slice of scamorza cheese, roasted red peppers, half a head of roasted garlic, and black olives). Others could be lobster-corn fritter with red pepper coulis, spinach pasta with garlic-toasted pine nuts, and caesar salad with pieces of warm garlic toast. The half-dozen entrees when we were there were pan-flashed shrimp with ginger and snap peas, smoked pork chop with oyster mushrooms, osso buco with risotto milanaise, yellowfin tuna with basil and sun-dried tomatoes, tenderloin with black bean sauce, and rack of lamb with garlic and rosemary. Lee handles the desserts, things like fresh fruit tarts, black bottom pie, and frozen zabaglione with chocolate and espresso. She also put together the wine list, an entertaining photo album interspersing labels and personal pictures, and containing good values.

Dinner, Wednesday-Sunday 6 to 10. No smoking.

Stratton

Birkenhaus Restaurant, Stratton Mountain, Stratton. (802) 297-2000.
Continental. $16 to $19.60.

The decor of this institution at the foot of Stratton Mountain is early 1960s American-Tyrolean, comfortable but elegant in muted earth tones. The menu changes daily, but features wiener schnitzel, as befits the background of owners Jan and Ina Dlouhy, who specialize in French, Austrian and Czechoslovakian cuisine. Gravlax, blinis, confit of duck, and baba ghanoush might turn up on the appetizer list. Entrees could be muscovy duck breast veronique, calves liver with shallots, brook trout with shrimp butter and fresh rosemary, baked salmon with salmon roe beurre blanc, and veal scaloppine with shiitake mushrooms. Apple strudel, linzer and sacher tortes, creme caramel, pear helene, and homemade sorbets are worthy endings. Czech specialties are featured on Tuesdays.

Dinner nightly, 6 to 9; weekend brunch in summer, 11 to 2.

Jamaica

Three Mountain Inn, Route 30, Jamaica. (802) 874-4140.
American/Continental. $12 to $16.

By reservation, the public may join overnight guests in sharing innkeeper Elaine Murray's straightforward cooking in two fireplaced dining rooms dressed with pink and white linens and ladderback or bow chairs. The handwritten menu changes nightly. Favorites among the five appetizers are tomato-dill soup, a hot carrot vichyssoise and scallops maison, served in cream wine sauce with mushrooms and swiss cheese. Guests are partial to the seafood kabob, trout amandine, chicken paprikash, and veal parmesan among the five changing entrees, which usually include baked ham and filet mignon. Kahlua-mocha fudge pie, butter-pecan ice cream pie, apple crisp with Vermont apple ice cream, and a French gateau made without flour are in the dessert repertoire.

Dinner by reservation, 6 or 6:30 to 8:30 or 9.

Townshend

Townshend Country Inn, Route 30, Townshend. (802) 365-4141.
American/Continental. $7.95 to $15.95.

Down-home country cooking and good values are enjoyed by patrons of this farmhouse-turned-restaurant. Joseph Peters, formerly manager of the Yankee Pedlar Inn in Holyoke, Mass., picked up his culinary skills while observing the kitchen there. Wife Donna's festive seasonal decorations enhance the main dining room, with bare pine floors, white-linened tables, windsor chairs, and a fireplace mantel topped with striking German chocolate pots. The dinner menu offers something for everyone, from vegetarian platter and pasta to eleven house specialties topping out with filet mignon with bordelaise sauce. Baked scrod, Nantucket seafood casserole, baby coho salmon stuffed with crabmeat, pork gruyere, veal piccata, and roast Long Island duck are a few of the offerings. The dessert list features homemade sherbets, pies and Indian pudding. An old-fashioned Yankee buffet brunch with more than twenty items for $8.95 packs in the locals, as does the Friday night all-you-can-eat prime rib dinner for $9.95.

Lunch, 11:30 to 2:30; dinner, 5 to 9; Sunday, brunch 11 to 2:30, dinner 5 to 9. Fewer hours in off-season.

Windham Hill Inn, West Townshend. (802) 874-4080.
American. Prix-Fixe, $25.

Five-course dinners are served nightly at 7 "in dinner-party style" by innkeepers Linda and Ken Busteed at their elegant and remote inn out in the middle of nowhere on a hill overlooking the West River Valley. Guests gather for hors d'oeuvres in the parlor before adjourning to two large tables in the main dining room or to smaller tables in the Frog Pond Room looking onto the pond and lawns. When we were there, a spinach custard with tomato vinaigrette was followed by a mushroom bisque. A salad of leaf lettuce with dijon vinaigrette flavored with garlic and dill, homemade poppyseed rolls and a pineapple sorbet preceded the main course, a wonderful scallops provencale. Dessert was a linzer torte. The inn's repertoire for entrees includes chicken stuffed with white asparagus, shrimp with peaches and apples, homemade tomato pasta with lobster and fresh tarragon, individual beef wellingtons, and pork tenderloin with apples.

Dinner by reservation, nightly at 7.

Chester

* The Inn at Long Last, Main Street, Chester. (802) 875-2444.
Regional American. $16.50 to $19.

The route to Jack Coleman's "inn at long last" was circuitous, but the result was worth the wait. The former president of Haverford College, who created a stir with his experiences in the book "Blue Collar Journal," transformed the abandoned Chester Inn into a hostelry and dining room of distinction. The mirrored back of a twelve-foot-long bar obtained from a razed Maine hotel is the focal point of the dining room, which is dressed in pink linens. The dinner menu, which changes nightly, might start with a soup of four onions, veal terrine with hazelnuts and armagnac, smoked salmon with cucumber-dill relish, or a vegetable brochette with tofu and balsamic vinegar. Entrees could be filet of salmon with two bean sauces, duck breast sauteed with lime and ginger, and loin of lamb with roasted vegetables and thyme. Desserts include homemade ice creams, dark chocolate truffle torte, a tangy kiwi tart, and occasionally the innkeeper's favorite, a Shaker lemon pie made with whole lemons.

Dinner nightly except Monday, 6 to 8 or 9.

Rockingham

Leslie's, The Tavern at Rockingham, Route 103, Rockingham. (802) 463-4929.
Continental/American. $10.95 to $18.95.

You'd never know it today, but Rockingham once was known as the "Village of Seven Taverns," of which this was one, and boasted a race track across the street. Dating to 1760, the attractive white farmhouse with black shutters contains a cozy bar with an appetizer menu and a variety of dining rooms, cheery in white and pink with bare floors and deep blue wainscoting and trim on light patterned walls. Each table bears an unusual oil pottery lamp inside a hurricane globe. There's a large rear deck for summertime dining. Chef-owner John Marston and his wife Leslie change the menu seasonally. Main courses include swordfish with dill beurre blanc, sea scallops and chicken sauteed with seasonal vegetables over puff pastry, veal oscar, pork wellington, roast duckling with red currants, roast rack of lamb dijonnaise, and filet au poivre. Choice appetizers are chicken, spinach and cheddar cheese enrobed in phyllo, escargots with pernod, and mushroom caps stuffed with snow-crab and boursin cheese. Among dessert treats are black and white bit-

Southeast Vermont

tersweet chocolate torte, maple-walnut pecan torte, and grand marnier-cranberry cream torte.

Lunch, 11:30 to 2:30, June to mid-October; dinner, 5 to 9 or 9:30, Sunday 4 to 9. Closed Tuesday.

Windsor

Windsor Station, Depot Avenue, Windsor. (802) 674-2052.
Continental. $8.95 to $15.95.

Built in 1900, the golden-hued Windsor railroad station has been renovated into a good restaurant with most of the railroad gear, ticket windows and such enhancing the Victorian decor, and an occasional train still roaring by. The circular dining room, once the station master's room, has a beautiful Carolina hard pine ceiling, sandblasted to reveal its original grain. On the other side of the entrance is the cozy bar, where a choice of bar snacks is posted on a blackboard. Lunching once years ago with our children, we tried the station burger and cheeseburger, the broiled scrod, and the old English cheese delight (cheddar cheese over bacon, tomato and toast points); all were good, and the french fries were pronounced superb. The dinner menu has been upgraded and expanded to encompass five kinds of veal (from wiener schnitzel to oscar), scallops mornay, chicken kiev, roast duckling with apricot sauce, linguini with broccoli and shrimp, beef liver, and steak au poivre.

Lunch daily, 11:30 to 2:30; dinner, 5:30 to 9 or 10.

Brownsville

Ascutney Harvest Inn, Route 44, Brownsville. (802) 484-7711.
Regional American. $12.95 to $18.95.

The contemporary Ascutney Mountain Resort at the foot of Mount Ascutney's ski area contains a large and elegant dining room with windows looking onto the slopes and a rather ambitious menu in ski season. Candlelight dinners are served at formal, white-linened tables topped with gold-rimmed china. Entrees on the seasonal menu might include yellowfin tuna with honey-lime sauce, broiled salmon with beurre blanc, chicken citron, roast pork loin with granny smith apple glaze, and grilled sirloin au poivre. Starters are more limited, perhaps chilled melon soup, clam chowder, ceviche, and a smoked seafood assortment. The pastry chef shines with a chocolate mousse torte, kahlua cheesecake, apple-cranberry and maple-pecan pies, strawberry-banana torte, and chocolate eclairs. Dinner is served in the dining room nightly in ski season, on weekends the rest of the year; other times, in the pub.

Lunch in pub, daily 11:30 to 9; dinner, 6 to 9; Sunday brunch, 11:30 to 2.

Weathersfield

The Inn at Weathersfield, Route 106, Weathersfield. (802) 263-9217.
Regional American. Prix-Fixe, $25.95.

Innkeepers Mary Louise and Ron Thorburn are known for the food served in their 18th-century homestead and farm, just south of Perkinsville. The inn is a re-creation in architecture and spirit of the period from 1790 to 1860, though the food is considerably more up to date. The menu changes daily for the six-course, prix-fixe dinner that attracts patrons from hither and yon. A typical meal might begin with pumpkin-apple soup and smoked seafood with three sauces and Belgian endive or fettuccine with shiitake mushrooms, and a marinated tomato and leek salad on a bed of greens. Lemon or raspberry sorbet might clear the palate for the entree, perhaps peppered shrimp with hearts of romaine and fresh rosemary, poached salmon with marinated leeks and mushrooms, loin of pork with apricots, or pheasant with sauce chasseur. Homemade desserts and specialty coffees follow. Meals also may be ordered a la carte from $14.95.

Dinner, Thursday-Monday 6 to 9.

Springfield

The Polo Club, Clinton Street, Springfield. (802) 885-1144.
Italian. $8.95 to $16.95.
The luxurious Polo Club came to this factory town in 1989 and, but for its perch over the Black River, it would be quite at home in New York City. The establishment is literally built on stilts at river's edge, so most tables have a bird's-eye view through arched windows of the rushing river, which is spotlit at night. The inside is ritzy as can be: upholstered banquettes and armchairs with chintz-covered seats, shiny mahogany tables so rich that they are not covered with linens but rather red cloth mats, and burgundy carpeting. The far solarium room is outfitted in preppy pink and green with Caribbean rattan furniture. The front lounge has a marble bar; on one wall is painted a trompe l'oeil bookcase so realistic that people have tried to straighten the plate that's tipped on one shelf. The designer touch extends even to the men's room, with its striking wallpaper, rich paneling and dried flower arrangement. The owner, local realtor Richard Baueries, even painted the bridge outside green and covered the sewer pipe with wooden lattice-work to coordinate with his restaurant. In such a setting, the food is almost anti-climactic. The lengthy menu lists six veal, six seafood and five chicken dishes, all fairly standard, along with sirloin steak coated with peppercorns, sauteed and topped with goat cheese and madeira sauce. They come with house salad or fresh vegetable and a choice of oven-roasted potato, rice or ziti with marinara sauce. Start with goat cheese with roasted peppers and aioli or a smoked seafood plate with piemontese sauce. The dessert tray may harbor an Italian rum cake, strawberry-amaretto cake and Kentucky derby (chocolate nut) pie. The wine list is fairly sophisticated and pleasantly priced.

Lunch, Monday-Saturday 11:30 to 2:30; dinner, 5:30 to 10; Sunday, lunch 11:30 to 2, dinner 2 to 8.

Hartness House, 30 Orchard St., Springfield. (802) 885-2516.
Continental. $11 to $18.
The Hartness House is one of those landmarks that endures. Listed on the National Register, the rambling, turn-of-the-century brown wood and fieldstone structure on 32 acres off a residential side street was once the home of a Vermont governor and inventor-astronomer. His equatorial telescope is still in working order on the expansive front lawn and a five-room underground apartment that serves as a museum for the Stellafane Society has quite a history. The inn's public rooms are like those in a mansion. A pianist plays in the lounge, and the dining room is formal and to some intimidating — "as elegant for breakfast as it is for dinner," in the words of the innkeepers. The continental menu is reasonably priced and fairly standard: shrimp cocktail, stuffed mushroom caps and escargots for appetizers; sole neptune, shrimp amaretto, chicken parmesan, veal marsala, wiener schnitzel, and rack of lamb for entrees. Prime rib is the house specialty; this is the Vermont heartland, after all. Homemade desserts change daily.

Lunch, Monday-Friday noon to 1:30; dinner, Monday-Saturday 6 to 9.

The Paddock, 190 Paddock Road , Springfield. (802) 885-2720.
American. Table d'hote, $8 to $18.50.
A large rocking horse used to greet patrons inside the entrance to this immensely

popular restaurant, family-owned for 43 years and ensconced in a brightly lit barn with expansive windows at one end. But young new owners took over in 1989, and their predecessors took the horse with them. So that meant a change of logo as well as an alteration to the menu, the back of which traditionally listed the distances to the Paddock from every state and places as far away as Melbourne, Australia. Keith and Karen Labrecque added a downstairs waiting room and lounge for weekend use and updated the menu a bit. Complete dinners, from appetizer to dessert, are still remarkably priced and generous in servings. The limited menu holds few surprises, although regulars might be startled now by Cajun shrimp and the new combination plate of Cajun tenderloin tips and broiled or fried scallops. Traditionalists start with French onion soup or clam chowder from the soup bar, sample the rolls and relish tray, devour the salad before their roast turkey or ham steak, and finish with one of the homemade desserts like Indian pudding, kahlua pie or banana-chocolate chip cake.

Lunch, Tuesday-Friday 11:30 to 2; dinner, Tuesday-Saturday 5 to 9; Sunday, brunch 10 to 2, dinner 2 to 7.

Plymouth

Hawk's River Tavern, Route 100, Plymouth. (802) 672-3811.
New American. $13.95 to $19.95.

If you enjoy eating in bars, here's a first-rate one — a contemporary and airy place where you can sit beside windows and feast on a woodsy view along with your meal. Of course, you also can sit in one of the four small dining rooms that make up the restaurant of the Hawk Inn and Mountain Resort. The decor is sleek in burgundy and white, with upholstered chairs and white linens. Opening chef Peter Ryan gave the restaurant quite a reputation for nouvelle cuisine. His was a tough act to follow, but the subsequent menu featured entrees like braised salmon filet with champagne-dill beurre blanc, sliced pork tenderloin with fresh sage and grand marnier sauce, veal with fontina cheese and prosciutto, and tournedos of beef zinfandel. Starters could be Nantucket scallop and corn chowder, seafood ragout in a puff pastry shell, or stuffed mushrooms with spinach, sausage and three cheeses.

Dinner nightly, 6 to 10.

Tyson

Echo Lake Inn, Route 100, Tyson. (802) 228-8602.
American. $12.95 to $16.95.

Since Phil and Kathy Cocco took over this historic hostelry, the country-rustic dining room has been considerably upgraded, and on a winter's night the expansive, gabled facade illuminated by flood lights is positively enchanting. The dinner menu is up-to-date as well: a pasta trilogy of scallops, lobster and shrimp simmered in pernod and creme fraiche, orange roughy with leek sauce, veal medallions with artichoke hearts and garlic, chicken jardiniere and such. Changing appetizers could be cream of leek soup, a velvety chicken and herb pate, balsamic grilled beef salad with radicchio and endive, and escargots with sun-dried tomatoes and garlic over angel-hair pasta. The sourdough French bread and the salad dressings are acclaimed. Kathy's desserts are outstanding: look for the chocolate decadence with raspberry sauce, frozen zabaglione, fruit tartes, or orange bread pudding with bourbon sauce. In summer, the Coccos put on a lavish Friday night buffet "to get the locals out," and they cater to the discriminating with a fine wine list that is their pride and joy.

Lunch, 11:45 to 2, summer and foliage weekends; dinner nightly from 6. Closed in April.

Ludlow

★ The Governor's Inn, 86 Main St., Ludlow. (802) 228-8830.
Regional American. Prix-fixe, $35.

Dinner is a culinary drama in six acts, each worthy of applause, at this small inn that has raised dining to a fine art. Following drinks and hors d'oeuvres in the parlor, innkeeper-chef Deedy Marble seats each guest at tables set with sterling, Waterford crystal, antique bone china, and rare knife rests from the largest collection anywhere. A typical autumn meal begins with hot sweet potato vichyssoise and tortellini with marinated vegetables in the inn's own poppyseed dressing. A pink grapefruit sorbet prepares the palate for the main course of shrimp, scallops and crab in brandied lobster sauce. Other entrees might be native pheasant under glass, game hens grand marnier with orange-pecan stuffing, bluefish flambeed with gin, salmon with champagne sauce, or oysters Okemo with crabmeat and shrimp. Among desserts are vanilla cake with homemade caramel sauce, chocolate-walnut pie with ice cream and creme de cacao, and English brandy cake with hazelnut custard. The complete meal includes pre-dinner hors d'oeuvres and a "complimentary encore," a dessert wine and a parting gift. Chef Deedy changes her menu nightly; "I challenge myself all the time," says she. Husband Charlie plays host, mixes drinks and oversees a small but select wine list.

Dinner by reservation, nightly at 7.

★ Nikki's, 44 Pond St. (Route 103), Ludlow. (802) 228-7797.
Regional American. $9.95 to $19.95.

Expanding and evolving over the years with its neighboring Okemo ski area, Nikki's is as casual or formal as you like, in the funky bar and dark original dining rooms or the newer, high-ceilinged addition with slatted wood benches, pink-linened tables and remarkable arched, floral stained-glass windows. Bob Gilmore's latest addition is a large dining room above a glass-enclosed wine cellar and wine bar for the showcasing of fine wines. The dinner menu includes bistro fare (Brittany tenderloin tips, Indonesian satay, and breast of chicken Santa Fe with fresh corn and mild green chilies and jack cheese, for instance) as well as more substantial entrees. Among the latter are mixed seafood grill in a tomatillo beurre blanc, grilled swordfish with a salspicon tapas marinade, veal sauteed with forest mushrooms and light cream, and steak au poivre. The dinner specials are really special: an oyster stew and a scallop and fresh dill quiche for winter appetizers, a shrimp mousse with seafood cream and a fine pork tenderloin for entrees. Be sure to save room for the chocolate-mandarin entremet with hazelnut-praline sauce (it won a gold medal in a Taste of Vermont competition), maple creme brulee, or homemade ice creams and sorbets. The Sunday brunch from a blackboard menu — Mexican eggs ranchero, smoked salmon, grand marnier french toast, grilled swordfish and the like — is a triumph. The impressive wine cellar boasts the area's most extensive collection of domestic and imported wines.

Dinner nightly from 5; Sunday, brunch 11 to 3, dinner from 4.

Mount Holly

Harry's Mount Holly Cafe, Route 103, Mount Holly. (802) 259-2996.
Contemporary International. $8.95 to $15.95.

The old Backside Restaurant west of Ludlow was refurbished in 1989 into this casual, comfortable cafe by Trip Pierce, an inventive chef who opened his own restaurant after eight years on Block Island, including a recent cooking stint at the well-regarded Tiffany's there. A changing, handwritten menu incorporates Chinese, Mexican, Italian, and Thai cuisines as well as seafood specials a la Block Island. From what he calls his "wide, wild assortment" of starters, you might choose corn and oyster bisque with fresh dill, beef sauteed with spicy peanut sauce, mahogany chicken wings, Thai crab and fish cakes with pickled onions and jalapeno relish, or roasted provolone cheese with marinated peppers, chorizo and dipping croutons — likened to "a little cheese fondue happening at your table." Entrees could be chicken Tiffany (a boneless breast filled with ricotta seasoned with basil and pine nuts and wrapped in prosciutto and bacon), flauta (thinly sliced steak grilled and wrapped in a flour tortilla with jack cheese, salsa and sour cream), Thai curried vegetables and stir-fried tofu, and grilled hot Italian sausage on spinach and cheese tortellini with a basil-marinara sauce. The homemade desserts include an extraordinary chewy brownie, baklava, creme caramel, and hazelnut cheesecake. Trip says he's trying to invent a clientele for a general store of ethnic eating in an area where people drive 30 miles for takeout Chinese food.

Lunch, 11:30 to 2:30; dinner, 5 to 10; Sunday brunch, 10 to 2. Closed Wednesday.

Central Vermont

Norwich

La Poule a Dents at Carpenter Street, Main Street, Norwich.
(802) 649-2922.
Contemporary French. All Entrees, $17.

This cheery, casual restaurant created by two sisters who were into health and natural foods was acquired in January 1990 by Barry and Claire Snyder, previously at the Parker House in Quechee. They gave their new venture a French name, which means "chicken with teeth," an obscure takeoff on the saying, "as scarce as hen's teeth." Both trained at the Culinary Institute of America, the Snyders planned an elaborate, changing menu featuring such entrees as grilled Norwegian salmon on a bed of caramelized onions and red wine-butter sauce, roast duckling with green peppercorns in balsamic vinaigrette, chartreuse of pheasant with savoy cabbage and madeira, and Barry's all-time favorite dish, baby milk-fed lamb braised and sliced into medallions and served with candied oranges. For starters, you might find home-cured gravlax, spinach fettuccine with mushroom-duck salad and mustard-garlic cream, scallop mousse wrapped in an herbed crepe with lobster sauce and caviar, and assorted charcuterie, perhaps crepinettes of wild boar pate or liver mousse with cognac and truffles. For dessert, try one of Claire's tarts (reputed to be the best in town), assorted poached fruits in port wine with homemade cookies, or chocolate mousse inside two little meringue cookies with raspberries. The Snyders planned to serve afternoon tea in the post and beam, cafe-style dining area flanking a beautiful cherry bar. The more formal fare is better taken in the main dining room, crisp with white linens and dark floral wallpaper, which has a couple of recessed alcoves, barely big enough for two.

Lunch, Monday-Friday 11 to 2; tea, 2 to 4:30; dinner, Monday-Saturday 6 to 10.

Quechee

★♥ Simon Pearce Restaurant, The Mill, Quechee. (802) 295-1470.
Regional American. $13.50 to $22.

This restaurant that opened in 1985 has as much integrity as the rest of Irish glass-blower Simon Pearce's mill complex. The chefs all train at Ballymaloe in Ireland, and they import flour from Ireland to make their great Irish soda and

Ballymaloe brown bread. The decor is spare but pure: sturdy ash chairs at bare wood tables topped with small woven mats (linens at night), brown and white tableware and heavy glassware, all made by Simon Pearce and his family. Large windows grant a view of the Ottauquechee River, hills rising beyond. A new dining addition looks out onto the falls and, in summer, a canopied outdoor deck is almost over the water. We've lunched here frequently; the menu changes but there are always specialties like the delicious beef and Guinness stew and shepherd's pie. Hickory-smoked coho salmon with potato salad and a skewer of grilled chicken with a spicy peanut sauce are extra-good. The walnut meringue cake with strawberry sauce, a menu fixture, is crisp and crunchy and melts in the mouth. Cappuccino cheesecake also is super, as are bittersweet chocolate tart with an espresso sauce, chocolate-almond torte and homemade sorbets. At night, a candlelight dinner might start with some of the luncheon entrees as appetizers, like country pate with onion jam, hot shrimp souffle, or fettuccine tossed with roasted red peppers, scallions, cream, and cheese. Entrees could be chicken sauteed with spinach and cheddar cheese, poached salmon with saffron sauce, roast duck with mango chutney sauce, veal with a two-mustard sauce, medallions of beef with port and bearnaise sauces, and noisettes of lamb with shallots, rosemary and port wine sauce. The wine list ranges widely and, naturally, you can get beers and ales from the British Isles.

Lunch daily, 11.30 to 2:30; dinner nightly, 6 to 9.

Parker House, 16 Main St., Quechee. (802) 295-6077.
French. Prix-fixe, $30.

The food is creative and the atmosphere elegant in the three small dining rooms of this Victorian inn. Graceful chairs are at well-spaced tables topped by white over burgundy linens and fresh flowers. Hand-screened French wallpaper lends a touch of owner Roger Nicholas's native Brittany to the rear Fleur de Lis Room, which opens onto a balcony overlooking the Ottauquechee River (used for dining in summer). Chef Martha Dempsey changes her menu weekly. Begin perhaps with a homemade pasta, fresh Norwegian salmon or a seasonal soup. A vinaigrette-dressed salad precedes the main course, perhaps rabbit braised with wine and tarragon, medallions of venison with a green peppercorn sauce, Long Island duckling with fresh plums or beef tenderloin with a pesto sauce. Favorite desserts include hazelnut torte filled with chocolate mousse and topped with chocolate ganache, tarte tatin, and vacheron (meringue shells filled with vanilla ice cream, rolled in toasted almonds and served with chocolate-amaretto sauce).

Dinner nightly except Wednesday from 6; Sunday brunch.

Quechee Inn at Marshland Farm, Clubhouse Road, Quechee.
(802) 295-3133.
Regional American. $14.25 to $19.

A drink by the fire in the cozy living room-lounge sets the stage for dinner in the beamed, antiques-filled dining room. The lovely pink and blue stenciled borders on the walls are repeated on the covers of the menu, wine list and the Quechee Inn Dessert Cookbook, a wonderful collection of the recipes of the inn's baker and dessert chef, Erma J. Hastings, including her renowned French silk pie. The dinner menu changes seasonally. You might start with petite California snails in puff pastry, fresh fruit compote, poached shrimp with snow peas and tomatoes, scallops ceviche, or a house pate. The entree repertoire includes grilled halibut with pistachio-lime butter, baked chicken stuffed with goat cheese and sun-dried tomatoes, sauteed duck with lingonberries and cointreau, and grilled loin of pork with maple-apple puree. Innkeeper Michael Madeira's hobby is wine, as evidenced by the wine cellar and racks he built as well as the 100-plus offerings on the reasonably priced wine list notable for its narrative descriptions. The California house wines bear the inn's own label.

Dinner nightly, 6 to 9. Reservations required.

Woodstock

* The Prince and the Pauper, 34 Elm St., Woodstock. (802) 457-1818.
Creative Continental. Prix-Fixe, $26.

A new cocktail lounge with a wine bar and the shiniest wood bar you ever saw has freed up space for more tables in what many consider to be Woodstock's best restaurant. Tables in the expanded yet intimate L-shaped dining room (some surrounded by dark wood booths) are covered with brown linens, oil lamps and flowers in small carafes. The lamps cast flickering shadows on dark beamed ceilings, and old prints adorn the white walls, one of which has a shelf of old books. Chef-owner Chris J. Balcer refers to his cuisine as "creative continental." His soup of the day could be billi-bi or French fish provencale, the pasta perhaps agnolotto filled with pesto and tossed with red peppers, sweet peas, cream and romano cheese, and his pate a mixture of duck, pork and chicken livers flavored with grand marnier and served with cumberland sauce. There's a choice of six entrees, perhaps the signature dish of boneless rack of lamb in puff pastry with spinach and mushroom duxelles, shrimp dijonnaise, veal with sun-dried tomatoes, roast duckling with mango and currants, grilled salmon au poivre, and steak with wild mushrooms. Homemade bread, house salad and seasonal vegetables accompany. Desserts are extra: perhaps profiteroles, strawberry sabayon with triple sec, pears helene, or fresh fruit, topped off with espresso, cappuccino or an international coffee.

Dinner nightly, 6 to 9 or 9:30.

Bentleys Restaurant, 3 Elm St., Woodstock. (802) 457-3232.
International. $12.95 to $17.50.

Always crowded and lively, this casual spot at the prime corner in Woodstock is the flagship of an expanding food and retail operation that started as a greenhouse and plant store, added a soda fountain and now embraces locations in Quechee and Hanover, N.H. On several levels, tables are close together (set with small cane mats, Perrier bottles filled with flowers, and small lamps or tall candles in holders) amid old floor lamps sporting fringed shades, lace-curtained windows, large potted palms and walls covered with English prints and an enormous bas-relief. At lunch, we've enjoyed a great torta rustica, a hot Italian puff pastry filled with prosciutto, salami, provolone and marinated vegetables, and a fluffy quiche with turkey, mushrooms and snow peas, both accompanied by side salads. From the dessert tray came a delicate chocolate mousse cake with layers of meringue, served with the good Green Mountain coffee. Appetizers, salads, sandwiches and light entrees such as the torta rustica, chicken chimichanga and cold sliced marinated flank steak make up half the dinner menu. The other side offers such entrees as maple-mustard chicken, duckling with cranberry-bourbon glaze, veal romanoff, Jack Daniels steak, sesame seafood stir-fry, and four Cajun-Creole specialties.

Lunch, daily 11:30 to 2:30; dinner, 5:30 to 9:30; Sunday brunch, noon to 3.

Rumble Seat Rathskeller, Woodstock East, Route 4, Woodstock.
(802) 457-3609.
American. $9.95 to $15.50.

The cellar of the 1834 Stone House houses this casual-elegant little establishment with intimate nooks and crannies in three small dining rooms. The original stone and brick walls have been lacquered, gray linens are accented by cranberry napkins, and it's all more attractive than one might expect from the name. It's an informal place where you can order anything from a hamburger to steak au poivre and a wonderful caesar salad. Fans say the crab salad sandwich is out of this world. Dinner entrees range from orange-roasted chicken and crumb-baked scrod to veal and shrimp dijon. There's a choice of five dressings for the house salad. Baked stuffed artichokes and potato skins with different fillings are popular appetizers.

Open daily, 11:30 to 10 or 11.

Barnard

★ **Barnard Inn,** Route 12, Barnard. (802) 234-9961.
French. $21.50 to $29.

This handsome red-brick structure dating to 1796 is really out in the country, ten miles north of Woodstock almost at the "back of beyond." Fans of Swiss chef-owner Sepp Schenker consider the distance a mere trifle when they want to experience some of the best meals in Vermont. Inside are four small dining rooms that are the epitome of the style of an elegant, late Colonial inn. Round tables are spaced nicely apart and covered with white linen, heavy silver, fresh flowers in tiny porcelain vases, and white candles in big hurricane lamps. A zesty sherried cheddar cheese spread with crackers accompanies generous drinks. We'd choose one of Sepp's special soups — mulligatawny, Belgian cream of leek, curried pumpkin, Bermuda fish chowder, cold fiddlehead, or shrimp bisque — over an appetizer, since meals here are quite hearty and you ought to save room for dessert (although the shrimp potpourri, each with its own sauce, and the Russian seafood plate with caviar sorely tempted). Hot crunchy rolls and an exceptional salad including lamb's lettuce and fresh morels come with the meals. Entrees are heavy on the beef and veal side, with a few choices of chicken, seafood and the signature roast duck with sauce of the season. We chose the tournedo adriano with a rich sauce of heavy cream, brandy and green peppercorns, and the chicken breast with garlic, wine and tarragon sauce. Barely steamed broccoli stems cut like matchsticks, glazed carrots and one of the inn's trademarks — a potato shaped and coated to look like a pear with a clove at the bottom and a pear stem on top — made a hefty plateful. The dessert cart is laden with caloric wonders. One cake was decorated with whipped cream and candied violets, and Sepp is partial to his apple charlotte with raspberry topping, a mille feuille with hazelnut nougat, and cinnamon ice cream with apricot-apple topping. Besides growing his own herbs and planting new beds of lamb's lettuce each month, Sepp gathers his own fiddleheads and morels, and picks wild grapes that make a colorful sauce for his roasted duck.

Dinner, nightly 6 to 9 or 9:30 in fall, Tuesday-Sunday in summer and Wednesday-Saturday in winter. Closed mid-November to mid-December and month of April.

Stockbridge

Annabelle's, Route 100 at Route 107, Stockbridge. (802) 746-8552.
American/Continental. $10.95 to $16.95.

An interesting combination of a Colonial tavern, contemporary ski lodge and an airy greenhouse, this venture that started as part of the Hawk Mountain North resort also offers appealing fare. The sprawling establishment has always been luxurious to the nines: oriental carpets scattered with abandon, a garden room for lunch, a cozy tavern with fireplace and comfy chairs to sink into and, beyond, a serene dining room with brown linens and huge wine goblets. On our latest summer visit, the decor seemed a bit threadbare and the scaled-down menu not as interesting as it had been. We once enjoyed smoked muscovy duck and oysters baked New Orleans

Central Vermont

style as appetizers, and a memorable lamb persille and a crisp duckling roasted with currants, whole chestnuts and pears. Now the appetizers are things like stuffed mushroom caps and mozzarella sticks, the entrees broiled trout, scallops, beef stroganoff, New York strip, and surf and turf. A temporary or seasonal relapse, we trust.

Open daily except Wednesday, 11:30 to 9:30 or 10.

Gaysville

Cobble House Inn, Gaysville. (802) 234-5458.
Northern Italian/French. Table d'hote, $16.50 to $25.

This country Victorian inn from the 1860s serves locally acclaimed food at seven tables in two candlelit dining rooms. Innkeepers Phil and Beau Benson do everything themselves, offering an ambitious menu as "ideas for guests," says Beau, who then will prepare almost anything to order. The complete dinner starts with a vinaigrette salad and a choice among three appetizers, perhaps gazpacho, smoked salmon or mussels marinara over pasta. The fifteen to twenty main courses, each embellished individually, might be based upon the house specialty, organic veal — say, veal scaloppine milanese, saltimbocca or veal with prosciutto, cheddar and shallots. Other options include sauteed chicken dishes, filet of sole with maple-mustard glaze and tarragon, shrimp scampi, sauteed sweetbreads with leeks and white wine, steak au poivre, and rack of lamb with fresh basil. Most people don't make it all the way through dessert, but the Bensons offer a choice of three, perhaps fresh strawberry pie, bavarian cheesecake or maple-amaretto bread pudding. The dinner-party-style feast is taken at well-spaced tables flanked by windsor armchairs in two Victorian rooms lit by candles, lights over the artworks and the blazing hearth. Phil is partial to the Californias on his wine list.

Dinner, Wednesday-Sunday 6 to 9.

Bridgewater

The Corners Inn & Restaurant, Route 4, Bridgewater. (802) 672-9968.
Continental/Italian. $10.95 to $16.95.

The exterior is unassuming and the interior is plain ("our inn is old New England," owners Patti and Butch Gettis concede). But the food is exciting at this restaurant favored by locals. People rave about the garlic bread, the caesar salad and the warm red cabbage salad tossed with walnuts and prosciutto, both medal winners in the annual Taste of Vermont competition. You're off to a good start with these, before sampling one of the fine pasta dishes, perhaps assorted seafood, sun-dried tomatoes and yellow peppers over angel-hair pasta; linguini with shrimp, chicken and clams, or a house specialty, cioppino, served on a fish platter over linguini. Start perhaps with the cold antipasti plate or fettuccine alfredo with prosciutto. Shrimp and scallop scampi, Sicilian steak, veal with artichoke hearts, and roast duckling are other possibilities. The dessert tray harbors homemade goodies, and the wine list is considered one of the best around.

Dinner, Wednesday-Sunday 6 to 10.

Killington

★ **Hemingway's,** Route 4, Killington. (802) 422-3886.
New American. Prix-fixe, $36.

The fame of the restored 1860 Asa Briggs House has far transcended its locale since Linda and Ted Fondulas moved over from Annabelle's in Stockbridge in 1981.

They oversee a serene sanctuary of three very different dining rooms enhanced by locally crafted furniture, antiques, fresh flowers from Linda's gardens, and original oils, watercolors and sculpture. A European feeling is effected in the formal dining room with chandeliers and maroon velvet chairs, a garden room done up in white and yellow with a brick floor, wainscoting and pierced lamps on the walls, and a charming wine cellar with stone walls, lace tablecloths and elaborate candlesticks. Such are the settings for stylish, creative fare that has made it the only four-star and four-diamond restaurant in Northern New England, Linda notes proudly. The prix-fixe dinner includes choice of appetizer, sorbet, entree, and salad, cheese or dessert. A typical menu might start with bundles of applewood-smoked salmon stuffed with smoked shrimp, hand-rolled lobster ravioli, terrine of pheasant and duck with apple chutney, and cream of garlic or chilled honeydew melon and cantaloupe soup. Entrees could be saute of shrimp with tomato and fennel, pan-roasted salmon with sweet corn, scallops in pastry with lobster sauce, loin of lamb roasted in vine leaves, grilled breast of duck with potato pie, and tenderloin of beef with green herbs and garlic. Salad, an exceptional assortment of Vermont cheeses or desserts like peach charlotte, coconut-rum souffle, fresh fruit tartlet with maple-cider sauce, and homemade sorbets and ice cream in a cookie tulip complete the repast. Truffles come with the bill. There's also a nightly four-course wine-tasting menu featuring prizes from a stock of more than 150 wines, including an incredible collection of fine Californias.

Dinner, Wednesday-Sunday from 6.

✱ Claude's, Killington Road, Killington. (802) 422-4030.
Continental. $14.75 to $18.25.

Chef-owner Claude Blais oversees the Killington area's most elegant dining room, part of a complex that also includes his more casual restaurant, **Choices.** The setting in a contemporary shingled alpine building he helped design could not be more posh: gray and burgundy with gray-rimmed china, white linens, modern glass oil lamps, striking swag curtains on the windows, and stunning modern art. The velvet high-back chairs cater to the owner; "I'm a big guy and I wanted something I'd be comfortable in," he explains. Claude changes his menu every couple of months: you might find entrees like swordfish Creole, medallions of salmon piccata, beef wellington, and rack of lamb persille. Baked oysters in phyllo, smoked salmon raviolis with spinach fettuccine and baked mushrooms with a creamy artichoke filling are possible openers. Desserts could be chocolate ganache with white and dark chocolate mousse filling, mocha cheesecake, and white satin tart with fresh raspberries. The fairly expensive wine list starts in the high teens.

Dinner, Wednesday-Monday 6 to 10 in winter, Thursday-Sunday in off-season.

Choices, Killington Road, Killington. (802) 422-4030.
Regional American. $8.75 to $13.95.

This dining room shares the kitchen with Claude's, but there the resemblance ends. The room is casual and brighter, the white tablecloths and red woven mats topped by glass. Jazz plays in the background. Chef-owner Claude Blais designs his menu for grazing. Talk about choices! There are wonderful salads and pastas, sandwiches and a raw bar, as well as such entrees as California cioppino, Shaker-style pork chop and knockwurst, jambalaya and Minnesota Dutch stew. Desserts are simpler versions of the Claude's extravaganzas.

Dinner nightly, 5 to 11; Sunday brunch, 11:30 to 3. Closed Monday and Tuesday in summer.

Central Vermont

The Back Behind Restaurant and Saloon, Routes 4 and 100,
South Killington. (802) 422-9907.
American. $10.95 to $18.50.

A bright red caboose, an old Mobil gas pump and a Wurlitzer nickelodeon attract skiers and families to this lively establishment with dark barn siding, lots of stained glass and a huge stone fireplace. The menu lists steaks and seafood items (many dressed with asparagus, as in rainbow mountain trout, sole neptune and steak oscar). Specialties are Arabian leg of lamb, venison steak Jack Daniels, brace of quail and Texas spareribs, supplemented by blackboard specials. All come with the restaurant's special coleslaw in a crock, vegetable, potato, and bread. Homemade desserts could be mocha-amaretto torte, mint mud pie or eggnog cheesecake. Romantics like to sit at one of the two tables in the upper level of the caboose, away from the crowds.

Dinner nightly, 5 to 10; lunch-brunch, Friday-Sunday in season, 11:30 to 3:30.

Mendon

Countryman's Pleasure, Townline Road off Route 4, Mendon.
(802) 773-7141.
Austrian/German. $9.95 to $22.50.

The rambling 100-year-old rural house is truly a country pleasure for ebullient chef Hans Entinger, who grows his own vegetables and fruits, lets guests walk the flower-bedecked trails, bakes his own tortes, and serves up the Austrian-German fare of his childhood. He mixes European decor in six rooms in a Colonial farmhouse, all variations on a theme of dark woods, moss green print mats, candlelight, and fireplaces. Such specialties as wiener schnitzel, sauerbraten, paprika veal goulash, veal with morels, sea scallops chardonnay, and rack of lamb are served with four vegetables and three kinds of rolls. Hans is as proud of his Austrian beers and wines as he is of his famed tortes, glazed apple strudel and countryman's trifle.

Dinner, Tuesday-Saturday 5 to 9 or 10.

Rutland

Casa Bianca, 76 Grove St., Rutland. (802) 773-7401.
Northern Italian. $10.95 to $16.95.

Ask serious diners in Rutland their favorite local restaurant and most will name this 30-year institution in a small house near downtown. "What you see is what you get," says chef-owner Lee Bove Ryan, an Italian married to an Irishman, who mothers patrons at eight tables in the tiny dining room when she's not cooking out back in the tiny kitchen (last we heard, her son Peter Ryan was back in the kitchen here after brilliant stints nearby at the late Nicole's and Hawk's River Cafe). The blackboard menu lists a handful of entrees: veal parmigiana or piccata, chicken florentine, pasta piscatore, and shrimp scampi. A side order of pasta, tossed salad and rolls comes with. Service is solicitous and personable, and the candlelit atmosphere appealing. In summer, extra dining is added on an enclosed porch, accented with stained-glass windows. "We can't expand any more and don't want to," says Lee. "We cook everything to order on one stove."

Dinner, Tuesday-Saturday 6 to 9.

Ernie's Grill at Royal's Hearthside, 37 North Main St., Rutland.
(802) 775-0856.
American. $12.95 to $23.95.

Ask longtime visitors to this area their favorite restaurant and invariably they'll name this institution near the crossroads where Routes 7 and 4 meet. After a brief retirement, Ernie and Willa Royal returned to the restaurant they ran for 22 years, keeping up with the times by adding a mesquite grill in their 160-seat dining establishment. The traditional open-hearth specialties (grilled chicken, smoked ham steaks, sirloin steak, and prime rib) have been updated to include blackened salmon and lamb chops with ginger and rosemary on toast. All this comes with cheese and crackers, crudites, hot popover and fresh breads, and choice of salad, vegetable or potato. So you may not need appetizers, which are standard anyway — chilled tomato or cranberry juice, chowder, pate, marinated herring and such. Special desserts could be New Orleans bread pudding with whiskey sauce or fresh fruit sorbet. Imported wines predominate, but are remarkably low-priced; special wines are offered from the reserve cellars.

Open daily, 11 a.m. to 10 p.m., Sunday to 9 p.m.

The Back Home Cafe, 21 Center St., Rutland. (802) 774-2104.
Seafood/Italian. $7.95 to $12.95.

This complex includes a main-floor deli and bakery, the upstairs cafe with a mix of tables and booths, and an art deco nightclub called the Ritz, with a large dance floor and live bands on weekends. It's billed as "a little bit of Greenwich Village in the Green Mountains." Chef-owners Tom DeMartino and Jerry Vaughan offer prize-winning desserts and breads from their bakery, although we found the deli menu boring. For more than an ordinary sandwich you must go upstairs to a long dark room with Tiffany lamps, booths and a black and white floor. The enormous lunch menu is strong on burgers (one called pizza burger comes with tomato sauce and melted mozzarella) and sandwiches (from vegetarian to hot muffalata), plus a budget special including soup, entree and dessert. At dinner, the fare ranges from baked ziti and homemade lasagna to a chicken stir-fry, sauteed scallops and broccoli over fettuccine, and sirloin steak. Hot and cold antipasti, baked stuffed mushrooms and potato skins are among the starters.

Open Monday-Saturday, 11 to 9:30 or 10:30; Sunday brunch, noon to 3.

The Sirloin Saloon, 200 South Main St., Rutland. (802) 772-7900.
Steaks/Seafood. $6.95 to $14.95.

Perhaps the most appealing of the three Sirloin Saloons (others are in Manchester and Shelburne), this large, family-style steakhouse is a mix of Victorian and wild west decor. It's full of Tiffany lamps, etched glass, electic paintings, engravings, and Indian artifacts. You can get chicken, seafood and sirloin, alone or in combinations, mesquite-grilled or charbroiled. The family-style prices include fresh whole-grain bread, a bountiful salad bar, rice, or potato. Desserts are few but include mud pie and cheesecake made by the nuns of New Skete.

Dinner nightly, 5 to 10 or 11.

121 West, 121 West St., Rutland. (802) 773-7148. (802) 773-7148.
Continental. $9.95 to $16.95.

Red linens, white napkins, candles, and fresh flowers set the theme at this downtown restaurant of the old school. The appetizers are standard — stuffed mushroom caps, barbecued chicken wings and escargots. Entrees range from wiener schnitzel to grilled swordfish, from roast Long Island duckling with apple-raisin stuffing to lobster and shrimp casserole. They're supplemented by such specials as chicken cordon bleu, medallions of veal bordelaise, deep-fried oysters, and roast prime rib. Desserts run to homemade puddings, cheesecake with different toppings, strawberry shortcake, and ice cream parfait.

Lunch, 11:30 to 2:30; dinner, 5 to 9:30. Closed Sunday.

Fair Haven

♥ **Vermont Marble Inn,** 12 West Park Place, Fair Haven. (802) 265-8383.
Regional American. $12.50 to $17.50.

The effervescent innkeepers here are integral to their restaurant operation, but they leave the dinner meal to Don Goodman, an ex-New Jersey chef who calls his cuisine "gourmet American." Candlelight dinners are served in two high-ceilinged, pink and white dining rooms seating about 60. Among entrees when we dined were excellent braised duckling with port and raspberry sauce and a loin lamb chop grilled with garlic and served with onion-bell pepper salsa. Both were accompanied by snow peas and wild rice pilaf, with herbal and floral garnishes from the gardens out back. Shrimp sauteed with endive, julienned vegetables and champagne, veal loin sauteed in saffron oil and finished with chive pesto, roasted tenderloin of beef with peppercorns and a shallot-brandy sauce, and roast quail with wild mushroom duxelles were other choices. The mild country pate with leeks and grain mustard and the assorted smoked fish plate were appealing appetizers. Homemade rolls, a tossed salad and a small dish of sorbets — blueberry and seabreeze (grapefruit and vodka) — preceded the main courses. A strawberry and cream roll with pecans and a very rich chocolate pate on a hazelnut creme anglaise were delicious endings. Other possibilities are chocolate-kahlua torte and a mile-high pecan pie. Candies come with your bill, and if you are staying overnight, you will probably find chocolate-covered nuts and raisins in a chocolate cup on your pillow.

Dinner nightly except Tuesday from 6. Closed April and mid-November to mid-December.

Fair Haven Inn, 5 Adams St., Fair Haven. (802) 265-4907.
American/Continental/Greek. $8.95 to $15.95.

Ex-Connecticut restaurateur John Lemnotis moved to Vermont to retire but ended up running a restaurant in an 1837 structure that had been known as the Cottage Inn. Over two decades he has acquired such a following that in 1988 he added an enormous dining room geared for functions. The stucco and barnwood walls of the long, narrow main room are enhanced by pictures of Greece. White and blue linens, windsor chairs and candlelight create a setting more attractive than one might expect from the exterior. Seafood is the specialty, and chef John has a wholesale business that supplies other restaurants. The lengthy menu offers shrimp a la grecque, Grecian haddock, seafood kabobs, and such rare-for-these-parts fish as red snapper and grouper under catch of the day. Veal francais, lamb chops and lamb en brochette are among possibilities. Spanakopita, stuffed grape leaves and calamari sauteed in pure olive oil are good appetizers. Greek soup and salads and homemade pastas also are offered. An enormous dessert cart, containing all the coffee cups as well, is laden with cakes and baklava. The inn has a noisy bar, fortunately shut off from the dining room.

Dinner nightly, 5 to 9:30.

Wells

Blossom's Corner, Routes 30 and 149, Wells. (802) 645-0058.
American/International. $8.95 to $16.95.

This rustic barn of a place has an enormous and casual pub as well as a more formal dining room. Although it caters to the area's meat and potatoes tastes, you can get vegetarian dishes (eggplant parmigiana or Italian manicotti), fried or broiled sole or scallops, veal cutlet parmigiana, duck a l'orange, and teriyaki chicken with a spiced Vermont apple compote. Dinners come with relish dish, green salad, baked or fried potatoes or rice pilaf, vegetable, and homemade bread. Chocolate mousse, cheesecake and apple pie are dessert favorites. The decor is barn-typical, with tiny white lights, hanging dried herbs and flowers dressing up the dining room.

Dinner nightly, 5 to 10; closed Tuesday and Wednesday from November to Memorial Day.

Middletown Springs

Middletown Springs Inn, On the Green, Middletown Springs. (802) 235-2198. American/Continental. Prix-fixe, $20.

The public can join inn guests for dinner at communal tables in two high-ceilinged, Victorian dining rooms at this venerable inn. While innkeeper Steve Sax handles the cooking chores, wife Jane introduces guests over cocktails in a wicker-furnished sitting room next to the bar. When seated for dinner, they find a note with the dinner courses written in rhyme and everyone tries to solve the puzzle of each course before it is served. By the end of dessert, says Jane, strangers have become cohorts and friends. Dinner the night we visited started with cream of carrot soup and tossed salad with celery-seed and maple-syrup dressing. A blueberry sorbet primed the palate for the main course, chicken kiev served country style with baked potato and broccoli with oregano. Homemade cheesecake with cherries was a worthy finale. Other menu fixtures are corn chowder and cauliflower soup, baked herbed scrod and beef Victorian, and Jane Sax's rum torte and English trifle.

Dinner nightly at 7 by reservation.

Bomoseen

Ringquist's Dining Room, Route 30, Bomoseen. (802) 468-5172. American/Continental. $7.25 to $13.95.

An attractive small white house with black shutters has been home since 1976 to Gordon Ringquist's pleasant little Colonial dining room, a tavern where lunch is served, and a side deck with tables facing Lake Bomoseen across the road. The decor ranks among the fanciest in area restaurants. Eight tables are clad in white and brown, flanked by windsor chairs, and topped with oil lamps and blue and white china. Dinner entrees include roast turkey, roast loin of pork, baked sole with mushroom and celery stuffing, veal cordon bleu, and filet mignon. Start with Gordon's special clam chowder, barbecued chicken wings, marinated herring, or escargots.

Lunch, Monday-Friday noon to 2; dinner, Tuesday-Saturday 5 to 9, Sunday noon to 9. Open year-round, fewer days in winter.

Brandon

★ The Brandon Inn, 20 Park St., Brandon. (802) 247-5766. Regional American. $12.95 to $16.95.

This large brick inn facing the village green has been around for two centuries, but never more fetchingly so than since Sarah and Louis Pattis acquired it and started restoring its elegance. Indeed, the inn fetched three coveted awards in the 1989 Taste of Vermont competition, more than any other restaurant and raising many an eyebrow. "We were viewed as upstarts," Louis recalled, though he'd been a chef in major European hotels and handled the Brandon Inn kitchen alone until he hired Saxtons River chef David Deen in 1989. The pair prepared the winning entries: an herbal rack of lamb, a salad of bean, endive and radicchio with garlic-honey mustard dressing, and a seafood chowder so thick that it's offered as a main course. Their regular dinner menu is quite limited. Besides the award-winning chowder, the six entrees when we visited were shrimp and scallop provencale over linguini, blackened swordfish in a garlic sauce, pork medallions with apricots and walnuts in a grand marnier sauce, chicken breast stuffed with artichoke hearts and shallots in a tomato-white wine sauce, and New York sirloin and shrimp with peppercorn and brandy sauce. Starters were avocado and shrimp with a honey-garlic sauce, escargots en croute with mustard cream sauce, melon and prosciutto, and two soups, cream of garlic and chilled three-melon (watermelon, cantaloupe and honeydew). Desserts include flourless chocolate cake, apple strudel, black forest cake, and various mousses. Solid white pillars march down the middle of the large dining room, rather austere with tables set well apart and dressed in black and blue; a side porch is lighter in white and wicker. In summer, you may lunch on the front terrace, where exotic waffles and Ben & Jerry's ice cream are available in the late afternoon. This inn, you can tell, is a culinary happening in the making.

Lunch, Tuesday-Saturday 11:30 to 2; dinner nightly, 6 to 9. Closed for dinner Monday in off-season, also Tuesday and Wednesday in winter.

Middlebury

★ Otter Creek Cafe, Frog Hollow Mill, Middlebury. (802) 388-7342.
Regional American. $12.50 to $16.

You'd never expect to get a dish like this in a cafe in a mill beside a creek, one of us noted upon finishing an extraordinary roast duck saute — tender slices of breast sauced with red wine, honey and green peppercorns, a leg covered with mushrooms, and the skin fried until crackling and resting on top. Ben and Sarah Wood patterned their nifty cafe upon the restaurants with bakeries they knew in San Francisco. Sarah is the baker, who turns out the great sourdough and honey-wheat breads that come with dinner, as well as all kinds of goodies to go at their newly relocated bakery up on Main Street. Ben is the chef, who wears a baseball cap at the stove and whose considerable talents showed not only on the duck but also on veal scaloppine with citrus sections and dry vermouth, a cream of leek and garlic soup with melted Vermont cheddar, and an appetizer of rabbit-juniper and lamb pates and terrines served with salad and melba toast — almost a meal in itself. An assortment of five intense sorbets finished a memorable dinner. Since our first visit, the cafe's menu has become even more exciting, offering seasonal specialties such as ragout of sweetbreads and lobster with fresh asparagus, saddle of rabbit roasted with fennel and carrots, and breast of pheasant stuffed with red lentils and sauced with oyster mushrooms and madeira. With soft pink walls and candlelight, the ground-floor dining room of the old Frog Hollow Mill is pleasant and contemporary, and the creekside deck is idyllic in summer.

Lunch, Tuesday-Saturday 11 to 2:30; dinner, 5 to 9:30. Closed Sunday and Monday.

★ Swift House Inn, 25 Stewart Lane, Middlebury. (802) 388-9925.
New American. $14 to $23.

This exceptionally attractive and comfortable inn in an 1814 white clapboard manse that once was the home of a Vermont governor offers candlelight dining to the public by reservation. Two dining rooms are elegantly appointed with white linens and fine antiques in the manner of a private home. Innkeeper Andrea Nelson and her chef, Martin Holzberg, prepare a highly sophisticated menu that changes nightly. The autumn evening we were there, starters included smoked salmon and trout pate with sevruga caviar, seafood fritters with orange-ginger-bell pepper sauce, lemon-peppered smoked mackerel with wasabi horseradish sauce, and cream of carrot soup with leeks and ginger. The ten entree choices ranged from grilled swordfish with orange-basil beurre blanc and poached Norwegian salmon with pineapple salsa to blackened lamb loin over roasted red pepper puree and grilled buffalo rib-eye with sun-dried tomatoes and garlic butter. Grilled quails with cranberry butter, seared filet mignon with wild mushroom and garlic polenta, and smoked and grilled duck with red currant sauce were other tempters. Desserts were devastating: chocolate chip and pecan pie, corinthian champagne grape tartlets, chocolate marble cheesecake with raspberry coulis, and creme brulee. International coffees and fine cognacs are worthy endings.

Dinner by reservation, Thursday-Monday 6 to 9.

Woody's, 5 Bakery La., Middlebury. (802) 388-4182.
International. $7.95 to $17.95.

This contemporary, multi-level restaurant with enormous windows overlooking Otter Creek looks like a cross betweena liner and a diner. They call it a cruise ship, which is not so far-fetched. Railings like those of an ocean liner, mirrors and curves make this four-level affair a bit dizzying by day, but it is certainly glamorous by night, and the creekside deck is popular anytime. Decor is ever-so art deco in salmon, blue and stainless steel, the colors repeated on the covers of the various menus. Run by Woody Danforth, formerly of Mary's in nearby Bristol and the Ritz-Carlton in Boston, the place is California casual from a hummus salad, grilled chilies or stir-fried vegetables at lunch to bourbon shrimp with pasta or filet mignon with twin sauces at dinner. A New Year's Eve menu of seafood in puff pastry with saffron cream sauce, chicken breast wih corn pudding, grilled and roasted duckling with chambord-citrus glaze, and grilled and roasted loin of Vermont lamb with polenta and goat cheese is not atypical. Everything on the luncheon menu, last we knew, was under $5. There's a creative-cuisine menu for the health-conscious, and an ever-changing array of tasty appetizers, salads and light fare to appeal to the college crowd.

Open daily, 11:30 a.m. to midnight.

Morgan's Paisano Restaurant, 86 Main St., Middlebury. (802) 388-3385.
Italian/International. $6.25 to $13.50.

The first thing you may notice in this intimate little charmer with a couple of candlelit dining rooms is the photographs on the walls. They're the work of owner Ben Morgan, a professional photographer. Next you may notice the adjacent seafood market; you'll know the fish is fresh. That's what regulars consider its strength and why they tend to order simple broiled swordfish, shrimp scampi, shrimp or scallops provencale, or the chef's favorite, herbed shrimp with julienned vegetables over angel-hair pasta. There are plenty of other choices — veal five ways (including curried), tamari beef stir-fry, chicken sauteed in sesame cream sauce, good pastas, and college standbys like lasagna, cannelloni and veal parmigiana. Argentine lamb chops and steamed Alaskan king crab might be specials. All are served with a cup of soup (minestrone or du jour, perhaps French onion) or salad and excellent garlic bread, so you may not need an appetizer, though the thought of lobster and julienned vegetables flambeed with grand marnier intrigues. Grand marnier also flavors the Italian cheesecake; other dessert possibilities are chocolate-mint mousse, marsala zabaglione and a magnificent Black Forest cake. There's a pleasant little sidewalk cafe at the side for seasonal dining.

Lunch, Monday-Saturday 11 to 5; dinner nightly, 5 to 10 or 10:30.

$ The Dog Team Tavern, Dog Team Road, Middlebury. (802) 388-7651.
Traditional American. $8.50 to $14.95.

Trendy restaurants come and go, but the Dog Team goes on forever, serving enormous, Sunday-dinner-type meals to generations of hungry Middlebury College students and tourists from afar. Built in the early 1920s by Sir Wilfred and Lady Grenfell, it was operated by the Grenfell Mission as an outlet for handicrafts from Labrador until it became a restaurant of note. You order from the traditional blackboard menu as you enter and wait for your table, either in the delightfully old-fashioned living room filled with souvenir gift items and nostalgia like a collection of old campaign buttons, or in the large and airy lounge, where chips and dips are served with drinks. When you're called into the charming dining room with a view of the birches and a rippling stream, you eat (and eat and eat). We've been doing so here for more than 30 years, and are always amazed how they can still serve such huge amounts of food for the price, from the poor man's ham or chicken with fritters to the big spender's prime rib or boneless sirloin. The price of the entree includes an appetizer, an assortment of goodies from brass pails on the spinning relish wheel that's brought to your table, salad, bread sticks, the Dog Team's famous sweet sticky buns, and a multitude of vegetables like your mother used to make, served family style. For dessert, if you can face it, there might be homemade pies, chocolate delight or a Bartlett pear with creme de menthe. One of us feels that far too much food is served, but the other generally is up to the challenge.

Lunch in summer, 11:30 to 2; dinner year-round, Tuesday-Saturday 5 to 9, Sunday noon to 8.

Mister Up's, Bakery Lane, Middlebury. (802) 388-6724.
International. $9.50 to $15.95.
On a nice day or moonlit night, it's fun to sit on ice-cream-parlor chairs on the spacious, covered outdoor deck under the trees beside tumbling Otter Creek. Inside, a number of brick-walled dining areas are on several levels; the balcony has colorful, locally made stained-glass windows. It's just the right mix for today's college students, who revel in its mix-and-match menu as well as its mix-and-match atmosphere. The large menu embraces lots of snacky items and light items as well as full meals, or you can just go through the salad bar (which has sprouts, sunflower seeds and cherry tomatoes as well as about 101 other things) for $4.50, including bread. Dinner entrees include teriyaki steak, poached salmon, barbecued seafood New Orleans style, shrimp scampi, and marinated leg of Vermont lamb. There are pastas, stir-fries, fajitas, hot Bangkok salad, quiche, Cajun duck, and Creole gumbo.

Open daily, 11:30 to midnight.

Fire & Ice, 26 Seymour St., Middlebury. (802) 388-7166.
International. $10.95 to $14.95.
How many good restaurants can a small college town support? Off the beaten path but obviously popular (it opened in 1974 and lately has been greatly expanded), Fire & Ice is a handsome establishment with all kinds of lamps and accents of copper (lanterns in copper niches on the walls and a huge copper dome in the ceiling). The candlelit dining rooms with nooks and crannies offer entrees ranging from Chinese ginger shrimp and champagne chicken to filet mignon stuffed with lobster or oysters. The lunch and light-dinner menu is available all day, meaning you can dine on quiche lorraine or the salad and bread bar (there are two on weekends).

Open daily except Monday from 11:30 to 9:30 or 10.

East Middlebury

Waybury Inn, Route 125, East Middlebury. (802) 388-4015.
American. $10.95 to $15.95.
This rural inn dating to 1810 was our favorite place for special-occasion dining in our college days, when the Waybury and the Dog Team had a monopoly on the

fine-food business hereabouts. We're partial to the dark and cozy taproom out back, the prototype of an old New England pub (the outside of this inn is, after all, the backdrop for the Bob Newhart show). But the great London broil with mushroom sauce was missing from the menu at our last visit, and dinners and Sunday brunch were being served in the stenciled, pink and green dining room and on the enclosed porch. The menu offers a short selection of fish (Norwegian salmon, stuffed trout), veal, roast lamb with a rich gravy, cornish game hen, and beef (prime rib, steak au poivre). Appetizers are standard: French onion soup, clam chowder, stuffed mushrooms, and shrimp cocktail. The homemade desserts are similarly old-fashioned.

Dinner nightly, 6 to 9; Sunday brunch, 11 to 1:30.

Bristol

★ Mary's, 11 Main St., Bristol, (802) 453-2432.
Regional American. $10 to $17.75.
We'd gladly eat here once a month or oftener, if only we lived nearby. For Mary's, despite being a small and quirky place, has always had one of the more interesting menus and wine lists around. There are different flowered cloths on every table, old kitchen chairs, macrame covers over the lights, and striking prints on the walls, most of which we'd love to own. A jungle of plants is overhead at the window table, where we once sat for Sunday brunch. The tomato-dill bisque was sensational and the seafood crepes and stuffed french toast with raspberry glaze just fine. At dinner, chef Douglas Mack has a way with duck prepared three ways — the wing, southern fried and served with a honey-jalapeno sauce, the breast sauteed au poivre and flamed with a shiitake mushroom and cognac sauce, and the leg a confit on a bed of onions and red peppers. Start with a warm smoked bluefish and lobster cheesecake, chicken and spinach terrine or fireworks shrimp (which really is). Any of those with a loaf of the irresistible breads and one of the light entrees like New England crab cakes with a key lime sauce, garlic coleslaw and french fries make quite a meal. Or go on to the big treats: lobster and scallop saute in a lime-mint beurre blanc, grilled swordfish with garlic and black pepper butter, grilled rainbow trout with chile-hollandaise sauce and cornmeal hush puppies, veal marguerite, pepper-charred venison, or that great duck. Desserts like bananas foster, key lime pie, three-layer cheesecake, and Savannah peanut pie are to die for. Doug and partner Linda Harmon are carrying on just fine the tradition started by Mary Bolton and Woody Danforth.

Lunch, 11:30 to 3:30; dinner, 5 to 9:30; Sunday, brunch 10:30 to 3, dinner 4 to 9:30. Closed Mondays.

Vergennes

Painter's Tavern Restaurant, 5 North Green St., Vergennes. (802) 877-3413.
American/International. $9.95 to $14.95.
A suave and contemporary restaurant done up in beige and brown occupies part of the Stevens House facing the village green, built in 1793 and listed in the National Register of Historic Places. The airy, two-level main floor has five booths and ten tables amid an abundance of greenery and antique photos. The porch is popular with diners in summer. The chef is into what he calls American with ethnic twists, perhaps Thai-curried mahi-mahi, grilled Korean chicken and Cajun jambalaya, along with baked New England scrod, coquilles St. Jacques, grilled tuna, seafood alfredo, and stir-fries. His salad of marinated and grilled quail with cilantro-chile dressing was honored in the latest Taste of Vermont competition, in which Painter's Tavern also was recognized for its veal medallions in maple-bourbon sauce and a

timbale of smoked salmon, Vermont cheddar and sorrel. Homemade desserts include a perennial favorite, death by chocolate, plus fruit tortes and Vermont maple-walnut pie. A bar menu is available in the upstairs lounge.

Lunch, Monday-Saturday 11:30 to 2:30; dinner nightly, 5 to 9 or 10. Closed Sunday and Monday in winter.

Burlington Area

Shelburne

* Shelburne House, Shelburne Farms, Shelburne 05482. (802) 985-8498.
New American. $19 to $24.

The 100-room summer mansion of the late William Seward Webb and Lila Vanderbilt Webb has been refurbished into a grand inn of the old school on their 1,000-acre hilltop agricultural estate surrounded on three sides by Lake Champlain. The main-floor public rooms are a living museum, but the highlight for food connoisseurs is the formal dining room, its walls dressed in red damask, the marble floor in black and white, and tables with napkins tied in red ribbons, Villeroy & Boch china, candles in crystal candlesticks, crystal stemware and heavy, impeccably polished silver. Here, dinners of distinction and creativity are available to the public. Young Scottish chef David Taylor, who was head chef on the luxurious train, the Royal Scotsman, changes his menu daily. For starters, there could be lobster and corn chowder, a warm mousse of smoked salmon, or warm asparagus pastries served with a strawberry hollandaise, followed by a mixed green salad or something more exotic, like a salad of roast veal tenderloin with sun-dried tomato dressing or grilled duck with wilted greens and pepper-shallot vinaigrette. The five main-course choices could be filet mignon of buffalo or roasted pheasant with chestnut dressing, pan-roasted red snapper with smoked salmon mousse and bourbon sauce, sauteed veal with red pepper fettuccine and roasted garlic, and grilled breast of muscovy duck with a blueberry sauce. For dessert, you might try a hot apple and calvados souffle, homemade passion-fruit ice cream with fresh fruit, hazelnut-chocolate terrine with creme anglaise and fresh berries, or Shelburne Farms cheddar with grapes and crispy wafers. This is not inexpensive fare, nor is dinner here an occasion to be taken lightly. For a culinary splurge, however, Vermont has few better dining rooms.

Dinner nightly, 6 to 9. Open June to mid-October. Reservations recommended two weeks in advance.

* Cafe Shelburne, Route 7, Shelburne. (802) 985-3939.
New French. $11.90 to $18.50.

This little prize among small provincial French restaurants has been going strong since 1969, but never better than under new chef-owner Patrick Grangien, who trained with Paul Bocuse and came to Vermont as part of the short-lived Gerard's Haute Cuisine enterprise. Talk about happy circumstance: the cafe was up for sale in 1988, Patrick was available, and knowing diners seeking inspired food and good value have been packing the place ever since. In 1989, Patrick added a lovely covered, screened patio in the rear that looks like it's been there forever, such is the mix of lattice ceiling and grapevines all around. Patrick calls his cuisine "more bistro style than nouvelle," which is appropriate for the French bistro decor — a copper bar on one side, a dining room of white linens, deep blue napkins and black lacquered chairs on the other. Seafood is his forte (in 1988 he won the National Seafood Challenge and was elected best seafood chef of the year). Try his prize-winning filet of lotte on a bed of spinach and mushrooms in a shrimp sauce,

Norwegian salmon bouquetiere, homemade fettuccine with shrimp and sea scallops in a creamy mushroom sauce, or a classic bouillabaisse. Filet mignon tartare, tenderloin of pork in a ginger and lime sauce, roasted rack of lamb with garlic, and beef tenderloin in a green peppercorn sauce are other possibilities. The five soups are triumphs and more innovative than the appetizers. Among desserts are creme brulee, warm chocolate cake souffle, raspberry mousse in a raspberry sauce, chocolate marquise, Paris-brest, and frozen grand marnier souffle. The wine list is pleasantly priced and bears considerable variety.

Dinner, Tuesday-Sunday 6 to 9 or 9:30.

Francesca's, Route 7, Shelburne. (802) 985-8661.
Northern Italian. $7.95 to $16.25.

Founded on the mezzanine of the Jelly Mill Common, this highly rated establishment up and moved across the street in 1989 into the old Potting Shed restaurant. The new space is twice the size, giving chef-owner Scott Vineberg and his wife, Francesca Muratori, more room to exercise their considerable culinary prowess and more customers to impress. Longtime regulars weren't universally impressed with the move, expressing concern over lack of elbow room and an abbreviated menu. Both shortcomings were being corrected when we visited. Scott planned to add things like veal chops and duck to the dinner menu, which features charbroiled Norwegian salmon with choice of sauces, sea scallops in a lemon-garlic sauce, chicken with shrimp and artichoke hearts, veal marsala, and charbroiled veal rib steak. All pastas are made fresh daily at Francesca's Pasta-To-Go shop. At lunch, one special of mussels and tuna alla panna with tomato dill was enormously successful; a second of chicken and tomato in garlic sauce over black pepper fettuccine was less so — we had to ask for more sauce, and still there was little taste of garlic or pepper. The pasta pescatora with seafood in marinara sauce over linguini appealed at our last visit. The antipasto plate is much-acclaimed, and so are such desserts as cannoli, mocha-flavored chilled cream pie, and chocolate sponge cake layered with hazelnut-chocolate mousse and topped with a chocolate ganache. The largest rope of garlic we ever saw was draped over a beam in one small dining room. The main room has black lacquered chairs at handsome wood tables topped with straw mats and green napkins. Color photos of Italy adorn the walls, and the place sports a sleek new bar.

Lunch daily, 11:30 to 2:30; dinner nightly, 5 to 9 or 10. No lunch weekends in winter.

South Burlington

★ **Pauline's,** 1834 Shelburne Road, South Burlington. (802) 862-1081.
Regional American. $13.95 to $21.95.

One of the earliest of the Burlington area's fine restaurants (nee Pauline's Kitchen in the 1970s), this unlikely-looking place with twinkling white lights framing the front windows year-round has been expanded under the ownership of Robert and Pat Fuller. The original downstairs dining room is now an exceptionally attractive cafe paneled in cherry and oak, where you can make a mighty good meal of appetizers and light entrees. All is serene and white in the original upstairs lounge, which has been transformed into three small dining rooms. The printed menu, which changes nightly, is the kind upon which everything appeals, from Maine crab cakes with orange-basil sauce to roast Vermont partridge served with a fresh raspberry gastrique. Our spring dinner began with remarkably good appetizers of morels and local fiddleheads in a rich madeira sauce and a sprightly plate of shrimp and scallops in ginger, garnished with snow peas and cherry tomatoes. Steaming popovers and zippy salads accompanied. The entrees were superior: three strips of lamb wrapped

Burlington Area

around goat cheese, and a thick filet mignon, served with spring vegetables and boiled new potatoes. A honey-chocolate mousse and framboise au chocolat from Pauline's acclaimed assortment of desserts ended a fine meal. A pleasant little side patio is particularly popular for lunch.

Open daily from 11:30 to midnight, Sunday from 10:30.

Burlington

★ Five Spice Cafe, 175 Church St., Burlington. (802) 864-4505.
Asian. $6.95 to $13.95.

This spicy little prize occupying two floors of a former counter-culture restaurant produced one of our more memorable lunches ever. A spicy bloody mary preceded a bowl of hot and sour soup that was extra hot and a house sampler of appetizers, among them smoked shrimps, Siu Mai dumplings, Hunan noodles, and Szechuan escargots. The less adventurous among us passed up the red snapper in brown bean sauce for a blackboard special of mock duck stir-fry in peanut sauce (the vegetarian dish really did taste like duck, just as, we were assured, the mock abalone really tastes like abalone). Sated as we were, we had to share the ginger-tangerine cheesecake, which proved denser and more subtly flavored than we expected. Chef Jerry Weinberg has a loyal following for his multi-Asian menu of unusual and tantalizing dishes from India, Thailand, Vietnam, Indonesia, and China. The wide-ranging dinner menu boasts, quite endearingly, that some of the items and spices have been imitated locally but never matched. Start with Indonesian chicken wings, Tahi crabby pork rolls or Vietnamese calamari. Main courses range from Hunan noodles to four shrimp dishes, one an eye-opener called Thai fire shrimp ("until this dish, we had a three-star heat rating — now there's four"). A drunken chocolate mousse laced with liqueurs and a blackout cake drenched with triple sec are among favored desserts. The setting does nothing to detract from the food. Oil lamps flicker on each table even at noon. Flowers in pressed-glass vases and a different bottle of wine atop each table comprise the decor. Above the serving sideboard is a collection of Five Spice T-shirts emblazoned with fire-breathing dragons and the saying, "Some Like It Hot." Yes, indeed.

Lunch, Tuesday-Friday 11:30 to 2:30; dinner, Tuesday-Saturday 5 to 9:30 or 10:30. Dim sum brunch, Saturday and Sunday 11 to 3. No smoking upstairs.

Deja Vu Cafe, 185 Pearl St., Burlington. (802) 864-7917.
American. $6.25 to $23.95.

Whether outside on the Spanish-style courtyard or inside on many levels or in the elegant new Frank Lloyd Wright look-alike dining room, this is one beautiful restaurant (and so dimly lit that candles are lighted on the tables, even at lunch). The all-day menu features crepes, salads and light entrees. One crepe is filled with smoked sausage, apples, muenster, and maple syrup; another with smoked Norwegian salmon with spinach, mushrooms and Vermont creme fraiche. The soupe au pistou is great, but ask for extra pistou (basil, garlic and parmesan) if you like it as much as we do. There are also changing dinner specials, among them sauteed scallops with raspberries, Vermont pheasant galantine, and veal savoyardes at our visit. A frozen champagne mimosa granite, black Russian pie, creme brulee, homemade truffles, and ice-cream crepes are among the delectable desserts. The decor is striking with all the different lamps, including wonderful glass ones fluted like lilies, and the biggest copper container we ever saw, up on a hoist and filled with plants. Even if it's not open, try to steal a look at the magnificent Wright Room, used on weekends and for private functions.

Open daily, 11:30 to midnight, weekends to 1.

The Daily Planet, 15 Center St., Burlington. (802) 862-9647.
International. $11 to $14.50.
The name of this funky place reflects its "global fare — ethnic and eclectic," in the words of the manager. Casual, innovative and a favorite local watering hole among knowledgeable noshers, it has a large bar with a pressed-tin ceiling, a solarium filled with cactus and jade plants, and a lofty, sun-splashed dining room full of exposed pipes and the rotating works of local artists, where the oilcloth table coverings at noon are changed to white linen at night. The Daily Planet shines with celestial appetizers like Thai skewered chicken, smoked chicken hash with leeks and sweet potato, and Down East crab cakes wilth basil mayonnaise. Pastas could pair feta cheese with seafood or smoked salmon with vegetables. There are also vegetarian and catalan risottos. For entrees, how about chicken with sun-dried tomato pesto on a bed of spinach, Thai seafood stew poached in coconut milk, grilled lamb with orange-scented olive sauce on a tuscan white bean cake, or grilled filet mignon with a sauce of roasted onion, shallot, garlic, and madeira? Desserts change daily; you might find lemon roulade, Southern nut cake with bourbon creme anglaise, baked apples with figs and cranberries, fresh plum ice cream, and white chocolate-lemon cheesecake. The wine list, though small, is well-chosen and offers incredible steals.
Lunch, Monday-Saturday 11:30 to 3; dinner nightly, 5 to 10:30 or 11.

Bourbon Street Grill, 213 College St., Burlington. (802) 865-2800.
Cajun/American. $9.25 to $13.95.
Art and Manon O'Connor had never been to New Orleans when they opened this small and intimate cafe in 1988. You wouldn't know it from the decor (a comfortable and warm rendition of a Bourbon Street establishment, nicely outfitted in pink with a tile floor, artworks and plants). Nor would you know it from the menu, which is patterned after those of restaurants there. Chef Art had been dabbling in Cajun food as executive chef for the Mount Mansfield Corporation after restaurant stints in Connecticut. Here he went all out with appetizers like gumbo, jambalaya, barbecued shrimp, and Cajun flank steak, and entrees like Cajun chicken, seafood mixed grill, shrimp etouffee, and New Orleans bouillabaisse. The dessert tray yields bourbon-pecan torte, chocolate cheesecake and chocolate-praline crepes.
Lunch, Monday-Saturday 11:30 to 4; dinner nightly, 5:30 to 10; Sunday brunch, 10:30 to 3.

Ice House Restaurant, 171 Battery St., Burlington. (802) 864-1800.
American. $13.50 to $19.50.
Two open-air decks, an oyster bar, a wine bar, a gourmet shop called Food Discovery, and a straightforward menu with an emphasis on North Atlantic seafood are attractions at Burlington's first restaurant restoration, circa 1976. Inside the massive stone building that really was an ice house is a large upstairs lounge and dining room with huge rough beams and plush sofas and a downstairs dining room with fieldstone walls and nicely separated tables. We enjoyed grilled marinated lamb on a skewer and mussels tuscan style prior to a dinner of poached scallops with julienned vegetables in a butter and cream sauce, and stuffed chicken breast with leeks, wild mushrooms, balsamic vinegar, and red wine sauce. Grilled swordfish, salmon baked en croute with shrimp pate and sauce nantua, and grilled red snapper with lobster cream sauce are other choices. Desserts include chocolate-toffee torte, bourbon-pecan pie a la mode, and caramel vanilla boats in creme anglaise.
Lunch, daily 11:30 to 11; dinner, 5 to 10; Sunday brunch, 10:30 to 2:30.

Sakura, 2 Church St., Burlington. (802) 863-1988.
Japanese. $9 to $16.
Burlington's first Japanese restaurant has fared well since opening in 1987 in

quarters vacated by the urbane but short-lived City-Side restaurant. Gone is the trendy setting; bare blond wood tables are set with chopsticks tucked inside peach napkins. Cranes in flight painted on the walls look like shadows. Along one side is a sushi bar. In the center is a raised tatami room with two tables at which you sit on cushions and take your shoes off. A noontime treat is the Sakura lunch box, served with soup, salad, rice and fruit, and containing a California roll, assorted tempura and chicken teriyaki. At dinner, the easy-to-follow menu written in English lists upwards of 30 appetizers from sashimi to California maki to bean curd cooked in seaweed-flavored soup. The sushi bar has a dozen choices, including a deluxe assortment called sushi heaven. The usual other Japanese treats are available in a wide range of prices, accompanied by soup and rice. One of the more exotic is broiled eel and dark sauce served over hot rice in a Japanese-style box. Fresh fruit, yokan, tempura ice cream, and Japanese crepe are available for dessert.

Lunch, Tuesday-Saturday 11:30 to 2; dinner, 5 to 9 or 10:30. Closed Monday.

Sweetwaters, Church and College Streets, Burlington. (802) 864-9800.
American/International. $7.95 to $11.95.

Built in 1926, this brick bank has been turned into one of Burlington's more popular restaurants with dining on several levels around an enormous mural in an atrium, and outside on a canopy-covered sidewalk cafe that's always crowded in summer. Voted locally as having the best lunch in Burlington, Sweetwaters serves a casual menu all day, offering things like potato skins, cheese nachos, chicken bits, and beer-batter shrimp. Among the twelve salads are Italian pasta (winner in a Taste of Vermont competition), a hot Thai salad, a three-salad sampler, and three low-calorie offerings. At night, more substantial entrees ($7.95 to $10.95) include oriental chicken, scampi and New York steak. The Sunday champagne brunch consists of items like eggs sardou, huevos rancheros and french toast stuffed with ham and Vermont cheese.

Open daily from 11:30 to 1 a.m., Sunday from 10:30 to 10.

Winooski

Waterworks, Champlain Mill, Winooski. (802) 655-2044.
American. $8.95 to $14.95.

You can still see the huge pine beams from the American Woolen Co. building as you dine here on two levels overlooking the Winooski River rapids. One of two restaurants owned by the same outfit anchoring either end of the Champlain Mill, Waterworks takes full advantage of the view, from the canopied outdoor deck running the length of the restaurant to the cheery greenhouse with hanging plants. The casual all-day menu offers an abundance of appetizers, salads and sandwiches. Dinner entrees include chicken with brie, shrimp scampi, scrod au gratin, wiener schnitzel, New York strip steak, and three stir-fried wok dishes, plus nightly specials. The house dressing on the salad is an outstanding lemon-mustard-dill, and the seaside mary is a bloody mary ringed with four large shrimp. For dessert, try white chocolate-almond pie, amaretto dolce or creme brulee.

Lunch, Monday-Saturday from 11:30; dinner, nightly from 4; Sunday brunch, 11 to 3:30.

The Prime Factor, Champlain Mill, Winooski. (802) 655-0300.
Steakhouse. $9.75 to $15.95.

Where the Waterworks leans to seafood, its counterpart at the other end of the mill specializes in beef, as its name implies. Also on two levels and slightly more formal, all done up in rusts and greens, it offers six beef entrees, from prime rib to filet mignon; four chicken dishes, and enough seafood to come up with six combination platters. Beer batter shrimp is a featured dish. Appetizers include shrimp barbecue, escargots and clam fritter. Triple chocolate crepes and white chocolate silk pie are the desserts of choice.

Lunch, Monday-Saturday 11:30 to 3; dinner, nightly from 5, Sunday from 4; Sunday brunch, 10:30 to 2:30.

Essex Junction

Butler's, The Inn at Essex, 70 Essex Way, Essex Junction. (802) 878-1100. New American. $15.50 to $20.

Imagine finding an inn of this elegance — to say nothing of a restaurant of such stature — in the midst of a large field at the edge of Essex Junction. The restaurant is the newest venture of the New England Culinary Institute of Montpelier, which runs the food and beverage operation and a bakery for the new 97-room Inn at Essex, a Hawk venture that opened in 1989. Actually, there are two restaurants: the formal Butler's with a vaguely Georgian look, upholstered Queen Anne chairs, heavy white china and windows draped in chintz, and the more casual **Birch Tree Cafe,** where woven mats on bare tables, dark green wainscoting and small lamps with gilt shades enhance a Vermont country setting. The cafe was where we had a fine Christmas lunch: sun-dried tomato fettuccine with scallops, a wedge of pheasant pie and a salad of mixed greens. Although the portions were small and the service slow, we saw signs of inspiration, on the menu as well as in a dessert of chocolate medallions with mousseline and blueberries in a pool of raspberry-swirled creme fraiche, presented as a work of art. Two pieces of biscotti came with the bill, a very reasonable tab. Interesting dinners at bargain prices are served in the cafe at night. Dinner in Butler's, NECI's temple to haute cuisine, is a study in trendy food. The menu changes daily, but you might start with white bean soup with rosemary and lamb, warm rabbit sausage and duck terrine with raisin chutney, beef tartare on waffled potatoes with smoked salmon ravioli filled with tuna tartare, or warm salad of stuffed loin of lamb with balsamic vinaigrette. For main courses, how about grilled tuna with steamed mussels, shrimp and herbed tomatoes, or grilled filet of beef with zinfandel potatoes and blue cheese? There's considerable creativity in the enormous kitchen, thanks to executive chef Robert Barral (formerly of Boston's Four Seasons) and his aspiring student cooks.

Butler's, dinner, Monday-Saturday 6 to 10. Birch Tree Cafe, lunch, Monday-Saturday 11:30 to 1:30; dinner, Monday-Sunday 5:30 to 9:30; Sunday brunch, 11 to 2.

Colchester

Marble Island Resort, 150 Marble Island Road, Colchester. (802) 864-6800. New American. $15 to $22.

The sunken, 60-seat dining room in pale peach and green off the main lobby at this renovated resort is quiet and intimate. Meals are a treat, thanks to ambitious chef Chaz Sternberg, for several years at the Ice House in Burlington. For starters, try the changing pate, caesar salad with crispy fried oysters, or smoked Idaho trout with remoulade. Likely entrees include grilled yellowfin tuna with wasabi, New England seafood stew with saffron, roast duck with crackling, sauteed Vermont sweetbreads with calvados and green apples, grilled Vermont veal chop with roasted red pepper sauce, and, when we visited, grilled saddle of Vermont venison with two sauces. For dessert, we'd choose Chaz's specialty, a hot cheesecake that's as light as a lemon souffle, a raspberry cloud cake, or one of his fresh fruit tarts. Light meals are served in the adjacent Intrepid lounge from noon to closing.

Dinner nightly, 6 to 10. Closed mid-October to Easter.

Northern Vermont

Montpelier

✱ Tubbs, 24 Elm St., Montpelier. (802) 229-9202.
New American. $12.50 to $16.25.

Bet you didn't realize that Montpelier is becoming a culinary mecca of sorts. It's all due to the ambitious New England Culinary Institute, established only in 1980 but since then exerting influence and opening a large new operation in Essex Junction less than a decade later. Tubbs is the crowning glory, the final-year effort of students in the institute's two-year culinary program. And what a jewel it is: a restaurant fashioned from a former jailhouse with a soaring, two-story-high, painted tin ceiling with track lighting, tables set with balloon wine glasses, fine white china and pink and white linens, and accents of local artworks and pottery here and there. The setting is as inviting as the changing menu offered by creative student chefs, and the prices are inviting as well. The day's lunch menu might offer a hot chicken salad with mushrooms and walnuts in a crepe shell or cold smoked chicken breast with cappellini and spicy peanut sauce, and entrees like noisettes of lamb in potato crust served with rosemary ratatouille or grilled yellowfin tuna sandwich with pickled ginger and wasabi mayonnaise. A dessert pastry (prepared at the adjacent La Brioche bakery) makes a worthy finale for a memorable lunch. At night, look for up to ten main courses, perhaps galette of scallops with leek compote, trout with two-salmon mousse and cucumber sauce, magret of duck with raspberry and merlot glaze, and escalopes of veal with red vermouth, prosciutto and fresh sage. A cabbage, bacon and blue cheese soup and confit of duck with mixed greens and walnut vinaigrette might precede. The assortment of pastries and sorbets is enough to undo a dieter's resolve. The wine list is well-chosen and reasonably priced. Service, as at most culinary schools, varies but can be quite polished.

Lunch, Monday-Friday 11:30 to 2; dinner, Monday-Saturday 6 to 9:30.

✱ Elm Street Cafe, 38 Elm St., Montpelier. (802) 223-3188.
Contemporary. $7.50 to $13.95.

The first-year effort of New England Culinary Institute chefs appeals in a different way from Tubbs. It's more intimate and informal, and serves three meals a day at prices like those you may remember from your college student union, particularly at breakfast and lunch. Decor in several small rooms with polished wood tables is cafe-casual. Luncheon offerings run from the simple to the sublime: perhaps a huge, fluffy sausage and swiss cheese quiche, mouth-watering Icelandic shrimp and crab louis in an avocado half, pan-broiled swordfish with tomatoes and scallions, or grilled lamb steak chambord. Good cubed fried potatoes, crisp broccoli, and a green salad with Vermont maple and poppyseed vinaigrette might accompany. The short dinner menu also changes daily, but might yield such treats as roast loin of pork with maple-mustard glaze and cranberry-apple compote, grilled swordfish with black bean sauce and cilantro salsa, and linguini with shrimp, spinach and Vermont creme fraiche. Under lighter fare, you might find sauteed crab cakes with a caper-lime sauce and arugula salad. Chocolate truffle cake, apple spice cake with caramel sauce and chocolate dacquoise could be the dessert fare.

Breakfast, Monday-Friday 7 to 10, Saturday 8 to 10; lunch, Monday-Saturday 11:30 to 1:30; dinner, Monday-Saturday 5:30 to 9.

Chadwick's, 52 State St., Montpelier. (802) 223-2384.
American/Italian. $8.95 to $14.95.

Opened in 1988, this is a pleasant place done up in oak with gaslight fixtures, marble tables and seating for 40 beneath twelve-foot-high ceilings. The all-day menu is big on salads, burgers, and sandwiches, plus appetizers ranging from potato skins and chicken wings to homemade chili, fried mozzarella sticks and gorgonzola tortellini with pesto. For entrees at night, you could have chicken in three guises (teriyaki, piccata or parmesan), barbecued ribs, shrimp scampi, scallop saute over linguini, or top sirloin with three grilled shrimp. Dessert could be fresh fruit, cheesecake or chocolate-amaretto mousse.

Open Monday-Saturday, 11 to 9:30 or 10.

Stockyard Inn, 3 Bailey Ave., Montpelier. (802) 223-7811.
Steaks/Seafood. $8.95 to $15.95.
The Kiwanis Club meets here, and so does almost everybody else in the area, it seems; the large steakhouse even serves breakfast in the summer. There's an open grill in the paneled main dining room. Light lunches are available in the bar, part of it in a railroad car with round velvet-cushioned chairs for drinks. Stockyard specials are choice ribs and loins, including steak teriyaki marinated for 24 hours in a special sauce, filet mignon topped with a mushroom cap, and sirloin kabob. Scallops come baked or fried, swordfish is charbroiled, and crab is served in veal oscar, steamed crab legs, or as crab and sirloin. Meals include a salad bar.

Open daily, 11:30 to 10; from 8 a.m. in summer.

Calais

♥ **The White House at Kent's Corner,** Kent's Corner, Calais. (802) 229-9847.
Regional American. Prix-Fixe, $33.50.
Have your cocktail on the white wicker-furnished porch as you gaze at the English perennial garden, the goldfish pond or the hummingbird that visits the lilac hedge. Or have it on one of the plush velvet sofas in the library. The gorgeous 1825 house was painstakingly restored over five years by partners Leo Romero and Iory Allison (Leo also is associated with Casa Romero in Boston), who finally had it ready for business in 1985, and have been making it more glorious ever since. Feast your eyes on the oriental rugs over painted floors, the spectacular sunburst window, the vaulted ceiling, the collections of china and priceless antiques, the wonderful mix of formal and country, and the impeccable taste exhibited everywhere you look. You want food, too? Leo prepares a prix-fixe, five-course dinner that might start with country-style borscht with fresh dill or cream of sweet vidalia onion with lovage soup, followed by Eastern smoked salmon or fresh agnolotti and shrimp with a pesto-cream sauce. A choice of three entrees might be sauteed shrimp with shiitake mushrooms over linguini, roasted leg of local organic lamb served with an orange-ginger sauce, and grilled filet mignon with madeira and shallots. A mixed green salad with herbed vinaigrette follows the main course. Dessert could be a choice of chocolate marquise, raspberry cheesecake or homemade maple-walnut ice cream with assorted cookies. There's terrific piano music (light jazz, Broadway) on Friday and Saturday nights. The White House is way out in the country north of Montpelier, but well worth the trip. Now you can stay overnight in three guest rooms upstairs.

Dinner by reservation, Tuesday-Saturday 6 to 9; Sunday brunch, noon to 3. Closed January-April.

Warren

★ **The Phoenix,** Sugarbush Village, Warren. (802) 583-2777.
Regional American. $13.75 to $22.50.
Some people come here just for the acclaimed desserts, although chef-owner

Peter Sussman admonishes dinner patrons as he passes their table with luscious-looking pastries that "you can't have dessert until you eat your veggies." The multi-level restaurant has expansive windows filled with plants, twinkling lights even in summer, deep-blue linened tables bathed in candlelight, bentwood chairs, an enormous espresso machine, an old barber pole in one corner, and mirrors and greenery everywhere. If you're trying to save room for dessert, skip an appetizer and concentrate instead on the chewy rolls that are good enough to demand seconds. Entrees might be grilled chicken basted with a fresh rosemary-black pepper-shallot butter, scampi tossed with garlic and pine nuts, and veal with pistachios. We liked the grilled medallions of pork sauced with green peppercorns and apple puree and the roast confit of duckling with a homemade orange-pear-ginger sauce. With much fanfare, Peter wheels up two carts containing six desserts each. Our choices ranged from white chocolate mousse and napoleons to raspberry cheese souffle with raspberry puree and banana-kiwi tart filled with custard cream, all of which we sampled because each can order two half-portions — which turned out to be what most would consider full portions. All of his repertoire of 280 desserts are masterful.

Dinner nightly, 6 to 10 (closed Wednesday in non-ski season). Desserts also available in the bar.

♥ **The Common Man,** German Flats Road, Warren. (802) 583-2800.
  Continental. $10.95 to $17.95.
  A soaring, century-old timbered barn has floral carpets on the walls to cut down the noise and keep out wintry drafts. Six crystal chandeliers hang from the beamed ceilings over bare wood tables set simply with red napkins and pewter candlesticks. The French-Swiss-Vermont fare is exceptional, yet a basket of herbed bread is served without benefit of a side plate. Despite the incongruities, the whole mix works, and thrivingly so since its establishment in 1972 in the site we first knew as Orsini's. Destroyed by fire in 1987, it has been replaced by a barn dismantled in Moretown and rebuilt here by English-born owner Mike Ware, who operates one of the more popular places in the valley with an air of elegance but without pretension. The escargots maison "served with our famous (and secret) garlic butter sauce" is the most popular of appetizers, which include shrimp with remoulade sauce and smoked mackerel with a red pepper mayonnaise. Main courses run from sea scallops and shrimp over rotelli pasta to rack of lamb provencale. The fresh Vermont rabbit sauteed in olive oil, garlic and rosemary was distinctive, and the Vermont sweetbreads normande with apples and apple brandy were some of the best we've tasted. With dishes like venison saute and roast pheasant, this is uncommon fare for common folk. Among desserts are kirschen strudel, mocha-chocolate cake, meringue glace, and Ben & Jerry's ice cream.
  Dinner, weekdays 6:30 to 10, weekends 6 to 10:30. Closed Mondays in off-season.

Sam Rupert's, Sugarbush Access Road, Warren. (802) 583-2421.
  Continental. $12.25 to $20.75.
  The old Sugarbush Sugarhouse no longer serves pancakes and homemade syrup. It's now a much-expanded, elegant dining establishment in white and pink, with masses of flowers, well-spaced tables and a smashing greenhouse room that brings the outside in. The dinner menu is a mixed repertoire of fresh seafood (grilled turbot bearnaise and monkfish with shrimp the night we visited), chicken with shrimp and curry, veal rib-eye with five peppercorns, lamb steak moutarde, and basque duckling. On a summer visit, we liked the seafood on linguini and a fine roast pork tenderloin garnished with apples and flavored with apple brandy. The terrine of smoked salmon and Chinese pancakes with shrimp, celery and ginger are popular

starters. Finish with the house specialty, a frozen white and dark chocolate mousse pie, frozen peanut pie with hot chocolate sauce, or peach melba deluxe with kiwi fruit and strawberries. If you're as full as we were, settle for a cantaloupe sorbet.

Dinner nightly, 6 to 9:30; closed Tuesday and Wednesday in spring and fall.

Chez Henri, Sugarbush Village, Warren. (802) 583-2600.
French. $10.75 to $17.95.

The longest-running of the valley's long runners, Chez Henri is in its third decade as a French bistro with an after-dinner disco in the rear. It's tiny, intimate and very French, as you might expect from a former food executive for Air France. Henri Borel offers lunch, brunch, apres-ski, early dinner, dinner and dancing, inside in winter by a warming stone fireplace and a marble bar and outside in summer on a small terrace bordered by a babbling mountain brook. The dinner menu starts with changing soups and pates "as made in a French country kitchen," a classic French onion soup or fish broth, and perhaps mussels mariniere, smoked trout with capers or steak tartare "knived to order." Served with good French bread and seasonal vegetables, entrees often include sauteed quails with vinegar and shallots, frog's legs provencale, tripe in casserole, rabbit with thyme and mushrooms, veal chop calvados, and tournedos bearnaise. Creme caramel, coupe marrons and chocolate mousse are among the dessert standbys. The wines are all French.

Open daily in winter, noon to 2 a.m.; weekends in summer, hours vary.

Waitsfield

✦ **Tucker Hill Lodge,** Route 17, Waitsfield. (802) 496-3983.
New American/French. $14.75 to $19.

The Sugarbush-Mad River Valley area is known for outstanding dining, and this inn is the premier dining spot. The inner dining room is paneled and beamed; the outer addition is greenhouse-style, with skylights and brick floors. Quilts and watercolors decorate the walls, tables are white-linened and service is friendly. The chef is a stickler for indigenous Vermont products, deciding each morning what he will put on the night's menu. Among starters are interesting soups like lentil with smoked ham and scallop with cilantro, and homemade pasta with lobster and romano cheese, venison pate and wood-grilled Vermont quail. Entrees include wood-grilled swordfish served with a jalapeno-lime butter sauce and grilled avocado slices, yellowtail sole in parchment with shrimp and coriander, and maple-mustard chicken. We savored a roast sirloin madeira with porcini mushrooms, local chanterelles and fresh savory, and the medallions of pork loin with apples in a creme fraiche sauce with whole-grain mustard and honey. The vegetables that garnish each dish are wonderful and ever changing. Desserts change as well: among the possibilities, coffee-sambucca cheesecake, frozen frangelico mousse, strawberries sabayon, chocolate chip-hazelnut ice cream, and an orange genoise layered with apples, maple syrup and blueberry butter cream (deceptively called Vermont apple pie torte). In the downstairs lounge, the lodge offers flatbreads (gourmet pizzas) cooked in an outdoor stone oven Monday through Wednesday nights in summer. Tapas are served Thursday through Saturday nights in slow periods.

Dinner nightly, June-October 6:30 to 9:30; mid-December to Easter, 6 to 9:30.

Millbrook Lodge, Route 17, Waitsfield. (802) 496-2405.
Country Gourmet. $7.95 to $14.50.

This small, rustic inn with two dining rooms where the tables are covered with paisley cloths is considered a sleeper among the better-known establishments in the Mad River Valley. Chef-owner Thom Gorman and his wife Joan make their famed anadama bread, as well as pastas and desserts, from scratch. Start with mushrooms a la Millbrook, filled with a secret blend of ground veal and herbs. Entrees include a daily roast, veal roma (with Vermont veal), shrimp scampi, garden vegetarian lasagna, cheese cannelloni made with Vermont cheddar and fresh basil, and fettuccine Thom. There are also four dishes from the Bombay region, where Thom lived for two years. The badami rogan josh, local lamb simmered in all kinds of spices and yogurt and served with homemade tomato chutney, sounds wonderful. The luscious desserts include ice creams like chocolate-chocolate chip and brickle candy, coffee-crunch pie (coffee mousse in a nut crust), seasonal berry pies, and an apple brown betty that regulars can't get enough of.

Dinner nightly, 6 to 9. Closed Wednesday in summer and month of May.

The Waitsfield Inn, Route 100, Waitsfield. (802) 496-3979.
Regional American. $12.95 to $18.95.
A wide fieldstone path brightened by pink geraniums leads to the main entrance at the side of the Waitsfield Inn, where a stuffed bear greets patrons at the bar. The sprightly country look of the inn's five small dining rooms is embellished by Laura Ashley wallpapers, frilly curtains and woven mats atop patterned tablecloths. The main dining room opens onto a small outdoor patio, where weekend breakfast and brunch are served at tables under bright yellow umbrellas. Dinner entrees range from chicken with leeks, sweet onion and pine nut compote to tournedos of beef with artichoke bottoms. Fresh salmon with sun-dried tomatoes and cilantro butter in parchment and loin of lamb with wild forest mushrooms were specials the night we visited. Among desserts are strawberries romanoff, raspberry tart and chocolate truffle cake.

Dinner, Tuesday-Sunday 6 to 9; Saturday breakfast, 8:30 to 10:30; Sunday brunch, 8:30 to 2.

Stowe

★ Ten Acres Lodge, Luce Hill Road, Stowe. (802) 253-7638.
Regional American. $16 to $23.
The dining room and airy summer porch are classically pretty — and the menus on the daring and innovative side — at Ten Acres, which many consider the Stowe area's best restaurant. White-linened tables are set with Villeroy & Boch service plates and the atmosphere is rather hushed, as Vivaldi music plays softly in the background. Chef Jack Pickett, who's been with Ten Acres for a decade, stresses regional foods and produce on his menus, which change weekly. One of the inn's waiters gathers the mushrooms, cepes and chanterelles, and a local man grows the melons, which are perfumed like flowers and so juicy you'd think they were from Persia, says the chef. Crusty sourdough bread is served with generous drinks. Salads are special: one night, one of spinach, endive, radicchio, apple, and walnuts with port wine and stilton dressing; the next, composed of spinach, mushrooms, red onion, bacon, and quail eggs. The butterflied leg of lamb with preserved black currants and cracked peppercorns and the chargriled cornish game hen with tomato, basil and creme fraiche were outstanding. Other entrees could be a saute of grey sole, bay scallops and lobster with asparagus and chanterelles, veal loin chop with braised kale and fontina cheese, venison steak with wild mushrooms and roasted garlic, and roast duckling with blood oranges, red grapes and orange muscat wine. You could start with malpeque oysters on the half shell with lime vodka, rock shrimp with black bean cakes and tomatillo salsa, or pate of rabbit with prunes and armagnac. Great desserts include cherry ricotta pie, raspberry cheesecake, casaba melon sorbet, chocolate truffle cake, and hazelnut chocolate ice cream. The huge

wine list has a page of old and rare vintages, this being a place to celebrate special occasions.

Dinner nightly, 6 to 9:30. No smoking.

Green Mountain Inn, Route 100, Stowe. (802) 253-4400.
Regional American. $10.75 to $17.50.

The once-traditional **Number One Main Street** dining room is now country pretty with bare wood floors and nicely spaced tables set with white damask, candles, blue flowered plates, and heavy polished silver. Lanterns and watercolors by the late Vermont artist Walton Blodgett adorn the walls. The cooking is assertive, as in appetizers like shrimp quenelles on spinach with ginger-rhubarb sauce, smoked salmon with goat cheese and cucumber salad, and smoked chicken and honeydew melon with raspberry mayonnaise. The red bell pepper soup is flavored with brie. Among entrees are yellowtail sole stuffed with shrimp mousse and served with basil and a tomato compote, poached chicken with maple cream sauce and pear fritters, and loin lamb chop with rosemary sauce and mint jelly. For dessert, how about frozen amaretto souffle or "sac de bon-bon," a chocolate shell filled with mousse and fresh fruit? Downstairs is **The Whip,** smartly redecorated and striking for the whips in the wall divider separating bar from dining room and over the fireplace. The day's fare is chalked on blackboards above cases where the food is displayed. Many of the dishes are calorie-counted for those who are here for the spa facilities. Country pate with cornichons on toast points, smoked salmon with capers, Mexican vegetable soup, salads with dressings devised by the Canyon Ranch in Arizona, crabmeat on a croissant with melted cheddar, open-face veggie melt (184 calories) — this is perfect "grazing" fare. Main dishes like grilled blackened bluefish, poached salmon, grilled rib-eye, and sauteed veal with interesting presentations are chalked up at night. Frozen mocha cheesecake, oatmeal-maple pie, raspberry-rum sorbet, and very berry bread pudding are some of the ever-changing desserts.

Number One Main Street, dinner nightly, 6 to 9:30. The Whip, open daily, 11:30 to 9:30.

Isle de France, Mountain Road, Stowe. (802) 253-7751.
French. $14 to $21.

Formerly the Crystal Palace, this lavish restaurant opened in 1979 by French chef Jean Lavina shows its heritage, though some of it is a bit threadbare: cut-glass chandeliers, mirrors, gilt ornamental work around the ceilings, rose-bordered service plates with gold edges, heavy silver, and a single red rose on each white-linened table. The two dining rooms have plush round-back chairs and sofas for two. The cozy bar with apricot-colored sofas and a striking medieval chandelier features a menu of assorted specialties for under $10. Dining in the classical French style is serious business. You might start with escargots, smoked trout or clams casino. The twenty entrees are supplemented by nightly specials like poached salmon in beurre blanc or fresh venison with a foie gras sauce. Eight beef presentations vary from entrecote bearnaise to chateaubriand; one is slices of tenderloin with a creamy bourbon sauce. There are sweetbreads, frog's legs, dover sole meuniere, and many other French classics. Desserts range from frozen meringues chantilly and creme caramel to bananas foster, cherries jubilee and crepes suzette for two.

Dinner nightly except Monday, 6:30 to 10:30.

Foxfire Inn and Restaurant, Route 100, Stowe. (802) 253-4887.
Italian. $11.25 to $14.50.

A plant-filled enclosed porch and a large formal dining room are on either side of the bar at this inn known for some of the best Northern and Southern Italian cuisine in Vermont. Munch on homemade egg-glazed breadsticks as you await the hot antipasto (rolled eggplant, mushrooms and shrimp) or garlicked red peppers with cured beef, both popular appetizers. The menu offers a large selection of pastas, plus six veal, five chicken, three steak, and three seafood dishes. A house salad with a dressing of olive oil and vinegar is served after the entree to set the stage for dessert — Italian cheesecake, frozen lemon tortoni, a rum and coffee-flavored chocolate cake, cannoli, or gelato. In cooler months, diners like to take their cappuccino with amaretto or Foxfire coffee (with frangelico and Italian brandy, the whipped cream topped with an Italian flag) into the parlor to sit in front of the fireplace. The mainly Italian wine list bears excellent values.

Dinner nightly, 6 to 10.

Stubb's, Mountain Road at Edson Hill Road, Stowe. (802) 253-7110.
Regional American. $9.75 to $16.75.

Vermont lamb and veal are featured here in a candlelit setting of brass lamps, white linens and ladderback chairs. Entrees run the gamut from fettuccine with asparagus and asiago cheese to sauteed loin of veal with fresh chives. Grilled leg of lamb with sweet roasted pepper salad, sauteed Vermont calves liver, crispy fish with Szechuan sauce, and curried pasta with sea scallops and sun-dried tomatoes are other winners. Standouts among appetizers include spicy grilled lamb sausage with endive and black bean salad, duck and scallion dumplings laced with ginger, and grilled shrimp with spiced pecans on watercress and Boston lettuce. Homemade pastries and ice creams are the dessert fare. An appealing bar menu, including portions of the dining-room menu, is served in the lounge. We'd go there just for the lamb mixed grill — spicy sausage and grilled brochette, with garlic-roasted potatoes and pepper salad.

Dinner nightly, 6 to 10.

The Shed, Mountain Road, Stowe. (802) 253-4364.
International. $9.95 to $13.95.

The whole world seems to beat a path to the Shed, an institution among skiers for years. It has expanded from its original shed to include a greenhouse filled with Caribbean-style furnishings, trees and plants, and a menu offering something for everyone at all three meals. In the process, it may have lost some of its charm, but the variety and low prices keep it filled day and night. The food is straightforward and with-it, from nachos to cobb and chalupa taco salads, from barbecued ribs to scallops persille. You can get seafood strudel, linguini verdi, shepherd's pie, lamb bourbon, prime rib, and goodness knows what else. The omelet and Belgian waffle buffet ($8.50) had folks lined up outside for Sunday brunch on Labor Day weekend.

Breakfast, 7:30 to 11:30; lunch, noon to 4:30; dinner, 5 to 10; late-night menu from 10 p.m. on holidays and weekends.

Restaurant Swisspot, Main Street, Stowe. (802) 253-4622.
Swiss. $7.95 to $14.95.

Every ski resort area ought to have a place specializing in fondues, and this is one of the few that does. It's a small and enduring place, brought to Stowe in 1968 after its incarnation as the restaurant in the Swiss Pavilion at Expo 67 in Montreal. The classic Swiss cheese fondue with a dash of kirsch made a fun meal for our skiing family. Also good is the beef fondue oriental, served with four sauces. There are six different quiches and a handful of entrees like bratwurst, manicotti, chicken florentine, and sirloin steak with a butter and herb sauce. The dessert accent is on Swiss chocolate, including Swiss tobler chocolate mousse, Swiss waffles, and a chocolate fondue with marshmallows and fruits for dunking.

Open daily, noon to 10. Closed April to mid-June and mid-October to mid-December.

Jeffersonville

★ Le Cheval D'Or, Main Street, Jeffersonville. (802) 644-5556.
French. $16.25 to $19, or Prix-Fixe, $28.

Imagine finding a great French restaurant in the middle of tiny Jeffersonville, particularly in the well-known Windridge Inn, a 30-year institution that seems much older. Yves and Carole Labbe have created a restaurant of uncommon style. It's a cozy, beamed room with barn siding on two walls, a stone floor, spotlit oil paintings on the walls, and tables set with pink linens, white china, fresh flowers, and candles in hurricane lamps. The proprietor opened his own restaurant in 1989 after a decade or so as executive chef at the esteemed La Vielle Maison, a five-star restaurant in Boca Raton, Fla. Now he's pleasing North Country palates with his exceptional cooking, available a la carte or in five courses at a bargain fixed price. The limited menu changes seasonally. Start perhaps with a pate of pork and veal stuffed with Vermont smoked ham strips, escargots with small vegetables, hot or cold leek and potato soup, or a soup of chicken and vegetable under a pastry crust. Main courses could be poached salmon with a fresh basil sauce, braised rabbit with whole garlic cloves and shallots, chicken tarragon flamed with brandy, pan-roasted quails wrapped in bacon, and tournedos bearnaise. The signature dessert is maple crepes souffle, but you also might choose black currant cheesecake, chocolate mousse or creme caramel. The short wine list starts in the low teens and rises rapidly.
Dinner nightly, 6:30 to 8. Reservations required.

Chez Moustache, Mountain Road, Jeffersonville. (802) 644-5567.
International. $7.95 to $14.95.

A large old gray barn houses an attractive restaurant decked out in big brass and glass ceiling lanterns, candles in hurricane lamps, ladderback or captain's chairs, and plant-filled windows framing stunning mountain views. Chef-owner Mark Brahmstedt, who caters to a local clientele, cooks all kinds of dishes but is especially proud of his Vermont veal and lamb. Moussaka and roast leg of lamb with celery dressing and hunter's sauce might augment such regular items as lamb souvlakia, veal schnitzel, Swiss charcuterie, baked stuffed sole with shrimp and crabmeat, chicken boursin, and roast Vermont duckling in a sauce of mandarin oranges and grand marnier. Light dinners include pastas, crepes, German meatballs, and knockwurst with sauerkraut. Among appetizers are smoked Norwegian salmon, escargots in mushroom caps and cheese raviolis. Popular desserts are lemon mousse pie, chocolate mousse pie and brownie a la mode.
Dinner nightly, 4 to 10.

Champlain Islands/The Heroes

The Sandbar, Route 2, South Hero. (802) 372-6911.
American. $7.95 to $15.95.

The locals are partial to this homey place, freshened up with new rose carpeting in 1989. The windows look onto Lake Champlain and the Green Mountains, and at night it is especially attractive by candlelight. The food is good and straightforward, from roast turkey and baked ham to seafood newburg, chicken cordon bleu and sirloin steak with sauteed mushrooms. The "Green Mountain Surprise," a homemade spicy preserve, is served as an appetizer over Vermont cream cheese with crackers and is sold by the jar. Dinners come with salad, homemade soup — the split green pea is hearty and good — and a bread bar with four choices, among them herb and whole wheat. Our New York strip steak and filet mignon dinners were so filling we had no room for dessert. The Sandbar also serves excellent breakfasts and Sunday brunch.

Breakfast daily, 8 to 11; dinner, 5 to 9. Closed late October to May.

Shore Acres Inn & Restaurant, Route 2, North Hero. (802) 372-8722.
American. $8.95 to $16.95.

The pine-paneled dining room dressed in blue and white linens and fresh flowers has a stone fireplace and looks out onto the lake. The limited menu offers entrees like marinated scallops, deep-fried shrimp and scallops, Yankee pot roast, sirloin steak, and charbroiled smoked pork chop with homemade apple sauce, all served with homebaked bread, salad and seasonal vegetables. Appetizers are routine (Vermont cheese and crackers, stuffed mushrooms and clam chowder). Desserts include chocolate and other homemade pies, maple syrup sundae and lemon pudding. The wine list contains some incredible values.

Dinner nightly, 5 to 9. Closed mid-October to mid-May.

North Hero House, Route 2, North Hero. (802) 372-8237.
Regional American. $13.95 to $15.95.

Chef and part-owner John Apgar is back in the kitchen of this historic Lake Champlain hostelry, which he runs in the summer with partners from his Old Timbers restaurant in Randolph, N.J. His short menu changes nightly. A typical dinner might start with pan-fried artichokes, a duet of pates, and sour cream, potato and chive soup. Garden salad with homemade raspberry-maple or honey-bacon vinaigrette dressings precedes entrees like poached salmon atop sauteed spinach and topped with a fresh tomato compote, roasted duck roulade stuffed with apple sausage, and roast loin of pork sauced with pineapple. Accompaniments could be roasted red potatoes, local swiss chard and maple-glazed summer squash. Maple-walnut pie and apple pie with a wedge of Vermont cheddar are signature desserts. All this is served up in a greenhouse dining room decked out in gold and red linens, Villeroy & Boch china and hanging fuschias. At lunch in one of two circular screened outdoor gazebos off the lounge, we enjoyed a roast beef sandwich on sourdough bread and pie of the day (a shrimp, tomato and brie quiche, served with pasta salad and coleslaw). Everyone enjoys the Friday night buffets served picnic-style on the boat dock, featuring Maine lobster or honey-mustard roasted chicken.

Lunch, noon to 1; dinner, 6 to 8; Sunday brunch, 8 to 11. Closed mid-October to mid-June. No credit cards.

Montgomery Center

♥ **Zack's on the Rocks,** Hazen's Notch Road, Montgomery Center.
(802) 326-4500.
Continental. All Entrees, $18.

Drive along a back road up a hill into the middle of nowhere to find this mountaintop fantasyland on the rocks and a dining experience that draws the cognoscenti from miles around. Ring the sleigh bell at the entry and you'll likely be greeted by Jon (Zack) Zachadnyk, attired in wild jewels and a purple caftan. Purple is Zack's favorite color (and wearing it prompted a goodbye kiss from one of us). It extends from the purple wood stove to the pillows all around, the tablecloths, the purple-edged plates, the wine lists encased in purple velvet, the waitresses' long skirts and, for the holiday season, a Christmas tree with 3,000 purple lights shimmering amidst the tinsel. Gold napkin rings, hanging flowers over each table, gold foil over the bar, a marble-top piano, and actors' masks of tragedy and comedy are about the only breaks in the prevailing purple. "I saw this view and went crazy," Zack said of his hilltop aerie on the rocks, which he built himself nearly 30 years ago. "Now people come here for the special occasions in their lives, because we put on a performance. You've got to do crazy things to get people out here." The performance begins in wife Gussie's After the Rocks bar, where patrons sip cocktails as they study the menu, handwritten on a paper bag that has been burnt to look like parchment. You're called by a cow bell to your table beside large windows overlooking the trees, in a 38-seat dining room illuminated by candles and a fire in the hearth. Your appetizers await: perhaps marinated herring or escargots bourguignonne, French onion pie or mushroom and barley soup. Purple goddess, among other choices, could dress the salads of hearts of palm, spinach and bacon, grapefruit and avocado, or Vermont cheddar and vidalia onion. About a dozen entrees are offered, ranging from chicken banana and calves liver saute to veal scaloppine au gratin, lobster and scallops with Johnny Walker scotch over pasta, filet of sole with asparagus and mushrooms, rack of lamb, and tournedos bearnaise. Zack, who does the cooking, offers a few desserts, including a hot fudge sundae called Jay Peak in honor of the nearby ski area, key lime pie and chocolate mousse. A pianist is at the keyboard on weekends to add to the already lively performance.

Dinner nightly except Monday by reservation, 6 to 9.

Black Lantern Inn, Route 118, Montgomery Village. (802) 326-4507. Continental. $9.50 to $17.

With pretty wallpaper, low beams and old pine floors, a country look pervades the pleasant, candlelit dining room at this inn owned for ten years by Rita and Allan Kalsmith. Everything is homemade and the handwritten menu changes weekly. Starters might be sausage-stuffed mushrooms, hummus with pita bread, herring in wine sauce, seafood chowder, and Vermont cheddar cheese soup. Entrees range from Mediterranean scallops and walnut-crusted sole to lamb marguerite and grilled salmon steak with cilantro butter, roast duck with bing cherry sauce, and chicken normandy. Among dessert choices are French chocolate cake, chocolate torte in a nut crust, and strawberry amaretto.

Dinner nightly, 6 to 9.

Newport

The Landing, Lake Street, Newport. (802) 334-6278. American. $8.95 to $17.95.

Hard to find and seemingly hard finally to get to, the Landing is worth the challenge. And surprise: the chef is Michael LaCroix, who once had the fabulous little Michael's restaurant in Derby Line before closing and turning up temporarily in Burlington. This is a venture of a different kind. A huge place seating 200 amid nautical decor right beside beautiful Lake Memphremagog, it boasts a fine view of the lake through expansive windows and from a popular open-air deck beyond the Quarterdeck Pub. The sunsets are almost magical. The Sunday champagne brunch buffet served in the enormous Captain's Dining Room is popular; so is the salad bar fashioned from a boat that once plied the lake. Waitresses in blue wrap skirts adorned with boats serve an array of seafood from haddock in a pouch and fried clams to broiled coho salmon with a four-peppercorn beurre blanc and crab imperial. Michael's influence shows in the nightly specials and on the meat side of the menu, things like barbecued spring lamb glazed with fresh apple-tarragon and garlic, roasted game hen stuffed with long-grain wild rice, and veal with a different preparation daily. The dessert menu encompasses parfaits, homemade cheesecake, mousse, key lime pie, and fried ice cream. A pub menu is served from 2 to 9.

Lunch daily, 11:30 to 2; dinner from 5; Sunday brunch, 11 to 2.

Coventry

★♥ Heermansmith Farm Inn, Heermansmith Farm Road, Coventry.
(802) 754-8866.
American/Continental. $11.95 to $15.95.

This bucolic retreat is a couple of miles out in the country beyond Coventry, along dirt roads and past a few farms, amid strawberry fields, haystacks and pastures of grazing sheep. When we arrived, the chef was in the living room chatting with the innkeepers and guests as he sorted through the watercress he'd just picked for the cucumber and cress mayonnaise that would dress the smoked salmon for dinner. This is a low-key, personal place, the family home of Louise and Jack Smith, part of the Heerman family who had been dairy farmers here for five generations. The Smiths started serving ice cream to people who came to pick their strawberries; someone suggested they should offer cross-country skiing in the winter, and then the skiers wanted something to eat. So in 1982 the Smiths opened their 1860 home to guests in a 30-seat dining room separated from the living room by a huge central fireplace. Oriental rugs, white linens, candles, fresh flowers, and books all around make guests feel as if they're dining in a private home. Leisurely dinners start with such appetizers as sherried mushrooms in puff pastry, escargots with roasted sweet red pepper and garlic, sausage-stuffed mushroom caps, or soup of the day, perhaps sweet potato, cream of leek or chilled blueberry. The half-dozen entrees range from shrimp dijonnaise and pecan chicken topped with raspberry butter to veal piccata and the house specialty, roast duckling enhanced with a strawberry and chambord fruit sauce, all accompanied by garden salads, fresh broccoli, and herbed rice or oven-roasted potatoes the night we were there. Desserts could be strawberry shortcake or torte, hazelnut cheesecake, puff pastry with lemon cream and fresh raspberries, and pecan pie.

Dinner nightly except Tuesday, 5 to 9.

Westmore

The WilloughVale Inn, Route 5A, Westmore. (802) 525-4123.
New American. $12.95 to $17.95.

This brand-new inn with modern amenities overlooking picturesque Lake Willoughby includes a dining room of local distinction. Polished wood tables are set with fanned, moss green napkins and a fire blazes in the hearth on cool evenings. The view looks down the lake toward Mount Pisgah, rising precipitously from water's edge, and the sunsets across the lake are awesome. As well as standards like prime rib and rack of lamb, the seasonal menu might include poached sea scallops with orange-ginger beurre blanc, poached salmon with roasted red bell pepper sauce, boneless trout with cornbread and crayfish dressing, braised Vermont veal with apple wine, venison with apples and cider sauce, and tortellini with pesto and cream sauce. You might start with smoked trout with horseradish creme fraiche, corn terrine with tomato sauce and lobster, or pumpkin soup with leeks. Finish with creme caramel, strawberry cake or chocolate cake with pistachio nuts. The Vermont Sunday brunch buffet already has become the talk of northern Vermont, so popular that we couldn't get in and had to settle for smoked trout and a roast beef sandwich from the bar menu in the taproom.

Lunch, Monday-Saturday 11:30 to 2, June through mid-October; dinner nightly, 5 to 9 or 10; Sunday brunch, 11 to 4.

Lyndonville

The Wildflower Inn, Darling Hill Road, Lyndonville. (802) 626-8310.
American/Continental. Prix-Fixe, $18.95.
The dining room is charming with stenciled strawberries, quilts on the wall and wreaths of dried flowers. But go beyond to the enclosed porch, which has a view that won't quit. Perched on a hilltop with seemingly half of Vermont below and beyond, inn guests and the public dine on excellent cuisine prepared by George Willy, a European who had his own restaurant locally until he was wooed away in 1989 by energetic young innkeepers Mary and Jim O'Reilly when they decided their dining room should go public. The set menu changes nightly. Leisurely meals begin with help-yourself hors d'oeuvres (maybe crab cakes, marinated herring and a wheel of brie) on a sideboard to go with drinks on the landscaped rear patio with its 180-degree view or, in cool weather, in the cozy living room near a wood stove. Traditional soups like split pea, mushroom or onion au gratin are followed by tossed or cucumber-dill salads and a blackberry or cinnamon-rhubarb sorbet. For entrees, there's a choice: perhaps prime rib or beef wellington, chicken marsala with chanterelles, broiled coho salmon, marinated leg of lamb, or raviolini (pasta stuffed with cheddar and walnuts). Vegetables could be parslied new potatoes and beans amandine, or mashed turnips with maple syrup and Vermont butter. Blackberry cobbler, fresh fruit compote with kirsch, and homemade ice cream or sherbet complete the feast. A complimentary glass of wine comes with. The entire wine list, in fact, is available by the glass.
Dinner by reservation, Tuesday-Saturday 5:30 to 8.

East Burke

The Old Cutter Inn, Burke Mountain Access Road, East Burke.
(802) 626-5152.
Continental. $7.95 to $14.25.
Swiss chef Fritz Walther and his wife Marti share innkeeping duties at this renovated farmhouse, a cozy inn and restaurant of the old school. The dining room with exposed beams and fireplace is popular with skiers from Burke Mountain; so is the adjacent rustic tavern with semicircular bar and round tables, where light fare and sandwiches are available. Fritz's extensive restaurant background ensures a consistency in such standards as veal piccata, rahmschnitzel, stuffed rainbow trout, tournedos of beef served on a crouton with a piquante bearnaise sauce, and riz casimier, pork loin sauteed with mushrooms, finished in a mild curry sauce and served in a rice ring. Rack of lamb and beef wellington can be ordered in advance; the dinner menu also offers an omelet, served with potato and vegetable of the day. Roesti potatoes are extra, but salad comes with. A Sunday champagne brunch featuring eggs benedict, crepes and homemade pastries is one of the area's more popular.
Dinner nightly except Wednesday, 5:30 to 9; Sunday brunch, 11 to 1:30. Closed November and April.

The Pub Outback, Route 114, East Burke. (802) 626-5187.
American. $8.50 to $13.25.
Housed in a barn behind Bailey's Country Store, this is a lively, casual place beloved by skiers. Focal points on the main floor are a long, rectangular bar in the center and two solariums used as waiting areas. Above the bar is a free-standing dining loft, open on all sides with beams overhead and barn artifacts here and there.

Northern Vermont

Tables are custom-inlaid with local memorabilia, and it's all unexpectedly airy and contemporary. Bowls of homemade popcorn stave off hunger as diners pick from an all-day menu of appetizers, salads and sandwiches, or what the menu calls "light entrees" but are large enough portions to sate hungry skiers. These could be baked haddock provencale, scampi primavera, sauteed chicken with scallions and mushrooms, chargrilled sirloin steak, or halibut en croute, baked with an almond rum butter and served with island chutney. Each is accompanied by homemade breads, green salad and rice pilaf or baked potato. If you're not up to a full meal, snack on the likes of nachos, chili, taco salad, or the pub chicken sandwich, grilled with boursin on a homemade roll.

Open daily from 11:30; dinner, 5 to 9 or 9:30.

Danville

The Creamery, Hill Street, Danville. (802) 684-3616.
American. $9 to $16.

There are no set menu, no signs and no advertising for this former dairy-turned-restaurant, perched on the side of a hill just north of the heart of Danville. Run by the Beattie family with five generations in the dairy business, it's the favorite restaurant of many area residents. Beyond a funky waiting area with old stuffed chairs is a large dining room and an enclosed porch, converted from a deck. Photos of Lake Willoughby abound, tables are covered with dark green cloths and woven mats of all colors, vases contain field flowers, and it's all rather country charming, especially if you get a table on the rear porch with a view. Good food, simply prepared, is the Creamery's hallmark. Lobster and shrimp cocktails are the most pricy of the appetizers. The blackboard menu may offer fresh halibut or swordfish, sole with lobster sauce, chicken cordon bleu, baked stuffed shrimp, and sirloin steak. Manager Tom Beattie's mother makes all the pies — Yankee magazine wrote up her maple cream pie. Raspberry shortcake and black raspberry pie are summer specialties.

Lunch, Monday-Friday 11:30 to 2; dinner, Monday-Saturday from 5.

St. Johnsbury

Aime's Restaurant, Route 2 at Route 18, St. Johnsbury. (802) 748-3553.
American/Creative Game. $7.95 to $15.95.

This pine-paneled restaurant associated with a motel of the same name has been run by the Bisson family for 50 years. It takes its name from Aime Bisson, father of the current chef, who stresses healthful foods and rare game dishes, carves and paints ducks, and runs chef's ski races at Waterville Valley. The regular menu is standard, from spaghetti and fried clams to roast leg of lamb, baked seafood imperial and steak au poivre. All meals come with soup and salad bar. More than half his business comes from his creative game menu, the chef says. Among the options are game pie (duck, venison and rabbit topped with a homemade biscuit), medallions of New Zealand venison, charbroiled Colorado buffalo steak, smoked Vermont duckling with a three-mustard sauce, stuffed quail and sea scallops, and broiled mako shark. One wall of wine bottles indicates a large selection of wines to go with.

Open daily, 7:30 a.m. to 8:30 p.m. Closed November-March.

Lower Waterford

Rabbit Hill Inn, Lower Waterford, Vt. (802) 748-5168.
Regional American. Prix-fixe $25.

The doors of the dining room here are kept closed until dinner, since innkeeper Maureen Magee is a believer in the theatrical. She wants first-time guests to appreciate the drama of a room lit mostly by candles, even on the chandeliers. Silver gleams on burgundy mats on polished wood tables, and napkins fold into pewter rings shaped like rabbits. Porcelain bunnies on each table and a spinning wheel in the center of the room add to the charm. New chef Russell Stannard, who trained with Boston culinary whiz Frank McClelland when he was at the Country Inn at Princeton, offers the area's most exciting food, with a choice of appetizer or soup, three to five entrees, salad and dessert. Our dinner began with cream of celery soup with pimento and chives and smoked pork tenderloin with roasted garlic aioli and mustard greens, delicate salads with a creamy dressing, and a small loaf of piping-hot whole wheat bread. Sorbet drenched in champagne cleared the palate for very spicy red snapper and a tender breast of chicken with a spinach, cheddar and wild mushroom duxelle, served with a double-mustard sauce and fried pancetta. Desserts of bourbon-pecan pie and chocolate crepes with grand marnier sauce were accompanied by brewed decaf coffee with chocolate shells filled with whipped cream to dunk in — a delicious idea. At other times you might find sauteed coho salmon with lime-scallion butter and roasted red peppers, served with a couscous salad; sauteed duck breast with marinated onions and a sweet potato puree, and beef tenderloin with a pistachio red wine sauce and apple-turnip puree. Maureen, a classical flutist, often plays during dinner. No detail has been overlooked to produce a fulfilling meal and evening.

Dinner nightly by reservation, 6 to 9.

What the symbols mean:
Three symbols are used to point out places of exceptional merit:
* ***** exceptional food.
* **♥** exceptional atmosphere.
* **$** exceptional value.

Southwest/Monadnock

Chesterfield

* Chesterfield Inn, Route 9, Chesterfield. (603) 256-3211.
New American. $17 to $20.50.
Here is one of those up-and-coming restaurants that you dream of. Innkeepers Phil and Judy Heuber set out to create an imaginative dining experience as the focal point of their elegant inn. They brightened up the original sunporch dining room and added three small dining rooms in the parlors of the original house, as well as a fourth to the rear. Judy made the quilts that adorn the walls of the largest room, which has beamed ceilings, patterned rugs, Hitchcock chairs and tables set with striking Dudson china, big wine globes, and oil lamps. Chef Carl Warner works in an open kitchen through which house guests must pass to get to the dining rooms; he's grown accustomed to chatting as he cooks. His menu changes every two months. A complimentary starter like smoked salmon pate is on the table when guests are seated. Start with one of the exceptional appetizers, perhaps fettuccine with smoked sea scallops in a dill-cream sauce, oyster bisque, or baked zucchini stuffed with pine nuts, shallots and parmesan cheese. Continue with Asian shrimp with scallions and sweet red peppers, pork tenderloin with apples in sharp cheddar sauce, loin of lamb with curried lentils, or grilled and braised duck with cranberry-port wine sauce. Snow peas, green beans, scalloped potatoes, or wild rice might accompany. The walnut pie, pumpkin cheesecake and warm apple crisp with ice cream are outstanding desserts. The wine list is as well-chosen as the rest of the fare.
Dinner, Tuesday-Saturday 5:30 to 9 (nightly in foliage season).

Keene

Henry David's, 81 Main St., Keene. (603) 352-0608.
American. $9.45 to $17.95.
They say it takes two fulltime workers just to trim and water all the plants, so prolific is the greenery in this spacious contemporary establishment named after Henry David Thoreau, whose maternal grandfather built part of the now-restored structure in 1775. On the main floor there are plants all around the bar and in the two front greenhouses, bow-window affairs with coveted tables facing the sidewalk. Upstairs are more plants among tables on three sides around a central atrium, filled with hanging greenery and lit by skylights. The food amid all the brick, brass and beams is consistently good for what it is, a glorified sandwich shop gone haute with salads, quiches, straightforward entrees and a few specials. The burgers and sandwiches, named after area towns (Suave Swanzey, Harrisville Tweed) are enormous and come with chips, pickle and potato salad or coleslaw. Dinner entrees run from filet of catfish to salmon with dill hollandaise, from oriental or Mexican chicken to prime rib and loin pork chops teriyaki. Chocolate mousse au cointreau and toasted coconut and almond cream pie are among desserts. Several flaming international coffees compensate, perhaps, for a severely limited wine list.
Open daily from 11:30 to 11.

The Bench Cafe, 222 West St., Keene. (603) 357-4353.
American/Mexican. $5.50 to $14.95.
Adjacent to the Colony Mill Marketplace, this light and airy place seems to change hands and names every time we stop by. Now it's owned by the people who have the Park Bench Cafe (rechristened Bench Cafe) in Manchester, Vt. The same

attractive decor remains, all pink and green with white brick walls and abundant greenery. The new restaurant is faster-paced for faster turnover, according to insiders. With more than 100 items on the menu, they guarantee you'll find something you like. Start with what must be New Hampshire's yuppiest assortment of "great beginnings" like Irish nachos, Buffalo wings and peel and eat shrimp. Then you'll find burgers, sandwiches, salads, Mexican specialties, Cajun dishes, "pastabilities," grilled entrees from prime rib to steak kabob and the house-specialty baby back ribs, and "finishing touches" that include confections from Mother Myrick's in Manchester. Somehow in such a sophisticated setting the smoked seafood, bouillabaisse, shrimp scampi and veal saltimbocca of former incarnations seems more appropriate. But alas, those didn't last. This could.

Lunch daily, 11:30 to 4:30; dinner, 5 to 10 or 11.

Westmoreland

Major Leonard Keep Restaurant, Route 12, Westmoreland. (603) 399-4474. New England. $12.95 to $17.95.

Many longtime Keene residents think the area's best restaurant is the Major Leonard Keep, a small house with an intriguing atmosphere in a country setting. The traditional Yankee menu is big on old-fashioned appetizers and salads (tomato juice or soup, jellied salad), but the list of main courses contains a mix from roast stuffed turkey and chicken pie to baked stuffed shrimp and filet mignon. The specialties are Yankee pot roast and fresh fish, in straightforward presentations. Homemade pies and ice creams are featured desserts.

Lunch, 11:30 to 2; dinner, 5:30 to 8:30, Sunday noon to 7. Closed Tuesdays and February.

Peterborough

♥ **The Boilerhouse at Noone Falls,** Route 202 , Peterborough. (603) 924-9486. New American. $9.95 to $18.95.

The setting and the scenery in this restored textile mill and powerhouse are great: an expansive, second-level dining room with white-linened tables and black lacquered chairs facing huge windows onto the waterfall, with an umbrella-shaded outdoor deck at the side. We suffered through a mediocre lunch one lovely autumn day, but continue to hear good reports about the place, especially for dinner. Votive candles flicker at night, when you might feast on entrees like shrimp and sun-dried tomatoes, medallions of veal sauteed with almonds and pine nuts, or the house specialties, medallions of venison with red and black currant sauce and braised chestnuts, and a rack of lamb roasted with garlic, bread crumbs and dijon mustard. A saute of fresh fish might be black bass, pompano or drumfish. Appetizers include havarti and mushroom duxelle and sherry-battered shrimp with straw mushrooms and ginger. Among desserts are interesting homemade ice creams, poppyseed parfait served with blackberry, kiwi and mango sauces, frozen grand marnier souffle and white chocolate pate served on blackberry sauce. The extensive, pricey wine list won an award from Wine Spectator in 1989. There's a pleasant Copper Bar downstairs and outside the entrance in the Boilerhouse arcade is owner Sandy King's popular little **Cafe at Noone Falls.** It was standing-room-only the last noontime we visited while the restaurant was surprisingly empty.

Lunch, Tuesday-Friday 11:30 to 2; dinner, Tuesday-Saturday 5:30 to 9; Sunday brunch.

✦ **Latacarta,** 6 School St., Peterborough. (603) 924-6878. Creative Cuisine. $9.50 to $14.75.

There's a decided New Age feel about this restaurant, owned by Japanese master

Southwest/Monadnock

chef Hiroshi Hayashi, in the old Gem Theater. He moved to Peterborough from Newbury Street in Boston where "I never had to serve meat, but I do here," he says. Serving what he calls an "epicurean collage," he is a student of cosmic philosophy (explained on the back of the menu) and gives seminars in natural-foods cooking at his home. Latacarta is a simple place, with bentwood chairs, mulberry walls on which are some sensational Japanese prints, track lighting, lace cafe curtains, and many plants. A gorgeous kimono made by Hayashi's wife is spotlit in a niche. A lunchtime taste of the two soups of the day, cream of butternut squash and a chunky fish chowder, made us wish we could stay on for dinner. Many specials augment the regular evening fare, but you'll always find vegetable or shrimp tempura, ginger chicken on linguini, enchiladas served with brown rice, pasta of the night, fresh fish like baked red snapper, and a colorful vegetarian dinner. Hummus served with pita bread is a popular appetizer. A large salad is topped with tofu, which the chef calls "sage's protein." Using little salt and sugar, he and his staff turn out desserts like mocha custard, fruit crunch and Aunt Mary's chocolate cake. Among items on the lunch menu are harvest lasagna, linguini with sauteed vegetables and dill sauce, and a Yankee hamburger — "out of this world," says the chef. A typical dish at an elaborate Sunday brunch is linguini wih smoked salmon, snow peas, broccoli, zucchini and mushrooms with a fresh dill sauce. A light menu is served most of the day in the adjacent bar/cafe. Nibble on a hummus and cheese platter or fish and chips while you listen to the New Age music or, on some nights, live music (filling a void left by the closing of Peterborough's venerable Folkways). The short wine list is more sophisticated than you might expect.

Lunch, Tuesday-Friday 11 to 5, Saturday noon to 5; dinner, 5 to 9 or 9:30; Sunday brunch, 11 to 5. Cafe open daily except Monday for cocktails and light meals, 11:30 to 9.

Temple

$ **The Birchwood Inn,** Route 45, Temple. (603) 878-3285.
American. Prix-fixe, $14.95 to $17.95.

Murals by Rufus Porter adorn the walls in the candlelit dining room of this homey, historic inn run very personally by Judy and Bill Wolfe. Their country breakfasts and four-course, prix-fixe dinners are so reasonably priced they attract a loyal following of locals as well as inn guests. "We do everything ourselves — that's how we can keep these prices," Bill Wolfe explains. Meals generally start with relishes like cottage cheese with horseradish and curried kidney beans and a choice of juice or soup, among them minestrone, French onion, chicken noodle and black bean. The blackboard menu usually offers three entrees, perhaps seafood Chautauqua (a medley of shrimp, scallops and lobster in herb butter sauce over rice), roast duckling with grand marnier sauce and tournedo of beef madeira. House favorites are she-crab soup and lobster bisque served on weekends, the homemade breads from a repertoire of 100, and, among desserts, chocolate hazelnut torte, apple raspberry cobbler, cream-cheese pecan pie and a Temple trifle — a hot milk spongecake with raspberry jam, custard and whipped cream.

Breakfast, Tuesday-Sunday 7:30 to 9:30; dinner, Tuesday-Saturday 6 to 9. BYOB.

Wilton

★ **The Ram in the Thicket,** Maple Street, Wilton. (603) 654-6440.
International. $14 to $17.50.

This creative restaurant is housed in a Victorian mansion owned by the Rev. Dr. Andrew Tempelman (the innkeeper-bartender, whose religious background inspired the inn's name) and his wife Priscilla. The intriguing menu is a heady mix that changes seasonally and includes dishes with Greek, Mexican, Indonesian and Korean accents, among others. The bread basket always contains surprises, as do the salads — for instance, one of greens and a mass of slivered carrots notable for a Korean sweet and sour dressing, another of cauliflower florets in a pickled ginger marinade, and a surprising combination of garbanzo beans, sauerkraut and chopped vegetables in a marinade on a bed of lettuce. Another appetizer might pair apples and cabbage, baked with garlic, cranberries, cinnamon and white wine. All the entrees entice, from the seafood stew provencale to veal jimella (with mushrooms, pears and a cranberry puree). The oriental pork tenderloin might be roasted with strawberry-raspberry-cointreau glaze; the Moroccan shrimp seasoned with garlic, cumin, cinnamon, ginger and harissa. Priscilla seeks out the new and rarely repeats an item, so she no longer serves the spicy Indonesian beef sate and the Greek gypsy lamb in a huge parchment pocket that we so enjoyed. Desserts might be double chocolate rum cheesecake, a trifle with kiwi and pear, an acclaimed Indian pudding and praline mousse. Pink napkins and calico cloths, along with oriental rugs, a crystal chandelier and reproductions of the old masters, dress the country-homey dining rooms. This is a fun, relaxed place where, says host Andrew, every night's a dinner party — and a mighty good one at that.

Milford

Elisha's, Route 101-A, Milford. (603) 673-8764.
American/International. $5.95 to $13.95
An explanation of who Elisha is leads off the lengthy menu at this casual decade-old restaurant. Elisha Towne was the builder of the 1770 house that forms the nucleus of the establishment, since expanded into an appealing mishmash of plants, hanging baskets on the walls, and booths and cane-back chairs seating 100. There's a separate bar, as well as a loft upstairs to handle the overflow. The cutesy menu begins with two pages of finger foods, potato skins, "souper soups" and "a lotta salad." Then it goes into numbers for burgers (13), wieners (5), omelets (11), steaks and seafood, pizzas, stuffed potatoes and such. Recent additions include teriyaki steak, grilled chicken breast, Mexican club, and grilled prime rib. Popular desserts are carrot cake, chocolate cake, and oreo ice cream pie.
Open daily 11 to 9, to 10 on weekends; Sunday breakfast, 8 to 11:30.

$ Mile Away, Federal Hill Road, Milford. (603) 673-3904.
French/Swiss. Table d'hote, $12.25 to $16.95
A mile or so southeast of town via a circuitous route that's hard to follow lies a large complex with a green farmhouse in front, a white house in the rear and stone fences, stacked-up logs and gardens all around. Swiss-born chef Josef Zund acquired the historic property (the barn was once the recreation room of the Hood family of Hood Dairy fame) in 1967. He and partner Ernest Kehl have been running their restaurant with a sure hand since. "We have the same customers as twenty years ago," Josef says; "that's when you know you're successful." They keep coming back for his veal dishes, frog's legs provencale, sweetbreads and mushrooms in white wine sauce, and tournedos with white asparagus and hollandaise. He makes all the dessert pastries, breads, and even his own bratwurst and fleischkaes. The trockenfleisch appetizer is his own creation, made with air-dried beef. Table d'hote dinners include a selection of appetizers, salad and desserts. The rustic atmosphere is comforting: captain's chairs at white linened tables, wide board floors, pine walls, a huge hearth and a wagon-wheel chandelier.
Dinner, Wednesday and Thursday 5 to 9, Friday and Saturday 5 to 10, Sunday 4 to 7:30. Closed January and July.

Dublin

★ Del Rossi's Trattoria, Route 137, Dublin. (603) 563-7195.
Italian. $9.95 to $12.95.

A pretty Colonial house is the scene of some fine Italian fare, cooked up by chef David Del Rossi, co-owner with his wife, Elaina. The two Jaffrey natives also run a music store, which is probably why they feature live music (mostly folk) on Friday and Saturday nights. The main dining room, with its wide-plank floors and post and beam construction, is plain and comfortable; there are two or three smaller rooms including a sunlit porch. Here you may begin with polenta topped with a fresh tomato and basil (from the chef's garden) sauce and melted mozzarella, or marinated mushrooms, go on to a pasta — all made in house — like spinach and cheese gnocchi, then enjoy an entree like delmonico steak scaloppini, chicken breast stuffed with ricotta, spinach and prosciutto, or scallops broiled in a wine sauce topped with bread crumbs and grated pecorino romano. "Once you try my Sicilian cake, you want it again and again," says the chef. Homemade pound cake has creamy cheese chocolate filling between its layers and couldn't be more lush. The lunch menu changes every day; there are always two salads, a frittata, a quiche and a pasta. Our quiche of smoked oysters and cheese with a generous salad and a PLT version of a BLT (prosciutto, lettuce and tomato on grilled garlic bread) were super. Here is what we call a "true" place. The wine list is most reasonable and beers are a bargain.
Open Tuesday-Saturday, lunch 11:30 to 2, dinner 5:30 to 8:30.

Bennington

Petite Maison, Bennington Square, Bennington. (603) 588-3000.
Continental. $9.95 to $17.95.

This really *is* a small house with two stenciled dining rooms, beamed ceilings, white linens and murals of the town painted on the walls. Chef-owner Richard Ranno terms his an international menu with "a little Italian and a French flair." Veal oscar, wiener schnitzel, shrimp provencale and rack of lamb dijonnaise are among the choices. A strong point is what the chef calls his bouquetiere of vegetables, things like poached cauliflower with mornay sauce, butternut squash with fresh chives, sauteed carrots with sesame seeds, twice-baked potatoes, and pommes cordon bleu — red bliss potatoes hollowed out and filled with a puree of ham and cheese. Along with the classic French desserts are a flambeed fruit du jour and the changing terrine Petite Maison, a mix of egg whites and heavy cream with perhaps peaches, hazelnuts and frozen schnapps. A chocolate-covered strawberry comes with the bill. Richard and Gina Ranno also own a new restaurant, **Cafe at the Atrium,** in downtown Manchester.
Dinner, Tuesday-Thursday 6 to 9, Friday and Saturday 5:30 to 9:30, Sunday 4 to 8.

Powder Mill Pond Restaurant, Route 202, Bennington. (603) 588-2127.
International. $12 to $15.75.

A cheery dining room of unusually vivid hues, a smaller room, and a screened porch facing Powder Mill Pond are the settings for what owner Jerry Willis calls "country classics and contemporary foods." The cooking has an oriental flair, as in appetizers like egg rolls and chicken sate with java dressing and in main courses like stir-fried shrimp with Chinese vegetables, crispy seafood Shanghai, Chinese pork roast with peapods, and beef stir-fried with peapods, mushrooms and bok choy. There are down-home favorites — pot roast, baked scrod, and English beef steak with gravy and thin fried onion rings — as well as continental touches: medallions of beef diane, seafood fettuccine, scallops parisienne, and veal marsala. Meals come with the house's special sticky buns. Desserts are more limited than the rest of the offerings, this being the land of bread puddings and chocolate sundaes.

Lunch, Tuesday-Friday 11:30 to 1:30; dinner, Tuesday-Saturday 6 to 9; Sunday brunch buffet, 11 to 1:30.

Francestown

Maitre Jacq Restaurant, Mountain Road at Route 47, Francestown. (603) 588-6655.
French. Prix-Fixe, $13.25 to $21.

The former Grandmother's House at the foot of Crotched Mountain has been grandly transformed by chef-owner Robert LeJacq into a classic French provincial restaurant favored by those partial to gourmet food and wine. Two beamed dining rooms seat 60 at tables set with white linens, pink china and small oil lamps. The menu is classic French, though M. LeJacq now eschews some of the old-style French dishes he used to cook for lighter, more healthful fare. Dinners are prix-fixe, including appetizer, salad and dessert. You could start with veal pate with cognac and herbs or herring filet in white wine and sour cream (a surcharge fetches fancier items like prime smoked scotch salmon). The dozen or so entree choices on the seasonal menu could include chicken roasted with leeks, boursin and snow crab, bouillabaisse provencale accented with pine nuts, medallions of pork loin with artichoke hearts and bearnaise sauce, and "the three tournedos" (beef, veal and pork, sauteed and served with sauces of bearnaise, bordelaise and mustard). Veal and stuffed roast duck are menu mainstays in changing presentations. Robert's wife Mary Beth touts proudly a new specialty from Brittany, coquilles Marie-Louise (his aunt's recipe for scallops, cream, shallots, carrots and leeks in puff pastry). The chef makes all his desserts, from a popular apple torte and fruit sorbet to frangelico cheesecake and chocolate mousse with curacao. Salad greens, herbs and vegetables come from the chef's garden outside. The award-winning but affordable wine list is one of New Hampshire's more extensive. The chef circulates through the dining room at meal's end, and hosts multi-course dinners and wine-tastings six times a year for members of Les Amis de Maitre Jacq.

Dinner, Tuesday-Sunday 5 to 9:30. Closed Sunday in winter.

The Inn at Crotched Mountain, Mountain Road, Francestown. (603) 588-6840.
American/Continental. $10.95 to $17.95.

Innkeepers Rose and John Perry are both schooled in the restaurant business and their dining room is highly regarded in the area. The nightly specials are often more interesting than the regular menu. Things like baked stuffed sole with scallops and crabmeat, pork tenderloin with apricot glaze, and roast duck with apple-- cranberry dressing may supplement the regular shrimp scampi, chicken teriyaki, calves liver and filet mignon bearnaise. Meals include cream of chicken or apple curry soup, garden salad with one of the inn's homemade dressings and homemade breads. Appetizers like wine-smoked mackerel, artichoke hearts and Indonesian chicken wings are extra, as are desserts. Guests eat in two dining rooms or at a couple of tables set up in a huge living room with fireplaces at either end. A display case holds jars of the Perrys' homemade goodies for sale.

Dinner, Wednesday-Saturday 6 to 8:30, weekends off-season. No credit cards.

Antrim

The Antrim Inn, Main Street, Antrim. (603) 588-8000.
American. $9.50 to $15.

Almost too elegant for words is this recently restored inn. Its spacious, beamed dining room is dressed in pink linens crossed by rose runners, with dark blue napkins in the stemware matching the candles in the hurricane lamps. Rose balloon curtains enhance the windows and worn oriental rugs cover the floors. The dinner menu offers something for all tastes, from appetizers (wings 'n things, Cajun chicken and escargots) through light fare (chili, Greek salad and seafood pasta) to entrees. Among the latter are Aegean Sea shrimp, baked sherried scallops, sole cardinale, chicken picatta, veal with mustard-cream sauce, and grilled lamb kabob. Surf and turf (shrimp scampi with club steak) is the best-seller, according to innkeeper Richard Reddig, followed by breast of chicken stuffed with an herb-dill cheese blend. The homemade desserts include key lime pie, chocolate mousse pie, chocolate brownies with mint chocolate chip ice cream, and grapenut and bread puddings.

Dinner nightly except Tuesday, 6 to 9; Sunday, brunch 10 to 2, dinner 1 to 7.

Hillsborough

★ Stonebridge Inn, Route 9, Hillsborough. (603) 464-3155.
Regional American. $10.95 to $16.95.

Just from her list of appetizers, we can tell that innkeeper-chef Lynne Adame is our kind of cook: mulligatawny or cream of pumpkin soup, camembert en croute, sherried mushrooms, pate du jour, and country-style tortellini stuffed with spinach, mushrooms and gruyere. The afternoon kitchen aromas almost overpowered us as we studied the main courses, perhaps seafood strudel, chicken savannah, and pork tenderloin with cherry sauce along with the locally ubiquitous prime rib. Her repertoire for veal includes one named Polonaise after a favorite, long-gone Boston restaurant. Accompaniments might be roasted new red potatoes with garlic and herbs or twice-baked stuffed potatoes, the latter so popular that some people reserve them while making dinner reservations. Standby desserts are a frozen chocolate mousse torte, apple shortbread tart, walnut pie, and Lynne's "ninth deadly sin," a Palm Beach brownie with chocolate ice cream, whipped cream and homemade chocolate sauce. Dining is in a main room done up in brown and gold or a Terrace Room with fancy wrought-iron chairs. Lynne lately has become a part-time restaurant management instructor in the New Hampshire College culinary program, so her dinner schedule has been curtailed, much to the disappointment of her guests.

Dinner, Friday and Saturday 6 to 9, Sunday 5 to 8.

Henniker

Colby Hill Inn, The Oaks, Henniker. (603) 428-3281.
American/Continental. Table d'hote, $12.95 to $21.95.

The unusual little college town of Henniker has acquired its share of restaurants lately, although the Colby Hill Inn has been around awhile. But new owners and a new chef have given a facelift to the menu and the presentation, while maintaining old favorites. Theirs is a charming country dining room with pine furniture, pewter plates, and views of vivid green lawns and fields to the west. There's a quaint small bar at the entrance. Dinner prices include such appetizers as smoked trout pate, marinated artichoke hearts and split-pea or vegetable soup, tossed or spinach salad, rice or potato, and beverage. Among entrees are a lobster and crabmeat pie so popular as a special that it's become a fixture, shrimp diavolo, poached Norwegian salmon, chicken dijon, veal oscar, and steak au poivre. Desserts obtained from a nearby baker are primarily cakes and pies, among them apple crumb pie, grand marnier torte and the signature chocolate cake with vanilla-butter cream frosting and a wedge of chocolate on top saying Colby Hill.

Dinner, Tuesday-Saturday 5:30 to 8:30; Sunday in season, 4:30 to 7:30.

The Meeting House, 35 Flanders Road, Henniker. (603) 428-3228.
Italian/Continental. $9.50 to $16.95.

Lovely stained glass and a sunburst on the door greet patrons to this interesting inn plus "solar recreation area" (hot tub and sauna) plus restaurant. With a good view of Pat's Peak ski area, the solar greenhouse lounge appeals with its purple velvet cushions and tiny white lights on the plants, even in summer. Something unique (at least we've never seen anything like it) is the collection of sand, shells and stones in labeled zip-lock bags tacked up all around the room, brought back by friends and customers from vacations to all kinds of exotic places. Innkeepers June and Bill Davis pick the wildflowers that adorn each white and burgundy-linened table in the main dining area in a 200-year-old barn, which is warm and homey and unusually appealing. The food, all prepared on the premises in an open kitchen, is rather sophisticated, from veal lorenzo and breast of chicken basque to brandied seafood beurre blanc, Bermuda lobster with sherry and pepper sauce, and beef wellington. Start with a pork and veal pate with pistachio nuts wrapped in puff pastry; end with chocolate brownie pie, the house favorite, or fried cinnamon apples flamed with apple brandy. Bill Davis mixes a mean bloody mary from scratch and his son-in-law, Peter Bakke (from Minnesota and a Garrison Keillor look-alike), is the personable host.

Dinner, Wednesday-Saturday 5 to 9:30, Sunday 4 to 8.

Daniel's, Main Street, Henniker. (603) 428-7621.
American. $9.50 to $15.25.

Over the years, Kevin Daniel has expanded this restaurant, which has a long narrow dining room with windows onto the river, an attractive lounge of stone and brick, and an old printing press retained from the days when the old building housed a printer. Now fresh flowers are in Perrier bottles and the menu offers everything from Buffalo wings and spud skins to shrimp provencale and baked chicken with apple-walnut-sausage stuffing glazed with maple cider. Chicken saltimbocca, veal marsala and twin tournedos are other offerings. Swordfish, bluefish and tuna were specials the last time we visited. The light entrees available all day include Louisiana crab cakes with cole slaw, turkey burrito and chicken teriyaki brochette at family prices. Homemade cheesecakes (perhaps coconut-almond) and chocolate-raspberry layer cake are the desserts of note.

Lunch, Monday-Saturday 11:30 to 3; dinner nightly, 3 to 10:30; Sunday brunch, 11 to 3.

Country Spirit, Route 114, Henniker. (603) 428-7007.
American. $8.95 to $15.95.

Proud to be located "in the only Henniker on earth," as the menu proclaims, this establishment celebrates Henniker in photographs in the lobby, in the artifacts in the large bar, and in all the old plates, mirrors, quilts and baskets of dried flowers in the dining room (there's even a wagon filled with flowers on the roof). The menu emphasizes certified angus beef, barbecued ribs and chicken, charbroiled steaks and lamb chops, fried clams and fish, and prime rib ("while it lasts"). A Sunday feature is roast leg of Western lamb. The meal price includes homemade breads, potato, coleslaw or salad, and endless coffee. Many patrons like to start with the sampler of barbecued beef, pork and chicken; mud pie and oreo cookie ice cream pie are favored desserts. The limited wine list is more interesting than some in the area.

Lunch daily, 11 to 3; dinner, 5 to 9 or 10.

Southern New Hampshire

Nashua

The Country Tavern, 452 Amherst St. (Route 101-A), Nashua.
(603) 889-5871.
American/Continental. $10.95 to $15.95.
A barn-red, restored 18th-century farmhouse encompasses an incredible ramble of beamed dining rooms with pink linens and hurricane lamps plus a bar surrounded by a loft. It's the suburban version of the owners' Common Crossing restaurant in Nashua, and the menu is updated accordingly. Here the lengthy menu starts with the locally coveted prime rib, followed by things like rack of lamb dijonnaise, tournedos B&B (one each with bordelaise and bearnaise), chicken oscar, shrimp scampi, teriyaki chicken, and scallops mornay. Salad, vegetable and potato or rice come with, but homemade fettuccine and garlic cheese bread are extra. Potato skins and fried zucchini join clams casino and escargots on the list of appetizers. And desserts? Why cheesecake, chocolate mousse, mud pie, carrot cake, and kahlua snowball crepe, of course.

Lunch, Monday-Friday 11:15 to 2:30; dinner nightly, 5 to 9:30 or 10, Sunday 4 to 9.

Merrimack

★ **Country Gourmet,** 438 Daniel Webster Hwy., Merrimack. (603) 424-2755.
Continental/International. $12.95 to $18.95.
Somehow we expected this much-heralded restaurant to be a gourmet mecca out in the country. It's a mecca, all right, but not really in the country nor really gourmet in the sense of culinary adventure. Jo Baker and Peter Massardo founded it in 1978 in an 18th-century house and tavern as "a place of refreshment and relaxation, a refuge from the ordinary." That it is, with four small, formal dining rooms dressed with white linens and service plates, banquettes of light blue and burgundy stripes, curtains arranged in the shape of an hour glass, and oil hurricane lamps. Oriental prints, an antique Chinese rice chest and other artifacts convey a vaguely oriental motif. To the side of a large bar and lounge is a newer dining room with burgundy velvet and chrome chairs. The original chef and much of the staff are still here and so are most of the menu items. You'll find a couple of unusual pork dishes (pork chinoiserie and pork tenderloin in sour cream-walnut sauce), Portuguese steak and shrimp, and chicken in a banana-coconut curry amid such classics as scampi, seafood wellington, filet mignon, steak au poivre, and tournedos served on a wild mushroom-potato pancake. The chefs experiment a bit with a couple of nightly specials, perhaps sesame-coated swordfish with orange Szechuan sauce or veal alsatien with spinach, wild and domestic mushrooms, and a riesling wine-cream sauce. Lots of spices and herbs enhance the interesting vegetables that accompany. Among appetizer choices are a Turkish dish of marinated eggplant, peppers and tomato and a Spanish version of broiled cheese with chorizo sausage. Desserts are simple, save for the chef's special — "for chocolate lovers only" (two layers of chocolate ganache with chantilly and chocolate mousse), the night we were there.

Lunch, Tuesday-Friday 11:30 to 2; dinner, Monday-Saturday 6 to 9:30 or 10; Sunday, brunch 10:30 to 1:30, dinner from 2:15.

♥ **Levi Lowell's,** 585 Daniel Webster Hwy., Merrimack. (603) 429-0885.
Continental/American. $12.95 to $18.95.

A green and white canopy, lovely landscaping and a sign for valet parking greet visitors at this widely acclaimed restaurant, now expanded with a nearby function center. It was started in the original barn of the Levi Lowell homestead by his great-grandson Mark Haseltine, though you'd never detect a barn heritage from its ultra-elegant trappings. Dining is at well-spaced tables on two levels with bentwood chairs and the occasional leather wing chair, white over blue cloths, and candles in hurricane globes. Several equally deluxe rooms are used for overflow or private parties; the most striking is the upstairs Starlight Room, all glass and glamorous with twinkling ribbed lights but with a heating-cooling problem that often renders it off-limits. Nightly piano music in the bar adds to the aura of special-occasion dining. The menu is predictable, offering consistently good seafood en papillote, beef wellington, braised Norwegian salmon with pistachio butter, Long Island duckling, and tournedos au poivre. The roast pork tenderloin served with a spiced cranberry compote and the Kennebunk sole blended with crabmeat, roasted corn and nutmeg and topped with a lobster-apple brandy sauce are the most unusual dishes. Among starters are a wild mushroom and marsala strudel, chilled duck and apricot pate, oysters stuffed with fiddleheads and fennel and topped with lobster cream, and Brittany lamb chops with stilton and port wine. Desserts are chocolate creme caramel, white chocolate mousse, and changing cheesecakes and pies.

Dinner, Tuesday-Saturday 6 to 9.

Anni Etelli's, 550 Daniel Webster Hwy., Merrimack. (603) 424-2448.
Italian. $8.75 to $11.95.

Amid the pretensions of its luxurious neighbors and the mediocrity all around is this cherished little place, funky but true. A wall of wine bottles by the door masks the cozy interior, a mix of barnwood, stucco and timbered walls, booths and tables with checked cloths, ropes of garlic, a collection of small watering cans, and graters on the wall with lights inside casting neat shadows. Hostess Di Canavan put together the mostly-Italian wine list, a charmer of a book with personal descriptions. Husband David mans the kitchen, putting out an ambitious menu embracing four chicken and six veal dishes along with three steaks, many pastas from shells to lasagna, and more than a dozen appetizers. Locals pack the place to partake of its down-to-earth food and friendly intimacy. Desserts include chocolate pie, zuccotto, ice cream crepes, spumoni and Italian ice.

Dinner, Monday-Saturday 4 to 10.

Hannah Jack Tavern, Daniel Webster Highway, Merrimack. (603) 424-4171.
Steaks/Seafood. $9.95 to $15.95.

"We have ghosts here," the ebullient waiter said of this historic house dating to 1780 when it was the home of New Hampshire's signer of the Declaration of Independence, Matthew Thornton, and his wife Hannah Jack. They also have consistently good, simple food of the steakhouse ilk and a warm, historic atmos-phere drawing locals and travelers alike. One of the Thornton sons maintained the house as a tavern, and the wainscoting in the front rooms, two bake ovens and the fan window remain. The food is updated Yankee, from prime rib, various steaks and teriyakis to crab-stuffed haddock, crab rolled in sole, shrimp lorenzo, lobster-stuffed scallops, Alaskan king crab, and veal oscar. You get the idea, but have you ever seen so many create-your-own combinations — a bar graph with seven times five possibilities? There are most of the usual appetizers (except no potato skins or nachos), but few bother when they can fill up at the salad bar, feast on homemade breads, and dig into a hearty steak with baked potato and fresh veggies. With candlelight in the six small dining rooms and a few ghost stories, you might think you're back in the 18th century.

Lunch, Monday-Friday 11:30 to 2:30; dinner, Monday-Thursday 5 to 9:30, Friday to 10:30, Saturday 4:30 to 10:30; Sunday, buffet brunch 10 to 2, dinner 1 to 9.

Nickel's, 4 Continental Blvd., Merrimack. (603) 424-0888.
American/International. $6.95 to $13.45.

Go here for the bar scene, the incredible jumble of decor, the blaring music, the huge portions of food. Don't go here for peace and quiet, or for fine dining. This large new establishment opened by the owners of the adjacent Appleton Inn just off the Everett Turnpike makes a handy stop for travelers and families. It's a multi-level mix of booths and tables, plants and brass, bric-a-brac and more to look at than you can take in, including the largest men's room we ever saw. We liked the pleasant prices, a special Chinese dumpling appetizer, hefty salads, and enormous platters of angel-hair pasta with chicken and vegetables and chicken dijon topped with ham and cheese over spinach, both so generous they went home in doggy bags for supper the next night. We did not like the music, or being overlooked by the staff after being greeted so warmly by the hostess at the entrance.

Open daily, 11:30 to 11 or midnight, Sunday from 10:30.

Litchfield

Shorty's Mexican Roadhouse, 450 Charles Bancroft Hwy. (Route 3A),
Litchfield. (603) 424-0010.
Mexican. $4.95 to $12.95.

This re-creation of a 1940s roadhouse has gone upscale, with neon signs, a slick Southwest look and a bright and airy atmosphere. It's the work of local restaurant impressario Rick Loeffler and chef Terry Rodriquez, a California-Mexican woman who prepares everything from scratch. The all-day menu offers salads (grilled chicken fajita, cobb and taco), five kinds of enchiladas, Colorado and Arizona burritos, fajitas and combinations. Dinners include chicken mole, citrus chicken sangria, grilled fish with salsa fresca, chili relleno with homemade chorizo and shrimp barbecued in a spicy Corona beer sauce. Deep-fried ice cream, kahlua cheesecake and margarita mud pie are favored desserts.

Open daily from 11:30, Sunday from 1.

Amherst

Lord Jeffrey's, The Meeting Place, Route 101, Amherst. 673-7540.
Continental. $10.95 to $19.95.

Lately taken over by a couple of Chinese men, this used to be part of the group that owns the family-style Sir William's restaurant almost across the street and the Greenhouse Cafe not far away. It was the group's most ambitious effort then, and so it remains — if anything, improved, according to regulars. The beamed and carpeted dining room, with curtained windows and cathedral ceiling, seats 80 in restrained elegance, the tables topped in beige and blue. The menu ranges widely, from seafood fettuccine and scallops sauteed with vegetables through steak diane and chateaubriand. The menu lists seven favorites, five of them veal dishes, one chicken in port wine sauce and the last, rack of lamb lyonnaise. Start with smoked trout, mushrooms and artichokes Copenhagen, or shrimp and cheese in phyllo. End with grand marnier creme bavarian, raspberry-walnut cheesecake or toblerone mousse with frangelico. Be sure to check out the striking local murals drawn on the barroom walls.

Lunch, Monday-Friday 11:30 to 2:30; dinner, 5:30 to 9:30, Saturday 5 to 10, Sunday 4 to 9.

Greenhouse Cafe, Route 101A, Amherst. (603) 889-8022.
Continental/American. $8.50 to $17.50.

Billed as "class under glass," this is the kind of contemporary suburban place that's proliferating everywhere, including New Hampshire. There are a busy bar, a rear dining room with white woven mats atop pine tables, a greenhouse looking onto an outdoor patio, and lots of hanging greenery. There also are, front and center, pictures of the owners with George Bush, a few framed tributes and a salad bar. Area residents go out of their way for things like schnitzel gastronome, paupiette of veal and shrimp, supreme of chicken mille feuille, and filet mignon. More contemporary tastes are served by pecan chicken, chicken jambalaya with blackened shrimp, sauteed linguini forestiere (with pesto, sun-dried tomatoes and shrimp), and rack of lamb dijonnaise. Diverse tastes appreciate the homemade tortes, the wicked ice cream pie, french-fried ice cream, the toblerone chocolate fondue, and the profiteroles au chocolat for dessert.

Lunch, Monday-Saturday 11:30 to 2:30; dinner, 5:30 to 9 or 9:30; Sunday, brunch 11:30 to 3, dinner 11:30 to 8.

$ The Black Forest, Salzburg Square, Route 101, Amherst. (603) 672-0500.
American/International. $7.75 to $11.75.

Chef Bruce Walters, who trained in France, and his wife Martha took over a family-style cafe that had a not-so-good reputation to overcome. Locals said they were succeeding in spades. And why not? Good, interesting food, casual surroundings and reasonable prices were their answer. Split-pea soup, tomato-salmon quiche, baked potato with ham and peppers, and a Canadian bacon and sausage sandwich could be the lunchtime fare. The weekend dinner menu changes weekly. For main courses, you might find sauteed shrimp in a spicy tomato-cream sauce over fettuccine, grilled pork chops with homemade apple chutney, braised breast of veal stuffed with wild mushrooms, or New York sirloin bearnaise. Crab empanadas, curried chicken skewers, crostini, and curried scallop bisque make good starters. The dessert display includes strudels, linzer torte and pumpkin pie. All this is available in a bright, country-fresh dining room with stenciling and lace half-curtains.

Breakfast and lunch daily, 7 to 5; dinner, Thursday-Saturday 6 to 9:30. Beer and wine only.

Bedford

* Daffodil's, Route 101, Bedford. (603) 472-8646.
Contemporary American. $9.95 to $15.95.

The landscaping at Daffodil's makes us think of restaurants in California, what with huge rocks jutting up and railway-tie steps — all very attractive. So is the inside, where a warm and bright feeling is conveyed by three rear solariums, antiqued stucco walls, dividers of faux marble and glass blocks, and white-linened tables at booths and banquettes. And great news! Restaurateur Rick Loeffler, an ex-stockbroker, is back, restoring his original Daffodil's at a site that had been taken over, expanded and folded by the restaurant Italia and its owners who built the Bedford Village Inn. While the first Daffodil's was mainstream continental, the new one that opened in late 1989 offers a contemporary grill menu with much California flair — dishes like grilled swordfish, salmon and mahi-mahi accompanied by light sauces, fresh salsas and chutneys, and grilled vegetables. Among wide-ranging entrees are steamed Thai scrod, Sonoran seafood stew, prairie grilled chicken with mustard tarragon, baked chicken with pears and cider brandy, grilled duck with New England baked beans and brown bread, veal marsala, prime rib, and grilled cowboy steak with onions and barbecue sauce. Plus — they must be kidding — something called the ultimate peanut butter and jelly sandwich (prime rib, two baked stuffed shrimp, spring roll, a split of champagne, and a PB&J sandwich for $34.95, negotiable, according to the menu). Appetizers are just as diverse, and desserts include bread pudding with whiskey sauce, cheesecake, sundaes, and creme brulee.

Lunch, 11:30 to 3; dinner, 5:30 to 10 or 11.

♥ **Bedford Village Inn & Restaurant,** 1 Old Bedford Road, Bedford. (603) 472-2001.
Regional American. $11.75 to $19.75.

This new inn and restaurant in a converted 19th-century yellow barn is luxurious to the max, and has the awards to prove it. Unfortunately, all that opulence took its toll, the original owners having been foreclosed in 1989 and a new corporation trying to make a go of it. Despite the cloud hanging over the restaurant's head, there were plenty of lunchers when we were there, attracted no doubt by its magazine designation as "best atmosphere statewide" and its reputation for special-occasion dining. The several dining rooms are a picture of elegance with pink fanned napkins atop pedestal tables, reproduction Chippendale chairs and oriental rugs. Chicken and pecan salad, a farmer's market salad and baked scallops with a lobster crumb stuffing appealed from the lunch menu. At night, a lengthy list of specials augments the regular fare. You might find scallops and mussels over pasta, medallions of veal sauteed with pears and leeks, stir-fried smoked duck breast with vegetables and peanuts in an orange-ginger and soy sauce over rice, and medallions of pork tenderloin with herb cheese and pecans. The regular menu ranges from grilled honey-mustard chicken and poached Atlantic salmon with sweet mustard-dill sauce to lobster and asparagus fettuccine and roast rack of lamb. Apple cider sorbet and chocolate-grand marnier fondue were desserts at our fall visit.

Lunch, 11:30 to 2; dinner, 5:30 to 9:30 or 10; Sunday, 3 to 9.

Manchester

The Millyard Restaurant, 333 North Turner St., Manchester. (603) 668-5584.
Steaks/Seafood. $9.95 to $22.95.

In part of a long, three-story red brick factory building (the 160-year-old Amoskeag Millyard warehouse) is this popular establishment, long synonymous with the best food in town. Like many restaurants in the area, it was in financial difficulty in 1989 but was regrouping to weather the storm. You can get light items from the menu in a large bar-lounge. The rest of the restaurant is a series of rooms that seem to go on forever, all red brick, rough wood, plants and fans. There are salad and soup bars all over the place. Entrees are mostly steak, seafood and chicken and combinations thereof, like scrod or scallops with sirloin, Cajun halibut with swordfish, seafood and chicken riesling with lobster, and halibut with a seafood sampler. Variations run from a chicken cordon bleu croissant to salmon oscar. The "grazertizers" are predictable; desserts like kahlua-chocolate truffle mousse, Bailey's Irish Cream mousse and grand marnier cheesecake aren't. In the reorganization stage, lunch was no longer served and a pianist entertained on weekends.

Dinner nightly, 5:30 to 9:30 or 10, Sunday to 9.

Gateway of Manchester, 50 Phillippe Cote St., Manchester. (603) 622-4663.
Continental. $11.95 to $16.95.

This welcome addition to the Manchester restaurant scene is housed at the south end of the miles-long Amoskeag Mill, on the east bank of the Merrimack River almost beneath the Granite Street bridge. It's worth the search to find, given its two-level dining room with an elegant, modern decor and views of the rushing river out back. Upholstered burgundy chairs are at well-spaced tables dressed in white linens; brick walls, rich wood, hanging ribbed glass lamps, and plants enhance the setting. The menu caters to local tastes and then some, from potato skins and prime rib to broiled scallops wrapped with bacon and peapods and filet wellington. The dessert tray includes cheesecakes, fresh cobblers and hazelnut torte. The restaurant closed unexpectedly in 1990, and its future was uncertain as this book went to press.

Lunch, Monday-Friday 11:30 to 2:30; dinner, 5 to 9:30. Closed Sunday.

High 5 Restaurant & Night Club, 555 Canal St., Manchester.
(603) 626-0555.
American. $10.95 to $16.95.

No one in Manchester knew quite what to make of this glamorous new establishment on the 17th floor of the Wall Street Towers shortly after it opened in 1989. Nor did we. There's no denying its sophistication in black, silver and teal, all windows, strip lighting and silver ceiling. And there's no denying the view. But the name? It comes from the height, the address and the sports background of owner Peter Telge (the establishment was sponsoring a biathlon bike-run the Sunday after our visit). There's a large, airy lounge and an upstairs club; the long, narrow two-tiered dining room seats about 200. Downtown business people favor the place for lunch, and the manager assured us that it should be taken seriously for dinner. Specialties are veal parmigiana over pasta, surf and turf, and lamb kabob. The rest of the menu is a mix of prime rib and filet mignon, chicken cordon bleu and Long Island duckling, blackened red snapper and shrimp scampi. The homemade desserts include apple cheesecake, pumpkin-spice cake, chocolate-grand marnier fudge cake, and mudslide pie with kahlua and Bailey's Irish Cream. With flourishes like these, bring on the music.

Lunch, Monday-Friday 11 to 4; dinner nightly, 5 to 10 or 10:30; Sunday brunch, 11 to 3:30.

Goffstown

Travers Tavern, 7 High St., Goffstown. (603) 497-3978.
Continental. $12.95 to $16.95.

Head through a lively bar to the dining rooms, one done up in blue and white and notable for leather banquet chairs, silk flowers and a grand piano in the corner, and the other more intimate with a beamed ceiling, lace curtains amd captain's chairs. Through a succession of chefs, the food has been highly rated. Appetizers include steamed mussels, spinach-stuffed mushroom caps finished with boursin sauce, and lobster ravioli. Entrees range from shrimp and vermicelli saute and grilled salmon with diced tomatoes and scallions to veal diablo with cayenne and filet mignon bearnaise. Among desserts are crepes l'esperance, liqueur parfaits, peach melba, and bananas foster for two.

Dinner, Tuesday-Saturday 5:30 to 9:30 or 10.

Hopkinton

The Horseshoe Tavern, Route 103, Hopkinton. (603) 746-4501.
Continental. $11.25 to $18.95.

"Elegant country dining" is the theme in this century-old house at the edge of historic Hopkinton, with rear windows onto a pond. It's here that a chef of our acquaintance heads on her nights off when she wants a meal like she'd have at home without having to cook it herself. Chef George Merritz and his wife Chris run a warm, personal place. The paneled main dining room on two levels is attractive in white and pink, with accents of yellow oil lamps. Meals include soup (perhaps lavender and corn or seafood bisque), tossed salad with choice of dressings and homemade breads, so you may wish to skip the appetizers, which are fairly standard. Main dishes include lobster and scallops chardonnay, frog's legs forestiere, lobster thermidor en casserole, shrimp jardiniere over pasta, roast duckling with grand marnier sauce, streudel of veal dijonnaise, tenderloin tips chasseur, and steak au poivre. Chateaubriand and rack of lamb for two can be ordered 24 hours in advance. For dessert, try the English toffee torte, grasshopper-mint pie, hot Indian pudding, or profiteroles with ice cream. Some exceptional egg dishes are featured at Sunday brunch.

Lunch, Tuesday-Friday 11:30 to 2; dinner, Tuesday-Sunday from 5; Sunday brunch.

Concord

Thursday's, 6-8 Pleasant St., Concord. (603) 224-2626.
International. $5.95 to $12.95.

With a name like Thursday's, co-owner Judith Graves says people have "a one in seven chance" of remembering her restaurant. The name has served well, for Thursday's has been going strong since 1978 in downtown Concord, an area not known for distinguished restaurants. Part of its appeal is its casual atmosphere: shiny pine tables with calico napkins, black chairs, oak walls, low lattice dividers, and changing art exhibits featuring local craftsmen. But its forte is its food, especially the breads, soups, stews, quiches, crepes, and vegetarian specials. Everything is homemade, and Concordites say you can't get a better spinach and bacon quiche, an onion soup au gratin, a clam and artichoke heart chowder, a chutney lamb stew, or a shrimp salad oriental for lunch. Dinner choices tend to the light side, as opposed to heavy: chicken mandalay, sweet and sour shrimp and vegetables, veal and artichoke marsala, and liver Twilly — a saute of liver, bacon and onions. You can get vegetable-cheese strudel, four kinds of crepes, a seafood croissant, and a Mexican burrito. The breads and salad dressings are homemade and varied, as are desserts like pumpkin cheesecake, strawberry crepes and New Hampshire maple-walnut parfait. The bar offers an impressive array of imported beers.

Open Monday-Thursday, 11:30 to 3 and 5 to 9; Friday and Saturday, 11:30 to 10; Sunday brunch, 10 to 2.

Vercelli's, 11 Depot St., Concord. (603) 228-3313.
Italian. $10.25 to $14.50.

Named after a small town near Milan, this became the capital city's hottest eatery upon opening in 1989. "Excellent," two departing businessmen proffered as they saw us eyeing the menu in the window one lunchtime. Randy Jones, the chef attired in a Celtics baseball cap, and partner Douglas Milbury tired of going to Boston and recognized a need for a good Italian restaurant in the area. Theirs is an airy place in pink and black, accented with deep green floral cafe curtains and black lights hanging from the high black ceiling. A display case at the entry contains homemade pastas, desserts and other goodies to go. If you stay for a meal, you'll have a choice of six chicken and six veal dishes, along with seafood like scampi, lobster fra diavolo and swordfish steak, and steak florentine or Italiano. The saltimbocca and grilled veal chop are highly recommended. Homemade desserts include cassata, chocolate decadence cake, strawberry zabaglione, caramel flan, spumoni, and gelato. If it's all rather predictable, at least it's the real thing. So is the Italian music in the background.

Lunch, Monday-Friday 11 to 2:30; dinner, Monday-Saturday 5 to 9 or 10.

Hermanos Cocina Mexicana, 6 Pleasant St. Extension, Concord. (603) 224-5669.
Mexican. $2.50 to $10.50.

Concord has not one but two Mexican restaurants, and this has been rated the best in New Hampshire. Here is authentic Mexican food doled out by Bruce Parrish in delightful surroundings: sombreros hanging on the walls, a counter with revolving stools, and a dozen tables amid colorful Aztec and Mayan artworks. The margaritas are made with fresh lemons and limes and the Mexican beers come with a wedge of lime. Chips, crispy as could be, came with salsas described as "mild" (red) and "hot" (green), both of which left one of us gasping for water. The taco pastor with chicken and the enchilito with chicken, vegetables and yogurt made an exceptional lunch, ending with a marvelous frozen kahlua pie — like a mousse on a graham cracker crust. The taquito is an unusual spiced pork concoction in a deep-fried corn tortilla. Eight kinds of tequila and seven Mexican beers are offered. Hermanos's Mexican grocery store and takeout next door is heaven for those who like to cook Mexican.

Lunch, Monday-Saturday 11:30 to 2:30; dinner, 5 to 9 or 9:30. Closed Sunday.

Tio Juan's, 1 Bicentennial Square, Concord. (603) 224-2821.
Mexican. $6.95 to $12.95.

The former Chuck's Steak House has been converted into a Mexican restaurant, steakhouse style. Ensconced in the old police station, the expansive restaurant on several levels offers very private tables in the old jail cells, a pleasant reception area with fireplace, glass-covered or bare wood tables, and a large circular bar. The reasonably priced menu is typically Mexican, including a giant "super burrito," a taster platter and combinations. New York strip steak is offered "for 100 proof gringos who would have rather gone to Chuck's," and steak and two enchiladas "for 50 proof gringos." Cinnamon ponsonita and margarita pie are among the desserts.

Dinner nightly, 4 to 10 or 10:30.

Sunapee-Hanover Region

Sunapee

✦ Seven Hearths, Old Route 11, Sunapee. (603) 763-5657.
Regional American. Prix-fixe, $28.

The suave, handwritten menu changes nightly for the prix-fixe dinner at this elegant inn. Candles, lanterns and recessed lighting illuminate the dark main dining room, pretty as a picture with pink and plum linens accented by vases of fresh flowers. Meals are preceded by cocktails and complimentary hors d'oeuvres (brie with crackers and hot cheese quiche strips, very good and very filling, the night we dined) in the inn's large living room. Dinner begins with soup, possibly chilled Georgia peach with sour cream or tomato-cumin bisque with jalapeno sour cream, or an appetizer like fresh asparagus flan over a tomato-basil coulis or sauteed shrimp and calamari over rice timbale. Entrees might be roast duckling with green peppercorn sauce, roast loin of Vermont lamb with a tomato herb concasse, and chicken breasts with mushrooms, scallions and artichoke hearts dijonnaise. We thought the last was excellent, as was a spicy shrimp dish with such bite as to leave the mouth burning. A green salad with aioli-herb vinaigrette follows the main course.

Sunapee-Hanover Region

Two desserts are offered, perhaps chocolate-chocolate ganache torte and steamed apricot genoise with sauce anglaise.

Dinner, Wednesday-Sunday 6 to 8:30, Thursday-Saturday in winter. Reservations required.

The Inn at Sunapee, Burkehaven Hill Road, Sunapee. (603) 763-4444.
American. $12.95 to $16.95.
Sophisticated country dining is the goal of the country-pretty dining room at the Inn at Sunapee, which affords views of the lake and mountains through bay windows. It succeeds with entrees like shrimp dijonnaise, grilled Norwegian salmon with mustard sauce, chicken kiev, and steak au poivre. Culinary Institute-trained chef Bill Kerwood changes the menu often, but you might start with wild mushroom soup, smoked salmon, gallatine of chicken, or crabmeat in artichoke bottoms. He teams with new innkeeper Susan Harriman on the desserts, perhaps cheesecake, Indian pudding, apple pie, and strawberry shortcake. The wine list is small but serviceable.

Dinner nightly except Monday, 6 to 8:30.

New London

★ New London Inn, Main Street, New London. (603) 526-2791.
New American. $13.50 to $19.
This inn's comfortable dining room, with its windows yielding full-length views of the colorful gardens outside, has been vastly upgraded lately by new innkeepers Maureen and John Follansbee. Their son Jeffrey became chef when Mary Richter moved on to Washington, D.C., shortly after she provided one of the best meals of our travels. He's continuing the tradition she launched, changing the menu nightly to feature such entrees as grilled Norwegian salmon served with vegetable florets and a yellow pepper butter, broiled Atlantic tuna with a petite sirah sauce and fried pasta, roasted loin of pork stuffed with apples and sage with turnip puree and maple-mustard sauce, and roasted rack of Wyoming lamb with a squash and leek timbale and oregano sauce. Our memorable meal started with a zippy garlic puree served with crostini and tiny nicoise olives, an assortment of breads, and a picture-perfect green salad garnished with raspberries and edible nasturtiums. We most remember the main courses: grilled lamb medallions with a smoked tomato coulis and roasted eggplant, and grilled Maine rabbit with a spicy mole sauce and cornflower pasta. Vegetables came family-style: green beans with bacon and potatoes with balsamic vinegar, in our case. Desserts include a marvelous peach clafouti with vanilla-bean ice cream, maple-spice torte with maple-butter cream frosting and praline pecans, strawberry mousse in chocolate shells with strawberry sauce, and pear sorbet with a hint of clove and two berry sauces. A complete change of silver with each course is part of the flawless service.

Dinner nightly, 6 to 8:30; Sunday brunch, 11 to 1. Closed Sunday and Monday in winter and spring.

Millstone Restaurant, Newport Road, New London. (603) 526-4201.
American/Continental. $12.95 to $17.95.
A lofty cathedral ceiling with skylights lends an airy feel to this candlelit, casually elegant place that is popular with the Colby-Sawyer College crowd. Owned by Tom Mills, who used to run another Millstone in Concord, it has a pleasant, canopied brick terrace for dining in the summer. Entrees on the large and varied dinner menu run the gamut from pasta dishes, Swiss-style veal and Bavarian schnitzel to pork tenderloin with mushrooms and white zinfandel, sweetbreads mimosa (glazed in an orange-champagne sauce) and charbroiled New Zealand venison with juniper

berry-coriander sauce. Worldly appetizers are grilled Carolina quail on Texas toast and hummus served with Syrian bread. Desserts include profiteroles aux chocolat, pecan flan, Belgian chocolate mousse pie, and maple syrup-cream custard.

Lunch daily, 11:30 to 2:30; dinner from 5:30; Sunday brunch, 11 to 2:30.

Plainfield

Home Hill Country Inn & French Restaurant, River Road, Plainfield. (603) 675-6165.
Nouvelle French. Prix-fixe, $28.

Frenchman Roger Nicholas, a former chef in California, thinks he's at home in the Loire chateaux country in the 163-year-old white brick Federal house he opened as an inn and restaurant beside the Connecticut River. The two dining rooms and a lounge are a mix of French formal and country looks. Dinner is prix-fixe (dessert excluded), typically starting with Norwegian salmon with a watercress sauce or sea scallops sauteed with vermouth and sun-dried tomatoes, leek and potato or acorn and butternut squash soups, and a salad of imported lettuce with a vinaigrette dressing. Main courses could be Peking duck with lingonberries, rabbit braised with wine and tarragon, chateaubriand of New Zealand venison, and veal with wild mushrooms, madeira and cream. A chocolate terrine with pistachio sauce and a "sinking island" — islands of chocolate mousse sinking in an ocean of grand marnier mousse — are favorite desserts. The wine list is worthy of the rest of the fare.

Dinner, Tuesday-Saturday from 6.

West Lebanon

River Cafe, The Powerhouse, Route 12A, West Lebanon. (603) 298-8813.
American. $8.95 to $13.95.

Formerly the Mascoma River Water Works, this restaurant in the Powerhouse Marketplace was taken over in 1988 by a partnership that includes Chris Balcer from the Prince and the Pauper, across the river in Woodstock, Vt. That should insure success, but outstanding cuisine does not necessarily travel. Anyway, the emphasis here is on more casual fare and musical entertainment, the latter an assignment that Balcer was concentrating upon. The cafe is on two floors, the main level an airy melange of bricks and beams with huge ficus trees lit by tiny white lights. The lower level includes a long, narrow room with windows draped in colorful swags framing glimpses of the Mascoma River. The dinner menu offers something for everyone, from appetizers and salads to entrees like beef chimichanga, grilled seafood brochette, Cajun swordfish, cannelloni florentine, veal parmesan, and open-face steak sandwich. Blueberry country cobbler, double fudge chocolate cake, cheesecake, and creme de menthe parfaits are among desserts. A tavern menu offers light fare, including hearth-baked gourmet pizzas. Interesting visiting entertainers perform on Fridays and anyone can perform on Wednesdays, "open mike night."

Lunch, 11:30 to 3:30; dinner nightly from 5; Sunday brunch, 11 to 3:30.

Hanover

The Ivy Grill, Hanover Inn, Main Street, Hanover. (603) 643-4300.
New American. $9.25 to $17.

The upgraded Hanover Inn bills itself as a "small, fine hotel." We like it for its trendy new Ivy Grill, which would be quite at home in New York. On two levels it has sleek lacquered chairs and murals of seasonal Dartmouth scenes. The fare has adventurous twists, among them such starters as quesadillas with two purees, game-bird pate with rhubarb and tawny port, grilled duck salad with roasted anaheim peppers, and house-smoked scallops with roasted chile and garlic mayonnaise. Sea scallops are sauteed with walnuts, scallions, stilton, and cream; Atlantic salmon is grilled with leeks and pinot noir, and roasted Moroccan chicken is served chilled on preserved lemons with couscous salad. The five-spiced rack of lamb comes with cucumber-red onion chutney and falofel. Desserts include white chocolate-cashew cheesecake and warm apple crisp with whipped cream. Lunch brings interesting salads, burgers, sandwiches, and entrees, and a light menu is available between meals. More formal meals are served in the inn's vast **Daniel Webster Room**. In summer, menus from both restaurants are available on an expansive outdoor terrace overlooking the Dartmouth green.

Lunch, 11:30 to 2; dinner, 5:30 to 10.

Cafe la Fraise, 8 West Wheelock St., Hanover. (603) 643-8588.
French. $15.95 to $22.50.

A French country look prevails in this 1823 house harboring two stylish dining rooms, a select gourmet shop and an upstairs lounge. The dinner menu opens with appetizers like scotch smoked salmon japonnaise, shrimp ravioli with fresh basil and cream sauce, and carpaccio with raw oysters. For main courses, how about grilled red snapper with tomato, garlic and basil coulis, sweetbreads with wild mushrooms and brandy cream sauce, roast New Zealand venison with tart black currant sauce, and breast of Peking duck with port wine and ginger sauce? A basket of warm and crusty French bread, lightly cooked fresh vegetables and a crisp salad accompany. The gorgeous desserts (also available from the pastry case out front) might include a pear and almond tart, coconut pound cake with hot buttered rum sauce, or pineapple-nut custard tart with whipped cream.

Dinner, Monday-Saturday 6 to 9.

Bentleys, 11 South Main St., Hanover. (603) 643-4075.
Eclectic. $4.95 to $17.50.

This more formal adjunct to the original Bentleys in Woodstock, Vt., has the masculine aura of an English club or library. Its darkness is relieved by floral banquettes in the back room and a ficus tree adorned with tiny white lights growing toward a skylight, but the bar and the small room facing the street remain clubby. Light, eclectic fare as well as full meals are available at both lunch and dinner. At lunchtime we enjoyed a house specialty, torta rustica, and a fluffy turkey quiche, both accompanied by side salads. Bentley's big burger, served with lettuce, tomato and hand-cut Idaho steak fries, is a standout. The dinner menu is supplemented by entrees like Jack Daniels steak, Jamaican pecan chicken and lemon-champagne veal. Out front is a gourmet shop, which has good soups, salads, chili, pastries, and sandwiches available for takeout. There's also a window onto the street where Ben and Jerry's ice cream is dispensed in waffle or regular cones.

Lunch daily, 11:30 to 2:30; dinner, 5:30 to 9:30.

Molly's Balloon, 43 Main St., Hanover. (603) 643-2570.
Mexican/American. $8 to $11.

A California-Mexican menu suitable for the entire family and a cheery decor commend this bright, amiable place in downtown Hanover. A greenhouse out front has a bar in the center and booths with upholstered green backs and slatted wooden seats, all set on a tile floor. Helium-filled balloons are handed out to youngsters. Snacky dishes like fritto misto and stuffed potato skins from the many-paged, brightly colored menu are good anytime. On various occasions, we've enjoyed a steaming crock of good onion soup, filling salads (neptune, spinach and taco), a giant tortilla, chicken wings, potato skins, chicken enchiladas, and hefty Mexican burgers with green chilies, guacamole and sour cream. At night, entree supplements include marinated sirloin, seafood fettuccine, barbecued pork ribs, chicken oscar and such. Popular desserts are Southern pecan pie with whipped cream and saucy bananas sauteed in kahlua over ice cream.

Open daily from 11 to 11, Sunday 11:30 to 10.

Lyme

✱♥ D'Artagnan, 13 Dartmouth College Highway, Lyme. (603) 795-2137.
New American. Prix-fixe, $33.

Certain dining establishments stand out like beacons. D'Artagnan is such a place. The atmosphere is historic and pleasant, the service friendly and flawless, and the food is exceptional, thanks to the French-trained chef-owners, Peter Gaylor and his wife, Rebecca Cunningham. Sixty diners can be seated in a pristine, pretty room in the brick and beamed basement of the reconstructed 18th-century Ambrose Publick House, which has windows onto the bubbling Hewes Brook out back. The menu changes nightly for the prix-fixe dinner of four courses (a special tasting menu provides a pre-determined sampling of this innovative team's work). You might begin with an outstanding mussel soup with saffron and garlic, superb hot oysters on a bed of rock salt, a salad of rabbit filet with endive and hazelnut oil, and a subtle duck pate with armagnac and madeira. A champagne-cassis sorbet clears the palate for the main course, a choice perhaps of sauteed tuna with snow peas and shiitake mushroom-cilantro-sherry vinegar sauce, escalope of veal grenadin, beef with green peppercorn sauce, rack of lamb with rosemary-shallot sauce, and usually a game dish, such as pan-roasted leg and filet of rabbit with a riesling sauce, leeks and mushrooms. A salad of ruby lettuce and slivered carrots with hazelnut oil dressing follows the entree. Save room for Rebecca's glorious sweets. You couldn't ask for more than her raspberry tartlets in a pool of creme anglaise with raspberry coulis, her three sorbets of grapefruit, strawberry-banana and lime, or her hazelnut dacquoise, a fancy ice cream and meringue concoction. Complimentary hors d'oeuvres precede dinner, and two homemade chocolate truffles come with the bill. The expanded wine list numbers about 100 offerings from California and France.

Dinner, Wednesday-Sunday 6 to 9:15; Sunday lunch (a lighter meal, $18 to $21), noon to 1:15.

The Lyme Inn, Route 10, On the Common, Lyme. (603) 795-2222.
Continental. $12 to $16.

German and Swiss specialties are offered by chef Hans Wichert at this 1809 country inn facing the common. Choices include wiener schnitzel, hasenpfeffer and a hunter-style veal as well as prime rib, Alaskan king crab, beer-batter shrimp, and loin lamb chops basted in red wine and garlic. Also available are "light supper" items such as seafood crepes with vegetable and beverage. French onion soup is a menu staple, and appetizers include marinated herring and escargots. Three spacious candlelit dining rooms are outfitted with 19th-century art and artifacts, including Hitchcock chairs, embroidered samplers, baskets, and old maps. There's a collection of early hand tools in the fireplaced tavern, which retains its rough pine walls and original floorboards.

Dinner, 6 to 8:15 or 8:45, Sunday 5 to 8.

Lakes Region

Center Barnstead

★ Crystal Quail, 628 Pitman Road, Center Barnstead. (603) 269-4151.
American/Continental. Prix-fixe, $35.

Only twelve lucky diners a night may make the trek to the "back of beyond" to sample the zesty cooking of Cynthia and Harold Huckaby, assisted by their two teenaged daughters, who have run a very personal restaurant in their small farmhouse (built just after the Revolutionary War) since 1975. Two to four tables in the tiny dining room, with its wide-plank floors and shallow fireplace, are set with delicate china and embroidered napkins on the polished bare wood. Game is always one of the three entrees in the five-course, prix-fixe dinners — perhaps quail atop a nest of shredded potatoes or marinated rabbit with mustard sauce (the Huckabys, who have a large garden that provides them with their own herbs and vegetables, even grow two kinds of mustard seed to make their dynamite mustard). Meat and fish are the other choices, perhaps veal scallops accompanied by a sauce of tomato and dried black olives, or filet of salmon with parsley sauce. A typical fall dinner offered cabbage soup with sausage, pheasant pate, a salad of shredded clorita squash with nasturtiums, homemade double-eight knot rolls, potatoes Champs Elysees (layered with mushrooms and shredded cheese and baked), crisp zucchini sauteed with garlic, and petite gateau, a small vanilla cake with candied cranberry filling, butter cream icing and coconut. The frangipane cake made with almond paste has a hollow filled with pastry cream, topped with raspberries from the garden and glazed. No wonder most customers here are repeaters, and they bring their own fine wines to go with the extraordinary food. Book two weeks in advance to be assured of a table. Be sure to ask for explicit directions; there's only a small mailbox out front.

Dinner by reservation, Wednesday-Sunday 5 to 9. No credit cards. BYOB.

Tilton

$ Chalet Rouge, 321 West Main St., Tilton. (603) 286-4035.
French. $10 to $16.

Although this unassuming little prize has been around for a dozen years, few know it — not the woman in the nearby information booth, not the restaurateurs in Ashland, and, amazingly, not even some of the merchants in downtown Tilton. But English innkeepers in Andover steer guests to their favorite French restaurant, and regulars come from Concord, the Winnipesaukee area and even Boston. "We turn away more people on most Saturday nights than we serve the rest of the week," laments chef William Prescott. He and partner Rosita Wiggins lived and studied in France, and run a true French country place, despite their non-Gallic backgrounds. Two small dining rooms in their old home have bare drop-leaf tables topped by red napkins and fresh flowers in Perrier bottles. Worn oriental rugs on wide-board floors, watercolors of Paris scenes and French music are the backdrop for a classic French meal at prices from yesteryear. Start perhaps with sorrel soup, chestnut soup, billi-bi, or winter squash chowder, depending on the season. Appetizers could be escargots, mussels mariniere and pate maison. The blackboard lists such main courses as trout amandine, frog's legs, cotes d'agneaux, entrecote aux champignons, and steak au poivre. Vegetables like baked tomatoes with garlic butter, squash, beans, and rice pilaf might accompany. Favored desserts are chocolate and grand marnier mousse, tarte au citron and cheesecake. The all-French wine list is one of New

Hampshire's better. Lunch here is a positive steal (spinach and ricotta tart, pork persillade, steamed mussels — all under $6), yet some days there are no takers.

Lunch, Tuesday-Friday 11:30 to 1:30; dinner, Tuesday-Saturday from 6.

Bristol

The Homestead, Route 104, Bristol. (603) 744-2022.
American/Continental. $9.50 to $15.95.

A good-looking white house with blue canopy and trim is home to this popular restaurant, now in its second decade. Five dining rooms seat a total of 180. A large quilt adorns the wall of the original house, since expanded. Pots of house plants grace tables in the new greenhouse, while a large rear dining room has striking floor-to-ceiling walls of rocks. The interior dining rooms are more old-fashioned, including one all in blue, in keeping with the Homestead's motto of "fine dining in a Colonial tradition." Entrees run from broiled scrod to seafood wellington, from chicken parmesan to steak or veal oscar. There are a couple of pasta dishes, as well as teriyaki steak, barbecued tenderloin tips and a hearty broiled sirloin steak. Lobster cocktail and escargots are the appetizers of choice.

Dinner nightly from 4:30; Sunday brunch, 11 to 2.

Bridgewater

The Pasquaney Inn, Route 3-A, Bridgewater. (603) 744-9111.
French/Belgian. $12.75 to $22.

This restaurant overlooking Newfound Lake met quick success after it was taken over by chef-owner Bud Edrick, who trained at the French Culinary Institute and formerly was at Flamand Restaurant in New York City. The main floor offers a cozy bar, an intimate dining room with pretty green and peach wallpaper and matching curtains, and a much larger dining room used on busy nights. The seasonal menu, written in French with English translations, is short but sweet: perhaps a medley of poached fish with sorrel sauce, sweetbreads madeira, veal chop in gin and beer sauce, and tenderloin of beef with truffle sauce. Two quails with grapes and port wine sauce were the most expensive item when we visited. Dandelion salad with sauteed bacon was an innovative appetizer. Belgian touches show up in such desserts as dame blanch (vanilla ice cream with melted Belgian chocolate) and croustillant aux pommes (sauteed caramelized apples in phyllo on creme anglaise).

Dinner nightly except Monday, 6 to 9; Sunday brunch, 11 to 2.

Laconia

Hickory Stick Farm, R.D. 2, Laconia. (603) 524-3333.
Traditional. $9.95 to $16.95.

Out in the country a couple of miles of winding roads southwest of town, this rambling red farmhouse with white trim and nice gardens — and the sign, "Hop, Skip and Jump" — is known for its duckling. In fact, owner Scott Roeder says, fully 70 percent of the meals served are roast Wisconsin duckling with orange sherry sauce, roasted slowly til the skin is crisp and the meat is fork-tender, a quality to which we can attest, since we bought one to have at home. The farmhouse is notable for huge fireplaces, including one within a fireplace, and a duck motif, from lamps to the guest book, and a good gift shop. Polished tables are set with pewter service plates and woven mats. There's a screened gazebo for outdoor dining. Duckling comes in five sizes — from one-quarter pound to whole roast for four. Other choices include baked scallops, individual beefsteak pie, sirloin steak, filet wellington and vegetarian

Lakes Region

casserole. You can get fried duck livers as an entree or appetizer, along with duck soup, homemade duck liver pate, and hickory-smoked rainbow trout. Meals come with cheese and crackers, orange curl rolls and choice of molded pineapple or green salad. Many of the specialties date back to the restaurant's founding by Scott Roeder's parents in 1950. Finish with a raspberry-peach pie, blueberries in custard sauce flavored with grand marnier, or a frozen Hickory Stick, French vanilla ice cream rolled in chocolate cookie crumbs, served on hot fudge sauce with toasted almonds. As the menu says, "atmosphere is traditional, with good food additional."

Dinner nightly except Monday, 5 to 9, Sunday noon to 9. Open Memorial Day-Columbus Day. Reservations required.

Summerfields, 1106 Union Ave., Laconia. (603) 524-3111.
American. $8.95 to $16.95.

A high-ceilinged barn open to the second level, this place is filled with Laconia memorabilia, Tiffany-style lamps, butcher-block tables, early skis on a crossbeam, a corner with a fireplace, and an old victrola in the center of the room. Much the same menu is available all day; it's huge in scope as well as size. Dinnertime adds things like steak, prime rib, veal piccata, shrimp dijon, sole a la Ritz (with Ritz cracker stuffing), chicken divan, and baked stuffed shrimp. At lunch, try chicken salad St. Moritz with a slab of chicken breast and artichokes, a kitchen sink burger (make up your own) or beef burritos. Your server might recommend Winnipesaukee River pie (graham cracker crust, coffee ice cream and hot fudge) or the Teddy Bar (orange sherbet with hot fudge, which does not sound like a great combination to us). We didn't ask about the blackout cake.

Lunch, Monday-Saturday 11:30 to 5; dinner, 5 to 10; Sunday, brunch 10 to 3, dinner 5 to 9.

Ashland

The Common Man, Ashland Common, Ashland. (603) 968-7030.
American/Continental. $9.95 to $15.95.

Hailed for food that is the most consistent in the area, this long-runner founded in 1971 by Alex Ray draws enormous crowds and has spawned many other restaurateurs, Jane and Don Brown of the Corner House among them. The vast place is full of memorabilia, from old sheet music and Saturday Evening Post covers to an upstairs lounge with buckets and lobster traps hanging from the ceiling. There's even a jigsaw puzzle in the works at the entrance. The rustic, beamed dining room is separated into sections by dividers topped with books. The dinner menu is straightforward and priced right, from chicken kiev and crab and scallop pie to roast pork tenderloin and veal oscar. Prime rib and "a grate steak" big enough for three are specialties. Desserts vary from hot Indian pudding to mud pie and white chocolate mousse. The house wines are Craftsbury Creek, bottled specially for the restaurant.

Lunch, Monday-Saturday 11:30 to 2:30; dinner, 5:30 to 9, Sunday 5 to 9.

Holderness

The Manor, Route 3, Holderness. (603) 968-3348.
Continental. $11.95 to $19.95.

The Squam Lakes area's most luxurious inn also contains its most sumptuous dining room, a picture of elegance from its leaded windows and tiled fireplaces to the crystal chandelier hanging from the beamed ceiling covered with rich floral wallpaper. A second dining room off the lounge is less formal. Hot popovers and a house salad of greens dotted with peanuts and mandarin oranges preceded our entrees, nicely herbed lamb chops dijonnaise and heavily sauced steak diane. Other choices range from shrimp neopolitan and scallops citron to roast duckling with plum sauce, and three veal dishes. Appetizers run the gamut from escargots and mushrooms stuffed with ricotta and sausage to baked brie en croute. Mocha ice-cream pie and chocolate-grand marnier torte are good desserts.

Dinner nightly, 5:30 to 9:30; Sunday brunch, 11 to 2:30.

Meredith

Mame's, Plymouth Street, Meredith. (603) 279-4631.
American/Continental. $7.95 to $14.95.

The menu in this restored brick house and barn is standard steak and seafood with a continental flair, from seafood diane and lobster-scallop divan to steak medici and veal pierre. The prices are gentle, and the atmosphere intimate and romantic. A meandering series of three dining rooms on the main floor is topped by a large lounge and three more dining rooms on the second. The lobby is the only new part of the building, which dates to 1825. Owner John Cook also is a partner in the Millworks, a casual, multi-level establishment in the nearby Mill Falls Marketplace.

Lunch daily, 11:30 to 3; dinner, 5 to 9 or 9:30; Sunday brunch, 11:30 to 2.

Center Harbor

Red Hill Inn, Route 25B, Center Harbor. (603) 279-7001.
American. $7.95 to $21.95.

The kitchen here is the special preserve of Elmer Davis, a chef of the old school who worked in long-gone American Plan hotels and never takes a day off. He makes everything from scratch, including the twelve dressings that grace the house salads. The extensive menu ranges from old-fashioned (marinated herring) to contemporary (curried shrimp on angel-hair pasta) for appetizers, roast Long Island duckling to chicken with lemon and pepper for entrees. Roast pheasant and Alaskan king crab are featured. There is a good selection of dishes for the vegetarian. A rich chocolate silk pie, amaretto cheesecake and berry pies are among the popular desserts; one area restaurateur says she'd kill for the raspberry pie. Colorful china, fresh flowers and candles in hurricane lamps are on the pink-linened tables in two dining rooms and an airy sun porch.

Lunch in summer and fall, Monday-Saturday noon to 2; dinner nightly, 5 to 10; Sunday brunch, 11 to 2.

Center Sandwich

★ **The Corner House Inn,** Center Sandwich. (603) 284-6219.
American/Continental. $10.95 to $17.95.

Dinner is by candlelight in a rustic, beamed dining room with blue and white tablecloths and red napkins, or in three smaller rooms at this highly regarded establishment run by chef Don Brown and his wife Jane. Dinner entrees range from vegetable primavera to tournedos normandy, and include raspberry-orange duckling, veal oscar, shellfish saute from an original recipe, and lobster and scallop pie. One diner reports the double two-inch-thick broiled lamb chops were the best she'd ever had. Salad and homemade rolls and zucchini bread come with. Dessert could be cappuccino cheesecake, frozen chocolate-kahlua pie or pina colada sherbet. Lunches are bountiful and bargains; we saw some patrons sending half of theirs back for doggy bags. We, however, enjoyed every bite of the Downeaster, two halves of an English muffin laden with fresh lobster salad (more than you'd ever get in a

Lakes Region

Maine lobster roll costing nearly twice as much), sprouts and melted Swiss cheese. We also tried a refreshing cold fruit soup (peach, melon and yogurt, sparked with citrus rinds) and an interesting crepe filled with ground beef and veggies.

Lunch, Monday-Saturday 11:30 to 2:30, dinner nightly, 5:30 to 9:30. Shortened hours and closed Monday and Tuesday in winter.

Moultonboro

The Sweetwater Inn, Route 25, Moultonboro. (603) 476-5079.
Continental/Northern Italian. $9.95 to $16.95.

Veteran restaurateurs Mike and Donna Love moved from a Northern Italian eatery in Red Bank, N.J., acquired the old Stone Hearth, rechristened it the Sweetwater Inn and have garnered a good reputation. The large and comfortable dining room, its two levels done up in beiges and browns amid beams and plants, would be quite at home in New Jersey. The Loves make their own pastas for such dishes as lobster ravioli and fettuccine jambalaya. Main courses include two versions of paella and an Italian shellfish medley, four veal and three chicken dishes, blackened fish and steak au poivre. In 1989, the Loves added to their menu a page of items under $10, including pasta primavera, individual pizzas (shrimp and scampi, andouille sausage are two) and oriental stir-fries to appeal to those who don't want to come here just for special occasions. Donna prepares a wonderful pecan pie, raspberry cheesecake with hazelnut-almond meringue and a white chocolate mousse with fresh raspberries.

Dinner nightly, 5 to 9.

The Woodshed, Lee's Mill Road, Moultonboro. (603) 476-2311.
Steaks/Seafood. $10.95 to $17.95.

This atmospheric old barn in the middle of nowhere packs in the crowds for prime rib, which, in the Woodshed's terms, is "aged beef" and "rib-eye." The main dining room with white cloths and green napkins is huge; some tables are on a balcony as well. Up a ramp are two more large dining rooms and a back room with still more seats. Like the farmhouse and barn that opened in 1978, the restaurant just grew and grew. We understand the Woodshed serves 560 people on busy nights. Abundant barnwood, moose heads, a Dartmouth banner, boxing gloves and old skis comprise the decor. Baked onion soup and a cheese sampler, the traditional starters, are supplemented by items from a raw bar. Prime rib comes in three sizes, and you can order filet, lamb chops, barbecued ribs, steak teriyaki, a crab feast, shrimp kabob, grilled fish and more. House salad, hot bread, grilled vegetables and starch come with. Nobody goes home hungry, especially after the ice cream desserts or Indian pudding.

Dinner nightly, 5 to 10, Saturday to 11, Sunday 4 to 10.

Wolfeboro

★ $ East of Suez, Route 28 South, Wolfeboro. (603) 569-1648.
Asian. $10 to $13.

Although Charles Powell and his family, some from the Philippines, have operated this restaurant for twenty summers, it seems to be almost a secret except for devotees of Asian food. Once part of a camp, it's an almost rickety house with a big side porch, set in a field south of Wolfeboro. Decor is spare oriental, with a mishmash of chairs, tables and paper globe lamps. Out of the enormous kitchen comes a parade of interesting food, available prix-fixe or a la carte. To start, poached scallops with crab in miso sauce and the Philippine egg rolls known as lumpia are standouts.

The day's soup was clam chowder, almost like a New England version, but curiously spicy. All the entrees sound so good that it's hard to choose. The Japanese tempura includes a wide variety of fresh vegetables and a ton of shrimp. Another great dish is Szechuan shrimp and cashews, stir-fried with snow peas. Korean bulgogi (steak with spicy pickled cabbage), Philippine pancit (curly noodles sauteed with morsels of shrimp and pork with oriental vegetables), and Philippine adobo (the islands' national dish) are enough to draw Asian food addicts from near and far. Leche flan and a rich cashew and meringue torte are worthy endings. You might skip lunch beforehand, since portions are huge.

Dinner nightly except Monday, 6 to 9:30, June through Sept. 10. No credit cards. BYOB.

The Cider Press, 10 Middleton Road, Wolfeboro. (603) 569-2028.
American. $7.95 to $15.95.
There's a cider press at the door, and apple trees are out back. Hence the name for this rustic restaurant that has been expanded several times by Robert and Denise Earle. They now seat 165 diners by candlelight in three country-pretty barnwood rooms and a lounge with a three-sided open hearth. Chef Bob Earle considers baby back ribs and golden fried shrimp the specialty; they're listed on the menu as "the odd couple." Among straightforward entrees are chicken parmesan, seafood gratinee, shrimp scampi, and rump steak with herb butter. Specials when we were there included roast duck with orange-grand marnier sauce, double-thick lamb chops with mint butter, and salmon with lobster-bearnaise sauce. Parfaits, Boston cream pie and ice cream crepes are favorite desserts. A few house wines are offered, but the spiked hot apple cider is more popular.

Dinner nightly except Monday, 5:30 to 9, Sunday to 8.

Lakeview Inn, 120 North Main Street, Wolfeboro. (603) 569-1335.
American/Continental. $13.95 to $19.95.
Locally regarded as the town's best restaurant, the Lakeview is country elegant with wallpaper of flower baskets, swagged curtains, crystal candlesticks and fresh flowers from the inn's garden. An appealing menu is served in a somewhat ersatz Colonial setting. Among starters are the owner's favorite Portuguese soup from her mother's treasured recipe. Nightly specials augment a wide-ranging list of entrees, which roam from London broil and lamb chops to lobster thermidor, langoustines en papillote and a specialty called filet boursin wellington. Desserts might be peach cobbler, chocolate mint torte, ice cream puff, or hot Indian pudding. Light fare is served in the adjacent lounge, and there's entertainment nightly except Tuesday.

Dinner nightly, 5:30 to 10.

Wolfeboro Inn, 44 North Main St., Wolfeboro. (603) 569-3016.
American. $10.95 to $18.25.
Vastly expanded in 1988, this inn has a nouveau-elegant dining room graced with an authentic Rumford fireplace and 230-year-old paneling from Daniel Webster's birthplace, as well an inviting tavern full of atmosphere out front. Nicely spaced tables in the dining room are flanked by windsor chairs and a couple of loveseats and are dressed with fine china, burgundy and white linens and vases of freesia. The menu embraces standards like sherried mushrooms and oysters rockefeller among appetizers, prime rib and stuffed breast of chicken with havarti cheese as main courses. Specials are sometimes inventive, as in a salad of warmed goat cheese on beet greens with a ginger vinaigrette, chilled stuffed veal breast, salmon en papillote, and basil ravioli stuffed with lobster. Desserts include raspberry linzer torte, frozen grand marnier souffle and tirami su. Featured in the lounge is "hot rock cooking," where patrons cook their own meals at the table on a slab of granite heated

to 500 degrees. The cozy **Wolfe's Tavern** combines three of the inn's oldest common rooms and offers 72 menu items with an English theme and a list of 43 beers from around the world.

Dinner nightly, 5 to 9:30. Tavern, daily from 11:30.

The Bittersweet, Route 28 and Allen Road, Wolfeboro. (603) 569-3636. International. $9.50 to $16.50.

This rambling yellow structure east of town has an airy barnlike dining room with mismatched chairs, all colors of napkins on refinished tables, farm artifacts on the walls, and a fairly innovative menu. The rear lounge with a small wood stove is rustic and priced for value-seekers. For openers, the french onion soup might be laced with vermouth or the almond shrimp flamed with amaretto. Lamb and cider pie, stir-fried seafood, beef liver and onions, veal oscar, and Norwegian salmon with a seafood mousse in puff pastry are favorite entrees. Chef-owner Garry Warren's nightly specials are unusual for the area: grouper en papillote, haddock topped with julienned vegetables, halibut with dill butter, and bouillabaisse. The lounge menu offers snacky appetizers, salads, sandwiches and entrees. Desserts like grapenut pudding and raspberry pie are homemade.

Open Monday-Friday noon to 8:30; Saturday 5 to 9; Sunday, brunch 11 to 2, dinner 5 to 8.

West Alton

The William Tell Inn, Route 11, West Alton. (603) 293-8803. Swiss. $9.50 to $15.95.

We know traditionalists who say this is the only restaurant worthy of serious consideration around Lake Winnipesaukee. Built in the Swiss chalet style, it's certainly authentic, from its stone entrance to its main dining room done up in brown and beige, with stucco walls, paneled ceiling and Viennese waltzes playing in the background. Added bonus: from the rear windows you can catch a glimpse of the lake. Wiener schnitzel, four other veal dishes, bratwurst and roesti, roast duck montmorency, chicken kiev and tournedos madeira are typical fare, though the chef offers a fish special, a fresh vegetable plate and "zurcher ratsherren topf," charbroiled filets of beef, veal and pork served with assorted sauces. And you can order cheese fondue. Appetizers and desserts are authentic as well. The bound wine list offers a couple of Swiss vintages.

Dinner nightly except Monday from 5; Sunday brunch from noon.

Mount Washington Valley

Chocorua

★ **Stafford's in the Field,** Off Route 113, Chocorua. (603) 323-7766. French/Country Gourmet. $10.50 to $17.95.

Since Ramona and Fred Stafford opened their dining room to the public (it had been for inn guests only for years), it has become a destination for people who like interesting food. Here's a rural place with personality plus: a country cozy dining room with fireplace, old wood stove, copper pots, an old sleigh seat and kitchen artifacts, among them butter molds and an antique peeler "that I use all the time," says Ramona. Developing many of her own recipes, she uses fresh and seasonal ingredients and leans on her California background for Mexican specialties and "some California tastes that are hard to outgrow." Dinner usually involves a choice of three entrees that change nightly: beef tenderloin with armagnac sauce, breast of chicken with raspberry and garlic and poached salmon the night we were there.

The meal begins with soup, perhaps curried pumpkin, tomato-bourbon or chilled avocado with salsa, and salad with caesar or blackberry-walnut dressings, followed by champagne-grapefruit sorbet. Dessert could be apricot ice, nectarine and cream pie, a flourless chocolate cake with raspberry creme fraiche, blueberry-brandy pie, or gingerbread cake with bananas and whipped cream. The interesting wine list is reasonably priced.

Dinner by reservation, Tuesday-Sunday 6 to 9.

Eaton Center

The Inn at Crystal Lake, Route 153, Eaton Center. (603) 447-2120.
International. Prix-Fixe $23.
The exotic metal sculptures on the walls and the metal flowers springing from crystalized rocks on the dining tables are the work of innkeeper Walter Spink. There's artistry as well in the kitchen, where this former geology professor-turned-innkeeper and his wife, Jacqueline, prepare fixed-price, four-course dinners for inn guests and the public. Walter apprenticed for three months with Jean-Pierre Tardy, former executive chef at Philadelphia's acclaimed Le Bec Fin, to learn the restaurant business first-hand. Our dinner began with fresh fruit cup and a good salad with Walter's piquant French dressing. The highlight was roast loin of lamb dijon for two, served with rutabagas, green beans, broccoli and rice pilaf, followed by New Jersey peach pie with blueberry sauce. Other entree choices (some or all of which might be available on a given night) are chicken brie, shrimp poached or Cajun style, veal piccata, roast duckling and filet mignon. Jacqueline handles the service with aplomb, and the dining experience is very personal and endearing. Victorian crystal, china and lace enhance the three-level room, once the auditorium of a former school.

Dinner nightly by reservation, 6 to 8:30.

North Conway

The 1785 Inn, Route 16, North Conway. (603) 356-9025.
International. $15 to $20.
Located at the Scenic Vista north of town, this inn claims the best view of Mount Washington — from the rustic chairs facing the Presidential Range outside on the lawn and from window tables in the dining room. The inn is named for the year its original section was built, and retains Early American charm throughout the public rooms. Hitchcock chairs are at tables set with pale blue cloths, gleaming glassware and off-white china; an open-hearth fireplace is the focal point of the beamed dining room. The fairly steadfast menu leans to interesting game dishes: pheasant with peach sauce, sherried rabbit, raspberry duckling and venison, along with tournedos bordelaise, chicken chinois, veal with crabmeat, scallops in cream sauce and shrimp capri. Start with duck pate, escargots in red wine, cinnamon-spiced shrimp or smoked salmon raviolis. Desserts like frozen chocolate velvet mousse laced with grand marnier, raspberry-strawberry bavarian and mocha mousse with raspberry sauce accompany espresso and cappuccino. This is dining with a flair that won it the "best restaurant" award in a local newspaper poll. Innkeeper Charles Mollar is also proud of his wine list, which contains more than 200 selections and won an award of excellence from Wine Spectator.

Dinner nightly except Monday, 5 to 9 or 10.

Stonehurst Manor, Route 16, North Conway. (603) 356-3113.
Continental. $16 to $22.50.
A more regal setting is hard to imagine: four dining rooms full of leaded windows

and Victorian stained glass, fan-back wicker chairs on plush green carpeting, and tables set with two wine glasses and a cut-glass water tumbler at each place. Especially remarkable are a lovely stained-glass wreath and an entire stained-glass door with a dogwood pattern. The gardens in back are illuminated at night, and the effect is quite magical. You could readily imagine yourself a guest at one of the parties given at the turn of the century by the heiress to the Bigelow Carpet fortune in this many-gabled, three-story English country manor home. Tuxedoed waiters serve the fare from a wide-ranging menu, from shrimp and oyster stew, dover sole and chicken bombay to six veal dishes, beef wellington, steak au poivre madagascar, and rack of lamb and chateaubriand for two. Fresh vegetables with a sour-cream dip, assorted rolls and a starch come with; everything else is extra. Lobster ravioli and scallops ceviche are favorite openers. The chef's wife makes German chocolate layer cakes, pear streusal pie and other delectables reflecting her German heritage. The house wines are imported specially from Germany. The Library Lounge and an outdoor terrace are popular for cocktails.

Dinner nightly, 6 to 10. Reservations required.

The Scottish Lion, Route 16, North Conway. (603) 356-2482.
American/Scottish. $12.50 to $18.95.
There is plaid everywhere at this large, well-lighted spread long favored by tourists. It's on the walls of the entrance to the old inn, on the floor of the lobby and up the stairs, on the walls of the Black Watch Pub, and on the waitresses' kilts. Homemade Scottish oatcakes and rumbledethumps are served with all meals. The menu features such Scottish specialties as highland game pie (pheasant, beef, hare, venison and goose in a puff pastry crust), Scottish steak and mushroom pie, and roast beef with yorkshire pudding and horseradish sauce. Veal oscar, roast duck au poivre, salmon en croute and roast lamb are other possibilities. Finnan haddie and pate lapin (with veal and pork) served with lingonberries and gherkins are popular appetizers.

Lunch daily, 11:30 to 2; dinner, 5:30 to 9 or 9:30; Sunday brunch, 10:30 to 2.

Horsefeathers, Main Street, North Conway. (603) 356-2687.
American. $3.50 to $12.50.
For a change of pace, try this casual establishment in the heart of town, the flagship of a small chain. The Western-looking facade conceals a fairly plain interior with red oilcloths on the tables, ladderback chairs, hanging lamps and old signs for decor. At lunch, we enjoyed a tuna melt duxelle with pasta salad and a Philly cheese steak sandwich with horsefries — some thick, some paper-thin, but all the best we've ever had. We understand the chain goes through four tons of potatoes each week. The all-day menu is a happy mix of appetizers, soups and salads, sandwiches, light entrees and pastas, and the blackboard specials are usually enticing. The "lasagna of legend" is the traditional Italian version, meaty with marinara sauce and imported cheeses.

Open daily, 11:30 to 11:30.

Glen

* The Bernerhof, Route 302, Glen. (603) 383-4414.
Swiss. $13.95 to $21.50.
A superb kitchen and the Taste of the Mountains cooking school create a culinary dynamic that sets this turreted Victorian inn apart, thanks to the efforts of owner Ted Wroblewski. Meals are served in three dining rooms amidst pine paneling, beamed ceilings, crisp white linens, a piano and a Swiss stove. The Zumstein Room cocktail

lounge has an oak-paneled bar and a limited taproom menu. At lunch, we enjoyed a platter of memorable duck, trout and seafood-vegetable pates and a generous serving of smoked salmon around a salad in the middle, much enhanced by the melba toast that, upon request, the chef prepared from good French bread. At dinner, the specialty is Delft blue provimi veal, used in wiener schnitzel, emince de veau au vin blanc, piccata a la Suisse, and schnitzel cordon bleu. Other entrees include veal steak persillade, veal chops with pears, filet of salmon with shrimp, and scallops provencale. A changing monthly menu is more innovative: perhaps avocado and caviar salad, pistachio fettuccine with cilantro, chicken breast with truffled veal mousse, and lamb noisettes with sweet red pepper and garlic sauces. Among delectable desserts are profiteroles au chocolat, chocolate silk pie made with Myers's dark rum, and chocolate fondue for two. The predominantly French wine list is extensive by New Hampshire standards.

Lunch, Monday-Saturday noon to 3 in season; dinner nightly, 5:30 to 9:30; Sunday brunch, 10:30 to 2:30.

The Red Parka Pub, Route 302, Glen. (603) 383-4344.
Steaks/Seafood. $7.95 to $15.95.

This is the perfect place for apres-ski, from the "wild and crazy bar" with a wall of license plates from across the country (the more outrageous the better) to the "Skiboose," a 1914 flanger car that pushed snow off the railroad tracks and now is a cheerful dining area for private parties. Somehow the rest of this vast place remains dark and intimate, done up in red and blue colors, red candles and ice-cream parlor chairs. The menu inside the Red Parka Pub "Table Times" features hearty steaks, barbecued ribs, teriyakis and combinations thereof, plus baked stuffed shrimp and kabobs. The salad bar offers 30 items and breads. Homemade desserts include mud pie and Indian pudding. Next door is the pub's new **Black Diamond Grill,** a casual American grill featuring burgers in six sizes, hot dogs, shakes and fries for lunch or dinner.

Dinner nightly, 4 to 10.

Jackson

★ **The Restaurant Ansonia,** Nestlenook Farm, Dinsmore Road, Jackson.
(603) 383-4106.
Regional American. $10.75 to $18.75.

After three years in the area at the Inn at Thorn Hill and a similar period at Stonehurst Manor, New York-trained chef Hoke Wilson and his wife Claudia opened their own restaurant in 1989. It's part of the multi-million-dollar transformation of Nestlenook Farm into a Victorian fantasy inn in peach and green. Their delightful room with gray-green walls and pressed-tin ceiling seats 32 diners at tables dressed in white striped linens with small chess pieces as the centerpieces. But it is the artfully conceived and presented food that's packing in the customers. Nicknamed "Hoke cuisine," it's a personal statement raised to high art, which is appropriate to his background as a graphic designer. The menu changes nightly, but typically could begin with a choice of spiced scallop bisque with julienned vegetables, chile and cumin linguini with cheese and tomatoes in sesame and scallion butter, pan-fried shrimp on watercress, crab cakes with spinach, sweet corn and lemon, and poached oysters with cilantro and mustard butter. A salad of the night could be grilled eggplant with shredded duck and endive dressed with ginger and garlic. For entrees, how about grilled chicken with black bean and vegetable saute with roasted red pepper and basil sauce, pan-seared peppered swordfish with cucumber-peanut relish, sauteed lobster with steamed vegetables and lobster chive-mint sauce, tournedos on a fresh tomato coulis topped with pistachio-garlic cream, and sauteed duck with braised onion and fennel sauce? Claudia does the breads and desserts, including a dynamite plum and ginger tart, chocolate floating island with orange custard sauce, white chocolate mousse with pomegranate and bitter chocolate, fresh minted raspberry ice cream, and assorted sorbets, in our case blackberry, cantaloupe and banana. Theirs is the stuff of which culinary dreams are made. The California-Australia wine list is as well-chosen (and fairly priced) as the rest of the fare.

Dinner, Wednesday-Sunday 6 to 9:30. Closed most of May. No Smoking.

Wildcat Inn and Tavern, Route 16A, Jackson Village. (603) 383-4245.
American/International. $9.95 to $16.95.

Food is what this inn is known for. The old front porch had to be converted into dining space to handle the overflow from the original two dining rooms, cozy and homey as can be. The exceptional cream of vegetable soup is chock full of fresh vegetables; that and half a reuben sandwich made a hearty lunch. We also liked the delicate spinach and onion quiche, served with a garden salad dressed with creamy dill. Dinner choices are a mix from lasagna and bulgogi to lamb kabob, shrimp and scallop scampi, filet oscar and lobster fettuccine. The desserts slathered with whipped cream are too rich to be believed. In summer, dine out back in the attractive tavern gardens.

Lunch daily, 11:30 to 3; dinner, 6 to 9 or 10.

Christmas Farm Inn, Route 16B, Jackson. (603) 383-4313.
American. $14.25 to $16.95.

Food is a focal point of this established, Christmasy inn where the large, candlelit dining room is decked out in red, green and white. New chef William Zeliff III, son of the innkeepers, has returned the menu's emphasis from a brief fling with new American to favorite New England fare. Among entrees are poached salmon with mushrooms and basil, saute of scallops with tomato concasse, saute of trout with almonds and lemon, chicken kiev, grilled lamb kabob, and baked pork chops with apple chutney and red cabbage. Starters could be crab ravioli, terrine of wild mushrooms and escargots. The pastry chef is known for decorated tortes and gorgeous cakes.

Dinner nightly, 6 to 9. No smoking.

Thompson House Eatery (T.H.E.), Route 16 and 16A, Jackson.
(603) 383-9341.
International. $9.50 to $13.50.

An old red farmhouse dating from the early 19th century holds a rustic restaurant full of cozy rooms and alcoves, flower-bedecked decks and an old-fashioned soda fountain. "Handcrafted food presented in an artful manner" has been the byword since the 1970s of chef-owner Larry Baima, who offers original fare with Italian and oriental influences. He's created so many unusual dishes that, legend has it, he had no room on the menu for hamburgers or french fries. Instead, sandwiches have flair, as in turkey with asparagus spears, red onions, melted Swiss and Russian dressing. Salads are creations: curried chicken, almonds and raisins atop greens and garnishes. Dinner entrees include "Baked Popeye," a remarkable spinach casserole with mushrooms, bacon and cheese and an option of scallops. Other artful choices include chicken saltimbocca, pork tenderloin lorenzo, heart and sole (with artichokes), chicken and sausage parmigiana, pastas, stir-fries and much more. Swiss chocolate truffle, wild berry crumble and Dutch mocha ice cream make great desserts. There's a beer and wine license.

Lunch daily, 11:30 to 4; dinner, 5:30 to 10. Closed November to Memorial Day.

Gorham

Via Sorento, 152 Main St., Gorham. (603) 466-2520.
Italian-American. $5.95 to $14.
This family place was run for twelve years by the Saladino family before they leased it to Douglas and Lorraine Loring in 1989. That accounts for the variety of names (Saladino's, La Bottega Saladino and Via Sorrento) that we encountered on signs and menus at our visit. The change also may account for lackluster (no, make that catatonic) service; it took over an hour to get lunch on a slow summer Saturday, but the pesto boboli and antipasti Mediterranean were worth the wait, we guess; the family with several youngsters at the next table was making such an incredible mess which, after they left, no one cleaned up, that we found it all rather distracting. The decor is a mishmash of banquet chairs, baskets and plants, but white tablecloths turn the atmosphere more elegant at night. Everything is homemade. There are eight pastas at dinner, though strangely none at lunch. The nighttime menu also calls for roast of the day, grilled sirloin steak capri, Italian mixed grill (chicken, veal and sausage), veal marsala, grilled chicken Mediterranean, sauteed shrimp and scallops, and baked stuffed shrimp Mediterranean. Baklava joins the parade of Italian desserts. The Italian market at the entrance is quite good.
Lunch, Monday-Saturday 11 to 4; dinner, 5 to 9. Closed Sunday.

Northern New Hampshire

Plymouth

★ **Glove Hollow,** Route 3, Plymouth. (603) 536-4536.
Regional American. $12.95 to $19.95.
"Refined, stylish dining" in an expansive 19th-century farmhouse is the billing for this unusual joint venture between the owners (and friendly competitors) of two of Central New Hampshire's better-known restaurant operations. In partnership with Alex Ray and Diane Downing of the Common Man in Ashland, Jane and Don Brown from the Corner House in Center Sandwich serve upscale American cuisine in a fancy Victorian setting in an area that once was the site of a glove factory. Striking murals — one of an old-fashioned couple walking in a field, the other of a country lass — enhance two of the three small country-charming dining rooms, each with well-spaced tables set with pink or white napkins billowing from the wine glasses. Ladies' white gloves hang from lamps and bookshelves; Victorian hats are on a wall. Chef Steve Witek, who used to be at the Corner House, oversees the menu. The lobster bisque with a flaky crust is a signature starter. Chicken sauteed in Moet Chandon champagne, Maine crab cakes, freshwater catfish, veal tenderloin wrapped around a dumpling and topped with bordelaise sauce, medallions of pork tenderloin finished with apple brandy and diced apples, and rack of lamb coated with dijon, garlic and rosemary are beguiling entrees. Desserts could be chocolate mousse, white raspberry torte, chambord torte, pecan pie, and creme caramel. The Sunday brunch is one of the best around.
Dinner, Tuesday-Sunday 5:30 to 9:30 (Thursday-Sunday in winter); Sunday brunch.

Suzanne's Kitchen, 36 South Main St., Plymouth. (603) 536-3304.
Natural Foods. $7.95 to $9.50.
The wholegrain bakery is the draw here, or is it the dessert showcase, the heaping sandwiches, the vegetarian dishes, the Syrian pizzas, the veggie burgers? No

matter. Suzanne Samyn has attracted quite a following to what she calls he "combination restaurant-coffeehouse-diner" since she first opened a snack bar (now expanded into Suzanne's Kitchenette & Deli) in 1976 in nearby Ashland. Twelve wholegrain breads and desserts are made from flour ground on the premises and only honey, molasses and maple syrup are used as sweeteners. We drooled over the strawberry whipped cream kiwi pie and the maple pound cake made with tofu and a cream cheese topping. But the conga bar we bought was tasteless except for the chocolate chips on top. The menu lists many items as egg-free, dairy-free and-o without cholesterol. The atmosphere is nil (bare tables and bentwood chairs), but there's an artists' wall and an open stage for "kitchen concerts" of folk music on most Wednesday and Sunday nights.

Open daily, 7 a.m. to 9 p.m. Lunch, 11:30 to 5:30; dinner, 5:30 to 9. Beer and wine. No smoking.

The Backyard, 105 Main St., Plymouth. (603) 536-1994.
Italian. $11.75 to $16.95.

Around back and downstairs from the Trolley Car diner-restaurant is this little prize a refuge of five booths and three tables separated by trellises. Small grapevines have been stenciled on the white walls; white formica tables are set with pink mats and napkins shaped like flowers atop white plates. Italian music plays in the background and it's all quite romantic. Homemade pastas and classic Italian dishes like veal marsala, shrimp scampi, shrimp and clam fra diavolo, chicken parmigiana and steak ala pizziola make up the small, no-nonsense menu. Chef Mario Hache who once worked in New Orleans, had added chicken gumbo and shrimp Creole as specials when we visited. The all-Italian wine list is a good one by New Hampshir standards.

Dinner, Wednesday-Sunday 5 to 9.

The Downunder, 3 South Main St., Plymouth. (603) 536-3983.
American/Continental. $7.50 to $13.95.

Everything's homemade from rolls to dessert at this college-style establishmer popular with students from Plymouth State, owner Mike Hanley's alma mater. started out in a different location "down under" Blake's restaurant, but says Mike "we're not down under any more," except perhaps for the aquarium "with 89 gallon of fish down under." There's a photo mural alcove in the foyer, and the place i outfitted with cane and chrome chairs, butcherblock tables and skylights. The far is a collegian's delight, from potato "heads," loaded nachos and Cajun fried chicke salad to veggie kabob, Sicilian chicken and veal parmigiana. The chef sometime gets adventursome with things like sole Key West (with melons and kiwi), Hungaria goulash and wiener schnitzel. The wine selection is dreadful, but no one seems t care.

Lunch, Monday-Saturday 11:30 to 5; dinner nightly, 5 to 9:30.

North Woodstock

The Woodstock Inn, Route 3, North Woodstock. (603) 745-3951.
Continental. $12.25 to $19.25.

This century-old Victorian home serves what many consider the best — an certainly the most ambitious — food in the Lincoln-Woodstock area. Floral china crystal and deep green and white linens are the setting in the formal Clement Room an enclosed wraparound porch. The attached section known as Woodstock Station was originally the Lincoln train station, sawed in half and moved here in 1984. Th freight room became the bar, and the passenger area is a dining room. Here, ami theater seats and sewing machine tables, you can get a wide variety of snacks and heavier fare from burgers and pastas to stir-fries and seafood wellington at pleasing prices. Veal is the specialty in the Clement Room, offered in nine presentations, from provimi prime veal legs handcut in the kitchen. The menu is wide-ranging, from coquilles St. Jacques and shrimp osceola to six chicken dishes (including a curried nasi goreng), beef wellington and steak diane. Meals come with a house appetizer like seafood chowder or tortellini with pesto or marinara, salad, sorbet and the like, but plenty of extra appetizers are offered as well. Homemade desserts include apple cake, chocolate mousse orgy and ice cream puffs.

Dinner nightly, 5:30 to 9:30; Sunday brunch, 11 to 3. Station, 11:30 to 10.

Truants Taverne, Main Street, North Woodstock. (603) 745-2239. Casual. $8.75 to $12.95.

A "Please Seat Yourself" approach and paper placemats that serve as the menu set the theme for this establishment fashioned from an old millyard. A desktop bar, polished pine tables with straightback chairs, maps on the walls and shelves of books for the truants are the backdrop for such prerequsites as muchos nachos and chicken fingers, electives like the school nurse (spinach) and school master (chef) salads, and dean's list entrees like baked scrod, chicken parmigiana, veal marsala and chicken cordon not so bleu. Sandwiches, a chimichanga and barbecued ribs are listed under fine arts courses. For detention's delight, how about Belgian chocolate cake? Fine dining it's not, but neither is it the school cafeteria.

Open daily from 11:30 until 10:30.

Lincoln

Tavern At the Mill, Millfront Marketplace, Main St., Lincoln. (603) 745-3603. International. $7.25 to $16.50.

The Lincoln-Loon Mountain area is a-boom, and this contemporary establishment on several levels of the east end of a shopping area is the largest and most ambitious of all the new eateries. There are a cozy lounge with an open brick hearth, an upstairs lounge with entertainment, an outdoor deck and a sunken, beamed and raftered dining room with windows onto the lawn. The last is pretty in pale pink and white, with blond windsor chairs at angled tables and plenty of vines and plants. The enormous menu has something for everyone: nachos, potato skins, Cajun mako shark, medallions of stuffed calamari, lemon pepper shrimp, Shanghai chicken, barbecued ribs, veal oscar, steak au poivre, six pasta dishes — you get the idea. There's even an American sushi bar in season. Desserts lean to things like cannoli, chocolate-peanut butter pie and sundaes.

Lunch daily, 11:30 to 3; dinner, 5 to 10 or 11.

Eugenio's Italian Cuisine, Lincoln Center North, Main Street, Lincoln. (603) 745-6798. Italian. $6.95 to $15.25.

Unexpectedly pleasant in gray and cranberry is this sleek little establishment in a shopping plaza storefront. Red mats and bud vases holding carnations top the inlaid gray and oak tables. Tiffany-style lamps, lovely stenciling and etched-glass dividers complete the decor. The menu offers plenty of pastas, plus chicken in seven presentations and veal in eight. Shrimp scampi, sauteed scallops, steak pizziola and steak au poivre are other possibilities. We'd splurge for the seafood pesto — scallops, shrimp and lobster in a basil and pine nut cream sauce over fettuccine. Much of the same, along with sandwiches and burgers, is available at lunchtime.

Lunch daily, 11:30 to 4; dinner from 5.

Franconia

Lovett's by Lafayette Brook, Profile Road, Franconia. (603) 823-7761.
American/Continental. Table d'hote, $20.
Longtime chef Peter Tavino's offerings continue to please a coterie of regulars. After cocktails in a small lounge with a marble bar from a Newport mansion, patrons are seated in three beamed dining rooms for three-course table d'hote dinners. Unusual soups include such summer offerings as cold bisque of fresh watercress with chervil, cold black bean soup with Demarara rum and wild White Mountain blueberry soup. Among more conventional standbys, entrees might include curried lamb with Lovett's grape chutney, sauteed Colorado trout, poached Norwegian salmon, and chicken with apples and calvados. Desserts are extravagant, from hot Indian pudding with ice cream to meringue glace with strawberries. We remember with gusto the chocolatey Aspen crud we tried almost twenty years ago and, yes, last we knew it was still on the menu. Such endurance is reassuring.
Dinner nightly by reservation, 6:30 to 7:45.

Franconia Inn, Easton Road, Franconia. (603) 823-5542.
American/Continental. $14.95 to $21.95.
For special occasions, area residents head for this venerable inn's handsome dining room with well-spaced tables and small-paned windows looking out toward the mountains. The limited menu changes frequently and is considered locally a bit pricey. Dinner could begin with escargots in puff pastry or herring with sour cream and capers. Entrees include seafood pernod, veal oscar, lamb chops dijon, spicy ginger shish kabob, filet mignon with pink peppercorn sauce and, for the vegetarian, sauteed vegetables served in a pastry shell. Fancy after-dinner drinks and coffees compensate for the lack of exciting desserts, which include pies and fruit melbas.
Dinner nightly, 6 to 9.

Littleton

★ Tim-Bir Alley, 28 Main St., Littleton. (603) 444-6142.
Eclectic. $13 to $16.50.
This tiny establishment named for its owners, Tim and Biruta Carr, is really down an alley and hard to find, but well worth the effort. The food is the most sophisticated and inventive in the area. Seven tables, plus a few stools at the counter, seat about 25. Antique lace tablecloths are under glass, walls are hung with posters and macrame, and classical music plays at night. The dinner menu changes weekly, usually offering one soup, two appetizers and a pasta dish, and five entrees. An outstanding scallop mousse with fresh dill and dijon vinaigrette is more than enough for two as an appetizer. The house salad is an interesting mix of greens, mushrooms, red peppers and Swiss cheese, dressed with a piquant vinaigrette. The mixed grill combines lamb chop with rosemary and feta, veal scaloppine with banana, rum and cream, and tournedo of beef with choron sauce — all beautifully presented around asparagus spears, red caviar on sour cream over roast potatoes, and bits of asparagus and zucchini in the middle. A smoky flavor pervaded the linguini with duck, scallions, tomato and smoked swiss cheese, another memorable combination. Other entrees could be fresh swordfish with papaya salsa or pork scaloppine with plums, brie and brandy cream. The lunches are just as good: an appetizer of shrimp mousse with two caviars and a bountiful seafood and citrus salad lately.
Lunch, Wednesday-Friday 11:30 to 2; dinner, Thursday-Sunday 6 to 9; Sunday brunch, 9 to 1. Winter, dinner on weekends only.

Edencroft Manor, Route 135, Littleton. (603) 444-6776.
   Continental. $9.95 to $17.50.
   Dining in this inn with conference facilities is in two formal, candlelit rooms with classical music as a backdrop. Five presentations of veal (including one with shiitake mushrooms) and three of shrimp, filet of sole with peanuts, lamb chops with chutney, and two fettuccines are among the choices. Appetizers include shrimp cocktail and oysters rockefeller. The dessert cart is laden with innkeeper Maryann Frasca's pastry creations, among them praline and double chocolate cheesecakes, key lime pie and a variety of mousses.
   Dinner, Tuesday-Saturday 5:30 to 9, Sunday 5:30 to 8.

The Clam Shell, Route 302, Littleton. (603) 444-6445.
   Seafood. $8.95 to $16.95.
   It's not where we'd think of heading for seafood, this outpost beside the interstate in the northernmost reaches of northern New England. But hundreds do, judging by the cars packing the parking lot at all hours and the several dining rooms full of nautical memorabilia and an aquarium. The restaurant has a fish market adjacent, and seafood arrives three or four times a week from Portland or Boston, so you know it's "as close to fresh as we can get," as the owner said. The no-nonsense menu goes along with the paper mats and gold-colored water glasses. The fish comes fried, baked or broiled, from seafood newburg to scallops parmesan, an original creation served over linguini. The fried oysters, when available, are said to be out of this world. For non-seafood eaters, there's an admirable prime rib among black angus beef items. And, of course, a salad bar.
   Lunch, Monday-Saturday 11:30 to 4; dinner, 5 to 9. Sunday brunch, 11 to 2.

Seacoast Region

Rye

The Carriage House, 2263 Ocean Blvd. (Route 1A), Rye. (603) 964-8251.
   American/International. $9.75 to $14.25.
   The decor is simple and homey in this Cape house with a restaurant history dating back 70 years. Candles flicker and classical music plays amid wainscoting, bare wood floors, Victorian-style lamps and tables set with dark green mats. Dinners begin with a plate of raw vegetables and a mild curry dip, and include excellent tossed salads or an interesting tomato and onion concoction dressed with oregano, garlic and parmesan. Dinner entrees range from calves liver, Szechuan chicken and curry of the day to salmon en papillote, veal marsala, marinated grilled lamb racks, Sicilian rabbit, and steak au poivre. Among the tasty desserts is a hot tuaca sundae normandie — apples sauteed with cinnamon, brown sugar and nutmeg, flamed with butterscotch liqueur and topped with ice cream.
   Dinner nightly from 5; Sunday brunch, 11 to 3.

Saunders at Rye Harbor, Harbor Road, Rye. (603) 964-6466.
   Seafood. $12.95 to $20.95.
   Go past the lobster pools at the entrance and head to the rear room with picture windows onto the water or, better, the breezy brick patio at the side flanked with geraniums and the area's best harbor view. The setting compensates for the food, which reflects the institutional mentality of "we've been successful for 60 years, so why change?" Oh, they have added baked brie as an appetizer for two, but most opt for Dorothy Saunders Tucker's lobster stew. For it is lobster in many guises, from saute to newburg, that packs in the crowds. Seafood offerings include broiled

Seacoast Region

haddock, scallops, scampi, shrimp pescatore, seafood brochette, and haddock pizziola. Chicken and steak dishes also are available. At lunch, try the lobster club sandwich, a half pineapple stuffed with shrimp, or seafood and asparagus salad.

Lunch daily in season, noon to 3; dinner, 5 to 9 or 10; closed Tuesday in off-season.

Hampton

Ron's Beach House, 965 Ocean Blvd., Hampton. (603) 926-1870.
Seafood-Continental. $9.95 to $15.95.

A lovely Colonial house with an unlikely name holds what many consider the best restaurant between Newburyport and Portsmouth. Owner Ron Boucher has built a devoted following for tablecloth dining in three main-floor rooms and more casual meals in an upstairs lounge with canvas deck chairs, a bar with tables facing portholes, and a sunny side deck with an ocean view. Homemade pastas and seafood are featured, with the day's catch listed on a card and available baked, charbroiled, blackened or poached with sliced tomatoes and cucumbers and served on a bed of spinach. The regular dinner menu ranges from baked finnan haddie topped with a light caper-lemon sauce to cioppino and baked lobster stuffed with shrimp and clams. Grilled citrus chicken, veal scaloppine and filet mignon au champignon are available for those who prefer. Desserts prepared by Ron's mother include a notable lemon lust, frozen mousse pie and raspberry trifle. The lunch and brunch menus offer a broad range to appeal to diverse tastes.

Open daily from 11 to 10; Sunday brunch.

New Castle

Marina Cafe, Wentworth Road, New Castle. (603) 433-5019.
New American. $12.95 to $18.95.

The vision of the rebuilt Wentworth By the Sea resort rising again in New Castle was first reflected in this cafe, the first stage of which opened in 1989 on the rocky shore. The small round room is sleek in gray and white, with an uncluttered look and a sunny outdoor deck beyond. Unfortunately, when we stopped for lunch the manager said he lacked the staff to serve outside; the inept service inside did not compensate. The mussel-clam soup harbored a fishy substitute for clams, and the shrimp and barley salad was mostly barley, oily and devoid of seasoning. The day's pasta of mushroom fettuccine with tomato, fennel and feta cheese was garnished with a marigold and ferns — very arty and tasty, but a niggardly portion. Yet hope springs eternal: others were enjoying oversize burgers and sandwiches, and the dinner menu tempted. Braised lobster in drambuie cream with fresh basil, roast duckling with apricot-ginger sauce and filet of beef with braised onions and port wine sauce might be on the changing menu. Even the lowly haddock is dressed up here with sauteed onions and fresh mint. For starters, try oysters ceviche or a salad of sea scallops and arugula. Ginger-brandy cheesecake sounds like a good dessert. Although prices are high and portions small, the kitchen has promise. An upstairs addition to double the restaurant's size was planned for 1990.

Lunch, Monday-Saturday noon to 2:30; dinner nightly, 6 to 9:30 or 10; Sunday brunch, 11 to 3. Closed Monday and Tuesday in winter.

Portsmouth

* Strawbery Court, 20 Atkinson St., Portsmouth. (603) 431-7722.
New American. $20.95 to $22.95.

This is tops for consistently fine dining in a city known for fine dining. Elegant, restful and refined, it has eleven well-spaced tables in the large dining room of a brick 1815 Federal House that's home to talented young chef Douglas Johnson and his dentist-partner, Dr. Frank Manchester, who came here with many of their staff in 1983 from their acclaimed L'Armagnac in Columbus, Ohio. A rose on each table, a few spotlit oil paintings and a large bouquet of gladioli on the service table provide color amid the prevailing white and platinum-gray colors, softly illuminated by track lights and candles. Dinner can be ordered prix-fixe or a la carte. For openers, we're partial to the souffle of coquilles St. Jacques, Norwegian smoked salmon garnished with caviar, and the colorful house salad composed like a painting. The chef mixes such seasonal specialties as pheasant normande and loin of venison with classics like tournedos with three peppers and sweetbreads sauteed with orange zest and cointreau. Between the medallions of lamb, served with pimento (red) and pesto (green) sauces, comes a ribbon of whipped potatoes; on the side is a bundle of crisp white asparagus tied with red pepper. The desserts are worth every pretty penny: perhaps a delicate cheesecake laced with armagnac and grand marnier on a layer of genoise or a chocolate-chestnut terrine on raspberry coulis.

Dinner, Tuesday-Saturday 6 to 9.

Seventy Two Restaurant, 45 Pearl St., Portsmouth. (603) 436-5666.
French/New England. $14.95 to $21.95.

Young chef James J. Miceli moved around the corner from his original success, 72 Islington, into a onetime Baptist church. It's an incredible space, with a high rusty red ceiling, tall arched windows and well-spaced tables pretty in white and pink. Over the kitchen in a balcony that must have been the choir loft is a cocktail lounge, decked out with an ornate metal banister, tables, piano, and a sofa seating a family of stuffed bears from the owner's collection. Service can be slow, but few quibble with the fare — "French food with a New England flair" is how self-taught chef Miceli describes it. The ambitious menu might list octopus, chilled lobster remoulade and veal sausage with shallot-cream sauce among appetizers, and French brie with sherry or oyster stew for soups. Entrees could be roast duck montmorency, veal oscar, shrimp scampi, and saute of quail in chambord and raspberry vinegar for entrees. The vegetables are artfully presented and the portions so filling you may have to pass up the hazelnut torte or frangelico cheesecake from the dessert cart.

Dinner nightly, 6 to 10; Sunday brunch, noon to 3.

$ L'Auberge, 96 Bridge St., Portsmouth. (603) 436-2377.
French. $12 to $18.

This one-room restaurant in the French provincial style is run very personally by Francois Rolland and his wife Kathy — he in the kitchen and she out front. The decor is unpretentious: hurricane candles and brown linens, pretty beveled windows and stained glass. All the French classics are offered, from cold vichyssoise and frog's legs provencale to beef wellington and dover sole meuniere. Tournedos rossini, sweetbreads, roast duck, and linguini with clam sauce are among the possibilities. Dinners include crusty French bread, potato or rice pilaf, vegetable and caesar salad. The French wines are a bargain, and the crepes suzette and cherries jubilee outstanding. Lunchtime is a particular bargain, when you can follow pate or French farmer soup with shrimp Creole or filet mignon and get out for less than $10.

Lunch, 11:30 to 3; dinner, 5 to 10; closed Sunday and Monday, plus June and part of July.

The Library at the Rockingham House, 401 State St., Portsmouth.
(603) 431-5202.
American/International. $7.50 to $18.50.

Books fill the shelves of three dining rooms and even enclose booths for intimate dining in this ornate, mahogany paneled restaurant on the main floor of a hotel-turned-apartment-house. For dinner, Thailand beef salad, Middle Eastern eggplant dip and broiled pork with peanut curry sauce are among provocative appetizers at bargain prices. Entrees run the gamut from mussels mariniere and oriental chicken to tournedos oscar and rack of New Zealand lamb with mint-apricot sauce. We like the sound of chicken gaiyang with a hot and sweet sauce. The fennel and gruyere quiche, a super-good spinach salad with a mustard dressing and homemade croutons, and the mussels made a wonderful lunch, topped off with a strawberry cheesecake at least three inches high. The owners of the Library also run The Toucan, a with-it downtown cafe at 174 Fleet St. with a mix of Mexican, South American and Cajun fare.

Lunch, 11:30 to 3; dinner, 5 to 11 or midnight; Sunday brunch, 11:30 to 4.

Karen's, 105 Daniel St., Portsmouth. (603) 431-1948.
International. $11.95 to $17.95.

In an unassuming little place with bare floors, stenciled walls and perhaps a dozen tables, Karen Weiss offers some of the most creative food in town. How about one fall dinner that started with spicy jalapeno quesadillas with blackeyed pea salsa or Indonesian chicken sate with cucumber relish and spicy peanut sauce? Main courses were grilled shrimp on jalapeno pasta with three-pepper salsa, fresh tuna with putanesca sauce, and veal medallions sauteed with pancetta, oyster mushrooms, shrimp, and cilantro lemon demi-glace. If you can't get in for dinner, settle for lunch, perhaps a hot eggplant sandwich, Mexican chicken club sandwich, grilled swordfish kabob, chicken fajita or pesto quiche and salad, or a memorable breakfast.

Breakfast and lunch, Monday-Saturday; dinner, Friday and Saturday 6 to 10; Sunday brunch, 8 to 2. BYOB. No credit cards.

Guido's Upstairs Trattoria, 67 Bow St, Portsmouth. (603) 431-2989.
Northern Italian. $13 to $14.

Healthful cooking with natural foods and authentic ingredients is the theme of Peter (Guido) Yosua, a young chef who hones his style during trips to Italy. The dozen white-clothed tables, set amid beamed ceiling and brick walls, are flanked by windows onto the harbor. Interesting pastas like porcini-stuffed tortellini in a roasted red bell pepper sauce are available as appetizers or entrees. The changing entrees might include veal stewed in a white wine and sage broth, jumbo shrimp redolent with garlic and olive oil, or tenderloin of beef braised in chianti. Sample tirami su or fresh fruit and Italian cheeses for dessert as you finish up a bottle from the all-Italian wine list.

Dinner, Tuesday-Saturday 6 to 10. No smoking.

Anthony's Al Dente, 59 Penhallow St., Portsmouth. (603) 436-2527.
Italian. $12 to $17.

Dark and grotto-like with stone and brick walls and slate floors, this local institution in the Custom House Cellar is usually jammed. A lengthy menu combines both northern and southern Italian specialties, and while it appears expensive, patrons are expected to share. The small antipasto, for instance, is enough for four and such a work of art that some hesitate to disturb it. Twelve pastas are meals in themselves, although most diners continue with "second main courses" of veal, chicken and seafood, supplemented by daily Italian specials featuring beef, lamb or game. Everything costs extra (remember, you're supposed to share), but don't pass up a dessert like ricotta cheesecake or almond cake with amaretto whipped cream.

Dinner, Tuesday-Saturday 5:30 to 10, Sunday 5 to 9.

Sakura, 40 Pleasant St., Portsmouth. (603) 431-2721.
Japanese. $7.25 to $15.50.

Portsmouth's first Japanese restaurant is in the old Post Office building, with a long sushi bar, blond wood tables, stucco walls, hanging lamps and screens. The two sushi chefs work magic. For lunch, we enjoyed a plate of beautifully decorated sushi, miso soup and tea. At night, sushi comes in several dishes. "Heaven" is comprised of twelve pieces and two rolls of sushi and ten pieces of sashimi. You can try broiled eel on rice, lobster broiled with egg yolk, baked halibut with soybean sauce, breaded cutlets, sukiyaki, teriyakis and tempuras. Enjoy a Sapporo beer with your meal, and finish up with ginger or green tea ice cream.

Lunch, Monday-Friday 11:30 to 2:30; dinner nightly, 5 to 10 or 11.

Blue Strawbery, 29 Ceres St., Portsmouth. (603) 431-6420.
Contemporary. Prix-Fixe, $36.

Chef James Haller and the Blue Strawbery inspired Portsmouth's restaurant renaissance when they opened in 1970 in a restored ship's chandlery across from the waterfront. The restaurant is known far and wide, better regarded nationally than locally and considered to be resting on its reputation. Longtime chef Phillip McGuire, who cooked during Haller's frequent absences, was still on board, but Haller had left and the last of the original partners had the restaurant up for sale. Some say the food is as good as ever, but increasing numbers of people have been disappointed. Prix-fixe dinners of six courses are served at two seatings. The choice of entree includes one each from land, sea or air, perhaps swordfish stuffed with hearts of palm and served with a tomato-rice sauce, breast of turkey with shrimp in sherry-port wine sauce, and tenderloin of beef with green pepper and sparkling burgundy. For appetizers, you might find mushrooms in chocolate-brandy cream sauce and chicken livers in a sauce with brandy and allspice. Waiters recite ingredients of each dish and deliver them with a flourish on huge platters to all diners at once. Although the menu changes nightly, the house dessert does not: fresh strawberries for dipping in sour cream and brown sugar.

Dinner by reservation, Monday-Saturday 6 and 9 p.m., Sunday 3 and 6 p.m.; single seating at 7:30 Tuesday-Thursday from Columbus Day to Memorial Day. No credit cards.

Lila's at Penhallow, 16 Penhallow St., Portsmouth. (603) 427-0177.
Regional American. $16 to $24.

Taking over an abandoned building dating to 1814, chef-owner Bill Martin did a remarkable restoration and opened this elegant eatery in 1989. Named for his late mother, whose portrait hangs in the main dining room, it's pretty as a picture in deep blue and white, with bare polished floors, twelve-foot-high ceilings, sheer flouncy curtains and a lovely curved arch between two dining rooms. Soap operas from Argentina and 1930s music may play in the background. Interesting soups like swiss chard and lobster bisque come with dinner in tureens topped by hens, but save room for the house pate of veal, pork, juniper berries and black peppercorns. For entrees, try grilled swordfish with black olive butter, lobster thermidor, medallions of pork with black currant and walnut sauce, pheasant hunter style or tournedos of venison with fruit compote. Desserts, also included in the price of the meal, might be peach shortcake, chocolate or strawberry "zephyrs" (light as a mousse and served in chilled silver goblets), and chocolate raspberry torte. The lunch menu is less ambitious.

Lunch, 11:30 to 2; dinner, 5 to 10; closed Monday.

The Metro, 20 High St., Portsmouth. (603) 436-0521.
American/Continental. $10.95 to $14.95.

This art nouveau bar and cafe is pleasantly decked out with brass rails, stained glass, old gas lights, mirrors and dark wood. It's especially popular with the locals. The clam chowder once won first prize in the New England competition at Newport. Dinner is a mix of lamb chops and haddock casino, steak diane and veal oscar. Desserts, attractively displayed on a fancy old baker's rack, include baklava, walnut pie and caramel custard.

Lunch daily, 11:30 to 3; dinner, 5:30 to 9:30 or 10; closed Sunday.

Exeter

The Starving Chef, 29 Water St., Exeter. (603) 772-5590.
International/Thai/Indian/Szechuan. $10.95 to $16.95.

These folks aren't starving; in fact after ten years in funky quarters, they planned to move in April 1990 to a larger space in an historic building at 237 Water St. How could they starve, with a mouth-watering menu billed as "creative cuisine" and a receptive following in the academic community? Chicken with brussels sprouts, dates, figs and cashews and lamb bhuna, both served on basmati rice, are menu fixtures. So are spanakopitas and shrimp kaho phat. Nightly specials might be Szechuan beef stir-fried with every vegetable in the book and sauteed tuna mellowed with honey and apples. Presentation here is secondary to taste, which is as it should be. Ditto for the atmosphere. Try one of the mango desserts: mousse, mania (layers of mousse, vanilla ice cream and sherbet) and magic (mousse with orange sherbet and chocolate mousse). Raspberry cream cake and Italian pudding with ricotta cheese, walnuts, berries, apples and raisins are other stunners. Soups, many salads and sandwiches are chalked up on the blackboards for lunch, along with beer and wine specials.

Lunch, Monday-Friday 11:30 to 2:30; dinner, Tuesday-Saturday 5 to 9 or 10.

The Loaf and Ladle, 9 Water St., Exeter. (603) 778-8955.
American. $4.95 to $7.95.

Open cafeteria-type service at the entrance characterizes this lovable, enduring place that lives up to its name. Of course there are wonderful soups (perhaps chilled strawberry with sour cream and chablis), "meals in a bowl" like chili, salads (Greek, India and spinach) and delectable breads. But nighttime brings a couple of dinner specials from the chef's repertoire of lemon chicken, baked haddock, pastas and seafood crepes, served with bread and salad for a wallet-pleasing $7.95. The rambling establishment has a couple of dining rooms with bare wood tables, a large bar with live entertainment and a shady outdoor deck by a tumbling river in back.

Open Monday-Wednesday 8 to 8, Thursday-Saturday to 9, Sunday 11 to 9.

The Inn at Exeter, 90 Front St., Exeter. (603) 772-5901.
Regional American/Continental. $12.75 to $19.50.

Despite a high advertising profile, "this is the best-kept secret along the Seacoast," said the host at the entrance to the Terrace Room that serves as the public dining room at this venerable inn. "Everyone thinks it's the private preserve of Exeter Academy," its owner. The small yet airy room, dressed in preppy pinks and greens with twinkling lights in the ficus trees, is a quiet refuge for an interesting meal. Consider veal with morels and key lime sauce, chicken and shrimp casimir, seafood en papillote or tournedos au poivre for dinner; curried sole with pineapple, beef and shrimp brochette or cobb salad for lunch. Fresh raspberry cheesecake, key lime pie and kahlua black bottom pie are favored desserts. Despite a formal, clubby atmosphere, the inn advertises "casual dining" and updates its menu. Sunday brunch is a local institution — all three dining rooms are opened up to crowds waiting to feast on a sumptuous buffet ($11.95) that straddles the hours from breakfast to Sunday dinner and changes accordingly.

Lunch, 11:45 to 2; dinner, 5 to 9; Sunday brunch, 10 to 2.

Durham

The New England Center, 15 Strafford Ave., Durham. (603) 862-2815. Continental/American. $11.95 to $16.95.

Hard to find and hard to access (a lengthy walk over a pedestrian bridge from street and parking lot), this is worth the effort. An architectural gem set in a pine grove in the midst of the University of New Hampshire campus, it's a hotel, conference center and award-winning restaurant that hums with activity from morn to night. The dramatic, two-story dining area with 60-foot-high windows is known for its huge stone fireplace and forest view, which is magical on a snowy winter's night. Glazed brick, dark reflecting glass, bold steel columns and an upper-level art gallery provide a contemporary backdrop for a wide range of cooking. At lunch, try chicken Trinidad, a Yorkshire popover salad, a fruit salad with finger sandwiches of whipped cream cheese on banana bread, frittata Roma or shrimp Barcelonaise. Dinner entrees could be smoked apple salmon, scallops yangtse, shrimp with a tomato concasse, roast leg of lamb stuffed with minted pesto, and New Hampshire's obligatory prime rib, in this case with Yorkshire popover and horseradish cream. Desserts are something else: mint chocolate chip mousse, galliano parfait, strawberry-banana ice cream pie and baked alaska, among many. The Sunday brunch ($9.95) is billed as a family dining event.

Lunch, Monday-Saturday 11:30 to 2; dinner, 5:30 to 9 or 10; Sunday, brunch 11 to 2, dinner 4 to 8.

Lee's Chinese Restaurant, 55 Main St., Durham. (603) 868-1221. Chinese. $5.25 to $9.95.

This Ma-and-Pa Chinese operation is popular with the University of New Hampshire crowd. "New style" Mandarin and Szechuan dishes are featured on the abbreviated menu, including bird's nest chicken (the house specialty), orange-flavored Szechuan beef and peking ravioli. Begin with one of the excellent hot and sour or wonton soups. Then try the pu-pu platter served native style with flaming hibachi delights, a bargain $15.45 for two when we were there.

Lunch, Tuesday-Friday 11:30 to 2; dinner, Tuesday-Sunday 5 to 9.

Dover

Firehouse One, 1 Orchard St., Dover. (603) 749-3636. American/Continental. $11.95 to $19.95.

Its brass pole and arched windows intact, the old Central Fire Station has evolved into Dover's most deluxe restaurant. Beyond the striking rust-gray brick facade lies a Victorian interior of colorful yellows and reds, with a lofty pressed-tin ceiling and highback red leather chairs. The menu is wide-ranging, from fried potato skins to escargots for appetizers, broiled haddock to tournedos au poivre and crabmeat imperial. Veal comes four ways, and many dishes (including fish) are offered in petite, regular and king sizes. The dessert cart might harbor coconut-tequila and black forest cakes.

Lunch, Monday-Saturday 11:30 to 4 (no lunch Saturday in summer); dinner, 5 to 9 or 10; Sunday, brunch 10 to 2, dinner 2 to 9.

Seacoast Region

The Work Day Cafe and Texican Grill, 487 Central Ave., Upper Square, Dover. (603) 749-0483.
Cajun/Southwest. $5.85 to $11.25.

The "Texican" aspect sets apart this casual, lively place that originated as one of the Horsefeathers chain. The decor of brick, paneling and plants remains in the long and narrow upstairs dining room above the bar, where live entertainment is the rule. The food is a bit different: a duck burrito, catfish and shrimp etouffee, a special of deep-fried 'gator and desserts like tortilla torte and banana-chocolate chimichanga. The Texican grill features beef, lamb, chicken and seafood, served with grilled veggies and rice. The rest of the menu is more predictable, covering the usual bases of Cajun and Mexican specialties, from crawfish etouffee to fajitas, plus interesting pastas.

Open daily from 11:30 a.m. to 11:30 p.m.

Newmarket

Riverworks Restaurant and Tavern, 164 Main St., Newmarket.
(603) 659-6119.
Regional American. $8.50 to $14.50.

A not particularly auspicious facade masks an authentic, 170-year-old Federal interior with seating downstairs in a charming, brick and bookshelved rear alcove off the bar and in two candlelit dining rooms upstairs. The original attic was eliminated, turning the second floor into an unusual spot with vaulted, two-story ceilings. Stenciling and beams complement the floral tablecloths covered with glass. Chef-owner Mary Robertson's dinner menu stresses seafood, alone as in Cajun blackened red snapper or snapper vera cruz, or in combination with shrimp and scampi over linguini or spicy steak and scallop stir-fry. Sauteed chicken frangelica and teriyaki london broil are other offerings. Daily specials like Italian vegetable quiche and oriental shrimp and chicken with peanut soy sauce supplement the lunch-tavern menu. The dessert list is pedestrian, but the small wine list is better than most in the area.

Lunch, Monday-Saturday from 11:30; dinner nightly, 5 to 10.

Kingston

The Old Swiss House, 143 Main St., Kingston. (603) 642-4465.
Swiss. $8.95 to $15.95.

Pictures from the area around chef-owner Paul Wahlen's native Berne accent the cheerful beamed dining room. White linens, candles in mismatched candlesticks, pretty china (also mismatched) and fresh flowers enhance the country look, and a small windowed alcove lets the daylight filter in. Wiener schnitzel and chicken wellington are the house specialties, although you can order anything from beef paupiettes and sauerbraten to pork tenderloin with chanterelles, and cheese fondue. Baked shrimp, scallops with lobster sauce and chateaubriand round out the menu. Entrees come with house salad, roesti potatoes or spatzle, and no one leaves hungry. Tobler sundae, chocolate fondue and fried apples with cinnamon in beer batter topped with ice cream highlight the dessert list.

Lunch, 11:30 to 2; dinner, 5 to 9 or 10; Sunday, brunch 11:30 to 2, dinner 11:30 to 8. Closed Tuesday.

The Kingston 1686 House, Main Street, Kingston. (603) 642-3637.
American/Continental. $10.50 to $21.95.

The oldest house in Kingston, now in its fourth century, has been greatly expanded since it became a restaurant in 1972. But the main house retains its original wide-board floors, nine-over-six windows, Indian shutters, beehive bake-oven, pulpit staircase and hand-cut beams. Seven dining rooms range from quaint and intimate to elegant and airy in the new solarium. The menu ranges widely as well, encompassing all the predictable items served in traditional ways, from chicken divan to veal cordon bleu and Alaskan king crab. Lobster and steaks reign. Cheese dip and crackers, an olive and relish plate with a couple of hors d'oeuvres, salad with classic dressings, bread, starch and vegetable come with. Appetizers like Greek meatballs and a hot spinach and feta cheese pie reflect the Speliotis family's Greek heritage.

Dinner, Tuesday-Saturday 5:30 to 9:30 or 10, Sunday 3 to 8:30.

♥ **Pond View,** Route 125, Kingston. (603) 642-5556.
   American. $14.50 to $21.50.
   There's more than a hint of Disneyland at this large establishment blessed with a view of — what else? — a pond. Not to mention the floating gazebo, swans, paddleboats and more. It's not unlike what you'd expect to find in Florida, except this is New Hampshire. All is on view from the rear decks, an outdoor terrace and window tables in a melange of dining rooms on two floors. As if the outside weren't enough, the interior is colorful as can be. Assorted chairs, from arm to wicker, surround tables dressed in a rainbow of cloths and napkins, each folded in a different design and held together by a napkin ring capped with an artifical flower. No wonder the Pond View was voted "best atmosphere" by a regional magazine. The same poll also gave it "best prime rib," advertised as the largest portion in the Northeast. The rest of the menu is standard, from a platter of continental seafood and boiled king crab legs to fried chicken and pot roast. Desserts like strawberry crepe flambeed tableside are a cut above.

Lunch, Monday-Saturday 11:30 to 3; dinner, 3 to 10; Sunday, brunch noon to 3, dinner noon to 10.

What the symbols mean:
Three symbols are used to point out places of exceptional merit:
* ✱ exceptional food.
* ♥ exceptional atmosphere.
* $ exceptional value.

South Coast

York

★ **Cape Neddick Inn,** Route 1 at Route 1A, Cape Neddick. (207) 363-2899.
New American. $16 to $23.

This intriguing combination of restaurant and art gallery is almost everyone's favorite in the York area for innovative cuisine. The setting is artistic and the menu creative. Well-spaced tables set with mismatched china are on two levels in the dining room. Potted palms, flowers in vases, fancy screens, paintings and sculptures enhance the feeling of dining in a gallery. The limited menu offered by chef-owners Robbie Wells, Pamela Wallis and Glenn Gobeille changes every six weeks. Nightly specials revolve around duck, fish, chicken, veal, and tournedos — the varying preparations not decided by the three chef-owners until that afternoon. Swordfish might be grilled with ginger and gin; the haddock baked with saffron-cucumber sauce; the chicken sauteed with pecan pesto. Our Korean-style lamb kabob came with sesame sauce and a spicy vegetable relish, and the remains of our special fettuccine with chicken breast were enough for supper the next night. A complimentary plate of raw vegetables with dip accompanied drinks, followed by salads swathed in creamy bacon or cucumber-dill dressings. The changing desserts from a repertoire of more than 500 are sensational.

Dinner nightly in summer, 6 to 9, Wednesday-Sunday in winter; Sunday brunch, noon to 3, mid-October to May.

Pipers Grill & Oyster Bar, Route 1, York Corner. (207) 363-8196.
New American/International. $11 to $13.

The emphasis at this small, one-story house with a jaunty outdoor deck, a busy cocktail lounge and a sparely furnished dining room is not on decor but on interesting food at reasonable prices. The fare includes mesquite-grilled burgers and all kinds of pizzas (one topped with shrimp, sun-dried tomatoes and pesto), crabmeat fritters with a sesame and ginger dipping sauce and spicy chicken quesadilla. There are such assertive entrees as Chinese barbecued tenderloin of pork with hot honey mustard, soft-shell crabs with cilantro pesto and fresh corn cakes, and skewered Thai beef with spicy peanut sauce. How about the night's special of grilled tuna with tomato-cumin and chile pepper sauce? Like the menu, the wine list is limited but chosen with an eye to price.

Lunch, Monday-Saturday 11:30 to 2:30; dinner, 5 to 10, to midnight Friday-Sunday; Sunday brunch, noon to 3.

York Harbor Inn, Route 1A, York Harbor. (207) 363-5119.
American/Continental. $12.95 to $21.95.

Three of the four charming, old-fashioned dining rooms here catch a glimpse of the ocean across the street. The menu features Yankee seafood with contemporary accents. An appetizer called Tatnic Bay Treasure mixes scallops, shrimp and crabmeat in a creamy veloute sauce. The recipe for veal swiss was requested by Gourmet magazine; pasta with shrimp and scallops, and chicken stuffed with lobster and boursin cheese are other specialties. Some of the food is rich, as in Yorkshire lobster supreme baked with parmesan cheese and the medallions of tenderloin with asparagus and crabmeat topped with bearnaise sauce, but a few items bear hearts for the health-conscious. The Toblerone Swiss chocolate-walnut confection is a favored dessert.

Lunch, Monday-Friday 11:30 to 2:30; dinner nightly, 5:30 to 9:30 or 10:30; Sunday brunch, 10:30 to 2:30.

Ogunquit

★♥ Arrows, Berwick Road, Ogunquit. (207) 646-7175.
New American. $19.95 to $24.95.
Two young chefs who worked with Jeremiah Tower at Stars in San Francisco came East in 1988 to take over this up-again, down-again restaurant with such potential. They have succeeded in spades, presenting some of the most exciting — and expensive — food in Maine. The setting is hard to beat: a 1765 Colonial farmhouse in a rural area west of the Maine Turnpike. A lavish display of figs, lemons and other California produce awaits at the entry. Through large leaded panes reminiscent of mission windows, patrons in the spacious rear dining room look out onto colorful gardens spotlit at night. Surrounded by trees, fields and flowers, they feast on the view of jaunty blackeyed susans and a sea of zinnias as well as inspired, beautifully presented fare that is remarkably sophisticated. Formally clad waiters in black and white take orders without making notes, quite a feat considering that the menu changes nightly. For starters, we liked tea-smoked quail with a garlic-ginger vinaigrette and red chile mayonnaise (the description does not do justice to its complexity) and a salad of gold and red cherry tomatoes on mustard greens with a medallion of goat cheese. The roasted duck with molasses glaze, wild rice, snow peas, and a macadamia nut vinaigrette was a triumph, and the only dish we weren't crazy about was the grilled tenderloin of beef, which had a too intense smoky taste. But the accompaniments of fire-roasted red onion, green and yellow beans, tarragon mayonnaise and the best thread-thin crisp french fries compensated. A dessert of pineapple, peach-plum and mango sorbets, each atop a meringue and each with its own distinctive sauce, was a masterpiece. Personable chef-owners Clark Frasier and Mark Gaier make the rounds at the end of the evening and like to talk about food. Clark, who studied cooking in China, is from California. Mark trained with Madeleine Kamman and was executive chef at the late Whistling Oyster in Perkins Cove. At Arrows, they make an exciting team. The tab is steep, but worth it.
Dinner nightly, 6 to 10, late April through late October.

Maison Charles, Route 1, Ogunquit. (207) 646-7082.
Regional American/International. $16.50 to $21.
Restaurateurs Charles and Loretta Jones moved Maison Charles from its former site near the Ogunquit Playhouse in 1989 to spanking new quarters rear and center in the luxury Gorges Grant Resort Hotel. A few steps down from the lobby, it's an airy, contemporary and pretty space, all cranberry and mauve with green upholstered chairs, large windows onto the pool area and a grand piano at the entry. "A very beachy atmosphere" — as in Florida or the Caribbean — is how Charles describes it. Here's a plush setting for what he calls international and imaginative cuisine with an emphasis on grills and sautes. Swordfish is grilled with Creole spices and tuna with soy, garlic and lime. The roast duckling comes with brandied peach sauce, the scaloppine of veal with wild mushrooms and the New York strip steak with green peppercorn sauce. Penne with sweet Italian sausage, saffron and cheese is a good starter, as is the warm goat cheese salad with belgian endive, watercress and raspberry vinaigrette. Because this is the dining room for the inn, Charles finds himself serving breakfast as well.
Breakfast daily, 7:30 to 11; dinner, 5:30 to 10.

Hurricane, Oarweed Lane, Perkins Cove. (207) 646-6348.
American/International. $10.95 to $18.95.
Some people love this trendy place that keeps changing with the times; others

don't. It's owned by the folks who run the Horsefeathers restaurant chain (Portland, North Conway, Freeport, and Marblehead), but there the similarity ends. Two small summery rooms are beside the ocean; most appealing is the enclosed but breezy porch. Although it's too close for some tastes, how can you not like the food, unless you're attuned only to tourist (as in boiled lobster and stuffed shrimp) tastes? The menu ranges from grilled chicken with scalloped bananas and peaches to skewered barbecued lamb with rice pilaf. The grilled duck breast is accompanied by caramelized onions, apples and walnuts topped with sharp cheddar cheese. The frogmore stew offers shrimp, sausage and corn on the cob in a spicy broth. To begin, try the deviled lobster cakes with fresh tomato and cilantro salsa or the grilled veal sausages with roasted sweet peppers. Appetizers, soups and salads are the same at lunch, when you can order grilled lamb salad with spinach and feta cheese.

Lunch, 11:30 to 3; dinner, 5:30 to 10:30; Sunday jazz brunch. Closed Tuesday.

The Cove Garden, Shore Road, Ogunquit. (207) 646-4497.
Northern Italian. $6.95 to $12.95.

There is no more charming and pretty setting for dining in Ogunquit than the deck or the dining room with views over the lovely gardens onto Perkins Cove, with a straight shot out to sea. Built as a teahouse in pagoda style, the interior is exotic and almost Mediterranean, with a lattice ceiling, an end wall open to the trees, interesting art, white ladderback chairs at red tables with mats and, in the middle of it all, a large lighted tree bearing shelves that display the wines. The rear deck with round red tables and white chairs is a fine place for a drink. Move inside to partake of the Genoese cuisine. The limited menu (perhaps three appetizers, four pastas and five entrees) is reasonably priced and the pastas are the star of the show.

Dinner nightly, 6 to 10.

Jonathan's, 2 Bourne Lane, Ogunquit. (207) 646-4777.
International. $12.95 to $19.95.

A crazy red sign greets visitors to this houseful of rooms, all different and intriguingly decorated in blue and white. Jonathan West's decade-old establishment is whimsical and his menu wide-ranging, from jaeger schnitzel to tournedos of beef au poivre over toast points with a mushroom duxelle and three-pepper sauce. Jazz is presented nightly, and the place is popular for after-theater snacks and desserts (it's right around the corner from the Ogunquit Playhouse). Huevos rancheros is a popular breakfast offering; another is — would you believe? — champagne and boiled lobster with muffins for two.

Breakfast daily, 8 to 11; dinner, 5:30 to 10 or 11.

Gypsy Sweethearts Restaurant, 18 Shore Road, Ogunquit. (207) 646-7021.
American. $9.95 to $15.95.

Breakfasts are the main attraction in this old house with an upstairs lounge in the heart of town. Try the Mexican eggs with salsa and cheddar cheese, the shirred eggs with swiss cheese, and blueberry crepes with sour cream. Or get anything from cinnamon toast to eggs florentine. Seafood with a twist — perhaps sole meuniere with pine nuts, sauteed scallops with sun-dried tomatoes and scallions in a lemon beurre blanc, and filet of haddock coated with honey butter and almonds — is featured at dinner. You can sample desserts and special coffees upstairs.

Breakfast daily, 7:30 to noon; dinner, 5:30 to 10.

Kennebunkport

★♥ Seascapes, On the Pier, Cape Porpoise, Kennebunkport. (207) 967-8500.
New American. $14.95 to $23.95.

The table settings are smashing at this elegant restaurant opened by Angela and Arthur LeBlanc of the Kennebunk Inn in 1988 in the waterside space that formerly held Spicer's Gallery. In fact, they won the national tabletop competition sponsored by Restaurant Hospitality magazine in 1989 as "the prettiest tables in America," a distinction of which Angela is justifiably proud. The plates and candle holders are of handpainted Italian pottery in heavenly colors, and the striking wine glasses are fluted. At lunchtime, we liked the pasta of the day, with red and yellow peppers, feta cheese and sprigs of coriander, and thought the Maine crab cakes with crispy outsides and a tomato-rosemary sauce even better than the ones we've had in Maryland. They were served with crisp potato bits and beets cooked in red wine vinegar. For dinner, the grilled seafood sausage appetizer was a winner. Salads and sorbet preceded our entrees, a classic cioppino and a breast of chicken coated with pistachio nuts and filled with scallops. Blueberry cheesecake, coconut-macadamia nut torte, chocolate decadence, and polenta pound cake with berry sauce are among desserts. At brunch, look for a salad of chicken and strawberries in a fresh pineapple boat, lobster or smoked salmon benedict, or Maine shrimp fritters served with a spicy salsa. In 1990, the LeBlancs acquired Tilly's Shanty, a rustic lobster pound to the rear of Seascapes, and planned to take over its operation in 1991.

Lunch daily, 11:30 to 2; dinner, 5:30 to 9:30 or 10; after Labor Day, closed Tuesday and at 9 p.m. Closed January and February.

★ Cape Arundel Inn, Ocean Avenue, Kennebunkport. (207) 967-2125.
Regional American. $15.25 to $21.95.

Dine at a window table here (with a bird's-eye view of George Bush's Walker Point compound) and watch wispy clouds turn to mauve and violet as the sun sets, followed by a full golden moon rising over the darkened ocean. The sea and sky provide more than enough backdrop for a plain but attractive dining room on two levels, newly outfitted with gray and aqua linens. After sampling a warm pheasant salad on radicchio with Thai dressing, you might try sweetbreads with a tart pear sauce, coho salmon sauteed with mushrooms and white wine, or saute of duck with apricot and ginger. The roast rack of lamb, accompanied by rice pilaf, crisp ratatouille, and julienned carrots and turnips, is a masterpiece. The dessert tray harbors interesting indulgences, a chocolate-almond torte and brandy pound cake among them. A Portland caterer of our acquaintance thinks the breakfasts here (open to the public and especially popular on weekends) are the best this side of home. We're partial to the fried codfish cakes served with baked beans and grilled tomato, a standard on the menu, and on our latest visit, liked a delicious omelet generously strewn with wild mushrooms.

Breakfast daily, 8 to 10:30, Sunday to 1; dinner, Monday-Saturday, 5:30 to 8:30 or 9. Open mid-May through October.

♥ White Barn Inn, Beach Street, Kennebunkport. (203) 967-2321.
Regional American. $14.95 to $23.95.

Soaring up to three stories with all kinds of farming artifacts hanging from beams and pulleys, the White Barn is almost too atmospheric for words. The tables are set with silver and pewter, linen and oil lamps, and the colorful impatiens on the deck beyond the large rear windows are spotlit at night. With candlelight flickering and classical music playing, the setting is heavenly. So are such appetizers as bacon-wrapped sea scallops with maple-mustard cream and escargots in puff pastry, heady with garlic. Among entrees, the grilled breast of chicken is enlivened with a tomato-mint salsa, the two stuffed quails with a grand marnier-orange butter, and the blackened tuna with peaches, brandied cream and Cajun spices. A fine house salad and hearty whole wheat rolls come with the meal. Cheesecake with raspberries, sweet potato pie and banana mousse are good choices from the dessert tray.

Dinner nightly, 6 to 9:30; Sunday brunch, 11:30 to 1:30. Closed Mondays off-season.

* Kennebunkport Inn, Dock Square, Kennebunkport. (207) 967-2621.
Regional American. $14.95 to $22.95.
The pristine and formal dining rooms on either side of the inn's entry are extra pretty, with fringed valances, lace curtains, stenciling, and hurricane lamps on well-spaced tables. Innkeepers Martha and Rick Griffin, who travel to France for new ideas, have garnered quite a culinary reputation. Good crusty rolls and excellent mixed green salads precede such main courses as grilled paillard of capon with sun-dried tomatoes, escalopes of veal with pancetta and roasted shallots, grilled swordfish with lobster butter and crabmeat, and tournedos of beef with a five-peppercorn sauce. The grilled duck breast with a piquant raspberry sauce is artfully presented and the mustard-ginger rack of lamb is extraordinary. An ethereal key lime pie and a white chocolate mousse with strawberries in kirsch are choice desserts.

Dinner nightly, 6 to 9; closed November-March.

The Olde Grist Mill, Mill Lane, Kennebunkport. (207) 967-4781.
American/Continental. $14.50 to $28.50.
The last remaining tidal mill in the country, this historic structure was built in 1749 and has been in owner David Lombard's family ever since. His mother opened it as a tea room in 1940 and it evolved into a full-scale restaurant, lately renovated and expanded with an immense cocktail lounge as posh as can be and a rear dining room all in pink, with windows opening onto the tidal river. With the transition, the restaurant has become more serious (and pricey) and is decidedly popular with the locals. Among the choices are salmon en papillote, jaeger schnitzel, baked stuffed shrimp with macadamia nuts, sea scallops with an amontillado sherry sauce, veal cordon bleu and roast duckling chambord. Don't be surprised that in such fancy surroundings a full shore dinner with lobster and all the trimmings is $32.50.

Dinner nightly from 5:30. Closed Monday in spring and fall, and January-March.

The Schooners, Ocean Avenue, Kennebunkport. (207) 967-5333.
Regional American. $11.95 to $18.95.
This handsome, crescent-shaped dining room with a wide-angle view of the mouth of the river and ocean beyond has had its ups and downs since the luxury inn opened in 1986. New ownership in 1989 steered it off its northern Italian course into the American mainstream. Baked brie with poached pears and smoked trout with creme fraiche, capers and toast points are interesting starters. A three-citrus hollandaise sauce tops filet of sole with crabmeat stuffing; veal medallions are sauteed with oyster mushroom sauce. Soup or salad and homemade rolls accompany. Homemade chambord and amaretto ice creams, cheesecakes, tortes, and cakes are the dessert fare. The food may be upstaged by the setting: burgundy linens, sleek black lacquered chairs, marine art on the walls, and balloon curtains on the windows framing those spectacular Maine sunsets.

Dinner nightly except Sunday, 6 to 10:30.

Kennebunk

Kennebunk Inn, 45 Main St., Kennebunk. (207) 985-3351.
American/Continental. $12.95 to $18.95.

This cheerful-looking 1799 inn has an esteemed hotel-style dining room with upholstered chairs, pink and white linens, candles in hurricane lamps, and Tiffany-style stained-glass windows. The food is creative and consistent — considered a compelling virtue in the area — and reasonably priced. Owners Art and Angela LeBlanc and their children are very much in evidence on the menu and in the dining room of this family-run place. The featured dishes (two veals, seafood fettuccine, shrimp, chicken, surf and turf, and duck) are named for family members, all of whose names begin with "A." Arthur's mother lends her name to Ma Mere's scallops and a dessert of trifle. One reviewer called the seafood chowder the best he'd had in Maine, period, and the escargots and shrimp with pernod "a perfect dish." The pretty gingersnap basket full of kiwi, raspberries, strawberries and whipped cream for dessert is an example of the LeBlanc style. A courtyard off to the side of the inn is attractive for lunching.

Lunch daily, 11:30 to 2:30; dinner, 5:30 to 9 or 10.

Old Orchard Beach

Joseph's By the Sea, 57 West Grand Ave., Old Orchard Beach.
(207) 934-5044.
French. $9.95 to $16.95.

Here is a culinary beacon amid a sea of fish fries and amusement arcades. You might suspect that owners Joseph and Mariette Dussault cater to the French-Canadians who make Old Orchard theirs for the summer (and why not?), but Joseph's has a strong local following as well. Son Paul Dussault, a chef since he was a teenager, attributes some of his creative instincts to having cooked in Waterville Valley and Vail. He makes his fresh fruit vinegars, steams fish in lettuce leaves and has a sense of whimsey, as in his "scallops overboard" — sauteed scallops and almonds in a sailboat fashioned from half a zucchini, with a carrot stick for the mast. A tangy shrimp moutarde is among the seafood specialties. There are things like veal marengo and steak au poivre for those who prefer. Start with escargots sauteed with wine and seaweed; finish with profiteroles or a banana praline crepe. The food is the match for the setting, which is formal with gold linens and crystal chandeliers. When the moon rises over the ocean, it's the most romantic spot around.

Dinner nightly, 5 to 10. Closed November to Easter.

Saco

Cornforth House, Route 1, Saco. (203) 284-2006.
American/Continental. $10.95 to $16.95.

The 19th-century brick Colonial homestead of a working dairy farm was converted in 1987 into a country-style restaurant of some elegance in the midst of the automobile-dealer and fast-food row several miles north of town. Owner Lee Carleton, who opened the restaurant after going to culinary school at age 50, greets guests in the waiting parlor full of old farmhouse-type furniture, stenciling and wreaths. Pink linens grace the tables, most covered with glass, in six intimate, candlelit dining rooms. Dinner starts with crackers and a complimentary spread of cream cheese with garlic or sun-dried tomatoes. Homemade veal sausage in puff pastry is a stellar appetizer. Among entrees, the three veal dishes, pecan chicken, rack of lamb, steak au poivre, and baked haddock stuffed with scallops and shrimp are recommended. Lee makes all the desserts, including profiteroles, chocolate-grand marnier mousse and raspberry cream pie.

Dinner, Tuesday-Sunday 5:30 to 9:30; Sunday breakfast, 8 to 11:30.

Portland Area

South Portland

Snow Squall, 18 Ocean St., South Portland. (207) 799-2232.
American. $9.95 to $17.95.

Go here for the view and for the Sunday brunch. A vista of the waterfront is offered from this California-style, brick and brass, fern and glass establishment overlooking a marina and named for a clipper ship that was built nearby. A large terrace with umbrellas is as popular as the amiable bar. The main dining room is a comfortable setting for a varied menu from fried clams to trout grand marnier. Specials like grilled monkfish with walnuts, olives, capers, and yellow tomato relish supplement the standard lunch menu. The prices are higher than expected (they help pay for the view). But the Sunday brunch buffet ($10.95) is a stunner of fresh fruits, smoked seafood, breakfast dishes, seafood, roast beef, and desserts.

Lunch, Monday-Friday 11:30 to 3; dinner, 4:30 to 9; Sunday, brunch 11 to 2, dinner 2 to 9.

Portland

★ **Brattle Street,** 19 Brattle St., Portland. (207) 772-4658.
Contemporary French. $14.50 to $24.50.

Chefs up and down the coast praise the cuisine and the elan emanating from this 1850 townhouse that Tom Ester saved from demolition in 1982. It now serves some of Portland's most acclaimed food under the description, "Restaurant Gourmand." Bare floors with oriental rugs, cane and chrome chairs, and interesting art create a contemporary setting on two floors. The limited menu is changed monthly by chef Dale Gussett, who joined Brattle Street after closing his own French restaurant in Portland, L'Antibes. The appetizers here particularly intrigue: perhaps lobster with red pepper coulis, pepper-roasted tenderloin of beef with aioli and sun-dried tomatoes, chilled roast cornish hen with plum and cinnamon sauce, or smoked salmon with corn crepes and jalapeno creme fraiche. Among entrees are such standouts as sweetbreads grenobloise, medallions of veal with brie, poached salmon with cucumber-dill sauce, boneless lamb loin with roasted garlic sauce, and roast duckling with raspberry vinegar sauce. The fish of the day might be lobster with pernod sauce or steamed halibut with chervil-orange butter sauce. Pink grapefruit sorbet, a green salad and good French breads accompany. End a memorable meal with marquise au chocolat, raspberry-hazelnut tart, grand marnier mousse cake, or such unusual ice creams as Dutch chocolate and French roast coffee. The presentation is artistic and the service flawless.

Dinner, Tuesday-Saturday 6 to 9:30.

★ **Cafe Always,** 47 Middle St., Portland. (207) 774-9399.
New American/International. $12.95 to $18.95.

One of our most exciting meals ever was served in this smart, new-wave-style cafe with an ever-so-with-it decor of slick yellow oilcloth table coverings, triangular shaped black rubber mats, napkins tied with black bolos, and changing art exhibitions. Boston-trained chef Cheryl Lewis changes her menu daily. It's adventuresome, the kind on which everything appeals (at least to us). The green salad tossed with sun-dried tomatoes, toasted pine nuts, sweet peppers and parmesan cheese and the grape leaves stuffed with goat cheese, lamb and walnuts were sensational preliminaries. The roast pork tenderloin, stuffed with sun-dried tomatoes and spinach in a red wine sauce, was a masterpiece. Ditto for the Thai chicken sauteed in red chile oil and served with a curried coconut cream sauce so spicy it brought tears to the eyes. The trio of intense sorbets and ice creams made a refreshing dessert. Recent offerings included veal and pork pate with pistachio nuts and black mission figs, a salad of swiss chard tossed with almonds and a warm curried bacon vinaigrette, grilled salmon served with polenta and grilled plum tomatoes, and chicken breast sauteed with arugula, roasted garlic and goat cheese. It all lives up to the cafe's logos: "No Food Rules" and "A Close Kin to Art."

Dinner nightly, 5 to 10. Closed Monday in off-season.

Madd Apple Cafe, 23 Forest Ave., Portland. (207) 774-9698.
Regional American. $8.95 to $15.95.
An American bistro with a Southern accent is the way Martha and Jim Williamson bill their sprightly place beside the Portland Performing Arts Center. Jim grew up in the South, which explains the barbecue items from secret family recipes and the fresh catfish, crawfish, pompano, cornbread, bananas foster, and sweet potato pie that turn up on the changing menu. Typical dinner entrees are pan-fried crawfish cakes with remoulade sauce, boudin blanc (Cajun sausage), pork tenderloin sauteed in cilantro and lime juice and served with black bean sauce, Carolina chopped pork barbecue, frog's legs meuniere, and chicken chasseur. Bourbon-pecan cheesecake and key lime pie are favorite desserts. Caribbean and Creole salads, chicken livers madeira, fettuccine alfredo, and interesting sandwiches are on the lunch menu. All this is offered in two small, unpretentious rooms with lace curtains on the windows, striped pastel cloths on the tables and changing art on the walls.

Lunch, Tuesday-Friday 11:30 to 3; dinner, Wednesday-Saturday from 5:30.

Back Bay Grill, 65 Portland St., Portland. (207) 772-8833.
New American. $13.75 to $23.95.
Is this Back Bay Boston or New York's Soho? No, it's downtown Portland, as evidenced to by the twenty-foot-long mural painted by owner Steve Steve Quattrucci, an artist and former maitre-d' at the Ritz Cafe in Boston. High ceilings, white walls, antique mirrors, architectural embellishments, modern chairs, white linens, and a stainless steel bar comprise the uncluttered "now" decor. The menu changes daily and features grilling, as in Atlantic salmon with wasabi butter, shrimp with green curry broth, barbecued chicken with cilantro and red onions, sirloin with roquefort and beet chips, and eggplant with roasted red peppers and aioli. Even the lobster is grilled. Pastas are another strong point. Local organically grown produce is served. Creme brulee, wild blueberry and peach pie, and chocolate raviolis filled with hazelnut ricotta are outstanding desserts.

Dinner, Tuesday-Saturday, 5:30 to 9:30 or 10.

Luna D'Oro, 41 Middle St., Portland. (207) 774-2972.
Regional Italian. $10.95 to $16.95.
Other chefs consider the home-style Mediterranean-Italian food here the best of its type in town. Forty diners can be accommodated in three small, candlelit rooms with red and white checked tablecloths and striking art on the walls. Chef-owner Alain Hasson, who cooked in France and Florence, had the place up for sale in 1990. He has been known for his provimi veal dishes, among them marsala, piccata

and parmigiana. The scampi alla griglia over pasta and the New York sirloin with dijon cream sauce, black peppercorns and cognac are highly rated. House pasta, salad and bread come with. But you might start with baked broccoli with three cheeses or one of the specialty pastas. Save room for the homemade desserts, especially the puff pastry filled with gelato and chocolate-brandy sauce. The all-Italian wine list boasts some that are rarely seen even in Italy.

Dinner, Tuesday-Saturday from 5:30.

The West Side Cafe, 58 Pine St., Portland. (207) 773-8223.

New American/International. $10.95 to $15.95.

Ensconced in an area of brownstones west of downtown, this convivial cafe with a canvas-covered outdoor patio is popular with locals. Chef-owner Aaron Park puts out a notable selection of appetizers plus salads, crepes, omelets, stuffed croissants, and light dinners. How about a crepe of snow peas, leeks and gruyere, or the day's pastry, scallops and basil in phyllo? The changing entrees are notable for exceptional sauces: perhaps pork tenderloin with glazed apples and sage, loin lamb chops in a coriander-pepper glaze with cucumber relish, chicken with a cassis-raspberry vinegar and fresh raspberry cream sauce, even tofu with roasted garlic, sun-dried tomatoes and pesto. They come with saffron brown rice or new potatoes and salad. The lunch menu is equally varied, as are the breakfast and brunch offerings. Local beers and bargain wines are available.

Breakfast, 7 to 11; lunch, 11:30 to 2:30; dinner, 5 to 10; Sunday brunch, 9 to 2:30.

Alberta's Cafe, 21 Pleasant St., Portland. (207) 774-5408.

American/International. $8.95 to $15.95.

This funky cafe, named for the mother of one of the owners, was voted "most bohemian" by a local magazine. When we stopped in, co-owner Tom Russell, who hails from Cambridge, volunteered that he didn't think the restaurant was bohemian at all; on the other hand, the bartender was wearing a black shirt accented by a silver tie. The decor is plain as day: two levels with bare tables set with paper napkins topped by cutlery and flanked by small white side plates, a few photos and, on the wall behind the cash register, a marble fountain with a nude carved by a friend of the owners. The atmosphere is such that the food has to be good. The eclectic menu changes weekly. For dinner, you might try an appetizer of warm cornmeal crepe torte with spinach, cream cheese, mushrooms, and fresh herbs served with grilled tomato coulis, or ravioli stuffed with lobster and scallops. Move on to a mixed grill of chicken and butterflied leg of lamb with assorted vegetables, seared tuna with cucumber relish, grilled swordfish with wasabi dressing, or pan-blackened rib-eye with sour cream and chives. "Death by Chocolate" (a chocolate terrine with layers of hazelnut meringue) is the signature dessert, followed by strawberry-peach brulee and lemon-poppyseed cake with raspberry sauce and creme anglaise.

Lunch, Monday-Friday 11:30 to 2:30; dinner nightly, 5 to 10:30 or 11.

Hugo's Portland Bistro, 88 Middle St., Portland. (207) 774-8538.

American/International. $10.95 to $14.95.

This lively newcomer along Portland's burgeoning restaurant row is named for the young son of owners Johnny and Caitriona Robinson, both from Dublin. The room is a pleasant hodgepodge of deep green cloths, pale pink walls, mirrors, and bird cages, with a red column in the middle and a prominent shelf of tag sale bric-a-brac. Caitriona does the cooking, mixing French, Italian and American with a bit of Spanish and Moroccan. For dinner, start with hot carrot and orange soup with fresh thyme or sweet red pepper mousse with melba toasts. Main courses could be breast of chicken en croute with coriander and garlic, poached salmon with pesto sauce, and tenderloin of pork with glazed apples and a maple-garlic vinaigrette. At lunchtime, feast on moussaka, poached salmon salad in aspic or savory cauliflower cheese pie with potato crust. Among desserts are chocolate mousse, fresh fruit sherry trifle, black raspberry cheesecake, and homemade ice creams.

Lunch, Monday-Friday 11:30 to 2; dinner, Monday-Saturday 5:30 to 10.

The Oyster Club Raw Bar & Grill, 164 Middle St., Portland. (207) 773-3760. Steaks/Seafood. $10.25 to $15.95.

One of the newer restaurants in the Old Port Exchange, this is also one of the more consistent and thus favored by locals. The downstairs dining room is clubby in dark green, brass, paneling, and hunting prints; the action is at high tables and stools in the main-floor raw bar. Oysters are served on the half shell or as an appetizer, rockefeller style, but lobsters reign supreme here in various guises, among them an acclaimed lobster pie. The dinner menu also ranges from baked haddock and herbed scallop casserole to chicken dijon and steak au poivre. The enormous lunch menu is designed to appeal to diverse tastes as well.

Open daily, 11:30 to midnight.

Hu Shang Exchange, 33 Exchange St., Portland. (207) 774-0300. Chinese. $6.75 to $14.

When Portland's first Chinese restaurant of note opened in 1979 in a hole-in-the-wall setting on Congress Street, local diners flocked to the scene. When it moved in 1983 to a large brick structure on Brown Street, the crowds followed and grew. The newest Hu Shang establishment in the Old Port is considered by many to be the best of the lot. Some of New England's finest Szechuan, Hunan, Shanghai, and Mandarin fare is served all day long in an unexpectedly trendy, brick and plant-filled setting. The prodigious menu runs twelve pages, offering appetizers from Peking dumplings to sesame shrimp puff, numerous soups, seven bean curd dishes, and so many chicken, beef, pork and shrimp selections that the choice is difficult. Noodle, rice and vegetarian dishes including Buddha's Delight are reasonably priced.

Open daily from 11 to 9:30 or 10:30.

Thai Garden, One City Center, Portland. (207) 772-1118. Thai. $4.95 to $13.95.

Many of the town's chefs go here on their nights off, and marvel at the freshness and spiciness of the food. With inside and outside dining but not much in the way of decor except for the Thai art on the walls of the two-level dining room, it's the food and the reasonable prices that draw. The seafood dishes are the more expensive items. Try shoosee tuna, a filet with red curry, lemon leaves, pineapple, green and red peppers, tomatoes and cucumber, or seafood curry, a mixture of shrimp, scallops, squid, and fish filet. The papaya salad contains carrots, tomatoes, ground peanuts, and ground dry shrimp in a hot sweet and sour sauce. Start with shrimp tempura or a Thai roll mixing ground pork, black mushrooms, onions, carrots and bean thread noodles. Curries, noodle and fried rice dishes are at the low end of the price scale. For dessert, cool off with coconut custard or homemade Thai ice cream. There's a great list of beers, the best beverage to go with Thai food.

Open Monday-Friday 11:30 to 9, Saturday and Sunday 5 to 10.

Falmouth Foreside

The Galley, 215 Foreside Road (Route 88), Falmouth Foreside. (207) 781-4262. Seafood. $11.95 to $16.95.

An outdoor deck allows you to eat with the water on two sides at this popular restaurant, which serves an astonishing variety of seafood, at the Handy Boat Service Marina. The view is grand, although you'll likely have to wait for a window table inside. Seafood comes fried, in crepes, baked, broiled and in salads. Haddock is prepared thirteen different ways and scallops seven. The sailor's egg benedict at lunch includes broiled tenderloin on an English muffin plus the works.

Lunch daily, 11:30 to 3; dinner, 5 to 9. Closed mid-October to mid-April.

Yarmouth

The Cannery, Lower Falls Landing, Yarmouth. (207) 846-1226.
American. $10.95 to $13.95.

This old shrimp processing plant reopened in 1988 as a restaurant in a new waterfront commercial complex and marina alongside the Royal River. From a breezy side deck, the view is more of boats than water. Inside all is crisp and contemporary with a high ceiling, dining on two levels, soaring windows, tree-size plants, and a large bar in the center. The ample napkins resemble dish towels. Two of the three principals own the Waterfront restaurant in Camden, so similarities like the great salads should not surprise. The dinner menu offers bouillabaisse, chargrilled salmon, chicken saltimbocca, crab cakes, haddock tahini and, for the landlubber, garlic-grilled sirloin. Locally marinated herring, Ducktrap River Farm smoked seafood sampler and a delicate lobster stew are good starters. Among desserts are chocolate fudge cake, linzer torte and lemon charlotte.

Lunch daily, 11:30 to 2:30; dinner nightly, 5 to 9 or 9:30; Sunday brunch, 11 to 2:30.

$ Moonlight Roasters, Westcustogo Inn, Route 88, Yarmouth. (207) 846-5797.
American/Barbecue. $6.95 to $11.25.

Native Mainer Ralph Clemons thinks his is the only wood-fired brick oven in the state. From it emerge acclaimed roasted meats, including pork, chicken, turkey and lamb, accompanied by hush puppies, vegetables and potato or rice at not-to-be-believed prices. Daily specials might include prime rib, brisket and cornish hen roasts, old-fashioned pig roasts, and shore dinner bakes. Ralph says his pork and beef barbecues are done in the Kentucky style, the recipes acquired on his frequent travels there. Dining is at oilcloth-covered tables in a spacious room with a beamed ceiling and ample evidence of its life as a hunting lodge since early in the century. At lunchtime, stop in for a roast sandwich, seafood pouch, salad, soup or stew. Chocolate-mocha cheesecake and raspberry-almond pie give the lie to the idea that all the desserts here are cobblers, pudding and jello. The Friday and Saturday night buffets offer all you can eat for $9.50. As if they needed a loss leader.

Lunch, Monday-Saturday 11:30 to 2:30; dinner, 5 to 9, Sunday 11:30 to 3.

Mid-Coast

Freeport

✱ Sebastian's, 15 Independence Drive at Route 1, Freeport. (207) 865-0466.
New American. $8.95 to $17.95.

Area foodies give high marks to this innovative eatery that opened in 1988 in a rural homestead across from the vast L.L. Bean headquarters on the east edge of town. Dining is at wood tables in small rooms with bare floors, sprightly wallpapers and high-back wooden chairs or, our choice, at outdoor tables topped with Poland Spring umbrellas on a small deck ringed with flowers. Classical music was the background for a lunch of gazpacho and a zesty spinach salad with a choice of currant vinaigrette or buttermilk-roquefort dressings and a pasta salad laden with grilled vegetables, enhanced with glasses of the house McDowell chardonnay. The lemon slice in the ice water showed Sebastian's was current with all the niceties, and the changing menu showed distinct flair. At dinner, look for grilled bluefish with tomato salsa, poached turbot with mustard and chive cream, baked salmon with toasted pine nut and savory butter, grilled chicken with warm citrus-leek vinaigrette, or tournedos of beef with wild mushroom and roquefort sauce. There's the ubiquitous lobster, but it's steamed, grilled or sauteed in puff pastry with brandy and thyme. Start with grilled eggplant and sweet red pepper terrine, grilled summer fruits with boursin-cream sauce or wild mushroom timbales with herbed bechamel sauce. Finish with a chocolate terrine with raspberry sauce or a hazelnut torte with ice cream. Here is a kitchen that dares to be different amid a sea of sameness.

Lunch, Monday-Saturday 11 to 3; dinner nightly, 5:30 to 9.

Harraseeket Inn, 162 Main St., Freeport. (207) 865-9377.
American/Continental. $13.95 to $24.

Three handsome dining rooms with black windsor chairs and tables topped with delicate pink-stemmed wine glasses and vases of alstroemeria await patrons at the Harraseeket, lately enlarged from a small B&B into a full-fledged, 60-room inn. A chef from the owners' other venture, the Inn at Mystic in Connecticut, oversees an ambitious menu, from broiled salmon steak au poivre with lime butter and rainbow trout nantua to roast duckling with peach glaze, chicken with white asparagus, loin of pork braised with maple syrup, and veal cutlet with basil cream and artichoke. Fettuccine alfredo, rack of lamb, beef wellington, and chateaubriand are prepared or carved tableside. Two clams, two shrimp and two oysters make up the Freeport cocktail; the lobster crepe, pate in aspic and oysters in champagne sauce are other starters. Desserts from an exotic list include pecan pie, banana-pistachio mousse, praline ice cream cake, cheese strudel, chocolate fondue, and bananas foster. Flaming coffees top off an elegant meal. A huge, more casual menu is available downstairs in the **Broad Arrow Tavern.**

Lunch daily, 11:30 to 2:30; dinner, 5:30 to 9:30 or 10:30; Sunday brunch buffet, 11:30 to 2.

Jameson Tavern, 115 Main St., Freeport. (207) 865-4196.
American/Continental. $9.50 to $16.95.

The first of the large new restaurants to emerge with the outlet explosion in booming Freeport, this properly historic-looking structure claims a 1779 heritage and packs in the crowds at all hours. Cheek by jowl with L.L. Bean, the building was the signing place of the papers that separated Maine from Massachusetts. The four dining rooms with a Colonial atmosphere seat 125, and light meals are served in the tavern. The chef caters to the tourist crowd, from shrimp cocktail and crab-stuffed mushroom caps as appetizers to mud pie and carrot cake for dessert. The two dozen entrees include chicken cordon bleu, broiled haddock amandine, prime rib, bacon-wrapped filet mignon, Cajun scallops and sausage, and six steak and seafood combos. Entrees include all the salad and rolls you desire, but vegetables are extra. Light meals are available all day in the lounge.

Lunch, Monday-Saturday 11:30 to 2:30; dinner, 5 to 10 or 11; Sunday brunch, 11:30 to 3.

Crabby Lobster, 10 School St., Freeport. (207) 865-9606.
Seafood. $9.95 to $15.95.

Born as a seafood market and restaurant in Santa Barbara, Crabby Lobster moved east in 1984 to fill a niche in Freeport. Decor is shanty-style with red oilcloths on the tables, but all kinds of fresh seafood are served at reasonable prices. Pig out on chowders, pastas, salads, sandwiches, fish and chips, hickory-smoked barbecued ribs, steaks, and lobster. About the only crab we found was in the crabmeat alfredo.

Mid-Coast

There's an outdoor deck with umbrella-covered picnic tables. The sign says "dress code: hardly any, just wear some type of shirt and shoes." 'Nuff said.

Open daily in summer, 11 to 10.

Brunswick Area

★ 22 Lincoln, 22 Lincoln St., Brunswick. (207) 725-5893.
Regional American. $8.95 to $24.

Chef-owner Sam Hayward turned a small Victorian dwelling a block off this college town's main street into one of Maine's better year-round restaurants, with an innovative menu and an extensive wine list. The main-floor dining room seats 30 patrons for candlelight dining, while an identical one upstairs is used as a cafe adjunct to the rear lounge. The menu, which changes nightly, is a la carte or prix-fixe, the three-course price varying ($16 to $19) with the meal listed. Here is a place for a splurge: a layered terrine of fresh noodles, foie gras and chanterelles, or a charlotte of smoked salmon, lump crabmeat and ossetra caviar for starters; flounder filets with salmon mousseline, riesling sauce and chervil or baby Maine pheasant with tarragon and wild mushrooms for main courses. If you really want to splurge, go for Sam's new nightly Maine menu of six or seven courses for $43 to $49. On one winter's evening, the succession of small dishes produced Pemaquid oysters, shrimp cakes, a firepot of Maine seafoods, and venison with black trumpet mushrooms, followed by fresh raspberries with soft New England chevre and a bittersweet chocolate marquise with praline-espresso cream. We'll never forget the strawberries romanoff and a moist sour-cream cheesecake with fresh raspberries in which we indulged. The **Side Door Lounge** at the rear, with cathedral ceiling and wicker furniture, serves up drinks, supper fare from $5.95 to $15.95, and live jazz or folk music from 5 to midnight.

Dinner, Tuesday-Saturday from 6.

The Great Impasta, 42 Maine St., Brunswick. (207) 729-5858.
Northern Italian. $6.95 to $10.95.

Contemporary Northern Italian fare is prepared at this crowded, intimate restaurant by a chef whose training at the Culinary Institute of America shows. The pastas are great, especially the tortellini with broccoli and garlic and the linguini with seafood. Or go for shrimp layered on a bed of creamed spinach topped with tomatoes and cheese or haddock sauteed with zucchini, tomatoes, onions, and cream. Veal and chicken are prepared creatively, too. A canopy fronts the open kitchen at the rear, where wicker shades soften the kitchen lights. In front, hurricane candles flicker on the linened tables and striking art is hung on the walls.

Lunch, Monday-Saturday 11:30 to 4:30; dinner, 4:30 to 9 or 10. Closed Sunday.

The Stowe House, 63 Federal St., Brunswick. (207) 725-5543.
American. $9.45 to $16.95.

Harriet Beecher Stowe and her husband lived in this Federal house while he taught religion at nearby Bowdoin College, his alma mater. Today, one of the first designated National Historic Landmarks in Maine has the requisite taproom and an original Victorian saloon. History looms important in the large beamed and paneled dining room where plates line a high shelf, wingback chairs flank the pine tables and the windows are full of hanging plants. The menu is billed as innovative regional, but not too innovative. The ragout of scallops comes in a puff pastry basket, the grilled swordfish with chunks of lobster and truffles, and strips of lamb are sauteed with peppers and chanterelles in a honey-mustard sauce. If these are too much, the menu advises, you can get a plain broiled version of "simply seafood." Oh yes, there's a very large salad bar.

Lunch daily, noon to 2; dinner, 5:30 to 9, Sunday to 8.

Rock Ovens, Route 24, Bailey Island. (207) 833-6911.
American. $12.95 to $19.95.

Who'd guess that this established, highly regarded place started as a seafood shack, serving lobsters and clams through a window? Georgene Schuster, daughter of the original owners, has upgraded the food and enclosed the once-open deck over the water to create a rustic, two-level dining room full of delightfully mismatched chairs she acquired at tag sales. The room is right over the water — "you sit here and get seasick," Georgene's mother quips. The chowders and lobster stew are exceptional, and the mainly seafood entrees are straightforward but stylish. We liked the sea scallops baked with white wine, mustard and honey glaze and the sauteed seafood over pasta. The salads and homemade breads are fine. Desserts include cheesecake, deep-dish apple pie and bread pudding with a rum-butter sauce.

Dinner nightly except Tuesday from 5:30. Open late May to mid-October.

Bath Area

Kristina's, 160 Center St., Bath. (207) 442-8577.
American/International. $8.50 to $15.95.

When we first met Kristina's, it was a tiny bakery with a few tables and a glass case where such things as sticky buns were displayed. You can still get sticky buns, but now there are two dining rooms, a front porch with tables and chairs, and, upstairs, **Harry's Bar,** an attractive room that is all blond wood and deck chairs, with lots of windows looking out onto green trees. Jazz groups often play here at night. You can still take out many good things from the display cases, but now you can sit down for breakfast, lunch or dinner. A Sunday brunch on the shady front deck produced the best huevos rancheros ever, groaning under salsa, sour cream and scallions, along with a super asparagus and crabmeat omelet. The food compensated for distracted service (which seems to be a recurring complaint of locals). At dinner start with a chilled seafood gazpacho or country pate with cognac and green peppercorns. Changing entrees might include chicken sate, Cajun crab cakes, and Thai shrimp and saffron scallops. Most dishes have interesting touches, like homemade apricot chutney on the grilled halibut. Desserts from the bakery case are gorgeous.

Open daily from 8 a.m. to 9, 9:30 or 10:30 p.m. Harry's Bar, with light menu, open to 10 weekdays, midnight weekends.

Desert Flower, 1 Elm St., Bath. (207) 442-8431.
Mexican. $5.95 to $8.95.

Formerly the Grapevine, then the Second Course, among others, the latest incarnation of this second-floor loft is Mexican and we hear good things about it. The setting and decor haven't changed much — the airy two-story room has large arched windows from which you can catch a glimpse of the Kennebec River. Banquettes line the walls and the tables are covered with red cloths on which are woven mats. Fajitas are topped with chili con queso and guacamole and served with corn and a green salad. Chimichanga, burrito plate and quesadilla are other choices. Combinations of tacos, mini tostadas, mini burritos, and enchiladas are popular. Start with one of the six nacho dishes (maybe with shredded chicken), gazpacho or albondigas. The soups, nachos and salads like chicken-avocado or taco are also served at lunchtime. Sangria comes by the pitcher, Mexican beers are on the docket, of course, and desserts include sopapillas, flan and Mexican chocolate mousse.

Lunch, Tuesday-Friday 11:30 to 2; dinner, Tuesday-Sunday 4 to 11.

Truffles Cafe, 21 Elm St., Bath. (207) 442-8474.
International. $2.75 to $3.95.
Ellen Spiegelman and Stephanie Redfern, both with lots of cooking experience in New York, took over Trifles in l989, renamed it, and now serve breakfast and lunch in a cozy tearoom setting filled with incredible little dolls (made by a Wiscasset woman and for sale) and wall hangings. Have the omelet of the day or roasted crunch with fruit and/or yogurt for breakfast; have a tabouli and hummus salad or a spicy chicken salad sandwich for lunch. Desserts of the day could be pound cake with berries and whipped cream, peach cake, or butterscotch brownies with vanilla ice cream. The owners were contemplating opening for dinner on weekends.

Open daily, 7 to 3. No smoking.

★ The Osprey, Robinhood Marine Center, off Route 127, Robinhood.
(207) 371-2530.
New American. $14.50 to $20.
From the open deck, an enclosed porch or an interior dining room above an out-of-the-way marina, the sight of Riggs Cove on two sides and a view of a pair of osprey nested atop a green channel marker are idyllic on a summer's afternoon or evening. The decor during its ten-year existence has been upgraded to one of simple, yet sophisticated summer charm. Chef Michael Gagne presides over a new American menu remarkable for its range (it's so extensive and the type so small that it makes for difficult reading by candlelight). He makes his own breads, pastas, sausages and ice creams, and turns out more than two dozen dinner entrees as well as a delectable array of appetizers and salads. At lunch, the cold cucumber soup with dill is thick, garlicky and has a real bite, the perfect foil for a a smoked sausage sampler. The fettuccine with Maine clams and garlic is terrific. A basket of hot bagels and corn muffins laced with corn kernels comes with. Dinner is assertive as well, perhaps a gutsy scallops nicoise in puff pastry or grilled chicken over fettuccine, both so ample as to require doggy bags — that is, if you want to have room left to sample the trio of ice creams — grasshopper, raspberry swirl and childhood orange at our latest visit. With food like this and a salubrious setting, it's little wonder that people drive from miles around, although we find it more appealing by day than after dark. And somehow the Poland Spring mineral water, which could be a nice regional touch, doesn't make it in place of plain water.

Lunch, noon to 2:30; dinner, 5:30 to 9; Sunday brunch, 10 to 2:30. Closed Tuesday and December to mid-May.

Wiscasset

Le Garage, Water Street, Wiscasset. (207) 882-5409.
American. $8.95 to $15.95.
It really is an old automobile dealer's garage, but the expansive interior illuminated entirely by candlelight is positively magical at night. The view from the airy, wraparound porch of the Sheepscot River and the huge rotting hulks of two schooners is cherished by photographers and anyone else who eats at Le Garage. Despite its French name, the menu features an enormous array of American fare that rarely changes from year to year, except for the prices — and those not by much. Owner Cheryl Lee Rust, who presides at the front desk of her decade-old establishment, wants "people to relax and enjoy themselves." No fewer than 36

entrees are listed at dinner, which starts with hot biscuits and a house salad. Our marinated lamb and garlic lamb kabobs were perfect, and we remember fondly from years ago a ham, chicken, artichoke heart, and cheese casserole that's still on the menu. Seafood and steaks come in many variations, most simply but well prepared. A baker's surprise tops the dessert list each day. The young staff outfitted in denim shirts with big plaid bow ties fits into the spirit of the place.

Open daily, 11:30 to 3 and 5 to 10 in summer. Closed Monday in winter.

Newcastle-Damariscotta

Newcastle Inn, River Road, Newcastle. (207) 563-5685.
New American. Prix-Fixe, $28.

Single-entree, prix-fixe dinners are served to inn guests and the public at this venerable inn, lately upgraded by Chris and Ted Sprague and offering a glimpse through the trees of the Damariscotta River. Following a cocktail hour with hors d'oeuvres at 6, guests gather in the 24-seat dining room for a five-course feast. A typical menu might start with scallops in puff pastry, red and yellow pepper bisque, and a green salad with cream biscuits. The main course could be rack of lamb with chive cream sauce, wild mushrooms, sauteed cherry tomatoes, and beet greens. For dessert you might find frozen white chocolate mousse with chocolate sauce and chocolate leaves. Chris, who was a pastry chef and ran a gourmet food store on Cape Cod, varies each course nightly. Other entrees over the seasons could be grilled salmon with butter diablo, Greek lamb with kaseri cheese, pork tenderloin amandine, and roast tenderloin of beef with wild mushroom sauce.

Dinner by reservation, nightly except Monday at 7. No smoking.

Backstreet Landing, Elm Street Plaza, Damariscotta. (207) 563-5666.
American/Seafood. $8.95 to $15.95.

Pleasantly casual and with a great view of the placid river behind, this is a particularly good spot for a waterside lunch on the enclosed porch with dark gray oilcloths and pink napkins. We enjoyed good fried clams with potato salad and coleslaw, and a crabmeat salad roll (which turned out to be a hard bun) again with coleslaw. Dinners get a bit more complex — just a bit, as in scrod au gratin, scallops sauteed with ginger and peapods, shrimp a la grecque, cioppino, and teriyaki beef kabob. The specialty is seafood bake: haddock, scallops and shrimp with wine in a creamy cheese sauce.

Lunch daily, 11 to 2:30; dinner, 5 to 9; Sunday brunch.

Salt Bay Cafe, Main Street, Damariscotta. (207) 563-1666.
American/Seafood. $7.95 to $12.95.

The front solarium add-on belies the rustic interior of dark paneling, booths and a rear bar. Chef-owner Scott Devlin offers a bit of Tex-Mex (nachos, tostada salad), Italian (linguini with clam sauce, chicken florentine), trendy (potato skins, barbecued pork tenderloin), and standard (mixed grill, fried clams and fisherman's platter). The lunch menu is down to earth, and we found a breakfast of grilled muffins and a western omelet, speedily served by a pro of a waitress, a downright bargain.

Breakfast daily, 6 to 10:30; lunch, 11 to 4; dinner 4 to 9, Sunday to 8.

Boothbay Harbor Area

Russell House, Route 27, Boothbay Harbor. (207) 633-6656.
American/Continental. $11.95 to $21.95.

The fanciest dining in the Boothbay area has been offered since 1984 by Jocelyn

Oakes in a handsome white New England farmhouse set on a rise well back from the Wiscasset Road. The candlelit side dining room with a latticework divider and tables topped by blue calico overcloths over pink linens is a picture of sophistication. Jocelyn's menu is enormous but relatively simple, a repertoire she can prepare easily for a variety of tastes, from rack of lamb to Cajun pan-blackened lamb steak. The emphasis is on veal and chicken dishes, but the most popular items are bouillabaisse, roast duck and lobster Russell, sauteed with herbs and garlic and tossed with fettuccine, heavy cream and parmesan cheese. Desserts like chocolate truffle mousse and kahlua-pecan pie are to groan over.

Dinner nightly except Sunday, 5:30 to 9:30. Closed Monday in winter.

Lawnmeer Inn and Restaurant,, Route 27, West Boothbay Harbor. (207) 633-2544.
American/Continental. $9.95 to $17.95.

Long revered for its home cooking and waterside views at the head of Southport Island, the Lawnmeer was upgraded in 1989 by new owners who hired as chef Patrick Dorr, who had helped put Kristina's in Bath on the map. The large pine-paneled main dining room with windows onto the cove has been redone in burgundy and white with green napkins that match the carpet. It's an inviting setting for food that is presented in exceptionally attractive style. Traditional nightly specials like Yankee pot roast, roast turkey and poached salmon with egg sauce have been augmented with more fancy offerings like almond chicken fettuccine and steak diane. The seafood pasta is a delectable array of mussels, shrimp and scallops topped with crisp vegetables and the drunken lobster is ever-so-nouvelle with a rich, wonderful sauce. Three kinds of hot rolls, salads with raspberry vinaigrette and dijon dressings, and red potatoes and zucchini accompanied our feast. It concluded with a sublime key lime pie.

Dinner nightly, 5 to 9; Sunday brunch, 8 to 1. Open May-October.

Ristorante Black Orchid, 5 By-Way, Boothbay Harbor. (207) 6323-6659.
Italian. $8.50 to $19.95.

Downtown Boothbay Harbor's lackluster dining scene has been enhanced since 1987 by chef-owner Steven DiCicco's two-story eatery in the heart of town. The colorful, can't-miss facade leads to an unpretentious interior done up in black and white, with pink stenciling on the walls, beams strewn with odd-looking grapevines and baskets of fake hanging fuschias. The upstairs **Bocce Club** caffe and raw bar overlook the downtown harbor action. The food is generally considered excellent. It's a heady mix of Italian favorites like pastas, veal marsala and lobster diavolo, and the locally obligatory broiled haddock and fried scallops. The shrimp dishes are especially appealing. Amaretto bread pudding and chocolate-chambord torte are favorite desserts.

Dinner nightly, 5:30 to 10:30. Open mid-May to mid-October.

Henry's Fine Dining, 152 Townsend Ave., Boothbay Harbor. (207) 633-6555.
Continental. $9.95 to $18.95.

A free-standing adjunct to the new Flagship Motor Inn complex on the road into town, this unlikely looking place with a parent of the same name in Allentown, Pa., has been drawing accolades for food well above the average hereabouts. The decor is elegant motel: airy and light in blue and white. The lengthy menu begins with classics like escargots in garlic butter, fettuccine alfredo and mushroom caps stuffed with crabmeat. Sauteed veal with lobster, blackened sirloin, grilled swordfish copenhagen, steak au poivre, and wiener schnitzel are some of the entree highlights.

There's a section devoted to fried seafood. The dessert list does not seem to be up to the rest of the menu.

Breakfast, lunch and dinner daily from 7 a.m. to 10 p.m.

McSeagull's, On the Wharf, Boothbay Harbor. (207) 633-4041.
American/Seafood. $10.95 to $18.95.

You can't help but be attracted to a place with a name like this, and McSeagull's has been drawing folks for food and fun by the water since 1976. Besides a couple of dining rooms with bright red cloths and white napkins and a large bar, there's a waterside deck. Planters of cascading petunias and geraniums and sea-blue deck chairs present a colorful scene as you lunch on seafood salads, crepes, steamed mussels or clams, shrimp and, of course, lobster. Some of the dinner entrees have a bit more kick, perhaps sole florentine, shrimp scampi, veal with shrimp and avocado, or lobster fettuccine with newburg sauce. Swordfish, halibut, scallops, and steaks are charcoal-broiled; the only fried fish is a seafood platter. Frozen grasshopper pie is a great dessert, and the wine list is better than many of its ilk. If you like quiet dining, don't even think of eating here after 9 when the entertainment begins.

Lunch, 11:30 to 3; dinner, 5:30 to 10. Closed January and February.

Pemaquid Point Area

The Bradley Inn, Route 130, 361 Pemaquid Point, New Harbor.
(207) 677-2105.
American/Continental. $10.95 to $19.95.

When locals want to go out a fancy meal, they don their Sunday duds and head for the Bradley, an inn and restaurant of the old school. Personally run by Ed and Louine Ek, the old-fashioned dining room is made colorful with cranberry linens and summery views through the windows onto lawns and fields. Clear glass service plates are at each setting, awaiting the arrival of appetizers like baked brie, carpaccio and baked stuffed clams. Main courses on the limited menu include a couple of pastas, and range from chicken with shallot-sour cream sauce and baked scallops en casserole to veal marsala, steak diane and rack of lamb. Green salad, rolls, vegetables, sorbet, and beverage come with the meal.

Dinner nightly, 6 to 9; Sunday brunch, 11:30 to 1:30; weekends, October-December. Closed January-May.

Pemaquid Chart House, beside Fort William Henry, Pemaquid Beach.
(207) 677-3315.
Steaks/Seafood. $8.50 to $17.50.

A nautical setting (a ceiling draped with fishing nets) and windows onto the harbor commend this casual place with a steak and seafood menu. Potato skins and nachos are available for contemporary tastes, but most start with clam chowder or lobster stew before chowing down on fisherman's platter, shrimp and scallop saute, broiled haddock, baked crabmeat au gratin, or surf and turf. Lobster comes five ways, and the steak prices are from yesteryear. Out back is **The Pemaquid Pier,** where you can order anything from lobster rolls to picnic-style shore dinners for eating under cover or at tables on the pier.

Open daily, 11:30 to 9:30, Memorial Day to Labor Day.

Shaw's Lobster Wharf, Route 32, New Harbor. (207) 677-2200.
Seafood. $6.50 to $11.95.

Few places can match the setting of the rooftop deck of Shaw's, right beside the water and with a glorious view of New Harbor and, beyond, Muscongus Bay. There's

Mid-Coast

a mallet on each table for cracking the lobsters that are de rigeur, any time of day or night. The sunny Sunday afternoon we were there, almost everyone was feasting on lobster dinners, featuring "single, double and triple lobster specials," the triples going strong. We settled for a lobster roll and a clam roll, washed down with a couple of bottles of Geary's dark ale from Portland, and agreed with the slogan on the menu — "Maine: The Way Life Should Be!" There are plenty of tables inside the rustic self-service restaurant (place your order and take a number). Downstairs at an open-air tavern along the dock, you can enjoy cocktails and a raw bar right beside the harbor.

Open daily 11 to 9, seasonally.

Port Clyde Area

The Black Harpoon, off Route 131, Port Clyde. (207) 372-6304.
Seafood. $9.95 to $13.95.

The ads tout "possibly the best seafood restaurant with the most interesting menu on the coast of Maine." It isn't, but the extensive menu that comes on a greasy, much-used paper bag does have its moments, as in seafood in parchment, bouillabaisse, cioppino, China shell (crabmeat, scallops, vegetables and rice), and shellfish over linguini. The steaks come in two sizes, and sauteed or fried vegetables may be ordered on the side. Cajun scallops and deep-fried squid rings are among the starters. Spumoni with claret sauce and New York cheesecake with strawberries are possible desserts. The restaurant, on a side street a few blocks from the public landing, is a melange of small rooms with lime-green oilcloths on the tables and ceilings covered with fish netting holding all kinds of hanging buoys. Character it's got in spades, although the location is nil.

Lunch daily, noon to 2:30; dinner, 5 to 9 or 10; dinner only, Wednesday-Sunday in spring and fall. Closed Columbus Day to Mothers Day.

The Craignair Inn, Clark Island Road, Clark Island. (207) 594-7644.
American/Continental. $10.95 to $14.95.

Go past the granite quarries to the end of Clark Island Road and a seaside settlement out of the past, in which the dominant structure is the Craignair Inn, a former boarding house for quarry workers rising beside the rocky coast. The menu is one of the area's more interesting, and the homey country dining room is refreshing in peach and blue, picked up from the colors of a lovely oriental rug in the center. Prolific ferns hang in the windows and blue plates and pottery decorate high shelves. Field flowers and candles grace the tables, and windows yield a distant water view. The dozen entrees range from scampi and bouillabaisse to veal oscar and lemon-pepper seafood kabob, which was honored in the Maine chefs' seafood contest in 1989. Herbed rabbit in wine sauce is a local specialty. Desserts include bourbon-pecan tart, grapenut custard and chocolate creme brulee.

Dinner, Monday-Saturday 6 to 9:30.

Rockport-Camden

Sail Loft Restaurant, Rockport Town Landing, Rockport. (207) 236-2330.
New England/Seafood. $7.50 to $19.50.

Immensely popular, this large, traditional establishment relies on straightforward seafood and lots of it, plus a view of the quaint Rockport harbor made famous by the late Andre the Seal. The decor is pleasantly nautical, and the most choice tables are those by the water; be advised that if you're landlocked in the interior, you could be anywhere. Don't expect any surprises on the menu, which is loaded with classic and safe seafood dishes as well as beef and poultry. The chef varies the menu slightly a couple of times a year, but predictability and consistency are the Sail Loft's chief virtues.

Lunch, 11:30 to 2:30; dinner, 5:30 to 9, Sunday noon to 9.

★ The Belmont, 6 Belmont Ave., Camden. (207) 236-8053.
New American. $17 to $22.50.

New chef-owner Gerry Clare took over in 1988 from the owners of Aubergine, a pioneer in nouvelle cuisine on the Maine coast. He and partner John Mancarella changed the cuisine from French to American, but otherwise repeat guests are hard-pressed to tell the difference. Floral china and field flowers in tiny clear-glass vases provide color in a quiet dining room lovely with white linens and aubergine carpet; the adjacent sun porch has pristine white tables and chairs. The limited menu changes every three days. Start perhaps with a plate of exotic pates or grilled Thai shrimp with tamari beurre blanc and cucumber relish. Entrees could be lobster risotto, roast duckling with ginger-peach sauce, and medallions of veal and sweetbreads. These come with interesting vegetables like a puree of broccoli with sour cream and horseradish, carrots braised in grand marnier, and garlic-cheese grits. Among desserts are bete noir (a dark chocolate cake filled with beach plum preserves and chocolate ganache), fresh raspberries with champagne sabayon, and amaretto cheesecake.

Dinner nightly, 6 to 9:30. Closed November-April.

Cassoulet, 31 Elm St., Camden. (207) 236-6304.
Country American. $12.95 to $15.95.

Tiny, cute and very colorful is Cassoulet (the former Secret Garden). Less flamboyant than their Texas predecessors, Bob and Sally Teague feature classic country cooking. Lots of seafood is offered on the interesting menu, including halibut broiled with pesto, shrimp a la grecque and bouillabaisse. Fresh halibut and clams poached in olive oil, wine, garlic, shallots, and herbs appealed at our latest visit. The traditional cassoulet is made here with lamb, pork, sausage, and white beans. Desserts change nightly; the flourless chocolate-raspberry torte is a specialty. All this is served inside or in a secluded rear garden.

Dinner, Monday-Saturday 6 to 9:30.

The Waterfront Restaurant, Harborside Square off Bay View Street,
Camden. (207) 236-3747.
American. $10.95 to $16.95.

There's no better waterside setting in Camden than this appropriately named establishment with a large outdoor deck shaded by a striking white canopy that resembles a boat's sails. You can watch the busy harbor as you lunch on chilled minted peach soup with ginger, lobster salad in a tomato, a Greek or Mexican corn salad, crabmeat rarebit, smoked salmon with toasted bagel, or seafood on a toasted roll with remoulade sauce. Many of the luncheon salads — known for outstanding dressings — also are available as entrees at dinner. Apricot chicken, Mediterranean seafood stew, sole boursin, New England crab cakes, and poached haddock with artichokes and hollandaise are favorites. All kinds of shellfish are at the raw bar.

Lunch daily, 11:30 to 2:30; dinner, 5 to 10.

Mama & Leenie's, 27 Elm St., Camden. (207) 236-6300.
Cafe/Bakery. $3 to $6.

A small cafe with a cheery atmosphere and a side patio, this opens at 8 a.m. for breakfast (how about blintzes with fruit and sour cream?) and continues with lunch and light dinner. At lunch you might order Mama's special peasant soup with beef, kielbasa and vegetables, or a caesar salad with daughter Leenie's homemade croutons. Bring your own wine for dinner, when you might find Indonesian marinated chicken on a skewer or a bowl of chili with homemade bread. Leenie is a master baker, as evidenced by the apricot strudel with coconut and walnuts, the double chocolate fudge brownies with orange zest, the pure butter shortbread, and the pineapple upside-down cake. The fresh berry pies with real whipped cream are masterpieces.

Open 8 a.m. to 9:30 p.m., Sunday 8 to 4, fewer hours in off-season.

Searsport

★ Nickerson Tavern, Route 1, Searsport. (207) 548-2220.
Regional American. $11 to $17.
Everybody from Camden to Bangor sings the praises of the restaurant housed in this white Colonial captain's homestead dating from 1838. Folks from miles around come for fine meals served in a pleasant, beamed dining room, which has windsor chairs at bare polished wood tables, lace curtains and fresh flowers. Chef-owner Tom Weiner likes to combine meats and fruits in intriguing ways. His raspberry hazelnut chicken (breast of chicken coated with crushed hazelnuts) is a favorite, as are veal with cider and apples, shrimp etouffee, lamb with pesto, and roast duckling glazed with fresh pear and cointreau sauce. He makes his pate of veal and pork with dried fruits and nuts, and serves a spicy Indonesian shrimp satay and scallops ceviche among appetizers. The dessert cart is laden with fresh fruit tarts, and you can choose dacquoise, white chocolate mousse, or homemade ginger ice cream.

Dinner nightly, 5 to 9.

Belfast

Penobscot Meadows Inn, Route 1, Belfast. (207) 338-5320.
American. $12.95 to $17.95.
This attractive country inn at the entrance to Belfast is the home of locally renowned cuisine. Start with cocktails on the deck with a glimpse of Penobscot Bay before adjourning to cozy dining rooms and a turn-of-the-century setting of gleaming woodwork, antique furnishings and quilts. The kitchen is known for delicate sauces, artistic presentations and generous portions. Seafood ceviche, tomato-cognac soup, and lime-grilled chicken with ginger and soy are among the specialties, and the seafood crepes are out of this world (one recent version paired shrimp with green peppercorns and sweet red peppers). Angus sirloin may be grilled with tarragon butter or red wine and shallot butter, or butterflied and sauteed with a green peppercorn, cream and brandy sauce. Veal herby is served with grilled vegetables and lots of herbs. Nightly specials supplement the dessert list, which features homemade ice creams and even a banana split.

Dinner nightly, 5:30 to 9:30. Closed Tuesday and Wednesday in off-season. No credit cards.

$ Darby's, 105 High St., Belfast. (207) 338-2339.
International. $8.25 to $12.95.
If only we'd known about this casual and pure little spot before suffering through a mediocre lunch at a better-known downtown cafe that here shall remain nameless. Self-taught chef Sheila Costello knows her food and changes her menu seasonally. The lunchtime options when we stopped by included seven salads, eight sandwiches (including California chicken with avocado and aioli), black bean

enchilada, and lamb stew. At night, the atmosphere turns more elegant, with tablecloth dining in a quiet upstairs dining room above the informal pub. Entrees, including salad, homemade bread and vegetables, could be lemon-cashew chicken, ginger chicken spa style, basque-style lamb steaks, and shrimp and smoked mussel pasta. Start with Chinese style eggrolls or shrimp wontons, but be sure to save room for one of the spectacular desserts, perhaps blackberry cheesecake, blueberry mousse or glazed raspberry pie.

Lunch, 11 to 4; dinner nightly, 5 to 9 or 10.

Harbor View Restaurant, Route 1, Belfast. (207) 338-5225.
Seafood. $5.95 to $22.95.
Tourists love this large place, part of the struggling Haymarket North complex, with a smashing view down a hillside to the water. The main-floor dining room in green and beige has all the ambience of an ersatz Colonial-style motel; the circular room upstairs with large windows and a beamed octagonal roof is better. Go here not for ambience but for traditional seafood and that water view. Lobster is served in eight guises, and haddock and scallops in five each. The presentations are simple and forthright. Steak, prime rib and chicken cordon bleu are available for the landlubbers. Lemon mousse pie is the house dessert. On warm days, the five outside tables on the rear porch are the first to go.

Lunch, 11:30 to 2:30; dinner, 5 to 8 or 9. Closed Monday.

Brooks

Calico's Ridge House, Route 7, Brooks. (207) 722-3666.
American. $12.95 to $17.95.
"A tradition returns," said the ads proclaiming the 1989 reopening of the Ridge House, a contemporary frame structure hidden in the woods near out-of-the-way Brooks. After running one of the state's better restaurants, the original partners split and the Ridge House had been closed for a few years. New owners from the South opened with a limited but appealing menu embracing veal applejack, poached salmon with ginger-lime sauce, Cajun fish, roast pork stuffed with raisins and apples in puff pastry, and breast of chicken filled with spinach, herb cheese and walnuts. Early reports were that the service and presentation were a bit stiff for those used to what had been a relaxed, ski-lodgey atmosphere. Entertainment is featured at the Sunday champagne brunch, also a local tradition.

Dinner, Tuesday-Sunday 5:30 to 9:30; Sunday brunch, 11:30 to 2:30.

Bucksport

L'Ermitage, 219 Main St., Bucksport. (207) 469-3361.
French. $11.95 to $15.95.
The original owners departed and ex-Connecticut residents Ginny and Jim Conklin took over in 1989. Although Ginny had never cooked in the French style before, she had wanted to own a B&B. She trained for two weeks under the founders and retained their menu. Soon she was offering specialties that had won acclaim under the previous owners: veal forestiere, lamb chops provencale, medallions of pork with apples and raisins, and steak chasseur. The house salad is an interesting blend of spinach, lettuce, walnuts, and bacon bits. Desserts include strawberry timbale, amaretto bread pudding, wild blueberry trifle, and sherry-chocolate cheesecake. The decor in the three small dining rooms is simple and homey.

Dinner, Tuesday-Sunday 5:30 to 9.

Western Lakes

Gorham

Gorham Station, 29 Elm St., Gorham. (207) 839-3354.
American/Continental. $9.95 to $17.95.

The one-time Gorham railroad station has been extensively renovated into a popular steak and seafood house decked out with old railroad posters, photographs and memorabilia. Swordfish grilled with a mustard-basil sauce is a specialty, along with the locally ubiquitous prime rib on weekends. Seafood entrees run from broiled haddock and haddock oscar to scallops with sauteed vegetables and lobster pie. Veal comes three ways and various steaks are offered, sometimes in combination with seafood — scallops and steak for instance. Salad, served family style in a large bowl, is available as a meal at dinner or lunch.

Lunch, Monday-Friday 11:30 to 2:30; dinner nightly, 5 to 10 or 11; Sunday brunch, 11:30 to 3.

Naples

The Epicurean Inn, Route 302, Naples. (207) 693-3839.
French/New American. $15.95 to $19.95.

This vivid pink Victorian house built in 1845 as a stagecoach stop was an instant winner following its opening in 1986 to a four-star review. Chef Paul Charpentier changes his menu weekly in partnership with co-owners Scott and Patti Sparks — he the pastry chef and she the overseer of 30 choice seats in a rear dining porch, a formal dining room for six and an intimate front room with four tables. Paul adds unusual touches to classic fare, perhaps a seafood provencale soup or Moroccan chicken and cashews in phyllo for appetizers, shrimp curry in a spicy sauce, chicken praline with pecans and sweet bourbon glaze, roast pork tenderloin with a mustard-flavored hollandaise sauce, or tournedos with stilton in a rich port wine sauce for entrees. We hear great things about the veal sauteed with sun-dried tomatoes and oregano in lemon and white wine. A sorbet precedes and salad follows the entrees, the latter tossed perhaps with maple-curry or raspberry-walnut dressings. Assorted cheeses and fruits are complimentary, fancy pastries are available, and the check comes with fresh strawberries dipped in chocolate. Amaretto-almond crepes are among the Sunday brunch treats.

Dinner nightly except Tuesday, 5 to 9:30. Hours vary off-season.

Bridgton

Black Horse Tavern, Route 302, Bridgton. (207) 647-5300.
Steaks/Seafood. $8.95 to $17.95.

A big hit in the Bridgton area is this new restaurant in a barn behind a gray house with a front porch straight out of Louisiana. The two structures are joined by a large bar. Most of the dining is in the rear portion, where all kinds of horsey artifacts hang from the walls and stalls have been converted into booths. The chef acquired a Cajun flair while cooking in Texas and Louisiana, which explains the chicken and smoked sausage gumbo that's a must starter for lunch or dinner. Steaks, prime rib, pan-blackened sirloin or swordfish, chicken Creole, and scallop pie are among the dinner entrees.

Open daily from 11 to 10, weekends to 11, Sunday from 12:30.

South Paris

$ Maurice, 113 Main St., South Paris. (207) 743-2532.
French. $8.50 to $14.50.

This longtime beacon in a culinary wilderness has been rebuilt by local restaurant impressario John Tisdale following a fire and continues to do very nicely, thank you. Although some of the soul is missing, the French flair lent by the late Andre Maurice remains in the vastly expanded establishment, now four dining rooms, and in an award-winning wine list heavy on margaux but with a bevy of values under $10. The bargains we cherish — a broiled haddock dinner for $4.95 less than a decade ago — are still affected only slightly by inflation. The top-of-the-line item, rack of lamb, was a mere $14.50 at our last visit. The menu is in French, with English translations and only a few compromises for plainer tastes. The chef's pate, rough and hearty with pickled onions and capers, is ample for two with the warm, crusty French bread. A lemon sorbet with champagne sauce cleansed the palate. The rack of lamb turned out to be eight small and tender chops dressed in blue ruffles, served with creamed potatoes and crisp zucchini and yellow squash. The tournedos with bearnaise were good if a mite thin. Try the veal flambe, grilled lamb chops or duckling bigarade, and take your salad after the entree. The seasonal dessert of diced local canteloupe on a bed of frozen cream cheese and lemon is perfection. The dining rooms are pleasant in red and blue or rust and tan, and lacy white curtains cover the windows. If it's not France in South Paris, it's the next best thing.

Lunch, Monday-Friday 11:30 to 1:30, Sunday 11 to 2; dinner nightly, 5 to 9.

Waterford

★ Lake House, Routes 35 & 37, Waterford. (207) 583-4182.
Regional American. $14.95 to $19.95.

A changing menu of creative regional cuisine, flaming desserts and a remarkable wine list are offered by proprietors Suzanne and Michael Uhl-Myers. The two dining rooms are pretty as a picture, but we like best the narrow front porch on a warm night, even though it's too brightly illuminated for our tastes. The Rhode Island squid sauteed with spinach ravioli and a garlic sauce is an excellent starter. A dollop of kiwi sorbet precedes the entrees, in our case a generous portion of sliced lamb sauced with curry and vodka, and roast duckling in a sweet sauce of blackberries and raspberries. Sliced potatoes, cucumbers, tomatoes, and pickled corn accompanied. Served after the entree, the salad of fresh fruit on a bed of lettuce was so refreshing we didn't need dessert. Apples normandy, bananas foster and crepes suzette are flamed tableside for two, a task that keeps Michael hopping on busy nights.

Dinner nightly, 5 to 10. Closed Tuesday and Wednesday in off-season.

Olde Rowley Inn, Route 35, North Waterford. (207) 583-4143.
American. $10.50 to $15.95.

Three candlelit dining rooms in this 1790 roadside stagecoach inn could not be more historic or romantic. Copper wall lanterns illuminate the hand-stenciled wallpaper in one room, and old baskets and dried herbs hang from the beamed ceiling in another. New innkeepers Meredith and Brian Thomas, he the chef, have maintained the tradition launched by Pamela Leja. Their menu starts with deep-fried Monterey Jack cheese with dill sauce, stuffed mushrooms, a scallop tart, and wonderful cream soups — the carrot bisque and mushroom laced with cognac being standouts. Entrees include hunter's chicken, veal piccata, haddock provencale, roast pork normandy, and sirloin steak. Desserts are triumphs: trifles with raspberries and peaches, walnut-bourbon pie, Indian pudding, and a four-layer French chocolate cake filled with rum mousse.

Dinner nightly, 5 to 10; sometimes closed one or two nights a week in winter.

Fryeburg

★ The Oxford House Inn, 105 Main St., Fryeburg. (207) 935-3442.
Regional American. $16 to $19.
This 1913 country house is run very personally by John and Phyllis Morris, whose creative cuisine has garnered a wide reputation. Dining is on a rear porch with a stunning view of Mount Kearsarge North, in the former living room and along the screened front piazza. Tables are set with delicate pink crystal, heavy silver and Sango Mystique peach china, with napkins tied like a necktie and candles in clay pots. The changing menu comes inside sheet music from the 1920s. Dinner begins with complimentary homemade crackers and a cream cheese spread, and a salad of fresh greens and fruits. Among entrees are scallops in puff pastry, poached salmon pommery, turkey waldorf splashed with applejack, pork with pears and port, and veal madeira. John does most of the cooking, but the desserts are Phyllis's: fruit trifles, amaretto-chocolate cheesecake and an acclaimed bread pudding with peaches and blueberries.

Dinner nightly, 6 to 9; Sunday brunch, 11 to 2.

Center Lovell

Center Lovell Inn, Route 5, Center Lovell. (207) 925-1575.
Northern Italian. $9.95 to $17.95.
Chef-owner Bill Mosca grew up with the heritage of five generations of Italian cooks, and the result is what draws patrons for serious dining at this farmhouse-turned-inn overlooking Kezar Lake. Two small, plain dining rooms are cozy in winter; in summer, eat outside on the wraparound porch as the sun sets over the Presidential Range across Kezar Lake. The milk-fed veal marsala and veal margarita are outstanding among entrees. Shrimp is baked and stuffed with crabmeat or sauteed in olive oil with spices and wine. Baked filet of Maine hake is stuffed with shrimp and flavored with sherry. Six pasta dishes are listed after the entrees. Bill's wife Susie makes the desserts, among them spumoni and a rich Italian cheesecake.

Dinner nightly, from 5.

Auburn-Lewiston

Poppies, 88 Main St., Auburn. (207) 784-7455.
Seafood/International. $8.95 to $14.95.
The folks from Slates of Hallowell branched out with Poppies in 1988, none too soon for the artists and intelligentsia who pack its main-floor bar-cafe and upstairs dining room nightly. The menu changes daily but is patterned after that of its eclectic parent. The cooking has flair: the haddock might be stuffed with crabmeat, the scrod baked with brie and blueberries, the shrimp pan-blackened with jalapeno mayonnaise, the salmon or mahi-mahi available with garlic and herbs, a strawberry-mint puree or creamy leek, lemon and pernod sauce. Even the vegetable saute comes "with many nuts," according to the hand-written menu. The tenderloin was available four ways — diane, au poivre, boursin with mushrooms, or grilled with jalapeno mayo — when we were there. The Cajun sampler makes an appealing starter, paired with a main dish of oysters florentine. Some choice wines are available by the glass at

a bargain price. The changing desserts might include chocolate cheesecake, bourbon-tollhouse pie, apple-raspberry pie, and chocolate-kahlua mousse.

Lunch, Tuesday-Friday 11:30 to 2:30; dinner, Tuesday-Sunday 5:30 to 9 or 9:30; Sunday brunch, 10 to 3.

No Tomatoes, 36 Court St., Auburn. (207) 784-3919.
American/Continental. $8.95 to $15.95.
We don't understand the name, but do know this is a versatile restaurant. The main dining room has white brick walls, a high ceiling and sailing prints. The Garden Lounge, with a light menu, sports bentwood chairs amid many plants and trees. The lunch menu is bigger than many a dinner menu. Here the nighttime menu calms down to a more manageable two dozen offerings, from baked stuffed haddock and shrimp wellington to veal oscar and steaks with a choice of sauces. The house specials are three chicken dishes, tenderloin tips with shrimp or chicken oriental, steak and shrimp, and steak and scallops. Favored desserts are raspberry mousse pie and cheesecakes by Izzy of Portland, who once was chef here.

Lunch, 11:30 to 4 or 5; dinner, 5 to 9 or 10.

Marois Restaurant, 249 Lisbon St., Lewiston. (207) 782-9055.
Greek/French/American/Italian. $8.25 to $18.95.
Unbelievable. An oversize, eight-page menu divided into Greek, French, Cajun, American and Italian cuisines, any one of which would be enough for most kitchens. Serving from 6 a.m. to 11 p.m. seven days a week. A long, narrow and bordering-on-the-gaudy dining room of booths, wrought-iron dividers, colored lights hanging from the ceiling, fabric walls, murals of sea and lake. And is this "the best-kept secret in town," as its card proclaims? "We've been here since 1919," said owner-hostess Antoinette Orastis of the place her grandfather founded. Her chef produces 70 appetizers, 100 entrees and blackboard specials like roast duckling with raspberry glaze with generally good results. "He's always creating something new," his boss explains. The marinated hare, stuffed squid and lamb shish kabob appeal from the Greek menu, which includes most of the classic dishes and wines. The pricier French menu has too many choices; ditto for the American, which offers ten chicken dishes including a couple repeated from the French side. The Cajun menu is perhaps the most tempting, and the anything-but-haute Italian specials are probably best skipped. Other restaurateurs have the highest regard for delectables from the European dessert cart on display near the entrance.

Open daily, 6 a.m. to 11 p.m.

Lita's, 114 Lisbon St., Lewiston. (207) 783-1883.
Oriental/Vegetarian. $5.50 to $10.95.
Lita Cabelin, who immigrated here from the Philippines with her obstetrician-husband in 1963, started with an Asian grocery store. Then she gave cooking lessons in the store and started serving food. Finally she got rid of the store and expanded the space into a colorful restaurant, all in mauves and rose with tiled floors and bright green and shocking pink banners. The cuisine is light and spicy as you wish — mild, medium and hot. Mandarin, Cantonese, Szechuan/Hunan, Philippine, Indonesian, Thai, and vegetarian specialties are offered. Seafood curry, Philippine pork and chicken adobo, lamb curry, sauteed beef with snow peas and broccoli, and Cantonese roast duckling are among the offerings. The special tasting menu is a bargain at $16 each for four or more. Desserts are exotic: macadamia pie, banana fritters, coconut mousse, and homemade ice creams in ginger, mango, green tea, young coconut, and even avocado flavors.

Open Monday-Thursday 10:30 to 9, Friday and Saturday to 10.

Greene

$ The Sedgeley Place, Sedgeley Road, Greene. (207) 946-5990.
American. Prix-fixe, $14.95.

Five-course meals are served at an astoundingly low price in this two-century-old Federal house with four dining rooms in rural Greene. The homey old-timer has been lovingly run for twelve years by Philip Wilbur and his wife Lorraine, who started with 30 seats and expanded gradually to 120. The two-hour meal could begin with a choice of baked French onion or creamed broccoli-zucchini-sweet potato soup, followed by a garden or spinach-mushroom salad. Then comes a changing choice of four main courses: always prime rib, fresh fish (perhaps haddock stuffed with crameat, mushrooms and scallions with hollandaise sauce), poultry (stuffed or sauteed chicken or roast duck with peaches, apricots and brandy), and a changing special of shellfish (maybe scallops baked in beer and parmesan cheese sauce), veal or lamb. Homebaked breads and two vegetables and potatoes are served family style. The dessert choice could include puff pastry with raspberries and whipped cream, hot Indian pudding with ice cream, peach melba, and key lime pie. If you want a *real* bargain, consider the half-price specials (a set entree, perhaps breast of chicken stuffed with rice, homemade sausage and cheese, plus all the trimmings) at the 5 and 6 o'clock seatings Tuesday through Thursday nights.

Dinner by reservation, hourly seatings nightly except Monday 5 to 9, Sunday 5 and 6.

Hallowell

★ Slates, 167 Water St., Hallowell. (207) 622-9575.
International. $8.95 to $13.95.

A varied menu is served up morning, noon and night in this appealing establishment, named for the slates on its front. The first time we stopped, one of us peeked in the dark and noisy bar in the late afternoon and ventured no farther. The second time, the other marched on through to find Sunday brunch in several dining rooms beyond, subtle in beige and brick with paintings for sale from changing art exhibitions. The brunch menu is an incredible treasury of omelets, quiches, croissants, and every kind of egg dish we'd heard of and then some; you could have a year's worth and never repeat, and not go broke, either, although you may have to wait up to two hours to get a table. The lunch specials are just as tasty, perhaps shrimp pesto over pasta with green salad, grilled salmon with fresh salsa, red potatoes and green salad, or a Mideastern plate of hummus, tabouli and marinated veggies. The dinner menu is handwritten daily, offering such fare as sole with brie and toasted almonds, pan-grilled coho salmon with smoked shrimp and jarlsberg cheese, jumbo shrimp with peapods in Chinese garlic sauce, cashew chicken, tenderloin boursin with mushrooms, and spicy vegetable saute. The appetizers lack the appeal of the other offerings, but the desserts are to die for: kahlua mousse, peanut butter-chocolate swirl cream pie and raspberry-cream cake, for example. Chef Wendy Larson, a part-owner, obviously knows her stuff.

Breakfast, Monday-Friday 7:30 to 11; lunch 11:30 to 2:30; dinner, 5:30 to 9 or 9:30; weekend brunch, 9:30 to 2. Closed Sunday and Monday nights.

Gardiner

Dr. Sylvester's, 1 Church St., Gardiner. (207) 582-4810.
Continental/American. $9.25 to $15.95.

Named for Dr. Sylvester Gardiner, the town's founder whose family still summers here in a home that's described as a castle, this is a sprightly restaurant with two rooms of Victorian furnishings and French fare cooked by chef-owner Michel Tessier. Old pictures of Gardiner, bentwood and cane chairs, a few booths with lattice work, dark green and brass lamps, white candles in brass candlesticks, and light green linens comprise the decor. The menu lists such specialties as stuffed cornish game hen, braised veal, jambalaya, and shrimp and scallops sauteed with garlic, peapods and linguini. The smoked seafood sampler is generous enough to be shared by two, as the menu recommends, and the special strudel — sausage and cheddar cheese wrapped in phyllo — is renowned. The flourless chocolate cake, French vanilla cheesecake and cappuccino mousse are among the winning desserts for which Michel is known.

Lunch, Monday-Friday 11:30 to 2; dinner, Monday-Saturday 5:30 to 9:30.

Augusta

The River Grille, 333-A Water St., Augusta. (207) 623-1767.
American/International. $8.95 to $14.95.
Only the address is the same as when we last supped here on Italian food when this was Guido's Wine Cellar. Since 1988, it's been the River Grille, aiming (and claiming) to be new American but trying to be all things to all people and ending up a mishmash that defies categorization. The enjoyment of the Kennebec River view from the ground-level deck is marred by a parking lot and the sound of a large air-conditioner. But we lunched there anyway (beside a bunch of black leather-clad motorcyclists) on a heaping fried clam platter with french fries and coleslaw and a special of chicken pesto topped with a ton of cheese and accompanied by good, fresh potato salad and coleslaw. The view of the river is better from the window tables upstairs in two dining rooms with red brick walls done up in green and white. An all-day menu lists soups, burgers, salads, light bites, and "the best pizza on the banks of the Kennebec." Dinner offerings include homemade pastas, oriental stir-fries, Cajun chicken, veal oscar, sirloin au poivre, mixed grill, and a trio of grilled lamb chops served on gingered apples. Oh, yes, a special menu features lobster in seventeen guises. Now the wine list *is* nouvelle — well-chosen with some rare-for-these-parts Californias, many of them available by the glass.

Open Monday-Friday 11 to 10, Saturday and Sunday 4 to 10.

Oakland/Waterville

Johann Sebastian B, 40 Fairfield St. (Route 23), Oakland. (207) 465-3223.
German/Continental. $11 to $21.50.
"As Bach to the ear, so we to the palate," says Hubert Kueter, a Colby College German professor who got talked by friends into opening a restaurant with his wife, Nancy Dahl, in their home in nearby Oakland, much to the delight of Colby faculty and parents. His German background is evident in such specialties as jaeger schnitzel, veal cordon bleu, bratwurst, kassler rippchen, sauerbraten, Swiss fondue, and a variety of crepes, including a choice combination of any four. Four chicken dishes, three versions of halibut and shrimp madagascar round out the interesting menu. Dining is in four small rooms and the porch on the main floor of a quirky Victorian house (the back room is called the Bach Room); the old oak floors are polished and the walls hung with interesting art, done by a fellow Colby professor and for sale. Classical music (not Bach) played in the background as our party started with a sampling of four salads (curried lentil, herring, potato, and tabouli) before feasting on pork tenderloin with dumplings and sauerkraut, wiener schnitzel with rice and a cheese sauce, and chicken cordon bleu. The spiced salmon soup

was a bit odd, but the black forest cake, the specialty sundaes, and the coffee with grand marnier and whipped cream were the real thing.

Dinner, Wednesday-Saturday 6 to 9 in summer, Friday and Saturday rest of year.

$ The Last Unicorn, 8 Silver St., Waterville. (207) 873-6378.
International. $8.50 to $9.95.

"Creative and intriguing cuisine" is the billing for this appealing spot, lately double in size with two dining rooms, bare blond-wood tables, good artworks, a couple of aquariums, and a bar. Healthful foods and vegetarian fare are featured on the all-day menu, with plenty of specials but nary a meat dish beyond two chicken presentations and tortellini with smoked ham on the menu. All Waterville seems to lunch here on hefty sandwiches like a vegetarian dagwood or avocado with green chilies, and wonderful salads dressed with such creations as Hunan multiple spice, sweet and sour French, Greek lemon, and California hot sauce. Appetizers include an excellent pate and cheese plate, a hummus spread on Syrian bread, and boursin and chips. Among specials when we visited were Mexican quiche and chicken with apricot and ginger. Desserts of the day were Swedish cream, chocolate delight and blueberry pie.

Open daily, 11 to 10.

Silver Street Tavern, 2 Silver St., Waterville. (207) 873-2277.
American. $7.50 to $16.95.

Just what a college town needs was first provided by this downtown establishment, an offshoot of the Old Port Tavern and Deli in Portland. The ceiling is pressed tin, Gibson Girl prints hang on the brick and stucco walls, bentwood chairs are at tables covered with floral oilcloths, and stained glass is all around. The menu ranges widely from coquille St. Jacques to broiled seafood platter, from loin lamb chops to teriyaki beef kabob. The appetizers are fairly traditional — stuffed mushroom caps, rather than potato skins or nachos. The salads are interesting, the steak fries exceptional and the steaks tasty. All's well for the Colby College crowd.

Lunch, Tuesday-Friday 11 to 2; dinner, Tuesday-Saturday 5 to 10, Sunday to 9.

The Carousel, Common Street at Castonguay Square, Waterville.
(207) 873-4755.
American/Continental. $5.95 to $12.50.

A beautiful antique carousel horse is poised under the canopy covering the front section of this new downtown restaurant. Youngsters in particular head for the carousel-like sitting area edged in mirrors and tiny white lights. There's more restrained seating in the rear or at the sidewalk cafe. The carousel theme is carried out in the special ice cream drinks, served with a small carousel horse as a swizzle stick. The menu continues the amusement theme ("starting gate, the mid-way, main event"), but happily the food is not so cutesy. Dinner entrees range from three versions of scallops and three of chicken to veal oscar and steak alaska. California sole (with avocados and tomatoes, topped with a bearnaise sauce) is a new one on us. Homemade ice cream pie and ice cream puff are the obligatory desserts.

Lunch, Monday-Saturday 11 to 2:30; dinner, Tuesday-Saturday 5 to 9; Sunday brunch, 9 to 2.

Northern Maine

Bethel

* Restaurant Francais at the Four Seasons Inn, 63 Upper Main St., Bethel.
(207) 824-2755.
French. $14.95 to $22.95.

Innkeepers Sandy and Jack Mahon seek to have the best formal French restaurant around and, word has it after their first year, they're approaching their goal. A chef from the Ritz-Carlton Hotel in Florida, a tuxedoed staff and the finest appointments portend a memorable experience. Forty-five patrons can be seated in three dining rooms, dressed in pink linens with comfortable Queen Anne chairs. Look for knowing touches such as blue napkins fanned in a lotus design, delicate pink-stemmed glasses, and no silverware on the table (the appropriate utensils are brought with each course). There's much tableside service, from chateaubriand and rack of lamb for two to Maine apple crepe flambe and bananas foster. The menu is classic French, from onion soup and escargots bourguignonne to beef wellington and bouillabaisse. The plates are works of art: the salmon rolled around fresh spinach and sliced in pinwheel fashion, and crisp vegetables carved into flower shapes. The short but sophisticated wine list is pleasantly priced. Chocolate-covered strawberries come with the bill. Earlybird specials from 4:30 to 6:30 attract the locals.

Dinner nightly, 4:30 to 9. Closed Monday and Tuesday in winter.

$ Mothers, Upper Main Street, Bethel. (207) 824-2589.
American. $8.95 to $14.95.

Owner Susan O'Donnell and a partner started this thriving place in 1977 and named it for themselves — "with seven children between us, we weren't feeling too imaginative at the time," she recalls. Three dining rooms in an old gingerbread house are outfitted as you might expect: walls lined with shelves of old books, mismatched chairs, real table lamps, lace mats, and white paper napkins. There's a spiral staircase in one room, a mannequin in a Scandinavian costume in another. The ash trays are little pails, and it's all rather endearing. A porch and a deck are available in summer. Lunch and supper are served at down-to-earth prices. Even dinner is a steal: charbroiled rainbow trout, chicken cordon bleu, veal marsala, or steak for about $12. There are nine kinds of salad, overstuffed sandwiches and desserts like mother used to make. Bet she didn't make the nachos and potato skins and carrot cake that Mothers does.

Lunch, 11:30 to 2:30; dinner, 5 to 9:30; closed Wednesday in off-season.

The Bethel Inn & Country Club, On the Common, Bethel. (207) 824-2175.
Traditional American. $11.95 to $17.95.

More than 230 people can be seated in two formal dining rooms and a screened terrace in this restaurant that's elegantly comfortable like, well, a country club. Enormous windows look out across the manicured grounds toward the mountains beyond. Barn swallows perch on an old tree just beyond the dining terrace and perform from late afternoon to dusk, often competing with a classical pianist who plays five nights a week. The menu mixes roast duckling with sweet and sour sauce and Yankee pot roast, crabmeat casserole and sole florentine. The prime rib is the best north of Durgin Park, the inn claims. There are few surprises — there can't be, when you may serve 50 or 500 a night, the owner says. Come dessert, look for the lemon ice box cake, for which everyone wants the recipe, or try the brandied orange-nut cake and crunchy peach pie.

Lunch daily, noon to 3; dinner nightly, 6 to 9.

Farmington

Fiddleheads, 23 Pleasant St., Farmington. (207) 778-9259.
International. $7.95 to $12.95.

A stained-glass fiddlehead on the wall greets patrons in this restaurant in an old red grist mill. The airy, square room is softened by tapestries, ladderback chairs and a neat brick fireplace, and a rear screened porch was in the works when we visited. The fare is what chef-owners Lynn and Chet Beard call upscale gourmet. For starters, try baked brie in phyllo or a hearty seven-layer dip consisting of pinto beans, onion, tomatoes, black olives, jack cheese, sour cream and salsa with tortilla chips. Salads are dressed with homemade herbed garlic vinaigrette or creamy yogurt dill. Among main courses, Lynn's specialties include filet mignon chester, veal saltim-bocca, chicken with a grand marnier sauce, and jumbo shrimp and sea scallops sauteed with fresh vegetables and finished with garlic cream. Pastas, five types of stir-fries and four of charbroiled skewers also are available. Sour-cream apple pie and cheesecake with peach glaze are among seasonal desserts, and wedding white chocolate cheesecake won an award. Appetizers and desserts are available in the upstairs lounge.

Dinner, Tuesday-Saturday 5 to 9.

F.L. Butler Restaurant & Lounge, Front Street, Farmington. (207) 778-5223.
American-Italian. $5.95 to $14.95.

This brick and frame structure has a Victorian air, from its bentwood chairs to its etched glass. A bright violet glass window casts a violet light across part of the room. Carved birds are on the window ledges and there's a stone hearth at one end. The lounge is notable for a brick bar and leather chairs fashioned from barrels. A ketchup bottle is on every table, the better to enhance five versions of burgers and the Mexican fiesta salad. We chose not to use it on the cheese and cauliflower pie or pasta primavera, served in a bowl with soft French bread and foil-wrapped butter. Broiled seafood, steaks and Italian dishes — from newburg of the day and shrimp amaretto to lemon chicken, ham steak and baked lasagna — are the fare at dinner. Baked apple pudding, chocolate-walnut pie and parfaits are dessert favorites.

Lunch, Monday-Friday 11 to 2; dinner, Monday-Saturday 5 to 9.

Skowhegan

Old Mill Pub, On the Riverbank off Water Street, Skowhegan. (207) 474-6627.
Steaks/Seafood. $5.95 to $10.95.

An attractive riverside deck and a rustic decor of brick and barnwood, hanging plants and old pictures commends this establishment on three floors. Go past the open bar at the entrance to the rear deck or to the upstairs dining room, but check the blackboard menu first — that's where the culinary action is. The regular menu packs no surprises, except perhaps for a cobb salad and the house specialty, chili. The day's specials might be broccoli-mushroom quiche, french vegetable ragout, tarragon chicken, and parmesan haddock for lunch; lobster scampi, Swiss scallops, Italian stuffed sole, and sirloin steak for dinner. Everything is made on site, and the chef says she's always trying something new — like amaretto cheesecake and tollhouse pie for dessert.

Lunch and dinner, Monday-Saturday 11:30 to 9 or 10, to 11 summer weekends.

Rangeley

Rangeley Inn, Main Street, Rangeley. (207) 864-3341.
American/Continental. $8.95 to $17.

This handsome Victorian structure run by the Carpenter family in downtown Rangeley is known for its food. Daughter Susan oversees the fare served in an elegant, hotel-style dining room dressed in pale pinks and greens with a high tin ceiling and reproduction Chippendale chairs. Lights from the crystal chandeliers and candles reflected in the large windows create an unexpectedly urbane scene at night. The glass of Mondavi house wine turned out to be a small carafe, enough to last through the appetizer of escargots en croute, a zesty plateful laden with garlic, shallots and mushrooms. Good bread and enormous house salads with excellent dijon vinaigrette and celery-seed dressings followed. There was barely room left for the main courses, grilled pork tenderloin with a plum-ginger sauce and peaches, and a sirloin steak said to be marinated with coriander, jalapeno and green chilies but which we found unseasoned. Tangerine chicken, sauteed scallops with sun-dried tomatoes, and lemon-garlic shrimp were other possibilities. We relished the dish of three intense sorbets. Desserts like brandied raspberry mousse cake and praline tulip cups draw people back, as does the Saturday night buffet in ski season.

Dinner nightly, 6 to 8:30. Closed mid-April to mid-May.

The Owl and the Pussycat, Main Street, Rangeley. (207) 864-2093.
American. $7.95 to $12.95.

New in 1989, this casual place offers a long, L-shaped candlelit dining room in green and beige and a rear deck overlooking a park beside the lake. The large menu offers something for everyone, from six kinds of burgers to dinner entrees like New York strip steak, chicken Creole, stir-fries, and Cajun shrimp. Salads and interesting pita pockets are featured at lunchtime. Desserts could be peanut butter-chocolate pie and hazelnut torte.

Lunch and dinner daily, 11:30 to 10.

Kingfield-Sugarloaf Area

✱ One Stanley Avenue, l Stanley Ave., Kingfield. (207) 265-5541.
Maine/Regional American. $13 to $23.

This Queen Anne-style Victorian, listed on the National Register of Historic Places, is a trove of elegant Victoriana. It is the food, however, for which it is deservedly known far and wide. Chef-owner Dan Davis, a native Mainer who is self taught, applies classic techniques to indigenous products and has come up with a true regional cuisine for Maine. Amazingly, he does all of the cooking, with assistance from his teen-aged daughter, serving ambitious fare to upwards of 65 people in two small dining rooms and an enclosed porch all decked out in pink. On one autumn night we dined, entrees included a renowned maple-cider chicken, veal and fiddlehead pie, dilled lobster on zucchini, roast duck with rhubarb glaze, and pork loin with juniper berry and port wine sauce. A remarkable alluvial chicken was served with fiddlehead ferns and two-rice pilaf. Even more memorable was the succulent mound of sweetbreads with applejack and chive cream sauce. A loaf of good whole wheat bread with sweet butter, green salads, coffee, and orange sherbet come with the price of the entree. Raspberry creme celeste and chocolate Maine Guide cake are signature desserts.

Dinner nightly except Monday, 5 to 9. Closed Oct. 20-Dec. 22 and Easter to July 4.

♥ **Hug's,** Route 27, Carrabasset Valley. (207) 237-2392.
Northern Italian. $5.95 to $12.95.
Here's a place with character. The character is provided as much by chef-owner Jack Flannagan as by his rustic, tiny restaurant transformed in 1986 from a sauna. Starting with half a dozen glass-covered tables (since expanded), a tiny kitchen, hearty northern Italian cuisine, and more than a dollop of humor, Jack and his wife of French-Canadian descent, Hug (for Hugette), pack in a coterie of devotees year-round. Jack jokes with patrons between stints in the kitchen where he whips up a dynamite pesto-pizza flat bread, some ethereal pasta dishes, shrimp scampi, chicken limone, and veal scaloppine or francaise. A full salad comes with. As for dessert, Jack says, "if they have room, I'm really upset." Then he offers a chocolate truffle mousse. The cafe atmosphere is cozy, and the place is fun.
Dinner nightly from 5.

The Inn on Winter's Hill, Kingfield. (207) 265-5421.
American. $11.95 to $19.95.
At our last visit, new owners from Newport were pouring pots of money into this landmark inn and restaurant, built by merchant A.G. Winter, whose son Amos began the Sugarloaf development. The interior of the 1898 Georgian Colonial Revival mansion was gutted in the summer of 1989, and fifteen guest rooms were added in a rear barn. Chef Gary Hubert was wooed from the Sugarloaf Inn to oversee the kitchen, three formal dining rooms called Julia's and the new Hilltop Cafe. The atmosphere was planned to be elegant in keeping with the inn's grace and style, but affordable. Meals are served casually weeknights in the cafe and weekends in Julia's. Innkeeper Diane Winnick planned a cafe menu to appeal to local residents, rather than the skiing gourmands who used to frequent the inn. It ranges from sandwiches to sirloin steak for two for $13.95. Entrees in Julia's include shrimp and scallop mornay, poached salmon, baked stuffed pork loin with apple-sage dressing, charbroiled lamb chops, and pheasant with raspberries. Chocolate bread pudding with vanilla ice cream is the signature dessert, but you'll also find warm fruit compotes, seasonal pies and an item called Winter's Hill: a brownie with vanilla ice cream, hot fudge, whipped cream, and walnuts. The inn was planning to serve lunch and Sunday brunch in the summer.
Dinner nightly, 6 to 9.

Arabella's, Sugarloaf Mountain Hotel, Carrabasset Valley. (207) 237-2222.
New American. $11 to $21.
Against a backdrop of green linens, polished wood and rattan chairs, this casually elegant, contemporary restaurant in the hotel at the foot of Sugarloaf Mountain serves an ambitious — some say pretentious — menu. The young CIA-trained chef's range goes from filet of sole with grapes and champagne sauce to seafood fettuccine "aroused" with cilantro and a jalapeno cream sauce. Grilled chicken with field greens and mustard, mahi-mahi with saffron-scallion beurre blanc, and swordfish with green peppercorns and Chinese vegetables are other possibilities. The pastry chef alters the dessert selection daily. The wine list is quite expensive by Maine standards.
Dinner nightly, 6 to 9 or 10.

The Truffle Hound, Village West at Sugarloaf, Carrabassett Valley.
(207) 237-2355.
Continental. $11.50 to $14.50.
Long established in the Sugarloaf village, this is a favorite among skiing gourmands, although purists say it lacks soul. The restaurant, with three rooms done up

in beige and blue and lit by tiny candles at night, is a peaceful respite from the crowds at the nearby base lodge. The traditional menu runs the gamut from marinated pork kabob to petit filet au poivre, from veal piccata to shrimp and scallop saute. Desserts include English trifle, baked Alaska, chocolate-hazelnut cake, and triple chocolate terrine with grand marnier sauce.

Winter, lunch 11:30 to 3, dinner 5:30 to 9:30; summer, dinner Thursday-Sunday 6 to 10.

$ Longfellow's, Main Street, Kingfield. (207) 265-4394.
Italian/American. $4.75 to $10.95.

With no apparent connection to the writer, this is a rustic, casual place with polished wood tables, beamed ceiling, homespun curtains, old glass lamps, and plenty of local color coming and going at the bar. It also has a second dining room upstairs with an outdoor deck overlooking the Carrabasset River. It's something of a find for an inexpensive lunch. We enjoyed a hearty vegetable soup with a tabouli salad and a vegetable quiche with garden salad for a bargain $6.50 for two, plus tip. Another occasion brought a stellar shrimp and basil soup, a bean burrito and again that fine tabouli salad, as well as an odd but tasty hot pasta salad of shells, veggies and tomato sauce. For dinner, the extensive menu is divided into Italian, garden, seafood and "some of our favorites" sections, and you know what that means: spaghetti with meatballs, stir-fry vegetables, seafood scampi, and Cajun chicken, among others, from Mexican to Polynesian. Quite a list of desserts and liqueured coffees concludes both lunch and dinner menus.

Lunch daily, 11 to 5; dinner, 5 to 9 or 9:30.

Eustis

The Porter House Restaurant, Route 27, Eustis. (207) 246-7932.
American. $7.95 to $16.95.

A small white house with a wraparound porch is home for the fine dining offered by Jeff and Beth Hinman, he formerly a chef of note in the Rangeley area, who brought a following with him to this outpost of the north. There's a charming country feeling to the four dining rooms, where nicely spaced tables are graced with white linens, green napkins and white china. A hefty, twemty-ounce porterhouse steak is featured on the menu because of the restaurant's name, but Jeff is partial to offerings like chicken madeira fettuccine, grilled chicken dijon, haddock stuffed with seafood and baked in a cheddar-mushroom sauce, and specials like fresh tuna with balsamic vinaigrette and salmon with a cucumber-caviar sauce. Vegetables are served family style, and the celery seed dressing is a favorite on the house salad. Demi-loaves of oatmeal, whole wheat or anadama breads precede the meal. For dessert, try Beth's homemade ice creams, peach melba or maple-walnut cheesecake.

Dinner nightly, 5:30 to 9.

Bangor

Pilots Grill, 1528 Hammond St. (Route 2), Bangor. (207) 942-6325.
Steaks/Seafood. $9.95 to $13.50.

A low-slung building that just grew and grew houses what many consider the area's best restaurant. It was born 50 years ago in a small place next to the airport; runway expansion forced the structure's move to its present site, and additions on all sides attest to its popularity. Owner Bill Zoidis proudly shows the original Knotty Pine Room, dark and intimate with interesting lighting on the ceiling and outlining the original windows. Combined with the brighter Skyview and Camelot rooms, the place seats 250. The oversize menu runs the gamut from fried clams to lobster saute, from broiled scallops en casserole to baked stuffed shrimp on toast. Twin lamb chops are the priciest item on the menu; pork chops with apple sauce, broiled hamburg steak with mushroom sauce and grilled ham steak with pineapple ring are the lowest. Food like that was served 50 years ago, and the Zoidises have found no reason to change.

Open daily, 11:30 to 10.

Seguino's Italian Restaurant, 735 Main St., Bangor. (207) 942-1240.

Italian. $9.95 to $15.95.

Colorful flowers surround the white house marked by red awnings in a commercial strip south of downtown. Inside, chef-owner Stefano Antonio Seguino oversees an equally colorful ramble of rooms notable for vivid wallpapers, white over red linens, walnut tables, and cane chairs. The Venetian Sun Room is the largest and most airy; there's also a covered outdoor patio. The enormous menu (no fewer than eleven veal dishes, from piccata to saltimbocca) reflects the family's Neapolitan origins. Seafood is their forte, generally served on a bed of pasta, but regulars say you can't go wrong with anything from lasagna, manicotti and gnocchi to chicken cacciatore. Desserts include cannoli, espresso cheesecake and profiteroles.

Open Monday-Friday 11 to 10, Saturday and Sunday 4:30 to 10.

The Greenhouse, 193 Broad St., Bangor. (207) 945-4040.

American/Continental. $9.95 to $16.95.

More than 400 plants help this large establishment under the Bangor-Brewer bridge live up to its name. The Living Room Lounge has attractive sofas and upholstered chairs, the main dining room is in pink and green, and a large outdoor deck with glass tables overlooks the Penobscot River. Locals think the food has slipped a bit since it was taken over by new owners. The chef mixes traditional American with classic French fare on the formal, oversize menu. Among the choices are delicacies not often seen hereabouts, like frog's legs, charbroiled quail and steak tartare as appetizers. Veal marsala, steak diane, prime rib, chicken frangelico, grilled duck New Orleans, and local seafood dishes are among the main courses. Fresh strawberry pie and grand marnier cake may be available on the dessert cart.

Lunch, Tuesday-Friday 11 to 2; dinner, Tuesday-Saturday 5 to 10.

Gourmet to Go, 25 Central St., Bangor. (207) 942-4642.

Deli/Take-out. $3.95 to $7.50.

If you despair of finding a nice little place where you can get a good lunch in the Bangor area, try this fine food shop, marked in season by four small tables on the sidewalk in front. You might hit a cold cream of blueberry soup, a veggie and havarti quiche, a sandwich called the Dowser (Maine crabmeat and cucumber on whole grain bread with a creamy dill dressing) or the Pioneer, smoked turkey with cranberry relish, mayo and sprouts on anadama bread. If you're on the run, Gourmet to Go will pack a picnic of maybe lemon fried chicken and potato salad or shrimp, scallops and veggies with rotini pasta in a fresh basil dressing. Or how about a pate, cheese and fruit tray? Why not end with a margarita mud pie, lemon cheesecake with gingersnap crust or a chocolate-macadamia brownie? Or maybe you'll just settle for a cup of decaffeinated raspberry tea.

Open Monday-Friday 10 to 6, Friday to 7, Saturday to 3, Sunday 11 to 3.

Lucerne

The Lucerne Inn, Route 1A, Lucerne. (207) 843-5123.

Continental. $10.95 to $18.95.

Commanding a hillside location high up over Phillips Lake out in the middle of nowhere, this country mansion is a welcoming and imposing retreat on the road from Bangor to Bar Harbor. The setting above a lake surrounded by mountains reminds some of Lucerne, Switzerland — hence the name. Established in 1814, it has a newer feel to it, at least from its stark white exterior all lit up at night. But the main dining room and two dining porches with windows onto the view are properly rustic, even with their art posters and red tablecloths at night. The continental menu, heavy on beef and veal, lists more than two dozen items, including Maine lobster. Among the favorites are beef wellington, rack of New Zealand lamb, veal oscar, and shrimp stuffed with provolone cheese, wrapped with prosciutto ham and baked in garlic butter. The all-you-can-eat Sunday brunch brings the usual plus such extras as chicken cordon bleu, kugel and strawberry crepes. The house band plays music for dancing, oldies but goodies, every Saturday night.

Lunch in summer, Monday-Friday 11:30 to 2:30; dinner nightly, 5 to 9 or 10; Sunday, brunch 11 to 2:30, dinner 5 to 8.

Dover-Foxcroft

The Dover House, 15 East Main St., Dover-Foxcroft. (207) 564-3248.
French. $10.25 to $14.95.

The renowned Thistles on Monument Square, whose reputation far transcended its remote location, closed in 1988 and reopened a year later with a new name and in new quarters up the street. Ex-New Yorker Leslie Thistle seeks to emulate the kind of classic restaurant she found on her European travels. An imposing old home with high ceilings, antique furnishings and an elegant white and green decor is the showcase for Leslie's culinary talents. Her changing entrees could be pecan-breaded chicken, medallions of salmon with shrimp and hollandaise sauce, pork medallions with amaretto-apricot sauce, tournedos, North Carolina quail, and local rabbit. Desserts include chocolate mousse, delice au chocolate and chocolate-walnut torte. A broader menu from quiche to quesadillas is offered at lunchtime.

Lunch, Tuesday-Saturday 11 to 2; dinner, 5 to 9.

Down East Maine

Castine

★ The Pentagoet Inn, Main Street, Castine. (207) 326-8616.
Regional American. $25, prix-fixe.

All is calm and sophisticated in Virginia and Lindsey Miller's refurbished and expanded dining room. Five-course dinners with a choice of three entrees are served nightly at 7 after a communal cocktail hour with hors d'oeuvres. Well-spaced tables are draped in white linens, each formal place setting containing pretty blue and white Staffordshire Finlandia china, two wine glasses and a crystal water glass. Occasionally there is live harp and flute background music. The chefs have a large new kitchen in which to prepare their changing fare. A typical menu might begin with Cajun-style blackened chicken breast and vegetable-barley soup. Main courses could be a choice of lobster with a dilled hollandaise, scaloppine of veal in a port wine sauce and chargrilled salmon steak with scallion butter. A salad of fresh greens with a dijon vinaigrette follows. Grand marnier-chocolate cake could be the dessert. Lobster is always one of the entrees; others could be grilled halibut steak hollandaise, veal saute with fresh basil, garlic and tomato concasse, and filet mignon bearnaise. The Millers are sticklers for detail, and everything about the leisurely meal is considered as perfect as the rest of their inn.

Dinner by reservation, nightly at 7.

The Castine Inn, Main Street, Castine. (207) 326-4365.
Regional American. $12 to $18.
Striking new murals of the Castine landscape as it surrounds you grace this inn's lovely dining room (even the posts are part of the scene). Innkeeper Margaret Hodesh, an artist and author of note, completed her masterpiece in less than two months in 1989. With aqua woodwork and a view of the water beyond a side porch furnished in teal wicker and wrought-iron, the setting is summery and nautical in a gentle, Castine kind of way. It's the perfect foil for the cooking of Mark Hodesh, whose menu changes daily. There's usually a choice of six entrees. Steamed lobster and chicken and leek pot pie are standbys; roasted duck with wild rice griddle cakes and apple chutney, broiled salmon with asparagus and egg sauce, fettuccine with sea scallops and basil, and roasted loin of pork with black beans and barbecue sauce come and go. Among starters are smoked trout with cucumber salad, crabmeat cake with mustard sauce, and warm pasta salad with lamb, tomatoes and Vermont cheddar. Biscuits, a mixed salad with sherry vinaigrette, and vegetables accompany the entrees. Dessert options could be rhubarb crisp with vanilla custard sauce, chocolate souffle cake, and nectarine and blueberry shortcake, and all are worth the indulgence.
Dinner nightly except Tuesday, 5:30 to 8:30. Closed Columbus Day to Memorial Day.

Dennett's Wharf, Sea Street, Castine. (207) 326-9045.
Seafood. $9.95 to $15.95.
This bustling, casual oyster bar and seafood restaurant right on the water below Sea Street has gone a bit upscale since Gary Brouillard acquired the old sail and rigging loft from his brother, Paul. Beneath the vaulted ceiling, a banner over what's billed as the world's longest oyster bar proclaims the annual Maine State Oyster Eating Championship in August. A shoulder-high partition divides the bar from the restaurant, its tables inlaid with nautical charts and many claiming views of the water (the rear deck with its umbrellaed tables is even better). Fish chowder or mussels steamed in wine and garlic make good lunches. The dinner menu is a melange: deviled lobster, fried clams, seafood lasagna in a white lobster sauce, broiled scallops parmesan, and chicken teriyaki. Chocolate-peanut butter pie and hazelnut torte were desserts at our visit. New since 1989 is a side deck where, daily between 11 and 5, you can pick your own lobster for steaming and feast on a limited menu of steamed mussels, clams and corn on the cob.
Lunch daily, 11:30 to 3:30; dinner, 5 to 10. Open April-October.

The Manor, Battle Avenue, Castine. (207) 236-4861.
Regional American. $12 to $17.50.
Now assisted by a chef, energetic and peripatetic Paul Brouillard (former owner of Dennetts Wharf, prospective owner of more local inns) cooks up a storm here at his original restaurant. Trained in France, he has a range as wide as his interests, and when he's in the kitchen (which is too rare these days), the results are dynamite: creamy mussel and garlic soup or crab cakes with a mustard sauce for appetizers; duck breast armagnac, roast pheasant with champagne and truffles, or Atlantic salmon with a sauce of fume, sorrel and creme fraiche for entrees. The Manor's latest menus seemed more mundane and the food reports mixed. The two small dining rooms are pretty at night in white and peach. End your meal with cordials at the elegant bar, surrounded by a multitude of carved birds.
Dinner, Tuesday-Saturday 6 to 8:30.

Deer Isle

★♥ Pilgrim's Inn, Deer Isle. (207) 348-6615.
American. Prix-fixe $25.

Inn guests as well as lucky outsiders feast on the island's best meals at the historic Pilgrim's Inn. Following cocktails and appetizers at 6 in the common room or on the deck beside the enormous new barbecue, a single-entree, prix-fixe dinner is served at 7 in the former goat barn. Here you're surrounded by candlelight, fresh flowers, farm utensils and quilts on the walls, mismatched chairs, and ten outside doors that open to let in the breeze. Innkeepers Jean and Dud Hendrick host the evening very personally, giving free reign in the kitchen to new chef Cameron Forbes, who was first in her class at the French Culinary Institute and who's "an unbelievably good cook," according to Jean, herself no slouch in the kitchen. Each meal starts with soup and is followed by salad with a special topping, perhaps shrimp, goat cheese, slivers of roast duck, or fritters. Entrees depend on the night: Tuesday, fresh seafood; Wednesday, poultry; Thursday, lobster (for house guests only); Friday, salmon; Saturday, rack of lamb, and Sunday, beef or free-range veal. All are done with inspiration and light, masterful sauces. Among desserts are homemade ice creams and sorbets and fresh fruit tarts. Never will we forget our dinner of salad with goat cheese, homemade peasant bread, a heavenly paella topped with nasturtiums, and a sensational raspberry-chocolate pie on a shortbread crust. The inn varies its menu annually and according to whim, but whatever is served, you can expect it to be a treat.

Dinner by reservation, nightly except Thursday at 7. Open mid-May to mid-October.

$ The Fishermen's Friend, School Street, Stonington. (207) 367-2442.
Seafood. $6.50 to 10.95.

The outside is unprepossessing and the interior decor is zilch: a front room with booths and tables, a smaller back room with windows onto a field, and tables covered with oilcloth, paper mats and fake flowers. Down-to-earth food is featured at the lowest prices around. For lunch, two of us had a good clam chowder and a shrimp stew, plus a superior crabmeat roll laden with meat and the best fried clams ever for a mere $14.50. At dinner, after an appetizer of Port Clyde sardines served on lettuce with saltines, try broiled Atlantic salmon, a seafood platter, ham steak with pineapple, or roast beef. They come with a salad bar and "real mashed potatoes" or french fries.

Open daily, 11 to 9. BYOB. No credit cards.

Bayview Restaurant, Sea Breeze Avenue, Stonington. (207) 367-2274.
Seafood. $5.95 to $11.95.

There's not much in the way of decor — pressed-tin ceiling and walls, linoleum floor and mismatched Scandinavian cutlery, blue mats and an arrangement of wildflowers at each table — and despite the name, there's not much of a view. But at night, the mats give way to tablecloths and candlelight, and the food is fresh and reasonably priced. We like Nellie's sauteed lobster meat served on toast points ("a la Nova Scotia, from an old family recipe," according to the makeshift menu). You can get almost any of the local fish fried, broiled or baked.

Breakfast from 6, lunch 11 to 3, dinner 5 to 9 or later. BYOB.

♥ Firepond, Main Street, Blue Hill. (207) 374-2135.
New American. $12 to $18.75.

A more enchanting setting than the dining porch beside the stream at Firepond is hard to imagine. Its garden-type glass tables are lit by candles and topped by woven mats, water ripples below and spotlights illuminate the gleaming rocks. It's almost magical, and more appealing than the inner dining room. The food of is often magical as well, and promises to continue, even with a sudden change in ownership that had the entire area buzzing in late 1989. New owners Lisa and Rod Hotham, Bangor business types who had frequented the place for years, pledged to continue it just as it had been and hired as chef John White, who had been sous chef and done most of the cooking the two previous years. They even were considering keeping it open year-round. If the past is an indication, start with the selection of pates, or a souffle made with local sea urchins. Continue with a sensational chicken with creme fraiche and mustard, a fabulous dish of veal sweetbreads with oysters in a lime-- butter sauce, or medallions of lamb with wild mushrooms. The roast duckling with mangoes and ginger and the tournedos with roquefort and lingonberries are fixtures on the menu. Desserts are few but select, among them a silken praline cheesecake, grand marnier-chocolate mousse, fresh fruit tarts, and mango or ginger ice cream. Some of the excellent wines are organic, and their prices are so reasonable you think they're a mistake.

Dinner nightly, 5 to 9:30, Memorial Day through December.

✱ Jonathan's, Main Street, Blue Hill. (207) 374-5226.
   Mediterranean/New American. $11.50 to $16.50.
   The front room is somewhat close and intimate, but a large rear addition with rough wood walls, bar, bow windows and pitched ceiling is airy and open, a fine place for an assertive summer meal. Our latest visit produced an appetizer of roasted elephant garlic with local chevre, served with ripe tomatoes and grilled French bread, and a remarkable smoked mussel salad with goat cheese and pine nuts. We also enjoyed a special of scallops sauteed with mint and tomatoes, and Jonathan's signature dish, shrimp flamed in ouzo and served with feta on linguini. A tasty Greek lemon soup and a fish provencale soup with cumin came with dinner. Chocolate- cointreau mousse and frangelico cheesecake are super endings, as is the white chocolate mousse with big fresh raspberries. The reasonably priced wine list is exceptional, and chef-owner Jonathan Chase is known for hosting special wine-tasting dinners in conjunction with Bartlett Winery of Gouldsboro.
   Lunch, Monday-Friday 11 to 2:30; dinner nightly, 5 to 9:30.

✱ Blue Hill Inn, Union Street (Route 177), Blue Hill. (207) 374-2844.
   New French. Prix-fixe, $25.
   This small, venerable inn has been drawing culinary acclaim lately, thanks to the arrival of chef Jim Rondinelli, who aspires to the French cooking style of Jacques Maximin, with whom he studied. Guests gather on the lawn or in the inn's living room for cocktails and hors d'oeuvres, a plateful of assorted fruits and cheeses when we were there. Then they adjourn to the rear dining room for a six-course dinner, the menu for which is written daily. One night's meal started with a mild lobster bisque glazed with cognac cream and green pepperorn-cured salmon with peach coulis. Kiwi sorbet cleared the palate for the main course, a choice of beef tenderloin with grain mustard or salmon filet persille. Garden greens with champagne vinaigrette followed. Dessert was an espresso-cognac mousse. Other entrees could be North Atlantic tuna with smoked bacon and local beans, and a tian of sea scallops in the style of Jacques Maximin.
   Dinner nightly in season at 7; weekends and holidays, mid-October through May. Reservations required by noon.

368

Ellsworth

✱ The Carrying Place Restaurant, 64 Pine St., Ellsworth. (207) 667-6127.
Regional American. $14.95 to $16.95.

A tan clapboard house on a side street just off Route 1 provides an elegant, comfortable setting for stylish regional food applauded by locals with adventuresome palates. Chef-owner Mardie Junkins painted the colorful oak leaves on the ceiling of one dining room and the maple leaves in another. Different-colored mats atop blond tables, dhurrie rugs on the floors, deep rose walls, and Mardie's fine paintings create an attractive decor (check out the monkey painted on the wall of the ladies' room). Most entrees are named for Maine places, which suggests a regional theme in cooking as well as in buying. They run the gamut from Pemaquid scallops sauteed with sherry and fennel to Katahdin game hen roasted with mushrooms and walnuts and served with a claret sauce. Burnt Coat veal is sauteed with garlic and mushrooms in marsala sauce; Penobscot pork, braised with a mustard-sherry sauce and apples. Mardie serves flounder three ways (one with lobster and another with crabmeat and creamy pesto sauce), and her Acadia beef wellington is a masterpiece. The best appetizer is the Carrying Place special, often oysters baked with bacon. Lobster comes steamed or chimney-smoked with seasoned breadcrumbs. Among desserts are trifles, butterscotch puff and key lime pie.

Dinner nightly except Monday, 5 to 10; Sunday brunch.

Trenton

Oak Point Lobster Pound Restaurant, Route 230, Trenton. (207) 667-8548.
Seafood. $6.95 to $15.95.

Off the beaten path, this lobster pound-turned-restaurant boasts a spectacular view of the mountains of Mount Desert Island from across Western Bay. Some think it has the best lobster in Maine. The shore dinner includes a 1 1/4-pounder surrounded by steamers and mussels, served with chowder, french fries, coleslaw, and hot rolls. You also can get broiled sole and scallops, baked stuffed shrimp, fried seafood and, for landlubbers, sirloin steak and chicken teriyaki. The stews and chowders are renowned, as are the blueberry pie and flaming cherries jubilee. There's seating inside and out, buoys hang from the ceiling, and red geraniums are all around. This is quite a cut above an ordinary lobster pound, with a full liquor license and a good wine list.

Dinner nightly in season, 4:30 to 9.

Mount Desert Island/Bar Harbor

✦♥ George's, 7 Stevens Lane, Bar Harbor. (207) 288-4505.
Greek/American. $10.95 to $18.50.

This summery restaurant run by a school teacher in a small Southern-style house behind the First National Bank has gone considerably upscale — make that glamorous — with redecoration and a sleek addition with a grand piano smack in the middle. It offers what is generally considered the best and most creative food on Mount Desert Island. White organdy curtains flutter in the breeze in several small dining rooms, a wild rose on the table matches the walls, Greek music plays on tape, and everything is served on clear glass plates atop pink-linened tables. Hot, crusty French bread and the best little Greek salads ever precede such favorites as seafood strudel, mustard shrimp and cioppino, and specials like smoked scallops on fettuccine or shrimp on a fresh tomato sauce with feta cheese, rice pilaf and New Zealand spinach with orange juice and orange zest. Duck breast with sauteed honey-rum mango and lamb tenderloin with mint pesto and raspberry ketchup were great on our latest visit. The appetizers are assertive — seafood sausage with lobster sauce, fresh crabmeat with aioli, and the assortment of smoked bluefish, marinated mushrooms, scallops ceviche, and garlicky tarama. A glass of retsina wine, with its faint taste of turpentine, was the perfect foil for the latter. Desserts are first-rate, from marjolaine and tirami su to a delicious homemade blackberry ice cream and an irresistible fresh blueberry and peach meringue.

Dinner nightly in summer, 5:30 to 10; lighter dishes until midnight. Open late June to mid-October. Reservations essential.

✴ The Porcupine Grill, 123 Cottage St., Bar Harbor. (207) 288-3884
Regional American. $12.50 to $17.95.

There's nothing pretentious about this new grill, even though the owners concede it may look it. Terry Marinke and her husband had an antiques business here, which provided the furnishings and impetus for the restaurant, whose name comes from the nearby Porcupine Islands. "Everything is real," she says, showing the assorted antique oak drop-leaf tables and Chippendale chairs, the rugs on the honey-colored wood floors, and the Villeroy & Boch china. Different fresh flowers are scattered about the dining rooms on two floors, and it's all very stylish. Antique bulls-eye glass dividers and period sconces help create a cafe atmosphere in the main-floor bar area, where many regulars prefer to sip champagne cocktails pairing French sparkling and Maine raspberry wines or Porcupine punch (rum and fruit juices) before snacking on crab cakes, homemade chicken and veal sausage, grilled vegetables with salad greens and roasted garlic mayonnaise, and a smashing caesar salad topped with garlic-fried clams. With appetizers like these, the main courses could be anti-climactic. But they aren't: grilled swordfish with pineapple salsa, grilled lamb with a cabernet sauce and onion marmalade, porterhouse steak smothered with caramelized vidalia onions and homemade french fries, and scallops with sweet bell peppers and leeks on homemade spinach pasta. Like everything else, the desserts are made here: white chocolate cheesecake with blueberry sauce, peach-pecan ice cream with cinnamon-bourbon sauce, a triple layer chocolate fudge cake. "Good old American cuisine — no surprises," says Terry. Who does she think she's kidding?

Dinner nightly from 5:30, May-October.

✴ La Cadie, 137 Cottage St., Bar Harbor. (207) 288-9668.
American. $11.95 to $16.95.

The changing site of some of Bar Harbor's most interesting small restaurants (once Betty Jean's, then Poor Boy's Gourmet) became La Cadie in 1987. Kathleen Mulligan, a local caterer, offers in her pine-paneled room five booths and six pine tables with woven mats, illuminated by tiny oil lamps and some too bright overhead lights. Homemade carrot bread and parmesan cheese rolls tide you over until the arrival of starters like cream of carrot and cashew soup, baked mushrooms stuffed with crabmeat and mussels diablo. The "scampi in love," sauteed with garlic butter, wine, cashews and snow peas, is worth falling for. So is seafood boursin, scallops and shrimp tossed with plenty of garlic and madeira on angel-hair pasta with a rich boursin sauce. The charbroiled Cajun lobster inspires raves. The accompanying zucchini with wine butter and tarragon was so good we asked for the recipe. Try the grand marnier-custard fruit tart or cappuccino cheesecake for dessert.

Dinner nightly, 5 to 10. Open May-October.

Hampton Court, 102 Eden St., Bar Harbor. (207) 288-5029.
American/Continental. $14.95 to $19.95.

The old Garden of Eden, an English-looking garden cottage of a restaurant along the road into Bar Harbor, gave way in 1987 to Hampton Court under the auspices of Bangor restaurateur Bill Murphy. Tall flowers and vines, gingerbread trim and small-paned, leaded windows make it look like an enchanted cottage out of the Cotswolds. A couple of small dining rooms and the main-floor bar are pleasant, but most choice is the upstairs Garden Room, almost like one in a miniature dollhouse, illuminated mainly by candles. The oversize French menu carries English translations. Appetizers seemed mundane and expensive for the area, so we made do with good hot monkey bread and a green salad dressed in mustard vinaigrette with baked goat cheese on a crouton. The sauteed breast of duck came with fettuccine and onion marmalade; the scallops in puff pastry with a rich lobster sauce and asparagus, new potatoes and carrot puree. The sign out front advertised lamb, but didn't mention the sky-high price ($25). Among other possibilities are four variations of lobster including thermidor, poached salmon with three sauces, and roast chicken with chestnut and pear sauce. A good dessert is the Hampton Court sorbet: champagne sorbet in a brittle chocolate cup atop a raspberry coulis.

Dinner nightly, 5:30 to 10:30. Open May to mid-November.

124 Cottage Street, 124 Cottage St., Bar Harbor. (207) 288-4383.
Seafood/American. $10.95 to $17.95.

Its crowded scene and "gourmet" salad bar — with 40, 50, 60 items (from nuts to gum drops), depending on the year — tend to turn us off, but everyone in town loves this place. The enclosed front porch, the rear courtyard and several cozy dining rooms inside the converted house are usually jammed. The eight-page menu is described as artful and with-it. An acclaimed clam chowder is among starters. Seafood dishes include lobster, the house specialty shrimp scampi, Szechuan shrimp, seafood marinara, scallop scampi, a fried platter, and stuffed haddock. There are stuffed potato skins, charbroiled steaks and Bombay chicken for those who prefer. Homemade desserts include oreo ice cream pie, blueberry pie with French vanilla ice cream, and "wall to wall chips," a cookie crust filled with chocolate-chip ice cream and smothered with hot fudge.

Dinner nightly, 5 to 11.

The Fin Back, 78 West St., Bar Harbor. (207) 288-4193.
Regional American. $9.95 to $15.95.

Skylights and track lighting illuminate this small and intimate newcomer with pink napkins standing tall like tulips in the wine glasses. Pink and white material billowing along the peak of the ceiling creates a beachy effect. Chef-owner Terry Preble claims his is Bar Harbor's only "full scenic restaurant with a smoke-free environment." It's a healthful setting for some inspired cooking. Among entrees are lobster and asparagus coquille, charbroiled scallops with cilantro-lime butter, duck breast with blueberry sauce, chicken stuffed with cilantro pesto and goat cheese, lamb grilled with port wine, and pork tenderloin stuffed with chorizo sausage. Cilantro quesadilla, shrimp ravioli, seafood sausage, and a concoction of goat cheese encased in a mixture of sun-dried tomatoes and basil, baked and served with French bread, are tempting starters. So is the crabmeat bisque with curry and apples. Cheesecake is the signature dessert.

Dinner nightly, 5 to 10; weekend brunch, 10 to 2. Seasonal. No smoking.

Down East Maine

♥ **Jordan Pond House,** Park Loop Road, Acadia National Park. (207) 276-3316.
American. $9.50 to $19.50.

After the old Jordan Pond House with its birch-bark dining rooms burned to the ground in 1979, this well-known restaurant was rebuilt in strikingly modern style, its ceilings high and its windows huge. The incomparable setting remains the same, however, with green lawns sloping down to Jordan Pond and the Bubbles mountains in the background. The dinner menu is fairly standard, with lots of lobster dishes, steak, chicken, and fish of the day, accompanied by a relish tray, popovers (a house specialty) and vegetables. We prefer lunch on the "porch," which is more like a covered terrace, where we enjoyed a fine seafood pasta and a curried chicken salad. If you can't dine here, come at least for afternoon tea on the lawn (two popovers with butter and strawberry preserves and tea), a Bar Harbor tradition.

Lunch, 11:30 to 2:30; tea, 2:30 to 5:30; dinner, 5:30 to 9. Open mid-June to mid-October.

Mount Desert Island/The Other Harbors

Asticou Inn, Northeast Harbor. (207) 276-3344.
American. Prix-fixe $25.

Come here for the lavish Thursday night buffet dinners that draw up to 300 people in peak season to this posh dining room of the old resort school. The pillared room is decorated with handpainted murals of trees and flowers on the deep yellow walls, a brass chandelier, oriental rugs, lovely flowered china, and tiny plants in clay pots. Most coveted — and hard to get — seating is in the adjacent enclosed porch, with wondrous views onto the harbor beyond. The mimeographed menu for the prix-fixe dinner changes daily. Typically there are three entrees, from broiled scallops, baked stuffed shrimp and boiled lobster to prime rib and broiled lamb chops. Meals begin with assorted relishes, breads and perhaps fish chowder, shrimp cocktail or lobster and shrimp in phyllo, and include a salad. Desserts could be frozen chocolate mousse or key lime pie.

Lunch, 12:30 to 2; dinner, 7 to 8:30; jackets required. Open mid-June to mid-September.

The Claremont, Clark Point Road, Southwest Harbor. (207) 244-5036.
American. $13 to $15.

Views on three sides down the lawns to Somes Sound, consistently good food and excellent service make the dining room in this century-old hostelry immensely popular with summer residents. Come early for drinks at the **Boathouse** (which also serves sandwiches and salads for lunch) and then head into the high-ceilinged dining room, elegant in pink and green. The appetizer du jour is often the best choice on the limited menu. Native crabmeat baked in a ramekin with artichoke hearts, sherry sauce and gruyere cheese is a specialty. Other entrees range from shrimp and sole baked in parchment to veal rib chop and rack of lamb. The produce comes from the inn's gardens and the baked goods from its bakery. The homemade desserts include cheesecake and lemon ice with Claremont cookies.

Lunch at the Boathouse, noon to 2, mid-July through August. Dinner, 6 to 9, late June through Labor Day; jackets required.

Clark Point Cafe, Clark Point Road, Southwest Harbor. (207) 244-5816.
American/Continental. $10.95 to $15.95.

Right up against the street in "downtown" Southwest Harbor, this storefront cafe fills a niche between the formality of more elegant eateries and the rustic seafood houses all around. The menu ranges widely: entrees like pasta of the day, seafood stew, poached Norwegian salmon, Granny Smith chicken, veal francaise, and lobster thermidor, plus nightly specials. The last include chef-owner Vance

O'Donnell's inspirations like roast duckling with Jack Daniels mint julep glaze and red currant and apple chutney, seafood strudel with thermidor sauce, and bluefish with basil, tomatoes, garlic, wine, and feta cheese. A section of the menu called lighter fare includes baked haddock and shrimp and lobster salad.

Dinner nightly from 5

Drydock Cafe, 108 Main St., Southwest Harbor. (207) 244-3886.
International. $8.95 to $16.95.
The Drydock has upgraded its decor and prices since it opened a few years back. For lunch try one of the burgers served on English muffins. The fajitas here are delicious; choose between grilled steak or chicken served with all manner of toppings. Dinnertime brings an extensive mix from mushrooms stuffed with crab-meat and fettuccine alfredo to a broiled seafood platter, chicken boursin, blackened scallops, and steak au poivre. The dessert tray might bear Kentucky Derby pie, cheesecakes, mousses, and truffles.

Lunch, 11:30 to 3:30; dinner, 5 to 10. Open May to October.

$ Seafood Ketch, On the Harbor, Bass Harbor. (207) 244-7463.
Seafood. $8.95 to $12.95.
If you didn't know, you probably wouldn't stop at this rustic shanty, but it happens to be many people's favorite restaurant on this side of Mount Desert Island. It's the real thing — a delightful, Down East place run by Ed and Eileen Branch with lots of fresh seafood and everything homemade, to the last loaf of crusty French bread served on a board with pats of butter. Dining is by candlelight with white linens at tables in the rear room beside the water, each decorated with a bottle of wine. Speedy service produces garden salads with homemade blue cheese or creamy Italian dressings and entrees like baked lobster-seafood casserole and the night's special, stir-fried halibut on rice. A fresh raspberry pie with ice cream is a superb ending. Among regular desserts are Ed's secret mocha pie and, according to the menu, "the world's best carrot cake" — Ed says so," and he does all the baking. An outdoor deck is popular before the bugs set in at twilight.

Open daily from 7 a.m. to 9:30 p.m., May to November.

Hancock

Le Domaine, Route 1, Hancock. (207) 422-3395.
French. $16 to $18.25.
A red frame building hidden behind huge evergreens, this wonderful place that looks as if it's straight out of provincial France purveys classic French cuisine and fine wines. Founded in 1945 by a Frenchwoman, Marianne Purslow-Dumas, Le Domaine is run now with equal competence by her daughter, Nicole Purslow, a graduate of the Cordon Bleu School and an advocate of country French haute cuisine. Beyond a delightful wicker sitting area where French magazines are piled upon tables is the long, narrow, L-shaped dining room, dominated at the far end by a huge stone fireplace framed by copper cooking utensils. The menu changes frequently and takes advantage of local produce, including herbs that grow by the kitchen door. The half dozen entrees could include veal with wild mushrooms and cream, sirloin grilled with tarragon butter, and fresh vegetables wrapped with grey sole, but we'll return any time for the marvelous sweetbreads in lemon and caper sauce, grilled salmon with fennel, and a house specialty, rabbit with prunes. The French bread is toasted in chunks and the garlic bread is really garlicky. A salad of impeccable greens, including baby spinach, might be tossed with goat cheese and walnuts. The cheesecake on raspberry sauce is ethereal, as is the frozen coffee

mousse. The experience is best enjoyed if you're staying overnight in one of the seven adorable guest rooms upstairs.

Dinner nightly, 6 to 9 (closed to public on Sunday). Open May-October.

Crocker House Country Inn, Hancock Point. (207) 422-6806.
American/Continental. $12 to $16.

"A little out of the way but way out of the ordinary" is how this restaurant advertises itself. It's located across Frenchman Bay from Mount Desert Island. Beyond an unprepossessing exterior is a Victorian parlor notable for its paintings and a rear dining room, which has leaded glass windows overlooking a forest of green. Chef-owner Richard Malaby likes to experiment with creative dishes. The blackboard menu might list "untitled chicken" (stuffed with caraway cream cheese and wrapped with bacon), poached salmon florentine and filet au poivre. Mocha mousse, chocolate-walnut pie and strawberry-rhubarb pie are some of the desserts.

Dinner, nightly 5:30 to 9 in summer. Closed Tuesdays in May and after Columbus Day, Monday-Wednesday in November.

♥ Tidal Falls Lobster Pound, Hancock. (207) 422-6818.
Seafood. $3 to $7.

What an idyllic setting for a lobster pound, on a grassy lawn with well-spaced picnic tables beneath shade trees right beside a tidal river's saltwater rapids. Unlike most lobster pounds, there's plenty of room for privacy and a big plastic bucket fastened to the end of each table keeps the place pristine. There's an enclosed pavilion for inclement weather. You order a la carte, anything from coleslaw to lobster. We savored a midday repast of mussels with garlic butter and a good, overflowing crab roll with a bottle of the elegant pear wine from nearby Bartlett Winery.

Open daily in season, 11 to 8.

Machias

Five Water Street, 5 Water St., Machias. (207) 255-4153.
Regional American. $9.95 to $18.

It's billed as serving nouvelle cuisine, and the address raised our hopes for a light and airy place with an ocean view. Not so. The rustic facade of an old building across the street from the Machias River backs into a a dark — some would say dingy — interior that conveys a barroom feeling, at least on the crowded late afternoon we stopped by. Dinner offerings include oriental shrimp, veal scaloppine, seafood spaghetti, salmon steak, and chicken curry. The seafood is particularly good here.

Open daily, 11 to 9, Sunday 5 to 9.

Lubec

Hillside Restaurant, Route 189, West Lubec. (207) 733-4323.
Seafood. $5.95 to $8.95.

This place started in 1979 as a takeout stand and added a dining room with a counter in 1986. It's so casual that we sat at the counter, along with three local geezers who came in for ice cream sundaes, and had a Saturday night dinner of an excellent seafood chowder, a lobster roll, and a plate of fried clams with french fries and coleslaw. It's so Down East and so utterly unpretentious that we didn't even mind the purple bug zapper or the lack of beer or wine (Lubec is a dry town). You can get a hot dog or baked haddock with lobster sauce. The fresh fruit pies are said to be great, and we found the strawberry shortcake simply yummy.

Open daily except Tuesday, 11 to 9.

Dennysville

* Lincoln House Country Inn, Dennysville. (207) 726-3953.
American. Prix-fixe, $17.50.

The pub is where the locals go, but the finest meals between Machias and Eastport are served in the 30-seat dining room of this out-of-the-way inn built two centuries ago. People drive for miles, and no wonder. An aura of history is conveyed by the prim white room with tan trim and wainscoting, narrow-board floors, a few prints and wreaths on the walls, and tables set with green cloths, floral napkins and pewter cutlery. Innkeeper Mary Carol Haggerty's menu is thoroughly up to date. She serves a full-course, prix-fixe meal, the single entree changing nightly — perhaps shrimp provencale, lobster, veal amelio, roast loin of beef with bearnaise sauce, or chicken "every way — piccata, diana, apricot glaze, or the chef's way." Soup, salad, vegetables, and homemade breads accompany. A special dessert is fresh blueberry pie, but the repertoire includes upside-down date cake, rhubarb-custard pie and strawberry pie. "I do whatever I feel like that's in season," Mary Carol says of her desserts, and the same goes as well for the rest of the meal.

Dinner by reservation, nightly at 7.

Eastport

The Cannery, North Water Street, Eastport. (207) 853-4800.
American. $8.50 to $17.95.

Right on the waterfront at the ferry landing, this complex of restaurants includes the Pickling Shed bar and the **Clam Kibben** for light meals. The main dining room in the Cannery is distinguished by its full-length wall of boulders covered with lobster traps, bare floors and large wood tables. Dinner entrees run toward items like baked salmon or swordfish, scallops en casserole, and linguini with scallops and clams in mornay or white sauce, and chicken with orange-mustard sauce. Splurge for reef and beef (a one-pound lobster and half a pound of beef). Fish chowder and scallop cocktail are bargain appetizers. Tables on the wharf are available for patrons of the Clam Kibben, where you can order steamers, lobster, crab or seafood rolls and salads, fish and chips, sandwiches and such. Both establishments are fully licensed.

Clam Kibben, open daily 11 to 7; Cannery, nightly 5 to 9:30; open June-September.

Flag Officers' Mess, 73 Water St., Eastport. (207) 853-6043.
Steaks/Seafood. $8.95 to $15.95.

A million-dollar-plus restoration went into an old, four-story waterfront building in 1989 and the result is a restaurant that looks like a million bucks. When he and his father bought the abandoned brick building, owner-manager Bernie McGoldrick said, "you could stand in the basement and look up to the stars." Now, patrons dine on three floors amidst rich mahogany and brick, blue tablecloths and candlelight, and admire the view of Eastport's inner basin through wall-to-wall, floor-to-ceiling windows. Interesting colorations and shadows are created by indirect lighting through the post and beam construction. The menu is limited and basic, Bernie concedes, although it's supplemented by nightly specials. Shepherd's pie is the signature item. Standards include lobster, salmon smoked or broiled in white-wine butter sauce, various steaks, and scallops broiled or in newburg sauce. Additions could be swordfish, tuna, veal parmesan, or pasta primavera. Start with sauteed scallops with ginger and garlic or rolled salmon stuffed with cream cheese, cucumber, horseradish, and chives. Finish with homemade blueberry pie and cakes.

Lunch daily, 11 to 3; dinner nightly, 5 to 8:30 or 9:30. Closed Monday in winter.

Index to Restaurants

Index to Restaurants

Index to Restaurants

Index to Restaurants

380

Index to Restaurants

Index to Restaurants

Index to Restaurants

Index to Localities

Index to Localities

Massachusetts

New Hampshire

Rhode Island

Index to Localities

Index by Symbols

Index by Symbols

Exceptional Atmosphere